Anti-Semitism in the Soviet Union:

Its Roots and Consequences

Anti-Semitism in the Soviet Union:
Its Roots and Consequences

Edited and with a Preface by Theodore Freedman
Foreword by Kenneth J. Bialkin

Freedom Library Press of the
Anti-Defamation League of B'nai B'rith
New York
1984

Published as a Cooperative Project of
The Anti-Defamation League of B'nai B'rith
The Hebrew University of Jerusalem
The Center for Research and Documentation of
Eastern European Jewry
The National Conference on Soviet Jewry

Freedom Library Press

Library of Congress Cataloging in Publication Data
Main entry under title:

Anti-semitism in the Soviet Union.

Bibliography: p.
Includes index.
1. Antisemitism—Soviet Union—Addresses, essays,
lectures. 2. Jews—Soviet Union—Persecutions—
Addresses, essays, lectures. 3. Soviet Union—Ethnic
relations—Addresses, essays, lectures. I. Freedman,
Theodore. II. B'nai B'rith. Anti-defamation League.
DS146.S65A56 1984   305.8'924'047   84-8038
ISBN 0-88464-051-5
ISBN 0-88464-052-3 (pbk.)

The publication of this book was supported by
the Memorial Foundation for Jewish Culture,
New York and the Society for Research on
Jewish Communities, Jerusalem

Table of Contents

Foreword

This is an important book and a disquieting one. It is disquieting because of the contrast between the style of these essays—scholarly, lucid, dispassionate—and the devastating picture they present of a society gone mad on anti-Semitism. And it is important, because the value of scholarly research, not just as an intellectual endeavor, but as a contribution to the moral climate of our times, has never been better demonstrated than in this volume.

Simply put, there is no way that a fair-minded person can avoid drawing anything but the most ominous of conclusions after reading these essays. Writer after writer describes in meticulous, graphic detail the manner in which anti-Semitism pervades every aspect of Russian life. From the days of the tsars to the present, Jews and Judaism have been the focus of an almost obsessive concern: in religion, politics, social life, foreign policy, even the arts. Frequently, anti-Semitic campaigns have been instigated or controlled by whichever government happened to be in power. But, it is also true that government-inspired action couldn't be so successful if it didn't exploit an ugly phenomenon that has deep roots in the Russian psyche.

Paranoia, xenophobia, nationalistic chauvinism: One can cite a whole host of explanations for Russian anti-Semitism. For the moment, though, I would like to discuss a problem of more immediate concern. Regrettable as it may be, the current Soviet leadership still uses anti-Semitism to terrorize its Jewish population. Under the specious guise of "anti-Zionism," Soviet authorities have cracked down on refuseniks, would-be émigrés and ordinary men and women whose only crime is the desire to better themselves. It is also dismally clear that the Soviets haven't hesitated to use a full range of sanctions against the Jews in their power: character assassination, loss of jobs, imprisonment and forced labor.

It is, I think, the willingness of Soviet authorities to use anti-Semitism as a weapon against a powerless group of people which lifts the book in hand from the world of scholarship into the political arena. I have no doubt that people of good will will be outraged by what they read in these pages, and this outrage will, I hope, serve as an incentive to learn more and to become more active in the struggle for a freer Soviet Jewry. Perhaps I'm being too sanguine, but I hope not. The situation is grave, the victims labor under a terrible burden and time is running out. If we don't act, the consequences, as suggested in this quietly forceful book, are frightening to contemplate.

—Kenneth J. Bialkin,
National Chairman,
Anti-Defamation League
of B'nai B'rith

Preface

Readers of these pages may well experience an overwhelming sense of déjà vu—seized by a feeling that they have reentered a world which we all thought we had left behind. That old world is full of dreadful ghosts here reconstructed as a reality of our present time by careful scholarship and placed in context by thoughtful analysis. The contributors to this volume describe a world in which anti-Semitism is once more a political weapon, and where the setting, the thinking, the machinations, and the purposeful manipulations raise anew those ghosts of yesteryear.

Readers who have grown to maturity in the twentieth century are all too familiar with those ghosts, but might have hoped that the tactics and stratagems which visited so much pain and suffering on our world would have disappeared with them. They haven't, and in that sense these pages are disillusioning. Yes, the old practitioners are gone, but they have been replaced by some apt learners, and so the tactics and stratagems which use anti-Semitism as a political weapon still flourish.

Thus, the importance of this book lies in its reminder value as well as in the menace it describes, because there are many who have been lulled by the illusion that politically motivated anti-Semitism has disappeared.

In the aftermath of the Holocaust, it is easy to lose sight of the fact that the fashioning of anti-Jewish attitudes into a potent weapon was first achieved by repressive Russian regimes. The tsars found endemic anti-Semitism a useful instrument for deflecting political unrest and social anger from themselves. Jews were convenient scapegoats; pogroms an effective instrument of political policy.

The inventiveness and the cruelty of the tsarist government were far surpassed by Hitler and his evil empire, but as the studies in these pages clearly show, the Soviet Union has been working diligently since World War II to reclaim its supremacy in this sordid field. It has, through the years, manipulated anti-Semitism at home for political purposes—as the tsarist regime did—but it has also refined it as an instrument in the Soviet arsenal for international aggression. The directions Soviet anti-Semitism takes always reflect the political problems a particular regime faces.

During the years when Stalin sought rapprochement with Hitler, Jews were expelled from government positions; when the economic shoe pinched, they lost jobs in the professions, in education, and in industry; when an internal scapegoat was needed, an "anticosmopolitan" campaign was pressed or a "doctors' plot" produced. Show trials, resistance to Jewish participation in the nation's cultural life, and the development of a distinctly Jewish culture all brought forth anti-Semitic manifestations, expulsions, incarcerations, and exile to Siberia.

But nowhere is Soviet paranoia more obvious, or anti-Semitism as a policy of state practiced more diligently, than in international relations. Confrontations with the West have always heightened anti-Semitic policies; the easing of relations with the West brings an amelioration of anti-Jewish tactics. Jews are seen, not as Russian citizens, but as outsiders under Western influence. The ultimate use of anti-Semitism as a political weapon has come in Soviet Middle East policy, the wooing of Arab support against the West. Out of the Soviet Union has come the propaganda line that Zionism is racism and a reversion to Nazism. Therefore Zionists (read Jews, who are all inclined to be Zionists) become "enemies of the people." The contributors to this volume delve into these matters in greater depth and understanding than ever before.

There is indeed both irony and tragedy in the Soviet Union's increasing use of anti-Semitism as an instrument of government. The irony derives from the historic reality that the Soviets learned and adopted their tactics from their greatest enemies—first, as indicated, the tsarist regime against which they fought their revolution; and then the Nazi invaders who nearly engulfed and destroyed the Soviet Union a quarter of a century later. The tragedy lies in the fact that the Soviet Union is perpetuating what it allegedly fought against and that, indeed, it has turned upon those who were the greatest victims of tsarist oppression and the Nazi Holocaust.

One must never lose sight of the fact that Russia is the land that invented the big lie of a secret Jewish world conspiracy—the forgery known as the "Protocols of the Elders of Zion"—and was perhaps the first government in modern times to bend endemic anti-Semitism to political use. Soviet anti-Semitism is therefore no accident. It derives from Russian history and political opportunism. How deep its roots are is revealed in the chapters that follow.

—Theodore Freedman,
Director,
Intergroup Relations Division,
Anti-Defamation League of
B'nai B'rith

PART

I

Proceedings of the Seminar on Soviet Anti-Semitism Jerusalem, April 7–8, 1978

Introduction

THE ROOTS AND consequences of anti-Semitism in the USSR were the subject of a seminar held in Jerusalem on April 7–8, 1978, by the Hebrew University's Center for Research and Documentation of East European Jewry. The papers and reports given at the seminar are presented in the pages that follow. Although most of the seminar's participants are not primarily involved in research on anti-Semitism, their familiarity with the subject, derived from personal experience and from knowledge of pertinent materials published in the USSR, makes their reports authoritative and authentic.

A seminar of this kind inevitably acquires political significance because of the participants' desire to provide the educated sector of the populace in Israel and around the world with a correct understanding of the situation. Comprehension of the magnitude of the problem, it is hoped, will add to the protest against the rising wave of anti-Semitism in the USSR. Such comprehension should also help expose the Soviet fiction, all-too-often believed in the West, that anti-Semitism does not exist in the Soviet Union. Worldwide understanding can also help strengthen the spirit of Soviet Jews, the main victims of Soviet anti-Semitism.

Historically, anti-Semitism has openly attacked Jews, whether as a group or as individuals, in clear language which left no doubt as to its object. Soviet anti-Semitism, on the other hand, generally employs ambiguous formulas. These are immediately understood by Soviet citizens, who are well versed in decoding the language of official propaganda, but in the West, few are skilled in the art of deciphering the Soviet usage of terms like *cosmopolitanism, Zionism,* and *thirst for profit.*

In addition to the difficulty of deciphering Soviet propaganda, Westerners seeking to fully grasp the quality of Soviet anti-Semitism face another obstacle—the *Jewish credit* earned by the Soviet Union in the early period of its history.

3

Before and immediately following World War I, especially in Central and Eastern Europe, anti-Semitism was chiefly associated with the political right. The left, as a rule, opposed the evil of anti-Semitism. Although Zionists of all shades, as well as Jews of other ideological leanings, disagreed with the leftist movements over ways and means of solving the Jewish question, no one doubted that the left disavowed anti-Semitism.

The Bolshevik Revolution in Russia appeared to confirm this rule. Although there were many anti-Semitic excesses on the Red side too, the murderous Jewish pogroms were carried out by the Whites. The Red leaders restrained their own pogromists and appealed against such incidents. In addition, many Jews joined the ranks of the defenders and builders of the Bolshevik regime during its formative period in the 1920s. The impoverished and oppressed newcomers from the Pale of Settlement streamed into the political and economic life of the country. All legislative restrictions to which the Jews had been subjected in tsarist Russia had already been abolished by the democratic February Revolution. The leaders of the Bolshevik Revolution, headed by Lenin, publicly condemned the occasional outbreaks of anti-Semitism, and made efforts to create an organizational framework for Jewish participation in economic and social life. Foundations were laid for a system of education and culture in Yiddish in the spirit of the new regime. All of this overshadowed reports of the successive blows the Soviet government dealt to Jewish religious and national movements (including left-wing Zionists and the Bund), of the destruction of community life, and of the terror used against Jews designated as undesirable elements (property owners, religious figures, and intellectuals unwilling to adapt themselves to the new order). Such calamities were generally explained as unavoidable revolutionary excesses rather than as manifestations of anti-Semitism.

It would be difficult to single out a specific date or a concrete event which might be considered the turning point in the Soviet government's treatment of Jews. Nonetheless, by the 1930s, Jews with political insight were beginning to sense an upsurge of anti-Semitic tendencies. However, they possessed no incontrovertible evidence, and the optimists did not take them seriously. Such "blindness" is not surprising. The tremendous social changes that took place in the Soviet Union after the revolution were accompanied by ruthless purges of the top leadership and by sweeping ideological changes, but government propaganda invariably claimed that Communist revolutionary ideals were being realized by Stalin. The idea was persistently inculcated that there was not the slightest retreat from the Communist heritage, which included the principle of equality for all peoples. No criticism, however superficial, was allowed. Special styles and figures of speech were developed that became obligatory in all mass media, a kind of Orwellian language which included the slogan "the universal equality of the working people of all Soviet nationalities." In fact, this equality had long ceased to exist, as was most graphically demonstrated in 1945, when Stalin said that the Russian people occupied a preeminent position among the rest of the USSR's nations. This was in full accordance with the rule that all peoples are equal, but some are more equal than others.

Years later, during periods of rampant anti-Semitism, a few Jews always "decorated" the top ranks in the Soviet Union. Understandably, any analysis of Soviet anti-Semitism could be undertaken only as a strictly underground activity. Authors of such studies endure grave danger and have difficulties in obtaining reliable information. Western attempts to address this question are usually rejected with hypocritical indignation by the Soviet authorities. The West, in turn, is accused of slander, inflaming hatred, instigating the cold war, etc. Thus the Soviets succeeded in camouflaging their actions, although a few Western eyes were opened after the publication of an official Soviet announcement about the Doctors' Plot in 1953. If the Soviets had decided not to publicize the plot, this new anti-Semitic libel, more arrogant even than the Dreyfus and Beilis affairs, might well have remained unknown.

The preceding demonstrates the importance of a thorough investigation of the essence of anti-Semitism in the USSR. In order to understand Soviet Jewish policy it is necessary to investigate a wide range of phenomena, such as the purge of Jews from Soviet ruling circles, the popularity of "Jewish" jokes, the abrupt reduction in the number of Yiddish publications, the campaign against "cosmopolitanism," the publicity given to persons with Jewish names arrested for economic crimes, and the absence of any mention of the Holocaust in investigating Nazi war crimes. In addition there are allegations of "centers of speculation" existing in synagogues, the so-called racist essence of Zionism, the reactionary character of the Talmud, the "base motives" of those wishing to make aliyah, and the emphasis on pejorative literary figures with Jewish names. The abundance of anti-Israeli and anti-Semitic caricatures in the press, the criminal "verse" in some Belorussian publications, the "terror" of the "Zionist invaders" in the Middle East, and the opposition of Ukrainian authorities to building a monument in Babi Yar, round out the list. The study of these phenomena is, perhaps, even more important than the statistical data on the decrease in the number of Jews in Soviet scientific and cultural spheres, although these data, too, should not be neglected. All this research, including the study of the daily environment of individual Jews in the USSR, deprived of every kind of communal or social support, reveals the surrealist nature of Soviet anti-Semitism. It encompasses all the elements familiar to Jews of other countries and other eras. Yet at the same time is so different from other forms of anti-Semitism that it can only be fully understood by those who are personally exposed to it.

During and immediately following World War II, Soviet anti-Semitism was "passive." Jews were not mentioned in print. The press was silent about the role of Jewish officers and soldiers in achieving victory. Until recently, the press also remained silent both about Soviet victims of the Holocaust and about the complicity of Soviet citizens in exterminating Jews. Any mention of Jews was suppressed if it might evoke sympathy for their misfortune. Of course nothing was done to stamp out popular anti-Semitism. This reticence on the part of authorities and the press was interpreted by the masses as official approval of anti-Semitism.

The anti-Semitic campaign in the Soviet Union has been conducted without interruption for the last thirty years. The "rootless cosmopolitans" have been replaced by "murderers in white coats"—"hirelings of the imperialistic intelligence services of the United States, Britain and Israel." Khrushchev's exposure of Stalin's crimes did not mention the sufferings Jews endured. Jews were chosen as objects of Khrushchev's antibribery campaign, and Jewish names were prominent in almost all newspaper crime reports, and on lists of those sentenced to death or long-term imprisonment for theft, various unlawful machinations, currency offenses, etc. Special attention was given to religious functionaries and to Jews who were simply attending synagogues.

Attacks continue against the Jewish religion, represented as the source of all possible evil: "black reaction," "savage ignorance," "the preaching of vicious crimes," exploitation of non-Jews, etc. Soviet newspapers are full of caricatures which would have pleased the editor of Der Stürmer. The newspapers speak at length about the Jewish bourgeoisie in the western Ukraine as exploiting Ukrainian workers while under Polish rule and then cooperating with the Nazis. They also discuss the close relations in the 1930s beween the Zionists and the Nazis, about Chaim Arlosoroff, Levi Eshkol, and others, who rescued wealthy Jews from Germany and left Jewish workers to their fate. Similarly, Zionist activities are described, particularly in Ukrainian towns, where Zionist leaders allegedly betrayed workers to Nazi invaders. From spine-chilling stories about the activities of such secret organizations as the Mosad, Brikha, the Shin-Bet, and Israeli military intelligence it is easy to move on to the "crimes" of the State of Israel, both before and after its establishment.

What picture emerges of the Jew—his history, religion, and state—as a result of this thirty-year-long campaign? The Jew emerges as someone devoid of a historical past (there are no books published in the Soviet Union on the history of the Jewish people), who has inherited coarse mythology and prejudices from his ancestors. He supposedly sits on money bags in the offices of big New York banks or spins the webs of conspiracy in Tel Aviv, while nurturing, together with the forces of world imperialism, plans for enslaving other countries and nations. In the USSR he locks himself up in his flat full of riches acquired by robbing Soviet working people. Together with his traitorous friends, he plans to desert the country which has offered him all opportunities.

Desiring to suppress any national awakening in the USSR and to occupy a dominant position in the Arab world, Moscow unhesitatingly resorts to anti-Jewish weapons of every kind; even Lenin's disputes with the Bund are used as weapons against Zionism and the State of Israel. Starting with the Arabs, the Soviets have developed anti-Semitism into a commodity exportable to the Third World and even, especially after the United Nations adopted its resolution equating Zionism with racism, to Europe and North America. Today Moscow is the world's largest spiritual, technical, and organizational center for the dissemination of anti-Semitism.

Studying the nature of this anti-Semitic activity, deciphering its formulas, exposing the channels for the dissemination of this spiritual poison are all tasks of the utmost importance for Jewish scholars.

The seminar organized by the Center for the Research of East European Jewry of the Hebrew University has made a significant contribution in this field.

The Historical Roots of Anti-Semitism in the USSR

SH. ETTINGER

THE QUESTION OF the roots, origin, and character of anti-Semitism is very complicated. Up to the present, scholars have held different opinions on the reasons for the historical continuity of anti-Semitism.

Undoubtedly, certain elements link the anti-Semitism of the ancient period—in ancient Alexandria and Rome—with that of the Middle Ages, that is, Christian anti-Semitism, with Moslem anti-Semitism, and with modern anti-Semitism.

In Eastern Europe, in what became the Russiam Empire, relations between non-Jews and Jews, the attitude of the church and the social elite toward the Jews, indicate that already during the Kievan period tension existed. Although the Jews possibly produced their own religious propaganda, anti-Jewish propaganda definitely predominated.

Its roots were not only Russian. Anti-Jewish propaganda was also based on the anti-Jewishness and anti-Judaism of the Church Fathers, and continued the Byzantine tradition. Although we do not know much about the attitude toward Jews in Kievan Russia, it is clear that Russian anti-Jewishness and anti-Judaism in the eleventh to thirteenth centuries did not differ in any specific way from the parallel spiritual, religious, and social developments in Central and Western Europe.

In my opinion, therefore, the specificity of Russian or, more correctly, Muscovite anti-Judaism is rooted in the so-called *yeres' zhidovstvuiush-chikh* (Heresy of Judaizers), the spiritual and cultural movement which exerted such a powerful influence on the development of Russian self-consciousness and of Russian society in the late fifteenth and early sixteenth centuries.

Historical documents testifying to the extreme intolerance of the church and the rulers of Muscovy toward the Jews date precisely from that time.

This intolerance was so strong that the existence of one single Jew on Russian territory was considered unacceptable. We are referring to the period from the beginning of the sixteenth century until the partition of Poland in the last third of the eighteenth century, when Russia, which until then had been completely *Judenrein*, suddenly became the home of almost half of the Jewish nation.

There was, on the one hand, active anti-Semitism and negation of all things Jewish, while, on the other hand, there was nonrecognition of the Jews as a political or social factor. Even the most enlightened Russian rulers, such as Peter the Great and Catherine II, during the early years of their reigns could not afford to allow Jews to reside even temporarily on Russian territory.

The negative stereotype of the Jew in Russian literature and in the Russian collective consciousness probably evolved from this Russian situation and from the cultural tradition common to all Christian nations.

In Russian folklore and literature of the eighteenth and nineteenth centuries, everything connected with Jews, *Zhidovin, Zhidy,* is associated with something negative. This pejorative attitude toward the Jews existed, and, of course, exerted its influence. True, in one sense this influence was small because the Russian population of the time was largely illiterate. Therefore, what I have referred to applies only to a small group—the enlightened Russians who were influenced by these ideas and, of course, imbibed the negative attitude toward Jews.

There was also the influence of the Ukrainian national tradition. It developed, in a certain sense, along a special course, particularly from the time of Chmielnicki, in the middle of the seventeenth century. For various historical, political, and cultural reasons, the Ukrainian influence on Russian literature and social thought was enhanced by the influence of nineteenth-century romanticism.

Gogol, the literary master, developed the stereotyped Yankel in *Taras Bulba,* which inculcated a negative attitude toward Jews among the Russian intelligentsia of the first half of the nineteenth century. Only with the ascension of Alexander II and the Era of the Great Reforms did a change in the Russian attitude toward Jews become perceptible.

This change was related to Russia's development toward Western norms as a result of changes in the judicial system, press, local government, and *zemstvo.* In addition it was connected with the emergence of independent public opinion in Russia. Only beginning with the reign of Alexander II were the opinions of a segment of enlightened Russian society expressed independently. It should be emphasized that precisely because of the development of Russian public opinion in the 1860s differences in attitudes toward Jews became noticeable.

As I have said, Western ideas were developing. Western literature, concepts of personal emancipation, individual political independence, and new political forms all helped change the attitude toward enlightened Jews, or "useful Jews," as they were called at the time. A section of Russian society emerged which was prepared to accept Jews, or at any rate to give them some—or even full—civil rights. At any rate, under the influence of public opinion, Jewish emancipation, in principle, was placed on the agenda.

But the pejorative attitude toward Jews was developing at the same time. This was based on the bitter ideological struggle between Westerners and Slavophiles which began in the late 1840s, and was not based on religious or political traditions.

While both groups discussed their attitudes toward Jews, the Slavophiles used anti-Semitism as one of the main principles in their approach to particular problems of Russia's civil system, and to the general political and moral problems of Russian society.

By 1860, most of the extreme right-wing Slavophiles and originators of Slavophilism, such as Khomiakov and Konstantin Aksakov, were dead. Only the so-called epigones of Slavophilism, such as Ivan Aksakov, remained. Yet the radical Russian intelligentsia, which formed the anti-autocratic populist movement (narodnichestvo), agreed with the tenets of Slavophilism which existed in the reactionary Russian circles.

From both the right and the left there emerges the stereotype of the Jew as an exploiter, a plunderer, a parasite always living at the expense of others. Some Slavophiles thought this description reflected the Jewish nature, including the Jews' incapacity for productive work or creative activity, and was also connected with the existence of a special secret Jewish world organization—the World Kahal. Its seat was in Paris, and it was called the Alliance Israélite Universelle. This international Jewish alliance was the very same center which directed all Jews in their exploitation of all societies, with the eventual aim of world domination. According to the Slavophiles, this was the essence of Judaism.

The radical camp offered a somewhat different explanation: Jews are always inclined toward schematic thinking, which subjects them to Western influence. Therefore, in explaining social relations they are always prepared to support and follow Western ideas of sterile democracy and formal rights which are determined by books, rather than by the social essence of society itself.

They concluded that the Jews were the bearers of principles that were contrary to the Russian nature. More importantly, the populist camp depicted the Jews as the exponents of those ideas which were leading to the development of capitalism and the destruction of the village commune, or *mir*, the social foundation on which Russia must rest and which was intended to lead to the dominance of the Russian social order, which by nature would be different from Western socialist teachings and trends.

Russia's salvation lay in counteracting or negating capitalism, of which the Jew was the most extreme representative. The struggle against capitalism, therefore, was the struggle against the capitalist exploiter, principally the non-Christian capitalist exploiter, the *Zhid*. Jews were alien by virtue of their social nature, their outlook, and their society.

The resulting situation was a very distinctive one. The populist circles and those of the radical Russian intelligentsia differed on various issues, but shared the same attitude toward Jews, reflecting the Slavophiles' negative view. These views were clear to the few Jewish members of the radical intelligentsia active in the movements of the 1860s and 1870s.

In Slavophile circles, rightist circles, and those connected with official ideology, the whole revolutionary movement was the result of a Jewish conspiracy. After all, nihilism was a Russian phenomenon, they argued, but the secret head of this movement was that very same universal Jewish alliance which was working out plans for the destruction of the world. Russian nihilism was only the first stage of the Jewish plan for world domination. A paradoxical situation arose toward the end of the 1870s, when official policies were somewhat more moderate than the policies of radical groups on the right and the left.

They, at any rate, regarded the Jews as subjects of the Russian Empire who would eventually have to become part of Russian society and the Russian state. For this reason Jews needed to be integrated into Russian culture and social life.

While the issue was discussed by bureaucrats and in the newspapers, right- and left-wing papers viciously attacked the Jews. They claimed that it was out of the question for Jews to become Russian citizens, because Jews had their organization and their Talmud, and until they began "eating with us," until they celebrated the same holidays that "we" do, "we" would not be able to integrate them into Russian society.

Consequently, at the beginning of the 1880s, when anti-Jewish pogroms began in dozens of Ukrainian towns and villages, the major part of the Russian press and of Russian public opinion explained this anger as the exploited masses' uprising against their exploiters. The *Zhidy* were parasites and exploiters. When the people's patience grew thin, they smashed their enemies. Only a few members of the intelligentsia dared to express the opinion that the cause of the pogroms was to be sought not in "Jewish exploitation," but rather in the social and political structure of the Russian state.

In a sense, Ignatjev, Gotovtsev, and the officials who prepared the anti-

Jewish decrees were using this opinion and sentiment of Russian society on the Jewish question more than they were creating it. That is, they adapted themselves to the existing anti-Jewish sentiments which were spreading through society.

The first sign of a shift in the intelligentsia's approach to the Jews began appearing in the late 1880s and 1890s. By that time it had become clear that a regime had been established which left no room for public opinion to influence either the government, the administration, or the behavior of those in power. The intelligentsia recognized that their views not only differed from the government's but were in conflict with them. It became clear that at least a segment of the Russian intelligentsia realized that by supporting anti-Semitism they were supporting governmental policy. People began to realize that whoever wanted to oppose the government would have to have a different opinion on the Jewish question.

As a result, a comparatively rapid transition occurred from the markedly negative attitude toward the Jews to a more sober view of things. While refusing to recognize Jewish "separatism," and even criticizing the Jewish social order, they began to explain the Jews' condition not by their character or by their secret conspiracy, but by the governmental policy which, by its restrictive nature, forced the Jews to take the path of exploitation and separatism.

During the 1890s it became clear to the greater part of the Russian intelligentsia that a radical change in the official policy toward the Jews was necessary, and that granting them political and civil rights was the only way to change the structure of Jewish society, thereby incorporating Jews into Russian social and cultural life. A new approach to the Jews developed in the late 1890s, at the same time that a liberation movement arose, bringing with it political groups which proposed struggle against the government. Most of the intelligentsia vigorously dissociated itself from anti-Semitism. This does not mean that they were prepared to recognize the Jews' right to national self-determination or their right to regard themselves as an ethnic or national group. What was considered natural for the Finns, Poles, Georgians, and Armenians was considered a manifestation of Jewish separatism, of some pathological idea about the existence of a Jewish nation. These members of the intelligentsia felt that because Jews were part of the society and culture they must also be part of Russia. Anyone suggesting that Jews must become a separate nation was under the influence of some reactionary Utopian ideas.

Therefore the greater part of the Russian intelligentsia of the time, except for the Socialist Revolutionary party, which was organized later, had a negative view of the Jewish national movement and Zionism, and followed traditional Russian centralist politics. Both the Constitutional Democrats and the Social Democrats followed the principles of Russian political centralism and could not recognize the right of the Jewish people to national self-determination. Even the liberal and radical intelligentsia maintained a suspicious attitude toward the Jews. They felt that Jews were too involved in Russian political and cultural life. A further increase in their proportion of journalists, actors, and artists would hinder the expression of Russia's creativity. To protect Russia, it was certainly not necessary to endorse anti-Semitism but what Peter Struve termed "a-Semitism."

A-Semitism means a cautious attitude in relation to the Semitic influence. The Jews must have equal rights, they must be citizens of Russia, but too many Jews are like too much salt. We must guard against Jews participating too actively in Russian cultural and social life.

Everything changed after the February Revolution of 1917. I wish to emphasize that formal, official equality was given to the Jews by the democratic February Revolution, not the socialist October Revolution. A few days after its formation the Provisional Government declared civil equality for the Jews, and there was almost no noticeable dissatisfaction with this proclamation.

Even the rightist forces in the spring and summer of 1917 did not speak against Jewish equality. There was a kind of thaw in relation to the Jews on the part of, more or less, all social strata.

After the October coup a new tendency became noticeable. The old state apparatus was destroyed because of the new regime's terror practices, and because of the boycott by Russian officialdom and the Russian intelligentsia. Consequently, a large proportion of Jews, both educated and semieducated, began flowing into Russian state positions and into the cultural and social life.

At the same time Russian society showed the first signs of reaction—in relation to the Jews. Although they could not discuss it openly, in the preceding twenty or twenty-five years Russian intellectuals could not be known as being anti-Semitic. However, deep down, some moderate and left-oriented elements of Russian society as well as the rightists disapproved of this "Jewish plague." When the results of the Russian Revolution first came to light, it looked as if all strata of society were the losers.

The economic and political situation deteriorated, culture was in a state of decay, and the only winners, the only people who had been "nothing" and became, to say the least, "almost everything," were *Zhidy*. Formerly they had been forced to live within the Pale of Settlement, they had been denied the right to be employed in the state apparatus, and they could not be teachers in state universities. Suddenly they appeared everywhere. Moscow was full of them, universities were full of them, the state apparatus was full of Jews, and then the intensively anti-Semitic campaign of the 1920s began.

This campaign was particularly strong among the Russian intelligentsia.

Both economic competition and the old cultural, literary, and religious tradition played a role. However, because of the grandiose plans of Russia's reconstruction, because of the five-year plans, because of the acute shortage of educated people and specialists, this question did not, during the 1930s, assume the character of a very acute social problem. This was especially true after the beginning of Stalin's ruthless terror, when it was impossible to express any opinion at all, let alone criticism, on the Jewish question. For this reason, the inclusion of tens of thousands of Jews in Russian professional groups, in the technocracy, in the economic leadership proceeded more or less painlessly. At least it proceeded without social excesses and much more peacefully than in any other society where a similar integration of Jews took place, such as in the United States or Western or Central Europe.

A new anti-Jewish campaign began in 1936–37, when the first signs of Stalin's rapprochement with Hitler appeared. During that period Stalin made his first attempts to reach an agreement with Hitler. A side effect of this effort was the expulsion of Jews from the state apparatus, the diplomatic service, the Central Committee, and Stalin's personal secretariat.

Apparently Stalin had possessed anti-Semitic inclinations much earlier. He tried to implement them occasionally during the interparty strife of the 1920s, when he was fighting Trotskyism and the opposition. In the late 1930s these inclinations became quite open. By various means, Jews were removed from the Central Committee, from the leading government organs, from the army, and from other important party and state bodies. This continued through World War II.

At the same time, as political terror diminished, new paths for the expression of public opinion increased. One such expression was the rapid rise of anti-Semitism, which now occurred in the highest echelons of the government. For example, Central Committee Secretary Shcherbakov surrounded himself with a whole group of anti-Semites who made their fight against Jews an important factor in their social and political activities.

This stood out with particular poignancy when Soviet Jews themselves began to realize their plight. As a result of the Holocaust, even the most assimilated upper crust of the Jewish intelligentsia began to think: Why should it be us? In this way national consciousness first appeared even among people who had been divorced from anything Jewish for several generations. It is after the Holocaust that Pavel Antokolskii proclaims in agony, ". . . the whole universe calls: "Shema Yisrael!"[1]

There are many such examples.

The anticosmopolitan campaign which served as a cover for the official party and state anti-Semitic campaign followed as a reaction.

This led to extreme excesses in many facets of life and, as has been proved beyond doubt by now, to the elaboration of a plan for evicting Jews (as well as some other national groups) from the European part of Russia. This was anything but new to Stalin's national policy; he had previously expelled a number of groups from their native lands, including ethnic Germans from the Volga zone, Kalmyks, Crimeans Tatars, and others. Then the plan emerged to evict the Jews from the European part of the USSR to Siberia and Kazakhstan. Only Stalin's death early in March 1953 kept it from being realized.

After the thaw and the liquidation of Beria and his henchmen, both Russian and Jewish circles expected a new policy to be adopted toward the Jews, a policy aimed at renewing Jewish culture, which had been completely destroyed during Stalin's last days. Jewish culture was so thoroughly crushed by the murder of Jewish writers, and the arrests and the destruction of cultural institutions, that in a collection of Engels's writings on military subjects where he quoted something in Hebrew (he knew a few Hebrew words), the quotation had to be reproduced by hand. Evidently, at that time Hebrew type could not be found even for publishing Engels's writings.

Khrushchev's secret speech at the party's Twentieth Congress in 1956 ended hopes for a basic change in the new Soviet rulers' attitude toward the Jews. Clearly, the new rulers were not going to change the old Stalinist approach based on negating the very right to the existence of Jewish culture and to any positive expression of Jewish national identity. On the contrary, the relative liberalization in Khrushchev's time, albeit weak, brought out strong public anti-Semitic feelings.

At that time, it became apparent that Jews were needed in the economy, in science, and in a number of industries in order to restore the normal conditions of life which had been ruined by World War II. But it also became equally apparent that there could be no rehabilitation of Jewish culture under Khrushchev. Khrushchev insisted that Jews wanted to establish their own anti-Soviet republic in the Crimea. He openly expressed his anti-Jewish views, particularly when meeting foreign delegations.

The main factor, of course, rather than Khrushchev's personal sympathies or his personal approach, was the growth of contradictions in Soviet society as a result of the easing of political terror. It was a time when all the centrifugal tendencies within Russian society became more prominent. Minor nationalities were struggling for better representation in the Soviet administrative organs, for national representation, for *national cadres.* The easiest way to satisfy the wishes of Ukrainians, Belorussians, Moldavians, and others, was by giving these national cadres positions occupied by Jews, not Russians. Thus began the systematic drive for the removal of Jews from leading positions in various fields. That was how the "comradeship of Soviet peoples" was interpreted: by displacing Jews from their positions in the state administration and in social life to please the "national cadres."

Another important point is that Stalin's purges and terror created a rapid change in the composition of Soviet society's elite. The Russian intelligentsia and the intelligentsia of other Soviet nationalities, which took a long time to develop and were so indispensable to the Russian state, were systematically eliminated several times. After Stalin's purges, therefore, the vitally important branches of Russia's national economy were headed by people with very limited cultural or professional experience.

The Russian villager, the *muzhik*, devoid of any deep-rooted elements of Russian culture or, indeed, universal culture, was promoted to leading positions in the Soviet state. This obviously influenced various aspects of life in the Soviet Union, including Jewish affairs. Tendencies which had persisted in certain circles were now manifested on both the political and the social plane because members of these groups rose to leading governmental positions.

I would say that in principle, the Soviet period as well as the preceding period (the second half of the nineteenth century) is characterized by one unmistakable tendency with respect to the Jews. Those population groups which are inclined to cooperate with the West, to accept Western influences, and to imitate Western social, cultural, or political forms, display a more moderate and often positive attitude toward Jews. The intensification of nationalistic tendencies however, and of a desire for distinct Russian national "originality," for a struggle against the West and Western influences, is accompanied by the intensification of anti-Semitism.

This yardstick may assist in revealing the attitude of Russian society and the Russian authorities to the Jewish question. The main sources of Russian anti-Semitism are to be found here. The growth of Russian (Soviet) nationalism and the intensification of the confrontation with the West which began immediately after the end of World War II inevitably led to an outburst of anti-Semitism.

So long as there is a trend toward cooperation with the West, anti-Semitism becomes more moderate, declines, and is restrained. As the relations deteriorate, anti-Semitism intensifies with some regularity.

Note

1. P. Antokolskii, "Teraiutsa sledy" [Tracks are lost], from the collection *Na odnoi volne: Evreiskie motivy v russkoi poezii* [On one wave: Jewish motifs in Russian poetry] (Tel Aviv, 1964), p. 48.

Contemporary Soviet Anti-Semitism Form and Content

R. NUDELMAN

IN RECENT YEARS Soviet anti-Semitism has increased dramatically. Its most important feature at the present is that it has turned into a phenomenon of international dimensions and has become a threat to the existence of Jewish people. The other special feature is that internationally, Soviet imperialism, Arab and Afro-Asian nationalism, and left-wing anti-Zionism combine with Soviet anti-Semitism to provide the *ideological base* for an all-out attack against Zionism, the State of Israel, and Jews in general.

In the first decades after the establishment of Soviet rule, official anti-Semitism was unknown in the USSR, and manifestations of popular anti-Semitism were severely suppressed. This situation had two causes. First, since Communist ideology was internationalist at the time, it did not include any specific anti-Jewish elements. The official policy line of the regime in relation to Jews was that of "voluntary assimilation," proclaimed in Lenin's works. Second, these decades saw the formation of a close alliance between the Soviet regime and the Jewish working masses freed from the Pale of Settlement. A disproportionately high number of Jews took part in the revolution, occupied appropriate positions in the Soviet state and party machine, and more importantly, replaced the old intelligentsia, recruited from the gentry and nongentry *(raznochintsy)* of Russian society, which had been thrown out of the country by the revolution. One may speak of a new "Russian-Jewish" intelligentsia which was formed during these decades and until recently played a leading role in Soviet life.

The revival of anti-Semitism took place during World War II. It proceeded simultaneously from the top and from the bottom. The Communist party, which during the war years had no choice but to rely on patriotic-national feelings for support, aimed at transforming the country into a nationalist-imperialist state. This necessitated displacing Jewish elements from the

17

leadership of industry, technology, science, and above all, ideological and cultural areas. The new course found support in popular anti-Semitism, which was revived during the war under the influence of German propaganda. The 1948–53 period was marked by an all-out offensive against Soviet Jews under the guise of the anticosmopolitan campaign culminating in the Doctors' Plot.

During these years Soviet anti-Semitism still had a purely internal character and was directed against Soviet Jews. Attempts to link the "cosmopolitan" and "murderous" doctors with world Zionism had a strictly propagandistic purpose and were intended primarily for internal consumption. Internationally the Soviet Union supported the State of Israel because of foreign policy considerations. Even the typical Communist hostility to Zionism as a non-class-conscious bourgeois movement was toned down.

Without attempting to delve into the reasons for subsequent changes in Soviet external and internal policies, it will be sufficient to name them:

• The changing international situation, the consolidation of the Soviet bloc, the break with China, the search for new partners in an anti-American and anti-Chinese coalition, an alliance with new African, Asian, and Arab political forces.

• The changed political situation in the Soviet bloc, including disturbances in Hungary, East Germany, Poland, and Czechoslovakia, the growth of nationalist movements in Soviet borderland regions, the emergence of the dissident movement, the growth of Israel's prestige after the Six-Day War, and the birth of the mass movement for aliyah.

All of these factors contributed to the development of internal processes which could already be detected in the USSR in the postwar years. At present the Soviet regime is quickly divesting itself of the remnants of Marxist and internationalist ideology. It is turning increasingly into a genuine nationalist-imperialist, Russian great-power regime whose totalitarian character is consistent with Russian historical tradition. This is suitable for accomplishing the internal social and cultural tasks set by ideology and for rallying around Russia similar genuinely nationalist-totalitarian regimes. The process is twofold: the USSR is the world's largest supplier of armaments and of a new model of society for developing nations; these countries, in turn, tend to accelerate internal changes in the USSR.

Viewed against this historical background, the escalation of Soviet anti-Semitism should be interpreted as anything but accidental or temporary. It could easily be demonstrated that each stage in the expansion of this process was accompanied by respective changes in the character of Soviet anti-Semitic propaganda and practice. Moreover, by observing the escalation of anti-Semitism, one could follow the various changes in the nature and policies of the Soviet regime. Anti-Semitism thus appears as a vital constituent of the historical process, an important organic part of Soviet ideology which is constantly evolving in accordance with the requirements of the internal and external political development of the USSR and of the Communist regime. Several such requirements are:

• To replace the former "Russian-Jewish" intelligentsia with a new nationalist intelligentsia which will become a mainstay of the nationalist-imperialist regime in its fight with dissidents and national movements in the Soviet empire's outlying regions.

• To fortify the position of the Soviet regime in the Eastern European bloc in order to suppress national-dissident movements in socialist countries and to consolidate them into an effective military force.

• To undermine the positions of independents, such as dissidents, intellectuals, and nationally-oriented elements, in other Communist parties in order to turn them into a reliable force in the struggle for hegemony in Europe.

• To win over anti-Western national-totalitarian Afro-Asian regimes in order to create a unified camp in the struggle against the United States and China.

The first of the above requirements dictates a massive and final onslaught on Jewry inside the USSR. The second adds to it the task of weeding out Jewish-dissident elements in the satellite countries. The third demands that the anti-Jewish crusade be combined with antibourgeois propaganda, so attractive to the rank and file in Western parties, to Western youth, and to leftist intellectuals. This might be stated in reverse: to give antibourgeois propaganda a clearly anti-Jewish, concrete character. The fourth requirement adds Zionism to this ideological complex as the banner under which it is particularly easy to rally Afro-Asian anticolonial regimes.

Consequently, Soviet anti-Semitism inevitably assumes a total ideological, political, and practical character within the USSR and of necessity extends beyond its borders, thus becoming an important part of Soviet international politics.

As pointed out by M. Domalskii, one of the investigators of Soviet neo-anti-Semitism, contemporary anti-Semitism is still secret; that is, it resorts to various kinds of camouflage, of which anti-Zionism is the most common.[1] This is both true and untrue. It is true that Soviet propaganda goes out of its way in official statements to refrain from any wholesale accusations against all Jews. But on the level which escapes the notice of the Western public, such as lectures on current events, administrative activity, and belle lettres, this limitation is increasingly removed. The contention that anti-Zionism is no more than a camouflage for Soviet anti-Semitism is not true. As has been indicated, it plays an integral role mainly in international policy. It is in tune with general Communist ideology and finds a response and support in different circles of Western leftists and Eastern nationalists. The mainstay of internal anti-Semitism is formed by the nationalist new intelligentsia and the mass worker and administrative plebes in the USSR, and in satellite countries. Generally, one may note the formation of a broad alignment of various forces offering suitable ground for Soviet anti-Semitic propaganda. With every year of its escalation, the effect of this propaganda becomes more and more irreversible, resulting in irreversible changes both within and outside the Soviet bloc.

The main danger of modern Soviet anti-Semitism lies in the fact that, in contradistinction to the anticosmopolitan campaign of 1948–53, for example, it is now directed not so much against individual Jewish groups, but against the Jewish people as a whole. Secondly, the brunt of the attack is not directed against some specific aspect of Jewish existence, but rather against the Jewish people. Third, this attack is ideologically substantiated by introducing an outline of Jewish history and religion mendacious in essence, and fascist and racist in character, which repeats the most atrocious fabrications ever concocted by anti-Semites of all time—from Roman historians and early Christian apologists to the authors of the *Protocols of the Elders of Zion, Der Stürmer,* and the agitators of the Russian Alliance of Michael the Archangel. Soviet anti-Semitism is meticulously collecting in its arsenal all so-called doctrines and theories produced by anti-Semitism during the whole of its history: religious, historical, social, cultural, psychological, mystical, and irrational. It consolidates these elements into an all-embracing new ideology to suit modern conditions, and in this way becomes the chief originator of a new global model of anti-Semitism and subsequently its main supplier as well as the organizer and initiator of a world anti-Jewish front.

Soviet anti-Semitism began to acquire its present character immediately after the Six-Day War, the period marked by the growth of dissident and national movements in the Soviet bloc. In 1968 Soviet bloc propaganda for the first time openly declared that Jews were the main source of every dissidence as such. It was crystallized by the Polish party theoretician Andrzej Werblan in one of his articles, which said that all Jews without exception were "particularly inclined to revisionism, Jewish nationalism, and Zionism," and that for this reason wherever "there is a large concentration of Jews . . . a bad atmosphere is created."[2] In 1971 a Soviet author, V. Bolishukhin, wrote in *Pravda* that every person who becomes a Zionist automatically becomes an enemy of the Soviet people. "Enemy of the people" is the same official term that was the watchword during all of Stalin's mass reprisals in the 1930s. Finally, soon afterwards, G. Arbatov, an adviser of the Kremlin Politburo, said that 90 percent of Soviet Jews who remain in the USSR "appear in an unfavorable light," meaning that they are suspicious elements.

The logic behind these statements is obvious. All Jews by their nature are inclined to become Zionists. All Zionists automatically become "enemies of the people." It could be added that internal Soviet propaganda in the form of public lectures concealed from outsiders claims that Jews may become Zionists "without being conscious of it." Soviet Jews leaving for Israel are thus open Zionists, while those remaining—at least 90 percent according to Arbatov—are hidden Zionists, and therefore enemies of the people.

This new global doctrine of indiscriminate distrust toward Jews has become a theoretical basis for the systematic displacement of Soviet Jews from all spheres of social, industrial, and cultural life in the USSR, a process which has intensified and reached global proportions in recent years. The facts about this discrimination are widely known: a *numerus clausus* for Jews who wish to enter institutions of higher learning or who seek employment, limitations in social activities, in the sciences, in international contacts, and simply in trips abroad. Other examples include the ruthless persecution of the Jewish religion and culture as well as suppression of every attempt at Jewish self-expression, such as the trials of the Hebrew teachers Y. Begun and P. Abramovich, the closing of the Moscow symposium on Jewish culture, and extralegal persecution of the Jewish Samizdat journal *The Jews in the USSR*. It should be noted that although national discrimination in the USSR is also being intensified toward other nations and ethnic groups—dictated by the Soviet leadership's fear of the growing nationalism in outlying regions—only the discrimination against Jews has such a total character, and only this discrimination tends to turn into undisguised spiritual and cultural genocide, since the special position of Soviet Jewry, including the lack of territory, national institutions, and national representation, makes it defenseless in the face of total displacement from Soviet life. The situation of Soviet Jewish youth appears particularly dangerous in this regard.

This discrimination has received further theoretical validation in the writings of the Soviet sociologist Mishin, who has proclaimed that at the present stage of development of Soviet society, it has become possible to realize the Marxist principle of "equal conditions for all nations," and this, he argues, must be preceded by a preliminary "equalization of the level of development of all peoples in the USSR."[3] This artificial equalization in the case of the Jews is, of course, tantamount to artificial inhibition and limitation of their social and cultural development.

Meanwhile, the Soviet authorities prevent the Jews of the USSR from finding a way out of the present situation either through assimilation or through emigration.

Assimilation of the Jews in the USSR, which seemed possible, at least formally, during the first decades of Soviet rule, is absolutely impossible at present, since both the population and the administration have for many decades to come been deeply infected with morbid anti-Semitic alertness, suspiciousness, and readiness to expose Jews. It would be naive to think that the results of such education, which has already been inculcated in the second generation, could be eliminated by decree. Further, anti-Semitic social attitudes, while forcing Jews to disguise themselves and their children still more thoroughly, are meanwhile continually intensifying their own national awareness. Whereas during the first decades of Soviet rule the dominant desire was for total assimilation, today the desire for "outward mimicry" prevails among assimilationists.

Those Jews who decide upon the other alternative—aliyah—find themselves confronted with a system of obstacles consisting of direct refusals calculated to intimidate them. They also face an intensive propaganda campaign aimed at discrediting Israel and exaggerating out of all proportion the real and imaginary problems encountered by new olim in Israel. The scope of this campaign defies all description. According to Domalskii's estimates, during certain days or weeks, the total volume of this kind of misinformation about Israel in the Soviet media exceeds the aggregate of all other items of world news.[4] The Soviet propaganda apparatus daily fabricates lies about the Jewish state and the Jewish nation, including descriptions of torture in Israeli jails and reports about whole families in Israel using a single towel and obtaining water upon presenting a ration card. Regrettably, the absurdity of such falsehoods often prevents us from realizing the full extent of their influence on the Jewish population of the USSR, which is assaulted this way daily. Recent repatriates testify that such fabrications are widely believed in the Soviet Union. The systematic campaign of lies has succeeded in sowing seeds of doubt in the minds of many Soviet Jews with regard to foreign and Israeli press reports about Israel and Israeli life. Soviet Jews sometimes form unbelievably distorted and absurd ideas about the Israeli way of life. Finally, one should not disregard another result of this systematic brainwashing: the breeding of anti-Semitism among Jews themselves. The absence of national traditions and culture, a distorted image of Israel as a militarized, clerical- and poverty-ridden country, and unconscious Jewish anti-Semitism, are the elements of this mentality which to a large extent determine the growth of neshirah.[5]

On the whole, Soviet propaganda continually depicts a Jew who above all wants to flee once and for all from his Jewishness, a Jew who does not believe in the possibility of a normal Jewish existence. The condition of Soviet Jewry, living under an enormous and increasing double-pressure, is becoming objectively tragic and historically dangerous.

The main thrust of Soviet propaganda, however, is directed not so much at Soviet Jews as at the indigenous population of the USSR, the satellite countries, the leftist Western public, and the semiliterate Afro-Asian masses. Naturally, the scope and character of this propaganda should be evaluated, first and foremost, on the basis of that portion which is intended for internal consumption, since it is here that the government gives the finishing touches to the principal new elements of Soviet anti-Semitism before including it in the international version. There are, in fact, several international versions—varieties of Soviet international anti-Semitism which are meant for, let us say, leftist intellectuals, or for Afro-Asian states, or as ideological weapons for terrorist and extremist groups in different countries.

Modern Soviet anti-Semitism uses all means of mass brainwashing and is directed at all strata of the Soviet population. In each sector and in each direction it displays the aforementioned traits, including attempts to discredit the Jewish people by spreading lies about Jewish history, religion, culture, the national movement, the character and specific features of the Jewish people, and their role in world history, and modern times.

• *Cinema and television.* Mass circulation in the USSR of anti-Semitic books, articles, and brochures (by Kichko, Evseev, Ivanov, and others) is now widely acknowledged. The use of the mass media, such as cinema and television, for the same purposes is relatively new. On January 22, 1977, Soviet television showed a one-hour documentary, *Traders in Souls*. The program featured caricatures of Jews and Israelis portrayed in the spirit of Nazi newspapers and journals. A disgusting man with the traditional anti-Semitic Jewish look is shown giving five-pound notes to English people protesting the persecution of Soviet Jews. An American tourist interrogated by the KGB confesses to having tried to smuggle forbidden literature into the Soviet Union "on the instructions of Zionist organizations which might be connected with the CIA." Scenes showing aliyah activists embracing Israeli athletes beg the question: "How has it become possible that Zionist agents have appeared in our country?" Shown on the screen were photos of activists supplemented by their addresses and the following comment: "These people are Zionism's agents within our country and conduct their subversive activities here."

This film has been shown twice. Another film, *The Overt and the*

Covert, with a still more openly pogromist character, was not shown to mass audiences but according to available information, was screened in a narrow circle which included groups of Soviet officers.[6] This film begins with a revolver shot and the voice of the announcer saying, "That was how the Jewess Kaplan attempted to murder Vladimir Il'ich Lenin." This is followed by appropriately selected episodes from Soviet history. When German tanks are shown entering a Soviet city, the announcer says, "Hitler was brought to power by Jewish capital."

• *Anti-Semitic indoctrination in the army.* A new, alarming feature of modern Soviet anti-Semitism is intensified ideological indoctrination in the army. The previously mentioned film shown in officers' clubs may be included among the evidence of such activities. The same contingent—officers and propagandists on the army staff—is catered to by anti-Semitic articles by a certain Lev Korneyev, a "specialist on the Jewish question." His articles appear regularly in the principal military newspaper, *Krasnaia Zvezda*, and the main political organ of the Soviet armed forces, *Kommunist vooruzhennykh sil*. Both publications are obligatory for all army libraries, and compulsory reading for all officers and propagandists. During last year alone Korneyev published more than ten articles under such characteristic titles as "Nazism from Tel Aviv," "Zionism's Mercenaries," "Israel's Army—An Instrument of Aggression," "Raiders and Bandits," "Terror—the Weapon of Zionism," "The Espionage Tentacles of Zionism,"[7] "Zionism's Secret War,"[8] and "The Poisonous Weapon of Zionism." Korneyev claims that Zionists are at the head of the American Mafia and the Mafia chief Meyer Lansky received Golda Meir's personal invitation to settle in Israel. Quoting the Arab press, Korneyev further claims that the Israeli army recruits disguised criminals after they have changed their appearance, and that strikes in Israel are suppressed by a "Civil Guard Corps" numbering 50,000 men. He also reports that Zionists are in control of 158 out of 163 of the world's largest arms factories.[9]

• *Lecture propaganda.* One of the distinctive features of the Soviet propaganda system is the daily delivery of lectures and reports in thousands of schools, institutes, offices, and industrial plants. These lectures are usually the main source of additional information for the listeners, and the main source of information on new party directives and trends. The scope of this branch of Soviet propaganda is not secondary to that of newspapers, radio, and television, but it differs from the mass media in that it is concealed from outsiders, and the lecturers, therefore, feel at liberty to go further in expounding anti-Zionist views and "theories."

One such lecture delivered by Moscow party committee representative V. Emel'ianov, which arrived through Samizdat channels, may serve as an example of this propaganda. The lecture is entitled "Judaism and Zionism."[10]

Of all Semitic peoples the Jews are the youngest. The Bedouins, i.e., Arabs, are the most ancient. The principle of Judaism has been formulated in the Torah. The Torah is the blackest book in mankind's entire history. Its main theses are that the Jews are a chosen people and should seize the territories of others. Joshua is like Genghis Khan. Jerusalem is translated as "the city of peace," but in reality it is a den of thieves and criminals. The Jews have contributed nothing original, they have proclaimed the racist principle: Jews must not work, work is for the goyim. That was the origin of the division of humankind into humans proper—the Jews, and two-legged cattle—the goyim. All nations must become the Jews' slaves. The Zionists have planned to achieve world domination by the year 2000. But they lack cadres. And then appears freemasonry, Judaism's fifth column. The aim of freemasonry is to shatter the goyim's regimes. The converted Jew Loyola, under the pretext of fighting freemasonry, organized the Jesuit order, which created the Inquisition. The best goyish minds were burned at the stake by the Inquisition. The Zionists are supported by the Judeo-Masonic pyramid, by the economies of 80 percent of the capitalist countries, and by 90–96 percent of the information media, which dupe the people. There will be a struggle, but we shall be victorious. But victory requires sacrifices. This does not mean that we must distrust all Jews, but we must take into acccount the fact that 40,000 leave annually for a state which is not just capitalist, but fascist.

Scholarly guidance for lecture propaganda of this kind in the USSR is provided by a special Commission for the Struggle Against Zionism attached to the Presidium of the Academy of Sciences of the USSR.

In February 1976 this commission held its regular session, at which urgent problems of the ideological struggle against Zionism were discussed. The materials of this discussion became available to one of the Jewish activists and were published under the pseudonym of Sol'mar in Moscow in the Samizdat journal *Evrei v SSSR* and in Israel in the *Sion* journal. They show that timid attempts on the part of moderate scholars to give Soviet anti-Semitic propaganda at least a semblance of scientific character met with a fierce counterattack by the commission's leadership. The session vindicated the writings of the rabid anti-Semite V. Begun. It was declared that Begun's activities had the full approval of the Kiev city committee of the CPSU, that the Znanie ("Knowledge") Society had awarded him an honorary diploma for his book *Creeping Counterrevolution*, and that books and speeches of V. Evseev were fully approved of by the administration of the Institute of Philosophy of the Soviet Academy of Sciences.[11]

• *Fiction.* Works of fiction are used to teach the masses the false image of the Jew constructed by Soviet propaganda: the image of a Zionist, a spy, a money-grubber, and the enemy of the people and humanity. In a novel by the Ukrainian writer I. Vilde, *The Sisters Richinskii*, a Jew is represented as a lascivious sadist and a greedy usurer. In the novels of the well-known writer Tevekelian, *Granite Does Not Melt* and *Beyond the Moskva River*, Jews are depicted as avaricious underground financiers, money-changers, and crooks. But in the novels of the vicious anti-Semite I. Shevtsov, *In the Name of the Father and the Son* and *Love and Hatred*, Jews are painted in the most apocalyptic colors of all. The main character of the second book, a Jewish journalist named Naum Holtser, murders his mother, rips open her belly, wraps the corpse in the intestines, and covers it with bankbooks. He seduces Russian girls and, for fear of being exposed, kills them, and rapes their dead bodies. In Shevtsov's novels, Jewish writers own luxury dachas and cars, possess untold wealth and innumerable mistresses. They are connected with foreign intelligence services and spread Zionist literature in the USSR. Jewish scientists are spies who sell Soviet atomic secrets to American intelligence agents and kill a young Russian scientist for having "exposed" the relativity theory of the Jew Einstein.

This kind of literature is supplied to the wide reading public in a systematic manner, in amounts typical of a state-sponsored activity. Vilde's novel was quickly translated into Russian, while the novels by Shevtsov, which were sharply criticized by some readers, were nevertheless reprinted—the second and the third printings amounting to 200,000 copies each—by the central publishing houses Moskovskii rabochii and Voenizdat.

Quite recently, Soviet anti-Semitic literature has been reinforced by the publication of Ts. Solodar's *Wild Wormwood* in such journals as *Ogonek* and *Krokodil*, with circulations of five million and eight million respectively. Solodar's book is sufficiently well characterized by the author's statement, "The similarity between Zionism and Naziism has finally been proven by the inhuman practices of the State of Israel. . . . These facts make one reflect more and more on the deep spiritual affinity between the followers of Adolf Hitler and those of Theodor Herzl."[12]

• *Scientific criticism of Zionism and Judaism.* Antireligious propaganda is a permanent element of Soviet life. Recently, however, the portion of this propaganda that is devoted to "criticism of the Judaic religion" has assumed a plainly anti-Semitic character. Articles and brochures by such authors as Belen'kii, Skurlatov, Epshtein, and others systematically distort the true character and meaning of the Jewish religion and its basic texts. An article by Epshtein, a lecturer at the Kharkov Aviation Institute with a master's degree in history, appears in *Our Reply to Slanderers,* a collection published in Kharkov in 1976, and serves as an example.[13] In this article, "When Zionists Are in Power," each page is divided into two parts, one of which contains quotations dredged up from Jewish and Zionist literature, intending to prove the Jews' alleged claim to superiority and their racial conceit. These sayings are juxtaposed with quotes from Hitler.

Soviet propaganda widely uses scholars not only in the struggle against Judaism but also in its anti-Zionist attacks. The collection *Zionism: Its Theory and Practice,* produced by the Academy of Sciences, is a fundamental "theoretical" work aimed at providing a basis for the mendacious fabrications of Soviet anti-Semitic propaganda.[14]

Although papers on "the criticism of Zionism" were not previously accepted at Soviet institutes as suitable thesis topics for degree candidates, characteristic changes recently occurred in this sphere also. On December 28, 1977, the Academy of Social Sciences attached to the Central Committee of the CPSU confirmed Nikitina's doctoral thesis written as a book, *The State of Israel.* Some speakers who spoke during the defense proceedings openly called Nikitina's book "a specimen of anti-Semitism," but they were denounced by the majority of others as "dyed-in-the-wool Zionists" and "anti-Soviets," and the dissertation was confirmed by a majority of votes.[15]

It should be added in conclusion that the latest inventions of Soviet anti-Semitic propaganda are regularly transmitted abroad in a great number of broadcasts by the Soviet, German, and Arabic radio, or through publications for the foreign listener and reader and by other means.[16] Meanwhile, the Soviet press makes wide use of fabrications produced by Arab propaganda. This coordinated effort is exemplified by a book written by someone named Jahiya and published in Beirut and Damascus under the title *Zionism's Ties with Nazism.* Reports about this book have already appeared in many Soviet newspapers. The work is a rehash of the fabrications of Soviet anti-Semitic propaganda, but at this point the Soviets are using it as "independent evidence of authenticity" of their own concoctions.

As is known, the Soviet Union has succeeded, by using its voting strength in the United Nations, in having the organization adopt the scandalous resolution equating Zionism with racism. Since then this formula has become a conventional cliché of all Soviet anti-Semitic propaganda. At present this propaganda is intensively developing a new thesis, which is gradually coming into use as its regular tool: *Zionism is the fascism of today.*

Here are a few recent examples. *Korneyev:* The Jewish population of

Palestine was, as far back as the 1930s, infected with the fascist virus; the similarity between Zionist and fascist doctrines led to their lengthy cooperation from 1933 to 1945; "Zionism borrowed Hitler's methods of mass extermination of the civilian population"; Weizmann was making arrangements with Mussolini for the use of Jewish troops in the conquest of Africa in exchange for a promise that Hitler would help the Zionists to "rob the German Jews and bring them to Palestine by force"; the pogroms during Kristallnacht had been "agreed upon with Tsvi Grinberg, an agent of the Zionist secret service"; the World Zionist Organization and the Jewish Agency intentionally kept silent about the Germans' extermination of European Jewry, "because the Zionists helped the Nazis to murder Jews— women, children, and old people."[17] Weizmann was the chief Zionist murderer, having said, according to Korneyev, "Let the Germans burn and kill unnecessary Jews, we shall bring only the rich and young ones" to Palestine. *V. Begun:* "Collusion between the Nazis and the Hungarian Zionist leader Kastner, who helped the Nazis to send thousands of Jews to gas chambers, is now common knowledge. In Czechoslovakia, Kastner's role was played by Mandler. This highly placed official of the Zionist Center for Jewish Resettlement helped the fascists to fill German camps with Jews."[18] *Brodskii and Shulmaister,* the authors of the book *Zionism—a Tool of Reaction:* In Lvov's archives new documents have been found corroborating the fact of fascist-Zionist cooperation in the mass executions of Jews in the Ukraine in 1941; "In the Warsaw ghetto cooperation between the fascists and Jews had reached such proportions, and the number of Jews who were secret agents of the Gestapo was so great, that the Poles had to execute a few Jewish Gestapo men"; "the insurgents of the Warsaw ghetto were fighters against the fascist occupiers and the Zionist lackeys."[19] *Epshtein,* in the *Our Reply to Slanderers* collection: "Numerous facts have clearly and convincingly corroborated the fascist character of the ideology and policies of Zionism. Fascism is disgusting in any of its manifestations. Its Zionism version is no better than the Hitlerite one."[20] *Solodar,* in the book *Wild Wormwood:* "The Eichmann trial was designed to conceal the cooperation with the Nazis of such Jewish leaders as Weizmann, Ben-Gurion, Moshe Sharett, Levi Eshkol. It is immaterial just how many Jews were killed with the aid of Zionist leaders; it is, in any case, an incontestable fact that the founders of the State of Israel are covered with Jewish blood."[21] The newspaper *Sovetskaia Rossiia* of February 2, 1978, in its review of the above-mentioned book by Faris Jahiya: "Collaboration between the Zionists and the Nazis led to a catastrophe which cost the lives of almost six million Jews."

The most important new element of Soviet anti-Semitism, however, in our view, is the comparatively recent and increasingly frequent attempts to demonstrate that *Zionism itself and its "fascist content" are a natural and necessary outcome of the whole of Jewish history, which, in its turn, has been predetermined by the nature of the Jewish religion and the national character of the Jewish people as such.* This new trend in Soviet anti-Semitism appears to be of paramount importance because it provides all the other aspects with the formerly missing link that transforms isolated anti-Semitic inventions into a kind of *unified and global historical-religious doctrine* whose edge is directed not so much against Zionism or the State of Israel as against the Jewish people as a whole.

The first outlines of this new doctrine began to appear in the Soviet press following the Six-Day War, when, at the authorities' bidding, on the same day hundreds of provincial newspapers published the same article entitled "What Is Zionism?"[22] The article claimed, in the spirit of the *Protocols of the Elders of Zion,* that there existed a secret world Zionist conspiracy aimed at gaining world domination. This idea was developed in the lecture of Emel'ianov (1972). It has been further explored by a certain Skurlatov, a former important Komsomol official, expelled from the party in 1965 for fascist agitation, but since promoted to a position in the history department of the Social Information Institute of the Academy of Sciences of the USSR.

In his book *Zionism and Apartheid,* Skurlatov sketches the pattern of Jewish history from ancient times to modern Zionism.[23] Even in ancient times, he says, the world needed middlemen for trade, and in the course of centuries a trade clan or order formed whose most successful embodiment was the upper crust of ancient Jewish society. In ancient times this upper class had already turned into a "transnational Jewish corporation." From then on this "transnational Jewish corporation" has appeared under different guises in world history but always with a single purpose: to win supremacy over the world. With this aim in view, the corporation first created "the religion of the God-chosen," Judaism, a religion created by stealing, in its usual manner, "not only material but also cultural values, from other peoples." Judaism proved to be a very useful religion for gaining world domination, for it "very consistently generates a solid ideology of race superiority and apartheid." Later on, "Judaism's racial concept served as a prototype for European racism," first of all Catholic (because Catholicism posed as the "New Israel"), then Protestant ("Protestantism is a version of Christianity pregnant with racism"), and finally Masonic ("Masonry is secular Judaism"). In modern times "the racist God-chosen prescripts of the Jewish corporation proved even more compatible with the bourgeoisie." This was particularly evident in the United States: "The Judeo-Protestant influence made itself distinctly felt in the formation of American imperialist ideology." And now, having inculcated Judaic formulas of conduct throughout the world, "the international Jewish elite already knows no bounds to its world-power ambitions." But bourgeois ideologists, "although imbued with Judaic components," proved insufficiently useful for this purpose, writes Skurlatov, and so "the financial-monopolistic corporation of the Jewish bourgeoisie concluded that it was necessary to equip itself with a caste-exclusive doctrine, Zionism." Today, concludes the author, "because it considers itself God-chosen," this corporation "openly lays claim to world domination."

Soviet propaganda adds two aspects necessary to "complete" this scheme. On the one hand, this veritably Manichaean, irrational "theory" of a mysterious, eternal, and omnipresent "Jewish transnational corporation" in the role of world evil, with Zionism as its latest embodiment, is supplemented by an "exposure" of Judaism, i.e., the Jewish national religion, as the ideological inspiration for all rapacious Jewish ambitions. On the one hand, it is supplemented by an "analysis" of the essence of Zionism as an insidious and well-calculated plan for speedy attainment of world domination by the Jews.

An example of the first kind of supplement is V. Begun's new book *Invasion without Arms,* of which 150,000 copies have appeared, and which is sold at the cheapest, i.e., popular, price. In this book (which has recently arrived in Israel) Begun writes: "The apologists of Judaism extol this religion in every possible way. . . . It should, however, be noted that Judaism was basically borrowed from other peoples. As Engels points out, so-called Holy Scripture is a record of ancient Arabic religious traditions." Begun then characterizes Judaism itself: "The Judaic religion divides humanity into 'God-chosen' Jews and 'God-disdained' non-Jews. Judaic chauvinism and racism are already rooted in this division and date back to the most ancient times." Further, "Holy Scripture elaborates a double standard of morals," which, in relation to the gentile, is "shameless and inhuman." "It is quite understandable," Begun claims, "that the Judaic religion provoked the suspiciousness and enmity of other peoples" toward Jews. Thus, the Jews themselves are to blame for the pogroms.

The history of ancient, medieval, and Russian anti-Semitism is related by Begun in a chapter bearing the eloquent title "Tears That Should Not Be Believed." In it he writes, among other things, that before condemning the pogromists one must investigate what kind of Jews they were killing—poor or rich. The trouble with the Jews, according to Begun, is that they always follow the chauvinistic idea of world domination formulated in Holy Scripture. Later, while discussing the modernization of Judaism in recent times, Begun, in passing, characterizes Ahad Ha'am ("he reeks of dyed-in-the-wool fascism a mile off"), Bialik and Jabotinsky (they demonstrate "unsurpassed examples of racism and national egoism"), and other Zionist leaders.

Begun's task is to prove that Zionism is no more than a secular variation of Judaism, permeated with the same morality, ideology, and practical prescripts. What then are these morals and prescripts? Begun answers: "If one views the Torah in the light of modern civilization, it will appear as an unsurpassed manual of bloodthirstiness, hypocrisy, treachery, perfidy, moral dissoluteness—all base human qualities." Begun admits that other peoples have long ago given up their ancient religions, and only the Jews remain faithful to the Torah as a manual of modern conduct. He concludes: "Thus one can trace the links of a single chain: The Torah—ideological prescripts of Zionist theoreticians—aggression in the Middle East—corruption of minds both in Israel, openly, and in other countries, secretly—world domination, this is the dream of Zionist fanatics."[24]

That part of Soviet propagandist doctrine in which Zionism is represented as the logical result and the latest variant of the Jewish people's perpetual desire for world domination may be illustrated by an article published in the book *Our Reply to Slanderers* and entitled "Zionism, a Variety of Racism."[25] The author, Professor A. Zuban', Doctor of History, writes:

Zionism is the most blatant form of modern racism. Its ideological sources are the reactionary ideas of the Jewish religion, which substantiates the Jews' superiority over all other peoples [in this Zuban' joins Skurlatov and Begun]. It was not accidental that Zionist ideologists at first disagreed on the question in which country and in which part of the world to found the so-called Jewish state. At last they decided on Palestine, the country situated near the Suez Canal, an important military and economic artery. Palestine lay at the international crossroads between the West and the colonial East and promised great advantages. Therefore the Jewish imperialist bourgeoisie and all the Zionist ideologists dragged out into the light of day the Judaic dogma of the "Promised Land," supposedly promised by God to the Jews. While preparing for the seizure of Palestine, the Zionists started, even before the establishment of a state there, to develop theories about Palestine as some sort of a world center of Jewish culture. Today, the Israeli press writes that the Arabs must return to Israel the Sinai, Palestine, Jordan, Syria, the Lebanon, Iraq, and part of Saudi Arabia, because all these lands were promised by God to Abraham's descendants.

These statements about Jewry, Judaism, and Zionism pass from article to article, from book to book, from lecture to lecture.[26] The repetition shows that somewhere in the depths of the Soviet propaganda machine, work is in progress on collecting, testing, and polishing the elements of an all-embracing ideological doctrine which must convince the world that the Jewish religion preaches the slogan of world domination; that the Jewish people, therefore, has been consciously and methodically striving for such domination throughout its history; that to achieve its aims it has formed a worldwide secret conspiracy in the shape of a "transnational Jewish trade corporation"; that at present the chief instrument of this corporation is Zionism, whose methods and ideology are racism and fascism; that in their struggle for attaining world domination the Zionists helped Hitler to exterminate six million of their fellow Jews; and that Zionism purposely captured Palestine as the main springboard for the occupation first of all the Arab lands and then of the rest of the world.

It would seem superfluous to prove that this anti-Semitic doctrine, which includes all the former "achievements" of Soviet propaganda, is directed against the Jewish people as a whole and threatens the very foundations of Jewish existence. That is why we have to state that to date Soviet anti-Semitism is the initiator and organizer of a worldwide crusade against Jewry, Judaism, and Zionism.

Occasionally one hears it claimed that individual glaring manifestations of Soviet anti-Semitism do not represent government policy, that propaganda can be separated from the state which, allegedly, is not responsible for the excesses of the Beguns and the Emel'ianovs. If the above facts in their entirety are not sufficiently convincing to disprove so naive a conception, then another striking fact may be cited. We have at our disposal a memorandum that Emel'ianov sent to the Central Committee of the CPSU. In this memorandum, which arrived through Samizdat channels, he sets forth his wild "theory" of the worldwide "Jewish-Masonic conspiracy" and concludes by proposing a program of concrete measures to fight the "Jewish danger."

Here is this program (in excerpts): [27]

1. Widest publicity to the ultimate world-power aims of Zionism and Masonry and their common source, Judaism.
2. Wide-scale publication of works on the history of Zionism, its strategy and tactics (by Ivanov, Evseev, Zhukov, and others).
3. The creation of an Institute for the Study of Zionism and Masonry attached to the Central Committee of the CPSU.
4. A policy of cadre selection which would bar potential carriers of Zionist ideas from work.
5. Introduction of a compulsory course on "scientific anti-Zionism and anti-Masonry" in all high schools and institutions of higher learning in the country.

6. Introduction of a "scientific anti-Zionism and anti-Masonry" section into educational television programs.
7. Inclusion of this subject into the compulsory training program of the armed forces of the USSR.
8. Retraining programs on this subject in all agencies which are responsible for mass information programs and cultural and artistic phenomena.
9. Inclusion into the criminal code of articles providing stiff penalties for membership in Zionist or Masonic organizations; concealment of such membership must be viewed as infiltration of an enemy agent into our society.
10. Outlawing Zionism and Masonry.
11. Ruthless struggle against all kinds of organized Masonic-Zionist activities (the Sakharov Committee, Helsinki groups, the Solzhenitsyn fund, Amnesty International symposia on Jewish culture, etc.).
12. Since Masonry and Zionism are organizations of the radical bourgeoisie, the struggle against them must be conducted in a no less radical way, especially considering that the dissidents led by Zionists have switched over to acts of murderous terror against the civilian population in the metro. They planned these acts as far back as eighty years ago in the metro's early days.

This memorandum is dated January 10, 1978. The author's obvious paranoia would provoke only a smile but for the amazing fact that even the cursory analysis of Soviet reality offered above shows that all the items of the Emel'ianov program from the first to the eighth have in fact been realized or are in the process of being carried out in the USSR under state auspices. This means that the pogromist writings and speeches of Emel'ianov, Begun, and their ilk, rather than expressing their "personal" point of view, reflect a certain objective tendency which is gradually making headway in Soviet society.

What is this tendency?

It would be, of course, absurd to think that the Soviet regime is entertaining a "secret plan" for the extermination of the Jewish people. But it would be equally naive to think that current Soviet anti-Semitism is some sort of transient, temporary expression of Soviet foreign policy interests and can be "abolished" when the changing world situation warrants it. As has already been pointed out, the Soviet regime is now undergoing a nationalistic evolution in the course of which it becomes more and more "popular," or, in other words, takes on a more nationalistic, great-power character. The ideology of this process is provided by nationalistically-minded intelligentsia who are gradually gaining influence in Soviet official and unofficial circles, and closing ranks with the ever-more-entrenched official anti-Semitism exemplified by the likes of Evseev and Ivanov. (Vivid symbols of this link are the united stand taken by "intellectuals" and "official figures" at Nikitina's defense, and the public debate on "The Classics and Modernity," which took place a little earlier, on December 21, 1977, in the Central Writers' Club, where nationalistic intelligentsia openly attacked "ethnically foreign elements" in Soviet culture.) In this historic situation the role of the Soviet-Jewish—or, in a broader sense, "Russian-Jewish"—intelligentsia has come to an end. The time has come when the Jewish element in the USSR has become "superfluous" and "alien." And this is already irreversible. Soviet anti-Semitism of today, which goes hand-in-hand with the general anti-intellectual and antidemocratic campaign in the USSR, is an objective expression of this fact.

Undoubtedly, one must distinguish between anti-Jewish and anti-Semitic tendencies. Not every anti-Jewish statement is anti-Semitism. The desire of certain groups among the Soviet bureaucracy and intelligentsia to oust Jews and to occupy their positions is dictated by an entirely rational factor, competition. Anti-Semitism, on the other hand, is characterized by an irrational hatred for Jewry as such, the conception of Jewry as the "universal evil," the various sketches of a "worldwide Jewish conspiracy" dating from ancient times and stemming from the national peculiarities of the Jewish people, etc. These special features of anti-Semitism were most completely expressed in Nilus's *Protocols of the Elders of Zion* and in the anti-Semitic propaganda based on this book spread by the members of the Russian Black Hundreds organization of the nineteenth and early twentieth century. In tsarist Russia *this* anti-Semitism did not constitute an integral part of state ideology; the "worldwide Jewish conspiracy" scheme was not an officially proclaimed doctrine, but this is occurring in the USSR now: the schemes of V. Begun, V. Skurlatov, V. Emel'ianov, and others are proclaimed in the official press, sanctioned by *official* organs, and gradually are becoming part of the *state* ideology. These schemes are integrated into the official reigning Marxist ideology by using the thesis that Zionism is the contemporary expression of the "Jewish conspiracy." The struggle against Zionism is the point where the Begun-Emel'ianov "homemade" anti-Semitism emanating from "below" meets with Marxist anti-Zionism directed from "above."

This compels us to define the present tendency of official Soviet propaganda with respect to Jews as specifically *anti-Semitic* with all specific features and aims inherent in any form of anti-Semitism.

This tendency is being reinforced—irreversibly—by external circumstances. The world has arrived at a stage when nations with collectivist,

Eastern-oriented mentalities, traditionally inclined toward totalitarian types of society (Communist or religious despotism) have advanced onto the foreground of history. The Soviet model of society, which during recent decades has undergone radical changes, has proved similar to the mentality of these nations, and is widely borrowed by them. In the collectivist East's offensive against the individualist West, Soviet anti-Semitic theories of a "worldwide Zionist conspiracy" as an expression of Western imperialist plans play the same role on the international arena that the theories of "Jewish contagion" play in the nationalist offensive against the intelligentsia and intellectuals inside the USSR. Anti-Semitism has proven an effective instrument in consolidating all nationalistic forces, both internal and external, in the fight against the forces of democracy, liberalism, and humanism. Processes of this kind always need a vivid, concrete symbol. In times past, during the Crusades, it was the Holy Sepulcher; in recent times it was Vietnam; today it is Israel, Jews, Zionism.

Notes

1. M. Domalskii, "Psikhologiia nenavisti" [The psychology of hatred], *Vremia i My [journal]*, nos. 25–26 (1978).
2. According to Polish dissidents, Werblan's article was Moscow-inspired. See M. Khenchinski's remarks, below.
3. V. Mishin, *Sotsial'nyi progress* [Social progress] (Moscow, 1970).
4. M. Domalskii. *Novoe v antisemitisme* [New trends in anti-Semitism] (Jewish Samizdat materials in publications of the Center for the Documentation of East European Jewry).
5. *Neshirah* (Hebrew for "dropout"). Emigrants from the Soviet Union who, despite possibilities of going to Israel, opt to go to other countries.
6. According to other data the film was screened in large movie theaters in a number of cities, e.g., Odessa.
7. *Krasnaia Zvezda*, 1977; *Kommunist vooruzhennykh sil*, no. 24 (December 1977).
8. L. Korneyev, "Tainaia voina sionizma."
9. *Nedelia*, November 21–27, 1977; "Vozhdi-gangstery" [Gangster leaders], *Moskovskaia pravda*, February 16, 1977.
10. *Evreiskii Samizdat* 10 (1976) (reprint of *Evrei v SSSR*, no. 8; [1974]), published by the Center for the Documentation of East European Jewry at the Hebrew University.
11. *Sion*, no. 21 (1977).
12. "Sionizm bez maski," review of Ts. Solodar's book in *Ogonek* (Moscow), March 12, 1977.
13. *Nash otvet klevetnikam* (Kharkov: Prapor, 1976).
14. *Sionism—teoriia i praktika* (Moscow: Academy of Sciences of the USSR, 1973).
15. S. Lukin, "Novyi povorot staroi temy" [A new twist on an old theme] (Materials of the Jewish Samizdat at the disposal of the Center for the Documentation of East-European Jewry).
16. A T report for foreign countries in English, February 1, 1978. See also *Ogonek*, no. 2, January 1, 1978, a report on the translation into Arabic of Ts. Solodar's book *Byvshie* [Anachronistic people], which has been published by the PLO's United Information Center.
17. L. Korneveyev. "Mrachnyie tainy sionisma" [The dismal secrets of Zionism], *Ogonek*, August 1977.
18. V. Begun, *Vtorzhenie bez oruzhiia* (Moscow, 1976); *Polzuchaia kontrrevoliutsiia* [Creeping counterrevolution] (Minsk, 1974).

19. *Sionism—oruzhie reaktsii* (Lvov, 1976).
20. *Nash otvet klevetnikam* (Kharkov: Prapor, 1976).
21. See above, in Ts. Solodar's book, *Dikaia polyn'*.
22. See, for example, *Leningradskaia pravda*, July 3, 1967.
23. V. Skurlatov, *Sionizm i aparteid* (Kiev, 1975).
24. See above in V. Begun's book *Invasion without Arms*.
25. See above in the book *Our Reply to Slanderers*.
26. See, for example, *Aziia i Afrika segodnia* [Asia and Africa today], no. 12 (1978) for G. Nikitina's review of such books as *Sionism—orudie antikomunizma* [Zionism: A tool of anticommunism] by D. Soifer (Dnepropetrovsk: Promin', 1976), G. Fain, *Moral' iudaizma* [The morality of Judaism] (Odessa: Maiak, 1976). These books reiterate or are variations of V. Begun, V. Skurlatov, V. Emeli'anov, and A. Zuban'.
27. From the Jewish Samizdat materials now at the disposal of the Documentation Center.

The Character of Soviet Anti-Semitism

G. ILIN

IN A CERTAIN sense my report will be a sequel to the preceding one. I think that the greater part of the preceding report is an illustration of what I am going to say. We are all very worried by the new upsurge of anti-Semitism in Communist countries. It is both old and new. We have the feeling that anti-Semitism in Russia is somehow different from the anti-Semitism that existed in the world during the whole of the two millennia when Jews were forced to wander from country to country, from continent to continent.

Naturally, we are trying somehow to find an explanation for this. I was going to discuss a certain point of view which seems to me very reasonable, but it may in fact be far from true, because the system is very complicated, and we are limited in our ability to comprehend it. But the problem in itself is very serious; in my view, it is a very important scientific problem which is of great significance not only for us in Israel but also for the whole world. I shall try to substantiate this in my report.

I would like to start with an analogy which may seem unusual. As is known, in the last few years or perhaps since a decade ago, symposia and seminars have been conducted from time to time on communication with extraterrestrial civilizations. Science fiction writers have painted different models of how two intellects meet somewhere in the depths of the universe, or how a known civilization lands on a planet, and what then happens. Contact springs up between civilizations the consequences of which the authors usually depict as disastrous.

Situations are often described by Communist science fiction writers in which everything is very sugary, mawkish, and the two civilizations make contact and integrate with each other in every way.

What in fact is the contact between two civilizations like? Imagine some humanoid, like you and me, with hands, feet, two eyes, and other indispensable organs, meeting here on the earth with a small, tentacled, foul-smelling creature. It is clearly a living being, and contact is established between the two. In what case will the contact be favorable, and coexistence possible, and in what case will this be impossible? Quite obviously, should both these civilizations have the same or similar fundamental morals, the contact will be favorable, and coexistence, irrespective of external appearances and manners of thinking, will be possible.

If the concepts of good and evil in both civilizations are similar, then a dialogue is possible, contact is possible, without any fear that one civilization will overwhelm or destroy the other. If, however, these fundamentals are different, then the situation is, generally speaking, hopeless or, perhaps, even destructive.

I make bold to claim that sixty years ago there arose in Russia a civilization basically different from the Judeo-Christian civilization which existed at that time in Europe and America. The civilization that arose on the ruins of old Russia laid down relativism as its spiritual, ethical, and moral basis. It disavowed the absolute concepts of good and evil given to the Jews in the revelation at Sinai and later transformed and adopted by Christians.

This new civilization proclaims that the useful is good. In the final analysis, it declares as an ethical standard some kind of variant of "rational egoism." We weigh our advantages every time; morality is determined by what is useful and advantageous for us at any given moment. Sometimes killing will be the highest virtue, and helping an abstract, punishable sin. Perjury is necessary as it may be beneficial, whereas someone may be executed for speaking the truth, for truths may be terrible heresy. I want to draw attention to this: the absolute quality of the Judaic morality is a very subtle thing.

When the Lord gave His immortal commandments to the Jews, perhaps He did not mean they must necessarily be observed. It seems to me that something else was intended: that with these commandments the concept of conscience was formed in men, in their minds. In other words, every time you transgress this commandment you feel you have done something inadmissible, and this makes you suffer. You go on transgressing them again and again, but again and again you suffer.

Essentially, the whole Bible is an illustration of how the human personality tries to overcome its perhaps base instincts and needs in defending the indispensability of an absolute ethical and moral criterion.

It is interesting that Christianity has generally adopted these commandments. The important thing that Christianity did was to develop these commandments to the extreme. It thus intensified still more the feeling of sin in man, because it is much more difficult to fulfill the commandments according to the Christian rather than Judaic interpretation. Man is permanently in a state of sin. This principle is, in fact, the motivating force in the development of a Christian. These concepts—concepts of sin, conscience—are basically absent in that other civilization which I spoke of before. Hence, the existing world civilization collided directly with some kind of antipode—an antipode highly destructive to it. I think that in this respect Soviet anti-Semitism differs fundamentally from all previous anti-Semitisms.

Formerly, anti-Semitism was based partly on some kind of religious intolerance, and partly on racial motives which may be in some respect deeply inherent in man in general, as a biological object. With the emergence of the new Communist morality this confrontation assumed quite a different complexion. The utterings of V. Begun and others quoted in the preceding report vividly illustrate what causes this confrontation.

Why is it impossible to tolerate the existence of Jewish culture? For one simple reason: It is not just the opposite of that other, Communist culture; it disavows it, it is its most terrible enemy. One must, indeed, reach for the pistol.

It is a very broad question. I am not going to insist that Communist regimes are inimical to any culture; I am not at this point going to analyze the Communist regime in general. I am discussing only one single aspect. We are now interested in anti-Semitism.

In essence, my thesis is that the cause of this anti-Semitism in its present form is the confrontation of two civilizations. The question is much broader, since the Communist regime confronts not only the Judaic civilization but also Western civilization in its entirety.

But Judaism is the quintessence of that other, inimical civilization; it is the most consistent and least-corrupted civilization. Perhaps it is an entirely different question whether the Russian people is the real carrier of this "Martian" civilization inimical to us. Perhaps such a civilization could not have grown on a different soil, but at present it would seem that the cause lies not in the Russian people but rather in that other, fundamentally different ethical and moral basis which in this case this people expresses.

Apparently, and I quite agree with Nudelman, it would be wrong to speak only of Russia's rulers. It is incorrect to speak of Russia's rulers as the bearers of an idea. This civilization, with its relativist morality, has become firmly ingrained in the whole people. The entire Russian people including intellectuals profess this morality. Even many Jews profess this morality. (Perhaps that is the reason why those who leave Russia occasionally have such a hard time.)

And it is understandable why Jews are the fifth column under Communist regimes. They are a fifth column much as a disguised Martian would be in normal human society. He is alien, he is different, he is inimical, he is terrible, he must be destroyed.

What I have said may be one of the answers to the question which concerns us now. It is a very complicated problem. My answer may be wrong, but it is necessary to go on thinking about it. In any event, thank God that we have our country.

Anti-Semitism in Soviet Publications (Belles Lettres and Feature Stories)

Y. TSIGELMAN

A JEWISH ENCYCLOPEDIA published before the Revolution defines anti-Semitism as "hostility toward Jews." Anti-Semitism is fostered by the prejudice that Jews are an inferior, depraved race, with a hostile attitude toward other peoples; that their dogma is completely at odds with the principles of the Christian faith and civilization, that wherever they gain control, Jews allegedly exert a corrupting influence on the political and social structure of the countries where they live, and undermine the prosperity of the native population.[1]

From Ivan Bulgarin to Krushevan's *Russian Banner*, Russian literature forged the image of a criminal, shrewd, perfidious Jew ungrateful to the countries and peoples whose generous hospitality he enjoys. That segment of Russian literature—which can include even the works of Pushkin, Gogol, and Dostoevskii—created the image of the Jewish crook, spy, and murderer. This tradition lives on in contemporary Soviet literature.

Who reads anti-Semitic literature? Books by authors such as Shevtsov, Kolesnikov, and Solodar appear in mass editions running into hundreds of thousands of copies. They can be found in almost any public library. Each book will probably be read by at least twenty to twenty-five people, and simple multiplication provides an idea of their readership.

Nor should one forget that these books are recommended reading for the politicization circles spread all over the Soviet Union. The Soviet citizen is taught to believe the printed word, never doubting a story published in a newspaper, journal, or book, particularly if presented in a suitable emotional wrapping. Fiction, specifically the short story, is much more effective than a published article in that respect.

41

In the words of Domalskii, an underground (Samizdat) author, "Social consciousness in a totalitarian state is deliberately shaped through a strictly and systematically controlled specific, uniform, tendentious, and centralized propaganda."[2] In addition to newspapers, periodicals, and books, it also involves cinema, radio, and television. Wherever at least five Soviet citizens work, there is a politicization circle. These circles play a paramount role in Soviet social life and are instrumental in disseminating the ideas of the ruling clique.

Asked whether the Jews are to blame for all difficulties, such as shortages, the propagandist will never reply with a definite no. Instead the answer usually is, "I don't know." Accompanied by a smile, it invites the audience to understand that the lecturer knows but is not supposed to talk about it. There are any number of answers but never an outright denial of the Jew's culpability.

Moreover, the importance of rumors in a totalitarian state is well known. The propagandist's reply is likely to generate them. Through controlled rumors, the government can test the public's reaction to its measures. These three devices are fully and actively used in the Soviet Union by the government and party leadership.

Ivan Shevtsov's trend-setting novel *Love and Hatred*, published in 1970 by the military publishing house (Voenizdat), illustrates how the image of the Jew is being fashioned by anti-Semitic fiction. It occasioned a review in *Pravda*, which said that one cannot question the workers' judgment. *Pravda* preferred to ignore the book's clearly anti-Semitic undertones. There were attempts to prevent publication of the book, says Manevich, another underground author. Perhaps the authorities had second throughts about letting Shevtsov publicize his ideas and his supporters so openly.

Certain positive characters in the book are openly distrustful or even hostile to its central character, a postgraduate student, Dubavin.[3] "Our soviet film industry is finally coming of age," says Dubavin after seeing a Soviet movie made according to French patterns. This makes him a negative character because he not only likes Western things but also judges Soviet art by Western criteria. For the sake of objectivity, the author endows him with some positive features: "He can talk about any of life's problems, he's erudite, he knows literature, art, foreign politics." This can only arouse the average reader's envy and annoyance with a highbrow. "Dubavin can talk persuasively," writes Shevtsov, who cannot help but add: "but talks with an assurance that leaves no room for doubt."

"Dubavin accompanies each sentence with a convincing gesture with his long, fine fingers." See? No callouses—he's not one of us, implies Shevtsov, and makes his point clear in the following dialogue: " 'Say, do you have a flat in Odessa as well?' 'Yes. And a summer cottage,' added Dubavin. 'On the seashore.' " The reader is bound to reflect: Where do these intellectuals get their apartments and summer cottages from? They either make more money than us or are dishonest. And Shevtsov keeps exacerbating these sinister character traits. "Dubavin is ready to live and die in the beautiful Arctic region, although he hates it. He is generous and altruistic, but petty and greedy." You can't trust Dubavin, he's a sham, a pretender. Those who surround him don't really know him. Only the KGB agents know what kind of person he actually is; although he introduces himself as Arkadii Osta-povich, his real name, says KGB Lieutenant Kuzovkin, is—Arieh Osa-fovich.

So there you are. The repugnant intellectual turns out to be, in fact, a Jew. And here comes the last passage. Arkadii (sorry; Arieh Osafovich Dubavin) is standing on the shore, signaling with a flashlight, waiting for an enemy sub. And the brave, ever-vigilant Lieutenant Kuzovkin utters the absolutely wonderful sentence: "We know everything. We know why you're here, Mister Dubavin!" The fiend has been unmasked, everything is okay!

The whole thing should be over by page 150. But no: the author keeps flashing Dubavin through the following pages. Pretty soon, he has served his sentence for espionage, and a Jewish-intellectual friend lands him a job with a top-secret scientific research institute of the Soviet Academy of Sciences. A likely story! Straight from prison to a top-secret institute!

Such imbecilic trash can hardly be taken seriously. But simple-mindedness is Shevtsov's stock-in-trade. For he does not write for the intelligentsia, or for Jews. Intellectuals and Jews—like myself when I was in the Soviet Union—read him, laugh, and throw the book away. His books are meant for the unsophisticated multitudes, who have no use for subtle psychological portrayals and other such literary devices. The simpler, the better. The stupider, the more effective.

In the second and third parts of the novel, the protagonist, Andrei Yasenev, a former naval officer victimized under Khrushchev by being discharged from the navy, becomes a police captain. Working for the Criminal Investigation Department, he clashes with spies and bandits, most of them Jewish and members of the intelligentsia. An example: "a nineteen-year-old, well-fed, square-jawed, red-haired ogre with round, empty eyes, and impudent smile, self-confident gestures, and an unduly familiar tone of voice."

Apparently the Jew has changed, he has adjusted, but it's the same Jew. What's his life-style? First, the reader's (and Shevtsov's) stereotype: material affluence and total idleness. "They sat around drinking champagne and sampling the pressed caviar. . . . They ordered a bottle of brandy, one of champagne, two portions of chicken cooked just right—and one bowl of julienne." This listing is meant to, and does, arouse envy.

If a simple Soviet citizen wants to eat caviar and drink champagne, what does he do? He works, increases productivity, comes up with inventions and innovations and earns a lot of money, and only then enjoys himself. But the caviar is being exported to the depraved West, from where this gluttony was imported into Russia. In the Soviet Union, however, according to Shevtsov, only bandits and murderers live like that. They get money the same way Makliarskii does: he steals if from a cab driver after stabbing him with a long, sharp awl made from a bicycle spoke. How remarkably reminiscent of the tool allegedly used by Jews in days of old to drain the blood of Christian children to make the unleavened bread for Pesach! In the era of the scientific-technological revolution, the nail has been replaced by the bicycle spoke.

We shall come across this awl again in the novel, for the murderous villain Nahum Holtser uses this deadly Jewish national weapon to kill the unfortunate Russian beauty Sonia Surovtseva, whom he has seduced and turned into a drug addict.

More about Holtser later on. Let us first make the acquaintance of Makliarskii. The surname leaves us guessing whether he is a Jew or not. To remove doubts, the author enlightens us: "Remember yesterday's cabbie who fumed about the varmints he has to put up with? Well, let me tell you about such a typical varmint, and you'll understand the cabbie's justified indignation. . . . He killed a man for twenty-five rubles—to them, that's the value of a human life! Not their own, mind you; they'll save their own skin by hook or by crook." Later: "These varmints find ways to circumvent the laws, with which they are only too familiar." Or: "What's a human life to them?"—all this is the philosophizing of a policeman—"They only think about themselves and nothing else. To Makliarskii, all the others are sheep to milk, fleece, and slaughter." You see how adroitly the psychology of the killer is combined in one sentence with the individualist intellectual's way of thinking. Because individualism and personal freedom are seen by Shevtsov and his readers as irreconcilable with the way of life of the Soviet citizen. Shevtsov's novel thus fits in with the mass-education policy pursued by the Soviet government and the Communist party.

Let us now get back to Holtser. He, too, is embellished with a long list of qualities meant to arouse the reader's envious resentment. Holtser, only son of the holder of a doctoral degree in law, has inherited a fortune to last him for a lifetime. Although he went to college, he does not work. A good-looking lad, he is the Moscow students' heartthrob, comedian, and entertainer. A Russian soldier reading this, who has barely finished grade school and quails before the girls of his own hometown, has long been irritated by the mollycoddle, lavish intellectual life exemplified by Holtser. Shevtsov adds that Holtser has a car, and a summer cottage, and influential acquaintances in high literary, movie-making, theatrical, and scientific circles.

After inciting the reader to a high degree of abhorrence, the plot begins to unravel. Holtser is instrumental in the downfall of a well-intentioned but weak Russian, Marat Inofant'iev. He accompanies an American tourist, Davy, in his journeys around Moscow. Davy is the American version of our old varmint. He is suddenly found in possession of drugs and, of course, Zionist literature. Together with his Jewish and Russian intelligentsia friends, Holtser infiltrates Dubavin into a top-secret institute. The latter supplies Sonia Surovtseva with drugs and kills her, corrupts Soviet youth in the person of a juvenile delinquent, Igor Ivanov, etc. Finally the most horrid of Nahum Holtser's crimes is described. In order to lay hands on the inheritance, he murders his own mother. Her name is Zinaida Aleksandrovna, and she is, of course, Russian! Had she been Jewish, he would not have killed her! And he uses the very same procedure: he drives a sharpened bike spoke through her heart.

Nahum Holtser is aided and abetted by Western anti-Soviet circles. When he is arrested, the Western press publishes a report on repressions against dissident intellectuals: " 'The well-known writer Holtser was imprisoned in the USSR. The intelligentsia is protesting. Holster was due to arrive in our country,' writes Davy, 'to meet with film director Landers.' " Shevtsov thus ties up the loose ends: the Jews act hand in glove with intellectuals, Russian by birth but corrupted by the Jews and by Western propaganda. The Western press takes Jews and intellectuals under its protection. Those are the dissidents that the Western broadcasting services holler about! The conformity with the mass-education policy pursued by the Soviet government and Communist party is again obvious.

Shevtsov has worthy precursors. I take the liberty to quote an almost forty-year-old source: "Jews enjoy the protection of foreign, hostile countries. Their destructive role for our people needs no further proof. The Jews are the enemy's agents among us." Thus Goebbels wrote in 1941 in the newspaper *Das Reich*.

Other episodes connected with Jews are also scattered throughout the novel. The manager of a fish store debauches his Russian shopgirls; Dr. Paikin helps Dr. Shustov, a surgeon, to raise the death toll; American Professor Samuel Paitsik treats his students to marijuana, etc.

The anti-Semitic belletristic productions of Shevtsov's predecessors are written in the same manner and with the same pathos. Georgii Makhorkin's novel *Life Afresh* was published in 1964; 50,000 copies were printed.[4] It is the story of the Krauses, a Jewish family of traitors, Nazi collaborators, sadists, rogues, and murderers. Gavrutto's novel *Dark Clouds Over the City* (*Tuchi nad gorodom*) skillfully substantiates Khrushchev's fabrication about the Jew Kogan, interpreter for the German World War II General Paulus, and betrayer of the Kiev anti-German underground.

Similarly depicted Jews appear in A. Andreev's novel *Take Care of the Sun*,[5] in Oleg Smirnov's novel *The Northern Crown*,[6] in Irina Vil'de's novel *The Sisters Richinskii*, published and reprinted in 150,000 copies,[7] in Tevekelian's novels *Granite Does Not Melt* and *Beyond the Moskva River*.[8] These Jews possess enormous riches, are cultured and dress neatly. They are poor soldiers, greedy, thieves, profiteers, swindlers, sadists.

The Jewish revolutionary in I. Vilde's novel *The Sisters Richinskii* does not fare any better; he is described as a good-for-nothing loafer who fakes revolutionary zeal in order to draw money from the Red Aid.

According to Domal'skii, the famous case against Stalin's personal physicians, although inconclusive in court, was a psychological success. The populace responded promisingly to incitement. The masses were for the first time fed official lies about monstrous directives issued by American Zionists and reacted perfectly. It became clear; of all the enemies against whom hatred could be incited, Zionism was the most convenient.

"The Jews have betrayed Russia" is an age-old rallying cry. It has now been amended: "they have at the same time betrayed socialism." Between 1948 and 1968 the propagandistic formulation was finally perfected by adding the idea proclaimed during the days of the anticosmopolitan campaign. People then were readily branded "antipatriots," and their surnames were always mentioned to make it clear that they were Jewish. The new formulation no longer requires that. "Zionist" suffices, since everybody knows that only a Jew can be a Zionist.

Zionist Jews or Jewish Zionists are described by I. Beliaev in his novel *By the Back Entrance*, in which he gives a peculiar account of the Six-Day War.[9] Khaimov and Rakhmanov write about Jews in a short story.[10] Allow me to quote just a few excerpts.

What took place in the State of Israel? "Advocates of peace endeavored to build a State of Israel but the Zionists, supported by the Americans and the British, on the one hand, and by the King of Jordan on the other, started the war. Through bloody intrigues, Israel and Jordan divided among themselves the land of the Arab state recently established in Palestine."

Then: "Saturday in Israel is a day of rest, when the Jew says his prayers three times and prepares better food. There are such routines and customs here." "In blessed Israel Jews are divided into an upper class and a lower one. Members of the latter are always subjected to indignities, they are referred to as black Jews. Their fate is to dig ditches in the burning sun, repair roads, do hard but poorly paid work."

The author tells the story of a Bukharan Jew, David. He arrives in Jerusalem, where all sorts of misadventures happen to him. "Together with his family, David decides to leave this dreadful country based on lies." He turns, of course, to the Soviet embassy, where he finds somber people, very similar in description to KGB agents. "They dragged him away and the foursome soon disappeared in a dark basement. They gave him a silent, long, and fierce workout." Returning to Jerusalem, David cries his heart out on Mount Zion: "With great difficulty, he kept walking uphill, holding on to the rocks and stopping every now and then for a minute to catch his breath. Having arrived at the summit, he started praying fervently. This time it was a strange prayer. He did not ask for anything, he indicted Zion. 'Why don't you speak up? Why do those who call themselves by your name poke fun at us? Look at me, a poverty-stricken Jew; I am standing here in front of you. What am I to do? Why don't you answer?' It was quiet around him. With hanging head, David started on his way down. Once home, he lay down with a fever."[11]

Tel Aviv is described as follows: "Beautiful city. Right in the middle of it there is a square in the shape of a six-pointed star. Streets and squares are bordered by multistoried buildings. Only the rich can live in those wonderful houses. Not far from those rich homes, the destitute huddle together in the ramshackle shanties of the Shakhun quarter."[12]

When it was finally and precisely established that Zionists and Jews are one and the same thing, it became easier to practice anti-Semitism under the guise of anti-Zionism and to direct at Soviet Jewry the hatred for the Jewish state. Putting Jews and the Jewish state on the list of accomplices of imperialism helped compound this hatred with the class hatred for imperialism and the United States assiduously inculcated for many a decade.

Journalists and essayists rushed to the publicists' aid. Those with Jewish surnames or of Jewish origin figure prominently among them. This is not a new phenomenon. In the 1860s, the baptized Brafman wrote *The Book of the Kahal*, which anti-Semitic publicists relied on heavily. In our time, this tradition is continued by books such as Belen'kii's work on Judaism and the Talmud, the booklet *Trapped* by the Odessan Prakh'e, and the virulently anti-Jewish articles and books by Gorbunov, Ehrlikh, Solodar, etc.

Sovetskaia Rossiya last year published Solodar's booklet *Wild Wormwood (Dikaia Polyn')* in a 200,000-copy printing. In the first, shorter section, the author relates his personal remembrances and observations about Zionists; the second section draws a propagandistic picture of the Jewish state and of Soviet Jews who wish to emigrate to Israel. To believe Solodar, Petliura's thugs staged their pogroms at the instigation of the Zionists. Authentic Jews, i.e., Zionists, hate bolshevism. A Nazi prisoner of war in Solodar's work proposes ideas similar to Zionism. Zionists are then mentioned in the same sentence or paragraph with White Guardists, Petliura's thugs, Trotskyites, and others, i.e., those whom the Soviet citizen has long been taught to hate and detest.

In his reminiscences, Solodar calls Jews to witness: Dunaevskii, Samosud, Leib Kvitko. All three hated Zionism almost from childhood, but are all dead now and cannot raise objections. This is very convenient for Solodar. He then devotes a whole chapter to Israel and those who went there. The first page states clearly that they are all traitors. They all left with dozens of suitcases—an implication that Jews prosper in the Soviet Union, which cannot fail to arouse the resentment of the masses. Besides, Jews are petty by nature: one left because he could not stand the house director; another left because the factory director did not respond to signals for help from workers in the plant.

In other words, Jews are petty and ungrateful. The Soviet government gave them a good life, but they betray it by leaving for Israel. And Israel is a state that the Soviet citizen has already been conditioned to hate. Solodar is at his best when writing about Israel. He tells lies, retells them, and relies on them. He lies because he can't tell the truth about Israel, and could not if he wanted to. He retells the fabrications of those who returned from Israel and lied only too willingly in order to justify their action and to please the Soviet authorities. He relies on lies because he is a faithful servant of the anti-Israeli and anti-Jewish Soviet propaganda and couldn't miss the opportunity. Besides, like many other anti-Semitic authors he is also an ignoramus and lies from ignorance.

Here is a sample of these publicized misconceptions. In Israel permanent passports are not issued to everybody, and if so, not immediately. The Zionists, it is reported, only provide them to their like-minded fellows, known as Kavoovs. A passport is something of supreme importance to a Soviet citizen. Those denied a passport find themselves relegated to the position of second-class citizens.

Solodar stresses the relationship between those who emigrate to Israel and the dissidents. One of his heroes, a Jew, translates the word "dissident" as meaning "rejectionist" and says: "We rejected our native land, our own people with whom we grew up, studied, and worked."[13]

The fact that the Hebrew language lacks a polite form of the pronoun "you" is also ascribed by Solodar to Zionist scheming. He adds that the teaching of Yiddish and Russian in Israeli schools is strictly prohibited.

According to Solodar, every old man must bring with him some young people capable of providing Israel with cheap labor and cannon fodder. If he fails, the old man is relegated to the status of a second-class citizen. For every invitation mailed from Israel, the sender receives 200 Israeli pounds. Solodar composes an emotional dialogue with heartwrenching comments interspersed with exotic Hebraisms about a family which arrives in Israel at the invitation of a sister, who then refuses to take them in. Not an implausible story, but where is the Zionist scheming?

According to Solodar new immigrants must wait a long time for enrollment in an ulpan and are forced to study Hebrew. A young woman's hair turned gray after a ritual bath in the mikvah. Russian books are very much sought after: a boy had Turgenev's *The Hunting Sketches* and was offered a monetary deposit to borrow his book.

Children in Israel are pictured as afraid of officers, who walk the streets with haughty arrogance, as though underscoring their lofty standing.

One of Solodar's heroes says that those leaving for Israel are only people who were caught in the Soviet Union stealing, accepting bribes, or committing some other crime. This is worse than the other fabrications, for it is more frightening by far, since a certain attitude is thereby fostered toward those who have remained in the Soviet Union. All this is elementary and is meant for readers whose lack of knowledge reminds one of certain merchants from Ostrovskii's plays; they believe the fanciful stories of a worldly-wise wanderer who describes countries inhabited by dog-headed people. They'd believe anything because they know nothing.

The Soviet propaganda machine is geared to its public. The anti-Semitic and anti-Zionist propaganda has affected all publishing houses and the media: radio, television, and the press. If a documentary film mentions that Fanny Kaplan, who shot Lenin, was Jewish, or that Trotsky, whom Stalin made an object of rabid hatred, was Jewish, the unsophisticated spectator naturally assumes that Jews are enemies of the Soviet state, and that it's time they were taught a lesson. They only await the word "Go!"

If the television networks show the movie *Traders in Souls*, describing the activities of American intelligence services and stressing that spies in the Soviet Union are helped by the Jews, the same viewer understands that Jews were and still are the enemies of the Soviet Union. Wielding quotations from Ivanov and Evseev, the propagandists establish connections between these alleged facts and point an accusing finger at the internal enemy of the USSR—Jews, responsible for all the country's difficulties.

One method of Soviet (and anti-Semitic) propaganda is a special commentary on facts. Taking advantage of the reader's lack of information, it distorts facts beyond recognition. Soviet readers will never check the press of 1948 for information concerning the history of the relationship between the Soviet Union and the Jewish state. They swallow the pro-Arab and anti-Israeli propaganda provided by the Soviet media. Soviet citizens know nothing about Israel and can be lied to without any compunction.

As of 1967, Jerusalem was allegedly under the same occupation as Russia was in 1941.[14] In a book about the Munich Olympics, a subject of great interest to the average reader, the authors blame Israeli intelligence for the murder of the Israeli athletes.[15]

Telling half-truths is another method of Soviet anti-Semitic propaganda. In a passage in which Solodar quotes a letter by those who returned from Israel, there are some genuine facts, but they are intermingled with unmitigated lies. Reality is thus transfigured, truth lending credence to lies.

Speaking of Israel, Zionists, and Jews, Soviet authors employ complex terminology that Soviet propaganda reserves for everything concerning its enemies. The Soviet reader reacts by conditioned reflex to such established patterns of language. Among the phrases used are "the thirty pieces of silver," "they call themselves Zionists," "allegedly," "regulations over there," "winked slyly," "the Zionist rulers," "the plans of Zionism," "unfailingly infamous," "they ensnare," "Eshkol's flabby face" (Beliaev), "pitiful hireling of the Zionists," "Zionist bonzes," "Zionism's führers," "Judaic aphorisms." It's very effective.

When speaking about Arabs, the very method of portrayal used evokes sympathy and a favorable impression of them. In his book *Minarets and Skyscrapers* Koriavin, with the normal traveler's curiosity, describes his pilgrimage to Mecca and tells of Cairo street life. All this is normal, but his good-natured tone turns malicious, with the aforementioned derogatory words interspersed, whenever Israel is mentioned.

In his novel *By the Back Entrance* Beliaev deals with Israeli intelligence and the beginning of the Six-Day War. He characterizes Moshe Dayan as follows: "He served as a communications officer in Australia, and there he eagerly acquired military experience." It is not that Dayan studied military science, but that "he eagerly acquired military experience."

"From the age of fourteen, Dayan was a guard in the village." Note that Dayan is described not as the Hebrew *shomer,* or "watchman," but as a guard, because Soviet readers know that guard is a police rank.

In his footnote about Herzl, Beliaev writes: "Herzl, Theodor, an Austrian journalist, the author of a booklet, *Jewish State,* which attained notoriety in its time."

Arab officials are presented in a respectful and reserved manner; Israelis, however, are shown winking slyly, and are insidious and ruthless. The Arabs, in contrast, speak unhurriedly, and the genuine Arab is depicted as trustful, very reserved, and never malicious; this is why he fights Israel.

The real Arab is not fanatic but rather is inclined to be sociable. The Syrian frontier guard is a good-natured sergeant, while the Israeli soldier is a professional murderer.

One of the devices used by Soviet propaganda is the appearance of objectivity. We have already mentioned that authors of this sort are fond of speaking about Sverdlov or Uritskii. [16] The notorious news conference for television, arranged for the same purpose, featured Plisetskaia, Bystritskaia, Raikin, [17] and other prominent Jews.

In the same issue of *Znamia*, just after Beliaev's story, poetry of Isaak Borisov appeared, translated from Yiddish. [18] The editors are saying: Look how objective we are! Here you see Beliaev's attack on Zionism, and here you see our own good Jews, who write poetry, which we translate and publish in our journal.

Finally we encounter another Soviet propaganda device—blatant lies, a device already receiving much attention.

Where do anti-Semitic works most frequently appear? First in such journals as *Oktiabr'*, *Znamia*, and *Ogonek*. *Oktiabr'* has always been an extremely right-wing organ; from the time when it was the organ of the proletarian-oriented "proletcult" writers, it has expressed an extremist outlook. *Znamia* is the mouthpiece of the Defense Ministry. Safronov, the editor-in-chief of *Ogonek*, is known as a militant anti-Semite. In the liberal *Novy Mir* anti-Semitic works also appear, although not often, occasionally in the form of memoirs (for instance *Memoris of Dolmatovskii*), occasionally as reviews where it must be mentioned that Israel should by all means retreat to the borders existing before 1967. Nothing extraordinary, just to show participation in the campaign.

Inostrannaia Literatura is trying not to take part in the campaign, also for the same reason—to preserve, like *Novy Mir*, the reputation of a liberal organ. And if we see some anti-Semitic views on its pages, they are mostly eyewitness accounts of people like Felicia Langer and Ruth Lyublich, a member of the Central Committee of the Communist party of Israel.

Anti-Semitic materials appear invariably and in enormous quantity in *Neman*, *Vitchizna*, *Zvezda Vostoka*, and naturally *Ogonek* and *Molodaia Gvardiia*.

Soviet journalism's connection with different groups in the Soviet Union and the participation of Soviet journalism in anti-Semitic propaganda is, I think, a special topic for investigation.

Fiction, journalism, movies, and TV shows arouse anti-Jewish animosity. I would like to remind you of the definition in the *Jewish Encyclopedia*. The impression is created that Jews are vicious, hostile to other people, and their moral principles contradictory to universally accepted moral laws. They are said to strive to dominate everywhere, they corrupt the socialist foundations of Soviet society, and they undermine the well-being of the Soviet people. Fiction and feature stories have the greatest emotional impact on the Soviet citizen, whose totalitarian upbringing makes him susceptible to these emotions.

Soviet propaganda, using fiction and essays, creates the image of the Jew as a ruthless killer, treacherous and mercenary, a bitter enemy of all that is Russian, a traitor and a spy. The terminology is somewhat altered in compassion with the prerevolutionary era; from cowardly and pathetic, the Jew has been turned into an aggressor, a militarist, and an exploiter. The notion of "dirty Jewish mug" has been replaced by the notion of "villainous aggressor's face." From the tool of bolshevism and socialism, the Jew has been turned into the tool of imperialism and aggression.

Jewish Soviet citizens are presented by Soviet propaganda as inferior citizens; their loyalty is suspect. They elbow their way everywhere, demoralize the Soviet people, and most harmfully affect the intelligentsia and the youth, i.e., the most ideologically unstable or immature elements of society. The Jews, Soviet citizens, are suspect because they are Jews. Based on this image of the Jew, Soviet propaganda creates the corresponding image of the Jewish state as a militaristic and fascist state, a treacherous and ruthless enemy of all peoples, an enemy who especially hates Russia and Russians as the stronghold of communism.

The devices of Soviet anti-Semitic propaganda are essentially the same as the usual tricks of Soviet propaganda in general. It efficiently considers the psychology of its audience, interprets facts while turning them upside down, uses traditional propagandistic phrases and stereotyped portrayals, and displays "objectivity," using half-truths and outrageous falsehoods. The press, with a few exceptions, radio, television, cinema, and all party and state communications networks participates in anti-Semitic propaganda.

Notes

1. *Evreiskaia entsiklopediia* (1903–14), vol. 2, p. 638.
2. I. Domalskii, "Novoe v antisemitizme" [What's new in anti-Semitism] (Jewish Samizdat Archives, Center for the Research and Documentation of East European Jewry at the Hebrew University), p. 5.
3. Ivan Shevtsov. *Liubov' i nenavist'* [Love and hatred] (Moscow: Voenizdat, 1970), pp. 130–150.
4. G. Makhorkin. *I snova zhizn'* (Sovetskaia Rossiya, 1964).
5. A. Andreev, "Beregite solntse, *Oktiabr*, nos. 8–9, (1967).
6. O. Smirnov. *Severnaia korona* (Moscow: Voenizdat).
7. I. Vilde. *Sestry Richinskie* (Lvov: Kamenar).
8. Tevekelian, *Granit ne plavitsia*, Sov pisatel', 1963; *Za Moskvoi-rekoiu*, Sov. pisatel', 1963.
9. I. Beliaev. "S chernogo khoda," *Znamia*, nos. 9–11 (1971).

10. Khaimov i Rakhmanov. "Rasstoianie do schast'ia" [A distance to happiness], *Zvezda Vostoka*, nos. 5–6 (1971).

11. Ibid.

12. Ibid.

13. Ts. Solodar, *Dikaya polyn'* [Wild wormwood] (Moscow, 1977), p. 80.

14. M. Koriavin, *Minarety i neboskreby* [Minarets and skyscrapers] (Moscow, 1973).

15. Grigorev et al., *Miunkhen: Olimpiada i politika* [Munich: Olympics and politics] (Moscow, 1974).

16. Sverdlov—the first president of the USSR. Unitskii—Head of the Soviet secret police, murdered by opponents of the regime. Both of Jewish origin, presented in history textbooks as "heroes of the revolution."

17. All three prominent living Soviet artists of Jewish origin. The news conference condemning Israel and Jews who support Zionism took place in March, 1970.

18. I. Borisov, "Stihi raznyh let" [Verses of various years], *Znamia*, no. 9 (1971), p. 109.

The Reception of Anti-Semitic Propaganda in the USSR

D. TIKTINA (Shturman)

I WOULD LIKE to report on the impact of the official Soviet anti-Semitic propaganda on the various Soviet population groups.

First of all, allow me to make some remarks. The topic we are dealing with today is enormously complicated and could be approached from many different angles. First of all a purely *emotional approach* is possible. There are more than enough grounds for it. When discussing the topic it is almost impossible to eliminate an emotional attitude. The *factual and graphic approach* is possible and also quite feasible. This approach is valuable and scientificaly most reliable, most objective, because it is easier to take responsibility for a study containing exact facts.

The approach which I consider to be most comprehensive and sound is the *conceptual approach.* Yet I feel that while using this approach we should be extremely cautious, for the problem is very complicated and touches upon many other questions related to it. Any conception requires multifaceted, collective, serious scientific elaboration before it can be presented for public judgment. As we all know, we can produce an enormous number of models to explain any complex problem; there are many approaches to this problem too. And therefore, if we want to consider our discussion of anti-Semitism not only as a cultural undertaking for the masses but also as a way of reaching significant conclusions about our struggle against anti-Semitism, then we should examine our conceptions in a very subtle and thoughtful way.

For instance, I disagree with the view that the conglomeration of features constituting the Soviet regime (namely, the value system, the system of moral criteria, the system of social and economic relations) represents an altogether different civilization, to an exclusively Russian populist, national phenomenon. This approach is as limited as declaring that Marxism, communism, or socialism is a creation of the Jewish spirit. The prototype of the totalitarian order, with certain reservations, exists in the ancient utopia, in ancient philosophical literature, in the European social utopia of the sixteenth to the nineteenth century.

This prototype has been repeatedly realized under various national and historical conditions. This order might be viewed to some extent as the result of the constant presence of two utopias in men's consciousness: ideal centralism and ideal primitive equality. For centuries these utopias have, in a certain way, been affecting actual political processes.

We can put forward one more objection to the model of a "purely Russian civilization, alien to the principles of high morality." The Soviet regime, as we know, from the very day of its inception, has waged war against the Russian people and against Russia. This war was total and persistent; in the process the Russian peasantry was suppressed and colonized, the Russian intelligentsia of several generations destroyed. The old intelligentsia, the ideological and revolutionary-minded intelligentsia of the older generation, the Soviet one, born under Soviet rule, was destroyed irrespective of national origin or any other factor. Yet I do not suggest that what is happening now, the escalation of anti-Semitism, its blunt enforcement, is the result of unity established between the Soviet government and the Russian people. Obviously, Russia has undergone great changes over the last sixty years. The peasantry, in the prerevolutionary meaning of the term, was eliminated in 1933; the kolkhoz member and the sovkhoz worker are not peasants, just as the Soviet specialists of mass production are not "intellectual intelligentsia," to use the definition of G. Pomerants. The destroyed generations of intelligentsia were replaced by the "Soviet specialists"; the first generations came from the factory, from the suburb, from the village. This certified urban petty bourgeois is none other, roughly speaking, than the very same basic *zhlob,* or philistine (we are not speaking here of exceptions), akin to the *Bürger* on whom German fascism relied.

Fascism (irrespective of its political hue) always relies on this very stratum of semi-educated *Bürgers.* And I feel that all the anti-Semitic literature about which we have spoken here is designated specially for the standardized way of thinking of these *Bürgers*—"new specialists," and not for peasants.

Why not? The farther from the cities, the fewer the Jews, the fewer the chances of anti-Semitic literature getting there—the Shevtsovs and all that garbage. There, in the village, the person is more often treated and judged as an individual, rather than as a representative of a certain nationality, class, or rank. The suburb, the town, the city office of every kind, are the targets of that literature.

I gained a lot of experience in the fifteen years that I worked in four settlements. With regard to the intelligentsia, the genuine intelligentsia, we should keep in mind the biblical saying that one can forgive the sins of a whole city for the sake of one righteous man. Thus we should not disregard the existence in Russia of people who became neither anti-Semitic, nor antidemocratic, nor agents of the Soviet government. The official anti-Semitic propaganda repels these people and evokes their sympathy to Israel and Jews.

The most favorable soil for all this tendentious, primitive, overly repetitious, obtrusive misinformation is this average, powerful, primitive man, who is no longer virginally innocent, but has acquired only the thinnest cultural veneer.

Official anti-Semitic propaganda has been greatly intensified in the 1970s. I feel that the reason for this is not the unity of Soviet society but, on the contrary, the government's effort to nip in the bud the pluralism which has begun to develop since the 1960s and over which the Soviet government has no control. In Khrushchev's time, when the upper ranks attempted, among other things, to optimize socialism, in the process the pressure on society was slightly lifted.

When the pressure was lessened a bit, diversity, which is natural in any contemporary complex society, began to develop. Contemporary Russia displays uncharacteristic dissent for the Soviet period (nonexistent from Trotsky's exile until Stalin's death), limited and suppressed but still dissent: diverse groups, trends, movements, moods not planned by the government. The Soviet regime cannot tolerate such a situation for a long time. It must eliminate this diversity, this dissent, and harness it as was done in the past, but to do so now is an extremely complicated task.

Why is it so complicated? Dictatorship is essentially founded on three monopolies: the economic monopoly, which has been achieved completely (not taking into account the "black" independent economy, which continually exists and continually challenges this monopoly); a political monopoly, which is functioning powerfully; and an ideological monopoly, which has always been as complete as possible. Yet no matter how complete and total this three-sided monopoly is, no top-level control and repression can fully prevent all the alien interferences, distortions, and drifts which infiltrate the system's components. Khrushchev's epoch, by slighty relaxing the grasp of the supreme authorities on society, at the same time amplified all the erratic signals to a great extent and thus preconditioned the present response and the present trends in Soviet governmental propaganda.

Modern man perceives reality not only from direct contact with it but also from innumerable sources of information. Under Soviet conditions all official sources of information present one and the same model of reality—its pseudomodel. Those widespread semieducated strata discussed above are fed information only by this official source.

The general features of Soviet propaganda have been discussed here quite comprehensively. I would only like to stress some additional features. Let us turn to the founder of the Soviet state. In 1907, at the London Congress, Lenin was asked to report to the delegates on his being brought to the party court just before the congress. He was accused of slandering the Mensheviks (who then were together with the Bolsheviks in one party), Lenin claiming that they had been selling Duma parliamentary seats to the Constitutional Democrats.

While justifying himself, Lenin expressed his credo, his understanding of polemics. He stated the following (I do not quote, but give the precise meaning accurately): "When we dispute with our political adversary, and not with a party member, we are not doing this to elicit the truth. We are disputing not because we want to influence the opponent—we are quite indifferent to him and to all his arguments and tricks. Our purpose is only to destroy him. And I call such a dispute a destrutive one. Our polemics are addressed not to the opponent but to those who listen. We want our listeners to despise our adversaries before they even understand what the issue is about."

Lenin then gives the following example: The Bund[1] left the party. According to Lenin, history does not repeat itself. He was sure that the Bund would never leave the party again, yet if this happened, the Bolsheviks would have the complete right to attract the workers away from the Bund by saying that Bund leaders had been bought out by the world Jewish bourgeoisie. In the shorthand record of Lenin's speech it is literally stated: ". . . anyone who would prevent the Bolshevik from so saying would be no politician but a sissy schoolgirl, for in political polemics we are limited only by criminal law."

Thus Soviet polemics and propaganda are intended to be destructive and to discredit the object of the polemics; they are meant to evoke definite emotions in the listeners. The polemical object is replaced by a sort of life-sized plaster of paris mold, which contains certain similar features depending on the audience to whom the dispute is addressed. For Shevtsov's audience the plaster model could be very crude and fantastic.

If polemics are designated for Soviet educated *Bürgers*, then the parallel to reality must be greater. Without similarity the "mold" would not look so horrible and grotesque. And this model is taken by the collar, raised before the audience, abused, slapped in the face, spat upon.

This trick is interwoven with another one, about which Hertsen spoke bitterly in the final pages of his *Past and Thoughts*. The man who devoted all his life to propaganda confessed: "The people never listen to those who try to prove the truth in the same way we prove theorems. People listen only to those who dream their own dreams more vividly then they themselves dream them."[2]

Addressing those broad masses, fascist in their mentality and cultural level, in their demands and inquiries, Soviet anti-Semitic propaganda is amplified by tremendous proportions just because it "dreams their dreams more vividly than they are dreaming them themselves." It awakes in the masses what is inherent in them; their anti-Semitism is really of the following kind: a young mother, well-dressed, frightens her child on the city street with the words: "Hurry up, or the *Zhid* will take you away." The child perceives his mother's emotions before he begins to understand anything, before he ever sees a Jew. This stress on the emotional response, this appeal to a certain sort of listener, is a very strong side of Soviet propaganda, designed to affect the subconscious rather than the conscious.

I would like to say a few words about the way this propaganda influences the *Jewish philistines* in the USSR. I speak only about my own impressions, for I never studied the question thoroughly in the Soviet Union. The repetition of the phrase "Israel is guilty of everything" finds a widespread response among a certain group of Soviet Jews who are stimulated by anti-Semitism to hate Israel, to consider it the cause of anti-Semitism in Soviet policy. I encountered this response at the training center where I worked. A rather successful Jewish teacher, then academic head of the younger grades of the secondary school, once said a terrible thing in the teachers' room: "How good it would be to throw just one nice bomb on Israel, so that it would disappear from the face of the earth, and then it would be easier for us." Only those Jews who want to do so consider anti-Zionist propaganda as not wholly synonymous with anti-Semitic propaganda; such Jews unfortunately do exist. Another kind of Jewish response is exemplified by the phrase "Do not beat me please, I am one of yours!" His tactics are: never elbow one's way, never thrust oneself forward—never respond to abuse. I witnessed such a thing once when we lived on the first floor of an apartment house in an industrial district. Then, after returning from the village to town in 1963, I was confronted for the first time in my life with malignant anti-Semitism. Once I heard the children calling the Jewish boy a "dirty Jew." I came out to scold them. Then I called him and asked, "Why are you playing with them? Why didn't you answer them, why didn't you curse them?" He replied, "My mother and father told me: when you hear the word 'Jew,' get away at once!"

This response is quite understandable. I am not going to blame anybody for it. Together with it a national feeling awakens on a broad scale, the desire to understand who you are and what you are. It arises at unexpected moments and in different ways. The syndrome of feeling besieged develops, the fright and mistrust is transferred to all non-Jews. More than that: once my Russian friend, a very intellectual person remarked, "You know, when I become acquainted with somebody now, and I see that he is a Jew, I am relieved; at least he wouldn't be an anti-Semite." One less apprehension! Among the genuine intelligentsia anti-Semitism was always considered dishonorable, and it is so now. And naturally, the people who are genuinely moral, decent, and democratic, no matter what their nationality, will consider a dishonorable man and an anti-Semite as synonymous. Yet the syndrome of feeling besieged makes one not notice such people, makes one attribute to others the negative chracteristics ascribed to oneself.

The national feeling also develops in different ways. Pride and resolution can be part of it, but not always. The determination and desire to be a Jew in a demonstrative way has manifested itself in recent years. By the way, the idealization of everything that is Jewish, that is Israeli, has also occurred as a consequence of total disbelief in Soviet propaganda: if the propaganda says "black," then the truth is purest white. This kind of idealization, by the way, creates a very difficult situation upon arrival in Israel.

If a person goes to Israel in the hope of finding an ideal of absolute fraternity and a perfect flawless society, when he confronts the real Israeli society he becomes shocked. He has painfully to reconsider his position. Disillusionment does not produce such a devastating effect on the more stable and cautious minds.

Under the influence of anti-Semitic propaganda, Soviet Jews have launched on a serious and conscious search for national self-determination (and without the propaganda they probably would not have done it); most often they end up leaving for Israel. The problem of Soviet official anti-Semitism has one more aspect. Only a very insignificant part of Soviet Jewry has so far left for Israel. The impression, therefore, is that the majority will live in Russia for a long time, if not forever.

I do not mean to put forth too "sweeping a treatment of facts," as Katkov put it when speaking of Chernyshevskii. We should not think that everybody is anxious to go to Israel; we know it is not so. And the most striking thing is that the national feeling is also stirring in many who are not eager to go to Israel. Yet they do not start on the path of national self-determination; they do not try to fight anti-Semitism.

We do not see any national self-assertion or fight for cultural autonomy or for the right to exist as a national minority. Why? Evidently because those who leave know that sooner or later they will leave and think more about their future in Israel than about their present in Russia. For those remaining, life is more difficult, more frightful, if they choose to identify themselves. Probably their national consciousness has yet to awaken. I also feel it is important to undertake some preventive counterpropaganda, propaganda of Jewish self-dignity and cultural autonomy not dependent on emigration. I always felt that the Bolshevik motto "The worse the better" is immoral; no matter where people live they should fight to improve their situation. The active, manly response to anti-Semitism is as yet found only among future repatriates. Among those who stay in Russia, this kind of response is witnessed only in those connected with dissidents. On the whole, nobody except the potential *olim* ("emigrants") and dissidents ever brave anti-Semitism openly.

It should be noted that more intellectual and educated people also respond to a more subtle kind of anti-Semitic propaganda. And in solving the question whether to go or not to go, and if to go, then where, a more refined propaganda, more elegant in style, more scientific and decent-looking than the phrases cited above, plays a substantial part. There exists also a masked propaganda, less aggressive, allegedly defending Soviet Jews from the "Zionist schemes," and this kind of propaganda has a certain impact on intellectuals, Jews and non-Jews.

I would like also to point out that we should not think that this propaganda totally conquers all people, yet it sometimes deliberately escalates political psychosis, a kind of prewar escalation of hatred, reminding us of ideological artillery preparation. It literally recalls the phraseology the Third Reich used while preparing to launch Nazism beyond the German motherland. This thing could turn out to be much more dangerous than it appears at first glance; some fundamental study is needed, and not only semiemotional conclusions based on insufficient factual material.

Soviet propaganda, despite all its tremendous victories, sometimes suffers setbacks. Therefore, it is required to stop escalating misinformation and falsehood even for a few minutes. I happened to get into difficult situations indeed.

The teacher whom the audience trusts is confronted under Soviet conditions with an unbearable problem. If you are considered to be an agent of the administration, a propagandist of the Soviet system, a member of its rank and file and bearer of its ideals, then you will be asked no questions.

If you are trusted, you are asked questions which are impossible to answer in the classroom. Sometimes this happened to me when I gave preparatory courses for people who had served in the army or came from the village, i.e., utterly uncultured people. And their questions, due to their ignorance, were quite killing ones, considering that among them sat students from the police force and students who were working for the

KGB, but had no higher education, and were preparing to enter law school. And before them all, I was asked such questions as "What is your attitude toward freedom of speech?" or "What is your attitude toward the events in Czechoslovakia?" or "Have you read Solzhenitsyn?" or "What do you think, do they write the truth about Sakharov in the newspapers?" So you try to get out of a scrape as carefully as possible, and every time you think: did I lie enough or too much?! Did I tell the truth, or was it a little too thick? Could I now reach home safely? This is not an exaggeration! The situation is quite complex.

I would like to tell you that there are at least three methods by which the public tests the truth of Soviet propaganda. In every stratum of society there are thinking people, inclined to analysis, possessing a sort of spiritual and intellectual independence and the ability to create their own criteria. This feature distinguishes the intellectual from the specialist; the desire to maintain his own system of accounting, his own system of values and criteria. These people have at their disposal at least three methods to test the propaganda whose truth they are used to doubting.

The first method consists of comparing incompatible pieces of information. By comparing many lies, we expose their false nature. We all used this approach for our unofficial sociological and statistical studies.

The second method is an inductive one; we generalize from the facts and expose the propagandistic statements. The third approach is deductive; we apply the Soviet Marxist premises to reality, which they never fit. I sometimes saw the components of all those methods in my pupils' compositions. (They used to write me letters rather than compositions.) I regret that I never photographed them, as I did other material which I brought with me! I thought it tactless to betray their trust and publish their works. Sometimes they wrote such startling things that I had to tell them, "We'll speak when we meet, but, please, never write like that on your graduation exams. You should remember that the graduation exams are not the place for elucidating complicated problems."

And I still think that if we seriously think over the problem of what can counter anti-Semitic and anti-Zionist propaganda and whether we need some way of fighting it (and I think we should, not to win over the Soviet authorities, but the public), then we should find it quite possible to make a breach in the state information blockade.

Here is a simple example: consider that now we have no Jewish propaganda, as we had in tsarist Russia. Then the Jews were not shy about writing about themselves. Then we had non-Jewish members of the intelligentsia who wrote about Jews. And when we mention that leftist parties never favored Jews, we should not forget that from the 1890s until the 1940s a large number of the members of those parties were Jews who themselves despised everything Jewish, everything national. But in tsarist Russia there also existed some counterpropaganda against anti-Semitism, which is completely lacking in Soviet Russia.

All decent people somehow refrain from any disputes with the dregs, from even standing on the same ground with them, and this actually weakens their position. It is not necessary to argue with them, but only to appeal to the same audience whom they are conquering. I'll make it clear by a simple example.

When I first pronounced the word "Jew" to my young audience of all ages, from those graduating from senior grades of school to those of past-army age, they responded as if it were a curse or a dirty word. They tittered; some even blushed. They felt something strange in the air.

Since half of the audience was from rural areas, not everybody realized that their instructor was a Jew. To understand this you have to have some city experience. Whenever I had the occasion to mention Jews, everybody felt awkward.

We were studying "Poor Liza" by Karamzin, and I stressed the great thought that had struck the readers of the time, that the peasant girl was also a human being and had feelings just like her mistress. "Ha-ha-ha! What a great idea!" they laughed.

I asked them: "Tell me, please, would you think it strange if somebody would consider the Jews as human beings just like all who are sitting here? in our times?"

The effect was shocking, of course. Yet when in one lesson after another on any possible occasion you refer to this theme, introduce it into conversation, they then cease to view it as odious. You read to them from Korczak, introduce them to this and that notion, acquaint them with somebody. And then you see that nobody at all is acting in this direction. There is no hopeless audience. If it is large enough, certain leaders appear who manage to spread definite ideas among the listeners.

Those were the few things I wanted to say on the question.

Notes

1. Bund—*The General Jewish Workers Union in Lithuania, Poland and Russia* was part of the *Russian Social-Democratic Workers Party* (Marxist). Dispersed by Soviet authorities in 1921.

2. Hertsen, Byloe i Dumy, Soch. v 9–ti tomakh, vol. 6, p. 506.

The Reasons for Anti-Semitism in the USSR

A. Voronel

I AM NOT sure I will be able to discuss all the reasons for anti-Semitism in the Soviet Union, but I promise I will offer at least one reason. Before getting to that reason, however, I must begin many years ago. I hope you will forgive me.

I shall begin at an even earlier period than Professor Ettinger did. He began with the heresy of the Judaizers; I think we have to begin at the period when the Russian provinces were under the control of the Khazar khaganate. Then there arose for the first time the idea of the Jews as something dreadful, unusually powerful, far surpassing the average human being in their power and, all the mroe so, the average Russian. Curiously, although this idea was in no way borne out later on in history, it nevertheless grew stronger in the Russian consciousness, and the average Russian was sure that the Jews were more powerful than he was.

That is also the basis of the average Russian's mystical attitude toward the Jews. I would go further to say that thanks to this episodic incident in history (though perhaps not even connected with it—I do not insist on that), there are at least two totally different attitudes toward the Jews, based on different principles. One attitude is the mystical notion of the Jews as extraordinarily powerful and terrifying people, or rather creatures. Then there is a notion which I would tentatively call Polish-Ukrainian, based on a purely practical conclusion, insofar as the Poles and Ukrainians were always in contact with Jews. Since they were in contact with totally different Jews (not awe-inspiring warriors like the Khazars, but ordinary merchants and tradesmen), there arose a purely practical attitude toward the Jews, which differs sharply from the mystical one. I think that a division of this sort is more fruitful for an understanding of what we will now be discussing than a division into anti-Semitic and philo-Semitic. The

63

mystical attitude can be philo-Semitic and anti-Semitic, and the practical attitude likewise. Nobody has slaughtered the Jews as successfully and cruelly as the Ukrainians.

Nevertheless, the mystical attitude toward the Jews is not widespread in the Ukraine. They know quite well who the Jews are, they know how to kill them, and they know how to come to an understanding with them. They see the Jews as an alien tribe with whom, let us assume, they compete or have practical mutual relationships.

The attitude of Russians toward the Jews has a totally different character. At least there is some tendency in the Russian nation built on a mystical attitude toward the Jews. The Russian love of the Jews has its basis in mysticism, in the idea that the Jews undoubtedly know something and bear something within themselves, and that this something is super-human. Both anti-Semitism and Judeophobia also have a purely mystical character, and the Russians sense their inner weakness. That is why I had to bring this up, because in history, in Russian history particularly, these two attitudes periodically, in the pattern of a sinusoid, so to speak, return and disappear. What I mean is that somewhere before the nineteenth century the mystical attitude toward the Jews (I will call it the Russian attitude) predominated. For example, I saw an ukaz (tsarist decree) of the eighteenth century in which Karaite Jews were permitted to own taverns and collect liquor taxes in Lithuania. As a result, many Karaites are now living in Lithuania, or at least were, until the Second World War.

The explanation is given that the Karaite Jews are not as fearsome and dangerous a tribe as ordinary Jews, because Karaite Jews do not recognize the Talmud. The Talmud, as is well known, is a fearsome book, totally inaccessible to the normal man; the Jews, therefore, are a fearsome tribe. But the Karaites are a bit simpler, and so they can be allowed to do exactly what the Jews have always been accused of doing—owning taverns and collecting taxes on liquor.

There is Elizabeth's well-known resolution, which proclaimed, "I do not want to have any income from the enemies of Christ." This is a purely mystical fear and horror that some incomprehensible harm, which cannot be taken into account, can come from the Jews. This is not seen in the Ukrainians and Poles; they calmly made use of the Jews when they had to. So long as the Russian state was governed on the whole by Europeanized people, westerners (zapadniki), the purely practical attitude to the Jews subsequently triumphed; practical considerations guided the way in which Jews were used. The Jews had a sufficiently sound position in Russian society, although the old mystical tendency would arise from time to time. For example, in the nineteenth century a ukaz was unexpectedly issued banning Jews from living on the Riga coast and even from visiting there. I read the petition of the inhabitants of the Riga coast, in which they literally beg the Tsar to permit the Jews to live there, because without such permission they would be ruined. It seems that as early as the middle of the nineteenth century, the Jews used to go to the holiday resorts and were the principal visitors to the Riga coast. Thus this mystical horror sometimes seized Russian administrators despite economic benefit. I think this occurred under the influence of some acquaintances or high officials or something of that kind. What happened after the October Revolution? Whatever revolution there might be in Russia and however radical the changes it would make in the structure of society, in general it cannot escape the bounds of necessity dictated by Russian history.

Russian history remains the history of a people living in this territory under certain conditions. Therefore the Soviet regime also finds itself within the framework of the same necessity. The Soviet regime requires, as did the tsarist regime in its times, some qualified minority that is somewhat alien to the basic population. The tsarist regime always made similar use of the Germans, and so it did not have too much need for the Jews. The Jewish problem did not become problem number one at the state level. If you examine the political struggle in the nineteenth century, particularly the beginning of the nineteenth century, then you will see a gigantic polemic connected with the claim that the Germans have seized everything, the Germans get in the way, the Russian nobility is battling with the German nobility.

For example, even in the second half of the nineteenth century, Mendeleev, a sufficiently enlightened Russian, was nonetheless not ashamed to write in black and white that Russian science was in a bad state because the Germans were hindering it. This was at the time when Russian science was quite independent, and to a significant degree thanks to Germans like Euler and Lenz, peaceful men of science, of whom any country could be proud. Nonetheless, that kind of feeling, an ethnic feeling, existed. And this feeling I would still call constructive, insofar as the Germans were not acknowledged to have any mystical peculiarities. This was simply competition and as such it gave rise to certain exaggerations.

Something like that is going on just now. The Soviet regime has totally done away with the nobility, and even with the middle class. In addition to this, in the 1930s, it even wiped out its own party personnel, as a result of which it lost an immense source of manpower.

We know what a manager is. We also know how important and how difficult his role is in real work terms. For that reason the Jews, as well as the Armenians and other aliens, have moved forward in the Soviet Union into the ranks of this very skilled minority. The Europeanized state-oriented section of the party leadership has accepted them, usually only for supporting roles, but has accepted them nonetheless. And they work, they are working now. At the same time, since it is a large empire, in which many different excesses occur, a national ideology is developing in the country which believes that this skilled minority is capable of competing and is too powerful for leadership. This group is struggling with, as they call it, the dominance of the Jews. And it is struggling quite successfully, because this "dominance," as we know by the statistics, is weakening all the time.

At the same time there is superimposed on all of this real—I would say, Polish-Ukrainian—situation, the old or ancient one, the opposite which is ideologically tinted and is bound up with the mystical attitude toward the Jews as something invisible and fearsome. Here I want to emphasize that a period is now beginning when the constructive, or we could say, calm, attitude of the Russian state administration toward the Jews is changing to the cautiously mystical orientation prevalent in the eighteenth century. Why this is happening is another question, but I want to say that such a wave is beginning to form. At the same time, between the eighteenth and nineteenth centuries, the Russian mystical attitude was replaced by the Ukrainian-Polish practical one. It too was anti-Semitic, but totally practical. Then in the 1930s and 1940s it changed from philo-Semitic and anti-Semitic, but remained practical. Now, in the post-1960s, it is reverting to the mystical attitude holding that the Jews are something elusive and fearsome.

What is this based on, and with what is it connected?

Since I will deliberately express this in an exaggerated form, it will be easy to criticize me. But I do not insist on the wording; I want my formulation to emphasize that element which in my opinion is the basic one. But I understand that in a case such as state politics there are too many elements present and they all have some significance.

Using the strongest words I can, I would say this: The present anti-Semitic campaign in the Soviet Union has nothing at all to do with the Jews. It is not directed against the Jews. There is a struggle—and a very serious one—going on within the party in the Soviet Union. It is connected to the fact that the older generation is dying out and the elite in Russia is changing. Now there is a fight over the composition of the new group which will replace the old elite.

In the Soviet Union, as you know, few people dare to open their mouths and say frankly what they think. There was only a short period, the Khrushchev period, when almost everything was said. None of us, of course, doubts that in China, when a campaign begins against classical literature, the real target is not classical literature, not the ancient sixth-century novel *Peaceful Backwaters*. Rather, the question is who will succeed Mao Tse-tung. Something similar is occurring at the moment in Russia. An extreme faction inclined to nationalism is choosing a direction for its assault, which, given the social conditions in the Soviet Union, cannot be opposed. They create a grandiose anti-Semitic campaign, because they know that in the existing social conditions, not one influential party worker can openly criticize anti-Semitism.

In this way when someone who aspires to power comes out against the establishment, he has in his hands the perfect weapon. It is possible to oppose it only on anti-Semitic soil, and only if the authorities declare that they are even bigger anti-Semites. But it is impossible to be bigger anti-Semites than these extremists, because theirs is already such fanatical anti-Semitism. For the state this ceases to make sense; at that stage it is necessary to switch to direct pogroms or to something similar that destroys the state's normal life. A very strong group is advancing on the establishment, which like any establishment, any state, is interested in stability. This group proclaims more and more radical anti-Jewish slogans and is going further and further along that road. If they proclaim, for example, anti-Armenian or anti-Cossack slogans, they will quickly be defeated. Anti-Jewish propaganda is the only sure thing.

Turn your attention to the group of good-for-nothings who write, invent, and in general organize this mad anti-Jewish campaign. Take Emel'ianov, for example. He is not an obscure person, supposedly controlled by some power, but a well-known individual. There are a few people living here in Israel who know him; Iura Breitbart must know him, Misha Zand, and a few other people. He worked in the Institute of Oriental Studies. He suffered many times for his anti-Semitism, really suffered. They expelled him from the Institute of Oriental Studies, he had trouble with the KGB— he really is a dissident. Nonetheless, he is a dissident who possesses immense power. Later I will move on to the question of where that power comes from.

Another such person is Skurlatov. Many Muscovites know who Skurlatov is, a dissident and a fighter against the Soviet regime. The fact is that Skurlatov is a fascist, and at the moment I am using the word "fascist" not in an abusive sense but in a clear-cut ideological sense. He knows this and considers himself a Nazi. When he worked on the town committee of the Komsomol, he did not turn out Samizdat, as Rafail Nudelman accidentally said, but an official paper, of which thousands of copies were published. He worked at the University of the Young Marxist. This university distributes instructional material. Perhaps it is called Samizdat, but it is official Samizdat which is officially printed and distributed in Russia. This document had such a monstrous, fascist Nazi character, was so openly copied from Hitler's books, that he suffered, and they removed him from the town committee of the Komsomol. Now, as you see, he has found a new job for himself, and has turned out to be indispensable in this business.

These people really take risks, because they are waging a real political battle. You most probably know that there are underground nationalists in Russia who publish the magazine *Veche* and those who are open about their nationalism, who are on the Central Committee or at the Institute of World Literature or in the Writers' Center. Nudelman mentioned Polievskii, Kozhanov, and a few critics who are seriously developing a Russian nationalistic ideology. There are a few members of the Central Committee who go along with them, such as Polianskii, perhaps, and Ustinov, who is partially involved in this, and someone else; somebody who in one way or another supports them, but "under the table." When these people are put in prison, expelled, or punished, that never means that justice has been brought to bear on them in any concrete sense. It always means that the fate of these people like the fate of the Jews is not being taken into consideration in this campaign. It always means that a certain member of the Central Committee has given another member of the Central Committee a rap on the knuckles. One has stretched his hand out too close to the other's pocket and has received a reprimand. "To get a rap on the knuckles" means, for example, that they have put Osipov in prison for eight years. Or the publication of an article in *Literaturnaia Gazeta* against the Russian nationalists—against the nationalists who are openly anti-Soviet. But actually it means that there was in-fighting.

The KGB is also very strongly involved in this struggle, but I do not know on what side. Perhaps the KGB, too, is not united on this question. But what I am sure of is that we have a political game which is in actual fact a power struggle. What I have said sounds paradoxical; because I said that it has no connection with the Jewish people.

Now I will say the opposite. This is what completely determines the fate of the Jewish people. Polianskii's struggle with Brezhnev has no connection with Osipov, but it is Osipov who was sentenced to eight years and is in the camps.

In exactly the same way this power struggle can mean life or death for the Jewish people. For that reason what I am saying is even more dangerous than if it were really a state ideology which had come to replace the existing ideology.

I agree with Rafail Nudelman's report that in the present situation anti-Semitism is becoming to some degree the state ideology. I agree with this to the extent that the Russian empire, which has always been an empire, is really becoming more and more a nationalist state, and therefore its ideology is becoming nationalistic. But I do not agree that the closer some group is to the regime, the more it will be compelled to renounce a nationalist ideology, because an empire cannot be governed by purely nationalistic slogans. As such groups grow closer to the regime, they will give up their nationalist ideology. But there is one point in this ideology which they will preserve, and which they will retain with pleasure—anti-Semitism.

It does not offend any one of the colonies of this empire. In this way anti-Semitism is successfully located on the ideological map, as it is the only feature of nationalistic ideology which suits everybody; the right, the left, the nationalists, and the imperialist. Brezhnev, Kirilenko, Podgornyi—they are all like Ukrainians in their attitude toward Jews, and by the way, they are all from the Ukraine. That is not by chance. All of them have Jewish relatives. They are all anti-Semites, but for them the Jews are people with whom they can compete. They can allow them to leave or not, but they do so for purely practical reasons, and these practical reasons are sufficient.

Naturally, the nationalist group trying to overthrow them looks fanatical on the surface, but in fact, its leaders are, of course, far from being fanatics. This group has a mystic approach toward the Jews. It cannot allow the Jews to do anything that they want to. If the Jews want to leave, they must not be allowed to leave; if the Jews do not want to leave, they must be driven out. They will do all that is necessary in order to destroy the Jewish people. This is their idea. This is the compromise which will reconcile these groups, because it is impossible to conceive of Russia nowadays, and Russian politics in particular, according to the same criteria used in Stalinist times. In Stalin's time there was the impression (and it has been confirmed to a significant degree) that the country was governed by one will, and everything was decreed from above. However, even in Stalinist times there was initiative from below. Party workers who showed that kind of initiative risked their lives, but some won. Now it is almost entirely like that; not all Russian politics is planned from above, in particular anti-Semitism. Limiting the number of Jews admitted to institutes or given employment, the quota, and so on—of course, that is planned. But anti-Semitism as a paranoid ideology, anti-Semitism as an attitude which leads to the destruction of one's own practical interests, is not planned. This means that it is even more dangerous, because it is the only kind of ideological initiative which cannot fail to be supported. A party worker is obliged to support the initiative of these madmen in order to prove his loyalty and to display the qualities that will make him popular in certain circles. He may realize that it is stupid and can do him harm, but he must do it. In my practical work I have come into contact with two such types of practical workers. As I was a scientist and sufficiently qualified, I was in practical terms a useful person. In addition I was in charge of a laboratory which simply brought in a lot of money to my institute. So, for example, I had dealings with two assistant directors, one of whom rang me regularly and said in a drunken voice, "Voronel, get us another hundred thousand, you can do it, it's nothing to you." I would say to him, "Then can you fix it up for me that such-and-such a Jew will be taken on?" And he would reply, "All right, damn you!"

He was prepared to meet me halfway, because he understood that for money he had to do something.

When the other assistant director was in the same situation, he clearly formulated another position. When I told him about the useful topics I was planning, he would laugh in my face and say, "I don't need anything from you, I will do everything to spite you. Do you think you need to join this mission? No, you'll not go on this one; I'll only allow you on that one"—the one I didn't ask for. He tried to go against whatever I wanted. And what is more, I would not even have called him an anti-Semite in the literal sense of the word: he surrounded himself with Jews. But the curious peculiarity was that he chose Jews who were more stupid than he was; he liked foolish Jews. He found it indispensable to be convinced within himself that Jews were stupider than he, that they were not as fearsome as he thought. This was really a psychological necessity. He had a mystical fear of the Jews, and because he had ten foolish Jews, he looked at them at every moment and was convinced that there was nothing to be afraid of; he could still go on living.

Assistant Director Pisarev, who proposed a compromise in a drunken voice, always gave way to the other one, Koborov, for one simple reason: his compromise was always secret, and he could not admit that he had these secret relations with me, infamous relations, so to speak, with world Zionism. That was the agreement, because he was always in the weak position.

What I want to say is that this is the most dreadful danger threatening the Jewish people in the Soviet Union at the moment. Because even the establishment, even the relatively moderate group of party workers, has only one path in the struggle with this extreme right wing—the path of making concessions with regard to the Jews because, shall we say, they cannot make concessions with regard to Kazakhstan, they cannot make concessions with regard to some Armenians; nominally it is a republic, and they would have to alter their whole imperial policy, which in no short time would start to collapse if they started proclaiming purely Nazi slogans. That is something on which an empire cannot maintain itself. Not for long, at any rate.

That is why I think that to be able to analyze the situation, to see the trend, and to understand the prognosis, what it can lead to, what we can expect, we must understand that a change of policy or hesitation in connection with anti-Semitism is in fact immensely significant for the Soviet regime. It is not a minor matter which we can overcome or overlook; rather it is what determines the fate of two to three million Jews in the coming decade, and what is itself determined partly by the whole of world politics.

I also think that one of the factors in this struggle is, of course, international public opinion. Perhaps it is not the most important factor, but it is one of the most important. Therefore, if international public opinion attaches immense importance to this mad anti-Semitic campaign being conducted in the Soviet Union, and it becomes obvious that such an ideology is unacceptable on the international market, and that a real Soviet government cannot sell it, that will mean that we have bolstered the moderate wing (I call it practical because it is anti-Semitic as before) against the extreme. It also means that the exremists will go on to aggravate things even more as far as this question is concerned.

I said that Skurlatov, Emel'ianov, and others are dissidents who have suffered, who are not in the best positions, and who do not so much enjoy protection from above as much as they can suffer for their activities. That was exactly the case with Kichko. If you remember, Kichko published a terrible anti-Semitic book, and some petty repressive measures were subsequently taken against him. These repressive measures were slight, not because the Soviet regime or its leaders like him and do not want to apply more severe measures. I think that in the Soviet Union the cruelty of the situation is such that they would not even feel sorry about twisting his head off; but the fact is that his protectors are still sufficiently powerful, and it is simply impossible to deal with him.

I think that if we do not see the real trend within the party behind this anti-Semitic propaganda, we will not be able to understand occurrences there and the significance of anti-Semitic questions. I in no way believe that anti-Semitic propaganda has a purely ideological significance; I am sure that it is a weapon in the political struggle within the country. Not in the political struggle with Israel, insofar as Israel is a problem of foreign policy for Russia, and they already have the appropriate means of dealing with this. I am sure that they derive from purely rational reasons, and it is a weapon in an internal political struggle being waged between opposing forces within the Central Committee.

The Jewish Problem in Samizdat and the Emigration Press

E. SOTNIKOVA

THE TOPIC OF this lecture is the Jewish question in the opposition Russian press in Russia and abroad, i.e., in Samizdat and Tamizdat.

It must be said straightaway that this question cannot be resolved as simply as it was in the lectures which examined the official Soviet press, which is sufficiently well known for its anti-Semitic publications. We do not have to talk about the opposite, about philo-Semitic publications, in current official Soviet journalism.

A completely different picture can be observed in the statements of the Russian opposition. This picture is rather complicated and diverse.

The Jewish question was traditionally a problem of the day for all trends in the Russian opposition. This tradition took shape a long time ago, and it is possible to find some timely, pressing reasons for it for every moment in time. I suggest that the reasons for such a morbid attention to the Jewish problem on the part of the Russian intelligentsia, and of the opposition at all times in Russian history, bear more of an existential character. Insofar as these traditions have been preserved to this day, it would be interesting to observe how they are reflected in today's opposition press.

I will basically limit myself to the material that has been published in Samizdat, since the Samizdat was less accessible in Russia, and in the short time I have been in Israel, I have not yet managed to become sufficiently acquainted with the material of the emigré Russian press.

So, on the whole, my lecture will cover material published in unofficial Samizdat magazines in Russia.

Traditionally, the Russian intelligentsia's particularly tense, morbid attitude toward the Jewish question has been composed of two directly opposed solutions to this problem.

On one hand, anti-Semitism, from the zoological to the ideological, in its most varied manifestations, has changed rather little (if we examine it in retrospect). The basic structures, the basic ideological constructs have remained as they were. And on the other hand, there is the constant—I would say, chronic—feeling of guilt on the part of the Russian intelligentsia toward the Jews. I think not only that the philo-Semitic traditions in Russia have mystical roots, as defined by Professor Voronel, but that they are, of course, bound up with ethical problems which have always been very important for the Russian intelligentsia. The mental moral discomfort that anti-Semitism aroused in the milieu of the Russian intelligentsia could not leave it indifferent. Today the situation has remained practically unchanged, and these two positions can be quite clearly observed in all the material I have read in Samizdat.

The anti-Semitic traditions in Russia have very strong religious roots. It would, therefore, be interesting to observe how they are preserved in the contemporary Russian spiritual and ideological situation. This is interesting not only in order to clarify opinions but also for another reason. It is common knowledge that very few attempts to elaborate positive programs for the reformation of Russia are connected with her religious renaissance. One can talk as much as one wants about the utopianism of such programs; nonethless, they exist and have a definite influence on public opinion. Of course it is possible to proceed from the assumption that the Soviet regime is so solid and strong that these questions are not urgent, they are unreal, utopian, etc.

Nevertheless, we must examine some positive programs. The Russian opposition has such programs. As a rule, what they amount to basically is the religious renaissance of Russia. If that is to happen soon, we too need some prognoses for the future. It is important to ascertain what might await Russia and the Jews who live there in the light of these proposed transformations.

The religious Russian opposition is heterogeneous. It can be very tentatively divided into two branches—the extremist and the liberal. It must be noted that the voices of both these groups are presently resounding loudly both inside Russia and in the West. Practically all the publicists, philosophers, scientists, and writers who are disposed toward the opposition—all these who acknowledge that they are in one way or another opposed to the Soviet regime and Soviet ideology—seek not only a solution to the Jewish question, but also try to formulate and expose the basic roots of the global conflict with the Jews. And although the standard Christian formula, which defines the roots of this conflict as the Jews' guilt for the crucifixion of Christ, has now practically disappeared not only from the discourse of the liberals, but even from that of the extremists and the anti-Semites, nonetheless, the stumbling-block remains, as before, the religious and theological problems.

However, and not by chance, out of the whole spectrum the question of the Jewish nation being the chosen people is regarded as one of the most important questions in Russia at the present time. It is discussed at various levels, both by anti-Semites and by intelligentsia circles who are disposed to being pro-Jewish. The great attention focused on just this question is quite natural for Russia, where ideas about the special mission of the Russian God-bearing nation and its special place in Christian civilization have always been very popular. In the light of these ideas, Russian-Christian *Pochvenniki* (contemporary neo-Slavophiles) examine the problem of being God's elect. Samizdat (and particularly Jewish Samizdat) contains very interesting material on these questions.

Many people in Russia and the West know the name of the author of "Notes from the Red House" (*Zapiski iz krasnogo doma*), Gennadi' Shimanov. He sides with the most extreme opposition wing of the Orthodox Church in Russia. G. Shimanov offered an interview to the magazine *Jews in the USSR*.[1] In this interview he throws light on many of the problems of the Russian-Jewish conflict. He proclaims openly that he is an anti-Semite, tries to find a logical basis for anti-Semitism's right to exist, and dwells in great detail on the question of being the chosen people, which concerns him very sharply and morbidly.

This is what he writes:

It seems to me, however, that the Jews' being chosen by God was not revoked by God, but wasted away from within as a result of their rejection of Christ. I will add to this that the very concept of being chosen by God in the Christian period of history must become different, must become complicated by the fact that many nations were attracted to Christ. So that to claim some exclusive selection by God in the ancient Jewish spirit is hardly possible for any other nation.

Later he adds:

It does not concern the nations of the earth that Divine Providence denied the Jews that true faith and their homeland, undoubtedly not without wise intent, so that the Jews should not introduce into Christianity their ingrown haughtiness with regard to being chosen by God. . . . God denied the Jews the true faith and their homeland not only in order to humble them but also so that the nations of the earth might share both the one and the other with the Jews in a brotherly fashion. . . . 'leave your home empty': this was said so that the truth should no longer come into the world through the Jews, but so that through the world, that is, through the other nations, the truth should enter into the Jews.

At other points in his interview Shimanov specifies who are the other nations through whom the truth is to come into the world; it is first and foremost the Russian nation. Similar concepts of being God-chosen are very actively engaged in by contemporary Russian Orthodox anti-Semites. However, as I have already said, in the statements of the Russian opposition we do not meet the uniform anti-Semitism that we meet in the official Soviet ideology. In Samizdat material we see not only various approaches to the solution of the Jewish question, but simply mutually exclusive points of view. And if we feel it is important to ascertain the basic points in the ideology of contemporary anti-Semites, then it is no less important to examine the directly contrary ideas of the Russian opposition. The same problems of mutual relations with the Jews, the Jewish nation being chosen by God, and the reasons for anti-Semitism are touched upon in an interview with the magazine *Jews in the USSR* by one of the most famous of the Orthodox publicists working in Russia, Evgenii Barabanov (a participant in the collection *From Under the Rubble,* "Self-consciousness," the author of articles published in the magazines *Kontinent* and *Vestnik R. Kh. D*).[2] He formulates a totally different position in the solution of the Russo-Jewish and Christian-Jewish conflict.

Anti-Semitism is the greatest disgrace in the history of Christianity. It is . . . not only contempt for one's fellow man as a bearer of God's image— it is an indication of weakness and spiritual mediocrity, a symbol of religio-moral degeneration. Anti-Semitism always signifies de-Christianization and dehumanization, a return to paganism and base instincts. All the myths, about the world Jewish conspiracy, the "Elders of Zion" and "Jew-Masons" are engendered by an extremely low level of consciousness and culture. And these myths are humiliating not for those against whom they are directed but for those who convey them. Usually the aggravation of the "Jewish question" is an alarming symptom of a sickness of the national-state consciousness, a sickness of the nation itself. . . . I want to emphasize that this is not so much a question of the Jews, as a question of that nation and state in which it arises. The search for a secret enemy, the thirst for revenge, the aggravation of xenophobia are most often determined by an inferiority complex on their part, depression, a lack of freedom, spiritual decline.

E. Barabanov tries to find the roots of the religious conflict with the Jews, in order to overcome this conflict, in order to atone for the historical guilt of Christianity before the Jews.

To acknowledge, and hence also to overcome, one's historical sins will create the conditions for a real dialogue. Such a dialogue is first and foremost necessary for the Christians themselves, for it can lead to a new deepening of faith, which will acquire a new meaningfulness. In this connection, the initiative taken by the Catholics after Vatican Council II deserves particular attention. Unfortunately, the Orthodox Christians have so far done almost nothing in this direction.

There is no transgression of the dogmas of either Judaism or Christianity in this aspiration for dialogue. E. Barabanov states purely humanitarian positions; he is suggesting a dialogue on an ethical moral level rather than a theological one.

As for the decisions of the Second Vatican Council, they were very tumultuously discussed both in Orthodox circles in Russia and Catholic ones in the West. Would it be possible to find a way to overcome anti-Semitism through changes in the canonical religious texts of the Orthodox Church? This is a timely question in Russia, and has given rise to controversy both in the Samizdat press in the Soviet Union and in the Russian emigré press. The periodical *Jews in the USSR* published an interview with Father A. Men', author of important theological works and well known both in the West and in Russia as a leading representative of the liberal opposition Christian wing.[3]

Father Aleksander Men' was asked: "What is your position regarding the worship of the Russian Orthodox saints Gabriel and Eustratius, allegedly martyred by the Jews?" His reply was: "No official decision of the Orthodox Church has ever come out in support of the ritual slander of Jewry. I am confident that these saints will be decanonized. The decanonization process is known to the Russian Orthodox Church."

Logically speaking, there is a certain contradiction in Father Aleksander's reply. If no official decision of the Orthodox Church had ever supported ritual slanders, there would not be any need for decanonization. But we are now interested in something else. By fully supporting the initiative of the Second Vatican Council, Father Aleksander immediately provoked very strong reaction and sharp criticism. *Vestnik R. Kh. D.* (issue no. 120, 1977) published a rather brief but categorical rebuttal by Igor Shafarevich, a noted figure of the modern democratic movement in Russia, a well-known mathematician, and one of the major contributors to the collection *From Under the Rubble*. Shafarevich's reaction to Father A. Men's interview follows: "Coming from an Orthodox clergyman, this statement is painfully disappointing. Much of it is surprising; for instance, the facile and critical attitude to Christian saints, the suggestion that the saints be decanonized, that texts of divine service be altered 'when the time comes for them to be revised.' "

In the same interview given to the periodical *Jews in the USSR*, Father Aleksander Men' clarified one more question concerning a very important aspect of the interrelationships between the Russian opposition and Jewry: the Russian opposition's attachment to the land *(pochvenni-chestvo)*, as seen in periodicals like *Veche* (the name of a popular assembly in old Russia), *Zemlia* ("The Soil"), and *Moskovskii Sbornik* (the "Moscow Miscellany"), whose chauvinistic platform is fairly well known. Father Men' was asked: "What do you have to say about the resurrection of Russian chauvinism in unofficial Orthodox circles—in the periodicals *Veche, Moskovskii Sbornik, Zemlia?*" He answered: "All chauvinism has always been abhorrent to me, whether Russian, Jewish, or Chinese. For a Christian, it is, in general, disgraceful. As for the anti-Semitism of those Orthodox Russians calling themselves *pochvenniki* ('the ones attached to the soil'), this is an old tune. People never liked to talk about their own guilt, preferring to look for scapegoats, and there is no ground for this in Orthodox Christianity." This statement of Father A. Men' also irritated I. Shafarevich, who added: "Men' not only agrees with the questioner as regards chauvinism, he even adds his own charges of anti-Semitism. What forms do chauvinism and anti-Semitism take in these periodicals? Could it be that such views have been openly expressed by their editors? As far as I know, they have not."

Here again, it is not that important that Shafarevich misrepresents the openly chauvinistic views of the writers and editors of these periodicals. Shafarevich accuses Father Aleksander Men' of entering into unfair polemics; he has the right to state his views openly in the periodical *Jews in the USSR*, whereas V. Osipov, in his capacity as editor of the periodical *Veche*, is sentenced to eight years in camp. In this case, I. Shafarevich uses definitely "unbecoming polemical tactics." One could think that all the Russian nationalistic periodicals are being persecuted by the KGB, while *Jews in the USSR* has already been in existence for six years without any of its editors being sent to prison. The truth is that they have all been persecuted by the authorities and the Moscow D.A.'s office has for years been conducting an open criminal case against them. Could it be that the Soviet authorities view the Russian opposition more seriously than we usually do, and see it as a real ideological rival, a real internal enemy, while the Jewish movement has an outward direction? If so, all the more reason to present all the ideological nuances of this opposition.

It is not by chance that *Jews in the USSR* has opened its columns not only to Christian-liberals but even to those who are openly anti-Semitic. Aside from the purely ethical aspect,[4] there is also a practical side to it: the opposition wing in Russia exists and should express its opinions, and not just for the sake of self-expression. It is hard now to surmise what direction reformation in Russia will take. For the Jews, it is not a matter for indifference. The question is, whose voice will be heard there—the anti-Semites, the *pochvenniki*, Shimanov and Shafarevich, or the voices of such opposition figures as Men', Sakharov and Barabanov?

It is important that this be understood by the Jews who now live in Russia and will apparently stay there in the foreseeable future. It is also essential for those members of the Jewish intelligentsia who are straddling the fence between the democratic and the Jewish movements. Just yesterday one of the reports pondered whether Jews should participate in the democratic movement or have any contact at all with the democrats.

One can, of course, discuss whether this is good or bad, useful or detrimental. Evaluations are possible, but the inescapable fact is that Jews are still living in Russia, and not all are ready to leave. As long as the situation remains unchanged, the Jewish intelligentsia cannot ignore general Russian problems. They concern the Jews anyway, to say nothing of the fact that the Jewish movement for emigration is most tightly intertwined with the democratic movement. The views of the liberal Russian opposition wing are therefore of great significance for the Jewish movement. By the same token, the problems related to Jewish emigration concern the Russian opposition. It would seem that Russia has problems of greater importance than whether, or what kind of, Jews emigrate to Israel. Nevertheless, each figure of the opposition sees it as his duty to take a stand on this problem. It would be interesting to study which opposition opinions intersect with Zionist ideology and which with official Soviet ideology. For example, G. Shimanov in his interview says about the emigration of Jews to Israel:

> I don't think it would be worthwhile to talk about those who leave for the sake of better material well-being. . . . I am referring in particular to the unselfish Jews; if they are not disoriented, they are in every respect affected by the musty atmosphere now pervading the Jewish problem. I can't welcome their departure, for they haven't yet found their place here, in the joint Russian-Jewish movement, and they are even less likely to find a place in the international movement. I have mixed feelings about those who leave in confusion. I hope that their departure and a better acquaintance with Israel and the West will help them to get rid of many illusions and to love Russia from afar. I would welcome their return to Russia for really constructive activity.

This is what Shimanov, a dissident, writes. Let us now see what a titled Soviet personality, Academician Gafurov, director of the Institute of Oriental Studies, president of the permanent commission of the USSR Academy of Sciences for coordinating research on the critical examination and debunking of the history, ideology, and practices of Zionism, had to say about the departure of Jews, during a meeting of the Commission for Combating Zionism: "I would let the mercenary-minded fellows go. That would clean up the air in our country. We have little use for free artists and writers. Let them go, but it's a pity that specialists sometimes go."[5]

There you are: on the one hand, an official anti-Semite says it's a pity to let experts go; on the other, an oppositional anti-Semite would like to see Jews returning for constructive activity in Russia. Whether official or not, anti-Semites agree on one problem: they still need some Jews.

Another opinion is that expressed by one of the well-known opposition publicists, whose pen name is M. Skuratov. In his articles, he adopts a clearly anti-Semitic attitude. Writing about Jewish emigration he comments: "Most Russian nationalists welcome the emigration of Jews to Israel. Only Jews who proudly declare that they are Jewish and consider Israel as their homeland deserve respect, whereas Jews masquerading as Russians cannot expect anything but contempt and suspicion."[6] This is in complete agreement with Zionist ideology. After all, consistent anti-Semitism is not an instinctual syndrome, but an ideological system. As such, it aspires to self-contained forms and final solutions. Consistent anti-Semitism offers a final solution to the Jewish question.

But there is also another, I would say nonideological, ethical, and humanitarian attitude toward the Jewish question. One more quotation from E. Barabanov's interview:

Q.: What do you think of the emigration of Jews to Israel?
A.: I am definitely against the ideology of both emigrating and staying. The problem of emigration is a purely personal one and I couldn't solve it for anyone. Looking upon fully independent adults as though they were helpless youngsters waiting for our omniscient wisdom appears to me both ridiculous and tactless. As to those for whom the problem of emigration has been raised to the level of personal responsibility for the fate of human rights in our world, I have the greatest respect for them and bow my head before their manly struggle. I am also grateful to Israel, which helped in the departure not only of Jews but also of many Russians. It's sad, however, that not all of them deemed it necessary to thank the Jews who helped them out.

A glance at the platforms of the various Russian oppositional trends reveals an extremely variegated ideological picture. Although some recent attempts in Russia at finding an alternative to the Soviet regime may appear utopian, we must have a clear picture of what Russia can expect if any such platform proves viable (and that applies to the Jews as well, who may still be around for quite a while). We must clearly understand the ideological background of today's Jewish movement, without forgetting that there are forces in Russia that support it and voices that cannot be silenced, vociferous as the choir of Russian anti-Semitism may be.

Notes

1. *Evreiskii Samizdat*, no. 13 (reprint of the journal *Evrei v SSSR*, no. 2), *Sion*, no. 21 (1977).

2. The interview with E. Barabanov is published in the magazine *Evrei v SSSR*, no. 14, and in the magazine *Sion*, no. 20 (1977).

3. Interview with Father Men' in *Evreiskii Samizdat*, no. 12 (reprint of *Evrei v SSSR*, no. 11).

4. They are, indeed, being sentenced to terms in prison and camp, whereas we are only being dragged for questioning and having our places searched. No. 17 of *Jews in the USSR* has just been published, published by the Centre for Research and Documentation of East-European Jewry at the Hebrew University, and in which is certainly a record for Samizdat.

5. E. Sol' mar, "Otchet o zasedanii" [Report of a meeting] *Sion*, no. 21 (reprinted from *Evrei v SSSR*, no. 14).

6. M. Skuratov, "Russkii natsionalizm i sionizm," *Journal* 22, no. 7 (1978) (reprinted from *Evrei v SSSR*, no. 14).

The Attitude Toward Jews in the USSR

L. DIMERSKI-TSIGELMAN

To UNDERSTAND MODERN Russian anti-Semitism, I think one should view it in the general ideological context which took shape in Soviet society during the 1960s and 1970s. I fully agree with Professor Voronel and Dr. Nudelman that anti-Semitism is part and parcel of the ruling policy and ideology, and that the intensity and direction of the next anti-Semitic campaign depends largely on the struggle for power among the ruling groups. This must be taken into account when assessing the position of the Jews.

But in order to understand the overall situation it is also important to comprehend the attitude of other, nongovernmental circles toward the Jewish problem, and the reactions of the Jews themselves to a change in their living conditions. You won't easily find the answers to these questions in the official Soviet literature. During the 1960s, however, Samizdat first became a significant phenomenon in Russia's spiritual and political life; it reflects the views and attitudes of people and groups that are, to a greater or lesser extent, in opposition to the regime.

The founders of Samizdat and most of its readers were the intelligentsia and students of the country's capitals and large cities. These groups were the social and professional ambient of a large section of Soviet Jewry. This is readily understood if one takes into account the fact that 52 percent of the gainfully employed Jewish population is composed of specialists with college or secondary vocational training, 4.8 percent are students, and more than 70 percent dwell in large cities.

The attitudes of these groups—intelligentsia, students, etc.—was particularly important for those Jews who had already moved in the direction of assimilation, and for whom the break with Russia was extremely painful. I was one of them, and I know that one had to be convinced of the

81

unavoidability of emigration before deciding to depart. This is not a unique occurrence, nor is it just a detail of my own biography. For many, emigration required an evaluation of the general prospects of Jews in Russia. This evaluation had to be based not only on government policy but also on society's ability to oppose it.

The late 1950s and the 1960s still gave rise to expectations of liberalization. But the structure of the opposition in the 1970s increasingly repudiated such hopes, since new forces tended to support the government's chauvinistic drift. Even a superficial comparative examination of the official and Samizdat literature of the early 1960s and 1970s suggests that a change had taken place in their interrelationship. The relaxation of censorship which took place during the period of liberalization created wider possibilities for having things published officially in the mid-1950s. It also led to the publication of a number of exposés which revealed, among other things, occasional truthful information about Jews' participation in World War II and about anti-Semitism.

As the pressure of censorship increased, such works were gradually relegated to the pages of peripheral publications, finally to end up completely in the Samizdat, then the emigré press. But although the Samizdat initially published mainly exposés and democratic opposition works which definitely rejected the ideology of totalitarianism, the 1970s brought a change of course to a tone more in keeping with that ideology. The total contraposition of government-sanctioned and oppositional ideology, of official press and some publications of the underground press, became increasingly shaky.

The model of a spectrum of interrelated ideologies seems to me more realistic.[1] I had the unexpected opportunity to discuss this problem with A. Amalrik.[1a] Before my departure in June 1976 he visited Kiev to complete his farewell tour of the Soviet Union. From his point of view, the interdependence of ideologies is more clearly visualized by the "wheel" model, which can be found in the article "Ideologies in Soviet Society."[2] The prevailing ideology is represented by two positions: neo-Stalinist Marxism (the ideology of seizing and retaining power) and neo-Stalinist nationalism (the same, but based on Russian great-power nationalism). The idea of chauvinism unites this trend with neo-Slavophilism, which, in contrast to the official nationalistic ideology, does display humanistic features ("nationalism with a human face"). The most prominent representative of this trend is A. I. Solzhenitsyn; it can rely on the support of the urban and rural intelligentsia and semi-intelligentsia. The idea of messianism unites this trend with the social-religious ideology of populist origin. It strikes a deep chord in the heart of the intelligentsia, which, having become disillusioned with Marxism, is inclined toward populism. Its right wing is represented by the All-Russian Social-Christian Union for the Liberation of the People (VSKhSON according to its Russian initials), headed by I. Ogurtsov. According to Amalrik, the left wing of this ideology is purely ethical, and the idea of humanism unites it with the "liberal-democratic ideology." This ideology, developed under the influence of Western liberalism, favors a gradual transformation of the Soviet system into a pluralistic democratic society of Western character. The social base of this ideology is formed by part of the intelligentsia—all those whose education and energy are sufficient for achieving success in a free society. The most prominent representative of this ideology is A. D. Sakharov.

The idea of law and order links the democratic ideology with liberal Marxism ("socialism with a human face"). The social base of this ideology is a large section of the Marxist-bred intelligentsia, as well as part of the party functionaries and managers. This ideology is presented by Roy and Zhores Medvedev and Pyotr Grigorenko.

Liberal Marxism is a faith rather than a truth and is related to neo-Stalinist Marxism through the idea of building socialism. In this way, A. Amalrik closes his "wheel of ideologies."

His model can be a useful analytic tool, since it helps to present the attitude to the Jewish problem and Jewish ideology itself not as separate, uncoordinated reactions, but in the interrelationship that creates the overall climate for Jewish existence in the Russian empire of today. One essential correction is needed in the diagram: one must include in it the Jewish ideology and those of the anti-imperial national movements. By means of the "wheel" model, the anti-imperial ideologies can be presented as related to the ethical wing of the social-religious ideology through the Christian-democratic ideas they have in common. The idea of national and cultural autonomy unites the Jewish ideology with the anti-imperial national movements, and the ideas of humanism and law and order unite it with the liberal-democratic ideology.

But these are just connections which bring the Jewish ideology into the overall "wheel," whose purpose is to explain the forms of transition from one ideology to another. These are links of unification and interalliance. But we are interested in the whole complex of attitudes to the Jewish problem, not just in the ideologies that are close to or distant from it around the "wheel," particularly in those attitudes that are becoming increasingly significant and attracting increasing numbers of adherents in contemporary Soviet society.

It would be difficult to reject Amalrik's contention that, under present circumstances, the chances of success are better for those who are guided by totalitarian ideologies rather than by democratic ones, by half-baked Oriental rather than alien Western ones, and by purely political rather than politico-ethical ideologies. It is clear to us that only one ideology at present fulfills all three conditions: the neo-Stalinist Russian-imperial nationalism. But that ideology displays, particularly in its chauvinistic anti-Semitic realm, only the tip of the iceberg. Documents such as "Ivan Samolvin's Letter to Solzhenitsyn" (1971) and "A Russian's Notes Sent to the Periodical *Veche*" (1973), circulated through Samizdat channels, can give one an idea of the submerged, invisible part of the iceberg.

M. Agurskii, who published these documents in *Novyi Zhurnal* (no. 118, 1975), has every reason to consider their appearance as a sympton of the growing danger of neo-Nazism in the USSR. Some may contend that these are just two dull papers attesting to the paranoid disposition of their authors. But their position is too close to the officially acknowledged, widely circulated productions of Ivanov, Begun, Zhukov, and others, to be dismissed. On the other hand, their ideas are in keeping with neo-Slavophilism, which enjoys increasing popularity both in the country and among emigrants.

Just like the official publications that continue the tradition of the anti-Semitic classics, Samolvin's uncensored letter is based on the myth of the chosen people laying claim to world domination. Reproaching Solzhenitsyn for the historically dubious image of the more or less loyal Il'ia Isaakovich (in the novel *August 1914*), Samolvin quotes directly from the *Protocols of the Elders of Zion*. By repeating the Soviet zionologists' odious accusations that Herzl allegedly used the creation of a national homeland as a cover for his real purpose—rallying the Jews around the flag in the struggle for world domination—Samolvin tries to prove that Western nations have long been suffocating in the clutches of Jewish domination.

Everything in the West belongs to the wealthy Jews: (a) political power. . . . The members of all the Western governments are either Jews or freemasons. . . . During the last few centuries, there was no political crime that the Jews didn't have a hand in; (b) natural resources, gold, banks, factories, land. Everything referred to as capitalism in our political education system. . . . Part of the money extorted is spent on the support of the parasitic State of Israel, but most of it on the eradication of non-Jewish traditions, ways of life and thought, and spirit in order once and for all to disarm the other nations and bring the hour of Jewish domination nearer; (c) the press, radio, and television. Haven't you ever thought, Mr. Solzhenitsyn, why are they so anxious to print your works? Why doesn't anything but praise of the Jews ever reach the printing presses? Why are the traces of the murders being covered up?"

The blasphemous equation of Zionism and fascism is also migrating from the pages of the official press to the uncensored leaflets. Arguing with Solzhenitsyn, the author writes:

. . . before Hitler's accession to power, 80 percent of German industry was in Jewish hands. . . . And the Zionists were the ones who taught Hitler cruelty. A perusal of his book *Mein Kampf* will reveal the passion with which Hitler quoted from the *Protocols of the Elders of Zion* and how zealously he implemented all the wicked formulas contained in this program of the Jews for the seizure of gold and power, for the future control of the subjugated nations, etc. He only replaced the Jews with the Germans.[3]

The sacred figure of 80 percent also appears in the unsigned letters to the periodical *Veche*.

The international Jewish business establishment has concentrated in its hand 80 percent of the capital of the entire non-Communist world. This is more dreadful than the fascist plague. If they win, it will be the death of all, first of the Russians, whom they nicknamed "zoological anti-Semites," and all of whom they wanted to destroy physically. . . . We must therefore unite now in the fight against Zionism: to unmask and strike at all those who are with them to support and encourage all those who are against them. The attitude to Zionism is the touchstone that separates the patriot from the traitor. There is no in-between. Whoever is not with us is against us. Whoever is not against Zionism in all its manifestations is against the Russians, against the Slavophiles, against everything that is honest on earth.[4]

Commenting on the anonymous letter, M. Agurskii considers it a reaction to the unsuccessful attempt of neo-Nazi circles close to the government to turn *Veche* into their unofficial organ. Although this attempt may have failed, on the whole, the anti-Semitic tone of the periodical in many ways coincided with the government position, supported both by laymen and Orthodox believers, although many thought that the Christian faith would be the strongest bulwark against neo-Nazism, M. Agurskii, for instance, wrote that the position of Christian nationalists, such as V. Osipov, L. Borodin, and Archdeacon Varsonofii, would prevent racism. Here is an excerpt from an appeal to the archbishop and the members of the Great Council. Archdeacon Varsonofii (Khaibulin) was one of the three co-signers.

We cannot remain silent when the extraordinarily increased threat of the organized forces of widespread Zionism and satanism has become obvious to everybody. Silence in all cases as a pattern of behavior is not only ineffective but harmful, because it permits the vagueness to continue and sows distrust and suspicion in interrelationships. Taking advantage of it, the agents of Zionism and satanism cunningly create friction between church and government in order to weaken them both. . . . Through incitement and the spreading of pseudoscientific theories justifying immorality and misanthropy, they try to poison society, particularly the intelligentsia and you with ideas of anarchic liberalism and amoralism, to destroy the very foundations of morality, family, and government. . . . Many of these blasphemers and destroyers of our national, cultural, and spiritual values have now found shelter in the Zionist centers of the West, especially in the US. . . . where Satan's church is operating. . . . By accomplishing our sacred mission of saving mankind from sin and its consequences, the church is a moral force and a pillar of the state in its noble struggle against the forces of destruction and chaos. . . . One of the major tasks of our time is the search for practical ways of bringing church and government closer to each other on the basis of their mutual interests, patriotic duty, and complete noninterference in the internal life of the church.[5]

This appeal indicates that there were and are no arrests, no gatherings for prayer were broken up, no churches were plundered and destroyed, no believer was prosecuted judicially or persecuted extrajudicially. There were just "frictions" provoked by the agents of Zionism and satanism. But if it supports a united front against them, the church can become "a pillar of the state in its noble struggle against the forces of destruction and chaos," obtaining in return "noninterference in its internal life." We support the "general line" and you grant us "noninterference"—the platform for collaboration has been found.

The Russian Christian movement's attitude toward Jews is, of course, not confined to the positions of the archdeacon and his partners. Much will remain unclear in the process of the spiritual reformation of intellectuals— whether Russians, or Jews—if we do not take into account the influence exerted by the Russian religious philosophers N. Berdiaev, V. Solov'ev, S. Bulgakov, and O. Florenskii, whose writings are being read again, and if we don't see how attractive the thought of the inner unity of Judaism and Christianity and possible Russian-Jewish cooperation on the level of an overall spiritual-religious renaissance has become. But this problem is explained in greater detail by E. Sotnikova. I would like to show the strong rebuke against this trend from the more or less moderate and soberly thinking Russian nationalists. I think that the position of M. Skuratov, one of the principal contributors to *Veche*, is sufficiently indicative in that respect. In an interview he gave to the periodical *Jews in the USSR* he declares openly: "The Jews who have not yet lost their hopes of assimilating, but have switched from Marxism-Leninism and proletarian internationalism to the Orthodox church, are entertaining ridiculous illusions. For one can very frequently notice that Orthodox convictions get along just fine with anti-Semitism, even in its most extreme forms." The kinship of Christianity and Judaism, he says, is by no means a basis for their finding a common language, but rather the other way round. Both religions were born of Jewish thoughts, which strives to "bring the entire universe to some 'common denominator.'" These are the roots of the militant intolerance, typical of any ideology of Jewish origin. Hence the persecution and eradication of any dissident thought, the religious wars and the big purges, the Inquisitions and the Gulags, the fight of Christians against Jews, Marxists against Christians, etc."[6] According to Skuratov, this tendency to totality can explain why the Jews have "extended their hate for a few pogromists to the Russian people as a whole and, after seizing the reins of power, organized the deliberate and well-planned extermination first of the Russian intelligentsia, then of the Russian peasantry, i.e., of the spiritual flower of the nation and its main physical base. That was a policy of genocide in its purest form. After all that happened during the first decades, one shouldn't be surprised at the general prevalence of anti-Semitism in our days." Skuratov's conclusion: a physical separation in such cases is the first and indispensable step to take. "Most Russian nationalists therefore welcome the emigration of Jews to Israel. Only Jews who proudly declare that they are Jewish and consider Israel as their homeland deserve respect, whereas Jews masquerading as Russians cannot expect anything but contempt and suspicion."

Skuratov criticizes the government's Middle East policy for spending colossal sums on hopeless aid to the Arabs, instead of supporting Israel and encouraging Jewish emigration. This and the unwillingness of many Jews to leave the Soviet Union delays the final solution of the Jewish problem through emigration, he believes. They could even be pushed a little bit, but that would appear inappropriate in our enlightened country, thinks Skuratov. He suggests that the Jewish community in the USSR be offered the status of a Union republic with its own government, academy of sciences, and educational system. This would achieve a relaxation of the tensions between nationalities. Such a republic is, of course, a naive utopia, if only because "tension" regarding the Jews is a cornerstone of government policy.

But what is important is not the utopianism of Skuratov's suggestions.

He is a frank and intelligent spokesman for the increasingly popular opinions shared by intellectuals and students in Moscow and Leningrad. The same opinions are held by a large number of Russian emigrés, including Jewish right-wingers. They are especially noticeable among those who, for ideological or professional reasons, continue to deal there in sovietology and Russia and keep offering Russia new recipes for its salvation and improvement. Typical in this respect is the reaction of the émigré press to the volume of collected papers *Democratic Alternatives* (published by Achberg in West Germany in 1976). The volume is a reply to Solzhenitsyn's "Letter to the Leaders" and to his article written with Shafarevich and published in the volume of collected papers *From Under the Rubble*. It discusses an autocratic version of Russian history, most clearly stated in A. Ianov's article "Halfway to Leont'ev (Solzhenitsyn's Paradox)." In this and other publications Ianov, a scholarly historian and skillful writer, tries to demonstrate a cyclic pattern in Russian history and prove that each cycle recreates autocracy in some form or other.[7] In his opinion, the danger of a new autocracy, fraught with new Gulags, lies in the strengthening of the nationalistic fraction in the party leadership. This fraction pretends to be confronting the opposition nationalistic forces and their prophet Solzhenitsyn, whereas in fact it is their supreme ally. The road covered by Slavophilism from Ivan Aksakov to the League of the Russian People could serve as a warning signal for the spiritual-nationalistic opposition.

The publication of the collection revived the discussion about the nature of bolshevism: Is it a purely Russian phenomenon or an alien occurrence? Are communism's vices universal, or only typical of its Russian incarnation? The problem about the role of the Jews in the Soviet elite and the measure of their responsibility for the crimes perpetrated by the regime is solved accordingly.

The idea of the Russian origin of bolshevism met a friendly rebuff, although in 1937 N. A. Berdiaev had already written that the Bolsheviks had created a police state after the model of the old Russian state ("Sources and Meaning of Russian Communism"). V. Varshavskii, in his article "Bolshevism's Genealogy" (*Novyi zhurnal*, nos. 125 and 128), explains Berdiaev's position: "a national inferiority complex, the position of 'other'— either 'a desire at any cost to absolve Marxism of its responsibility for the Gulag Archipelago or going as far as turning into an anti-Russian racism the inveterate visceral hostility to any kind of Russia."[8] V. Varshavskii carefully avoids illusions that would give rise to discussions in the West about the Tartars' yoke, the cause and specifically Russian nature of communism. These misgivings are shared by E. Pirozhkova, professor of political science at Munich University.[9] While evaluating certain pessimistic prognoses concerning the fate of empires as a call for the dissolution of the Russian state, Pirozhkova suggests that V. Belotserkovskii, a contributor to the collection *Democratic Alternatives,* should turn to the Jewish people, specifically at Massada, where Israeli soldiers take the oath: "Massada will never fall again!"

The appeal to leave Russian history and take part in the history of one's own people becomes increasingly urgent. And behind those who take this viewpoint with a feeling of sympathy for Israel (the same Pirozhkova) loom Black Hundreds types like V. Orekhov, editor of the periodical *Chasovoi* ("The Sentinel"), an ideological counterpart of *Veche* abroad. V. Orekhov summons all Russian patriots to unite against "the ninth (highest) wave" carried by the third emigration. He is referring to "those Jews or half-Jews who fancy themselves oracles and speak in behalf of the 'democratic movement' which exists almost exclusively amid Jewish circles and which they have fostered with the aid of foreign capital. With exceptional assertiveness, these gentlemen hold key political positions in our ranks abroad. They can be found in broadcasting, the emigré press, and various organizations."[10]

What we have here is an attempt not only to bar Jews from the political centers of the emigration but also to discredit thereby the "partner" in the opposition (the democratic movement). Orekhov acts in accordance with a well-known formula, "Beat the Jews and the Communists," "Beat the Jews and the commissars," but restyles it this time into "Beat the Jews and the democrats." (The psychological infallibility of this formula is demonstrated by a joke: Try and expand the series by saying "Beat the Jews and the tractor-drivers." You will always be asked the question "Why the tractor drivers?" but never "Why the Jews?"). The Soviet authorities, on whom Orekhov wastes very little love, display the same desire to settle accounts with the democratic opposition by branding it Jewish. What else but a feeling of kinship could explain the fact that a recent issue of the periodical *Ogonek* spoke in openly sympathetic terms about the Russian émigrés who sometimes have to relinquish their patriotic positions in the struggle with the "dissidents"?

The deliverance of Holy Russia from Jewish dominance today unites the most dissimilar forces, from the Soviet government to the White émigrés abroad, turning former enemies into allies, and, if need be, into comrades-in-arms. On this basis the Russian emigration is now reassessing its values and is proclaiming that, in conjunction with *Veche* and the *VSKhSON*, national bolshevism is the force that will lead the country on the road to national and state progress. E. R. Sergeeva, in her article "The West's Failure to Understand Russia," formulates this thought more clearly then the others. She thinks that the West does not comprehend the potential of the Russian national movement and censures Ianov for his distorted picture of the right wing and atrocities the world could expect, were it to be victorious. Although national bolshevism (a military-industrial complex, in R. N. Redlich's definition) "is not free of dogmas connected to its present existence it has the potentialities of a Russian national state system. At least in the people involved in it."[11] Sergeeva is not mistaken. National bolshevism can count on the support of party and government officials of low and medium rank, of the military, and a significant number of executives in enterprises and institutions. Most of these officials are former peasants or sons of peasants and advocate an imperial policy of russification ("national-state development"), and try to solve problems connected with this policy through an intensification of anti-Semitism in the national republics. This policy is unreservedly supported by the leadership cadre of the native nationality groups. In the Ukraine, in Belorussia and Moldavia, the "half-baked imperial national-bolshevism" is strengthened by a rich historical tradition and strikes a deep chord in the "heart of the people."

But the opposition nationalistic circles (formed of intelligentsia and students), who are struggling against the imperial policy, seek an alliance with the Jews. They respect the Zionist aspirations of the Jews and their contribution to the struggle for freedom of national self-expression and for national culture. The need for mutual assistance between Jews and Ukrainians was stressed by the writers Antonenko-Davidovich and Ivan Dziuba in their addresses to the gathering on September 29, 1966, at Babi Yar. Less than seven years later the state security apparatus obtained from Dziuba a retraction and public self-criticism and let him spend the rest of his life a degraded and completely broken man. Most of his adherents are now imprisoned or banished; people like V. Chernovil and E. Svirstiuk will continue to support the prisoners of Zion and to advocate the Jews' right to emigrate freely.

To determine what the mutual relationships are within the triangle formed by Russian imperial policy, the anti-imperial movements, and the Jewish problem, it is interesting to examine the debate started in *Kontinent* by S. Rafalskii's article "Malady of the Century" on the national problem in the Soviet Union. According to Rafalskii the malady of the century is nationalism, which, in his words, is supported by false ideas of separatism and destroys the unity based on history, economy, and ethnography. Criticizing the anti-imperial tendencies of the Ukrainians and the centrifugal tendencies of the Poles, Rafalskii does not forget about the Jews either. He describes them as traitors who walk out on the only country which has offered them protection and higher education, good employment, and social positions.[12]

This was followed in *Kontinent* no. 13 by a reply from E. Oganesian. Analyzing the economic and social conditions in the Soviet Union, he demonstrates the inevitable emergence and growth of national movements. Oganesian is filled with indignation at Rafalskii's malicious attacks against the Jews who wish to build their own state. The experience of Israel, which was built up on a patch of land by "a handful of courageous patriots, inspires and instills hope into all the minority peoples." Using Zionism as a model, writes Oganesian, "my people called their own movement Araratism and made Herzl's *The Jewish State* their reference book."[13]

Oganesian sees the concern of a segment of Russian Jewry about supranational processes and problems as just a means of evading national difficulties, work, and responsibility. "In order to dedicate oneself to Israel's national problems, one would have to join the Israelis on the barricades. But in taking up general human problems we do not owe anything to anybody. As for Russia, some Jews are preoccupied by its problems because it is at the center of the political marketplace, and who is not concerned with it?"[14]

Vas. Mikhalchuk did not agree. He also sharply criticized Rafalskii's article "The Force of Our Days."[15] In his opinion, preventing the Jews from loving the land of their ancestors, the land where they were born, grew up, worked, and suffered, preventing them from thinking about the misfortunes of that land and analyzing its social situation, is not only undemocratic but even inhuman. As a Ukrainian, Mikhalchuk can only smile at Rafalskii's impotent hostility to the Ukraine and its people but cannot remain indifferent when scornful words are being said about his friends, when Jewish authors are being castigated for daring to condemn baseness, the oppression of people, and the persecution of nationalities that advocate the partition of the Soviet empire into independent national states.

For Mikhalchuk the Jews thus are "protesters," natural allies in the struggle against imperial claims.

We will not dwell now upon an assessment of the philo-Semitism of Ukrainian nationalism: it would lead us astray. Let us examine the liberal-democratic movement's attitude toward the Jewish problem, as revealed in their treatment of three issues of vital importance to Soviet Jewry: (1) free emigration, (2) renewal of national culture and national consciousness, (3) opposition to governmental anti-Semitism.

It is common knowledge that on all three issues the Jews have received the constant and fullest possible support of A. D. Sakharov, V. Chalidze, Iu. Orlov, A. Tverdokhlebov, V. Bukovskii, and many other members of the democratic and human rights movement. Every issue of *Khronika* ("Chronicle") includes material in defense of free emigration and in support of the prisoners of Zion. The struggle for the renewal of Jewish culture has been supported for several years now. A. D. Sakharov supported the December 1976 Moscow symposium on Jewish culture.

We have already seen that the democratic movement is sometimes equated with the Jewish movement. It would seem that the Jews were helping themselves. Indeed, there were many Jews among the active members of the democratic movement. The interesting problem is, however, not so much the proportions and interactions of people as the proportions and interactions of ideas. And on this level we find the differences in concrete goals that divide the two movements, and the community of initial principles that determine their profound consanguinity.

While the Jewish movement concentrates its efforts on defending the right of Jews to emigrate and to study their own language and culture, the democratic movement has a wider scope: respect for human rights, the right to civic and personal freedom. The mere stating of purposes shows that there is essentially one problem here: the first is the result of the other, and vice versa. This problem, the sovereignty of the individual, carries criticism of the system beyond the limits of political expediency and leads to the conclusion that the system is, in general, socially untenable. Indeed, it is a system which destroyed millions of human lives in its "historic" epochs, and in its comparatively stable periods totally corrupts personality by violating its rights and disregarding moral criteria. This is why the democratic opposition, by its nature rather an ethical protest movement than a political one, is nevertheless perceived as deadly hostile, and the authorities attempt to eradicate it completely, using accusations of "support of world Zionism."

To complete the survey, let us dwell briefly on liberal Marxism's attitudes toward the Jewish problem. Our brevity on this subject is due to the limited time at our disposal. Many old people, Jews included, retain a sentimental feeling for Marxism. "Liberal renewal" instills in them hope not only for the preservation of the former symbol of truth but also for the achievement of much-longed-for assimilation.

In protesting against patently anti-Semitic publications such as T. Kichko's *Judaism without Embellishment*, liberal Marxists, especially Roy Medvedev, defend the rights of the Jews. They consider equal rights to be most important and a guarantee of successful and organic assimilation. How strange it is to notice that M. Shimanov, a contributor to *Veche* and a leading author of the Christian underground press, also sees assimilation as a solution to the Jewish problem. He admits to being an anti-Semite.[16] The Jews are a permanent evil in Russian and world history. Their unification with Christianity, followed by their complete dissolution in it, is the only possible way of making them disappear bloodlessly. Liberal

Marxism believes that the best way would be social assimilation. The first is a religious utopia, the second is a social one, but the two solutions to the Jewish problem coincide. Though not through physical extermination, Jewry ceases to exist, in the first case in accordance with the laws of mankind's spiritual progress, in the second in accordance with the laws of its social, economic, and historical progress. Liberal Marxism criticizes the Soviet government's professed Marxism for its inconsistency in the pursuance of the Marxist-Leninist policy of assimilation.

The ideological circle is thus closed, and we can draw a number of conclusions. First that the area of social resistance to the Jews is expanding in the Soviet Union. The government's anti-Semitic policy is actively supported both by advocates of an intensified national-bolshevist direction and by the Russian nationalistic movement, whether Christian or secular. The former add nothing significant to the ideology of governmental anti-Semitism but only exacerbate it by scorning the mask of accepted terminology. But the nationalistic movement, in modifying the ideas of Slavophilism, proposes ideological plans that simply will not do for the creation of a united front. The combination of nationalism with moral Marxism, religious preaching, and Protestant pathos against the abuses of the authorities brings under its aegis the most diverse strata. The danger represented by the Jews—according to the nationalistic doctrine—turns these strata into natural allies of governmental anti-Semitism. This coalition is also joined by outside forces, the emigrés. In statistical terms, their number is insignificant, but increased propaganda contacts turns the emigrés' frame of mind into a factor influencing internal attitudes in the Soviet Union.

A second conclusion is that in spite of the official policy of opposing and defaming Jewish emigration, various circles, although for different reasons, do support their emigration. The Soviet petty bourgeois says: "Go away, go to your Israel—vacate your residences and your positions." Most of the Russian nationalists and many advocates of ethnic nationalism: "Only the Jews who consider themselves as Jewish and Israel as their homeland are worthy of respect." Some Judeo-Christians: "The time has come for the holy history of Israel to continue, and the Jew's place is in his spiritual homeland." Whether philo-Semitic or anti-Semitic, these attitudes in favor of emigration envelop the Jews in an atmosphere of expectation, sometimes tolerant and benevolent, most often intolerant and spiteful.

A third conclusion is that adherents of the liberal-democratic movement in the country and abroad unreservedly support complete freedom of choice, the right to live in the country or emigrate, the right to one's own language and culture. They also unreservedly condemn anti-Semitism, which they consider a base violation of human rights. Jewry's real and natural ally could therefore only be the democratic movement. It could, but this authentic antipode of the Soviet regime is subjected to the most ruthless persecution and is on the brink of complete annihilation. In terms of visible repression, it is in the same situation as the Russian national movement, whose representatives are also imprisoned or banished. But the ideas of the national movement are supported. Such periodicals as *Molodaia Gvardiia* ("The Young Guard") and *Oktiabr* are alive and gathering strength. Legal mouthpieces of the loyal anti-Semitic version of their ideas, such as I. Shevtsov, V. Chalmaev, P. Palievskii, V. Kozhinov, and A. Ivanov, prosper and flourish. As for the periodicals that dared "ad-lib" during the 1960s, they are now under the strictest control; the editorial board and the line of *Novyi Mir* have been changed completely. All we can do now is set our hopes on the self-sacrificing heroism of A. D. Sakharov's little group. Perhaps he has more adherents than we think.

An assessment of the situation of Soviet Jewry and a comparison of forces of social attraction and repulsion (sometimes rejection) suggests that (1) the forces of repulsion are already incomparably stronger, and their strength is increasing, and (2) their impulses originate not only from the "party, government, and people" but increasingly from intellectual circles.

How does the ideology of Soviet Jewry change along with the radical changes of their existence? It would be impossible to talk of a general ideology of Soviet Jewry, part of which show no inclination to leave the "prehistoric" homeland; others emigrate, and some go to Israel. It is difficult to talk even of the ideology of separate groups, because they are also highly heterogeneous. Two basic ideological trends can nevertheless be distinguished; they unite people who share each other's views and patterns of behavior in spite of their differences in personal attitude.

The first trend is connected with the revival of national consciousness in Zionism. The second embraces a wide range of assimilatory tendencies, which are turning into an ideology of national apostasy.

Sure enough, nothing new. We know all that, and it happens with astonishing regularity at every new turn of Jewish history. This regularity may be at least partly due to the fairly stable types of Jewish personality, molded by this very history.

The first type is the spiritually oriented personality, prone to asceticism and intellectual preoccupations if the social atmosphere is nonconformist in his fields of activity. His opposite is the consumer-oriented personality, prone to adaptive reactions. His pattern of behavior is dictated by the paramount importance ascribed to all forms of worldly comfort.

This is, of course, an idealization, and we can seldom find either one of these two types. More often than not they coexist in man as his potentialities; which one will eventually gain the upper hand depends on the strength of those potentialities and on which personal qualities are stimulated by the social environment.

We find that the conditions under which Soviet Jewry now lives (1) are destructive for its spiritual and intellectual forces, and (2) foster consumerism and adaptive patterns of behavior, conducive to the lowliest forms of national apostasy. This is borne out by the large number of those who drop out (they go to countries other than Israel) and by the growing participation of Jews in the present anti-Semitic campaign.

We are all witnessing how the Jewish movement in the Soviet Union, born in the late 1960s as an ideological, Zionist movement, turns increasingly into an emigration, a flight "from nowhere to nowhere." Understandably, in the choice between the USSR, America, and Israel, the leader in terms of standard of living and personal safety is America. The USSR comes second with its familiar native conditions, tenor of life, and physical safety. Those who choose Israel do so only out of lofty moral reasons, and not on the basis of pragmatic considerations. The strength of this motivation can be judged by the almost 100 percent rate of dropouts from the capitals and large cities of the Soviet Union. It is fascinating to observe how the attitude of Soviet Jews to dropouts is changing. In the beginning, when the reorientation had just started, those who made a "beeline" away from Israel felt somewhat like recreants: they either kept their plans a secret or did their best to justify them; but now those who go to Israel keep it quiet to avoid being regarded as fools. They are apt to hear admonitions like "Don't you know there's a war going on there? Didn't you hear about the inflation and the hard life? About corruption and religious intolerance?"

I do not intend to make appraisals. It is more important to understand what is going on, to understand that consumerism is a symptom and a consequence rather than a cause. And the cause is the urge to run, to escape one's Jewishness. In the average Odessan or Kievan (an employee in the service field or commerce, an engineer, etc.), reason and consequences are interwoven, resulting in a single complex of escapism and consumerism. The intellectual, however (usually a capital-city dweller), is given to idealistic justification of his behavior. Here, for instance, is the way Muscovite Iurii Glazov, a dissident historian, who in 1973 turned up in Boston and published a book titled *Narrow Gates: The Resurrection of the Russian Intelligentsia*, explains his choice: "I had to run away from Russia, where they wanted to kill me." Where to? "In Israel, I would have had to sit cross-legged and talk about the greatness of the Jewish people with my blood brothers, who scorned Mary's gentle son from Bethlehem. Abandon the Russian language, the culture that had become my own? Give up what belongs to me by right just because some people think that I have nothing to do with that culture. Start again learning a language which my distant forefathers spoke? No, there is not one nationalist bone in my body. I can't like some wild Moslem who despises all infidels. No, no, and no."[17]

What is characteristic of the statement of this undoubtedly gifted and spiritually inclined man? Two things:

1. He equates the Jewish national idea with a primitive-chauvinistic form of nationalism, while thinking that adherence to the Russian national idea would protect him from the narrow-mindedness and primitivism of nationalism.

2. He asserts his rights to the Russian culture, in defiance of the "opinion of some" that he has nothing to do with it.

Glazov's attitude is eloquent proof of the moral crisis that a significant number of Jewish intellectuals are now undergoing in their desperate attempts to remain "Russian." How else can one explain the blindness, not of an average man, but of a professional, a historian, who does not realize that the resurrection of the national idea has become a fact of contemporary history, that the distinctiveness and salutary diversity of national cultures are the only things today capable of resisting the overwhelming drive toward standardization of mass production and mass culture? Naturally, the resurrection of nationalism can also foster its primitive, chauvinistic, and egalitarian forms. But this is true of every nationalism, all the more of a nationalism reborn under a totalitarian regime. This is exactly what happened to Russian nationalism, whose cultural and spiritual elements are all being suppressed by government-supported chauvinism. Is it possible, without dropping the criteria of moral and professional judgment, to speak of Jewish nationalism as a chauvinism and thus make common cause with the forces that adopted the resolution with that interpretation of the United Nations?

Internationalists like Glazov, who still prefer to be not only citizens of the world but Russians as well, do not seem to notice that human and national dignity is indivisible, and that nationality, unfortunately, is not defined by the knowledge of the language, or belonging to the culture, or even the attachment to the country's nature and way of life. It is measured with a different yardstick: the sharing of historical destiny, which depends on the extent to which the given individual is involved in the history and destiny of his own people. Although for others, this measure of involvement is a given, for the Jews it is mainly a question of choice. But not an easy one, for no other people has had to prove throughout its history its right to exist. All the more reason for the moral man not to escape this choice and destiny in order to go over to the "camp of the strong and happy ones." The trouble is that Russian life shatters moral considerations, leaving only practical or abstract ideological criteria.

The practical criteria are becoming particularly important now that the Soviet society is turning into a special kind of consumer society, differing from its Western counterparts in its constantly growing shortage of an increasing number of goods. Their procurement is becoming a vital purpose in life, and their possession a substantial indicator of social prestige. The "hero" type, the social standard emulated by the conformist majority, is also changing. The "fighter" is being replaced by the one who "has made it," and this is perhaps the most typical phenomenon of the 1970s. The fighter as a social ideal was a prestigious figure at the time when people still believed in studying hard and had faith that a liberalization of the regime was possible. The one who has made it comes to the foreground now that they have lost faith in both beliefs.

These conditions facilitate the spread of consumerism among the Jews as well, because—although increasingly rejected by the Soviet society— they are still an integral part of it. Neither national-cultural nor spiritual values can counteract this development, for the simple reason that the Jews over the last sixty years have not only been torn away from them altogether, but owing to the tireless propaganda and their own ignorance, are also experiencing an increasing aversion to everything Jewish. What else can be expected when the editorials keep blaming all Jews for whatever the accursed Zionists and their Israel do? Their hostility to Israel and to their own Jewish stigma sometimes exceeds that of the sworn "experts" on Zionism and Judaism. All the same, it is becoming obvious that the son won't be admitted to college, the long-awaited promotion will never come, and being fired is also a possibility. Wouldn't it be better to resign? Besides, cousin Monia and colleague Iura, who have also ceased being Jewish a long time ago, write that with a little help from HIAS, you have nothing to worry about. Time to go, but in a way in which you lose no comfort, and stay away from "those" Jews. But suppose one nevertheless decides to stay? In that case, he will have to try his best in order to prove that he has nothing to do with "those" Jews whatsoever, and that he is the ideal patriot.

These circumstances explain the growth of the shameless national apostasy characteristic of the anti-Zionist and anti-Semitic public utterances of the Jews themselves, in scientific treatises on the reactionary nature of Judaism and Zionism (Belen'kii, Mitin, and their confederates), in the newspapers (Ts. Solodar and others), and in countless instances of personal testimony (press conferences, open letters, articles in periodicals). One sometimes gets the impression that this apostasy is assuming mass proportions and that the authorities have finally succeeded in achieving conformity between prototype and literary image, thereby providing the masses with the stereotypes of the selfish Jews, the Jewish traitor ("he betrays his own kind," that is the general impression left by the famous press conferences), the Jew as a kinless soul.

The pro-Soviet anti-Semitism of some Jews intensifies the hostility toward Jewry of others. By getting used to reading "something" from the underground press, they are becoming imbued with hatred for the Jews— the eternal renegades and subverters, guilty of staging the revolution that ruined Russia and of its grisly consequences. That is how A. Sukonik, a forty-five-year-old engineer and man of letters who emigrated in 1973 to the United States, describes these attitudes in his short-story "My Adviser Bolotin." Bolotin is a Jew, a high-ranking official, an influential man. If you make his acquaintance, you find it much easier "to trace back the sinister genealogy of the sons of Israel in our days. . . . Solomon begat the commissars . . . The commissars begat the people's commissars, who put them up against the wall. . . . The people's commissars begat, guess who, but of course him, Bolotin, who else."[18] Bolotin requires a field of activity where absolute evil and absolute destruction rule. "And the destruction must go on unceasingly. The same area of absolute destruction that Bolotin's precursors had acquired throughout Russia."[19]

Perhaps nobody but a Jew is capable of so completely identifying Jewry with universal evil, with absolute destruction. No wonder that such national self-flagellation and self-humiliation compounds the anti-Semitism of the "aliens," which is emotionally completely justified in such cases.

Widespread though the sell-out and apostasy have become, we should not forget that widespread does not mean universal. Real tragedies are very often brought about by apparent apostasy. To illustrate this point, here is a case describing the price that sometimes has to be paid for renouncing this apostasy.

When I was still a university student, one colleague was a very good friend of mine. She later held a job with an outfit that publishes scientific books. The security services in charge knew, of course, that she corresponded with a girl friend of hers who had emigrated to the United States and were aware of where her sympathies lay. She was invited to the bureau of the party and told that they knew all about her connections and acquaintances and that her own attitude was somewhat hard to understand, but she could explain her attitude to Zionism in an open letter to the press. She retorted that she had specialized in another field and, Zionism being a complicated problem that she was not familiar with, she would not write the letter. She knew that she risked losing her job, and took this as a great calamity, which it really was. At home, she and her husband had the habit of keeping nothing from the children (although this is far from being the rule in the Soviet Union). The girl was twelve and the boy fifteen years old. The boy, a talented musician, an intellectual, was very delicate and sensitive. The day after the incident at his mother's place of work, the boy's teacher found a sketch in his notebook, depicting Brezhnev in a not very flattering matter. She called up the boy and said, "Tell your parents to come and see me tomorrow. But I shall send this composition to their employers anyway." On his way home, the boy hanged himself. To keep his screams from being overheard, he first tied a kerchief over his mouth.

When I was about to leave the country, she told me, "I know you have a way with words. You know what this suicide means. If I ask you to explain what killed him, will you do it? If and when I ask you to do it, will you?" She never asked me, and this is why I cannot reveal her name.

Speaking of apostasy, I don't ask you unreservedly to "stigmatize" "condemn," "raise the flag," and go into the fray against the renegades. Naturally, I am not referring to Solodar and his ilk, but to those who, in one way or another, are being coerced to become renegades. We must understand the mechanisms of coercion, which offer a choice between two equally baneful alternatives: either the loss of your job and your social status or moral degradation and a break with your friends and colleagues. It is just another manifestation of the same destructive, hypocritical system where the right to exist must be paid for in human dignity. And the situation keeps repeating itself. For many, it has become the leitmotif of their life, and of its destruction. Were it possible for us to obtain statistical data on the incidence of mental disease among Jews, we should discover countless cases of broken lives for which nobody is willing to assume the responsibility. (A psychiatrist who studied conditions in Kiev's psychiatric clinics, told me about the disproportionate growth in the incidence of mental diseases among Jews.)

I presume that Russia's modern, consumerist society, with its typical decline in spiritual and social life, spells further destruction of the Jews' spiritual and intellectual potentialities. According to recent data, there is a deliberate drive to expel the Jews from their last intellectual stronghold: science and other fields of scholarly activity. This, under conditions where professional activity almost alone determines access to knowledge and culture, the range of personal interests, and one's social circle. The number of Jewish students has dropped to a third of what it was seven years ago, and the number of postgraduate students, according to I. Domal'skii's data, had dropped by 33.3 percent between 1970 and 1973. What can the Jewish youth hope for? Apparently the lowest-paid and least-prestigious jobs in the increasingly distant countryside. Those who are intellectually endowed to become first-rate physicians, engineers, managers, perhaps great scientists, musicians, writers, must instead become hairdressers, nurses, or industrial workers at best. The problem is not scorn for this kind of work. One must realize that after depriving them of their national and cultural roots and with the overall drop in spiritual and moral values, denying the Jews the last resort, the professional path toward an intellectual occupation and its corresponding milieu, is tantamount to sentencing them to social and spiritual degradation.

Under the circumstances, the only possible way for Russian Jewry to preserve its spiritual and intellectual potentialities is the resurrection of its national consciousness.

All the solutions that have been suggested concerning the adjustment to life in the Soviet Union under conditions of growing discrimination, adjustment to life in other countries (emigration), all the attempts at abandoning Jewishness and the inevitable adoption of the way of life of other peoples, even if these attempts were made in the name of universal human values, will in the long run only aggravate the reactions triggered by the sense of uprootedness and undermine the personality of those concerned. These solutions are destructive both for those still capable of perceiving the disgrace and discomfort of their new existence and for those so far gone as to have lost the criteria of moral evaluation and self-appraisal.

The resurrection of national consciousness was perceived by some Jewish intellectuals as a duty of national significance. Through their efforts the Jewish Samizdat, formerly consisting of scattered literary productions, appeals, and letters, has since the early 1970s started to acquire the form of regular publications, like the periodicals *Jews in the USSR, Iton,* and *Tarbut,* which go uncensored.

The Jewish Samizdat and the various Russian-language journals, such as *22, Sion, Vermya i My* ("The Time and Us"), *Menora,* and *Vozrozhdenie* ("Resurrection"), published in Israel attest to the intensity and variety of the processes of self-knowledge and self-consciousness now preoccupying Soviet Jewry, especially that segment of it which has chosen Israel. Could this choice be indicative of the narrow-minded nationalism so much shunned by the Soviet citizens of Jewish nationality? There are those Jews who think this is really the case. A desire for dialogue exists, but a real one, the two sides being free of coercion and enjoying equal rights. Only having found a place in the sun and having become actively involved in our own problems, can we *as equal partners* conduct a dialogue on spiritual values, world problems, and most urgent of all, on how to resist totalitarianism, violence, and the oppression of homo sapiens. By adopting a position all our own, we become competent allies in the struggle against oppression and terror. Standing with Sakharov in this struggle means to be with Israel and in Israel.

Upon accepting the honorary degree of Doctor of Philosophy from the Hebrew University of Jerusalem, Senator Daniel Moynihan said:

Israel has become synonymous with democracy. By the same token and to a higher degree, the unprincipled terrorist attacks on Israeli civilization have become synonymous with an all-out offensive against democracy and humanity, which is the key-note of modern totalitarianism. The Israelis' heroic resistance to terrorism gives us an example of the position that free people all over the world should adopt. . . .

The Soviet's hostility to the State of Israel is born of the same hatred for freedom and the same contempt for human rights that drive them to persecute Sakharov and those who help him in his heroic struggle. . . . For Sakharov is here, and those who are with him are also here. "We— this is Sakharov."[20]

Let us hope that the number of those "present," wherever they are, will keep growing.

Notes

1. We must keep in mind that we are applying the term "ideology" to a society where only one ideology is officially permitted, that represented by the one ruling party. The actual influence and social significance of other ideologies can be assessed only indirectly, because the criteria used for open societies (the influence and membership of the parties representing the ideology) do not apply to conditions in the USSR. The comments about ideologies are therefore inevitably hypothetical. The evaluations are made even more hypothetical by the campaigns against supposedly harmful ideologies, conducted from time to time by the authorities for reasons of expediency and covert purposes (e.g., the campaign against Weissmannism, linguistic concepts, cosmopolitanism). True, the situation now has changed somewhat, and the campaign—whether overt or covert—is directed against an actually existing opposition ideology. But the evaluation of these ideologies and their interrelationships is of an inevitably qualitative and hypothetical nature.

1a. Amal'rik, a well known Russian dissident, author of "Will the USSR survive 1984," died in emigration.

2. "Ideologii v Sovetskom obshchestve," *Arkhiv Samizdata*, no. 2536 (1976).

3. *Novyi Zhurnal*, no. 118 (1975), pp. 209–210, 213.

4. Ibid., p. 223.

5. *Veche*, no. 3.

6. See *Evreiskii samizdat*, vol. 16, pp. 99–113, and vol. 22, no. 1 (1978), p. 79.

7. A. Ianov, "Ivaniana," *Kontinent*, nos. 9–10 (1976); "Sud'ba russkoi idei" [The fate of a Russian idea], ibid., 22, no. 1 (1978).

8. V. Varshavskii, "Rodoslovie Bolshevisma," *Novyi zhurnal*, no. 128 (1977), p. 222.

9. E. Pirozhkova, *Novyi zhurnal*, nos. 126, 127 (1977).

10. V. Orekhov, "Evreiskii vopros v Rossii" [Jewish problem in Russia], *Inf. biulleten rossiiskogo natsional'nogo ob'edineniya*, no. 10 (Belgium).

11. E. R. Sergeeva, "Neponimanie Rossii zapadom," *Posev*, no. 12 (1977).

12. S. Rafalskii, "Bolezn' veka," *Kontinent*, no. 11 (1977).

13. E. Oganesian, "Ia nationalist," *Kontinent*, no. 13 (1977), p. 239.

14. Ibid.

15. "Sila nashikh dnei," *Kontinent*, no. 15.
16. Interview with *Jews in the USSR*; see *Evreiskii Samizdat*, vol. 13, pp. 175–188.
17. Yurii Glazov, *Tesnye vrata: Vozrozdenie russkoi intelligentsii* (Boston, 1973), pp. 9–10.
18. A. Sukonik, "Moi konsul'tant Bolotin," *Kontinent*, no. 3 (1975), p. 102.
19. Ibid., p. 106.
20. *Sion*, no. 21 (1977), pp. 97–98.

State and Popular Anti-Semitism in Soviet Lithuania

SH. HIRSH

I CAME FROM Kovno, Lithuania, several months ago. I would like to draw your attention to the anti-Semitic activities in Lithuania, one of the Soviet Union's Baltic republics.

You certainly know that in World War II Lithuania was a leader in Europe in terms of annihilation of the Jewish population. Jews were brought to Lithuania for extermination even from other European countries. After the war, when only a pitiful number of Jews remained in Lithuania and there was nothing left to plunder, the Lithuanian anti-Semites began to destroy Jewish cemeteries and the sites of mass executions of Jews. This continues today. The tombstones in Kovno's old Jewish cemetery were smashed in 1972. A group of Jews restored the broken monuments. Film showing the smashed monuments was smuggled out to the West. I was thereupon called to the KGB and told that the smashing of the tombstones was allegedly the work of Zionist agents provocateurs rather than of Lithuanian anti-Semites.

A monument with inscriptions in Hebrew and Russian was erected after the war in the small town of Zagare, where the local Jews and those from the region had been executed during the war. The authorities subsequently had the Hebrew inscription obliterated and replaced with a new one in Lithuanian and Russian. Similar acts were committed on many sites of mass executions in Lithuania: at Linkuva, where Jewish women and children were murdered; in the Atkocunai forest, where men were shot; near the Dvariukai forest, where a village of Jewish farmers had been before the war, a plaque announcing the erection of a monument was fixed in a specially enclosed place. They were all smashed. In spite of my repeated appeals to the local authorities and in the press, particularly in the

103

republic's newspaper *Sovetskaia Litva* which even published my letter, nothing has been done by the authorities so far.[1]

At the sites in the Kuzei forest of mass executions of Jews from Saulyai and vicinity, not only were the enclosures smashed but I even saw a dug-up ditch where skulls, bones, and remains of the footwear of our murdered brothers and sisters lay scattered about. Who knows, perhaps the grave robbers were after gold teeth? The authorities know about it but act as though they know nothing. I have the pictures.

On a vacation at Palanga in 1976, I was informed that the Jewish prewar cemetery had been destroyed by anti-Semites and that Moscow dissidents had contacted the authorities about it. I visited the cemetery and saw the smashed tombstones, the desecrated graves, the scattered skulls and bones of the Jews. My son took pictures with a movie camera. The film is now here in Israel.

Since our friends in Moscow had already contacted the federal authorities, I decided to turn to the priest of the Polish Roman Catholic church in Palanga. I asked him to admonish the congregation in his sermon not to defile the cemeteries of other faiths. He promised to do so.

Last year, I happened to be in Palanga once more and went back to visit the Jewish cemetery—or rather the site of the former Jewish cemetery, for all the graves had been razed to the ground, and the tombstones and monuments had been buried in the desecrated graves. This is the way in which the Soviet authorities solved the problem of the Jewish cemetery at the Palanga spa.

Earlier this year, before leaving for Israel, I visited the Jewish cemetery still in use in Kovno, to say goodbye to my dear departed ones, and I noticed that tombstones, mostly of those whose relatives had left for Israel, had been smashed with heavy rocks and sledgehammers. And that had happened while Soviet soldiers were watching, because next-door to the cemetery there are carefully guarded military food storehouses.

I have referred here only to a few cases of anti-Semitic mischief concerning Jewish cemeteries. But anti-Semitism in Lithuania and in the Soviet Union in general is a comprehensive topic which has been and will be much discussed. What I think we should do is bring these facts to the knowledge of world public opinion in order to compel the Soviet government to put an end to anti-Semitic activities, to prosecute the anti-Semites, and to respect the national minorities, especially the Jews.

Note

1. See the *Sovietskaia Litva* of September 21, 1971, and *Tiesa* of February 16, 1964.

Aspects of Anti-Semitism and the Fight Against It

M. AZBEL

I THINK THAT the growth of Soviet anti-Semitism is very closely connected with the rapid growth of anti-Semitism throughout the world. In terms of the scale and comparative scope of these phenomena, it is hard to tell which is growing faster. After World War II, being an anti-Semite was generally considered unbecoming, and people overtly dissociated themselves from anti-Semitism and covered up their anti-Semitism, but now it is becoming fashionable. Some countries are already openly proclaiming anti-Semitic policies. Governments like that of Argentina declare it in their printed organs and adopt in fact a Nazist program. It is no secret that the rate of immigration to Israel (aliyah) from the Soviet Union is now lower than that from some Western countries. We are now beginning to speak in real terms of an aliyah from England. Immigration from South Africa is growing fast. Immigration from Argentina is growing all the time. We have the right to think of an aliyah from France. In short, all you have to do is go to an ulpan (Hebrew-language program) or immigrant hostel and see for yourself.

Leftists and ultraleftists today are preponderantly anti-Semitic, pro-Arab, and pro-Palestinian. The further left a leftist is, the more openly he usually proclaims his anti-Semitism, whatever he may call it.

And what's the picture today with the young generation? Universities in England have recently played host to a number of discussions between "Zionists" and "Palestinians." I would assess the situation as fifty-fifty. This indicates a sharp tilt toward anti-Semitism, pro-Arabism, and pro-Palestinism. Furthermore, today's students are a sign of what will be in the world tomorrow.

I can quote figures proving the growth of anti-Semitism and the drop in Israel's prestige, a situation common all over the world. By and large, anti-

Semitism has rarely been confined to any one country. One country might be its breeding ground, but the sharp growth of Soviet anti-Semitism is, I think, largely due to increased permissiveness, or even encouragement, on the part of international anti-Semitism. (However, emigration from the USSR is viewed differently in the world, and that is why it is "tolerated" in the USSR as well.)

This disease, anti-Semitism, nearly always has exactly the characteristics of a pandemia, an epidemic of unusual strength and severity, a highly infectious disease spreading rapidly throughout the world and causing an enormous number of victims, not among anti-Semites, mind you, but among Jews. They become victims not only in a figurative sense but literally. This raises the question: What to do? How to fight this evil? How to contend with a situation that tomorrow may become catastrophic?

It must be stressed here that, although the nature of anti-Semitism is very aggressive and extremely effective, the struggle against it unfortunately is being conducted mainly among Jews. It is the same principle that holds for the classes on atheism in the Soviet Union. They are attended by people who don't believe in God anyway, whereas those who do believe never attend the classes. Our seminar is an excellent example.

Shouldn't we change this tradition? One can put together a hundred lectures, each of them contributing to the knowledge about the flu viruses or typhoid-fever microbes and the evil work they do, not knowing that they are harming not only the wicked people but also good, noble persons as well. One could explain how illogical their position is as inferior creatures, etc. Alas, I have a strong suspicion that it would not help too much in controlling cholera or typhoid fever, no matter how well-founded all the arguments were.

Explaining to people that cholera is a very bad disease, and cancer even worse, although cancer can take longer to kill, would be of equally little help, I'm afraid, in the control of any disease.

I have the impression that the struggle against anti-Semitism is usually conducted in the same manner, i.e., in vain. This is because the anti-Semites never read all the persuasive arguments, for the same reason that germs are indifferent to reasoning. Germs destroy us not because they mean to harm *us*, but because it is good for *them*. I think that anti-Semitism exists because it is useful. It is useful on a governmental level because the Arabs are very much needed, and it is very desirable to make friends with Soviet Russia, and being ultra-ultra-left brings prestige, and flirting with the ultra-ultra-left is very desirable.

Anti-Semitism is profitable and useful on the most trivial, most mercenary, most personal level as well. The anti-Semite asserts himself in the simplest and most accessible manner. By making someone else into a wretched, nasty, worthless, insignificant slob, the anti-Semite appears in a better light, he grows in his own eyes.[1] Besides, it offers so simple an explanation for all his misfortunes and troubles. Moreover, he gets an opportunity to loot every now and then, etc., etc. Now, if anti-Semitism is so profitable, why should he change his mind about it, why should he ever doubt that he's right?

It clearly makes no sense to try to persuade him that he's wrong. He has no desire to listen to you, he'll never attend your classes, he'll never read any of your books. That's it: *c'est la vie.*

If so, then what is the solution? Answering this question is rather difficult, since externally anti-Semitism appears to be perfectly correct and very reasonable, and takes into account with extraordinary accuracy the psychology of the masses. This, unfortunately, renders the struggle against it all the more arduous. The anti-Semite does not deliver a long lecture quoting logical, well-founded, and utterly boring arguments that Jews are bad. He never takes the trouble. He does not feel at all uneasy about the justice and truth of his arguments. And rightly so; a propaganda genius like Goebbels, still held in high esteem by anti-Semites, stated it very clearly: It is pointless to try and persuade those who demand proof. They cannot be persuaded. They should be shot if possible, ignored if not. It is necessary to act, to repeat over and over again, and never care a damn about logic, about contradicting today what you've said yesterday.

In the entire literature devoted to the struggle against anti-Semitism, there is, I daresay, nothing to match the immortal *Protocols of the Elders of Zion.* From the anti-Semites' standpoint, it is a brilliant book. It is a very tenchant, very precise, heavily emotion-laden best-seller of nightmarish acuity; it appeals to the lowliest instincts, for a strikingly clear purpose. It is not by chance that it is reprinted and sold all the time. I was told that one can see it displayed in shop windows in Mexico and Argentina, and the Soviet anti-Semites are now guiding themselves entirely by it. And it works! Nobody listens to the arguments that it is a forgery. Who wants to know?

If we really mean to make the struggle against anti-Semitism effective and not just a lot of hot air, we must first take into account the audience and what kind of arguments they are capable of understanding and accepting. Even the best argument is not worth a red cent if nobody is listening.

The anti-Semites keep dealing us trump cards. We must be (and we often are) thick-witted idiots not to play them and to continue on the tired beaten path instead. Let me give you an example.

The anti-Semites in the Soviet Union have declared that Protestantism is fascism, hardly anything but a variety of Judaism. This may not be a matter of complete indifference either for the United States or for Great Britain.

But pray tell, which American or Englishman has ever heard of it, or realizes that anti-Semitism in the Soviet Union is thereby coming dangerously close to antireligion of that sort? In the Soviet Union there are those who insist that the United States government, economy, press, etc., are controlled by the Jews. We immigrants from Russia know about this hoax and discuss it among ourselves. Statements like this by Emel'ianov have already penetrated the Soviet press, but who is going to tell the average American about it? The State Department sees no advantage in doing so, and we Jews are just too busy. We are involved in the much more subtle logical exercises of the struggle against anti-Semitism.

This is why the British students lose their arguments. The British Jews keep boring them with their own worries. But the students may be more interested in what is going on in Russia. We realize that today's Russian anti-Semitism is tomorrow's fascist onslaught on Britain. But no one has ever told the students about that, either. We are being asked why we come out in support only of the Jews or the refuseniks when there are so many more dissidents in Russia. Can we say that we are doing so because the Jews are more important? We rather dodge the question, but it has to be answered in a manner that would win the minds and the hearts of non-Jews. I don't want to go into any specific argument that may be true or false. My preferences are irrelevant here. What I am talking about is the approach, not the recipe. Some things are very simple and very clear to anyone who is willing to look and listen. How long are we going to keep trying to prove that Jews are not bad? This is a sterile approach. Show me one book in which the Jews are depicted the way they really are, the way we see them! It is good to remember the time when a turning point was almost reached in Russia with regard to the Jews: not after decades of Israel Radio broadcasts, but after the Six-Day War. The war was a weighty proof, after which it became far more difficult to maintain that the Jews are cowards, poor soldiers, perennial jailbirds.

Did anything happen in propaganda after the rescue operation at Entebbe or any other heroic action of the Jews? Of course not, deliberately not. The translations of *90 Minutes at Entebbe* like that of *Forged in Fury,* prepared by refuseniks, were snatched away and avidly read by Russia's Jews. But in Israel opinions are divided: is it necessary, or is it not? Well, it is! For the sake of aliyah! We have almost no book of compelling emotional appeal. Have you ever seen a captivating book whose message is not that the Jew is not too bad a guy, but that the anti-Semite is a pitiful, worthless character? This message must be conveyed not by logical arguments but by means of thrilling novels, movies, detective stories, television programs, where the anti-Semite is described as a complex-ridden person, in need of asserting himself. He should smell bad, rather than others saying bad things about him.

Sociological research has proven that achievements in sports give a country's prestige a bigger boost than its size, its technology, or its achievements in space. It is a fact. We can complain as long as we want that the world is not perfect, but this is the world we live in, and at least for the moment, we don't have any other choice. Half a dozen gold medals won by Jews in the Olympic Games can do more good in the struggle against anti-Semitism than 10,000 dreary books specially written for the purpose. But this demands understanding. It may even turn out that an investment in sports is the most effective way of spending money to fight anti-Semitism. We have been on the defensive long enough; this attitude is reminiscent of the Diaspora. Let us preserve only one thing from the Diaspora, the ability to understand what makes people listen, what can influence them.

Why shouldn't we be amused when it turns out that the lowly Jews are the ones who made the great history of great Russia's great people? Why shouldn't we throw light upon this inferiority complex? Maybe such anti-Semitism is becoming uncomfortable even to Solzhenitsyn, to say nothing of the Russian intelligentsia. We might flirt a little with the left. After all, the leftists aren't too enamored of Arab oil. All they need is ringing phrases. Couldn't we oblige?

I have, no doubt, expressed many debatable, even incorrect opinions. But there is one thing I don't doubt: The time has come for us to stop being on the defensive the way we have been throughout the history of the Diaspora, and to take the offensive, courageously! We should stop trying to prove that the Jew isn't really as bad as you think, that he is even a little better than you could imagine. No! We must prove that the Jew's place is not in the shop but on the field of battle! Proofs abound in our history. We have something to show for ourselves. But who knows about it? Nobody. Let's show it, not demonstrate it. Let's show by artistic not logical means what the anti-Semite is like, what a worthless character he is. This requires means, of course, this requires talent. But unless we get down to it now, Jews will be endangered in many countries, a new Holocaust may be in the offing, and Israel may yet prove to be just a gigantic ghetto.

The struggle enhances the dignity of a people, logomachy does not. This is the lesson that Israel teaches us.

Note

1. Asked if the English were anti-Semitic, Academician P. Kapitsa replied, "No, they don't consider themselves stupider then the Jews." Nor do I think that the English would accept the humiliating Russian idea that the authors of their history were Jewish.

Discussion

M. KHENCHINSKI: I lived in a province of the Soviet empire—in Poland; so I think that some of my observations would be of interest. On the whole, I feel that all the extremely valuable reports read here only partially explain what is happening in the countries of the Eastern bloc.

The problem of anti-Semitism is not only a problem of the Soviet Union, but a wider problem of the Communist and leftist movements. The Soviet Union is today the center of anti-Semitism, yet the weapon of anti-Semitism is used by all leftist and Communist movements. The Soviet Union has created a very rich and, we may say, even unbounded apparatus to influence the world. It is using its apparatus quite efficiently, and to undermine its efforts we also should establish our own apparatus no matter how small, but well organized and properly functioning. Unfortunately, at the present time in Israel we do not yet have an apparatus.

The Soviet Union, on a very large scale, is using its satellites in the anti-Zionist campaign. Therefore, we cannot analyze anti-Semitism, its methods and the methods of combating it, without taking into account countries like Poland, East Germany, and especially Czechoslovakia.

I would like to give you some examples from Polish life. Nudelman, in his very comprehensive report, noted that Werblan's article was the first manifestation of so-called theoretical anti-Semitism in the Eastern bloc. This is a mistake. Werblan's article, as I know for certain, was written on the initiative of the Soviet Union and the party Central Committee in Moscow and not in Poland. Poland was the first laboratory of official anti-Semitism in the Eastern bloc. The results of the work of this "laboratory" were then used on a very wide scale.

In the Soviet Union as well as in the countries of Eastern Europe, nothing happens spontaneously or accidentally. Everything is coordinated and directed from the single center, Moscow.

I would like to present two examples to describe the procedure. Recently a Professor M. Dziewanowski was invited to Jerusalem from Boston

110

University to give some lectures in Israeli universities. Mr. M. Dziewanowski is a Polish emigrant, an enemy of communism. M. Dziewanowski wrote a book published three years ago. The title is simplicity itself: *The Communist Party of the Soviet Union*. The book doesn't refer to the Communist party of Poland, yet M. Dziewanowski an anti-Communist, has twice been invited to Poland for a rather long time.

He lived there on Polish-government money and wrote a book dealing with contemporary Poland, but it was an anti-Semitic book. Harvard University Press published it. It contains things that make it really hard to believe the book could be published in the West. The author writes, for instance, that Gomulka's wife is a sort of Polish Rasputin. And you know quite well who Rasputin was in Russia. The Polish Rasputin is a woman, as is only natural for Poland. But she also acted like a "dirty Jew," conspiring against Polish interests. The same M. Dziewanowski wrote that Zambrovskii, Mints, and a third Jew, Berman, organized a gang which on the orders of world Jewry wanted to subjugate the Polish people. All this nonsense appeared in M. Dziewanowski book.

So the methods are quite sly. And it is impossible to expose them without establishing a special center to analyze not only the actions of the Soviet Union, the true breeding ground of anti-Semitism, but also its various manifestations in satellite countries. And this problem is very complex and important.

Another example: In 1963 a Russian delegation visited a military academy in Poland. It consisted of two generals, including the notorious Zheltov, and several colonels. They all were from Soviet military academies. In the Soviet Union, as usual, there was nothing to eat at that time. But in Poland food products were somehow available. By the way, now Poland is advancing on the path toward communism and there is no food there too. But those colonels and generals were greatly astonished that there was food in Poland but none in Russia.

We had a party, drank vodka, had nice hors d'oeuvres, and one of the Polish officers said, "But you had a drought." And he meant it quite seriously. But the colonels and the generals retorted, "What drought? The Jews have eaten everything up."

One more example: Three years ago in Poland the *Journal of the Academy of Sciences* published a work of a Professor Borkovski. Among other things he wrote about the prewar anti-Semitic incidents and recalled the pogrom at Przytyk, where many Jews were killed or wounded. But he assures us that the pogrom was not undertaken by Poles against Jews; on the contrary, the Jews started a pogrom against the Poles!

Why am I speaking about it at all? I would like to stress the great impact of Poland, East Germany, and Czechoslovakia, not only on their own population but also on Europe and the Arab countries. When speaking about fighting anti-Semitism, we should not disregard their influence.

Finally, allow me to express my deep satisfaction that such a symposium took place today. I hope this event will be a harbinger in the policy of the Israeli government. Otherwise some people might think that up to now the *olim* have not been encouraged to speak out about anti-Semitism in the Soviet Union and in Eastern bloc countries. I, for instance, am aware that a research worker at the Hebrew University was dismissed only because he wanted to write a book on Polish anti-Semitism.

I hope there will be no such occurrences in the future. I propose that all our reports and contributions to the symposium should be translated into English and published as soon as possible.

V. MENIKER*: It is very important to trace the historical roots of anti-Semitism, not only for our opponents but for ourselves, not only in order to fight anti-Semitism but also to understand what causes this phenomenon.

Soviet propaganda persistently states that Ben-Gurion allegedly said he would hire gangs of goyim who would harm Jews and thereby force them to emigrate to Israel. Surprisingly, this statement has never been refuted either in the Hebrew press or in the Israeli Russian-language press. What Ben-Gurion really said was never explained.

We should identify ourselves (though, as I know, there is opposition to this view) as part of those world movements fighting totalitarianism and fascism, and we should cooperate with other movements.

On the contrary, in Israel, there exists an official point of view that we have to separate drastically our movement from others, lest the Soviet government identify us with other movements. But it does so all the same! Clearly, we should first think of our own interests, and nobody would object to this; but the support of other democratic movements is also a matter for our concern, and no less important than defending the Zionist movement.

I would like to direct your attention to something in Mr. Nudelman's report with which I can by no means agree. He stated that the Soviet authority managed to become the governing power of all the nation, or managed by some means to identify itself with the people. I see here a confusion of ideas, for the power of the people is radically different from autocracy, that is, from the power of the few. The existence of the people, the existential nature of the people's souls exists in reality, and it is not simply for some sentimental reason that we speak about the existence of a

---

*Unfortunately the major part of the tape-recording of Mr. Meniker's report was spoiled (ed.).

national soul and national character. Those who speak for the people do not always express its existential essence; often other strata of society do so.

We can all remember not only expressions of sympathy by simple people, but also their profound emotional and rational responses, their display of philo-Semitic, pro-Israel feelings.

By the way, these expressions of sympathy mainly occurred (as it was correctly noted here) as a response to any proud, independent, confident behavior by Jews. We should think about this seriously when dealing with the establishment of Jewish education in the Diaspora.

A Jewish teacher I had when I was a little child once called aside four Jewish pupils just before they finished school and told them: "Well, children, I would like to tell you only one thing. You are going to enter institutes, and a very hard life is ahead for you. Fortunately, there is one tool at your disposal, namely, to be better than the others in all respects, in appearance, in morality, and also in the characteristics which most attract other people. It is the only tool to withstand the great pressure which will be imposed on you in the future."

This is roughly what he told us, in simpler words. And I think Jewish education in the Diaspora is completely lacking in that respect. Much is said about learning Hebrew or about the achievements of Israel, but attention should be given first of all to this aspect. Unfortunately, according to a saying, "Bad is the era which demands heroes." Our times are really difficult, and they demand from Jews daily heroism often consisting not of fighting with one's fists but of manifesting a strong will and determined character.

I only would like to add that in my opinion Israeli propaganda often uses primitive models and primitive propaganda devices. Our audience is not the kind to believe every word, whether spoken or written. I should tell you that for me, personally, Kishon's stories were the best education that spared me any disillusionment and helped me to understand Israeli society. Israel Borisovich Mints translated them, but I had already read many of them in English in the Soviet Union, and after reading them, no illusions were left. Yet I felt somehow a sympathy toward Israel, and I learned something from them that is most attractive to a Soviet citizen; I learned about the democratic nature of Israeli society, about pluralism in public life, that is incompatible with any social stereotypes.

Y. DEGIN: I am from Kiev and arrived here four and a half months ago. I understand that the discussion will take place tomorrow, so I do not want to express my views at length on the lectures we have heard, and hope that I will have the opportunity of saying a few words tomorrow.

But now, a few short remarks regarding the second-to-last lecture.

First, it was correct to say that anti-Semitic literature is intended chiefly for people who cannot read between the lines. But one should note that for the person who understands, who, let us say, understands the significance of equating the concepts "Zionist" and "Jew," there is also something to be read between the lines. So D. M. Tiktina was very correct in noting that there is such a kind of anti-Semitic literature. One example is the well-known book *Zionism: Theory and Practice* edited by Academicians Mitin, Mints, and others, whose tone really is kept very calm and which has an immense influence, in my opinion, on Jewish circles. I have very often heard the view expressed: "You know they all lie, of course, it's all propaganda, it's all lies; but then there still is five to ten percent truth in it." In general, all this is also intended for people who read between the lines.

Also, in my view, there is a very interesting example of anti-Semitic literature missing from the survey carried out by Y. Tsigelman. It is not fiction, not an essay, and generally, as far as I know, it has not yet been classified.

Here is what I am talking about. There is a person in the Soviet Union, if I might be permitted to say so, called Professor Aleksei Alekseevich Tiapkin, a physicist. For some reason he specializes in anti-Semitic literature, the main object of his criticism being Einstein. Unfortunately I am unprepared and cannot cite precise words, but they can easily be found. I remember the sense of them. Tiapkin maintains that in actual fact Einstein was not original, that he was a plagiarist, the theory of relativity was discovered by Poincaré and Lorenz. Einstein's popularity was fostered by Jewish scientists. In Germany, he says, the Jews were in a grave situation, and in order to make things easier, they had to produce a distinguished scientist from their ranks. And so they artificially put Einstein on the path to distinction.

There really is a good deal that can be said about this, but I simply wanted to direct your attention to similar "scientific" research.

Finally, a circumstance that is very sad, in my view. A man who is respected at the moment, and for whom we undoubtedly feel compassion, the Ukrainian writer Mikola Rudenko, has made his contribution to anti-Semitic literature. He is in a camp now. In his book *The Wind in Your Face* can be found the image of a totally repulsive Jewess, a gynecologist. She is an utterly disgusting character. I simply wanted to direct your attention to the fact that even the kind of man who sometime ago took part in really noble democratic activities could still turn out to be tainted by anti-Semitism.

I don't know how to explain it. Perhaps it is a tribute to the times, or an attempt to prove that "you see, I am a good boy as well." It is definite conformism, but it is a fact all the same, and we must keep that in mind.

I. MINTS: I do not intend to discuss the lectures we have been listening to; I just want to say this. I am very well aware of the power of the Soviet regime. For this reason everything that has been recounted here, particularly by Mr. Nudelman, is quite terrifying.

I have been in Israel for more than four years now. I still haven't read everything published in the Soviet Union, what Mikhail Zand called "Antisemitica Sovietica." I am sure that many of you have not read it either. We no longer have an idea of what is going on in that terrible, crazy world. I do not doubt that this dreadful force can bear down upon us. For that reason I want to express my gratitude to the Hebrew University of Jerusalem, and in particular to Mr. Kelman, for deciding to organize a seminar of this kind. I think that a seminar ought to be conducted not only among the Russian-speaking public, but also in many towns and settlements in Hebrew, and in the Israel Defense Forces. I often give lectures and talks there. Sometimes I am struck by the extent to which the army and other places, especially schools, lack what in Russian is called political studies or political literacy. People's perception has become dulled toward phenomena which become terrifying if you recall to what consequences they can lead.

It is a national necessity of the first degree to take up this question in real earnest. This is just as important as peace and all the rest. We are simply losing sight of a phenomenon which menaces our country.

M. ALTSCHULER. I want to limit myself to just a few points. The first is about Soviet Marxist ideology. I am not sure that there is such a thing. An ideology is something that has the air of politics about it, and it ought to serve politics.

The second point is that if we wish to make sure that it really is a question of anti-Semitism, we must, in my opinion, analyze what distinguishes Soviet propaganda directed against the Jews and that directed against Israel from that directed against others in the Soviet Union's enemy camp.

Not long ago I was reading Soviet newspapers from 1948, and interestingly at that time the Jordanian forces were called fascist forces. It was also said that thirty to forty Germans had been brought over from Germany in 1948 and were preparing gas chambers in order to exterminate all Jews.

Again not long ago, I saw what was written about Tito in 1948 and 1949. That was very close to what is written about us. In my opinion, only when we take into account all the international factors that lie at the basis of Soviet propaganda and politics can we generalize. That is one point.

Another concerns what the second lecturer spoke about. I think he knows exactly what Judaism is. Unfortunately, however, I cannot say that I know exactly what Judaism is—an idealistic or nonidealistic philosophy? I would say that we need to be a little more careful about things like that.

N. OLSHANSKII: The question has been raised here whether our links with the dissidents are necessary. They are necessary to the degree that the dissidents fight for democracy. And if the Soviet Union were to become a democracy, the situation of the Jews there would reflect such a change. They would be able to leave more quickly and more easily. One day in Moscow, before I handed my medals back to the Kremlin, one of my good friends (he is here, incidentally) said to me, "Don't go to Sakharov. He is a dissident; you're a Zionist." But I was at Sakharov's three times, and he wished me well on my trip to Israel. A wonderful man, a fine person who loves the Jews and Israel. I think it is always worthwhile being in touch with dissidents such as Sakharov. And when I rang Sakharov from Minsk and said that Colonel Davidovich had been summoned to the local military office, that the decision had been taken to reduce him to the ranks and to court-martial him, he asked, "Really?" I replied, "Yes. Andrei Dmitrievich, I am turning to you as an official representative. You are at the forefront of the democratic movement and of Amnesty International." "Nachum," he said, "I will try to come up with some adequate way of appealing to the appropriate bodies."

You know that Sakharov saved Davidovich for yet another year. Sick man that he was, after his fourth heart attack, he was not deprived of his pension. So that we need to maintain the link. That is my personal opinion, of course; it might be called into question, but that kind of link has helped me. It is true that I spent four years struggling, but I got to Israel.

Now about our counterpropaganda and anti-Semitism, and about Soviet propaganda in general.

I think, to use military language, that it is purely defensive in character. But we need to be on the offensive, without glancing back. To wage an offensive battle is to answer every anti-Semitic word in Russia with our powerful Jewish voice.

There is one more topic which is close to me, and it is very painful to recall. General Avidar asked me not long ago, "What's the anti-Semitism like in the Soviet Army?"

I served in the army for twenty years, and felt the pressure of anti-Semitism very strongly. For instance my friend Colonel Ovsishcher shot down eleven German planes. He was an ace pilot, and was severely wounded at Stalingrad. For his record he was awarded the title of Hero of the Soviet Union. Ovsishcher was recommended by his regimental commander for this highest decoration. But he was registered as Leibe Peretsovich. Ovsishcher—that you can get away with; it's suspicious, but not totally. But when they read the name Leibe Peretsovich, a shudder ran through their bodies and they left the recommendation aside.

He submitted a request to emigrate to Israel, and when we were being interrogated by the KGB, Georgii Ivanovich Nikiforov said to him, "Well, look here, Leib Petrovich, how did you dare take such a step—to go to Israel, when you were recommended for the title of Hero of the Soviet Union?" Leib Petrovich, very calm and restrained, said, "But I didn't get it. This is precisely why I'm going to Israel."

Anti-Semitism has permeated the whole Soviet state machinery, and cannot circumvent the Soviet Army. It suffices to tell you that after the war, from 1945 right up to the present, not one Jew achieved the rank of general. The rank of general is conferred by the Soviet of Ministers. The rank of marshal is conferred by the Supreme Soviet. Since the establishment of the Soviet regime, there have been 206 Jewish generals.

I consider Trotsky to have been a general as well, when he was Navy commissar. He held the post of marshal; his deputy was Ephraim Sklianskii.

Half a million Jews have fought in the Soviet Army, of whom 200,000 have lost their lives. The Jews in the Soviet Army who have been awarded decorations and medals number 176,000, of whom 142 are Heroes of the Soviet Union.

One can judge the hatred of the Jews by the following example. Maksim Luzhanin holds a very responsible position, chairman of the Draft-Bill Commission of the Supreme Soviet of Belorussia. Maksim Luzhanin is his literary pseudonym. He is supposed to submit laws prohibiting anti-Semitism, but in his own poem "The Dew on the Ears of Corn" he writes, "And we thought that they would all perish in the crucible of war, but they managed to dig themselves in at the commissariat depots and occupied Tashkent. And I am sorry that they did not all perish in that war."

That is what the chairman of a commission of the Belorussian Supreme Soviet writes. Begun wrote two books, *Creeping Counter-Revolution* and *Invasion without Arms*. This so-called author writes that pogroms in tsarist times were a protest against Jewish capital. That is how the anti-Semitic interior of a "progressive Soviet writer" manifested itself.

J. KERLER: We have just been talking about Soviet propaganda blaming the

Jews for the pogroms. This is what you would call laying one's own fault at someone else's door, and that is the main feature of Soviet propaganda. That is also why I think the Soviets write that Zionism is racism.

We have to clarify things: The Soviet system is a racism system. It was for just this reason that they put the sadly famous resolution through the UN, in order to shift the blame away from themselves. That is exactly the direction our counterpropaganda ought to take. And it is easy to prove that their whole system is totally racist, from beginning to end.

At one time there was a Jewish Anti-Fascist Committee in Moscow. As is well known, it was broken up and abolished. Many of the leaders were shot. Mikhoels was killed in Minsk.

I make a concrete proposal that we establish a Jewish Anti-Fascist Committe in Israel to fight Soviet propaganda and to explain to the whole world that the Soviet system is racist.

L. LURIE: I came to Israel over three years ago, but I have been here before. Fifty-two years ago I came here as a very young girl with the Hashomer Hatzair movement, which is why I can already speak Hebrew.

The reports we have heard here were very interesting. But no one mentioned neo-Nazism and its relation to neo-anti-Semitism. In my opinion, these two phenomena are closely interrelated, and I doubt that anybody would dispute that.

The Yad Vashem Institute has a remarkable worker, Dr. Kulka, who has for many years been investigating contemporary neo-Nazi trends. Neo-Nazis provide material to fill a small library; they have developed an enormous propaganda apparatus, all of it financed with Arab oil money, of course. This whole ghastly campaign, which is reaching the West, too, is being orchestrated chiefly in Moscow. Moscow waves the conductor's baton.

When I was still living in Moscow, I made the acquaintance of a very well-educated Arab gentleman, a doctrinaire. I had the occasion to meet him frequently. He was not aggressive, volunteered no opinion in favor of terrorism; he was gentle, very polite, spoke with me in Hebrew, and even strove to oppose anti-Semitic articles and anti-Semitic bias in general in Moscow. I was even present when he defended his quasi-scientific thesis on the development of the proletarian movement in Arab countries. This is a dangerous ideologue; he now lives in Haifa.

Getting back to the close relationship between neo-Nazism and neo-anti-Semitism, I agree entirely with the previous speakers that it is time we stopped the passive, cautious, considerate approach to anti-Semitism and anti-Semitic trends wherever they are displayed, but particularly in Russia.

The time has really come for us to raise our heads and hit back hard, I mean at the more emotional, more aggressive anti-Semitic elements.

In this connection, I would like to draw your attention to an excellent book published in the "Aliyah" series. It was mentioned here two or three times: *The Russian Jews Yesterday and Today.* The author's pseudonym is Domal'skii. If the author really is just one person and not a group, the book is all the more remarkable. I cannot understand why it hasn't been translated either into English or Hebrew, and nobody seems to know about it except our small circle. It was suggested to me that I read it, for it is going to be the subject of a discussion. Domal'skii has gathered an enormous amount of material, and his book is a polished scholarly work which must be translated into other languages so that all who struggle against anti-Semitism could benefit from it.

A. VORONEL: We are touching upon a very interesting question, but I'd rather reserve judgment. For now, I don't think any one of us has an immediate answer.

Professor Azbel's address, I think, contained a thought of paramount importance: that if we really want to make an impact, we have first to take into account the psychology of our public, and not what is conclusive proof to us. True, the entire campaign against anti-Semitism—rather, Jewish politics as a whole—is geared to what is convincing for us. It does persuade us, but we are not its target.

I think there is a passage in the preceding address that was very much to the point, that very few organizations or governments pursue a purposeful strategic policy. No democracy, including Israel, is pursuing a long-range policy that would coordinate action taken in Argentina and the Far East, for example.

However, since the world, or at least the Soviet Union, is as good as up in arms against us, we sense the urgency of a total strategic response. But we are a democratic state, and we, like the democratic world in general, in fact lack a real single-minded policy. There have been attempts to formulate such policy. Some of you know what I am talking about. By and large, these are no match for the KGB and Soviet global politics. And we shall always be torn between the need to devise a strategic plan for a total response and transient interests that, for some reason, always seem to run at cross-purposes with it.

The question I referred to in my opening words as yet has no answer, unfortunately: how to bring a strategic or total policy in line with freedom, democracy, an open society. If we are to remain a democratic nation, we must avoid such a strategic policy, but we can't do without it, either. We shall always struggle in the grip of this contradiction, and I'm afraid it is altogether inevitable. Each case will have to be tackled separately, and on a basis of compromise.

Sports representation is a case in point. The State of Israel could feed and train a dozen first-class athletes who would win a few gold medals in the Olympic Games. Wonderful idea, if it were feasible. But what about their military duties? Neither sportsmen nor physicists can be exempt.

THE CHAIRMAN: Getting back to the subject of our discussion. For a day and a half we have been trying to understand the reason for and structure of Soviet anti-Semitic propaganda, its impact on the Jewish and non-Jewish population, and its relation to the international situation, in order to come up with specific suggestions for a campaign against anti-Semitism. I don't mean a campaign run by the government, over which we have no say. We want at least to understand what we can do independently. I would like to invite Professor Ettinger to express his opinion on the matter.

SH. ETTINGER: We've heard here complaints that this seminar has been convened, as it were, in order for us to convince ourselves that Jews aren't that bad, after all. Were it really so, I still wouldn't see anything wrong with it. Anti-Semitism exists not only among non-Jews, but among Jews as well. Not only those who write *Creeping Counterrevolution*, *Wild Wormwood*, etc., but even among those who sit here and know everything about the level of Jewish culture, the incidence of cultural backwardness, etc.

A large section of the Jewish people is cut off from Jewish culture and Jewish roots today, and frequently appropriates the criteria of so-called public opinion, or even of anti-Semites. Very often those who try to erect bulwarks against anti-Semitism base themselves neither on the Talmud nor on Jewish philosophy nor on the thousands-of-years-old Jewish culture, but on heresay, on the ideas of Eisenmenger, Rolling, Shmakov, or others who write in German, English, or Russian about the essence of Judaism, about the hundred rules of the *Shulchan Arukh*, etc.

I therefore repeat: If we merely tried to understand the danger of anti-Semitism, it would be a meritorious effort. Even more so if we take into account (I think Dr. Nudelman did not mention it) that anti-Semitism and anti-Semitic propaganda affects Jews' souls. All you have to do is talk with the newly arrived immigrants to see that. The effect of anti-Semitic propaganda on Jews is therefore a very important problem. It wouldn't be a bad idea to devote a special seminar to this problem.

However, at the Center for the Study of East European Jewry we did not understand this task; we are trying to understand the reasons for the anti-Zionist, anti-Semitic campaign that has been going on in the Soviet Union over the last decades. Why are they doing it? To what purpose? For reasons of internal policy, because of a struggle between various groups or leaders? Or in order to achieve some international goal, to attract the Arabs or the blacks to their side?

The Soviet Union, or certain groups there, is devoting tremendous efforts to anti-Semitic propaganda, to anti-Zionism. Zionism is becoming one of the major enemies of humanity. Except for the extreme pathological cases, even anti-Semites do not view the Jews as so big an international power as to deserve so much energy spent on portraying them as Enemy No. 1. It was exactly the same with Titoism, Trotskyism, etc. The Soviet Union does carry on such campaigns. They claimed that Titoism was a threat to the Soviet Union, that Trotskyism was a tool of international imperialism. All that is poppycock, but it was done in order to achieve certain political, social, psychological, and cultural goals. We are trying to understand the purposes of the anti-Zionist campaign, but not merely in order to convince ourselves. We are analyzing extremely significant political, psychological, and social phenomena. I would, therefore, like something specific to be stated here in the spirit of the addresses by Professor Voronel, Mrs. Tsiegelman, and others, which advanced their own explanations and analyses of this phenomenon.

One more thing: Professor Azbel doubted the effectiveness of logical arguments in the struggle against anti-Semitism. He suggested that a number of other steps be taken to heighten the prestige of the Jews and the State of Israel, for instance by obtaining better results in various international sports events. This approach is not new. It was used by Nazi Germany and is now being used by the Soviet Union. As for Israel, the absorption of new immigrant athletes should be promoted just like that of all new immigrants, and not in connection with the struggle against anti-Semitism, which is a problem all by itself. Israel is a democracy, and the methods she uses to assert herself cannot be those used by totalitarian states. As a rule, we turn to public opinion. Personally, I can't think of a campaign that has so great an impact on world public opinion as the campaign conducted in the West in defense of Soviet Jewry. And that using just words, not blows. Of course, this has no effect on those who don't read or on the pathological anti-Semites; they stick to their guns. But it exerted a demonstrable influence upon a very large section of West European and American public opinion. It is still too early to discard logical arguments as useless.

THE CHAIRMAN: I am happy to see that the atmosphere of the discussion is gradually warming up. We have a number of reports and addresses that try to tackle anti-Semitism in the Soviet Union as a global, psychological, etc., phenomenon and several reports on the sociological analysis of anti-Semitism. Their common concept is that proposed by Professor Voronel. We also have several groups of suggestions concerning the struggle against anti-Semitism. They range from strategical ones similar to those put forward by Professor Azbel to detailed proposals to be decided upon on the individual level. Again, Professor Voronel proposes some interplay between these two approaches. As we continue with our proceedings, I think it would be appropriate to dwell upon the evaluation of the concepts and specific solutions proposed here.

A. ROZHANSKII: I think this seminar is an important event in our life here in Israel, and even more so in the life of those newly arrived from the Soviet Union. The level of discussions is very high, and the organizers should be congratulated on their success.

As for the problem itself, the reasons for anti-Semitism in the Soviet Union and the methods that we should, that we must, use in order to counteract the anti-Semitic campaign, I'd like to say the following.

At first glance, Professor Voronel's report is very appealing with its extremely clear, I should say mathematical, geometric plan. But such geometric plans are, generally speaking, very dangerous. They appear convincing because they are readily understandable. But they very often are deceiving in their clarity and simplicity. With all due respect to Professor Voronel, and in spite of the aesthetic satisfaction I derived from this logically simple, almost geometric plan, I cannot agree with its oversimplification. For what does the entire idea of this report boil down to? That anti-Semitism in the Soviet Union is not a campaign directed against Soviet Jewry at all, but just a trump in some card game called the struggle for power between the leaders of the Communist party of the USSR.

This is obviously an oversimplification. What are the socioeconomic causes of anti-Semitism in the Soviet Union? And where are the social problems that led and are still leading to the anti-Semitic campaign there? Under no circumstance should we agree with Professor Voronel's assessments. If we did, we wouldn't find methods to combat it. Neither we nor Western public opinion are in a position to interfere in this vile struggle for power among the leaders of the Communist party in the USSR.

The factors that generated anti-Semitism are not new. The main cause of anti-Semitism—and this is no secret—is the Diaspora, a foreign body which, owing not to its being God-chosen but to its natural talents and capabilities, competes successfully with the local population. This is the cause of anti-Semitism.

Should the Diaspora disappear, there would be no anti-Semitism. I know this is not a simple problem to solve. But we must, at least, try. This is the global solution to the problem of anti-Semitism. For anti-Semitism exists not only in the Soviet Union but all over the world. And, however strange and regrettable, I shall relate a case proving that it exists even among the world's democratic figures.

I happened to be a participant in November 1977 in the session of lectures in Rome dedicated to the nuclear physicist Andrei Sakharov. On the second day I already had the unpleasant surprise of discovering that not one report on anti-Semitism in the Soviet Union was scheduled among the reports concerning the struggle for human rights in general and in the Soviet Union in particular. Not one address. During the intermission I turned to one of the chairmen (guess who: Simon Wiesenthal) and requested that something pertinent be put on the agenda. He hesitated for quite a while, but acceded to my request. The next day, I received ten minutes on the agenda to present the problem. This intentional omission is indicative; let me tell you, moreover, that my address was received very coolly, in contrast to my first address, which concerned Sakharov's friend, Kovalev. They may be dissidents and democrats, but you could see that my subject bored them to tears. Now this is something to think about. What should we do to present the problem in a more interesting light? We can come up with specific suggestions instead of mere complaints. An exegesis of Soviet legislation can produce results. This is my professional opinion, and I shall easily prove it.

The Soviet leaders themselves provide us with the means to expose them. It is not generally known that the Soviet Constitution—both the old and the new one—contains a whole series of articles (I don't have the time to quote them *in extenso*) to the effect that anti-Semitism is unconstitutional and should fall under criminal law. The Criminal Code of the Soviet Federation contains Article 74 punishing direct or indirect incitation to conflict between nationalities.

What should we do, then? We must raise hell in every specific case of anti-Semitism and demand that the culprits be brought to trial. There are ways; we can exert pressure from here, from the West. There is a whole series of articles in the Constitution which permit one to request the establishment of Jewish schools in the Soviet Union; there are articles stating that one method of education in the Soviet Union is teaching in one's mother tongue in schools. I haven't heard any such demand to the Soviet government being made from here or from the Western countries, based on articles of the Constitution, on the legislation that they can't deny, much though they would want to. It is no secret, gentlemen, that Soviet legislation is, to a great extent, just a propagandistic tool, but no Soviet leader can now or will ever be willing to admit that!

Demanding that legislation be enforced and that the authors of slanderous anti-Jewish literature be brought to trial means referring to specific articles of law, naming names, enlisting the support of international public opinion. The Soviet leaders will have to answer.

I am suggesting this approach because it is germane to my profession. I don't claim to have all the answers, but I think that every weak point that exists in the Soviet reality, in Soviet legislation, should be exploited. Thank you for your attention.

J. LITVAK: Just two remarks. One concerns the origins, the roots and causes, of Soviet anti-Semitism. In view of our speakers' philosophy of life and undoubtedly very high level of education, it is only natural that, in accordance with historical materialism, they should stress rational factors, material and political interests, etc., without paying any attention to the irrational side of anti-Semitism.

Anti-Semitism is primarily an irrational phenomenon, and any purely rational explanation is necessarily one-sided and unsatisfactory. Anti-Semitism is a phobia, a mental disorder. It has its origins in certain psychopathological phenomena, such as hatred for strangers, hatred for intellectuals, the need for scapegoats. The last often turns out to be a rational necessity and has repeatedly been used by many regimes during our history, and it is still being actively used by the Soviet regime. But the need to find scapegoats can also be irrational, the manifestation of defense mechanisms of projection that transfer to others one's own shortcomings. This was wonderfully defined yesterday through the Ukrainian saying *"Shcho na mene, to na tebe"* ("What I actually intend to do to you, I say that you want to do to me"). All the vile, aggressive plans that the Soviets are contriving against us, they claim we are concocting against them.

Another explanation can be found in the social structure of contemporary Soviet society. Who belongs to the Soviet elite? Let us take just two well-known Soviet leaders, Stalin and Khrushchev. Against the backdrop of their origins and political training, hatred and feelings of inferiority appear only natural. Stalin already experienced them during his discussion with the Mensheviks, when he made the well-known "joke" that the problem must be solved through an anti-Jewish pogrom, inside the Party itself. He experienced this feeling of inferiority later on as well, when he had to contend with such intellectuals as Trotsky and Radek.

The term "Neanderthal man," used by Arthur Koestler in his *Darkness at Noon* to define the Soviet elite, helps us understand how powerful the irrational, diabolical forces are that drive them into hatred of Jews.

Secondly, what could be the purpose of this far-reaching campaign of staggering scope, intensity, and violence? For this campaign is being conducted only for the sake of lofty ideals. Professor Ettinger once said that what is most unfortunate is not that they talk about these things and conspire to implement them, but that they even believe in what they are saying. But this is not just a primitive, fanatical belief in absurd ideas engendered by the deepest psychological needs of these people, whether the elite or the masses for whom this campaign is tailored. What we have here is an unusually cold-blooded plan. What is its purpose, what are they trying to achieve? After careful examination of the very diverse forms of Soviet anit-Semitism, of its many and varied manifestations, a certain unique purpose is gradually emerging.

One could point out several characteristic features, which are too obvious to be ignored: Israel is a pirate state that perpetrates crimes more serious than those of the Nazis (take, for instance, the gas chambers allegedly discovered in the Sinai Desert). Israel is described as a state of robbers and murderers, representing a danger to the whole world and humanity itself, as the most dangerous enemy of the Russian people, the Soviet Union, and all mankind. The only remaining question is: what else could be done with such a state, except destroy it?

Who are the Zionists? They are all criminals and murderers, collaborators with the Nazis, and the very ones who drove the Jews to destruction. The fate of this gang is clear: it must be destroyed by progressive humanity, the fighters for freedom and friendship among nations, under the leadership of the Soviet Union, naturally.

Such statements can be culled from all domains of Soviet anti-Semitic propaganda, all aimed at preparing the ground for a second catastrophe. By preparing the ground I mean also the planning and legitimization of a new catastrophe. Vladimir Begun's justification of pogroms cannot be ascribed to excessive love for "scientific truth." It is meant to justify the future pogroms, not only past ones. Thank you very much.

M. AZBEL: The basic idea of my report was that we must take into consideration the psychology of our audience. What I said about the absorption of new immigrant athletes was consistent with that thought. It was just a suggestion which could be correct or incorrect, acceptable or unacceptable, and I stressed this point in particular. This suggestion of mine has aroused quite a number of objections. I think, however, that creating for athletes the absorption conditions available to many others is possible and wouldn't be too bad at all. Just as Voronel, V. Yakhot, Pyatetskii-Shapiro, Hochberg, Fein, Mil'man, Rabinkin, Levich, and dozens of other scientists come to Israel, and dozens more are making efforts to obtain visas, knowing that they'll have to serve in the army here, I am persuaded that there are many Jewish athletes in the Soviet Union who would gladly come to Israel and represent her. And they are not afraid of military service, if they only had the possibility and some means for absorption as Israeli athletes. But isn't it really necessary? Isn't it really important? There is no totalitarianism here.

To continue: Should we take into account, for instance, the fact that the rank-and-file Soviet Jew is unfortunately still not clear about what a kibbutz is, whereas he does know, at least vaguely, what a kulkhoz is? Should we take into account the fact that several issues of the magazine *Sion*, which has taken a new editorial direction, has been interpreted lately in the USSR as genuine anti-Jewish, anti-Zionist propaganda? Why? For a trivial reason, because in the Soviet Union any narrow-mindedness, anything smelling of being extremely categorical or limited judgment, is not accepted whether it's true or not.

Bringing Jewish culture into the Soviet Union would, of course, be fine, but perhaps something about Jewish culture should also be included in some written form to encourage reading.

There are many more specific problems. Continuous discussions are going on in the United States, Great Britain, and other countries; we must make our position clear and convincing not only to ourselves, but so that people would know what to answer. I have been there and seen how it goes. The example adduced by Mr. Rozhanskii should put us on the alert: we are becoming uninteresting, they don't want to listen to us. We must strive to make them yearn to hear us. It can be done! There are things of the utmost topicality, and I think that only by discussing them open-mindedly in such seminars can we come up with ideas on how to fight real anti-Semitism, particularly in Russia.

We need publications that people would snatch away from each other. I would suggest that we collect funds for an international competition for the best feature and documentary film, book, play, television program, etc., devoted to Israel, its history, aliyah, religion, culture, its people; or devoted to the Jews in the Diaspora, to the Jews in the struggle against fascism. We should advertise for and attract the best artists. The struggle against anti-Semitism requires professionals, not dilettantes.

M. KHENCHINSKI: I would like very briefly to give a pragmatic answer to Professor Ettinger's question: why the big upsurge of anti-Semitism after 1968? I shall deal only with the extent to which this upsurge helps the Soviet Union and its policy.

But first I have two points to make. Except for the Soviet Union, Europe after World War II remained almost without Jews. In terms of Soviet policy, this is a very important political phenomenon. Western Europe had had several million Jews. There was a political addressee for certain policies. After World War II, when these Jews had been exterminated in Western

Europe, that political addressee no longer existed. Now anti-Semitism does not have the defense which, let us say, it had before World War II.

I also am very much surprised that so well-known a historian of the Jewish people as Dr. Altschuler should compare the present wave of anti-Semitism with the wave of anti-Titoism and anti-Trotskyism, etc. These things aren't comparable, for several reasons. At the very least because neither in the Soviet Union nor in Russia was there any tradition of anti-Titoism or anti-Trotskyism. But there is a significant, old tradition of anti-Semitism both in Russia and the Soviet Union. The anti-Semitic propaganda conducted in hundreds of books and articles is sinking deep roots for the future. This is why a comparison with anti-Titoism and anti-Trotskyism cannot be taken seriously.

As for the pragmatic answer I promised, insofar as I can judge the facts I know, Soviet anti-Semitism pursues two purposes. The first is the destruction of the State of Israel. I know that very many don't agree with me, but the purpose of the Soviet Union is to correct the mistake made by Stalin in 1948, when he was (true, not for long) in favor of the establishment of our state. But destroying Israel now won't be easy, although they think they can.

The second purpose is to widen the Soviet Union's front of action throughout the world, but mostly in the satellite countries. I would like to adduce two examples from life in Poland. It is a well-known fact that there were disturbances there in 1966. Those were the first anti-Soviet disturbances. I don't have to explain to anyone present how much Poles love the Soviet Union and the Russians. It was necessary to find a scapegoat to blame for the outburst of hate for the Soviet Union. Poland then no longer had very many Jews, especially during the second stage, in 1967–1968, but the tactic worked nevertheless. And this the Soviet Union knows only too well.

It has to be stated here clearly that all anti-Semitic manifestations in Poland were organized from the beginning to the end by the KGB and the Soviet embassy in Warsaw. The Soviet Union understood that the anti-Semitism, which it sells to Poland, helps the Russians fight the Jews (not in Poland, for there aren't any left there) and find a common language with the new class that rose to power both in the Soviet Union and Poland as a result of the changes that took place after 1945.

Furthermore, anti-Semitism helps the Soviet Union create a united front with the so-called White emigration, It may cause wonderment, but both the Polish White emigration and the Russians began to look differently upon the Soviet Union from the moment it raised high the banner of anti-Semitism. They can say, "Soviet Russians, after all, are our own people; we could come to an agreement with them." As for the Polish emigration, it is clear that anti-Semitism helped find a common language both with Poland and the Soviet Union.

Anti-Semitism, therefore, turns out to be a very important political factor. And, finally, anti-Semitism is known to be able to help in increasing unity with the Arab world and in finding a common language with the young generation under the influence of the New Left. By being anti-Israeli the latter is also anti-Semitic.

When the State of Israel was created, anti-Semitism played a part by prodding the Jews to come and settle here, thereby strengthening the state. Today, anti-Semitism is directly mainly against the state of Israel.

D. PRITAL: The subject of our seminar is anti-Semitism in the USSR, i.e., in a Communist country. It would be appropriate, however, to examine anti-Semitic trends in the policy and practices of the Communist and socialist parties of the West. We find an ambivalent situation there. Time was when anti-Semitism made the Jews feel they were aliens, unable to occupy suitable social positions. This brought them closer to the proletariat and made them receptive to socialist ideas.

The coincidence in time of two events, the liberal emancipation of the Jews and the industrial revolution, made the native population identify the Jews with the middle class. You remember that Marx spoke of the Jew as the synonym for the bourgeoisie. Bebel saw anti-Semitism as a stage on the road to socialism. In part, this situation can be explained by the tense relationship between the Jewish intellectuals and party leaders on the one hand, and the workers' leaders of the Communist and Socialist parties, on the other. They were separated, first, by their different origins, secondly, by cultural traditions particularly by the Jews' inclination toward theorizing and insufficient practical experience in political activity.

In the book *The Jews and the Leftist German Organizations in the Weimar Republic*, Knipper describes the Jews as follows: first, they are different because they have just cut their traditional links with Jews without having in return been welcomed yet by the new society; secondly, the Jews are really incapable of making decisions; third, they are both selfish and excessively altruistic; fourth, they are torn by internal strife due to this tension; fifth, all these contradictions make them more nimble intellectually; sixth, their lack of discipline is due to their individualistic attitudes, which is why most leftist Jews free-lance in literature, theater, etc., where they can give their imagination free rein; seventh, Jews are nervous, which is typical of the big-city dweller. This characterized the ambivalence of the situation in the Communist parties of the West, and seems to have had far-reaching repercussions.

I. ELKIND: I'm glad nobody is poking fun at my surname. Which reminds me of something that happened to me in a Moscow suburb. I received a promotion in the presence of a lot of people who were attending a trade-union convention of the workers in governmental institutions. The announcement that Isak Shlomovich Elkind was being promoted was followed by a general outburst of laughter. I remember how embarrassed we all felt. We clearly were foreign bodies there.

You start thinking about the history of our people, and whichever way you look at it, whether mystically or factually, you feel like crying. Our life back there, in Russia, was full of tragic occurrences. Many are now imprisioned and have been refused visas, and many more have been through that. Some of those present here have served long sentences for having fought for their destiny, for their people. Speaking of anti-Semitism, we may argue with one another over what's more important from a theoretical point of view. But we must always remember that we have left behind two million hostages. Some have been waiting for their visas for five, eight, or even ten years. Others are serving long sentences, or are denied the opportunity to earn a livelihood. I know that V. Slepak has been out of work for nine years already. People are losing their professional standing. They encounter difficulties even after they arrive here. And we are sitting here, engrossed in an impassioned discussion of theoretical problems.

What we should be looking for are ways of getting them all out of there. When talking about specific things, we should therefore endeavor to present our case in the most sober manner, so that muddle-headed articles won't ever find their way to Russia. It is sometimes possible to obtain Israeli periodicals and newspapers. They are passed from hand to hand as something of great value. I once found the most incredible things in such an article. Such articles may not affect those who have long ago decided to go to that island of salvation, their own country. But they can influence the decision of those whose moral fiber is weaker.

How unfortunate that some Jews made harmful statements at that press conference. They said nasty things about their own people, who have endured so much for so many centuries. Those intellectuals know what our people have gone through and how they were saved. Each one of them declared that members of his own family had been killed by the fascists or that they themselves had fought against the fascists. To a stranger, they still appear unhappy. Why?

We now have our Jewish government. In this ocean of anti-Semitism we Jews now have our own state. What can be greater than living in it? A strong army has been created to defend it against the surrounding enemies.

Many give the Six-Day War as one reason for their coming here. It proved to them that Jews can defend themselves on their island of salvation.

What we need now is a strong propaganda apparatus. The right way to encourage awareness must be found. Simple stories about the State of Israel could do the trick. Israeli broadcasts are jammed and can hardly be heard in Russia. I was lucky. Although, or maybe because, a jamming station was right next-door, I sometimes heard transmissions very clearly. I can't explain it; I am a lawyer. The only unjammed broadcasts, those of the Communist states, say nothing good about Israel. But this may be the breach we need to get through and provide Soviet listeners with some information.

I am sure we all agree that each refusenik, each prisoner of Zion, needs concrete help, not just an outcry. Each one should be helped to get a lawyer, because they all get entangled in a legal maze of civil, administrative obstacles. This will also make it clear to the whole world how people are, for no apparent reason, prevented from leaving the Soviet Union.

Let me present to you a case in point. Scientist Eduard Nizhnikov is being prevented from leaving the Soviet Union. His job was to calculate yesterday's weather on a French-made computer, and his work was labeled top-secret. He was so informed when he was denied the visa. Doesn't that prove that such people are being held hostage? What more do you need for effective propaganda? Our seminar will have been a success if it is followed by a reorganization of our information abroad. We will then all be able to join forces and do something for our brethren.

M. ALTSCHULER: We are lucky that most people who write about the Jews don't speak Hebrew. They only seem to read Russian, German, and English. Had they been able to read the Jewish, Israeli press, they would certainly get more material to use against us.

Shall we stop printing unflattering information about ourselves only because it can be used by the anti-Semitic propaganda? Shall we forgo our freedom for the sake of more effective information abroad? This is the question. In this light we can understand the question asked by some new immigrants: why is there no agitation and propaganda department in the army? Perhaps if we had one, our propaganda would be more effective, since the newspapers would only contain positive things without saying a word about our shortcomings or revealing our weaknesses that could be exploited by the enemy. But then we would have to pay the price for that. I have the impression that some of the speakers do not realize what that price would be. We are an open society where the causes of negative phenomena are brought into the open. Of course the enemy can exploit that, particularly in totalitarian countries. All writing there is done by order. This is an important problem requiring careful consideration. We cannot turn on a propaganda machine that would show everything that is good here. What about the bad things? Won't we be showing them? We must show them for our own good, not for anybody else's. Are we willing to pay that high a price? This is something to ponder.

Conclusion

SH. ETTINGER

GENTLEMEN, I WOULD like to present some results of our seminar. As I have already said, this seminar is being held in order to elucidate the causes of anti-Semitism and of the anti-Semitic campaign and to discuss methods of fighting it. I think that the reports that have been read here have been carefully prepared and contain a number of interesting ideas. I think that their discussion was interesting as well.

For lack of time, we cannot go into the phenomenological problems of anti-Semitism. Our attention is focused on Soviet anti-Semitism. In my opinion, Soviet anti-Semitism is but one manifestation of worldwide anti-Semitism. Specialists and those concerned with the problems of anti-Semitism are carrying on a debate. The late Hannah Arendt, for instance, Bruno Bettelheim, and others consider there is no connection between contemporary anti-Semitism and the historic Judeophobia of ancient times or of the Middle Ages. I think the connection exists. Speaking in terms of anti-Semitism's phenomenology, we should distinguish three of its main manifestations.

The first manifestation is cultural-psychological. It is the centuries-old tradition whose origins are traced by many investigators back to the Jewish monotheism in the ancient pagan world during the Hellenistic and Roman periods. In a religious and cultural sense, Jews were really an exception, and this caused friction between Jews and non-Jews. The Christian church did not create Christian anti-Semitism but, in its efforts to set itself apart from Jewry and Judaism, took advantage of the already existing anti-Semitism to increase the popularity of its own groups. From that time on, we can indeed see a historical continuity of anti-Semitism. It grew particularly violent in the Christian Middle Ages owing to the stereotyped attitude toward culture. This is a very complex problem. Let me just say that the transmission of cultural values was stereotyped particularly during the early Middle Ages. They were concentrated in various formulas, brief,

132

compressed forms, and handed down from generation to generation. The negative attitude to Jews thus penetrated the consciousness of both Jew and Christian and was also passed on from generation to generation.

When actual conflicts arose between Jews and non-Jews, there already was a fertile ground of negative experience, negative stereotype. This stereotype was and is being carried on. Particularly during the nineteenth century, there were some who thought that the spreading of enlightenment would cause the situation to change, that people would start evaluating things by the essence of the matter rather than by stereotypes or by antiquated religious traditions. What actually happened was exactly the opposite. With the increase in the amount of information fed to him, modern man uses more and more stereotypes to absorb it. The cultural-psychological heritage, therefore, is a very important factor in the emergence and growth of anti-Semitism in the Soviet Union and everywhere in the world.

The second manifestation of anti-Semitism is social antagonism. Social contradictions, particularly among the better-educated social strata, are due to competition for positions, influence, opportunities, etc. And this competition is based on the same stereotyped, traditional hostility to Jews that is already there. It makes no difference who is a Jew. "I decide who is a Jew," said a Nazi leader once. It is important that such an image—sometimes satanic, sometimes sly—lies at the basis of the stereotyped representation of the Jew, and that image does exist. It has no relation to any particular Jew, only to the existing stereotype.

More has been said here about the third manifestation of anti-Semitism: its use, i.e., the use of the psychological-cultural tradition and social antagonisms, as a political weapon in a specific political campaign. Whenever some group tries to gain popularity, it uses anti-Semitism. This was done in tsarist Russia, this was done in the Weimar Republic, this was done in the United States from the 1920s to the 1930s, and this is being done now in the Soviet Union. They can use anti-Semitism as a political weapon because, as Professor Voronel said here, there is no monolithic entity, but only various competing individuals and groups.

It cannot be said that only one of these factors is the real basis of Soviet anti-Semitism. Soviet anti-Semitism consists of all three interrelated elements: traditional anti-Semitism, social conflicts and conflicts between nationalities (Jews are perceived as Russifiers in the national republics of the Soviet Union), and the intragroup and intraparty political struggle.

While stressing one aspect or another, one should always remember the overall picture of the development of anti-Semitism in general and Soviet anti-Semitism in particular.

None of the speakers here has stressed the effect of Nazi propaganda.

During the rapprochement of Stalin and Hitler and the German-Soviet cooperation mentioned in my report, strong elements of anti-Semitism permeated Soviet society. They increased under the Nazi occupation of exactly that part of the Soviet Union where most of the Jewish population was concentrated. After the Germans were driven back, the Soviet government did not find it necessary to counteract the influence of anti-Semitism. On the contrary, it started to conceal and cover up the plight of the Jews and their struggle against fascism. It also conducted an active but hidden anti-Semitic policy. On the one hand, there was increased anti-Semitic pressure on the man in the street; on the other hand, no action was taken to counter its effects, either by Jews, who were not allowed to speak up, or by the authorities, who had no desire to do so.

The anti-Semitic elements that emerged during the last years of Stalin's rule still exist, although there were brief periods during which they assumed different forms. They exist because nothing was done to prevent or oppose them. This is one difference between the Soviet Union and West Germany. There are neo-Nazis in the Federal Republic, there are many Nazis who continue to occupy important positions in highly influential circles, but in principle Nazism was and is condemned in schoolbooks, in the press, in court examinations. The trials of Nazis continue in spite of the fact that many of those who sit in judgment are former Nazis. This is why, in a certain sense, I don't fear the danger of neo-Nazism in Germany too much, although it also must be fought, counteracted, just like any other anti-Semitism. However, as a political or cultural force, neo-Nazism is not that important, in my opinion. I don't fear those dozens or hundreds of publications in Sweden and other countries; this is not the main enemy of the Jewish people now and should not be the main object of our attention.

In Germany, Nazism and, by the same token, anti-Semitism are, in principle, condemned. Maybe not sufficiently so, but they are. By contrast, in the Soviet Union not only is anti-Semitism not condemned but all the traditions established during the last years of Stalin's life are, in fact, being continued.

I don't believe that by publishing twenty novels depicting the anti-Semite as an odious villain could we influence public opinion in the Soviet Union. That would require a radical reformation of the Soviet system of education, of the morals there, but under the existing immoral regime that would be absolutely impossible.

What can we do? First, consolidate ourselves. I repeat, we are not as strong a bulwark against anti-Semitism as we think we are, neither those of us here nor world Jewry. The anti-Semitic arguments, the anti-Semitic influence permeates the Jewish milieu, undermines it. This is a very dangerous process and must be halted.

Secondly, there is, of course, public opinion in America, in Western Europe, even in the developing countries of Africa. It may be stronger in some countries and weaker in others, but it can be reached through suitable arguments and by addressing ourselves to emotional factors. I agree with Professor Azbel that emotional approaches are much more effective than rational ones. Everything possible must be done with that purpose in mind. One can get the impression here that nothing was or is being done in that direction. That is not true. I think that the campaign in defense of Soviet Jewry, against anti-Semitism, launched by American Jews and then taken up by European Jews, was one of the most important and most effective campaigns to influence public opinion. I, at least, don't know of any other, more effective campaign which so influenced the Western world. This does not mean that we should rest on our laurels and be content with what has been achieved.

Many improvements are still necessary, but the achievements are there, in spite of criticism. This is the point of departure for our future activity. A correct analysis of the political forces and social attitudes in the Soviet Union, of the psychological state of Jews there, should provide us with the necessary data for working out a specific program for the struggle against Soviet anti-Semitism. I hope that this seminar has created a certain basis for that analysis. This is only a beginning, but I am confident that all the participants, and those who could not be here with us, have received the necessary stimulus and will try to widen further the scope of our activities, in order to build possible models for it and develop feasible arguments for the rejection and condemnation of anti-Semitism. I think not enough has been done about analyzing anti-Semitic literature published in the USSR and counteracting it with morally and historically accurate arguments.

I know, for instance, that three or four years ago in Paris there was a trial when the Soviet governmental bulletin in Paris published an article about education in Israel. It contended that education in Israel is based on the *Shulchan Arukh*, which says that every goy must be killed. The Society for Combating Racism and Anti-Semitism in France sued both the publisher and the editor of the bulletin. The trial was held in a criminal court of law, and the Soviet embassy was officially stigmatized. Such actions are of paramount importance for Western public opinion and should be continued. Should anyone here come up with practical suggestions as to how to continue such efforts, I think that, on the basis of our theoretical analysis, we would be in a position to put them forward to those who take part in practical activities against anti-Semitism.

II

Proceedings of the
International Colloquium on
Anti-Semitism in the
Soviet Union
Paris, March 18–19, 1979

Introduction

ANDRE LWOFF

THE INTERNATIONAL COLLOQUIUM on Anti-Semitism in the Soviet Union took place in Paris on March 18–19, 1979, under the auspices of the French National Council for the Protection of Rights of Soviet Jewry. As a member of the council's science committee, I was given the honor of opening the meeting.

One might naturally ask why a scientist was chosen to open the conference. Perhaps it was because scientists, whether Jews or not, are among the privileged victims of the Soviet government. This persecution is probably due to the fact that scientists are among the most active supporters of the principles of the Universal Declaration of Human Rights and, more generally, defenders of the universal values of reason, justice, and truth. It is certainly also because they have started a struggle to defend or to free their colleagues, those guilty of having demanded the implementation of the Helsinki Declaration. Because of this, they have been interned in mental hospitals or sentenced to long terms of imprisonment.

Soviet anti-Semitism is a fact. The documents and analyses presented at the colloquium leave no doubt as to its reality and extent. The Declaration of Human Rights forbids all discrimination for racial or religious reasons. To defend the Rights of Man is, ipso facto, to fight against racism and to defend the rights of the Jews, whether they are Soviet or not.

History teaches us that national political needs have always transcended universal values, and that governments exploit religions or systems which have a universal appeal. It is, therefore, not surprising that those who fight for doctrinal purity are persecuted. The creators of several universal religious and sociopolitical systems have come from the Semitic peoples: Christ, Muhammad, and Marx. Moreover, fraternity, love for one's neighbor, respect for moral values, and justice are an integral component of religions and universal systems of Semitic origin. Perhaps it is here that we should look for one of the causes of anti-Semitism in totalitarian states—in addition to the fact that the latter are opposed to all religions. Soviet anti-Semitism would then be just one aspect of a nationalism pushed to the extreme by a government totally dominated by political needs.

The fate of the Soviet Jews is a serious problem, and it is essential to find means of assisting them. Scientists are doing much in this respect; they have launched a "refusal movement," i.e., a refusal to take part in conferences held in countries that flagrantly violate the principles of the Universal Declaration of Human Rights. This is an international movement—2,600 American scientists belong to it, as do more than 1,000 French scientists.

Numerous geneticists refused to take part in the International Congress on Genetics held in Moscow in July 1978. A number of physicists, mathematicians, and chemists have refused to take part in conferences in the USSR and refuse to accept Soviet scientists in their laboratories.

We know that this movement is a considerable annoyance to the Soviet scientific establishment. By expanding it, we are convinced that we are reinforcing respect for human rights, and thus for the rights of Soviet Jews.

The Status of Jews in Soviet Society

LEON DULZIN

IT IS SYMBOLIC that this prestigious gathering should take place in Paris, the hearth of the French Revolution.

This was the revolution which proclaimed full *civil* rights for Jews as individuals. More than a century later, in addition to these rights, the October Revolution of 1917 proclaimed *national* rights for the Jews and recognized them as a *people* in the Soviet Union.

A retrospective glance at Jewish life in the Soviet Union, however, leads to the conclusion that the "success story" of the Jews in revolutionary Russia was short-lived, and that the overall picture is, from the historical point of view, tragic.

It is true that immediately after the revolution, many opportunities beckoned to the Jews of Soviet Russia. They became administrators and scientists, politicians and economic experts, writers and engineers, teachers and army officers.

Institutes of higher learning were opened to them, along with branches of the economy from which they had hitherto been excluded—even agriculture. Jews were given a chance to move into areas previously closed to them, and their names began to appear as participants in all spheres of Soviet life.[1]

Unfortunately, anti-Semitism, as a persistent factor in Russian-Jewish life, did not disappear, even though the new Soviet regime condemned anti-Semitism and tried to create a new cultural foundation for the Jews by promoting Yiddish and by creating a Jewish Autonomous Region.

But in the context of the oppressive measures applied against all religions, the Jewish religious infrastructure and rich cultural heritage were fatally undermined; the Hebrew language was declared illegal, and religious leaders were persecuted and even murdered. Consequently, the

141

community structure was effectively destroyed. The real status of the Jews in the Soviet Union became very different from the picture Moscow has sought to portray.

There have been periods of remission. But during Stalin's last years Soviet anti-Semitism reached terrifying dimensions. It receded after his death, re-emerged under Khrushchev, then abated somewhat. Unfortunately, it is again reaching new depths; we all know that very few things happen in the Soviet Union without the knowledge and sanction of the authorities. We are, therefore, compelled to view the spate of anti-Semitic books, articles, cartoons, and films as having official approval. This propaganda, not the Soviet Constitution, is creating the anti-Semitic atmosphere that determines the true state of the Jews in Soviet society today.

Today, Jews are still tolerated in several sectors of the Soviet economy and in the Soviet cultural and social structure. But they are almost completely excluded from such fields as government administration, the army, the foreign service, and certain fields of research. Understandably, it is very difficult to uncover the numerical magnitude of these trends, as the Soviets are very reticent about making statistical data public.

Even today, they are very careful not to destroy the myth about the so-called equality of Soviet Jews. But we know the general picture.

In the Ukraine and White Russia, where hundreds of thousands of Jews live, they are not only excluded from many professions; in many cases, they are not even admitted into the secondary schools and universities.

Many Jews from the Ukraine and White Russia move to Siberia because of the restrictive quota and even total prohibitions that apply to Jewish students in their native regions.

A similar situation exists in the Russian Soviet Federated Socialist Republic, especially in Moscow and Leningrad. Thus the number of Jewish scholars, scientists, and university graduates in the Soviet Union is constantly declining. This has been confirmed by responsible publications in the West. There are verified reports of unexplained failures in exams, and clear evidence of blatant discrimination in employment.

Anti-Jewish incitement currently assumes various forms in the Soviet Union. It appears in the guise of campaigns against religion and Zionism, and accusations of so-called economic crimes. Their common denominator is the Jewish culprit; there is an odious similarity between recent anti-Semitic Soviet publications, the *Protocols of the Elders of Zion*, and Nazi German publications. Only the Soviet name for the culprit varies; in the early fifties the code name for the Jews was "rootless cosmopolitans," today it is "Zionists."

Yet even during the darkest days of persecution (the time of the so-called Doctors' Plot) the Soviets categorically denied the existence of discrimination against Jews.[2]

Today we hear of a Professor X who bears a Jewish name and is a member of the Academy of Sciences of the USSR, or a violinst Y, a Jew who plays in the Moscow Orchestra. But let us examine the facts; we are gathered here not to seek pretexts for conflict with the Soviet authorities but to report the truth, the true facts which must be acknowledged and acted upon. We know that there has been an increase recently in the number of exit visas granted by the Soviet authorities, and we express our appreciation for this new development. For despite intimidation, Soviet Jews are queuing up at emigration offices in Minsk and Odessa, Cherno-witz and Kishinev, Derbent and Leningrad. The number of requests for affidavits from relatives in Israel has reached unprecedented proportions.

But we are here today to examine the impending danger to the hundreds of thousands of Jews who are still in the Soviet Union.

History has taught us that anti-Semitism is a contagious disease—it has no frontiers. It endangers not only the Jews themselves but also the society in which they live.

I should like, in this regard, to quote Jean-Paul Sartre, whose absence today—due to illness—we deeply regret. In 1948 he wrote:

> What must be done is to point out to each one that the fate of the Jews is *his* fate. Not one Frenchman will be free so long as Jews do not enjoy the fullness of their rights. Not one Frenchman will be secure so long as a single Jew—in France or *in the world at large*—can fear for his life.[3]

This danger must be faced boldly.

Despite Soviet denials, the true facts should be made known not only to ourselves but to the world at large, whose business it is halt the danger in time. For, as always, when danger looms, it is incumbent upon people of good will to sound the alarm.

Notes

1. On the changes in the status of Soviet Jewry, see W. Korey, "The Legal Position of Soviet Jewry: A Historical Enquiry," *The Jews in Soviet Russia since 1917*, edited by L. Kochan, 3d ed. (Oxford University Press, 1978), pp. 78–105; A. Nove and J. A. Newth, "The Jewish Population: Demographic Trends and Occupational Patterns," ibid., pp. 137–167; M. Altshuler, *Soviet Jewry Today: A Socio-Demographic Analysis* (Jerusalem: Hebrew University, 1972), pp. 15–18, 122–164 (in Hebrew).

2. See N. Gribachev, "Obshchipany Joint" [The plucked joint], *Krokodil*, 1953, reprinted in *Jews and the Jewish People 1948–1953*, compiled and edited by B. Pinkus (Jerusalem: Hebrew University, Center for Documentation of East European Jewry, 1973), vol. 2, pt. 4, pp. 1765–1766, no. 2157.

3. J.-P. Sartre, *Anti-Semite and Jew*, trans. I. Becker (New York: Schocken Books, 1970), p. 153.

The Soviet Attitude Toward Jews Ideology and Practice

CHIMEN ABRAMSKY

THE JEWISH QUESTION in the Soviet Union is immensely complex and bedeviled in many essestials. This is due in part to the formal attachment by the leaders of the Communist party and the government to old definitions of Jews and anti-Semitism, as set forth in the writings of Marx-Engels and Lenin. Whether the current Soviet officials, writers, or journalists who indulge regularly in anti-Jewish diatribes really believe, or are interested, in ideology is largely irrelevant, since officially they claim to adhere particularly to the teachings of Lenin. To understand better the problems facing Soviet Jews today, it is essential to glance briefly at the views of Lenin, and to note how radically removed from his notions are the present policies regarding Jews.

Like Marx and Engels before him, Lenin considered civil emancipation a necessary stage in the fight for human emancipation from the exploitation of man by man. He thought that the social revolution and socialism would remove conflict and contradictions from within society. Hence the Jewish problem would disappear through the Jews' full assimilation in their countries of residence. Lenin was thus continuing the line initiated by Clermont-Tonnerre who, speaking in the famous debate on the granting of emancipation to Jews held by the French National Assembly in December 1798, proclaimed: "To Jews as individuals we give everything, to the Jews as a nation we give nothing."[1]

Many liberals, socialists, and Jews themselves shared the belief that assimilation was the answer to Jewish separatism, that once Jews were offered full opportunities to integrate themselves in society, in the social, cultural, and political sense, the Jews would shed their ethnic separatism and merge with the rest of the population. From this point of view, the Jews had ceased to be a nation long ago, since they lacked many of the

144

ingredients which make up normal nations, such as territory and a common language. For Jews living in Eastern Europe, where the majority spoke and wrote Yiddish, the transition to assimilation might be slower. But everything should be done to facilitate the removal of discriminatory barriers and to help them master the dominant languages of specific countries, so that the coming generations of Jews would gradually be absorbed and integrated, and play their part in the building of a socialist economy. Lenin repeatedly stressed that everything should be done to help the Jews in this transition to the supreme goal of total assimilation.

For Lenin, as well as for many other socialists before and after him, Jewish culture was a reactionary manifestation of "bourgeois-clerical nationalism."[2] "The Zionist idea of a Jewish nation is absolutely false and essentially reactionary."[3] Lenin fully endorsed Kautsky's view that "the Jews in Galicia and Russia are more of a caste than a nation."[4] From this followed the conclusion that the Hebrew language and the specific Jewish culture which the Jews created over the centuries were reactionary; the quicker opportunities were created for their integration in society, the better both for the Jews and for society. Lenin reached this conclusion, which was far from original, through an a priori mode of reasoning, without attempting to examine either Jewish history or the components of Jewish culture. Similarly, Lenin's notions of anti-Semitism as a diversion of the class struggle, and as a reflection of deep economic strata of rivalry and competition between Jews and gentiles, was a reformulation of earlier views put forward by Engels and by August Bebél. Moreover, according to this view, anti-Semitism appears only in backward countries, which still retain strong feudal remnants. For Engels, "anti-Semitism, therefore, is nothing but the reaction of the medieval, decadent strata of society against modern society, which essentially consists of wage-earners and capitalists."[5] In modern societies like England or America, "it would simply be ridiculed."

This rather simplistic view of anti-Semitism was passionately maintained by many people. However, it ignored old traditions, stereotyped outlooks, deeply ingrained religious prejudices, and all the irrational elements which make up the anti-Semitic imagination. According to this idea, once you remove class conflict in society, anti-Semitism will just wither away.

Like Engels before him, the only positive thing about Jews that Lenin saw was their enormous contribution to the revolutionary movement in Russia and in Europe: "The Jews furnished a particularly high percentage (compared with the total Jewish population) of leaders of the revolutionary movement. And now, too, it should be noted to the credit of the Jews, they furnish a relatively high percentage of internationalists, compared with other nations."[6] Engels, in April 1890, singled out a few Jews for praise—not Jews of the distant past, but of his immediate generation: "We owe much to the Jews. To say nothing of Heine and Boerne, Marx was of purest Jewish blood; Lassalle was a Jew. Many of our best people are Jews."[7]

Lenin's views about Jews and anti-Semitism were later incorporated into the Soviet legal system of the early twenties, and vast opportunities were opened up for Jews to move out of the old Pale of Settlement into Russia proper. In their thousands they rushed to take an active part in the building of the Communist party apparatus, the new bureaucracy of the Soviet government, and went to work in many of the new industrial enterprises springing up all over Russia as laborers, managers, economists, functionaries, and so on.[8] No field of activity was barred to them. Many in the Soviet Union and outside, Jews and non-Jews, sincerely believed that within a generation or two the Jewish problem in the Soviet Union would be solved, and that Jews would somehow gain acceptance, would lose their identity and assimilate.[9] These persons believed that those not sharing this superficial view were remnants of Jewish nationalists or Russian reactionaries, and treated them as a dangerous minority adhering to obsolete ideas.

Even after Lenin's death the same state of affairs prevailed. Outwardly, Stalin shared their optimistic view, at least publicly, until the outbreak of the Second World War, or to be more accurate, until Hitler attacked the Soviet Union in June 1941. In January 1931, Stalin gave an interview to a correspondent of the Jewish Telegraphic Agency in which he condemned anti-Semitism, "which is considered in the Soviet Union as deeply hostile to the Soviet system," noting also "that anti-Semitism is an extreme form of racial chauvinism, and appears as the most dangerous survival of cannibalism."[10]

All this began to change when a wave of Russian nationalism spread in the Soviet Union from 1941 onwards, a nationalism harking back to old Russian traditions, customs, and prejudices, and nurtured on Slavophile and religious sources.[11] This time the anti-Semitism met with immense popular support; not only was it not officially combated by the Communist party or the government, it was given the widest encouragement. This contrasted with the appearance of anti-Semitic agitation during the twenties, when the Soviet authorities had launched a bitter fight against many publications which espoused this poison, taking punitive measures to suppress the anti-Semitic activities. (It is still a debatable point whether Stalin employed anti-Semitism in his fight against Trotsky, as Trotsky and others claimed, and whether in the purges he killed more Jewish than non-Jewish Communists. The evidence for both points of view remains inconclusive.)[12]

One of the first manifestations of distrust of Jews emerged in a conversation between Stalin and Stanislaw Kot, the ambassador to the Soviet Union of the Polish Government-in-Exile, to whom Stalin remarked that the Jews would not make good or reliable soldiers.[13] The partisans in the Ukraine and in White Russia gave the Jews no help, and in many areas occupied by the Nazi invaders the local population assisted in rounding up and murdering the Jewish inhabitants. The Holocaust and the establishment of the State of Israel heightened Jewish consciousness, and the very fact that the government inspired anti-Jewish manifestations added considerably to the feeling among Soviet Jews that they were not wanted, were aliens. Soon after the war, Stalin and Zhdanov launched their ruthless campaign against Russian Jewish intellectuals, branding them "rootless cosmopolitans."[14] It is important to emphasize that this preceded Israel's establishment, so that the anti-Semitic approach is not necessarily linked with the rise of the Jewish state.

Since the war, anti-Semitism has assumed many forms, which are reflected in the descriptions of the Jews and of their activities. We shall first look briefly at the portrayal of Russian Jews in the past and in recent times by comparing it with the historical treatment of the Jews in earlier Soviet reference books. For this purpose I have made a comparative analysis of the relevant entries in the first *Great Soviet Encyclopedia* (*Bolshaya Sovietskaya Entsiklopedia*), whose publication was begun in 1926, the *Second Encyclopedia*, which appeared between 1949 and 1960, the *Literary Encyclopedia* (*Literaturnaya Entsiklopedia*), published between 1929 and 1939, and the new current *Historical Encyclopedia*. The results are striking. I have selected four areas of investigation:

1. The economic role of Jews in tsarist Russia, as described in the articles on towns in the Pale of Settlement, such as Kiev, Kharkov, Odessa, Minsk, Gomel, Vitebsk, Mogilev, Bobruisk, to mention only a few. The first encyclopedia gives the number of Jews and their economic activities. The later works have omitted almost all references to them; the Jews do not appear. Hence their contribution was nonexistent.
2. Jews in the Russian revolutionary movement.
3. Jews in the Russian Revolution.
4. Jews in the development of the Soviet Union and Soviet economy, their participation in fighting Hitler's armies, and the number of Jews who won distinction on the battlefronts against the Nazis. On all these points there is complete silence.

One has to remember that in 1930 the Jews officially formed the third-largest national component in the membership of the Soviet Communist party.[15] In a wartime Soviet publication, intended for readers abroad, the Jews came third in Soviet nationalities who received medals and honors for distinction on the battlefield.[16] Now rumors are current and widespread in the Soviet Union that the Jews came rather late to the revolution. If a Soviet person wishes to find out something about the Jews, he can discover only blanks or very negative views about the Jewish religion.

Anti-Semitism operates on another level, which is far more venomous and dangerous than the silence on Jewish achievement. These writings can be classified in the following categories: denigration, innuendo, and sheer falsification.

1. *Denigration.* The Jewish religion is portrayed as egoistic, racist, teaching the Jews to cheat gentiles ("goyim") and to hate them. Zionism is depicted as a world conspiracy linked to American imperialism, which is seeking to dominate the world. For the Zionists, all means, including murder, poison, and sabotage, are justified by the end. Israel is depicted as a demonic, oppressive, predatory state which tramples on the Arabs and is reminiscent of Hitler's Germany. The Zionists are viewed as the successors of Hitler. They are fascists who must be destroyed by any form of resistance, including the terrorist methods employed by the PLO, or any other form of struggle.

2. *Innuendo.* Novelists, short-story writers, and journalists have inundated Soviet publications with portrayals of people with distinctly Jewish names who avoided military service during the war, escaped to the rear, engaged in black-market activities, sought cushy, comfortable jobs, and, on the whole, were utterly untrustworthy and unreliable compared with the heroic Russian or Ukrainian peoples. This genre is more sharply reflected in fiction and plays, and is very widespread in cheap novels with a mass circulation.

3. *Falsification.* Jewish writings are distorted. False quotations from the Talmud, the Jewish codes, particularly the *Shulchan Arukh* of Joseph Karo, and other Jewish texts, appear regularly in the writings of Kichko, Ivanov, Yemelyanov, Bolshakov, Mayatsky, and many other prominent popular journalists who scribble on Jewish matters. Accusations against Jews of conspiring to dominate the world, to overthrow the Communist system in Eastern Europe, in Czechoslovakia, Poland, and particularly in the Soviet Union itself, appear very frequently. They use arguments or sometimes actual quotations from the *Protocols of the Elders of Zion,*[17] other time-worn anti-Semitic writings, such as Eisenmenger's *Entdecktes Judentum,*[18] or the so-called tsarist expert on Judaism, Shmakov.[19] Of course, all this is done without acknowledgment of the sources quoted. The old accusation of the subversive alliance of Jews and freemasons has been revived. Recently, the views of the prominent Israeli historian Professor Jacob Katz have been misquoted and distorted.[20] The vulgar anti-

Semitic writers mentioned earlier can publish their views in mass-circulation pamphlets, articles, and books without a single person receiving permission or authority to reply. A large number of ignorant Soviet citizens accept these views as true, and the writers are regarded as so-called unchallengeable experts. It is not surprising that among some of these anti-Jewish writers there are even Jews who deliberately indulge in lies and falsehoods for opportunistic reasons of self-advancement.

This is a familiar phenomenon well known to students of Jewish history in medieval Spain and Germany.

Since 1967, two hundred and twenty such publications have appeared in Russian, Ukrainian, and White Russian. This does not include publications in the languages of other Soviet nationalities. We are a long way from the days of Lenin or the late twenties. At the present time, however, no countermeasures have been taken. It is a one-sided campaign preaching hatred toward an ethnic-national minority, without any Jew having the right to reply. We are, on the contrary, further than ever from the ideal set by Lenin, that the Jews will assimilate and merge with the rest of the population. The Soviet system creates new Jews from those who considered themselves assimilated. The Jewish question will remain in the forefront as long as Soviet internal passports carry the words "Nationality—Jewish," and as long as discriminatory policies not only restrict the number of Jewish university appointments but also exclude Jews from the party apparatus and many government ministries. Today, as a result of the vicious anti-Semitic campaign, Jews may face even physical assault, particularly as a result of the recurrent economic difficulties and shortages in the Soviet Union. The future is full of foreboding for the well-being of the Jews.

Notes

1. Regarding this debate, see by R. Mahler, *A History of Modern Jewry (1780–1815)* (London: Valentine-Mitchell, 1971), pp. 32 and 699.

2. Lenin, *Polnoye sobraniye sochinenii*, 5th ed. (Moscow: Izdatelstvo Politicheskoy Literatury, 1959), vol. 24, p. 121.

3. Ibid., vol. 8, p. 72.

4. Ibid., vol. 24, p. 126.

5. Marx and Engels, *Selected Correspondence* (London: Lawrence & Wishart, 1936), p. 471.

6. Lenin, op. cit., vol. 30, p. 324.

7. Marx and Engels, op. cit., p. 471.

8. See M. Altshuler, *Soviet Jewry Today: A Socio-Demographic Analysis*, (Jerusalem: Hebrew University, 1972), pp. 235–243; J. A. Newth and Z. Katz, "Proportion of Jews in the Communist Party of the Soviet Union," *Bulletin of Soviet and East European Jewish Affairs* (London), no. 4 (1964), pp. 31–38.

9. The belief that a complete and final solution of the "Jewish problem" can be realized only in the Soviet Union has been expressed by many writers. We note only some of these: S. Agursky, *Der Idisher Arbeter in der Komunistisher Bavegung (1917–1921)* (Minsk,

1925), p. 21; S. Dimanstein (ed.), "Yidn in FSSR," Moscow, "Mezhdunarodnaya Kniga," and "Emes," 1935, pp. 15–25; A. Kirzhnits (compiler), Der Idisher Arbeter, vol. 4, 1917–1918 (Moscow, 1928), pp. 230, 244–247; I. Kantor, "Ratnboyung Tswishn di Yidishe Masn," Emes (Moscow), 1932, pp. 9–10; A. Tchemerisky, Di Alfarbandishe Komunistishe Partai (Bolshevikes) un di Yidishe Masn (Moscow, 1926), pp. 21, 74, 76; D. Zaslvasky, "Yevrei v SSSR," Emes (Moscow), 1932, p. 12; Bolshaya Sovetskaya Entsiklopedia, vol. 24 (1932), p. 157; Malaya Sovetskaya Entsiklopedia, vol. 3 (1929), p. 51; Malaya Sovetskaya Entsiklopedia, vtoroye izdaniye, vol. 4 (1935), p. 163; B. Z. Goldberg, The Jewish Problem in the Soviet Union: An Analysis and a Solution (New York: Crown, 1961), p. 10; S. Ettinger, "The Modern Period," in A History of the Jewish People, ed. H. H. Ben-Sasson (London: Weidenfeld & Nicolson, 1977), pp. 857–858; T. Leshchinsky, The Jews in Soviet Russia, from the October Revolution till World War II (in Hebrew) (Tel Aviv: Am Oved, 1943), pp. 7–8, 35–36, 145–163; S. Schwartz, The Jews in the Soviet Union (Syracuse University Press, 1951), pp. 107–108, 117, 119–120; Ch. Shmeruk, The Jewish Community and Jewish Agricultural Settlement in Soviet Belorussia (1918–1932) (in Hebrew) (Jerusalem, 1961), pp. 183–184.

10. Stalin, Works (Moscow: Foreign Languages Publishing House, 1952), vol. 13, p. 30. Also published in Pravda, November 30, 1936.

11. Istoriya Velikoi Otechestvenno voyny Sovetskogo Soyuza 1941–1945, vol. 1 (Moscow: Voenizdat, 1960), pp. 68, 430.

12. Following the Fourteenth Congress of the CPSU in 1925, official party agitators used an anti-Semitic approach in inciting workers against Trotsky and Zinoviev. See L. Deutscher, The Prophet Unarmed, Trotsky (1921–1929) (London: Oxford University Press, 1959), pp. 257–258.

13. S. Kot, Conversations with the Kremlin and Despatches from Russia (London: Oxford University Press, 1963), p. 153.

14. On the "rootless cosmopolitans" campaign, see Y. Gilboa, The Black Years of Soviet Jewry 1939–1953 (Boston and Toronto: Little, Brown, 1971), pp. 146–186; B. Weinryb, "Anti-Semitism in Soviet Russia," in The Jews in Soviet Russia Since 1917, ed. L. Leacham, 3d ed. (Oxford University Press, 1978), p. 322.

15. T. H. Rigby, Communist Party Membership in the USSR 1917–1967 (Princeton University Press, 1968), pp. 373–374; Altshuler, Soviet Jewry Today, pp. 235–242.

16. About the Jews in the war against Nazi Germany and about Jewish Heroes of the Soviet Union, see Jews and the Jewish People—Jewish Samizdat (Jerusalem: Hebrew University, 1978), vols. 9, 14.

17. The Protocols of the Elders of Zion purported to present a report about a secret resolution, supposedly adopted at the First Zionist Congress in 1897. The resolution supposedly was to promote the realization of the Jews' "cherished dream": seizure of the reins of power throughout the world. That the manuscript was a forgery was proved without doubt; it was also proved that the author's aim was to convince the Tsar of Russia, Nicholas II, that the Jews and Freemasons were undermining his throne. The first version of the Protocols formed part of Serge Nilus's work, The Great Within the Small: The Anti-Christ as an Imminent Political Possibility. The Protocols were published in dozens of languages and in numerous editions throughout the world. See S. Dubnow, History of the Jews, vol. 5 (New York: Thomas Yoseloff, 1973), pp. 911–915; J. Katz, Jews and Freemasons in Europe, 1723–1939 (Cambridge: Harvard University Press, 1970), pp. 171–173, 179–186, 193–196.

18. Johann Andreas Eisenmenger, (1654–1704), German theologian, author of Entdecktes Judentum (Frankfurt a.M. 1700), which exercised an important influence on modern anti-Semitic polemics. His charges against the Jews include the blood libel and poisoning of wells; see Encyclopaedia Judaica, vol. 6, cols. 545–546; S. Ettinger, Modern Anti-Semitism: Studies and Essays (in Hebrew) (Tel Aviv, 1978), pp. 44–45.

19. Aleksey Semyonovich Shmakov (d. 1916), jurist, a leader of the Russian Monarchist party, wrote several anti-Semitic books and brochures, e.g., Yevrei v istorii [Jews in history] (Kharkov, 1907); Mezhdunarodnoye taynoye pravitelstvo (Moscow, 1912). He took part in the Beilis blood-libel trial as a civil representative supporting the prosecution.

20. Katz, Jews and Freemasons in Europe.

The Soviet *Protocols of the Elders of Zion*

WILLIAM KOREY

MARX ONCE OBSERVED that history tends to repeat itself, first as tragedy and then as farce. The episode of the Doctors' Plot early in 1953, accompanied by a massive anti-Zionist campaign in the Soviet media, constituted a near-pogrom tragedy of monumental proportions for Soviet Jews. The current vast propaganda effort directed against Zionism has many of the elements of farce. Thus, the Camp David agreements have been portrayed as a cunning Zionist plot, which derives from its very name. And thus, the cellist Mstislav Rostropovich is stripped of his citizenship, according to official accounts, because of his contact with the "notorious Zionist," Leonard Bernstein.

But to highlight such farcical illustrations misses both the character of the campaign and the impact it exerts. The character of the campaign, content analysis makes evident, draws its inspiration from a document first published just over seventy-five years ago by a leading tsarist reactionary and anti-Semitic publicist, Pavel Krushevan.[1] The document purported to be the secret Protocols of the World Zionist Congress, held in Basle in 1897. Replete with what later historians would call "rank and pernicious forgeries," the so-called *Protocols of the Elders of Zion* was ultimately to exert a profound impact upon the mind of the bigot.[2] Generating virulent anti-Semitic movements, it triggered vast pogroms and ultimately provided the Nazis with the "warrant for genocide."

The principal themes of the *Protocols* merit special attention because, to an extraordinary degree, they have served during the past decade as the central element in a massive propaganda drive conducted by the Kremlin against Zionism. The five major themes of the "Protocols" are: (1) international Jewry, through the "chosen people" concept, aspires to world domination; (2) its aspirations are to be realized through guile, cunning, and conspiratorial devices; (3) an especially powerful mechanism for achieving world domination is Jewish control over international banking; (4) equally crucial as a mechanism of control and manipulation is the press; and (5) the deception is to be maximized by infiltration and manipulation of Freemasonry lodges. [3]

Each of the first four themes is either repeated or echoed or varied slightly in numerous articles and books published in the USSR. [4] The fifth theme has found expression principally in the speeches of a leading lecturer of the Znaniye society, Valery Emelyanov, [5] who appeared as a reviewer in a well-known journal of the Writers' Union in the RSFSR last August. [6] More significantly and ominously, the theme was articulated, although in circuitous fashion, in a long article in the organ *Komsomolskaya Pravda* as recently as September 13, 1978. [7]

The Kremlin's drive against Zionism was launched in the first week of August, 1967, with the simultaneous publication in the principal provincial journals of the USSR of an article entitled "What Is Zionism?"[8] Its opening paragraph struck the dominant note of the campaign: "An extensive network of Zionist organizations with a common center, a common program, and funds much greater than those of the Mafia 'Cosa Nostra' is active behind the scenes of the international theater." Stereotyped images of the Jew abounded in the paranoid portrait sketched by the author. The global "Zionist Corporation" is composed of "smart dealers in politics, finance, religion, and trade" whose "well-camouflaged aim" is the "enrichment by any means of the "international Zionist network."

Three more landmarks can be delineated in the evolution of the campaign. On February 18, 1971, *Pravda* carried a lengthy and definitive article by Vladimir Bolshakov labeling Zionism "an enemy of the Soviet people."[9] The phrase ominously echoed the language and terror of the great purges of the late thirties. In the autumn of 1974, the party's Central Committee adopted a seven-point Plan of Measures to Strengthen Anti-Zionist Propaganda and Improve the Patriotic and National Education of the Workers and Youth. [10] The Plan, which was sent to every district committee of the Soviet Communist party for implementation, called for "intensification of the struggle against the anti-Soviet activity of Zionism," and specifically asked for the selection of a special group of lecturers from the Znanie society "to give lectures on Zionist themes." The Central Committee directive is probably the only one concerning Zionism to be formally adopted by the party's policy-making body during its long history. It confirmed the unrestrained character of the campaign. As part of that effort, some forty books have been published since 1975 by various official publishing houses. Finally the Soviet leadershiop vigorously backed the adoption by the United Nations General Assembly, on November 10, 1975, of the resolution equating Zionism with "racism and racial discrimination." The Kremlin then mounted a synchronized and large-scale propaganda effort to interpret the meaning and significance of the UN decision in its own way.[11]

The culmination of the propaganda drive came in 1977–78. The entire media apparatus of the USSR was fully harnessed to the campaign. This concentration upon Zionism is extraordinary. It is equated with every conceivable evil—racism, imperialism, capitalist exploitation, colonialism, militarism, crime, murder, espionage, terrorism, prostitution, even Hitlerism. No ideology, no "enemy" today receives or has received in the past decade as much attention or been subjected to so much abuse. Even Maoism was perceived by the leading intellectual ideologists of the campaign as a threat of far less consequence.

What is striking about the Kremlin's perception of Zionism, as reflected in its propaganda, is the enormity of the power and evil with which it endows Zionism. As in the *Protocols*, this power is cosmic, bordering on the divine, although a divine that is Satanic in character. Diabolical and displaying transcendent conspiratorial and perfidious talents, Zionism strives for world domination. Poised to resist that aspiration is the great Soviet power. The world is perceived in Manichaean terms: the forces of darkness, representing Zionism, are locked in a final struggle with the forces of light, represented by the Soviet state.

The campaign but thinly masks overt anti-Semitism. Stereotyped images of the Jew dominate the paranoid descriptions of Zionism. Indeed, the distinction between Jew and Zionist has become blurred with time, and in many instances, particularly during the past two years, the words are used interchangeably. Moreover Judaism, especially the concept of the "chosen people," is seen as the root of the Zionist evil. The Torah and the Talmud are presented as works preaching racism, hatred, and violence. Fundamental Jewish tenets, appropriately distorted and vulgarized, are seen as the embodiment of inhuman aspirations.

The tone of the anti-Zionist propaganda drive was set over the past decade by several key ideological specialists—Evgeny Evseev, Trofim Kichko, Yury Ivanov, Vladimir Begun, Valery Yemelyanov, Vladimir Bolshakov, and most recently, Lev Korneev.[12] These seven horsemen of an apocalyptic vision are collectively the authors of the new Soviet *Protocols of the Elders of Zion*. Dozens of other writers and lecturers have been developing similar arguments and presenting similar analyses.

On various levels, the initiatives launched in 1977 and continued into 1978 constituted both the apogee of the decade-old drive and the point of departure for an even more ominous future. On one level, the audience for the media campaign was maximized. On a second level, the campaign catered to and exploited the deepest public fears and traumatic memories of the Soviet public. On a final level, and of the greatest significance, the campaign provided, for the first time, a Leninist rationale carrying the imprimatur of the prestigious Soviet Academy of Sciences.

Anti-Semitic volumes were now published in editions two to three times the size of even the large editions of previous years. Thus, 150,000 copies of Vladimir Begun's new book *Invasion without Arms* appeared.[13] Justifying the pogroms of the earlier tsarist epoch, it called the Torah "a textbook unsurpassed for bloodthirstiness, hypocrisy, betrayal, perfidy, and moral dissoluteness."[14] It contended that the Zionist objective is "mastery over the whole world" through "control of national governments" by Jewish bankers and the Zionists getting "into their hands the most powerful propaganda apparatus."[15]

An earlier and similar work by Begun appeared in an edition of only 25,000 copies. The largest previous anti-Semitic edition was Yury Ivanov's *Beware: Zionism!*, published in 1969 in an edition of 75,000 copies.[16] Another new book, Tsezar Solodar's *Wild Wormwood*, equated Zionism with Hitlerism, and the "chosen people" concept with Aryan racism, and was published in a special edition of 200,000 copies.[17] It was intensively promoted in a large number of Soviet journals.

Equally important was the use, for the first time in an unrestrained fashion, of the television medium. On January 22, 1977, Soviet television carried at prime time, 7 P.M., a newly produced hour-long documentary entitled *Traders of Souls*.[18] Replete with juxtaposed visual images of Jews and Israelis, it was obviously meant to evoke suspicion and hatred of Jews. An American Jewish tourist at Moscow Airport was shown confessing, during an interview, that he had attempted to smuggle anti-Soviet material into the USSR, and that he had acted on instructions from Zionist organizations which may have maintained "clandestine ties with the CIA." The Jew as moneychanger—"a trader of souls"—was the constant theme of the documentary. Activists were presented as subversive: "These people are all soldiers of Zionism within the Soviet Union, and it is here that they carry out their subversive activities." "Traders of Souls" served as the basis for extensive and enthusiastic commentary in Soviet newspapers and journals for several succeeding weeks. Because of "popular demand," the authorities decided to repeat the documentary on March 11.

To maximize the Soviet audience, the propaganda drive focused upon themes that stirred the deepest public fears—espionage, war, and Hitlerism. The weekly *Ogonyok*, with a circulation of two million, emphasized the espionage theme. On January 29, the journal charged that "Zionist agents" had succeeded in "directly penetrating foreign secret services" with the aim of exercising "influence" over the intelligence operations of "a sizable number of states," including the United States and England. The title of the article, "The Espionage Octopus of Zionism," is self-explanatory.[19]

The author of the *Ogonyok* article was Lev Korneev, who had recently moved into the front ranks of the professional peddlers of hate. A week later, on February 2, he applied his vitriolic pen to a new charge. Zionism was responsible for dumping arms on the world market in order to foil detente and foster racism. The militarism theme was again trotted out by Korneev on February 16.[20] He declared that in the United States, the military-industrial monopolies are "to a considerable degree controlled or belong to the big pro-Zionist bourgeoisie." "Many" of the oil companies, among the one hundred largest suppliers of the Pentagon, are "directly controlled by pro-Zionist capital." The following month, Korneev dilated upon his Zionist-war thesis in a long article in an important military journal.[21]

The Hitlerism theme emphasized in the Solodar book was expanded by Korneev in a two-part series for *Ogonyok* (August 20, 27). He "discovered" that Zionism was a covert ally of Nazism in the struggle against the Soviet Union. Their economic collaboration was held to be particularly pronounced. According to Korneev, "many banks and monopolies of the capitalist states (first and foremost of the United States) known as permanent donors to the fund of international Zionism or to be indirectly connected with Zionism and a part of the system of pro-Zionist capital, extended assistance to the Nazis and collaborated with them both before the latter came to power in Germany and in the period when the Hitlerites were making preparations for world war."[22]

Korneev then linked the Hitlerism theme with present-day military-industrial complexes in the West. In November 1977, he charged that "out of 165 of the largest 'enterprises of death' in the West, 158 are controlled or directly owned by the pro-Zionist bourgeoisie of Jewish origin."[23] During 1978, Korneev dilated upon this theme in an essay in *Ogonyok* (July 8). He flatly contended that Lockheed Aircraft is "controlled" by Lazard-Frères, "one of the largest finance empires, founded and directed by bankers of Jewish origin." McDonnell-Douglas was said to be controlled by the Rockefellers' Chase Manhattan Bank, "which constantly supports international Zionism and the ruling circles of Israel." General Dynamics was said to be "controlled by the financial supergiants among Jewish bankers—the Lehmans.[24] The list was endless.

What the decade-old campaign against Zionism lacked, despite its vastness, was a Marxist-Leninist ideological underpinning; only scattered scraps of Lenin's writings were available for use as an intellectual sanction. The founder of the Soviet state had referred to Zionism, according to his *Collected Works*, merely fifteen times. And only once did he offer more than some passing remarks on the subject. Moreover, an economic and historical analysis, drawing upon Leninist methodology and ideology, was lacking.

The requisite ideological legitimization finally came in the summer of 1977 with the publication by the prestigious Academy of Sciences of *International Zionism: History and Politics*.[25] This 176-page work consisted of articles by "scholars" from various institutes of the academy. It was trumpeted by Tass in a special release and commentary on July 22. The work echoed the themes of the *Protocols of the Elders of Zion* to a remarkable degree, even if the language appeared to have a Leninist ring. The central theme of the *Protocols* is that Jewry aspires to world domination by means of control over the international banking system. The same theme predominated in the new Soviet work, especially in the principal essay, written by V. Kiselev.[26] According to the latter, the "Jewish bourgeoisie," using Zionism as a cover, has sought "to enhance its positions in the economy of the largest capitalist states . . . and in the economic system of world capitalism as a whole."[27]

The *Protocols* propagated the well-known canard that Jewish magnates are intimately linked, family-wise, with one another in a vast conspiracy. This reflects the age-old classic notion of clannishness that, in the eyes of the prejudiced, stamps the Jew. The new Soviet study enlarged upon the clannishness thesis. "Among the Jewish bourgeoisie," Kiselev contends, "the use of all sorts of extra-market . . . kinship relations through 'one's own' . . . has always been practiced very extensively."[28] A related major theme of the *Protocols* which is reflected in the Soviet book is the Judaic concept of the "chosen people."[29] In the former it was perceived as the religious and ideological rationale for world domination. The current Soviet authors stress the same medieval perception; they contend that Judaism considers the "goy" (defined as a "non-Jew") the "enemy" against whom "violence" is required. They then build upon the theme by adding their own specious interpretation of messianism. The Judaic belief in the Messiah is supposedly inculcated so that Jews will aspire to "mastery over all mankind."

Finally, as in the *Protocols*, the Zionists are said to strive for the status of a "supergovernment," with Jews encouraged to become "fifth columns" throughout the world. Israel is characterized as merely the "connecting" link in the vast and monumental effort of "the big Jewish bourgeoisie" to achieve "the consolidation of their positions in the world of capital" and for acquiring "superprofits."

During 1978, two important academic journals gave strong endorsement to the Academy's book, reinforcing Tass's official approval;[30] a "scholarly" imprimatur had now been given to a refurbished *Protocols of the Elders of Zion*. A decade ago Andrey Sakharov publicly criticized the president of the Soviet Academy of Sciences for justifying anti-Semitic discrimination in personnel appointments. But such discrimination was mild compared with the endorsement of blatant and vulgar anti-Semitism. The capstone of the massive propaganda effort was now firmly placed. It constitutes a basic source for the future promotion of bigotry and hate.

The impact of anti-Zionist propaganda upon public attitudes in the USSR is difficult to measure. Yet there can be little doubt that, as reported by Soviet Jewish activists in Samizdat literature and in their appeals to the West, the level of popular anti-Semitism has been significantly raised.[31] Verbal abuse of Jews was particularly marked after the above-mentioned television documentary in early 1977 and following the trials of dissidents in 1978. Overt violence is, however, absent. To suggest that pogroms are just around the corner would be a serious misreading of the current scene. Yet the stirrings of the embers of hate could have, under combustible social circumstances, a fiery outcome.

International law bars "incitement" to racial hatred. Both the International Convention on the Elimination of All Forms of Racial Discrimination, in Article 4(a), and the International Covenant on Civil and Political Rights, in Article 20(1), prohibit "advocacy" of "racial hatred" by the contracting parties. The USSR ratified the former in 1969 and the latter in 1973, and is therefore bound by the treaty prohibitions.

The responsibility, both legal and moral, of the international community is clear. Its attention must ineluctably focus on the Soviet Union, which not only saturates its own people with a nonstop campaign of anti-Semitic books, articles, and television programs, but is also the world's largest exporter of anti-Jewish hate materials. The failure of an earlier generation to respond effectively to the *Protocols of the Elders of Zion*, which subsequently became a "warrant for genocide," continues to weigh upon mankind's conscience. The new and updated version of the *Protocols* must not become the basis for another "warrant for genocide."

Notes

1. Pavolakii, Krushevan, (1860–1909), journalist, publisher of *Bessarabets* and *Drug*, in Kishinev. Published a series of articles on "The Program for the Conquest of the World by the Jews." His articles were a contributory cause of the Kishinev pogrom in 1903. See *Materialy dlya istorii antiyevreiskikh pogromov v Rossii* [References on the history of anti-Jewish pogroms in Russia], vol. 1 (Petrograd, 1919), foreword by S. Dubnow, p. xi.

2. Regarding the *Protocols*, see above.

3. The Freemasonry movement was founded in the seventeenth century and was modeled after the craft guilds. The movement opposes all restrictions on freedom of religion, conscience, and thought, and rejects all connections with formal religions. Its attitude toward Jews was complicated, at least at the beginning, and for a long time Jews were not accepted

as members; sometimes the attitude toward Jews was anti-Semitic, especially where there was a strong Catholic membership. See J. Katz, *Jews and Freemasons in Europe, 1723–1939* [Cambridge: Harvard University Press, 1970], pp. 1–3, 7, 19, 21–25, 134, 147, 206.

4. These elements of the *Protocols* are recognizable in the works of V. Begun, Yu. Ivanov, V. Skurlatov, E. Evseev, and others. See below, n. 12.

5. This work of V. Emelyanov, "Who Is Behind Jimmy Carter and the So-Called Eurocommunists?", repeating the charges about the Freemasons, was published for the first time in a Jewish Samizdat publication, *Yevrei v SSSR,"* no. 16. It is reprinted below, p. 000.

6. The review *"Zionism Unmasked"* by V. Emelyanov from *Nash Sovremennik,* no. 8 (1978), is reprinted below.

7. V. Polezhayev, "Kovarny plagyat" [A crafty plagiarism], reprinted in the quarterly collection, *Jews and the Jewish People—Excerpts from the Soviet Press* (hereafter cited as *JJP*-quarterly) vol. 89, pt. II, no. 381.

8. Yu. Ivanov, "Chto takoye sionizm?" [What is Zionism?] in *Sovetskaya Latviya,* August 5, 1967. Also published in *Bakinsky Rabochy,* August 6, 1967, and in *Za rubezhom,* under the title "Sionizm bez rumyan" [Zionism without cosmetics], August 4–10, 1967, reprinted in *JJP-quarterly,* vol. 29B, nos. 1773, 1774, 1801.

9. V. Bolshakov, "Antisovetism—professiya sionistov" [Anti-Sovietism—the Zionist profession], *Pravda,* February 18–19, 1971, reprinted in *JJP-quarterly,* vol. 43A, no. 601.

10. Regarding the seven points of the "Outline of Measures to Strengthen Anti-Zionist Propaganda and Improve the Patriotic and National Education of the Workers and Youth," see Jews and the Jewish People—Jewish Samizdat (Jerusalem: Hebrew University), 1976, vol. 10, p. 271 (hereafter cited as *JPP—Jewish Samizdat*).

11. For example, E. Evseev, "Sionizm—eto rasizm" [Zionism is racism], *Selskaya Zhizn,* November 14, 1975, reprinted in *JJP-quarterly,* vol. 70, no. 141; V. Korotkov, "Sionistskaya svistoplyaska" [The Zionist witches' sabbath], *Gudok,* November 15, 1975, reprinted in *JJP-quarterly,* vol. 70, no. 142; Y. Valakh, "Sionizm—forma rasizma" [Zionism—a form of racism], *Pravda Ukrainy,* November 15, 1975, reprinted in *JJP-quarterly,* vol. 70, no. 145.

12. On Vladimir, Begun, see note.

Vladimir, Bolshakov assistant to the secretary-in-chief of *Pravda,* author of the book *Sionizm na sluzhbe antikommunizma* [Zionism in the service of anti-Communism] and such articles as "Kritika sionizma v sovetskoy istoriografii" [Criticism of Zionism in Soviet historiography], *Voprosy Istorii* review, 1973, no. 9.

Yury Ivanov, the author of the books *Ostorozhno: sionizm!* [Beware: Zionism!], published numerous editions and translated into many languages; *Ot Nila do Yefrata* [From the Nile to the Euphrates] in Estonian, and *Antikommunisticheskiye ustremlenya sovremennogo sionizma* [The anti-Communist aspirations of modern Zionism], 1970.

Trofim Kichko, Candidate of Philosophy. His anti-Judaic writing and published dissertation thesis was entitled *Modern Zionism and Its Reactionary Role.* He was engaged in research on Judaism and wrote two books on the subject: *Iudeyskaya religiya: proikhozhdeniye, sut'* [Judaism: The originals and the essence] (in Ukrainian) Kiev: Znanie, 1957); *Iudaizm bez prikras* [Judaism without embellishment] (in Ukrainian) Kiev: Znanie, 1963. Because of the extremely anti-Semitic nature of his books, they obtained negative reviews in the West, and consequently in the USSR, in particular, by the Central Committee of the CPSU. At the end of the sixties his publications appeared again.

Lev Korneev, Candidate of Philosophy, scientific worker in the Institute of Oriental Studies of the Academy of Sciences of the USSR. He is the author of a number of books and essays on Zionism. It is believed that his books have been published by the Novosty news agency in the West, the author being given the pseudonym Leo Korn (in *Insight: Soviet Jews,* vol. 5, no. 2, [1979] p. 78; vol. 6, no. 2 [1980], pp. 6–7).

Valery Emelyanov was well known as a lecturer on ideological matters, employed by the Moscow Party Commitee until 1976. He presented a memorandum calling for a "Final Solution of the Jewish Problem" to the 25th Congress of the Soviet Communist party in 1975. It is a new version of the *Protocols of the Elders of Zion.* See *JJP-Jewish Samizdat,* vol. 10, pp. 272–275; also note 5 above.

Evgeny Evseev, Candidate of Philosophy, author of many books, and prolific author of anti-Zionist propaganda. Since 1967 he has published many articles in all types of papers and periodicals, including *Pravda, Ogonyok,* and *Krokodil.* He is the author of *Fascism Under the Blue Star* and *Zionism: Ideology and Politics,* 1971. Employs the usual anti-Semitic arguments. Regarding his speech at the Academy of Sciences' Conference on the Problems of the Improvement of Methodology, Scientific Criticism, and Politics of Zionism, see the article by E. Sol'mar, "Protokoly antisionistskikh mudretsov" [The protocols of the anti-Zionist elders], *JJP-Jewish Samizdat,* vol. 16, pp. 130, 133–138, 141.

13. V. Begun, *Vtorzheniye bez oruzhiya* [Invasion without arms] Moscow: Molodaya gvardiya, 1977].

14. Ibid., pp. 40–41.

15. Ibid., p. 89.

16. Yu. Ivanov. *Ostorozhno: sionizm!* [Beware: Zionism!] (Moscow: Politizdat, 1969), p. 173.

17. Ts. Solodar, *Dikaya polyn'* [The wild wormwood] (Moscow: Sovetskaya Rossiya, 1977).

18. For reaction to this film, see L. Shvedov, "Telefilm *Skupshchiky dush*"[The traders in souls], in *Vechern ya Moskva,* January 1, 1977, reprinted in *JJP—quarterly,* vol. 80, no. 523. See also nos. 524, 527, 529, 536, 545.

19. L. Korneev, "Shpionsky sprut sionizma" [The Zionist espionage octopus], *Ogonyok,* January 29, 1977, reprinted in *JJP-quarterly,* vol. 80, no. 209.

20. L. Korneev, "Sionizm kak on yes't!" [Zionism as it really is!] under the heading "Vragi mira i progressa" [Enemies of peace and progress], *Moskovskaya Pravda,* February 16, 1977, reprinted in *JJP-quarterly,* vol. 80, no. 554.

21. L. Korneev, "Na mezhdunarodnyie temy—Laynaya voyna sionizma" [On international subjects—Zionism's secret war], *Kommunist vooruzhonnykh sil,* 1977, no. 6, reprinted in *JJP-quarterly,* vol. 80, no. 240.

22. L. Korneev, "Zloveshchiye tayny sionizma" [The malicious secrets of Zionism], *Ogonyok,* August 20 and 27, 1977, nos. 34 and 35, reprinted in *JJP-quarterly,* vol. 83, no. 335, See below.

23. L. Korneev, "Otravlennoye oruzhiye sionizma" [The poisonous weapon of Zionism], *Krasnaya Zvezda,* November 16, 1977, reprinted in *JJP-quarterly,* vol. 86, no. 599.

24. L. Korneev, "Samyi sionistskii bizness" [The most Zionist business], *Ogonyok,* nos. 28 and 29 (July 8 and 15, 1978), reprinted in *JJP-quarterly,* vol. 89, no. 383.

25. *Mezhdunarodnyi sionizm—istoriya i politika* [International Zionism—history and politics] (Moscow: Nauka, 1977).

26 V. I. Kiselev, "Sionizm v sisteme imperializma" [Zionism in the imperialist system] in *Mezhdunarodnyi sionizm—istoriya i politika* (Moscow: Nauka, 1977), pp. 5–28.

27. Ibid., p. 9.

28. Ibid., p. 7.

29. For example, M. A. Goldenberg, "Iudaizm na sluzhbe sionizma" [Judaism in the service of Zionism], ibid., pp. 88–98.

30. See *Novaya i noveyshaya istoriya,* 1978, no. 2, pp. 187–189, reprinted in *JJP-quarterly,* vol. 88, no. 384.

31. See also I. Domalsky, "New Developments in Anti-Semitism"; E. Sol'mar, "The Protocols of Anti-Zionist Elders," *JJP-Jewish Samizdat,* vol. 16, pp. 128–143; V. Brailovsky, "The Soviet Press on Zionism," *JJP-Jewish Samizdat,* vol. 21, pp. 455–462.

Anti-Zionism and Anti-Semitism in the USSR

STEPHEN J. ROTH

IT IS OFTEN stated, and not only by non-Jews, that anti-Zionism in the normal meaning of the word cannot be regarded as inherently objectionable. Zionism is a political concept that provides an interpretation of Jewish history. It is also an answer to the dual problem of how the long chain of anti-Jewish persecution by a hostile environment can be broken; Zionism is also an answer to the question of how the survival of Jews as a religious, cultural, and national entity can be secured in a friendly environment. Like all political concepts it can be accepted or rejected, and it can be neither proved nor disproved with the certainty of an exact science. Jews and non-Jews can, therefore, criticize the concept of Zionism (and indeed have) in a rational manner, and have offered other interpretations of the Jewish history and other answers to the Jewish problem.[1]

From the outset the Communists have been the foremost critics of Zionism. The idea that the Jews comprise a separate nation was reactionary according to Lenin.[2] Equally reactionary and contrary to the interest of the Jewish proletariat was, in the classical Communist view, the desire of Jews to survive as a national group when their national historical fate was complete assimilation.[3] Such assimilation will be possible in a classless society, wherein anti-Semitism will disappear. Zionism is a reactionary bourgeois-nationalist movement which fosters among Jews a spirit of hostility to assimilation, preaches interclass cooperation among Jews, and distracts working-class Jews from the common class struggle, including the struggle against Jewish bourgeoisie.

I regard this criticism of Zionism as erroneous and largely disproved by both the Nazi Holocaust and Soviet reality. Nevertheless, it is an arguable point of view, though I regret the violent tone in which the Communists often conduct such argument. But it is absurd to stigmatize this type of opposition to the political concept of Zionism as anti-Semitism, even though it endangers basic Jewish interests.

However, the anti-Zionism which we face in the Soviet Union at present is totally different. It does not argue, rationally and respectably, against Zionism as a political concept or as a movement that supports the State of Israel, the policies of which the Soviets, like others, are of course entitled to criticize if they see reasons to do so. But roughly since the 1967 Six-Day War, Soviet anti-Zionism has become completely irrational; were it not based on clear political calculations, one would have to consider it pathological. It regards Zionism as "the enemy" par excellence which occupies a prime place in Soviet propaganda, second only to that of China. The Zionism which the Soviet propagandists portray and attack often has no connection with the Jewish question at all; e.g., it is the greatest association of financial capital which "largely controls the economies of Western Europe and the United States" (Radio Peace and Progress, June 15, 1977); it "controls the banks in the United States" (B. Antonov, *Zarya Vostoka*, March 1, 1978);[4] it "controls and directly owns 158 of the 165 largest 'death corporations' in the West" (L. Korneev in *Krasnaya Zvezda*, November 16, 1977);[5] "20 percent of the periodicals in the United States and 80 percent of all television programs are enmeshed in the Zionist web, as are nearly a thousand newspapers out of the 1,811 published in the United States" (B. Antonov);[6] Zionism is supported by "monopoly capital in the form of banks, trusts, and corporations [which] does not necessarily appear as the capital of businessmen of Jewish origin [but] is frequently integrated into formally non-Jewish capitalist enterprises" like General Motors, Ford, General Electric, IBM, Mobil Oil, and Chrysler (Korneev, in *Ogonyok*, no. 28, 1978).[7] The Zionist organizations are the "tentacles" of the "predatory octopus" Israel; they "have enmeshed half the world and suck the lifeblood out of various countries" (V. Begun, *Invasion without Arms*).[8] Zionism "aspires to world power" (V. Skurlatov, *Zionism and Apartheid*),[9] its "main strategic goal [is to] establish dominion over the world" (Begun, op. cit.),[10] it is "a variant of ultra-imperialism";[11] it is an octopus of "espionage and subversion" operating like the Mafia (Korneev, *Ogonyok*, no. 5, 1977);[12] indeed the two are fused; it is "the Zionist Mafia of death" (Yu. Ivanov, *Komsomolskaya Pravda*, November 19, 1975);[13] "exerts influence on the secret service operations of a number of states" (L. Korneev, *Narody Azii i Afriki*, no. 1, 1976).[14] Zionism is, moreover, the "shock corps of imperialism" (L. Korneev, *Moskovskaya pravda*, February 12, 1978)[15] which is directed against the countries of the socialist bloc, including the Soviet Union (L. Korneev, *Krasnaya zvezda*, November 16, 1977),[16] and "against the world revolutionary, national-liberation, and Communist movements" (I. Migovich and D. Koretsky, *Liudyna i svit*, no.

1, 1978).[17] Zionism "has no equal among other bourgeois nationalist and anti-Communist tendencies and cohorts of world reaction" (V. Kiselev).[18]

Thus we are dealing here not with the Zionism of Herzl, Weizmann, or Ben-Gurion, but with a world-conspiracy myth, a Zionism as imagined in the infamous *Protocols of the Elders of Zion*. Indeed there is concrete evidence that Soviet propagandists consider the two terms interchangeable. L. Korneev, in an article in *Ogonyok*, no. 34, 1977, quotes a passage from Hermann Rauschnig's *Gespräche mit Hitler* in which the Führer describes that he learned political intrigue, techniques, conspiracy, subversion, and deception from the *Protocols of the Elders of Zion*; but in Korneev's version Hitler borrowed these "from the Zionists."[19]

The change in the Soviet interpretation of Zionism can be seen even if one ascends from the propagandistic depths to the scholarly heights. A survey of the treatment of this subject in various editions of authoritative Soviet encyclopaedias may serve as a useful yardstick. In the first and second editions of the *Great (Bolshaya) Soviet Encyclopedia*, the columns containing the entry on Zionism appeared in 1945 and 1956, as well as in vol. 7 of the *Small (Malaya) Soviet Encyclopedia* which appeared in 1930.[20] Zionism is criticized in this entry as a reactionary bourgeois-nationalist movement, a Jewish response to anti-Semitism supported by the Jewish petty and middle-class bourgeoisie. Based on the notion of a unified Jewish nation, Zionism preaches class cooperation and thereby distracts Jews from the revolutionary struggle. Its aim is the settlement of all Jews in Palestine. And without giving it much emphasis, the text also refers to a connection between Zionism and British imperialism. Lastly, it stresses that the USSR has solved the Jewish question and therefore there is no basis for Zionism in Soviet society.

Even the 1968 *Ukrainian Soviet Dictionary*, which briefly mentions the 1967 Six-Day War, sticks to the above definition.[21] But in the third edition of the *Great Soviet Encyclopedia*, which began to appear in 1970, and particularly in vol. 23 of 1976, we find the following definition of Zionism:

> Zionism is the most reactionary variety of Jewish bourgeois nationalism which became very widespread among the Jewish population of the capitalist countries in the twentieth century. Modern Zionism is a nationalist ideology, a far-flung system of organizations, with a policy expressing the interests of the great Jewish bourgeoisie, which is closely connected with the monopolist bourgeoisie of the imperialist states. The fundamental elements of modern Zionism are militant chauvinism, racism, anti-Communism, and anti-Sovietism.[22]

This contains many of the elements of the current propaganda campaign, viz., racism, anti-Sovietism, an extensive system of organizations, links with the monopolist bourgeoisie—all matters unrelated to the Jewish question.

Thus it would appear that at some point after the 1967 war, Zionism was redefined in the USSR. William Korey puts the date around August 1967, when an article appeared in the provincial press embodying the main themes of the current campaign.[23] But the new definition was not yet reflected in the 1968 *Ukrainian Encyclopedic Dictionary*, even though it refers to the 1967 war.[24] The most decisive turning point seems to have been the publication of Yury Ivanov's book *Beware: Zionism!* by the Moscow State Publishing House of Political Literature in 1969.

Apparently, therefore, we are facing a semantic problem in regard to Soviet anti-Zionism. The term has been used for ordinary political discussions of Zionist ideology, free from emotional components and prejudice (as was the case prior to 1967) and for a perverted, irrational attack on some imaginary world conspiracy, some Zionist monstrosity. Those who claim political legitimacy for the second approach misrepresent it, claiming it to be identical with the first, when in fact we have seen that the two are fundamentally different. It is a clever exploitation of a semantic confusion.

The question arises, however, whether this Soviet anti-Zionism, objectionable as it no doubt appears to all of us, is necessarily anti-Semitic.

Professor Shlomo Avineri advanced the view that the question whether an anti-Zionist statement is or is not anti-Semitic must be decided by Jews and not by the person who makes the statement. This is based on the analogous idea that if blacks find the term "Negro" derogatory or offensive then it is derogatory. In other words, racism or anti-Semitism is in the eye of the beholder *(Congress Monthly,* December 1975–January 1976).[25]

I accept Avineri's point that it may not be relevant whether the anti-Zionist perceives his anti-Zionism as anti-Semitic, and whether he admits that it is may be even less relevant. But I cannot agree that the anti-Semitic character of a statement depends entirely on how Jews react to it; it is possible for Jewish oversensitiveness to perceive as anti-Semitic a statement or act that non-Jews—and not only the "offender"—would fail to see as such. There should be no communication gap between Jews and non-Jews on this subject, and therefore we must try to find objective criteria for ascertaining the anti-Semitic nature of anti-Zionism.

The first such criterion is to be found in the fact that Zionists are almost by definition Jews. Occasionally a non-Jew like Winston Churchill calls himself a Zionist.[26] But in the perception of the ordinary reader of the Soviet press or anti-Zionist books, the Zionist will be identified as a Jew. In this respect the anti-Zionist camouflage of anti-Semitism reminds one of an earlier Soviet version of masked anti-Semitism, Stalin's and Zhdanov's anticosmopolitan campaign of the late forties and early fifties.[27] At that time "rootless cosmopolitan" and "the person without a home" were code words for "Jew." "Cosmopolitan" then and "Zionist" today are simply code words for "Jew," and very convenient code words they are, because anti-Semitism is usually regarded as being based on emotion and prejudice, whereas anticosmopolitanism and anti-Zionism sound like political views, something more acceptable to a Marxist-Leninist. But the anticosmopolitan campaign did not last as long as the current anti-Zionist campaign, now in operation for some twelve years, and the strictures against the cosmopolitans were not as virulent as the vilification of the Zionists.

This identity of Jew and Zionist, however, can give rise to confusion. In Soviet propaganda, practically every Jew who is not a faithful follower of the Soviet regime is labeled a Zionist, including Jews who are well known for their opposition to Zionism.

The second criticism is to be found in the equating of Zionism and Judaism, or at least in the stress on their common ideological roots. This is a recurrent theme of Soviet anti-Zionism. The Soviets ascribe what they call Zionist racism to the Old Testament concept that the Jews are God's chosen people. By implication, the charge of racism is made against the entire Jewish people, which was nurtured by Judaism and whose members, for the most part, respect their heritage irrespective of the degree of their personal observance of its rituals.

A third criterion is the application to anti-Zionism of the cliché, imagery, and phraseology of timeworn anti-Semitic propaganda.

1. This is most easily discernible in pictorial presentations, such as cartoons, films, and television programs, which often depict Zionists as the hook-nosed, thick-lipped, greasy stereotypes of Der Stürmer.[28]

2. Typical of verbal propaganda are anti-Semitic clichés, such as (and primarily) the allegation of a Zionist conspiracy aiming at world domination, which obviously derives from the conspiracy tradition of the Protocols.[29]

3. The reference to Zionist money power appears, for all practical purposes, as a repetition of one of the oldest anti-Semitic tocsins.

4. Another anti-Semitic pattern is the association of Jews with all kinds of evils, e.g., crime, moral degeneracy, avarice, prostitution, and also political vices, which in the Soviet vocabulary are primarily racism, imperialism, colonialism, capitalist exploitation, fascism, Nazism, neo-Nazism, and associated with the tsarist police, the CIA, and even Maoism. These are all attributed in Soviet propaganda to the Zionists. The most recent twist is the revival of the old anti-Semitic accusation of collusion with Freemasons.

5. Another device that identifies anti-Zionist propaganda as anti-Semitic is the stress on the obviously Jewish names of persons disapproved of or attacked, particularly when they happened to have changed their names,

the former Jewish name being added in brackets. This was a well-known technique of the Nazis, and it is often employed in Soviet anti-Zionist propaganda. (E.g., when Marcel Dassault is attacked as a representative of the financial oligarchy, he is described as "Dassault [Bloch]".)[30]

It is sometimes argued that the essential criteria of anti-Semitism are the emotional ingredients of hatred or contempt, the motives and intent of the perpetrator. I would reject these as criteria, not only because they are difficult to prove or disprove, and therefore cannot serve as reliable guides, but mainly because anti-Semitism must be measured by its effect. To use Marxist terminology, I am concerned with whether it is objectively, not subjectively, anti-Semitic. There is no doubt that whatever the motive or intent of Soviet anti-Zionist propaganda, its effect is anti-Semitic. If the propaganda is aimed at the Soviet population, the revival of traditional anti-Semitic images gives sustenance to old anti-Jewish prejudices in Russia, the Ukraine, etc., and may even turn previously unprejudiced persons against the Jews. If its purpose is to intimidate Soviet Jews, this is certainly anti-Semitic. And as far as the propaganda is meant for foreign consumption, its exportation is probably the most anti-Semitic feature of Soviet anti-Zionism.

Notes

1. E.g., the attitude of A. Toynbee in his argument with Professor H. H. Ben Sasson and Dr. Y. Herzog; H. H. Ben-Sasson, "An Israeli Historian's Analysis of the Challenge of Toynbee," *Iggeret Lagolah*, no. 76 (1967), pp. 31–40; "Mastema B'shita, Torato shel A. J. Toynbee" [Systematic hatred, theory of A. J. Toynbee], *Mussaf Davar-Massa*, no. 46 (204), November 7, 1974. *A People That Dwells Alone: Speeches and writings of Yaacov Herzog*, ed. M. Louvish (London: Weidenfeld & Nicolson, 1975), pp. 21–47. See, too, H. Arendt, *The Jew as Pariah: Jewish Identity and Politics in the Modern Age* (New York: Grove Press, 1978), pp. 18–36, 125–192.

2. Lenin, "Polozheniye Bunda v partii" [The Bund's position in the party], in *Polnoye Sobraniye Sochinenii* (Moscow: Politizdat, 1959), vol. 8, p. 72.

3. Ibid., pp. 73–74.

4. B. Antonov, "Pautina sionizma v Amerike" [The Zionist spider's web in America], *Zarya Vostoka*, March 1, 1978, reprinted in *Jews and the Jewish People—Excerpts from the Soviet Press* (hereafter cited as *JJP-quarterly*), vol. 87, no. 563.

5. See above.

6. Antonov, op. cit., p. 44.

7. See above.

8. V. Begun, *Vtorzheniye bez oruzhiya* [Invasion without arms] (Moscow, 1977), p. 22.

9. B. Skurlatov, *Sionizm i apateid* [Zionism and apartheid] (Kiev, 1975), p. 42.

10. Begun, op. cit., p. 44.

11. Ibid., p. 45.

12. See above.

13. Yu. Ivanov, "Vopreki mneniyu bolshinstva" [Against the majority opinion], *Komsomolskaya Pravda*, November 19, 1975, reprinted in *JJP-quarterly*, vol. 70, no. 300.

14. L. Korneev, "Sekretnye sluzhby mezhdunarodnogo sionizma i gosudarstva Izrail" [The secret service of international Zionism and the State of Israel], *Narody Azii i Afriki*, no. 1 (1976), reprinted in *JJP-quarterly*, vol. 72, no. 242.

15. L. Korneev, "Zapozdaloye prozreniye" [A delayed revelation], *Moskovskaya Pravda*, February 12, 1978, reprinted in *JJP-quarterly*, vol. 87, no. 549.

16. See above.

17. J. Migovich and D. Koretsky, "Neokhasidizm na sluzhbe reaktsii" [Neo-Hassidism in the service of reaction], *Lyudina i Svit*, no. 1 (1978), reprinted in *JJP-quarterly*, vol. 87, no. 4.

18. V. Kiselev, "Sionizm v sisteme imperializma" [Zionism in the imperialist system], in *Mezhdunarodny sionizm—istoriya i politika* (Moscow: Nauka, 1977), Vladimir Kiselev—Candidate of History, Institute of Eastern Studies, Academy of Sciences USSR.

19. L. Korneev, "Zloveshchiye tayny sionizma" [The malicious secrets of Zionism], *Ogonyok*, August 20, 1977, no. 34; August 27, 1977, no. 35; reprinted in *JJP-quarterly*, vol. 83, no. 335.

Korneev's quote from Hermann Rauschning: "He [Hitler] learned from the Zionists (and from the *Protocols of Zion*) political intrigue, conspiracy, revolutionary subversion, camouflage, deception, and organization!" Rauschning's version of Hitler's remark: "I learned a great deal from these *Protocols*; I've always learned much from my opponents. I learned revolutionary technique from Lenin, Trotsky, and other Marxists." In *Gesprach mit Hitler* (New York: Europa Verlag, 1940), pp. 225, 227.

20. *Bolshaya Sovetskaya Entsiklopediya*, 1956, p. 138. *Malaya Sovetskaya Entsiklopediya*, 1930, pp. 138, 513–514.

21. *Ukrainsky Sovetsky Entsiklopedichesky Slovar* (Kiev: Akademya Nauk Ukrainskoy SSR, 1968).

22. *Bolshaya Sovetskaya Entsiklopediya*, 3d ed., vol. 23.

23. See the article by Korey.

24. See above, n. 21.

25. Regarding Avineri's attitude, see also Sh. Avineri, "Aspects of Post-Holocaust Anti-Jewish Attitudes," in *World Jewry and the State of Israel*, ed. M. Davis (New York, 1977), pp. 3–10.

26. On the relationship of Churchill to Zionism, see M. Gilbert, *Churchill and Zionism*. (London: World Jewish Congress, 1974), pp. 26–27; J. Cohen, *Churchill and Palestine, 1939–1942* (Jerusalem: Yad Izhak Ben-Zvi Publications, 1976), pp. 12–14 (Hebrew sect.); *Encyclopaedia Hebraica*, vol. 28, p. 1000.

27. See above.

28. Y. Nir, *The Arab-Israeli Conflict in Soviet Caricature, 1967–1973* (Tel Aviv: 1976). For films and television programs, see above.

29. Regarding the *Protocols*, see above.

30. Regarding Marcel Dassault, see V. E. Kolomiytsev, "Gospodin Mirazh" [Mr. Mirage], *JJP-quarterly*, vol. 44, no. 472.

Israel as a Factor in Soviet Anti-Semitism

UMBERTO TERRACINI

THE TITLE OF my speech, "Israel as a Factor in Soviet Anti-Semitism," is designed to draw attention to a basic element in the history of all states, namely, the interdependence of their foreign and internal policies. In the case in point, this concept can be applied by formulating the question of whether, and to what degree, the creation and existence of the State of Israel and its position on the international scene can be correlated with the revival and sudden expansion of the anti-Semitic movement in the Soviet Union.

In my opinion there can be no doubt that the existence of Israel and its foreign policy are major causes of Soviet anti-Semitism. This, however, is not the fault of Israel. What has had, and continues to have, great influence over the foreign policies of all countries is the existence of two large opposing blocs characterized, among other things, by their differing institutional models and socioeconomic systems. One could, therefore, consider Soviet anti-Semitism as going beyond nationalism, although admittedly, the Soviet Union defines Jews as members of a nationally differentiated group for which the territory of Birobidjan was provided. And it is a violation of the Soviet Constitution to discriminate against any of the nationalities within the USSR's borders.

The Jews did not wish to migrate to the territory assigned them (and not only because of the discomforts of the area due to its geographical location and harsh climate). They preferred their traditional homes despite the fact that they had never enjoyed the opportunity to organize their lives according to their own laws and customs. [1]

There is no doubt that they welcomed the creation of the State of Israel (to which their native country, the Soviet Union, had contributed significantly) as an act of justice and a great achievement for civilization. By the same token, for a long time they also appreciated the Soviet policy in favor of the Arab struggle for liberation from colonialism, in accordance with the October Revolution's two basic strategic principles: the revolt of workers against class domination by the various national bourgeoisies, and the revolt of national groups against foreign imperialist domination.

I would like to note here that of these two driving forces of the socialist revolution, the latter has already fully achieved its objective. Colonial empires have fallen everywhere, and the capitalist system is now being assailed directly or indirectly wherever it is still in power in the great majority of states, old and new.

It is a fact, however, that the greater part of Soviet Jewry ignored the road leading toward Israel for many years, thereby proving that the bonds tying them to their native land were strong indeed.

But proceeding with my analysis, I wish to point out that anti-Semitism has been for centuries, hence long before the formation of the Soviet state, a basic characteristic of the peoples who comprise the USSR.[2] The Soviet government never really tried to eradicate it (except in the years immediately after the revolution). On the contrary, it has exploited this tendency time and again for the purpose of serving its internal or international policies. The lashing out against the Bund in prerevolutionary times is one example.[3] Even more obvious were the protracted conflicts which lacerated the Bolshevik leadership. The anti-Semitic aspects of these conflicts inevitably appeared because of the Jewish origins of many of the most-well-known opposition figures (Trotsky, Zinoviev, Radek, Kamenev, etc.).[4] Stalin in particular played the trump card of anti-Semitism in those often tragic conflicts, as in the notorious Doctors' Plot, wherein all the doctors turned out to be Jews.[5] Nor was anti-Semitism entirely extraneous to the infamous Molotov-Ribbentrop Pact, which was concluded between the Soviet Union and Germany just before the outbreak of the Second World War.

There is a complete absence of moral considerations in the Soviet Union's foreign policy decisions, to the point of her sacrificing the very ideological principles she declares to profess. This is obvious today in her close relations with the Arab states of the Middle East, which after their liberation from colonial domination, established political institutions and economic systems having absolutely nothing to do with socialism. They are, in fact, autocratic; and their enormous wealth and resources, especially oil, belong exclusively to those who wield governmental power.

It is, therefore, not for ideological or socioeconomic reasons that the Soviet Union (or rather its rulers, since the common people have no way of interfering with the political decisions of their state) invariably sides with the Arab states against Israel in international affairs.[6] The Soviet choice is based essentially on military strategy, not to speak of the neoimperialist imperatives inspired and nourished by the "great-power" politics of the Soviet Union.

In order to render the USSR's pro-Arab policies acceptable to the Soviet people despite the many burdensome sacrifices necessitated by arms expenditures, the Soviet government tells its people that their country is seriously endangered by the existence of the State of Israel, which is supported by all the Jews of the world, and therefore also by those who live in the Soviet Union. Anti-Semitism, perhaps rebaptized as anti-Zionism, thus becomes a tool serving the nationalistic maneuvers with which the Soviet leaders convince their people to support their choice of the Arab states. This frantic anti-Semitic campaign came as the greatest surprise to the Soviet Jews themselves.

After World War II they sincerely believed that their participation in the war and in the victory over the Nazis had finally assured them full and equal rights under Soviet law. This was one reason why initially so few of them sought or planned to move to the new State of Israel. The latter held little power of attraction for them. Nor does it attract them today; many Soviet Jews change their destination and proceed to some Western country instead of Israel after they arrive in Vienna, and after having obtained their emigration visas at the cost of difficulties and risks.[7]

What leads them to abandon the Soviet Union, in fact, is not a desire to return to the ancient homeland of their forefathers, to Zion, but to escape an oppressive regime. State-sponsored anti-Semitism as an internal policy and a pro-Arab foreign policy are thus two inseparable aspects of Soviet policy as a whole. Considering the long-range character of all international politics, one can therefore foresee that Soviet anti-Semitism is also destined for a long life. But this implies the danger that at a certain point the Soviet Jews will turn to some imprudent course of action (hopefully nonviolent) out of a desire for self-protection, and I say this not because I fear that the Soviet leaders wish to find a pretext for a new "final solution" modeled on the Nazi example.

I do not share the pessimistic predictions expressed today by various speakers. The mass physical destruction of Jews does not at all fit into the logic of Soviet politics. Moreover, the Soviet Jews are well protected by the solidarity of all the Jews of the world. I am encouraged in this belief by the "soft" techniques with which anti-Semitic persecution is being implemented in the USSR. This persecution is not based on specific laws or the use of direct or immediate violence against individuals; it uses the means offered by the ordinary laws of the land, which are, moreover, not at all based on respect for the freedom of the individual citizen. As we know, it is extremely difficult for Soviet citizens to obtain a passport to go abroad, or even to get the compulsory one for use inside the country. It is sufficient for the Soviet leaders to enforce existing laws with particular severity to make the lives of its citizens intolerable.

Thus, thanks to the law against so-called parasites (i.e., persons with no regular means of employment), the authorities merely have to deprive a person of his job under the most absurd pretext (which is what happens to Jews as soon as they ask for a passport to Israel). He may then be accused of parasitism, placed on trial, and convicted.[8] Likewise, a gathering of several Jews in a private home is subject to punishment as a "nonauthorized assembly" (especially if the gathering is for purposes of praying together or for studying Hebrew), and voila! the trial and sentence find "legal" justification.[9]

The methodical repetition of these punitive measures against individuals makes the burden even harder to bear; these vexations lead to despair, despite their relative mildness.

I have passed, via a chain of ideas, from a discussion of anti-Semitism in the Soviet Union to a discussion of a regime that is antilibertarian for all citizens. Only under such a regime is it possible to conceive of a policy of persecution against a religious group, professional category, or national minority. The causes and explanations offered are not important here. Persecution always offends the dignity of human beings and defiles the spiritual values which are the fruits of civilization and the heart and marrow of every person who considers himself free.

So while I express my solidarity with the Soviet Jews who are persecuted in their country merely because they are Jews, it is to the entire Soviet people that I would like to express my wishes for the achievement and enjoyment of complete freedom.

Notes

1. J. Levavi (Babitsky), *The Jewish Colonization in Birobijan* (in Hebrew) (Jerusalem: Historical Society of Israel, 1965), pp. 43–56; M. Altshuler, *Soviet Jewry Today: A Socio-Demographic Analysis* (Jerusalem: Hebrew University, 1972), p. 83.

2. See S. Ettinger, "The Jews in Russia at the Outbreak of the Revolution," in *The Jews in Soviet Russia since 1917,* ed. L. Kochan, 3d ed. (Oxford University Press, 1978), pp. 15–29; and S. Ettinger, *Modern Anti-Semitism: Studies and Essays* (in Heb.) (Tel Aviv, 1978), pp. 169–189.

3. S. Schwartz, *The Jews in the Soviet Union* (Syracuse University Press, 1951), pp. 46–55.

4. Ettinger, *Modern Anti-Semitism,* p. 181.

5. B. D. Weinryb, "Anti-Semitism in Soviet Russia," in *The Jews in Soviet Russia since 1917,* ed. L. Kochan (Oxford University Press, 1978), pp. 321–323.

6. J. B. Schechtman, "The USSR, Zionism, and Israel," in *The Jews in Soviet Russia since 1917,* ed. L. Kochan (Oxford University Press, 1979), pp. 128–130; J. Frankel, "The Anti-Zionist Press Campaigns in the USSR, 1969–1971: An Internal Dialogue?" in *Soviet Jewish Affairs,* 1972, no. 3, p. 5.

7. Z. Alexander, "The Emigration Policy of the Soviet Union (1968–1978): Cause and Statistical Data," in *Behinot: Studies on Jews in the USSR and Eastern Europe* (Jerusalem and Tel Aviv: Hebrew University of Jerusalem, Center for Research of Eastern European Jewry, 1979), nos. 8–9, p. 35.

8. For example, regarding the prosecution and conviction of Y. Begun as a parasite, see Dr. J. E. Singer, *The Case of Yosef Begun: Analysis and Documents* (Jerusalem and Tel Aviv, 1979), pp. 28–48.

9. *JJP-Jewish Samizdat*, vol. 17, pp. 109–153.

Historical and Internal Political Factors in Soviet Anti-Semitism

SHMUEL ETTINGER

AT THE END of the nineteenth and beginning of the twentieth century, tsarist Russia was notorious for the anti-Semitic attitudes and practices that permeated its government and public. The prevalence of anti-Semitism stemmed from the combined influence of the three major elements that have sustained and nourished anti-Semitism in a variety of historical settings. The constant one of these elements is the negative image of the Jew, or the negative Jewish stereotype, which is rooted in a long and stable religious, cultural, and social tradition. The dynamic elements are the political and social tensions that create a need to exhibit a villain—evil in intent and alien in demeanor and spirit—who is responsible for undermining stability. By manipulating these elements, rulers, demagogues, and politicians have been able to seduce the masses into supporting them and the attainment of their goals.

The vividness of the negative Jewish stereotype in Russia was demonstrated during the sixteenth to eighteenth centuries, when virulent anti-Jewish feelings were aired on a variety of occasions despite the fact that not a single Jew was allowed to enter the Muscovite state.[1] When Russia's armies conquered Poland, they persecuted and massacred Jewish townspeople.[2] The same was true of the Ukrainians during their short-lived attempt to achieve political independence during the mid-seventeenth-century Chmielnicki revolt, and in the framework of the popular, revolutionary Haidamak movement of the eighteenth century.[3] The portrayal of the Jew as an alien, exploiter, and enemy became part and parcel of the folklore and cultural traditions of the Ukraine and can be found in historical chronicles and ballads. In the nineteenth century, it even grew into an important motif in Ukrainian and Russian literature.[4]

In the second half of the nineteenth century, with the development of the

172

Slavophiles-versus-Westerners controversy among Russian intellectuals and politicians, this religious and literary tradition became an ingredient of a political ideology.[5] The Westerners claimed that in order to overcome her backwardness, Russia must adopt modern European forms of administration, economic life, and social development, while the Slavophiles sought the cure for all the country's ills in a return to ancient norms and the way of life traditional to Russia before the advent of Peter the Great. The paradox in Russia's political structure lay in the fact that both the right-wing Slavophiles and the radical, revolutionary populists (the Narodniki) were for the most part anti-Westerners. They rejected the capitalist economic system, opposed constitutional safeguards for individual liberties, and believed that the rural communal organization known as the *Obshchina* was the essence of the just society—a form of "Slavic socialism." As they saw it, Russia's salvation depended on her ability to prevent the development of a capitalist economy and evade the influences of the "rotten West." This attitude brought the Narodniki into close spiritual affinity with the Slavophile way of thinking. The result was that both movements were hostile to Jews and their allegedly destructive role in Russian life.[6]

The Jew was viewed as the capitalist par excellence—parasitic, rapacious, the bearer of economic, social, and moral damage to the "host nation" or "the basic population." Hence the Ukrainian democrats of the 1860s and 1870s dreamed of a general expulsion of the Jews from the Ukraine. The Slavophiles looked upon the pogroms of the early 1880s as a just punishment of the Jews by "the people," while the Narodniki saw in these pogroms the beginning of the thoroughgoing social and political revolution to come. The liberals in Russia were a small minority who were held in contempt. Only a few of them—and an even smaller number of radicals—were prepared to view the situation of the Jews in a more objective light. It was only at the end of the nineteenth century, when a "liberation movement" emerged in Russia to fight against the autocratic tsarist regime, that a sector of the Russian public began to look upon official anti-Semitism as a tool of reactionary policy. Within a short time, the small opposition parties and the majority of the Russian intelligentsia began to reject anti-Semitism. With this change in attitude, the "Jewish question" became one of the central issues in Russian political life, a litmus test for the supporters and opponents of the autocratic regime.[7]

For several generations, the Jews were culturally isolated from the mainstream of Russian life, politically passive, and loyal to the regime. Then the process of modernization in the second half of the nineteenth century and the emergence of new forms of political activity stimulated Jewish involvement in the liberal and revolutionary movements.[8] When the supporters of autocracy claimed that these movements were alien to the Russian spirit and tradition and the product of a Jewish and Polish plot, anti-Semitism turned into a hallmark of loyalty and patriotism:

The abrogation of all laws discriminating against Jews after the democratic revolution of February 1917 did not meet with opposition, even from the right-wing political parties and press. But during the Civil War, anti-Semitism again took hold among the White regimes and armies.[9] Since the opponents of the new Bolshevik regime depicted it as being dominated by Jews, strong measures were adopted against violent anti-Semites, and at the end of the 1920s the authorities instituted a broad educational program to combat anti-Semitism.[10] It is true that Stalin's supporters availed themselves of anti-Semitic arguments in party debates. But it was only during the latter half of the 1930s that Stalin's personal inclination toward anti-Semitism (of which there is definitive evidence) became a political factor. This reversal may have been bound up with Stalin's early attempts to come to an accommodation with Hitler; the elimination of Jews could have been a step toward achieving this goal. On the other hand, Jews played an outstanding role in Russia's economic, technological, and cultural life and were considered staunch supporters of the Communist regime. It is difficult to overestimate their contribution to Russian life during the 1930s and throughout World War II.

There is no clear-cut explanation for the launching of a strong anti-Semitic campaign during the last years of Stalin's rule, the period subsequently referred to as the black years of Soviet Jewry.[11] The campaign was ostensibly directed against "cosmopolitans," "people without roots in our soil," and the like. But its distinctly anti-Semitic character was an open secret among Jews and non-Jews alike. This campaign was the first expression of an official anti-Semitic policy in the Soviet era. It was marked by the arrest and execution of Jewish intellectuals, the mass dismissal of Jews from influential positions, and even a plan to expel all the Jews from European Russia and deport them to camps in Kazakhstan and Siberia. The exposé of the so-called Doctors' Plot portrayed "Jewish bourgeois nationalism" as a link in the worldwide anti-Soviet conspiracy, which embraced the government of Israel, the Joint Distribution Committee, and the CIA.[12] It was only Stalin's death that saved Soviet Jews from the harrowing consequences of this campaign.

The "thaw" that accompanied Khrushchev's rise to power spawned a self-contradictory policy toward the Jews. On the one hand, their talents were needed by the Soviet state; on the other, however, the very policy of liberalization afforded greater opportunities for the expression of popular opinion, which was not supportive of the Jews. A combination of historical anti-Semitism, the exposure of a large portion of the Russian population to anti-Semitic propaganda during the Nazi occupation of Soviet territory, harsh living conditions in the areas of the USSR devastated by the war, and the widespread feeling that the Russian people had borne the principal burden of the war against Hitler engendered an outburst of chauvinistic, xenophobic sentiment in which the suspicion and hatred of Jews was a prime ingredient. Khrushchev himself believed that the executed Jewish intellectuals had planned to establish an anti-Soviet Jewish republic in the Crimea.[13] He was imbued with many of the notions of popular anti-Semitism, and in the trials of so-called economic criminals he tried to pin much of the blame for the Soviet Union's economic difficulties on the Jews.[14]

The principal difference between Stalin's regime and that of his successor, however, lay in the growing influence of popular feelings and public opinion on the formulation of the official policy line regarding internal political questions, despite the government's firm control over the mass media. It appears, for example, that the secret instructions limiting the acceptance of Jews into institutions of higher learning and the employment of Jews in sensitive branches of the economy and sciences were dictated more by popular distrust and hatred of Jews than by the "national interest." At the same time, it must be remembered that due to Stalin's policy of eliminating many members of the Soviet intelligentsia and Russia's phenomenal losses during the war, a large portion of the Soviet bureaucracy (including people of the highest rank) and the country's professional class consisted of people from the lower strata of the population, with all their prejudices, anti-Semitism being hardly the least notorious of them. As a result, an accusation which had been widespread during the first years after the revolution—namely, that the regime favored the Jews, and that consequently they had the most to gain from the Soviet system—now reemerged in spite of the above-mentioned discriminatory regulations (which were not known to the lower strata of the Russian population).

It is not difficult to account for these feelings if we consider the yawning gap between the standards of living, incomes, social benefits, and educational opportunities of manual laborers (particularly the rural population) and of officials and professionals concentrated in the Soviet Union's larger cities. A fundamental change in the social structure of the USSR's Jewish population was engendered by the extermination of the Jews in Russia's small towns by the Nazis, and their destruction of Jewish agricultural settlements. An additional reason for this fundamental change was the sharp rise in the number of Jewish scientists, professionals, and students during the postwar years (and at a slower rate during the 1950s and 1960s; only at the end of the 1960s did this number begin to decline). Very few Jews engage in manual labor, and despite the discriminatory regulations, the Jews try by every means possible to provide their children with a higher education. To the above-mentioned social strata, the Jews therefore represented the hated middle class (which officially does not exist in the Soviet Union), and their "social enmity" is heavily mixed with anti-Semitic prejudices. At the same time, the professional intelligentsia and even scholarly and artistic circles look upon the Jews as potential rivals and impel the bureaucracy to implement the discriminatory regulations to the letter, especially in light of the fact that the Soviet Union has recently experienced a glut of technical and scientific intelligentsia and even hidden unemployment. Thus we can see that conditions of social unrest and fear in the USSR provide a favorable climate for exploiting the negative stereotype of the Jew. Such exploitation is particularly evident in the widespread anti-Semitic propaganda of the mass media, where any mention of Jews and Jewish affairs is exclusively negative.

Another source of unrest and tension that has a direct effect on the sharpening of anti-Semitic sentiment is the relationship between the Russians and the smaller nationalities and ethnic groups in the Soviet Union, particularly in the non-Russian republics. As a result of demographic changes, the proportion of Russians in the overall population of the USSR is declining (though I should add that the results of the latest population census, taken in January 1979, are still unknown).[15] Russians, however, still hold the key positions not only in the central government and party apparatus, but in those of the national republics as well. Published data indicate that the proportional increase of Russians among so-called scientific workers (a privileged group) is greater than the increase in their ratio in the population. It appears that this situation likewise holds true in other important fields. At the same time, the small national groups in the USSR have begun to press for greater representation in the government, the party bureaucracy, scientific institutions, and the arts—a demand connoted by the expression "national cadres." For a variety of historical reasons, even though Stalin expelled the Jews from influential positions in the government and the party, and Khrushchev completed the job by removing them from the bureaucracy at even the local level, the Jews continue to play an important role in the economy, technology, the sciences, and the arts, significantly exceeding their ratio in the population at large. It is convenient for the central authorities to satisfy the demand for national cadres by replacing Jews with members of local nationalities. The intelligentsia of the national republics not only compete with the Jews for jobs but regard them as bearers of the Russian language and culture into their national domains, since the Jews have for the most part assimilated into Russian culture. Hence in some of these republics, we find an additional reason for anti-Jewish sentiment—the Jew is perceived as a Russifier.

Due to the government's policy on the "Jewish question" and the social and national tensions within the Soviet Union, there have been both a sharp decline in the number of Jews holding important positions and an attendant intensification of anti-Semitic attitudes. This process has created a vicious circle: discrimination, which sharpened Jewish sensitivity, ultimately led to the creation of a group consciousness among many Jews—and in some even the arousal of nationalist or religious feelings—and impelled them toward thoughts of emigration. The most courageous went so far as to initiate an open struggle for the right to emigrate. At the very same time, however, this movement toward Jewish consciousness sparked off accusations of Jewish clannishness, heightened distrust of Jews on both the governmental and popular level, charges of disloyalty to the "socialist fatherland," and so on. The Six-Day War, which was perceived as a defeat for both the Arabs and their Soviet patrons, aroused anti-Semitic feelings among the military, intelligence quarters, and other ruling circles. It is not by chance that the most virulent anti-Semitic publications are sponsored by newspapers and publishing houses connected with the Ministry of Defense.[16]

It stands to reason that the intensive anti-Semitic campaign of the last decade—which includes the claim that world Zionism is the Soviet Union's most dangerous enemy, the systematic falsification of the Jewish past, the emergence of "specialists" in Jewish affairs, the use of anti-Semitic literature of the past, and attempts to incite and exploit anti-Semitic sentiment abroad—is designed to achieve specific political goals. That it is not merely political opportunism, that is, an attempt to exploit an existing mood, is clear from the fact that the USSR is today the world's principal supplier of anti-Semitic propaganda through the mass media, and a guiding hand is evident in the direction of the campaign.

There is reason to believe that this anti-Semitic onslaught is merely one aspect of a power struggle between opposing factions with the Soviet ruling elite. Its recent intensity is reminiscent of the situation during Stalin's last years, when his prospective heirs used anti-Semitism in their struggle for the succession. Today the struggle among Brezhnev's prospective successors is not limited to the party's inner circle alone, and appeals for the support of one section or another of the bureaucracy, or even of the public, become even more attractive when based upon ideological anti-Semitism disguised as the struggle against the "worst enemy," world Zionism. The hardliners and neo-Stalinists, who appear to be the most outspoken anti-Semites, can point to a "lack of vigilance" in the "ideological struggle" against the "Zionist enemy" as the reason for "going soft" in matters related to détente or other aspects of international relations, or in suppressing dissent within the Soviet Union. At the same time, attacks on the "reactionary Jewish bourgeoisie" can serve as a cover for the rise in the number of emigrants and justify those who call for the expulsion of "untrustworthy elements."

Whatever the reasons for the prevalence of anti-Semitism in the ruling circles of the Soviet Union, the Jewish historical experience has shown that when a world power exploits anti-Jewish sentiment for its own political purposes, the result can be a real and present danger to Soviet Jewry, the State of Israel, and the entire world.

Notes

1. S. Ettinger, *Modern Anti-Semitism: Studies and Essays* (in Heb.) (Tel Aviv, 1978), pp. 145–146.

2. S. W. Baron, *The Russian Jews under Tsars and Soviet*, 2d ed. (New York and London: Macmillan, 1976, pp. 10–12.

3. See S. Dubnow, *History of the Jews in Russia and Poland*, vol. 1 (Philadelphia: Jewish Publication Society, 1916), pp. 144–153, 182–187.

4. Regarding the Jews in Ukrainian and Soviet literature, see Ettinger, *Modern Anti-Semitism*, pp. 99–144.

5. Ibid., pp. 101–104.

6. L. Greenberg, *The Jews in Russia: The Struggle for Emancipation* (New Haven and London: Yale University Press, 1951), vol. 2, pp. 162–163.

7. Ettinger, *Modern Anti-Semitism*, pp. 176–177; also Baron, pp. 51–56.

8. Greenberg, vol. 1 (1944), pp. 146–159; vol. 2 (1951), pp. 138–159.

9. Baron, pp. 179–186.

10. Regarding political publications attacking anti-Semitism, in traditional form (a remnant from the past) and in contemporary Soviet Society, see *Russian Publications on Jews and Judaism in the Soviet Union, 1917–1967*, ed. M. Altshuler (Jerusalem: Society for Research on Jewish Communities, 1970), pp. 43 (Hebrew sec.), 51–66; also S. Schwartz, *Anti-Semitizm v Sovetskom Soyuze* [Anti-Semitism in the Soviet Union] (New York: Checkhov Publishing House, 1952), pp. 80–97.

11. B. J. Goldberg, *The Jewish Problem in the Soviet Union: An Analysis and a Solution* (New York: Crown, 1961), pp. 101–103; Baron, pp. 269–278; Y. Gilboa, *The Black Years of Soviet Jewry 1939–1953* (Boston and Toronto: Little, Brown, 1971), pp. 311–312.

12. "Shpiony i ubiytsy pod lichinoy uchyonykh-vrachey," *Izvestia*, January 13, 1953; V. Minayev, "Sionistskaya agentura amerikanskoy razvedki," *Novoye Vremya*, 1953, no. 4, pp. 13–16; P. Plotnikov and A. Lipatov, "Rotozei—posobniki vraga," *Pravda*, January 31, 1953, reprinted in *Jews and the Jewish People, 1948–1953* (Jerusalem, 1973), no. 2139, p. 1744.

13. S. W. Baron, pp. 272–273.

14. Regarding economic crimes, see S. Schwartz, *The Jews in the Soviet Union Since the Beginning of World War II (1939-1965)* (in Russian) (New York: American Jewish Committee, 1966), pp. 325–347; also B. D. Weinryb, "Anti-Semitism in Soviet Russia," *The Jews in Soviet Russia Since 1917*, ed. L. Kochan (Oxford University Press, 1978), p. 326.

15. Data on the results of the census appeared at the beginning of 1980. See the chapter on the structure of the population in the USSR, *Naseleniye SSSR po dannym vsesoyuznoy perepisi naseleniya 1979 goda* (Moscow: Politizdat, 1980), pp. 27–30.

16. These are some of the anti-Semitic publications in Voenizdat: I. Belyaev, *S chyornogo khoda: Dokumentalnaya povest* [From the Backdoor: Documentary tale], 1972; Yu. Kolesnikov, *Zanaves pripodnyat* [The curtain raised], novel, 1979; S. Krylov, *Taynoye oruzhiye sionizma* [The secret weapon of Zionism], 1972; N. Pokormyak, *Armia Izrailya-orudiye imperialisticheskoy agressii* [The Israeli army—a tool of imperialist aggression]. 1970; I. M. Shevtsov, *Lyubov i nenavist: Povest*, [Love and hate: Novel], 1970.

Soviet Anti-Semitism and Jewish Scientists

LAURENT SCHWARTZ

I SHALL SPEAK about anti-Semitism at the Soviet universities, with particular emphasis upon anti-Semitism in the field of mathematics. An anomalous development is taking place in this field which may serve to clarify the entire problem. Under Stalin mathematics was probably more secure than other branches of science, doubtless because it is less accessible. In physics, on the contrary, such fields as quantum physics were sometimes condemned as anti-Marxist, and in biology all progress was rendered practically impossible for twenty-five years because of Lysenko.[1]

At present, however, mathematics is the victim of anti-Semitism. Certain persons in this field are playing the same role that Lysenko assumed in biology. They are taking advantage of the general atmosphere to systematically discriminate against Jews, to the impairment of the development of mathematics in the USSR.[2]

Occurrences in this field cannot be equated with what is taking place in other branches of Soviet science, not only in regard to anti-Semitism, but also with reference to liberalization and to the nature of human relations.

Soviet mathematics is on the brink of destruction. To substantiate this assertion, the behavior of at least two Soviet mathematicians, I. Vinogradov and L. Pontryagin, must be mentioned.[3]

Vinogradov is known in the world of mathematics for his work in arithmetic. He is a director of the Steklov Institute, which is affiliated with the Academy of Sciences and brings together hundreds of persons engaged in research. Vinogradov openly espouses anti-Semitic opinions which are not even camouflaged with anti-Zionism. At present, he boasts that virtually no Jewish researchers are to be found any longer in the Steklov Institute.

Pontryagin has a more varied background. He is a renowned mathemati-

179

cian of deserved reputation despite the fact that he is blind, which has earned him both fame and sympathy. During the war and postwar years his personality changed. He became rigidly authoritarian in his relations with the scientific community in general, and a notorious and active anti-Semite. Until last summer he was a member of the executive committee of the International Mathematics Union. In this capacity he directed the National Committee of Soviet Mathematicians, which controlled the foreign travel of Soviet mathematicians. Pontryagin also heads several of the most important mathematical publications, such as *Matematichesky sbornik*. Consequently, when so influential a figure openly espouses anti-Semitism, the effects are not inconsiderable.

At the present time an anti-Jewish quota is being applied throughout the field of Soviet mathematics. This situation is exemplified by the changing content of *Matematichesky sbornik* (of which Pontryagin is chief editor). Out of 108 articles printed in 1970, for example, 43 were signed by Jewish mathematicians; in 1974 there was a decline to 33 out of 111; in 1975 to 12 out of 96; in 1977 to 5 out of 95. At present, no Jewish mathematicians can publish any articles, regardless of whether or not they wish to emigrate. Their writings are either flatly refused or shelved under various pretexts.

As for admissions to departments of science at the University of Moscow, in 1948 a third of those admitted were Jews. They comprised a much higher percentage than that of the Jews in the general population. And as late as 1964 Jews still comprised 84 out of 410 admissions. During the last few years, however, no more than 0 to 5 Jews have been admitted to the Moscow University science departments, out of an average of 500 admissions. In other words, a Jewish student in the sciences knows today that he has practically no chance of gaining admission to Moscow University. It is possible for him to go elsewhere, for example, to the Institute of Electro-Chemistry or to the University of Yaroslavl, which currently has something of a reputation as a refuge for Jews. Nevertheless, a young Jewish intellectual, even though brilliant, knows that he has no real future in the sciences and particularly in Soviet mathematics.

As for the situation in regard to doctoral theses, we may note, first of all, that there are two distinct doctoral-thesis levels: candidacy, which is inferior to the French thesis, and the doctorate, which is superior to it. There is a thesis examination committee called VAK.[4] It ignores all theses submitted by Jews. Thus a world-renowned mathematician like Margulis, who was awarded the Fields Medal at the last International Congress of Mathematicians in Helsinki, does not have a doctorate because VAK refused to permit him to defend his thesis.

Moreover, let us take, for example, the case of the Special Lyceum in

Moscow. I have visited this lyceum. It was a school in which, from the second to the last grade, the mathematical abilities of pupils were given particular encouragement. Thus the Special Lyceum was an arboretum for future mathematicians. It was a very successful institution. A great number of the younger Soviet mathematicians of today are its alumni, and it was a model for similar schools in Eastern bloc countries. Not surprisingly, many children from Jewish families attended the Special Lyceum, and many Jewish students who took the entrance examinations to the mathematics department of Moscow University were its graduates. Moreover, the children of liberals also found a haven at the lyceum; there is an obvious affinity among the persecuted—be they Jews or liberals. Hence, eventually the Special Lyceum appeared to pose so great a danger to the Soviet authorities that it was closed down. Thus was one of the finest preparatory institutions for Soviet mathematicians eliminated.

Restrictive policies in regard to Moscow University entrance examinations represent an even graver situation.[5] The examiners are usually mathematicians of considerable repute. Yet at present they are expected to exclude all Jewish applicants without saying openly that Jews are not being admitted because they are Jews. The examiners have a blacklist of persons to be excluded. It contains the names not only of Jews but also of non-Jews considered untrustworthy by the authorities. If the examiner is a conscientious mathematician, what is he to do when he is given such a blacklist? He cannot submit to its dictates, and those who still have any professional integrity have had the courage not to submit. But as a result they have been deprived of their role as examiners. In some cases the punishment has been more ominous: having refused to do what was expected of them, they may be looked upon as proto-dissidents. Consequently, today, entrance examinations to the University of Moscow are conducted by persons with no ethical or scientific qualms about barring blacklisted applicants. There is, of course, a price for this: what is currently taking place at Moscow University, a bastion of Soviet science, will determine the latter's future for the next ten or twenty years. The recruiting of top minds is therefore becoming increasingly difficult, and the entry requirements for the University of Moscow are visibly declining. This aspect of Soviet anti-Semitism is reminiscent of what occurred in Nazi Germany; i.e., anti-Semitism results in a contraction in the intellectual potentialities of the perpetrator.

Trips abroad and participation in international conferences are additional subjects worthy of comment in regard to Jewish members of the scientific community. We may note that at an international conference in 1970 in Nice, approximately two-thirds of the Soviet mathematicians who had been invited appeared in person. And the remainder were able to send reports which were presented by their colleagues. At the conference of 1974 in Vancouver, however, only half arrived, and no Soviet reports could be presented in absentia. This affected not only Jews but also philo-Semites, liberalizers, and others who were considered unreliable. At the most recent conference in 1978 in Helsinki (very close to Leningrad), only about 40 Soviet mathematicians participated, in contrast to about 300 Japanese, 300 Frenchmen, and 500 Americans. In other words, the Soviet presence was abnormally small because most of the Soviet mathematicians who were expected could not get permission to come. A public protest by participants in the conference was organized, and a breach ensued between the Soviet and international scientific communities. At present the breach is such that unaccustomed procedures are now current in the international mathematical world. Denunciatory articles, for example, are being published. Thus an article on mathematics in the Soviet Union and anti-Semitism, which dealt with Vinogradov and Pontryagin, appeared in the United States.

This article was written by two emigré Soviet Jewish mathematicians. Although the authors are anonymous, their integrity was "guaranteed" by the signatures of a dozen American mathematicians. The article was circulated in the international mathematics community and was publicized at an international conference in Helsinki. Such procedures had never before been used in the international mathematical world. But when one has to contend with Lysenkos, novel countermeasures become necessary.

Thus, an article denouncing Pontryagin's bigotry was distributed to the mathematicians present in Helsinki. This was a retributive act, as unprecedented as it was disheartening. The Soviet mathematicians avoided the table at which this article was being dispensed. In general these mathematicians, who were academicians and officials, were in a state of considerable trepidation. They sat near the exit of the hall at every session, prepared to leave at the least sign of criticism. All the mathematicians took note and deplored the fact that many of their Soviet colleagues were absent. There was a buildup of considerable tension. The Soviet mathematicians who were present were aware of another well-documented article about the situation of mathematicians in the USSR. (It was subsequently published by the French Committee of Mathematicians.) The Soviet mathematicians were obviously eager to read it, but did not dare to do so until one of their number availed himself of a copy and retired to his room. Thereupon, they all rushed to read it together. At present, copies of it are circulating among the mathematicians of the USSR. They know, therefore, what the international mathematical community thinks about them and their situation. And I have been told by many of them that the criticisms of the international mathematical community are justified.

Prior to the Helsinki conference, Pontryagin published an article in the important Soviet mathematical publication *Uspekhi Matematicheskikh Nauk* ("Achievements of the Mathematical Sciences"). He explained in this article that he was opposed to the naming of the American professor Nathan Jacobson, "a very mediocre mathematician and an aggressive Zionist," as president of the International Mathematics Union.

Actually, Jacobson, although Jewish, is by no means "an aggressive Zionist." He is a mathematician of world renown. Pontryagin's *ad hominem* animadversions indicate that we are returning to the cold war and that Soviet mathematics is abandoning its scientific integrity.

Some recent visitors to the USSR, who succeeded in talking with Soviet mathematicians, maintain that many of the latter are toying with the idea of leaving, as they no longer consider it possible to lead a normal professional life. One of them observed: "It is a pity that the 220 million inhabitants of the Soviet Union cannot emigrate; that would solve many problems." In short, there is disillusionment in the universities. The atmosphere within the latter is stifling. People are tense and irritable. And because of the anti-Semitism among the Soviet masses, the Soviet Jew probably senses it even from his janitor or local tradesmen. But is it possible to speak of university anti-Semitism? I do not know.

The anti-Semitism and anti-Zionism of Soviet foreign policy hold little interest for the average Soviet intellectual, who tends to dissociate himself from these problems. However, if a truly secret referendum could be held among Soviet scientists concerning their preferences between the State of Israel and the Arab states, I believe most would prefer Israel.

For mass anti-Semitism has long since ceased to exist among Soviet intellectuals. What does exist among them is first and foremost anxiety and a kind of individual paralysis. They are paralyzed by the *apparatchiki*, by governmental power. They fear contacts with Jews when such contacts might prove dangerous. No well-placed mathematician, for example will have relations with Alexander Lerner, Victor Brailovsky, Mark Azbel, or with the "Seminar of the Excluded."[6] I once asked Azbel: "What would such-and-such a non-Jewish mathematician do if I were to send him two copies of one of my articles and request that he give one to Victor Brailovsky?" Azbel thought for a moment and replied: "He would be very disconcerted, but would do nothing." In short, his conscience would suffer; he would tell himself: "This is not normal. I ought to be able to give this article to Brailovsky, but cannot. It is too dangerous."

Hence persons "excluded from science" can no longer go to the universities, cannot visit libraries, and have no further contacts with their colleagues. This is how their names are eradicated from publications. There is no longer any contact between them and their fellow scholars and scientists. Thus there is no contact between A. Sakharov and his former colleagues; self-preservation is the first law of human nature.

The Soviet intellectual community, like the rest of Soviet society, is fragmented and atomized. People face an uncertain future. Frank conversations are possible, for the most part, only with dissident Jews; the latter are, in a certain measure, already outside the Soviet Union. Among those who have emigrated in recent years I have met some who felt profoundly Jewish and who therefore went to Israel. Others, feeling less Jewish, went to the United States, France, or elsewhere. But all observed: "We have already been outside the Soviet Union for years, because we could do nothing there any more." They were outsiders. They no longer read any Soviet newspapers, they ceased to believe in Soviet politics, they listened to the BBC Russian-language broadcasts and read foreign magazines whenever they could be found. Mentally, they were outside the country.

I am not familiar with relations in general among scholars within the universities, with how pervasive anti-Semitism is within the latter. I believe there are Jews who feel persecuted by the authorities but not by their colleagues.[7] The Gelfond Seminar is the most well-attended seminar in Moscow. An extraordinary seminar, it takes place every week. Gelfond is a Jew, though not a full member of the Academy of Sciences. (He is merely a corresponding member.) His seminar is followed with interest by the entire mathematical community in Moscow. And none of the participants asks who is a Jew and who is not. Visiting foreigners are not asked such questions either. Moreover, when Russian mathematicians go abroad and talk to foreign mathematicians, they do not ask whether or not the latter are Jews. I look upon Soviet mathematicians as persons harassed by the authorities, people fearful of everything.

Much has been said about passivity vis-à-vis the Holocaust, and there is considerable passivity in the USSR. With the exception of those Jews who are different thanks to their desire to emigrate to Israel (and who thus consider themselves as being practically Israeli citizens), the Soviet population does not know how to react critically to events.[8] It is capable of extraordinary courage and audacity. With the exception of a very small minority of persons, like A. Sakharov, I. Shafarevich, and the physicist Yu. Orlov, it is imbued with passivity. The average Soviet citizen feels powerless; it is better to keep quiet and not get involved in things that do not directly concern one. Caution must be observed; if asked a question, it should be answered in an evasive fashion. However, I do not believe—though perhaps I am mistaken—that those Jews who remain in Soviet university communities feel that they are being subjected by their colleagues to anti-Semitism in its classical form.

Notes

1. Agronomist and biologist T. Lysenko became a member of the USSR Academy of Sciences in 1939. He championed the non-Darwinian theory that within species there is no overpopulation and no struggle for survival. In an address at the 1948 session of the Lenin Academy of Agricultural Sciences, he affirmed that "progressive biological science" was indebted to Lenin and Stalin. After Stalin's death many articles appeared in Soviet journals which condemned his methods. At an assembly of the Academy of Sciences, President Keldish, referring to Lysenko's unfounded theories, charged him with having impeded the development of Soviet biological science.

2. See the essay of G. Freiman on discrimination against Jewish mathematicians, below.

3. G. Freiman details charges against I. Vinogradov and L. Pontryagin in his essay, below.

4. VAK (Vysshaya Atestatsionnaya Komissiya)—Higher Certifying Commission. See below.

5. Entrance examinations to Moscow State University are discussed by G. Freiman, above. Academician A. Sakharov, in a letter published in *Khronika zashchity pray v SSSR* (New York), no. 35, July–September 1979, p. 17, charges the Mechanical-Mathematics faculty with "planned discrimination" against Jewish applicants.

6. For material about the Moscow seminar for "excluded" Jewish scientists, see "Arestovanny seminar" [Proscribed seminar] in *Jews and the Jewish People—Jewish Samizdat*, vol. 8, pp. 193–254.

7. On the situation of Jews in Soviet science, see M. Popovsky, *Upravlyayemaya nauka* [Manipulated science] (London: Overseas Publications Interchange, 1978), pp. 188–210.

8. See petitions in which Soviet Jewish scientists renounce their Soviet citizenship and declare themselves citizens of Israel: V. Rubin and I. Akselrod to the Supreme Soviet, May 15, 1974, published in *Jews and the Jewish People—Petitions, Letters, and Appeals from Soviet Jews*, 1974, vol. 8, no. 157; V. Raiz, "To the Scientific Public," June 13, 1975, ibid., vol. 9, no. 106; V. Slepak, A. Luntz, A. Lerner, and V. Rubin to the President of Israel Ephraim Katzir, ibid., vol. 9, no. 82; A. Lerner to the scientists of the world, ibid., vol. 9, no. 113.

The Slavophile Revival and Its Attitude to Jews

EMANUEL LITVINOFF

MUCH HAS ALREADY been said here about anti-Semitism in Soviet literature, politics, and society at large. I propose to draw attention to the effect on Soviet Jews of the powerful revival of nationalist feeling in Russia. Professor Ettinger has made my task somewhat easier by his learned analysis of Slavophilism in his talk this morning.[1]

The traditional schism between Slavophiles and Westerners has, of course, profoundly influenced the culture and politics of Russia over several centuries. Slavophilism in its positive sense draws strength and inspiration from the native character of the Russian people, the Russian Orthodox Church, and what it sees as the peasant values of integrity and simplicity—in short, from "the Russian soul." It is expressed with genius in the writings of Pushkin, Tolstoy, Gogol, and Dostoyevsky, and its most famous representative today is Alexander Solzhenitsyn.

In its cruder manifestations Slavophilism is characterized by xenophobic fear of foreign influences and an obscurantist insistence on the moral superiority of Russians and traditional Russian values.[2] Antagonism to Jews has been a major component of these characteristics, Jews being viewed with deep suspicion as agents of change and as possessed of some malevolent power. In the nineteenth century the political right wing, deeply impregnated by Slavophile ideas, tended to see industrial capitalism as the penetration of a "Jewish spirit" alien both to Christianity and to Slavic traditions. Seizing on the writings of German anti-Semites and of the notorious converted Jew and rabid anti-Semite Jacob Brafman, nineteenth-century tsarist Slavophiles evolved the theory that a sinister international Jewish organization, based in Prague or Paris, was plotting to obtain world domination through the control of banking, the press, and revolution.[3] The Jewish forces of evil were thus counterpoised in deadly

186

enmity against the sweetness and light of Christianity. The most extreme exponents of such ideas in tsarist Russia were the virulently anti-Semitic League of the Russian People and the pogromist Black Hundreds.[4]

The 1917 revolutions embodied the struggle between Slavophiles and Westerners in an approximate sense. The liberal February Revolution had affinities with the Westerners, and the Bolshevik seizure of power in October soon manifested the xenophobic tendencies of the Slavophiles. These were particularly evident when Stalin imposed an almost hermetic isolation on the Soviet Union and the very expression "admiration for the West" could signal arrest. The Slavophile element in Stalinism was most blatantly expressed in the anti-Jewish purge of "rootless cosmopolitans" soon after the Second World War when, together with the wholesale arrest and execution of Jews, there were chauvinist claims that Russians had invented practically every modern scientific amenity.[5]

A persuasive case can be made that from Stalinist times onwards there has been a massive retreat from ideology in the USSR. Communism remains the official creed to which everyone is expected to pay lip service. But national pride and patriotism find a much more genuine response in the population, as does the thirst for freedom and intellectual exchanges. And the old divergence is evident between Slavophiles (who now think of themselves as the "Russian" party) and Westerners.

Under Brezhnev, the struggle between these trends has become more acute. This has led to tighter censorship, the suppression of those urging democratic reforms, and the increasingly blatant propagation of primitive anti-Jewish prejudices, including the appearance of crude fascist-type racist fiction and poetry in influential journals. According to well-informed Soviet emigrants writing in the Russian-language emigré press in the West, neo-Slavophilism has been taken up by prominent members of the Soviet Writers' Union. Leading publishing houses and magazines have come under the control of proponents of this trend. The famous Samizdat journal *A Chronicle of Current Events*, no. 48, described a Moscow Writers' Union meeting in December 1977, in which the tone was set by critics and literary specialists "who belong to a grouping characterized by sharp hostility to 'modernism' and great reliance on the national traditions of Russian culture."[6] The subject of anti-Semitism surfaced obtrusively, and the poet Yevtushenko, who was present, argued that "the best of the Slavophiles never permitted themselves to exalt their own people at the expense of other peoples. Russian classical literature condemns anti-Semitism through the lips of Korolenko, and hatred of anti-Semitism 'remained an eternal heritage of the Russian intellectual.' "[7]

Unfortunately, it is not "the best of the Slavophiles" who are given a broad platform in the Soviet media, but the most ignorant and vituperative.

In pursuit of their obsession that the Russian people and the world at large are menaced by some diabolical Jewish conspiracy to enslave mankind, they do not hesitate to fabricate evidence or borrow such evidence from fabricators of the past. Thus the Soviet embassy in Paris was tried and convicted for publishing in its French-language journal a tract full of quotations from nonexistent Jewish religious sources that purported to authorize the extermination by Jews of people of other faiths. This tract was an exact copy, including spelling mistakes, of a 1906 anti-Semitic pamphlet used to instigate the bloody pogroms that took place that year. The only change was the substitution of the word "Zionists" for "Jews."[8]

Borrowing from prerevolution anti-Semitic writings has become the rule in the Soviet Union, for the instigators of modern Soviet anti-Semitism are direct descendants of the pogromists who flourished during the last decades of tsarism. Once again the Russian people is being warned of an unholy alliance between World Jewry (or Zionism) and Freemasonry, its secret vanguard for infiltrating the centers of power. The lecturer Valery Emelyanov, of whom we have already heard, closely adheres to the practice of updating his tsarist predecessors.[9]

Take the following example, published by G. Butmi in 1906.

England, through its agents, the Russian Masons, is promoting the internal enslavement of Russia by the Jews, by Jewish Zionists. . . . Agreement between the Zionists and the Masons on this subject was apparently achieved in 1900 on the initiative of Dr. Herzl, the founder of modern Zionism. Thus Jewish Zionism, working in Russia under the protection of Russian Masons, is well-organized and widespread in Russia through the treacherous agency of British foreign policy.[10]

Compare this with the following extract from Emelyanov's 1977 memorandum to the Central Committee of the Soviet Communist party:

And so the "struggle for human rights" (i.e., of Jews, because goyim are not human beings) is an integral part of the Masonic and Zionist strategy and tactics, which has been evident both in major and minor cases during all the years of the Soviet regime. . . . Carter assumed office on January 20, 1977, at approximately the same time as the start of the 29th World Zionist Congress in Jerusalem. This congress will once again specify the tasks confronting Carter and confronting all those directing the international Zionist-Masonic campaign against our country and other countries of the socialist camp in order to undermine us from within.[11]

Another Soviet specialist, V. Skurlatov, is the author of a book called *Zionism and Apartheid* which has been widely praised in the Soviet press.[12] Going back still further, Skurlatov derives inspiration from medieval myths. His thesis is that an international Jewish corporation has been striving for thousands of years under various guises to rule the world. Using the Jewish religion for this purpose, it extended its influence through the "secular Judaism" of Freemasonry. Thus American imperialism, South African apartheid, the ideology of racial superiority, and other evils were spawned by this incredibly ancient prebiblical Jewish conspiracy.

Political anti-Semitism is highly infectious, especially among Russians who have been reconverted to a belief in the transcendental virtues of Russian nationalism. This is true even among victims of the Soviet regime. Edward Kuznetsov, the young Zionist serving fifteen years who has published remarkable writings on Soviet imprisonment in his *Prison Diaries*, has reported that his Russian fellow-prisoners are convinced that Brezhnev, Kosygin, Andropov, and other Soviet leaders are Jews ("look at their Jewish mugs").[13] It is impossible, they maintain, for true Russians to treat their own people so cruelly.

Another prisoner, Michael Heifets, who served four years for his Samizdat writings on poetry, had similar experiences. His book about prison camps was published recently. A review of this book appeared in the Polish-language monthly *Kultura*, in Paris last June.[14] The review stated:

Russian nationalists with whom Heifets talked in camp reasoned very logically. "Why was agriculture destroyed in the year of the 'Great Breakthrough'? Why were the peasants killed? Why is there a national shortage of bread even though battles for the harvest are organized every spring and autumn? Why are new factories manned by prisoners? Why does the Soviet Union put its nose into everything, wasting billions in Cuba, Angola, and Iraq? The Russians . . . live with shortages, seeing no meat for months, at times there is no milk or onions. . . . Could any government treat its own people this way?" Heifets was asked by Piotr Sartakov, who was serving his fourth sentence in the camp within thirty years, "Where does such cruelty toward one's own people come from? . . ." For Piotr Sartakov and other Russian nationalists in the camp the answer was clear: the country is run by the Jews. The phenomenon that Heifets describes may be defined as a byproduct of official Soviet propaganda, for which anti-Semitism has long been an important element and, in the last few years, the most important. . . . It has been drummed into people's heads for years that the Jews are enemy number one. . . . All misfortunes come from the Jews—the Jews have become a synonym for *evil*. Therefore many Russians who become disaffected with the regime identify it with Jews. Russian prisoners showed Heifets newspaper photographs of Brezhnev, KGB chief Andropov, and Procurator-General Rudenko and said: "If you're an honest man, tell us if you can see anything Russian in these photos. Names can be invented, but faces can't be hidden!"

Far more sophisticated, and surely more dangerous, is the "cultured" anti-Semitism increasingly encountered among neo-Slavophile intellectuals. Last year the emigré journal *Syntaxis*, edited by Andrey Sinyavsky and M. Rozanova and published in Paris, printed an extraordinary interview by its Moscow correspondent, Oleg Dmitriev, with a man described as "a respected Soviet writer who wished to remain anonymous."[15]

In the editorial note preceding the interview, *Syntaxis* remarked that official Soviet anti-Semitism derived a certain amount of support from the population.

These flashes of summer lightning, which herald a future pogrom . . . flash more and more frequently and visibly. And among the advocates of such ideas today are certain intellectuals who may even be liberal and progressive . . . and moved by a concern for "national revival." . . . New ideological versions of Russian or Soviet fascism will issue from these ideas and modes of thought.

The anonymous "respected Soviet writer" was interviewed in his summer home near Moscow. He began by saying that the policy of confining Jews in the geographical ghetto of tsarist times, the so-called Pale of Settlement, was the right policy. It was necessary "so that this highly sensitive and, in its own way, great people—because of the complete purity of its blood—be restrained from causing too much evil and misfortune. . . . In spite of the restrictions imposed by nineteenth-century laws, newspapers, book publishing, and the press in general were already in their hands. I do not mention their financial power." He claimed that Rasputin was a tool of the Jews and that they had "crept into the mattress of culture," and into science and medicine. As for their role in Russian literature, it is true that "clever Jews who simulate other peoples" began to be successful after the revolution when a host of other Russian writers emigrated; Babel, Bagritsky, and Paustovsky are mentioned. However, many of the Jewish writers concealed their Jewish origins. In any case, since literature is written in a national language, it is the least accessible to "aliens." Therefore "these agile people," the Jews, produced only a second-class literature which in fact was not literature at all in the sense that fresh sturgeon must invariably be first class. "After all, the Russian language . . . is our national heritage, it can be neither sold nor imported. It is not a commodity like lumber or oil, and is more precious than fur, gold, and the oil being formed in the nation at some sort of molecular level. And it started to spoil and be sullied long before the revolution. . . . Very many Jews came from various cities and small towns and began to cast lots for the vestments of art." Speaking specifically of Isaac Babel, one of the greatest writers to emerge in postrevolution Russia, the "respected Soviet writer" declared that Babel's *Odessa Stories* and *Red Cavalry* are inimical to "the principle of morality, spirit, and everything else that comprises the heart of Great Russian literature."

He went on to make the astonishing assertion that 80 percent of the Moscow writers organization consisted of Jews. "Eighty percent, officially," he said. "It made no difference to them what they wrote about because this is apparently an easy way to make money. . . . Therefore very glib, bookish types who like to sit in offices, who are mostly people of Jewish nationality, are now taking up the writing of novels and stories. And when somebody takes note of and talks about it, he is regarded as a typical anti-Semite, as something of a pogromist." Nevertheless, our "respected Soviet writer" concedes that it was not only Jewish dominance that was leading to the suppression of Russian literature.

Although he believes that part of the Jewish population will assimilate, he is worried about "the problem of the half-breeds," or "half-rubles," as he picturesquely calls them, because they become either "some sort of fanatical Zionist or extreme anti-Semites. I am almost certain," he says, "that one of the authors of anti-Zionist brochures, and extremely crude ones, is doubtless Jewish in his entire physiognomic and psychological make-up; he is most probably a 'half-ruble,' But the greatness of the Jews is that they always have people in every camp, in all parties, so that in case of any clash some should be victorious."

In the course of a point-by-point commentary on this interview, Andrey Sinyavsky sardonically draws attention to the selection of Jews as scapegoats by those who share the views of the "respected Soviet writer." He depicts their approach in this fashion: "They arranged the revolution for us, they arranged Rasputin for us, 'pure art,' anti-Semitism, and medicine . . . and they destroyed our agriculture, and have spoiled our Russian language. . . . How unfortunate we are! We have seized half the world, but the 'Jew' still does not leave us in peace." As Sinyavsky points out, the writer expresses relatively mild, liberal, and cautious views compared with many others in Soviet official, unofficial, and even dissident circles and in the Russian Orthodox Church.

For national feeling to the point of extreme chauvinism has been steadily growing for a generation or more in the Soviet Union. As the "respected Soviet writer" put it, the Russian nation is reemerging with vigor. Moreover, the influence of the Russian Orthodox Church is expanding, and not, he believes, to the detriment of Communist ideology. But it is paradoxical that in regard to Jews, Soviet Russia has taken over and amplified some of the most negative aspects of nineteenth-century Slavophilism.

Notes

1. See S. Ettinger's presentation, above p. 172.
2. "Slavophilism, Its Expression in Contemporary Soviet Society," a collection published in *Insight: Soviet Jews*, ed. by E. Litvinoff, vol. 4, no. 12 (December 1978), and vol. 5, no. 1 (January 1979).
3. Jacob Brafman, a Jew who became a convert to the Russian Orthodox Church; he wrote *Yevreyskiye bratstva, mestnye i vsemirnye* [Local and world Jewish brotherhoods] and *Kniga Kagala* [The book of the Kahal], published in 1869, reprinted in 1875. *The Book of the Kahal* was a translation of the minutes of the committee of the Minsk community. Brafman's introduction to it contained the charge that Jews form a state within the state, and that they aspire to exploit and enslave the rest of the population. These books served as propaganda for Slavophile groups and anti-Semitic movements. See *Yevreyskaya Entsiklopediya* (St. Petersburg), vol. 4, pp. 917–922; S. Ettinger "The Modern Period," in *A History of the Jewish People*, ed. by H. H. Ben-Sasson, (London: Weidenfeld & Nicolson, 1977), p. 821.
4. Black Hundreds—armed gangs which appeared in the wake of the Russo-Japanese war of 1904–1905. They directed their attacks against Jews and revolutionaries with the help of the police and army and Cossack units. When Tsar Nicholas II issued a manifesto on October 17, 1905, guaranteeing the basic freedoms of his citizens, the Black Hundreds incited mass riots against the Jews, which resulted in the loss of hundreds of lives, Ben-Sasson, p. 887, also L. Greenberg, *The Jews in Russia: The Struggle for Emancipation* (New Haven and London: Yale University Press, 1951), pp. 80–81.
5. S. Ettinger, *Modern Anti-Semitism: Studies and Essays* (in Heb.) (Tel Aviv, 1978), p. 188.
6. *Khronika tekushchikh sobytii* [A chronicle of current events], no. 48 (March 14, 1978), p. 150.
7. Ibid., p. 151.
8. On the trial which took place in Paris in 1973, see *Soviet anti-Semitism—The Paris Trial*, ed. E. Litvinoff (London: Wildwood House, 1974); G. Svirsky, "Zalozhniki" [Hostages], *Les Editeurs Reunis* (Paris, 1974), pp. 446–461.
9. See lecture by V. Emelyanov, "Judaism and Zionism," *Jews and the Jewish People—Jewish Samizdat*, vol. 10, pp. 272–275.
10. See S. W. Baron, *The Russian Jews under Tsars and Soviet* (New York and London: Macmillan, 1976), pp. 66–67.
11. See below.
12. V. Skurlatov, *Sionizm i aparteid* [Zionism and apartheid] (Kiev: Politizdat Ukrainy, 1975), pp. 71, 118–119; about V. Skurlatov, see above.
13. E. Kuznetsov, *Prison Diaries* (London: Valentine-Mitchel, 1975), 256 pp.
14. See A. Kruczek, "W sowieckiej prasie," *Kultura*, no. 6 (1978), pp. 102–103; M. Heyfets, "Mesto i vremya (yevreyskiye zametki)" [Place and time—notes of a Jew], (France: Third Wave, 1978), pp. 80–81.
15. *Syntaxis—publitsistika, kritika, polemika* (Paris), ed. A. Sinyavsky and M. Rozanova, no. 2 (1978), pp. 36–62.

Anti-Semitism in Daily Life (A Personal Account)

SOFIA TARTAKOVSKY

I AM FACED with a task that is almost impossible, for I wish to tell you about things which are difficult to express in words. It is as hard to make someone else understand one's feelings as it is to explain a melody with words. Nevertheless, I shall do my best.

Anti-Semitism is as old as history. Nevertheless, it changes its form in every epoch and in every country, and I would like to draw your attention to its contemporary manifestations in the Soviet Union. Particular emphasis will be given to its consequences in the emotional, psychological, and intellectual spheres. I hope to make you feel the social climate in the Soviet Union.

Should anyone ask me what is the most terrible consequence of anti-Semitism, I would say it is the fact that abnormal phenomena turn into ordinary everyday phenomena.

Permit me to illustrate this with a few examples.

In the Soviet Union, my husband used to be head of a department in a faculty of medicine. Each time he wanted to hire a Jewish physician, he had to enter into negotiations with the rector of the faculty.

"I would like to nominate a Jew," my husband would say.

"But that is impossible, you already have three," the rector would answer.

"No, no," my husband would reply, "the third one is myself, and as a Doctor of Sciences I am already classified as a Jew under a different classification. Therefore I have only two."

I am quoting almost word for word a typical example of their conversations. My husband is a Jew. The rector is not an anti-Semite. He knows that my huband has no doubts on this score, and there were no witnesses to their conversations. It was therefore possible to speak frankly about practical matters. It does not matter that both knew very well that the Jewish quota is not specified in any written document. But both of them were distinctly aware that it is no less enforceable because it is not in written form.

To add the last brushstroke to the scene I have just depicted, let us imagine the voice of a Soviet radio announcer; he is lauding the firm, solid, and eternal friendship of the peoples of the Soviet Union. Or perhaps the announcer is saying the Soviet Constitution is the most democratic in the world, that it guarantees equal rights to all citizens of the USSR.

Similar scenes occur everyday all over the Soviet Union. Nobody, however, asks himself whether or not these are taking place in 1984. Poor George Orwell could not imagine how much Soviet reality has outdone his fiction. [1]

When my son was a child and was called a "dirty Jew" in class, he would hit his offender in the face without hesitation. I always encouraged this because I considered his reaction perfectly natural. But I was stunned when he did not dare to write a Jewish name in a composition he was preparing at home. To write a Jewish name he explained, "was not permitted." I realized that his soul had been poisoned and that an inferiority complex was being spawned in him.

The remedy I applied at that moment was a shocking one for the child that he still was: I told him the details of how the Nazis had murdered his grandfather. My son was then only about eleven years old.

One day after class his teacher confided to him when they were alone: "You have received only a passing grade. You must understand once and for all that, as a Jew, you cannot permit yourself to get just passing grades; even with excellent grades you will have enough problems in your life." Subsequently, experience taught my son that his teacher had spoken the truth. But at that moment I saw that this child was suffering as only someone much older could suffer.

One day in 1952, during the time of the Doctors' Plot, I noticed that the woman who was taking care of my son was crying. The first thought that occurred to me was that my husband had been arrested.

Fortunately this good woman was crying for an entirely different reason: her female neighbors were abusing her because she loved the child of a Jew, despite the fact that all the newspapers were proclaiming that Jews were "killers in white coats." Most paradoxical of all was the fact that this poor woman was crying because, as she explained it, she could not help loving the child of an enemy of the people.

The libraries in the Soviet Union are crammed with the crudest anti-Semitic propaganda, including books and brochures entitled: *Beware:*

Zionism!, *Zionism-The Poisoned Weapon of Imperialism*, etc. This propaganda is particularly repulsive because of its hypocrisy—the word "Jew" is not actually mentioned. But just as everyone is aware of the quota limiting the number of Jews in universities,[2] etc., everybody knows that this anti-Semitic literature is aimed at Jews, whom it calls "Zionists," "aggressors," "servants of imperialism," etc.

One day a friend of ours was asked to write one of these "masterpieces." On the one hand, he was appalled by the loathsomeness of such a request; but he was afraid (with good reason!) of being dismissed from his job. I saw the anguish in his eyes, but I can find no words to describe it. Crushed and distressed, he suddenly went on a vacation for a month. While our friend was away, a colleague of his agreed to execute this "social order." (Our friend has only his wife to be responsible for, but his colleague has a number of children.) All this might seem childish; instead of resolutely making a decision, instead of refusing or accepting a request, one takes a vacation for a month! It is true—life under a totalitarian regime is childish and also hideous!

Another example taken from life concerns the son of friends of ours. There is nothing Jewish about him, either physically, in his surname, or in his given name. This was why he was asked to handle something that was not supposed to be divulged—at any rate not to Jews. When he was a senior at the Higher Polytechnic School in Leningrad, he was asked to assist the commission responsible for preparing the files of new applicants. His job was to sort the files into two categories: Jewish and non-Jewish. A number of years have passed since this happened, but five days ago he received his visa for Israel.

A related incident about the sorting of files involved my own son. He was admitted to the University of Leningrad thanks to a non-Jewish professor who took the risk of removing my son's file from the Jewish pile and putting it on the non-Jewish pile.

Another episode from daily life occurred when one of my colleagues and I were drinking coffee in a cafe. A woman, dead drunk, appeared near the cloakroom shouting: "Down with the Jews, save Russia!"

My colleague, who is a Russian intellectual and an inherently decent person, was even more shocked than I and said to me: "Poor woman, it is not her fault. She is the victim of the dirty anti-Semitic propaganda." And he was right; she was only a victim. Anti-Semitism obviously afflicts the lives of Jews. But it also afflicts the lives of Russians. I have in mind Russians who do not wish to be accomplices in what Bruno Jasienski has called "The Conspiracy of the Indifferent."[3]

Anti-Semitism influences the souls of human beings in various ways;

sometimes it becomes a powerful stimulant that awakens Jewish national consciousness. As a result, we have the movement for repatriation to Israel.

On the other hand, however, anti-Semitism destroys souls. It pushes people into the rut of abject conformity. In his desire to adapt himself, to adjust (even if this desire is subconscious, as it is in typical cases), the Jew accepts an intolerable situation at any price.

I believe I have merely related to you some vignettes from life and that I have not told you about the problem in general. Generalizations, however, are made preferably by the people themselves and not by me. But you can find even in jokes a true reflection of people's thoughts. Thus, in one of these jokes:

A Jew is asked: "What nationality are you?"

He replies: "That's what I'd like to know!"

But I must confess to you today that, despite everything, I remain an incurable optimist.

In his poem "Babi Yar," Yevtushenko wrote: "Let the International sound the day when the last anti-Semite on earth is buried!"

The purpose of our gathering today is to bring the dawn of that day nearer.

Notes

1. George Orwell's satire *Nineteen Eighty-Four* was first published in 1949.

2. See note 5, p. 185 of Laurent Schwartz above.

3. Bruno Jasienski (1909–1941), Polish and Soviet Russian writer. Lived in USSR from 1929, began to write in Russian. Author of a number of books and plays; was repressed in 1936, and died in a camp hospital.

Jewish Samizdat on
Anti-Semitism

Introduction

PART III OF this volume provides some documentary background for the papers in Parts I and II. The two items included in this section are recent publications of the Jewish Samizdat (i.e., writings that are circulated privately in the USSR because they cannot obtain official approval and thus cannot be formally published and distributed through normal channels). The authors of both have been personally subjected to discrimination against them as Jews, but each adopts a different means of conveying this experience.

G. A. Freiman is a professor of mathematics in a provincial university. He tells of his own experiences, but he also depicts the attitude of the leading figures in Soviet mathematics to Jewish students and colleagues, and the discriminatory practices used to exclude Jews from institutions of higher learning, to prevent academic appointments of Jews, etc. There can be only one conclusion: this attitude demonstrates a deeply rooted anti-Semitic attitude to Jews.

Dr. Ruth Okuneva, a historian and an educator, examines the historical continuity of Russian anti-Semitism and its contemporary features. She compares quotations from pre-revolutionary Black Hundreds anti-Semitic writers with statements of Nazi German ideologists and recent Soviet anti-Zionist campaigners like Kichko, Begun, Evseev, Korneev, Emelyanov, and the like. The main conclusion is that, despite the official Soviet claim that these recent publications are anti-Zionist, in fact they are of a purely anti-Semitic nature, and do not differ from the earlier manifestations of anti-Semitism. Furthermore, in these recent writings, extensive use is made of earlier anti-Semitic materials, Russian, German and French, in an attempt to discredit Jews and Judaism. Appended to the study is a bibliographic list of the sources used by Dr. Okuneva.

Footnotes incorporated by the authors are given as they appear in the original. All editorial additions are given in square brackets.

I Am a Jew, It Turns Out

G. A. FREIMAN

1. PREFACE

The Prince and the Pauper

DURING THIS YEAR of 1976 I shall turn fifty. My chief occupation has always been mathematics. I studied it, found pleasure in teaching it, and organized group projects in it. Having finished one paper, I immediately went on to a second; having placed the final period in one book, I started thinking about the next.

But now, the train whose only idea was "forward along the tracks" has suddenly come to a halt. I am not organizing anything—but then, no one is asking me to—and I teach through force of habit. But the main thing is that I have no heart for solving problems, proving theorems.

The reason? Briefly, I feel I am being subjected to oppression in my work because I am a Jew, and that people around me, Jewish people, are also being subjected to oppression.

Thus has a worker's enthusiasm given way to sorrowful reflections.

Is it worth going on? Are my personal troubles of any general interest?

While reflecting in this way, I often "converse" with an imaginary interlocutor. I see my critic run up to me, a newspaper in his hand.

Critic: Are you really being oppressed? Have you been told "Jew, be off!"?

I: Well, no, they weren't that outspoken.

Critic: It's all clear: you've imagined it. But it's the facts that matter, isn't that so? Now, you went off to the war after finishing high school?

I: In '43, at the age of seventeen.

Critic: After the war you were given an opportunity to study?

I: Your question is so strangely formulated. Could it have been otherwise?

Critic: And you completed a VUZ[1] in 1950?
I: In '49.
Critic: Seven years later you defended your candidate's thesis?
I: Yes, in 1956.
Critic: And in 1965 a doctoral thesis?
I: Yes. But tell me at last, what are you driving at?

Instead of an answer he unfolded the newspaper.* I read the following:

I want to declare emphatically: In our socialist country there has never been nor can there be any oppression of any nationalities in general and of the Jewish nationality in particular. All citizens of our multinational country are guaranteed equal rights by law.

My own life can serve an example of how "oppressed" the Jews are in our country. After finishing high school, I went to the front. After the war I was given an opportunity to study. In 1950 I graduated from an institution of higher learning. Seven years later I defended a candidate's thesis, and in 1965 a doctoral thesis. How can anyone dare say I am being "oppressed"?"

I glanced at the signature: V. S. Etlis, doctor of chemical sciences, professor.

I sank into thought; my griefs and worries were suddenly swept up in a raging whirlwind rapidly rushing away from the unshakable ground of Professor Etlis's officially sanctioned formulas. The opposing poles of our statements abruptly pulled us in different directions. I found myself in the forest of life gone by, with glowworms of reminiscences illuminating with a glimmer the night of forgetfulness, and a very familiar road of thoughts leading to the horizon of my problem. Walking on this path, feelings of prejudice and bias left me. I remembered that some tiny particle of the emerging sun of truth can be claimed your opponent in this dispute.

On the Usefulness of the Written Word

"What exactly are the troubles that befall you and other Jews?" a foreigner might ask.

"Trouble at work: I was removed from the chair of a department at the university; trouble with scientific activities; the thesis of one of my pupils was rejected by the VAK;[3] it became difficult to publish; scientific trips

---

*Literaturnaya Gazeta, no. 7 (February 18, 1976), p. 9.[2]

abroad are not even to be dreamed about. Many IHLs do not accept Jews; it is hard to find suitable work."

"Why then don't you protest? If certain persons are guilty of an injustice, you must appeal to their superiors. There are laws against racial discrimination, so go to court; if you disagree with Etlis's newspaper article, write to the newspaper yourself. There will be an inquiry, the facts will become known to the public, and so truth and justice will triumph."

I became angry.

"You are like a blind man in a strange room. People are not admitted to an IHL because they fail to pass competitive exams; they are not given employment because there are no vacancies; a thesis is not approved because its quality is low. You will be ridiculed if you try to insist that the claimant's nationality could have been of any significance whatsoever. No court will investigate a case of oppression based on nationality, since there is no such thing here. Nor will you succeed in getting your case into the newspaper."

"What about freedom of speech?"

"It has been guaranteed by the Constitution, but you cannot maintain, can you, that something that must not be does in fact exist. *That* you will never be allowed to do. My sorrows increase a hundredfold because they are like a shameful disease; I cannot talk about them aloud. To do so would mean to put in jeopardy all my well-established, well-adjusted life. Work, scientific activities, family—all will fall into disarray. Freedom and life themselves will be threatened. To start talking, to leave the multitude of the silent, to rebel against society—for pity's sake, I want to live in peace, to work in peace, there is such a backlog of theorems to be proved—for pity's sake. I'm a coward, I'm simply afraid."

I spent long hours in reflections of this kind. How am I to act, what should I do? At last I came to a decision: I must record my life's experiences. The written word has often rendered invaluable services to the history of science, and helped to temper morals and customs. Perhaps this time, too . . .

2. STUDIES (PAST . . .)

A Documentary Poem

After graduating from the university I started working in an NII[4] even though what I really wanted was to take up mathematics. The work was exhausting, without fixed hours; toward evening it was hard to think straight. I began to go to bed at eight in the evening, and to get up at three or four o'clock in the morning. In this way I could put in four hours of mathematical studies after being refreshed by sleep. And so it went on every day for a year and a half.

This period—from the "unmasking of the cosmopolitans" to the notorious "doctor murderers"—was for me, a Jew, very difficult. Here are the documents, you can judge for yourselves.

Our No. p/260/ts, 1 August, 1951

To: The Rector of the Moscow State University,[5] Academician I.G. Petrovsky.

The N. Ye. Zhukovsky Institute[6] does not object to Comr. G. A. Freiman, member of its staff, being enrolled for extramural postgraduate studies at the MSU.

Deputy Chief of the Institute G. P. Svishchev

To: **Comr. Freiman**

By decision of the selection committee, you are barred from taking entrance examinations because of the absence of a work record. It is necessary to have worked three years.

Deputy Director Lidsky

To: The Rector MSU Acad. I. G. Petrovsky
From: G. A. Freiman, of CIA

Application

Please allow me to sit for examinations in Candidates' Minimum[7] in mathematics and the Mechanical-Mathematics Faculty.

16. 4. 1952   G. A. Freiman

Resolutions:

Examinations in mathematics may be arranged at the Institute of Mechanics and Mathematics. Please permit the examinations to be given.

A. Kolmogorov

I recommend enrollment for extramural postgraduate studies.

15. 5. 52   I. Petrovsky

To: The Rector MSU Acad. I. G. Petrovsky
From: G. A. Freiman, of CIA

Application

Please enroll me as a postgraduate student of the Mechanical-Mathematics Faculty attached to the Chair of the Theory of Numbers.

12. 6. 1952   G. Freiman

Kazan Aviation Institute, 8. 8. 1952, No. 2425

To: Comr. Freiman G. A.

We are returning to you your documents, since by decision of the competitive enrollment committee of Kazan Aviation Institute your candidacy has not been approved.

Deputy Director Docent[8] Yakovlev

Excerpt from Record no. 4 of the session of the Selection Committee of the Mechanics and Mathematics SRI, of the MSU of 16 August 1952.

Topic discussed:
Comr. Freiman, Grigory Abelevich, born 1926, Jewish, member of VKP(b).[9] Graduated from the MSU in 1949. Mathematician. Has been working in CIA for threee years as an engineer. Diploma without honors. (Intramural postgraduate studies)

Decision taken:
Recommend enrollment for postgraduate studies at CIA.

(Seal of Authentication)   Secretary of the Institute
                                                         Uspenskaya

To: The rector MSU, Acad. Petrovsky
From: Freiman G. A.

Application

In 1949 I graduated from the Mechanical-Mathematics Faculty of the MSU and was sent to work at CIA. I am a mathematician by education. This year, after three years' work at CIA I applied for postgraduate studies in mathematics at the MSU. The selection board has decided that I am to be "recommended to take up postgraduate studies at CIA." However, at CIA there are postgraduate studies in mechanics only. In view of the fact that I have received special mathematical education and have never during all these years ceased my scientific work in the field of mathematics, and since it is my wish to continue scientific work in the field of mathematics in the future, please reconsider my application and permit me to take entrance examinations for admission to postgraduate studies.

20. 8. 1952   G. Freiman

Resolved: I can see no reason for canceling the board's decision.

                                                                                                    I. Petrovsky

To: The Director, Kazan Pedagogical Institute
From: Freiman G. A.

Application

Please allow me to take examinations for postgraduate studies in mathematics.

20. 8. 52   G. Freiman

Resolved: To be refused: has no work record of schoolteaching experience.

25. 8.   [Signature illegible]

V. I. Ul'yanov-Lenin Kazan State University[10]
                                                                                          30 August 1952

Comr. Freiman G. A.,

You are admitted to entrance examinations for postgraduate studies at the KSU. The entrance examinations will begin on 1 September 1952.

                                                                          Director, Postgraduate Studies
                                                                          Kharlamova

                                                              912-3/11121, 29. 10. 1952

To: The Rector, V. I. Ul'yanov-Lenin Kazan State University, Prof. D. Ya. Martynov

The Central Universities Administration does not find it possible to enroll Comr. Freiman G. A. for postgraduate studies, following nonapproval of his application by the postgraduate studies admission committee.

                                                              Deputy Head, Central Universities Administration
                                                              S. Syomin

To: The Deputy Head, Central Universities Administration, Comr. Syomin
From: Freiman G.A.

Application

The letter you sent to the Rector of the KSU, Comr. Martynov, says that I was not to be enrolled for postgraduate studies "following nonapproval by the postgraduate studies admission committee." Considering that I passed all the entrance examinations with the grade of "excellent," and was enrolled for postgraduate studies by the KSU committee, please state the reason for the nonapproval of my application by the Ministerial committee.

19.11.52   G. Freiman

Note: No reply was received. G.F.

To: The Deputy Minister of Higher Education, Prokofiyev M. A.
From: Freiman G. A.

Application

In September 1952 I passed entrance examinations for postgraduate studies at the Kazan University, and my application was approved by a university committee. However, it was not approved in the Ministry. I have been trying—in vain—for two months to discover the reason for the refusal. According to Comr. Syomin and to Comr. Khitrov, who is directly considering my case, there are no documents to pinpoint the reason for the rejection of my application. Clearly, in this case the rejection is invalid.

In my view, there are no grounds for rejection since:

1. I passed all entrance examinations with the grade of "excellent";
2. I am the author of seven scientific publications;
3. I have the three-year work record which is required for admission to postgraduate studies;
4. I have received positive references from my place of work as a professional and as a party member;
5. and, lastly, it should be taken into account that I am a member of the KPSS[11] and participated in the Patriotic War.

The consideration of my case has been dragging on for three months now. I do beg you to intercede personally, to uncover the reason for the Ministry's nonapproval of my application, to cut the red tape in the consideration of my case, and finally, to approve my application.

25. 12. 52   G. Freiman

The V. I. Ul'yanov-Lenin Kazan State University encloses herein an excerpt from the order confirming your enrollment for postgraduate studies at the University.

Date of arrival: 20 January 1953.

Enclosure: excerpt from the KSU order.

Prorector, Scientific Studies
Prof. M. V. Markov

Today I am amazed at my persistence at that time, which stemmed from a deep conviction in the correctness of all that was going on; any deviation seemed to me no more than episodic and incidental.

But the amount of effort, energy, and time consumed by this protracted affair! In order to obtain a single covering letter or memo, one had to spend days and weeks, to register for reception in advance and stick it out for hours in queues.

And the references! Yura Vasil'yev, my superior, was a tough man who mercilessly exploited his co-workers. He did not want to let me go, and as a result, collective hair-splitting discussions produced the following typical remarks for inclusion in my references: "It must, however, be stated that Comr. Freiman G. A. does not always display a conscientious attitude toward work he is entrusted with. Should some task happen to be not to his liking, he performs it, whatever its importance, formalistically, without showing the necessary initiative"; ". . . expresses a persistent wish to enroll for postgraduate studies in pure mathematics to the detriment of his main work."

And the interview with Petrovsky!

The rector of the MSU Ivan Georgievich Petrovsky was a mathematician himself.

In the summer of 1943 he was the dean of the Mechanical-Mathematics faculty. I met him for the first time when I was transferred from Kazan University to the MSU. He made a most favorable impression; his conversation was unhurried, he showed interest in his interlocutor, in his affairs and plans. I remember him at that time as being lean, gentlemanly, subtle, and understanding.

So now Petrovsky agreed to listen to me after my teacher Alexandr Osipovich Gelfond[12] recommended me as a promising young man.

He received me in his spacious study in the old MSU building on Mokhovaya Street. I told him about my trials and tribulations, about my great desire to take up mathematical studies. Petrovsky listened attentively and—so it seemed—sympathetically.

"At present I am unable to change the decision of the admissions committee," he said.

"Let it be *extramural* at least," I interrupted him.

"No, this will not succeed either. Now listen," he said upon thinking a little, "you might take candidates' exams."

I saw that he was not going to render me any assistance whatsoever, this seemingly all-powerful man, a friend and classmate of my teacher, and what was more, a mathematician, a man of science, who of all people should be able to understand my acute desire to engage in an occupation we both loved.

"But look," I cried out bitterly disappointed, "when I go to the left, you send me to the right, but as soon as I go to the right, you send me to the left again, so I don't really know where I am!"

He did not understand what I was talking about and looked at me questioningly.

"You advise me to take candidates' exams while refusing to enroll me for postgraduate studies. But look at what you wrote when I did ask for permission to take exams in the Candidates' Minimum."

And here I placed before him my request for this approval bearing his note: "I recommend enrollment for extramural postgraduate studies. 15.5.52. I. Petrovsky."

He read it and said nothing. He just sat there without moving and did not utter a word. I, too, was silent—at first because I was so wrought up—and then, when I regained my composure, I waited, tensely, for what he would say after all. But he continued to sit motionless and silently. This went on for fully three minutes: an eternity. Then, in response to some unconscious impulse—for I did not wish this silent admission to be interrupted by some pitiful hypocritical babble—or, perhaps, acting out of a feeling of pity, I rose, took the piece of paper lying before him, folded it, put it in my pocket, and went out without a word. And still he sat like that, without stirring.

I saw him once again, just ten years later, when I came to ask for dormitory accommodations at the MSU. I found an entirely different person. He was stouter and older, but his main feature was that he appeared somewhat harried, nervous, and inattentive. He did not listen to his visitor, and did not delve into the matter. Having barely grasped what was being asked of him, he immediately refused, harshly, rudely, peremptorily, without any sense of communication whatsoever, without really seeing the visitor, instead concentrating feverishly on something that occupied him at that moment.

And, finally, that affair with the postgraduate studies at Kazan . . .

When the Ministry's letter informing me of the refusal reached me, I was dumbfounded, but it was an absolute certainty that I would prove my case. They just could not refuse me, and that was that.

At the Ministry, I was received by Khitrov, an official of the personnel department. He was a middle-aged man, gray-haired, with military bearing. There was no particular ill-will or hostility in his attitude toward me.

"The committee has not given its approval," he said, "You've been refused admission."

That was all that could be got out of him during both my first and my subsequent visit. There was a decision, but no explanations, no minutes of the discussion, not even my documents, since everything had been sent off. I had to return to Kazan; the case was closed.

"The case will be reconsidered," I declared with conviction, "there are no grounds for a denial."

He held his ground, but little by little things began to move. A request for my personal file was sent to Kazan; Khitrov reported about me several times at various administrative levels. Although everything remained as it had been, I began to overpower Khitrov psychologically. When he saw me, he became nervous, and, in a faltering voice, advised me to leave Moscow, trying to convince me that the case was hopeless.

"The committee has refused," he kept saying with emphasis. "Whatever you do won't get you anywhere."

For my part, I was quite composed and kept pointing out to him that since I was in the right, the decision, too, couldn't but be the right one.

At last, I succeeded in obtaining an interview with the Deputy Minister's private secretary. He heard me out in a room where some women were also sitting. Clearly, stubbornly, and loudly I laid out all my trumps: excellent results in the examinations, there had been no competition, published articles, and so on. Silence fell in the room; the women's backs were listening expressively to my narrative.

"I shall arrange for you a meeting with Prokof'yev," the private secretary said.

Prokof'yev listened attentively till I finished and said there would be a committee session the next day where the case would be reconsidered positively.

Two days later I called on Khitrov.

"Yes, they've reconsidered the case and adopted a decision on enrollment," he said in an embarrassed voice. "I'll prepare the text of the directive. How would you like it dated?"

It was the beginning of January 1952, and we agreed on the eleventh. Two days later, on January 13, the case of the "doctor murderers" was launched, and things became still more dismal, but it did not affect me much personally, for, having been enrolled for postgraduate studies, I left for Kazan and began to study mathematics in earnest.

Here I shall add a couple of vivid impressions of that period—for the benefit of those who will not understand or will pretend not to understand the purport of my narrative.

The Yellow Star

Misha Klyachko was short, plain, and slow, and spoke in a low voice. I remember him as a contrast to his wife, who was also a student in our year and was red-lipped, large, and conspicuous.

Misha's application for party membership was being considered at a party meeting. He had been through the war, becoming a candidate for membership at the front. There was nothing in his life's story that might provide cause for doubt, but there was a discrepancy in the documents. On his candidate's card—a party document—he was registered as Russian, whereas his identity card stated that he was Jewish. While he was speaking about himself, he was asked to explain this little discrepancy. Misha replied that upon his return from the military hospital, where he had recovered from a wound, he had registered as a Russian when his new Red Army card was made out.

"But why did you register as a Russian?" asked Ogibalov, a Mech.-Math. figure who then and later played a most dismal role in the life of the faculty. I remember his face, always sullen and hostile, his averted empty eyes, his dry, accusatory voice.

Misha faltered, began to mutter something, but despite the tough pressure exerted on him was unable to explain a thing. He fell silent, as a fantastic picture unfolded in his mind's eye: a German in SS uniform comes running into the room, drags him to the door—which is not a door at all, but a yawning gas chamber with a blazing, roaring Auschwitz oven behind it—while Ogibalov jumps off the table and pushes him, resisting, in the back.

There was a short debate. A young fellow with a luxuriant curly head of hair, creased trousers, and a full, good-natured face popped on to the rostrum. He made a hot, persuasive speech maintaining that there was no subject for debate, that there was no difference between people of different nationalities in our land, that it was equally honorable to be a Jew or a Russian, and he was therefore all for admission. Both the audience and the head table listened in polite and somewhat tense silence. Then a member of the party bureau took the floor saying that it was, of course, no more than a matter of formal disparities in documents, which it was necessary to correct, from which it followed that Klyachko should be denied admission. And this was duly agreed upon.

Not long ago I saw a new type of identity card which does not contain the entry on social origin that used to accord unequal rights to members of different classes in bygone times. The entry on nationality, which was absent during the early postrevolutionary years, has been retained in the new identity card. The incident described above provides an example of its ill-intentioned use. Can anyone explain to me in what way an entry of this kind could be used for the benefit of the noble ideals of the universal brotherhood of all men?

The Alliance of the Sword and the Plough[13]

When I was in my fifth year, an "anti-Soviet society" was discovered in our midst.

What exactly happened? There was a small group of young people who struck up a particularly close friendship in their first year. They often got together, went for walks in the streets, discussed works of art, disparaged Surov's play *The Green Light* (an important item of the accusation). They compiled facetious "regulations" for their association. (There's an organization for you!)

Nadya Gindina had an uncle who lived in Palestine. One day a book arrived by mail from that uncle of hers. It was a book on a scientific subject, something like botany or zoology, and was needed for her father's studies. I well remember the emphasis laid on this book by Gorbunov, the party bureau secretary, when he spoke at the fifth year's general meeting. What a sinister complexion he placed on this event; what a miasma of apostasy, of the intrusion of things alien, of spying, began to pervade the tensely silent hall.

A certain poem about Jews that no one was ever to see was used as the main pretext for attack.

The group consisted of twelve persons, of whom six were Jews, and the other six Russian. As in the anticosmopolitan campaign, the blows were directed not against the Jews only, but mainly against them, whereas the rest were attacked just for seeking their company, as it were, and in a milder fashion.

All the Jews were expelled from the Komsomol[14] and from the university. The others were merely penalized by the Komsomol organization.

The active organizers of the persecution—Ogibalov, Gorbunov, Gusarova—are still at work in the university—and prosperous.

3. STUDIES (. . . AND PRESENT)

Hardships of Higher Education

Am I perhaps raking up things past and gone? No. The story has no less significance today. Had I tried to enter postgraduate studies now, the experience would have been repeated.

What about admission to IHL?

The scientific-technical institutes MIFI[15] and MFTI[16] have always imposed severe restrictions. There have been restrictions for whole categories of IHLs: military, diplomatic (naturally), medical (with the exception of those in remote regions), technical with a military bias (aviation, electronic equipment); stricter limitations for specific localities (the Ukraine, Moldavia, Leningrad). This list is, of course, incomplete.

It may be argued that the Jews of Russia are far from having sunk into the mire of ignorance, that there are—relatively, of course—far more Jews with higher education than Russians, that the number of Jewish students is very great even now.

This kind of situation took shape at a time in the past when there were fewer restrictions, and is now rapidly changing "for the better."

At present, restrictions do exist and are being more and more intensified.

What is the mechanism through which they are implemented? For surely the acceptance of documents is not controlled along ethnic lines?

It is, with few exceptions. If one's future work involves secrecy, undesirable persons are advised not to submit documents. In this case even a high examination mark is no guarantee of enrollment. Thus, F. passed entrance exams at MFTI with the best results in his grouping and . . . did not find his name on the enrollment list. A notice was posted in the admission board's room stating, "Complaints on matters of enrollment are not accepted."

But this is still not the most dishonest thing. It is worse when someone who *must not* pass fails to get a passing grade irrespective of the high level of his or her answers.

"It's a strange thing: isn't a professor, a teacher, an independent person with a highly developed sense of professional dignity, with explicit professional standards? Would a person like that deliberately cheat, or juggle his evaluations? For goodness sake, can you imagine doctors who would deliberately destroy their patients?"

"I don't know about doctors, but there are teachers who are strangers to professional ethics and are guided by other, selfish systems of conduct."

"This opinion ought to be as well-substantiated as the very fact of the existence of restrictions."

"I have detailed knowledge of the situation in one field—mathematics. My graduation group at the MSU is that of '49. Jews constituted no less than a quarter of our course. Subsequently, in the fifties and sixties, this proportion hardly ever dropped below one-fifth. The other day, when I was at the MSU, I was looking through a list of students who had passed to the second year of Mech.-Math. I found *not a single* Jewish name in it. Two years ago, in the Mech.-Math faculty of Leningrad University, I discovered no more than two or three Jewish names in the list of admissions which contained several hundred names. The trend is distinct and undeniable. Should my reflections become a subject of discussion some day, let my critics make public the composition of the Mech.-Math faculty year by year, for the postwar period at least. This testimony is incontestable."

The above facts are of general significance, since MSU, the Leningrad State University, and the Novosibirsk University, where Jews are also barred, produce the lion's share of creative mathematicians.

"It would not be out of place to make a detailed check of these data. But look, what are you getting into now? Is it any of your business? Calculating percentages, leafing through lists, searching for certain names. You'd have done better proving your theorems."

"But aren't we human beings? With living souls?" I cried out indignantly. Take the *Quant* journal, where they publish, issue after issue, the names of schoolchildren who are the best at problem-solving. This is done objectively, since Shirshov and company have not yet succeeded in gaining full control of this journal. Try and trace the fate of these kids. How many of those who might become the glory of our discipline will in fact design model components in the central design bureaus of various industries? Will this country not lose something if some of these despairing youths leave it?

And what about science? What will become of mathematics? To cultivate talent, to create schools of science is a subtle task demanding many years of care and effort. It is like growing a forest.

He who cuts down a forest will live to see a desert.

The Mechanism of Denial

Some may ask where I got these claims of injustices at exams, since I was not there in person.

My first impression was formed from an accumulation of verbal testimony. Here are a few examples.

The son of the well-known mathematician K. was taking exams at the Mech.-Math.

"My son has a very decent knowledge of mathematics, so I'm not worried about that, but his physics is worse, he might get a 'four.' "[17] Well, his son got a "two" in physics.

Here it may be argued that parents always have an exaggerated opinion of their children's abilities, and that, possibly, the examiners had no ill intentions.

V. passed both exams in mathematics, receiving "fives," and received a "four" in physics in a very demanding examination. However, he got a "two" for his Russian composition, written without a single mistake. The examiner wrote the following explanation: "You have developed the theme of patriotism, not that of the Motherland."

You get the idea from a conversation such as this: "Jews are not admitted to Mech.-Math.,[18] it's true, but in this case, you know, it's too much. V., for instance passed . . . " The speaker was an MSU teacher, a Russian, and he was addressing someone who was not a close friend of his.

Z. received the first prize at the All-Union Mathematical Olympiad and a "two" in a competitive examination in mathematics.

Why do I think such a combination hardly probable?

The winner at such an Olympiad stands first among millions. The problems presented there are so difficult that not every professor will solve them, and then not in a short time.

I could multiply the number of these examples, I have hundreds of them. but let us, for the time being, limit ourselves to these. What sort of people are they who give students those "twos," those lowered marks? Why do they do it?

Scoundrels are always few. Honest people give the scoundrels a look of condemnation and . . . keep mum. How it is all done I learned for the first time from a conversation with R., who worked at the Novosibirsk University. His colleague, a member of the admissions committee, had a heart-to-heart talk with him at a faculty party. He dissociated himself, *he* did not do this. It was done by special persons who examined special groups where Jewish high-school graduates were concentrated.

The moral issue involved here is extremely grave. Can we base our conclusions on oral communications alone, however indisputable they might seem?

In August of this year I visited the Mech.-Math.[18] often, and watched the course of the entrance exams, and so I can give the results of my personal observations.

I have many acquaintances who work in the MSU or prepare high-school graduates for entrance exams at the MSU, and there is a lot of talk on the examination topics. One day before the oral exam I again heard the rumor that Jews were being concentrated in special groups. What then are the techniques for failing students? Outwardly, the examination proceeds in quite a normal way, everything is very simple. But the problems assigned to the examinees are somewhat more difficult than usual.

Now it is necessary to discuss in some detail what is a difficult and what is an easy problem, and how the degree of difficulty is to be measured.

In a field other than my own, in chemistry, for instance, I might appear in the role of a dismayed parent whose offspring complains that he was given an excessively difficult problem. The upset papa goes to the secretary of the admissions committee.

"A difficult problem?" says that person, "But this is a university, you know. Here one has to solve difficult problems."

"But the problem was *too* difficult," insists the parent, feeling like one lost in a fog. "They did not have to solve such problems at high school."

"No, it was not too difficult," the specialist explains with patient indulgence for papa's incompetence.

"The problem cannot be a standard one, for we accept only the best, not just anyone."

And so the parent goes off. Not that he is satisfied, but he sees that there is nothing he can say. In order to measure human potentialities one must have knowledge and experience.

Sometimes it is not so difficult to work out objective criteria after all. Let us, for example, estimate your physical development according to the height to which you can jump. Although neither you, reader, nor I, are experts, we are nevertheless capable of forming an opinion if the matter is simple.

If you cannot jump to—

125 cm: you have long since stopped going in for sports, and you consume a great deal at supper.

150 cm: Suppose you can easily get over.

Then you jump to

175 cm: Oh, this attracts attention; there is more than a little to build on.

200 cm: I can hardly believe my eyes! You are the hope of our sport; there are only a few such athletes in the whole country.

225 cm: No, this just doesn't happen; it's too good to be true.

Although everything seems simple here, an expert can see more. He will break up the test scale into centimeters, he will evaluate both technique and previous training, as well as future possibilities. He sees a slender youth flying easily over the bar, and the old coach's heart starts beating furiously in joyous anticipation: the long-awaited pupil. This talented youth will absorb all his many years of wisdom and experience and conquer a new height.

And suddenly, in place of the moving figure of an old teacher devoted to his science, we see quite a different character scrambling into view, gloomy and watchful.

"Your name?" he asks. "Ayrapetyan, Tsoy, Rozentsveig. (Oh, you Armenian bastard, you yellow-faced mug, you dirty Zhid.) Did you jump 175 cm at the written exam? Here's another little problem: jump 10 cm higher! You have? Well, just raise the bar above 2 meters, will you? Ah, you couldn't do that? You get a 'two.' Next!"

When criteria are not easily discernible, then the significance of the last evaluation remains a cryptogram.

What, then, is the degree of difficulty in mathematical problems? Can it be calculated? It can, although it is not easy. It is done by using the expert evaluation method. I, for instance, have examined thousands of school-children, taken part in and conducted Olympiads, composed problems for competitive entrance exams. And if I work out a difficulty scale to which honest specialists will agree, and make evaluations according to this scale, then the nonspecialists ought to believe them. I shall now try to provide illustrations of problems of five degrees of difficulty.*

1. Construct the graph of the function

$$y = /x/$$

2. Prove that

$$\log_2 3$$

is an irrational number.

3. Solve the equation

$$\sqrt{a + \sqrt{a + x}} = x, \ a > 0$$

4. Inscribed in a given triangle is a circle with a square described around it. Prove that more than half the perimeter of the square is contained within the triangle.

5. Numbers m and n have equal simple divisors. Numbers $m - 1$ and $n - 1$ possess the same property. Find out whether the set of such pairs of number m and n is finite or infinite.

A high-school graduate is given these problems and begins solving them.

1. There is the sign of the modulus here on the right, says the average high-school graduate. Let us use the definition. Thus:

$$y = \begin{cases} x, \text{ if } x > 0 \\ -x, \text{ if } x < 0 \end{cases}$$

And here is the graph: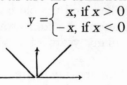

"We did this problem at school," he will say if asked. "I knew how to solve it."

---

*Those who find it hard to follow may skip the mathematical material, but some people will want to get to the heart of the matter without taking everything on trust.

Let us digress from the theme of these notes and ask ourselves the following question: How many of our high-school graduates will solve this problem?

"All the three million will," an inspector of the Education Ministry will reply, and will add, upon thinking a little: "There are schoolchildren whose level is below the syllabus requirements, but their number is, of course, small."

For years I have tried to overcome the low quality of instruction in mathematics, and I am well aware of how bleak the situation is. I think that

1. Two of every three high-school graduates in this country will fail* to solve a problem of this kind. †

2. Let us try a negative demonstration. A somewhat better prepared schoolboy will say, "The whole trick is in this sentence. After this it's quite simple."

$$\log_2 3 = \frac{p}{q}; \ p > 0, \ q > 0; \ 2\frac{p}{q} = 3; \ 2^p = 3^q,$$

with an even number on the left and an odd number on the right, a contradiction.

The average level of those who sat for entrance examinations to the MSU in the year 1976 was not high, and the degree of difficulty of most problems posed at oral examinations was identical to this. Except for special cases.

3. "Let us eliminate the radicals," says the schoolboy, beginning to solve the problem:

$$a + \sqrt{a + x} = x^2; \ \sqrt{a + x} = x^2 \ 1 \ a;$$
$$a + x = x^4 - 2ax^2 + a^2; \ x^4 - 2ax^2 - x + a^2 - a = 0$$

"I have arrived at an equation of the fourth degree," he says. "I don't know how to solve such equations."

"Try introducing a new variable," says a well-wishing teacher coming to the rescue. "Designate $\sqrt{a + x}$ by y."

To think of a trick like that is not easy. After that it is all very simple:

---

*Specialists will be surprised at this prediction. Checks by the Ministry of Education offer quite different—optimistic—results, but they are, as a rule, falsified.

†In order to screen out those who reproduce the solution from memory without realizing its meaning, the problem should be presented in a slightly different form, for example: 19

$$\overline{\sqrt{a + y} = x} \quad (x > 0, y > 0)$$
$$\sqrt{a + x} = y \quad y - x = x^2 - y^2$$

Since the relation $x + y = -1$ is impossible, then

$$y - x = 0, \ x = y, \ x^2 - x - a = 0, \ x = \frac{1 + \sqrt{1 + 4a}}{2}$$

How many schoolchildren could solve this problem?

A thousand, perhaps. Two thousand? Hardly likely.

The problem may be posed at entrance examinations to the MSU's Mech.-Math. faculty in the event of intense competition. It was posed in *special* cases.

4. The problem is quite out of the ordinary. There might be, perhaps, a few dozen schoolchildren in the entire country who could solve it.

I coped with it in three stages over a few days, and it was not clear at first how it was to be approached.

My colleague, a lecturer in geometry, worked on it for three days, and having finished, made a special phone call from Kalinin to let me know.

First one has to guess that the solution is obtained from the solution to the following subsidiary problem:

A square is given in which a circle is inscribed. How long is the longest section of the perimeter of the square which can be cut off by a tangent to this circle?

$2R$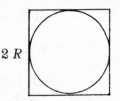

Using the extremum solution it can be proved that the maximum is cut off by a tangent perpendicular to the square's diagonal. This maximum equals $2(2 - \sqrt{2})R$. The length remaining inside the triangle will be > $4.45\,R$, i.e., more than one half ($\sim 3.55\,R$ being cut off).

It would take very unfair people to pose a problem like that at entrance exams. However, it was posed this year. In *special* cases.

5. The problem is one of incredible difficulty (for high school level). It is impossible to pose it even at Olympiads, of whatever kind. I could not solve it after spending about an hour on it. (I think I could cope with it, if I devoted a few days of systematic work to it.) It was supplied with the answer, without being told how it is to be arrived at:

$$m = 2^k - 1, \; n = (2^k - 1)^2$$

This problem was given in last year's Mech.-Math. faculty entrance examinations to Sasha Novodvorsky, whose half-brother had left for Israel not long before. Having received a "five" in the written examination, he got a "two" in the oral.

What was the average difficulty of this year's problems?

Gavrilova* was given problem no. 2 and also this type of problem: Demonstrate that $3 < \pi < 4$.

Gavrilov*: construct the graph of function $y = 2^{\log 2/x}$; construct a section whose length equals the distance between two intersecting straight lines; find the variation area of function

$$y = \frac{x}{x^2 + 1}$$

all of which belongs to the second category of difficulty.

Are these examples typical? Yes, they are. While the oral exam in mathematics was in progress, a crowd of high-school graduates and anxious, curious parents milled about the faculty. Those who emerged were immediately surrounded, the dismayed mothers asking again and again for each word and taking down the formulations of the problems. Here are the overall results of my observations, of which there were over twenty:

1. The overall mark in half the cases was higher than in the oral examination, never below.

2. The degree of difficulty in most cases was 2, occasionally 2.5, and never higher.

Now for the *special* cases.

Problem 4 of our list of specimens came to Rubinshtein at an oral exam. He had worked on it for about fifteen minutes, when the examiner came up, asked whether he had solved it yet (!), and suggested another problem which was a complicated version of Problem 3.

Both these problems were also given to Finkelshtein.

The results of an examination inflicted on several pupils of Mathematical High School no. 2, whose graduates are frequently accepted by the Mech.-Math. faculty, demonstrate our point well.

Brilliant reports about Yura Sorkin had reached me even before that. He had won first prize at an All-Union mathematical Olympiad, but did not attend an international Olympiad because of some odd administrative obstacles. Do you think Olga Korbut might fail to enter the Institute of Physical Culture because of poor results in the physical culture examination? There can be only one conclusion: enroll Olga Korbut, discharge the wretched examiners. Yura, however, did not pass, according to the competition results. At the oral exam he received three problems of the fourth degree of difficulty. Among them was one like this:
Which is greater—

---

*[A clearly Russian name.]

$$\sin \frac{8}{7} \text{ or } \frac{8\pi}{27}?$$

This problem Yura solved (this alone would be enough for an excellent mark). Another of the problems placed before him had been posed by Yugoslavia at an international Olympiad.

Also failing the competition were Beskin, Verkhovsky, Illarionov (Shapiro), Lipkin, and Fleishman. All the problems set them were of the fourth degree of difficulty. All except Fleishman also received the above-mentioned problem assigned to Sorkin. The numbers to be analyzed are equal to 0.910 and 0.931 respectively. How a schoolboy can distinguish between them without tables, I have no clear idea. It can be tackled only by a prodigy like Sorkin.

To conclude, there exists a *special* exam of the difficult-problems-for-the-Jews kind.

In the special cases, as a rule, the results of the oral examination were lower than those of the written one, never higher; while in the general cases it was the other way around.

A "Misunderstanding"

Yura Sorkin is a Russian; his father is only half-Jewish and is registered as a Russian on his identity card, while his mother is a noncounterfeit Russian.

The boy, however, was identified as Jewish and so was subjected to the corresponding procedure. At the faculty they knew about the mathematician Yuriy Isaakovich Sorkin and drew the necessary conclusions. For *this* is done by people who are deeply interested in what they are doing, who follow the "dictates of their hearts"[20] and display much initiative in their work. They will not let themselves be deceived by an entry on an identity card; they look at the photographs, listen to the sound of the patronymic, and make the necessary inquiries.

Upon hearing the results of the exam, Yura's mother went to see the chairman of the admissions committee. He refused to receive her. Sorkina, an indomitable woman (a former circus performer), broke into his office and shouted: "A misunderstanding! But it's impossible, it's a misunderstanding! My son is not a Jew at all!"

And she explained his entire genealogy. The professor turned purple and expelled her from the room while explaining the just principles of our existence.

Academician Kolmogorov wrote a personal letter soliciting Sorkin's admission, but even that did not help.

The Mechanism of Denial (Continued)

In order to check the principle on which examination groups are made up, I went up to the fourteenth floor of the MSU's high-rise building where the admissions committee's notices were put up. Here I was disappointed. There were no lists of names, the examinees designated by the number of their examination cards! What was to be done? I decided to carry out the check at another place where the practice, so rumor had it, was similar. I shall keep to myself the name of the IHL and the department in question, and confine my story to the results.

Near the door leading to the admissions office were three large boards with the lists of examinees who had passed the written competitive exam in mathematics, 1,160 in all.

The check could only be made according to the sound of the names. I wrote out some:

1. Erivansky Yuriy Konstantinovich	28
2. Liberman Valentin Isaakovich	53
3. Kushnir Valeriy Vladimirovich	53
4. Shtern Olga Davidovna	28
5. Konikov Arkadiy Bentsionovich	16
6. Grinbaum Semyon Matveevich	41

The number on the right represents the group number. Thirty-six names from my list were distributed in the following manner:

1 person in a group	—	8 groups
2 persons in the same group	—	6 groups
2 persons in the same group	—	1 group
6 persons in the same group	—	1 group
7 persons in the same group	—	1 group
		17 groups

If 36 persons are distributed in a random manner over 60 groups, then no more than one person out of our list will, as a rule, be found in any one group, occurrences of two or more being of low probability. But there was something else—and this was what I noticed at once.

In two groups (53 and 28) there was a denser concentration of Jewish names. Liberman—53, Kushnir—53, these names appeared one after the other, and I remembered the number. Soon, this group number turned up again: Pinchuk . . . Izrailevna—53, Zakharevich . . . Itskovich—53, Kogan . . . Yefimovich—53. These members of Group 53 followed almost successively, then the group was complemented by names which did not "grate on the ear." A similar situation was observed in the case of Group 28. A coincidence? At first glance, it was a somewhat vague picture. Then I remembered I was a mathematician and made an estimate of the probability. It turned out to be no higher than 10^{-19}. Can one guess five numbers out of thirty-six in the Sportlotto game three times running?

To conclude, the way those thirty-six names were allocated to groups turned out to be far from random.

Now for the results. Three of those on my list had succeeded in the competition. The probability of only one Jew in twelve passing, when on average every second person passed the examination, is one one-hundred-thousandth.

What then are the motives of those who bring about all this?

They are not new. What do you call it when socialism is not intended for all? In the MSU there is one who thinks this way, named Ulyanov.[21] Once, having had one too many after a drinking bout on the occasion of someone's thesis defense, he said aloud:

"You're a good chap, I've nothing against you, but we're at home here, and we don't want you."*

Doing first-year studies at the Kalinin University are two very bright and very nice young people: Olechka T. and Kostya N. I meet them every week. They take an interest in everything: solving difficult problems, listening to all sorts of things about mathematics. It is a pleasure to work with them.

However, is the effort worthwhile in this case? Is not Pyotr Lavren-tyevich Ulyanov, member of the American Mathematical Society, ready to worry about *my* children? Nonetheless, I shall continue with my work: perhaps after all there will be found such Russians who will curb him.

4. WORK
"You Want Work? Not Convincing."

Appointed head of a newly created computer center, G. began selecting his personnel and discussing the candidates with the group manager.

He selected about a dozen people to fill the vacancies of department heads, of whom two were Jewish. The manager looked through the documents in silence and pushed aside the files of Jewish candidates.

"Won't do," he said.

---

*One cannot help recalling here the utterances of His Majesty's minister Count Mentirov (to quote S. A. Stepnyak-Kravchinsky): "I am cordially disposed toward the Jews. The western border is kept wide open for you. So please, go ahead! Europe is at your disposal. Your place is there. There they love you. There your talents and abilities are needed. But of what use are they to us? We have enough of our own. What we want is the Russian spirit."[22]

"They are good specialists, Candidates of Sciences."

"Not *convincing.*"

"We want these people very much."

"*Not convincing*: We are selecting department heads, aren't we? We'll have to take them to conferences, to the Gosplan,[23] to the Council of Ministers. How can I put him at the same table? It's all written across his mug!"

Here is an example of a similar mentality. The philosopher Narsky, the author of *Istoriya zapadnoyevropeyskoy philosophiy*,[24] was a candidate for membership of the academy. He sent a letter to the president of the academy refuting the malicious rumors that he was Jewish and proved quite convincingly that he was a Pole. This wizard, however, did not get into the academy.

And here is what happened to a school headmaster in Kalinin: At a meeting of the school's pedagogic council he took to task a teacher named Nikolskaya. Her social level was evident from the status of her husband, a professor of philology. She lost her temper and in front of the whole honorable company called the headmaster a dirty Zhid. He went complaining to the party's regional committee, tried to get to the committee's first secretary, but failed. He was sidetracked to the regional department of education. A commission of inquiry came to the school, and Nikolskaya was mildly reprimanded for her unseemly conduct. As for the headmaster—well, he was freed of his duties for shortcomings in his ideological-educational work. It took him six months to find a teaching job somewhere in a suburb.

Recently, ten laboratories were shut down in an academy institute, eight of which were headed by Jews. There can be no question of coincidence; shortly before this, an article appeared in the institute's wall newspaper saying that "the management's personnel policy will be changed in view of the many instances of renunciation of Soviet citizenship." It is all true, but why is it that no one is worried by the feedback? Moreover, have not cause and effect changed places here?

A characteristic feature of the recent period: while the ticklish theme used to be treated by way of circumlocution, now the question is discussed quite often in a businesslike fashion.

A young university graduate arrives to take up his first job at an SRI of the Academy of Sciences. An official of the personnel department leads him along the corridor into the science department, in order to get to know him before completing the necessary formalities. The conversation is heard by all:

"So you are Russian, are you?"

"Yes."

"Your father and your mother, are they both Russian?"

"Yes, both."

"Is your wife Russian?"

"Yes."

"Then it's OK."

What I have related here are just some of the more amusing incidents, for it would be impossible to recount the innumerable ordinary ones. An exhaustive investigation is not my purpose. I just wanted to reveal another facet of this no-one-needs-you feeling of isolation.

X-Day and Birthday

At the beginning of 1972 I entered the carriage of a Kalinin electric commuter train, estimating how long it would take me to reach my home in Troparyovo from Kalinin. It looked like it would be about four hours. The tall houses of Kryukovo and Klin with their quite Moscow-like appearance, the deserted patch of a wood creeping up to the very station platform of Yarmuga, the snow-covered expanse of the Sea of Moscow on both sides of the railway track, the interlacing pipes of the Redkino chemical plant— henceforth I was to contemplate all that regularly twice a week.

I assessed the end results. I had made some independent achievements in mathematics. That was a plus. But almost twenty years of activity in the network of pedagogic education had led to a disappointment. The universally low quality of knowledge in mathematics would remain what it was, and no amount of personal effort would help. A minus. I had managed to move to Moscow, but no suitable work could be found for me in Moscow— another minus.

The rector of Kalinin State University could find no time for an interview, but he gave his instructions without seeing me: I was to be accepted. Later on I learned, in a roundabout way, that the rector had been in considerable doubt whether to take me on.

During the ensuing four years I had accomplished not a little, working energetically with reborn enthusiasm; there was a new field of activity opening up before me—organizational work in applied mathematics.

When I began, the students were only taught a small twenty-hour programming course. They practiced on an old discarded M-3 valve (tube) computer.

After four years:

There are about one hundred people in "my" line of activity. The KSU has a computer center with one ES-1020 and two M-220 computers in three big rooms. Orders worth one quarter of a million rubles. There is a chair of computer mathematics with a staff of adequately qualified teachers. A new speciality: applied mathematics, with hundreds of students.

Soon I was given a kick in the backside.

In the university everything is determined by the rector. He keeps all the strings firmly in his hands.

I think that his having avoided an interview when he accepted me was no accident: "Keep working in the meantime, but remember it was not I who took you on."

My opinion of him, formed from reports, was favorable: a clever, resolute man, unwilling to listen too much to recognized authorities, treating scientists (or, more precisely, doctors of science) with respect, "nationally" tolerant. Besides, he had given me good work, did not interfere in my affairs, and I was grateful to him.

But in January 1975 there came, abruptly, the rector's order on the separation of the computer center. Soon I also lost the scientific-research sector. A not inconsiderable amount of effort had been invested in it by my assistants, both of them retired colonels who were at odds with the intelligentsia of the chair and were very sensitive about questions of subordination.

Involuntarily, an incident from the past came to my mind. When I lived in Yelabuga, the curator of the Shishkin Museum, a local woman with a seventh-grade education, had been guiding an out-of-town excursion group.

"Shishkin is the greatest Russian landscape painter," she said.

"What about Levitan?" asked one of the excursionists.

The curator took offense.

"Levitan, as compared to Shishkin, is a pup," she said. "And a Jew into the bargain."

Now about X-day.

Our secretary had repeatedly conveyed to me a request to come to Section 2. When I finally presented myself, she told me that important work was going on.

It was necessary to put in order the curricula and syllabi on the occasion of X-day.

I promised to come and then forgot about this insane affair.

One day the word was passed to me that if I did not come, it would be reported to the rector. "Damn," I said as I tore myself away from my real business, collected the syllabi, and presented myself. We went to the end of the corridor, knocked on a small, closed window, and were admitted into a large room with gratings over the windows, in which was sitting a man with expressionless features.

A young female clerk brought a slip of paper from the next room. On the left-hand side, subjects were listed in a column, with the hours indicated on the right-hand side. I said that the task was clear to me. Then, suddenly, the man said, in a somewhat abstract way:

"We have decided, in connection with this, to register you while you are here."

A paper appeared in his hands, and he showed me where I was to sign.

I took the pen and was about to sign when I noticed that the paper was a printed one, and here and there the words "state secret" and "foreign citizens" caught my eye.

I took the paper from the hands of the head official and began to read it attentively, trying to ascertain what it was all about. I could see that it dealt with access to classified work.

I expressed my doubts as to the necessity of such a step, my work being very open indeed.

The head official said, in an ordinary voice, as of something that had been decided upon long before:

"We are registering all the heads of chairs, you have all been given access already."

"It states here: 'I promise not to divulge state secrets,' " I said, "but I know no secrets and don't want to know any. As for contacts with foreign citizens, I conduct an extensive scientific correspondence. And what about trips abroad? I am interested in scientific contacts."

"We shall consider it and give you special permission."

"Wouldn't it be still better not to start the whole thing at all? I tell you frankly, I have grave doubts, for this is a very serious document."

"Of course," he agreed, dropping his careless tone for the first time.

"So I want to think carefully before signing," I said, and laid the paper on the table.

"This will have to be reported to the rector," the official said.

"As you like."

I said goodbye and left.

We had both forgotten about the syllabi. They were not the point.

I made some inquiries among my colleagues and acquaintances; none of them had undergone this kind of experience. Could it be that the performance had been intended for a single observer?

And it so happened that not long afterwards, on one fine spring day, three ladies from my department came up to me and said:

"The local newspaper has printed a notice announcing a competition for the post of head of the computer mathematics chair. What can it all mean?"

I told a colleague about it.

"It is an outrageous and unprecedented act; I've never heard of anything like it. You competed for this post, didn't you?"

"Only a year ago, and I was accepted unanimously. They heaped praise on me, like sugar and honey: 'a first-rate organizer.' "

"Appeal it, and the competition will be canceled."

"So it will be, most likely, but it is not in my interest to protest," I said after thinking a little. "The rector will find a hundred pretexts for kicking me out all the same. Whereas I am interested in work, not in a position."

Following the next council meeting I approached the rector and said I wanted to talk to him. He hesitated, started to plead that he was very busy, but I insisted. He agreed and invited me to his office. The party-committee secretary entered behind him and sat down too, for support, but uttered not a word throughout the interview, maintaining a sullen silence.

I asked the rector what it could mean, the affair of the announcement.

"I will not make a secret of it, we did announce the competition to take on a new man. But you asked for it yourself. You told me you'd be glad to discontinue your work in applied mathematics and devote your studies entirely to your theory of numbers."

At this point, for the first time, I spoke out in a sharp tone and rebuked him:

"I never asked for anything of the sort. Yes, I was going to find a suitable person, a specialist, and transfer my work to him gradually. You have decided to remove me immediately. If you had talked to me beforehand, I would have vacated the post, transferred to another chair, and you could have announced a competition for the vacant post. As things are now, you are dismissing me as if I had not been up to doing my job, as if I made a mess of it. That's what everybody will think."

"Yes, we may have overlooked something here," the rector said. "If you like, I can take the floor at the next scientific-council meeting and explain."

You will hardly do that, I thought.

"Since you have already taken all the decisions for me, I don't want a confrontation. I would like to go to the Faculty of Advanced Studies from September."

And so the matter was closed.

What was the role of my nationality in what had taken place? A very substantial one. The number of Jews occupying leading positions is decreasing everywhere, including the KSU. There were about ten of them among the heads of chairs some five years ago, but there are only two or three at present. Would the rector have expelled me had I not been Jewish? Possibly. But it would have never been done in such a crude, peremptory manner, in violation of the law. He had clearly felt that he was dealing with a defenseless person. This person would not make a row, he had nowhere to go to, and you could do whatever you liked with him. This is one of the causes of my present dejection. I have come to understand this: you are kept on while they need you, but as soon as people who can replace you come into view, you will be expelled without regret that same moment, and it will be done as rudely as can be.

A short time ago I turned fifty. The day before my birthday, I was summoned to a party-bureau meeting by the newly elected secretary, Nikolay Yakovlevich Popov, my former deputy. He made a crushing speech and tried very hard to launch a "personal case"[25] concerning me. As he put it, I had long been behind in paying trade-union membership dues, and had absented myself from the meetings and the Marxist philosophy circle.

"You have completely broken your ties with the party," he said, concluding his sinister speech.

They treat me well at the faculty; it would be unfair to complain. It was agreed to confine the matter to discussion. Many happy returns of the day to you!

5. SCIENCE

What Makes Me Sorry

"Have you acquired enemies?" I was asked by someone who shares my views.

"There are people who persecute me, who seek my destruction. To try to flee, to oppose them has been of no avail. What am I to do?"

"Could you be more specific?"

"There is a group of very highly placed mathematicians who have joined forces in a conscious and purposeful effort to bring about the expulsion of Jews from the field of mathematics. They act in different directions and by all kinds of means. What is most outrageous, unprecedented, and dishonest in their activities is the practice they have adopted of thesis rejection."

"What sort of practice is that?"

"A paper defended in an IHL's scientific council goes to the HCC, where it has to pass scientific examination by experts. A specially selected reviewer, or 'black reviewer' as he is customarily called, writes a negative opinion on a competent piece of work which fully merits a scientific degree for its author. The Experts' Council conducts a biased discussion with a predetermined outcome, and takes a decision rejecting the thesis. All the participants in these proceedings are fully aware that the thesis is rejected for the sole reason that it is a 'Jewish' one. This practice has been in existence for quite a long time, about seven years or so. The number of theses turned down in this way has, by my estimate, exceeded one hundred, possibly a few hundred."

"How did you obtain this information?"

"While fighting. For almost two years I disputed the rejection of my pupil V.'s thesis. He wrote a very good paper, far above the average. I have studied the well-developed mechanics of rejection, met people who participated in the rejection, seen their motives. At the same time I came to know of dozens of similar cases. In spite of all my efforts, the thesis which is an integral part of my many years' work has been rejected by decision of the VAK college, of December 22, 1976. Now it must be clear to you: these events make me very depressed."

"You must lodge a protest. Those people must be stopped. Do you know them?"

"I know many of them personally, the names of others are also known. All of them are either members of the Experts' Council or members of expert groups, a close circle of reviewers. Since the examination procedure is strictly documented, a disinterested investigation could easily . . . But will it take place? People *did* complain, but there have been no results."

"What did they complain about?"

"As usual: The thesis has been rejected, but it is good, please reconsider and approve."

"But the real reasons?"

"They are never mentioned: no one wants to get involved in politics."

"What has politics got to do with it? A specialist writes an obviously false evaluation. He votes for the rejection of a thesis from purely racial motives. All this means a violation of the law. These people, who, as I can see from what you say, are not so very numerous, must be exposed, punished, or at any rate, prevented from committing lawless acts. This means that it is your duty to lodge a protest."

"Why me?"

"If you don't, who else will? How many times have you boasted that your thirst for truth is basic to your existence and said that you lose the very basis for existence if obstructed in your mathematical studies. But now you see emerging people who are out to tarnish truth, and push the foundation on which you stand from under your feet. Will you humbly submit? Are you afraid? Don't be afraid: you are dead already."

I wanted to answer but could not.

"Don't answer, I understand your feelings, your fears. Let us do it this way: You will state your protest in all due form, you will set out your observations. Then we shall think about it."

A Letter to the President of the Academy of Sciences

Comrade President,

You have recently taken up your high post. Now you are faced with the task of restoring justice.

By this I mean the elimination of militant anti-Semitism in mathematics.

This phenomenon, which has always been condemned by men of culture, is all the more intolerable today when "complete and final liquidation of . . . national oppression and race discrimination . . . is the optimistic perspective that Communists offer to the world," and is particularly the aim of scientists, whose lives are an incessant quest for truth.

This is not, as is usual in such cases, a matter of something shapeless and elusive. There are explicit addresses: The V. A. Steklov Mathematical Institute of the Academy of Sciences of the USSR, the Experts' Council on Mathematics and Mechanics of the HCC. And specific people. Of these I shall name only some, who are particularly active. They are Academician I. M. Vinogradov; Corresponding Members of the Academy of Sciences of the USSR A. I. Shirshov, Yu. L. Yershov, S. V. Yablonsky; Doctors of Physico-Mathematical Sciences A. A. Karatsuba and P. L. Ul'yanov. What they do is a crime against science, to say nothing of their motives, which apart from being immoral, are punishable under the Soviet Constitution and Soviet law.

Consciously and purposefully, acting via the VAK's Experts' Council, they arrange wholesale rejection of good theses whose authors are Jewish. This has passed all bounds of "moderation and decency": such rejected doctoral theses number dozens, while rejected candidates' theses run to many dozens or, perhaps, as an accurate count may show, to hundreds. This is unprecedented; nothing like it has ever taken place in the whole history of science.

So far have things gone that they do not even take the trouble to keep up appearances; of those summoned for chastisement to the Experts' Council sessions, two-thirds, three-quarters, and in some cases as many as one hundred (!) percent are Jewish.

When you start to look into the heart of the matter, and look into it one must for the sake of a sound future for our science and our society, you will discover a veritable cesspool of unscrupulousness in matters of science: negative opinions which are obviously mendacious, based on personal likes or dislikes, ignoring all norms of scientific criticism, virtually illiterate; sessions which in fifteen to twenty minutes sum up and reject the appraisal by numerous specialists of international repute. The taking of well-founded decisions in such conflict situations would presuppose prolonged, detailed analysis without any time limitation. But there it is: they discuss anything but the essence. Those taking part in the discussions have a very poor idea of the subject but are very loud in clamoring for rejection. Specialists are not admitted to sessions and must stay outside closed doors, even though they insist on their right to express their opinion. Why should they be admitted? A competent person would only impede the proceedings!

False pride prompts insistence on odious decisions which have provoked general indignation. An instance of this is furnished by the disgraceful decisions on the theses of Tsalenko and Winberg, during their second examination at the Steklov Institute. One cannot, indeed, help remembering the case of "that rascal D." in the second Military Council!

The responsibility is shared by all the members of the Experts' Council, by all the experts, albeit to different degrees. Many of them gave in to pressure, or did not want a conflict, or were unwilling to lose their privileges. Free them from compulsion, and they will tell you at once that they did not want it, did not know it, that they were coerced into doing it.

To sum up:

I accuse Ivan Matveevich Vinogradov of being the chief organizer and inspirer of anti-Semitism in our mathematical science. Let him, in his declining years, reflect a little on what he will see when he looks into the mirror of history: an outstanding creator, or a poisoner of the spirit of genuine scientific exploration?

I accuse Anatoliy Alekseyevich Karatsuba of having, in opposition to the general opinion, maligned and turned down fine, and even quite outstanding, papers on the theory of numbers, being guided solely by national antipathies. May his sick conscience give him no peace!

I accuse Yuriy Leonidovich Yershov and Anatoliy Illarionovich Shirshov of having created an intolerable situation in the field of algebra by persecuting people who do not share their own extreme views.

I accuse Pyotr Lavrentyevich Ulyanov of violating norms of equitable selection with regard to the process of admission to the MSU, and of contributing to the rejection of good theses at the MSU and in the Experts' Council.

I accuse Sergey Vsevolodovich Yablonsky of pursuing racist policies in the sphere of cybernetics.

I accuse the HCC's Experts' Council in Mathematics and Mechanics of dereliction of their official duties, which found expression in repeated rejection of theses by Jewish mathematicians that merited approval.

I accuse the Mathematical Institute of the Academy of Sciences of harboring that anti-Semitic and intolerant spirit which reigns supreme in and of poisoning all life in the sphere of mathematical science.

It is up to you to intervene and normalize the situation. Do not let yourself be deterred by considerations of the honor of the high institution which you head, for its honor will not suffer. Remember the ill-fated Vilio [?]!

It is necessary to:

Change completely the composition of the Experts' Council.

Pension off Vinogradov as an urgent measure.

Open wide all windows in the Steklov Institute, for it reeks of carrion there.

The words with which the man of great spirit finished his historic letter are also my words.

Standing, as you do, at the head of Soviet science, you must personify the high principles of scientific honor, of the search for truth and justice. So do your duty!

Please accept, Comrade President, assurances of my deepest respect.

Professor Grigory Freiman
Doctor of Physico-Mathematical Sciences

Now for a more detailed account.

Ivan Matveevich Vinogradov

". . . born on 14 September (new style), 1891. His father, Matvei Avraamievich, was a priest at the Milolub pogost of the Velikiye Luki uyezd,[26] Pskov Province. . . . his parents sent him . . . to an advanced technical school in Velikiye Luki (1903), where his father settled with his entire family after being appointed priest of the Pokrov church."*

It is possible that the impressions of his childhood years were the source of his hatred for Jews—one of the main and essential springs driving his dynamic nature to activity. His other main passions are a thirst for power and a love of mathematics. He was a brilliant mathematician, there is no disputing the fact.

Of his attitude toward the Jews, Vinogradov always speaks out loud, although he does what he does behind their backs.

During the period when N. was defending his candidate's thesis he spent much time in "Steklovka"[27] and met frequently with Ivan Matveevich. He testifies that when two or three persons of Vinogradov's entourage gather in his study, within fifteen or twenty minutes any conversation, whatever its starting point, is invariably channeled into the mainstream, and they begin to disparage the Jews with great gusto and animation.

The Nemchinovs lived in the academy township, and their dacha was next-door to Vinogradov's. He often saw them over the fence but never came up to them or said hello.

One day, however, he suddenly came up to Nemchinov's wife and said,

---

*V. Delone, *Peterburgskaya Shkola teorii chisel* [The Petersburg school of the theory of numbers] (1947), p. 321.

"How do you do, Mariya Ivanovna. You know, I thought you and Vasiliy Sergeevich were Jews!"

When a "higher-up" phoned Vinogradov to complain to him about Shafarevich,[28] he answered:

"Shafarevich is not a Jew."

"But he is such and such—"

"He's not a Jew, I checked it myself."

"No, but—"

"Shafarevich is not a Jew, and the rest is no concern of mine."

This famous anecdote seems to have some basis in reality.

When Vinogradov for some reason or other took a dislike to the mathematician Sabirov, he said:

"Don't call him Sabirov; he's Shapiro!"

I.M.'s name for my teacher Aleksandr Iosifovich Gelfond, behind his back, was invariably Sashka the Zhid.

A splendid administrator and politician, Vinogradov has held all the levers of control over the mathematical field firmly in his hands for several decades. All the material things—elections to the academy, prize awards, trips abroad—all this is done according to his decisions and under his supervision. The possibilities of other academician mathematicians, however famous, are insignificant. Mark Grigor'yevich Krein, for example, has for many years in succession been nominated as a candidate for the Lenin Prize award. Finally, Aleksandrov, Kolmogorov, and Petrovsky published an article in *Izvestia* insisting on the necessity of the prize going to Krein, but it was to no avail.

When I learned that Karatsuba was preparing to reject B.'s paper, I decided to see Vinogradov—for the third time in my life.

I first met him after making my report in his presence at the third Mathematical Congress in the summer of 1956. As soon as I had finished, he rose, came up to me, and said, approvingly:

"Not bad." Then he paused and repeated: "Not bad, not bad—" And left.

Our second meeting took place shortly before my doctoral defense, early in 1965. I came to "Steklovka" by invitation and had to kill a lot of time walking up and down the second floor corridor, near the director's office. At last, I.M. showed up at the end of the corridor—a corpulent, hulking figure, short and stooping, with a large shaven head inclined slightly forward, and long arms that seemed almost to reach the floor, hanging down the sides of his powerful torso, making him look rather like an orangoutang. We went into his study, and I was accorded a solemn reception which lasted for almost two hours. I gave I.M. all my publications, told him about my results, and received his approval. I.M. spoke unhurriedly, with digressions into the past, relating various incidents and jokes, which both added flavor to the conversation and provided time to consider serious matters.

I did not see him again; knowing his antipathies, I did not seek a meeting, although we have the same field of scientific interests, and I derived much from his work.

And so it was that just then, at that decisive moment, I conceived the idea of applying to him. Having turned it all over in my mind, I rang him up at home, introduced myself, and suggested that we discuss problems of general scientific interest. Vinogradov knew me at once, said that he was ill, and suggested that we meet when he got well.

For about three months, I had one meeting after another with Konstantin Vasil'yevich Borozdin, Vinogradov's personal assistant—not a mathematician, but a fairly intelligent and meticulous man, and a really great administrator.

Each time he listened to what I had to say and explained in an attentive and even quite affable manner why Vinogradov was absent or what he was busy with, and he then invited me to call at the institute or ring up the following week. I had almost lost hope, but one day Borozdin invited me to come on Thursday, saying that a meeting was being planned.

Going up the stairs on Thursday, I ran into three young Negroes who were accompanied by a responsible member of the institute's staff.

"I.M. was going to receive you, but just now he will be receiving Negroes—" K.V. was speaking in his most concise style, measuring out his words. Here he paused, thought a little, and added: "And Arabs."

"If so," I said, "I'll have to wait."

The Negroes proceeded into the study. There were no Arabs, and I saw that this was just a subtle joke of Borozdin's.

I did not get to see Vinogradov that day. Then, finally, the next Tuesday rolled around.

In an empty reception room the secretary politely asked me to sit down, entered Vinogradov's study, and invited me to come in. Vinogradov was sitting at a large writing table that stood by the wall on the left-hand side between two large windows. On the opposite side of the enormous study there hung a large blackboard. When I entered, Vinogradov rose, extended his hand, and invited me to sit down on a chair placed by the table on his right.

The talk started to unwind unhurriedly, which I had anticipated, remembering his manner. So the finale was the more unexpected.

I reminded him of our last meeting, of my studies in the general principles of the additive theory of numbers. Vinogradov said that he remembered it. I let him know that my ideas had proved to have applications in the theory of probability. Vinogradov then started to develop his favorite theme, on the relationship between form and substance in mathematical studies. It is an age-long controversy between two trends of mathematical thought, which in Bourbaki's *Architektura matematiki*[29] is expressed in the incompatibility of the strategic (form) and the tactical (substance) approach. What is more important—universality of application or the result? I think the result. Vinogradov held the same opinion.

I decided it was time to come to the point little by little.

"I have taken a great interest lately in the famous Markov problem on the arithmetical minima of quadratic forms, and I have succeeded in obtaining results which are, in my view, significant."

"So this problem, what is it," Vinogradov said falteringly, "is it not what was proposed by Delone?"

Like a flash of lightning, this sentence illuminated the entire state of affairs, rendering it perfectly clear. It told a lot.

The old man sat confidently and firmly in his chair. He spoke with clarity, his large shaven head, his broad figure, the leisurely movements of his big, outstretched hands—all this was imposing as never before. And yet I could see that his intellect was not quite as powerful, his memory failed him a bit, and it was harder for him to conceal what he was thinking.

He did not understand what the problem in question was, had forgotten it, although he could not have been ignorant of it in his time.

This is what Delone writes about the work of Markov: "This work, which has been very highly praised by Chebyshev, belongs among the keenest achievements of the Petersburg school of the theory of numbers or, perhaps, of all Russian mathematics."*

Vinogradov, a representative of the same school, did not recognize the famous Markov problem in Delone's reference, which he had discussed with someone. Who was that, what were they talking about?

It all became perfectly clear to me. It was precisely in the Markov problem that V. had achieved considerable progress, and it was this particular result that Karatsuba had discussed with Vinogradov, to whom he had reported it as progress in some trivial problem proposed by Delone.

I always knew that Vinogradov, for whom there was no such word as "trivial," kept every little thing under his control. This meant that Karatsuba had received detailed instructions from Vinogradov on V.'s thesis, and the rejection of his work was being organized according to his directives.

I nodded noncommittally in response to his question and said:

"If you will allow me, I'll briefly explain the merits of the result obtained."

Vinogradov nodding agreement, I got up and went over to the blackboard.

---

*B. N. Delone. *The Petersburg School of the Theory of Numbers* (1947), p. 144.

"A set of minima may be represented by points on a straight line, points of a spectrum."

I took a piece of chalk and drew a line on the blackboard.

"Markov found all the points of the spectrum to be fewer than three. The next important result was that of Marshall Hall, who proved that the spectrum included a ray. And what is its origin? B. N. Delone and his pupils proved that it lay to the left of 6.4, whereas my pupils and I, and Hall himself, obtained a refined value of 5.1."

I took a breath, for I was coming to the main point.

"A very important refinement, based on a new method, was obtained by V. His value is 5.04."

At this moment the secretary entered the room, came over to Vinogradov, and bent down to him. Carried away by my narrative, I paid no attention to this, but later, when I thought about what had taken place, I recalled clearly that he had said to her, briefly:

"Stay a while."

She sat down on the chair I had recently occupied.

I went on with my story.

"I have succeeded in refining V.'s result. I have found the exact value for Hall's ray: it turns out to be equal to 4.52 (to two decimal places)."

And I triumphantly placed this significant point on the straight line.

Abruptly, the situation in the room changed sharply. Peace and quiet were gone. The door was flung open and closed from time to time. In fact, there were only two intruders—Borozdin, and Mishchenko, the director's assistant—but the impression was that a whole crowd had burst in. They opened files, handed papers to Vinogradov for him to sign, and crowded around the table, so that I was immediately cut off from Vinogradov, so accessible before, as if by an impenetrable wall.

I did not immediately grasp what was going on, but felt instinctively that it was time to wind up.

"Those are all the essentials," I said and went over to the table, Vinogradov's satellites whirling around it in a mute dance as if in approaching I could do some harm to their beloved chief, and they were determined to defend him by blocking my way even at the cost of their own lives. I could hardly squeeze myself through. I took my books, which I had placed on the table at the beginning of our interview, and held them out to Vinogradov, pointing out the place where the sought-for value of the ray origin was given.

"I'll look, I'll look at it," Vinogradov said. "You'll excuse me, won't you."

And he pointed with his hand at the crowd, and at the papers awaiting his signature. As I made for the door, he rose from the table, a heavy, stooping, hulking figure, and extended his hand. I shook it, although to do so I had to squeeze my way again through the close formation of his vassals, and—left the field of battle.

Only in the corridor did I understand what had actually taken place. On hearing V.'s name, he had seen what I was driving at and had started frantically to press the buttons on his writing table summoning all his assistants, whom he had instructed beforehand how to act when the moment came to chuck me out.

Anatoliy Alekseevich Karatsuba

In times gone by I had often met Karatsuba at Aleksandr Osipovich's[30] seminar sessions. As a student under Korobov, he had specialized in the theory of numbers, then did postgraduate work under that same Korobov.

He was thin and shy, always wore a nice snow-white shirt, was very affable and benevolent toward everyone, went in a lot for mountaineering and held fairly progressive views.

During those years, B. also studied under Korobov and was fairly well acquainted with Tolya. For the first two years after Karatsuba went to Steklovka their relationship did not change. Whenever B. came to Steklovka, Karatsuba was very warmhearted towards him.

When Vinogradov drew Karatsuba into his circle, he changed very sharply, broke relations with his old university friends, and even stopped greeting them. Vinogradov and Korobov had a dispute over a question of priority. Karatsuba took a very active part when they set about expelling Korobov from the institute. Korobov is still going round the departments seeking reinstatement.

Karatsuba first espoused this new career during Feinleib's doctoral defense in the Lenin Pedagogic Institute. According to the general professional opinion, it was a good piece of work, quite up to the necessary level. Karatsuba came to the defense session, heaped wholesale disparagement on Feinleib's work, and the thesis failed to get the necessary two-thirds by just one vote. Feinleib is still not a Ph.D.

When B.'s thesis was being defended, I did not even think about whether it would be approved, whether any additional evaluations were needed or additional organizational work was necessary. For what purpose? The thesis was very good, and good work could not be rejected!

The examination, however, dragged on; we began to worry and to make inquiries. We succeeded in discovering who had received the paper in order to write an evaluation. The address: Dolbilin, Steklov Institute. We found out who the person was. Dolbilin was a young chap, about twenty-five, who had recently defended his candidate's thesis, and worked in Delone's section.

Here I felt for the first time that something was brewing. Why was the paper sent for evaluation to this young fellow, who was not even a specialist?

I rang up Delone. He knew nothing, but promised to find out. This set me thinking: Delone did not know that the thesis was being held by Dolbilin, a member of his own section; nor had Dolbilin informed his superior, although the paper had been with him no less than three months already.

It was when I spoke with Delone on the telephone a second time that I became aware for the first time of that distinct smell of putrefaction that has been my invariable environment for the last couple of years.

Yes, Dolbilin had been given the thesis in order to write an evaluation. Had just received it (!), so he'd had no time to make his report. He did not like the thesis. The questions discussed were so very special. And what particularly displeased him was that conditions of coincidence of the Markov and Lagrange spectra were obtained only within certain ranges, not everywhere.

"But these conditions are necessary and sufficient, so it's fundamental progress," I objected.

Arguments of the Dolbilin type are irrefutable: You are the first to swim the English Channel; this is very bad because you didn't swim the Atlantic, all the way to Africa.

Boris Nikolayevich Delone, reluctant as he was to get involved in conflicts, would have to tell the truth when obliged to speak up. He made an appointment for Tuesday week. He, Dolbilin, and I must meet and elicit the truth through scientific discussion.

On Wednesday I phoned Delone and reminded him of the forthcoming discussion.

"Kolya beat us to the punch (!)," Boris Nikolayevich said. "Today he sent the paper back to the HCC without an evaluation."

Only by degrees did I begin to grasp the motives of such actions. Karatsuba's reward, the piece of meat that Vinogradov dangled on a string above his head, was the title of Corresponding Member of the Academy. For Dolbilin, there was the defense of a doctoral thesis pending and a flat as an imminent prospect.

That was why he agreed to undertake the unsavory work; Karatsuba had told him to do it. But he failed to do it on the sly. Dolbilin saw that a scandal was imminent. Delone had learned of the entire affair. M. phoned him and asked for an explanation. To give a negative opinion would have meant to disgrace himself, for which he was not prepared, since, unlike Karatsuba, he had not yet burned all his bridges behind him. To give a positive evaluation was tantamount to losing his job (M.'s reaction). So the thesis was sent back without an evaluation.

"The work is weak—that is the reason, and all those nuances are a hallucination, they just aren't there!" Such will be the ear-splitting battle cry of the defenders of the "New Alliance of Truly Russian People in Mathematics."[31]

I have a witness. And that is Dolbilin himself. Not long ago, speaking in certain company, he produced his own and, to his honor be it said, truthful version of what had happened. Yes, that was a well-made piece of work, not invulnerable, but quite worthy of the degree. Therefore he had sent it back without an evaluation. There was no hope: the thesis would be rejected because Vinogradov and Karatsuba despised the author's professor.

No further trace of the paper could be found, and the next reviewer to receive it from Karatsuba remained unknown.

I went to see Delone.

At eighty-six, Boris Nikolayevich Delone is the oldest of the Soviet mathematicians. Even Vinogradov is one and a half years younger than Delone. The old man treats me well, although irony and causticity are always present in his conversation like spices in Oriental food. Now, after his wife's death, his health has declined considerably, his gray hair has thinned, his face has grown leaner, he has few teeth left. But not long ago he still looked quite vigorous.

It was a pleasure to look at his bronze-colored, weather-beaten, healthy face. He used to come to work in Steklovka in a blue woolen sweat-suit with a white champion's border. He was an outstanding mountaineer in his day and kept his form until very recently. On one occasion during winter he asked me nonchalantly if I was afraid to sit by an open *fortochka*[32] ("You Semites are wary of cool air"), climbed on to the window sill, banged the *fortochka* to, and jumped down—didn't climb down, but simply jumped, somewhat heavily, not very dexterously, but was very pleased for all that.

The old man was far from enthusiastic about getting involved in this whole squabble. I, as usual, spent many hours with him, and he again recounted all the events of his youth, all the mathematical jokes of Moscow. I had already heard that Pontryagin had written a negative evaluation of a very solid doctoral thesis by Winberg, defended in the MSU. Lev Semyonovich Pontryagin is a mathematician whose achievements have already become classic. A strange line of thought, not peculiar to him alone, led him during recent years to the conclusion that Jewish mathematics was bad mathematics and must be fought. They say that it was precisely on these grounds that he insisted that the two volumes of the historical review *Matematika v SSSR za 50 let*,[33] already set in type, be taken apart. This book never came out.

"Winberg came to me," Delone said, "and began to tell me with tears in his eyes, while producing some ancient papers, that his grandfather had headed a ministerial bureau in imperial Russia, held a high rank, and therefore could in no way have been Jewish, and that he himself was not Jewish but a Russianized Swede. On meeting Pontryagin, I told him about it, and he muttered, 'You don't say,' and looked very embarrassed. I had a close look at Winberg on meeting him, and thought that he was absolutely wrong in declining the honor of belonging to the 'God-chosen people.' "

Our talk went on in this way until I lost patience and put the issue point-blank: "If Boris Nikolayevich thought the thesis weak, let him say so; if not, then he, as the initiator of the study, must give an objective evaluation." Delone thought a little more, took his pen, and wrote a positive evaluation which was sent to the HCC.

In March 1976 there appeared a negative evaluation by the HCC's reviewer. I shall give a more detailed analysis of this important document below. At this point I shall confine myself to stating that it was an utterly mendacious piece of writing. During all that time I made no attempt to discuss the problem with Karatsuba personally; that he was purposely trying to organize the thesis's rejection was not at all my hypothesis. However, concrete evidence reached me through common acquaintances, and remarks of his were quoted, that left one in no doubt as to the hopeless outcome of the affair.

While visiting A. at the end of March, I was advised to meet Karatsuba anyway. All the same, however plain his position according to roundabout information, it would look more definite if asserted directly. Karatsuba's wife's telephone (they live not quite together and not quite separately) happened to be available. A phone call was made, and Karatsuba was unexpectedly found to be there. When I introduced myself, he was stunned and did not know what to say.

"I am not *au courant* with the affair," he said at last, "the evaluation has not yet reached me at the office. When I familiarize myself with it, a meeting can be arranged."

I phoned him in a week's time and another week later also, and got the same answer both times. I saw that he was acting like a nasty mouse gnawing assiduously under the floor but afraid to stick its nose out into the light of day. There was no seeing him until the very session of the expert committee where the material would go after he had fully prepared it for rejection.

After the thesis was rejected and, on my complaint, returned to the Experts' Council, I rang him up once again, and here it turned out that Karatsuba was—suffering pangs of conscience. I was staggered by the immensity of sterling human emotion that he put into the conversation this time.

"Anatoliy Alekseevich, it looks like we ought to meet in connection with B.'s work."

"You think so?"

There was an incredible amount of emotion in his voice, veritable agony.

I kept silent, waiting for a concrete answer. All the quotations here are authentic, I put them down immediately after the conversation.

"I don't know—" Here his voice was reduced almost to a whisper, vacillating at a peak of irresolution, and the chord was resolved in a painfully indefinite:

"Then when can we?"

"Whenever you like," I said.

He whispers something (yes, yes; it was a whisper as of someone turning his affairs over in his mind), then falls silent, silent for good.

I am waiting. It's all right. Silence. I am obliged to break it.

"We must talk, mustn't we though?"

He (in a lost voice): "I see."

A pause again. At last he regained his normal voice.

"The thing is that I'm going abroad, and everything is bound up with that."

We agreed to meet after his return.

After this conversation I decided not to ring him up again.

And yet our meeting and interview did take place not long before the final sitting of the Experts' Council, where Karatsuba did everything to have the paper turned down.

Our meeting took place by chance in a trolley-bus. I knew that Karatsuba's wife lived two doors from me, but I had never met him near the house. Now, one fine day, as I boarded a trolley-bus running along Vernadsky Prospekt, I discovered Karatsuba sitting right across from me. We saw each other at the same time and looked each other straight in the face, he somewhat expectantly; there are many people now who just cut him dead. I nodded, and so did he, and we both looked away.

Should we part thus without saying a word? No, there is nothing for me to be ashamed of or to conceal, I must go through with the talk, appealing to whatever vestiges of decency there were in him. If, however, as in the case of Vinogradov, all this should prove futile, we would both know where we stood.

"Anatoliy Alekseevich Karatsuba, since we have met anyway, let us have a talk," I began. "It's about V.'s paper."

"Oh yes, I seem to remember him," Karatsuba said. "He seems to have been at the MSU."

Just imagine! On seeing his own mother, this man is likely to say: "We seem to have met some place."

The trolley-bus stopped, we alighted and proceeded along the pavement, which turned toward his house in about 150 meters. I must manage to say all the essential things.

"I know this paper well. It is first-class."

"But the evaluation contains a criticism of the thesis, there are errors in it," Karatsuba said, as if remembering.

"The evaluation is not an objective one. There are no substantial errors in the paper. The study is very good. It is not this that I was going to talk to you about (you know all about it very well yourself). It is my personal appeal to you: please, don't kill this paper. You are a key figure in deciding its destiny—"

"Oh no, no—" Karatsuba said, defending himself.

"Yes, yes, you are," I said, interrupting him. "You and I may have had some sort of differences, but they are insignificant—"

"But we didn't disagree," Karatsuba corroborated.

"All the more reason why you should let this paper pass—it's a very successful result of many years' persistent work."

"But the evaluation does point out errors, so I recollect," Karatsuba repeated, his voice carrying great interest and insistence.

I think the reviewer and perhaps he himself had spent many a day trying to find at least some minor errors in the skillfully constructed paper, and he wanted to know my opinion concerning its substance.

"Yes, there is an indication of a single error which is not an essential one and can be corrected by a single line. As far as his other remakrs are concerned, the reviewer is mistaken."

Karatsuba made another inconsequential remark, we stopped, exchanged the last handshake in our lives, and parted.

I was wasting words and abasing myself for nothing. He could not disregard the task he had been entrusted with by Vinogradov, what with the forthcoming elections to the academy into the bargain, or, indeed, even consider doing so. But for all that, he showed an ongoing desire to minimize his participation in this dirty business, a desire to efface himself.

At the session in December, where he nevertheless succeeded in seeing the matter through and doing away with the paper, he sat with a fixed frown on his face, his hands on his knees, never looking B. in the face, even when asking him questions.

We Don't Like Him, He Came Too

Vinogradov and Karatsuba's attitude toward me, which Dolbilin spoke of, can be explained by reasons of general character. My charming contacts with Vinogradov have already been described here. Nor did I ever clash with Karatsuba, one minor incident excepted.

In 1971 an international conference on the theory of numbers took place in honor of I. M. Vinogradov's eightieth birthday. I was not invited to the conference, and this had nothing to do with inadequacy in rank, since my students and postgraduates were invited. Among those passed over were Levin, Pyatetsky-Shapiro,[34] and—need I say more?—even Gelfond. Erdesh and Turan were also absent.

Karatsuba was deputy chairman of the organizing committee. I came to its meeting, and on meeting him in the corridor expressed my resentment in a displeased tone of voice.

"It is too late to do anything about it now," Karatsuba said, "but you can attend the sessions and take part in the proceedings; I'll tell them to let you through."

"But why should it be too late?" I asked cheekily. "In my view, this mistake can easily enough be corrected."

But I got no answer from him.

Apropos of the present-day mathematical conferences—the organizational principles behind many of them are an eloquent illustration of the far-reaching cleavage within mathematical society along the lines of the Jewish question.

This spring a conference on discrete programming was held in the Republic of Georgia, organized by A. Fridman. It emerged that there also take place parallel (Yablonsky) conferences on purely Russian cybernetics, to which Jews are not invited. Nor are Russians who hobnob with Jews invited.

Principles of racial purity were strictly observed at the conference on the theory of groups (Krasnodar, 1976, Gorchakov).

The Kishinev conference on mathematical logic: The main theses of reports to be presented at the conference were already being typed (Shein received a letter in which he was pressed to hurry with the dispatch of corrections to his report) when suddenly some of those invited were notified that due to the great number of applications and the small number of hotel rooms their participation had been canceled. Among those who were thus denied participation were, for example, Shein, Grindlinger, Shneerson. The background of the affair soon became clear enough: members of the organizing committee, Shirshov, Yershov, and Adyan, had demanded that the organizing-committee secretary come to Moscow with a list of participants and had then set about purging this list.

When Shein was notified of the refusal, he sent a letter to Kishinev, pointing out that since the people who had been refused participation had only one characteristic in common, one could not but recall the incident in 1934 when Isaiah Shur received a letter from——in which his request for participation in a conference was denied, because he had failed to book hotel accommodations in due time.

Whether on account of Shein's letter or for some other reason, all the original invitations were soon confirmed.

Yershov, Shirshov, and Adyan did not go to Kishinev.

In order to convey better my present melancholy mood of loneliness and isolation, I shall describe at this point my "trip" to Hungary.

In the summer of 1973 a conference in honor of Paul Erdesh's sixtieth birthday was to take place in Hungary. Erdesh's scientific interests were very close to mine. I became closely acquainted with him and met with him many times when he came to the International Conference of Mathematicians in Moscow, in 1965.

It was then that I gave him my book. He leafed through it quickly and joked: "It is a very good book."

—???

"By definition: a good book is one in which you are quoted!"

I had been sent an invitation. I did not get it but realized that it existed when I read Semeredi's New Year's greeting: "Looking forward to our meeting this summer on the Balaton."

In my reply I asked that the invitation be sent to my office address. Soon the secretary of the faculty party bureau handed me an unsealed envelope with the invitation.

I went to the rector.

Komin told me without thinking much that he was not against my trip and would send me, provided he received a directive from above.

I went to the Ministry of Higher Education of the Republic and there, in its Department of International Relations, procured a form with a full description of the procedure for my projected trip: the institute was to recommend me, the ministry to enter the trip into its plan, and upon the latter being endorsed—off you went. Now back to the rector. My exhaustive explanation (so I thought) would inspire him to start making the necessary official arrangements. Nothing of the kind. He had to have a directive from the higher echelons. Another pass of the shuttle. Recapitulation.

I started for the reception office of the CPSU's Central Committee. There was a long queue consisting mainly of people who had come from outside Moscow. As far as I could judge from their conversation, most of the complainants hoped to solve their personal problems of housing, work, or various legal predicaments. I found the telephone number of the Science Department and explained that I wished to be received to discuss being sent abroad on a scientific mission. A female voice gave me the telephone number and the name. Y. took the receiver. I explained the substance of my request and introduced myself. Y. asked where I worked and to whom I had spoken at the ministry. Then he said (his voice was very polite, steady, his manner of speaking distinct and businesslike):

"I think there's no point in our meeting on this question. Apply to the deputy director of the Department of International Relations of the Educational Ministry (he named him). The director is not there at present, he is out of town. Phone number so-and-so, you will be received and your problem solved for you."

I thanked him and hung up. In the ministry (on Zhdanov Street) I found the deputy and stated my business. He was a young, pleasant chap who sat at a big table in a room he shared with other officials. I told him that I had been sent by I., that I was very interested in the theme of the conference, adding that there would be no expenses, since the hosts had promised to pay for everything.

HE: We draw up the plan for the trip in March, and we shall have ample time to include you, provided we get the recommendation early enough.

I: That is precisely the difficulty. The institute is not recommending me, because it is waiting for instructions from higher quarters.

HE: How can we issue a directive without having any information about you?

I: There's no sense in my going around in circles any longer. You, I understand, are authorized to *make the decision.*

HE: Speak to Dubrovina, deputy director of the Department of Universities in Lenin Prospekt.

I (IMPATIENTLY): But listen, you are again sending me to a lower official, but I need someone who will make a decision.

HE (RESOLUTELY): Speak to Dubrovina—she can and will solve your problem.

I went to Dubrovina and was charmed by her amiable, simple, and affable manner. She did not think my problem difficult.

"Komin, your rector, has been in our system only a short time, he's still not familiar with our rules. I'll ring him up tomorrow and settle the question of your trip."

She did not let me go quickly, asking me about my work in the educational system, about the Kalinin University. In a word, the conversation was a most pleasant one, a fairly rare occurrence.

I let one day pass to be sure, then went to the rector's reception room. Dubrovina had not yet phoned. I called her there and then from the reception room and reminded her about myself. This time her voice was not so friendly, it seemed somewhat dry and businesslike.

I shall phone Komin now," she said.

I strolled for half an hour in the corridor, then returned to the reception room, found out that the call had been made, and entered the rector's study.

"Vladimir Vasil'yevich, you asked for a directive from above," I said to Komin confidently, "so it must be all right now?"

"What do you mean?" Komin asked.

"I assume Dubrovina has just spoken to you," I said, half-interrogatively.

What Komin then said surprised me not a little.

"Yes, I had a talk with Dubrovina. So what? This talk doesn't mean anything. What I need is an *instruction*. Then I'll be able to send you."

"Wasn't this talk the instruction you need?" I asked, feeling quite at a loss about what this mysterious instruction was and in what form it was given.

"No, it wasn't. I must get an instruction."

At this juncture I saw (too late?) that the matter was closed.

Later on I was told that the rector had said: "Now, what's to be done if Freiman wants to go to Hungary, Ryzhak to Japan, and Freiburg to Yugoslavia?"

So nobody ever went anywhere.

The Negative Evaluation

The reviewer's evaluation of V.'s thesis was sent to him by mail. It took us about two weeks to prepare the reply. We worked on it together, and it was very convincing and well-grounded—only, as I found out later (and was struck dumb with amazement), nobody read this reply, not a soul looked at it.

I have this evaluation and our reply to it before me now, and what I am thinking is this: In submitting to the rules of mathematical dispute, we tried hard to show as clearly as possible that the reviewer's statements were wrong, that he had erred. But that was not what was important; he is simply, a conscienceless man, a liar, that reviewer.

In making his evaluation the anonymous reviewer, whom we shall call S.,* was quite consciously aiming at discrediting a very significant study made with the utmost care. This evaluation should exclude S. from the scientific community. But who will corroborate this? These mathematical materials are hardly intended for easy reading.

There are only a few specialists in the entire world who can grasp at once the substance of the problem. Other mathematicians will simply find no

---

* I have very substantial reasons for believing that his name does in fact begin with this letter.

time to spare. It is good, at any rate, that mathematical statements have the property of being immutable and do not admit of double interpretation, so the truth can be established quite unequivocally. My statements are not unsubstantiated; I placed in the balance my spotless scientific reputation, gained in a lifetime of work; as for the validity of what I am saying, it can be tested even in a hundred years.

Meanwhile, try to follow this dialogue:

REVIEWER: All these features provide nothing new, as regards the effectiveness of the definitions.

I: The definitions are ineffective, the features are effective.

R.: What is being demonstrated is the existence of very narrow ranges.

I: The reviewer makes persistent use of pejorative adjectives in order to create a psychological background conducive to the rejection of the paper: "really extremely narrow," "a very particular character," "quite a number of errors," "insignificant amplification." In this case the discovered ranges *are* narrow. Is that bad? And what is to be done if wide ranges with a given important property are altogether nonexistent? Imagine a physicist being reproached for the new elementary particle he has found being "too small"?!

R.: The thesis abounds in errors and misprints.

I: The analysis of these remarks has shown that what has been pointed out by the reviewer amounts to one error that can easily be corrected (which was, in fact, done in two lines of the reply) and a few slips. The paper has been carefully drawn up and presented with all due form.

R.: The thesis as a whole has a purely calculative nature and has no theoretical value.

I: The entire work has a purely theoretical character, with only paragraph 15 being devoted to calculation. What is developed in B.'s paper is a new method of investigating Hall's ray.* The work is one of great theoretical significance and has aroused numerous responses, including some from abroad.

---

* This sentence is borrowed from Delone's evaluation. All the rest is from the reviewer's evaluation and our reply to it.

Such dishonest, mendacious evaluations are not isolated occurrences. There have been dozens, hundreds of them already. How did it come to pass that such filth should crop up in mathematics, this most honest of all sciences?

This discussion could well be continued. The arguments of the parties are diametrically opposed, I am prepared to defend my statements in any public debate.

Sergey Ivanovich Adyan

I rang him up the day after B.'s thesis had been rejected at a sitting of the group of experts at which he, too, was present.

"Sergey Ivanovich?"

"Speaking."

The voice in the receiver was quiet and cultivated.

"Freiman speaking. You will have heard about me, Andrey Andreevich must have mentioned my name."

No, he didn't quite remember me, somehow. Which was, mildly speaking, not so, for only the day before he had personally mentioned my name several times.

"I work mainly in the theory of numbers, but some of my work is related to algebra. I would like to give you copies of my books, and to discuss the situation concerning B.'s paper, which now faces rejection."

"But I'm just leaving now for a meeting—"

"Oh, I don't insist on seeing you immediately. When will you be available?"

"I'll be at the Steklov Institute at two o'clock."

"Very good, I'll come by then."

"However,"—his voice did not sound enthusiastic about the forthcoming meeting—"I may be at some other place, too. You'd better ring me up then."

"Better still, I'll ring you up early in the morning so we can make a precise appointment."

"Good. But,"—he must have decided to forestall a possibly unpleasant talk—"had it not been for B. and his paper, you'd not have rung me up, would you?"

"Possibly," I agreed, "but it's a good stimulus for our meeting, and I'll be able to tell you both about my own studies and about V.'s paper, which is of a very high quality."

"The theory of numbers is not my specialty, and I am not very familiar with his result, but yesterday I had a chance to see him; he didn't sound convincing, he looked confused."

"Well, I have been working in this branch of mathematics for many years, and I know it well—"

"Yes, I've heard about it. You obtained some kind of result here—"

"So I can tell you quite explicitly about B.'s study, which, I repeat, is one of high quality."

I laid particular emphasis on the last words.

"But there are mistakes in it?"

"There are certain shortcomings, but they are not substantial."

"That's the point, you see"—his voice, which had sounded quite uncertain before, gained some strength—"I, for one, always take the trouble to see that a paper produced under my guidance is given a most perfect form."

"So I'll see you tomorrow," I said, thus ending the talk.

If he only knew how much effort I had put into giving that paper all the required polish.

Coming to Steklovka the next day, I found Adyan's office. Very politely, he asked me to come in, sat down by the window, and asked me to take a seat beside him.

Adyan was short, and had a swarthy, clever, expressive face, with his whole style of behavior evoking sympathy; I involuntarily yielded to his charm, to his efforts to make a good impression. Only afterwards did I begin to compare his words and his previous actions, trying to uncover their hidden meaning. But at that moment he simply charmed me. His behavior was simple, he listened very attentively, did not try to brush aside reasonable arguments, but tried, rather, to understand them. I began by giving him copies of my books, showing him the American translation of one of them; in a word, by presenting my credentials. Having shown him the book *Zadacha Markova*,[35] I immediately passed on to B.'s study.

"I think this study very good, and I view its rejection as a gross mistake in which I shall never acquiesce. Before giving you my opinion on the merits of the case, I should like to support it with some general considerations. I have addressed myself to this problem for many years, have achieved a number of substantial results, and can, therefore, define the importance of the study and the place it occupies. Now, I assert categorically that this is a solid piece of work, that the negative evaluation has been given by an incompetent and unconscientious person, and that the rejection of the paper is an act of ignorance and ill-will."

I went on speaking and, without being aware of it, raised my voice, as the accumulated bitterness of the preceding sleepless nights found expression, and harsher and harsher words, such as "prejudice," "injustice," "amoral grounds of unprincipled actions," began to appear in my speech, with others still more forceful and forthright already emerging.

My interlocutor immediately made a very persuasive gesture, said two or three words, something like "Oh come, why put it this way, this'll get you nowhere," and brought me back to a normal conversational manner at once.

This is precisely the paradoxical situation of our time, when everything is done by stealth. Formerly, on hearing the call "Thrash the Zhids!" you could at least cry "Help" and somehow make ready to defend yourself. Nowadays, even when speaking to a well-minded person, I must use the language of Aesop, both of us must make believe we are discussing purely scientific problems, while the true meaning of the case, which everybody grasps, comes out in euphemisms and hints.

"I understand your conviction," Adyan was saying, "but much depends on presentation. The work may be very good, but sometimes the aspirant wanders, speaks confusedly, is unable to explain satisfactorily the meaning of his work, and so it's rejected. I can see nothing particularly bad in that. He may defend it a second time at a later date and do it flawlessly. I know of such cases. As for your aspirant, he spoke rather poorly, unconvincingly."

I waved my hand discontentedly, sweeping aside this false argument.

"What new defense are you talking about? Any study, and this one in particular, is the result of many years' effort. So many difficulties have been overcome in connection with formalities, publications, the organization of a defense. He would, without doubt, have told you everything quite cleverly had he been given the opportunity, that is, if they'd given him time and had not interrupted him."

It will not be out of place to recount here the following incident: When people summoned to the council were awaiting their turn by the door, one of them, a resident of Central Asia, in discussing the high rank of the commission members, went into raptures over Adyan and exclaimed, shaking his head and puffing out his cheeks: "Oh-oh, Adyan, he's a real elephant in mathematics!"

Most of those summoned do not realize what castigation they are in for and get lost when confronted by a panel of luminaries who are overtly unfriendly and try hard to confuse them and lead them away from the essence of the matter. If, on the other hand, some of them keep their nerve, it does not affect the result and only leads to the debater being accused of self-conceit (Shein, Levin).

I continued:

"Let me tell you about B.'s subject and the results obtained. Judge them purely on their merits."

I rose, went over to the blackboard, took a piece of chalk, and began my explanation. Adyan listened attentively, asking questions from time to time. I introduced definitions, drew a line on the blackboard, marked points on it—in a word, did the same as during my visit to Vinogradov.

It was then that I became aware of a fact that was of paramount importance: Adyan was absolutely unfamiliar with the substance of the problem! Wht is more, he did not even know the basic definitions!

Nor was this discovery confined to Adyan alone: I saw the level on which the work of the experts' commission and the Experts' Council is carried on. As a rule, they base their judgment on the opinions of two or three of their co-members who are closest to the subject of the thesis under consideration (such as Karatsuba, Andrianov, Kostrikin, or Adyan in our case). The latter, however, do not familiarize themselves with the paper beforehand, but look at it on the spot, leafing through it in the course of the session (as they did also in our case), and plucking sentences from it and from the evaluation. To put it more briefly, the main body of the specialists look for guidance to an expert (in our case, the absent Karatsuba) and the reviewer, no one inquiring again into the essence of the problem.

In my subsequent interviews with Kostrikin and Andrianov, I was able to corroborate further and substantiate my impression. They, too, knew nothing about the Markov problem, with Kostrikin simply not knowing chalk from cheese in the matter, while Andrianov had only a very vague notion about it.

It follows that the judgment is formed by specialists in a given narrow field, with others trusting them. If, however, the one or two specialists, in total disregard of professional ethics, produce a mendacious decision in pursuit of some selfish aim, then God help the poor council, for how on earth will they get to know the particulars? In actual fact, anyone taking part in these activities is perfectly aware of the real state of affairs. Much may be gathered from the discourses of the aspirants themselves. And what about the flow of protests from specialists who, as a rule, are much more competent than the reviewers selected by the HCC? And the very fact that for some mysterious reason the authors of "bad papers" who appear before them one after another, day in, day out, happen to be Jewish—has it no message for "honest, decent" people* like Adyan, Kostrikin, and Andrianov?

Let us, however, get back to my interview with Adyan. I was still standing at the blackboard, explaining to him both the substance of the subject and the results.

"I shall try to explain briefly the importance of what has been accom-

---

* As reported orally by some mathematicians I know who are not familiar with the activities of the above persons in the Experts' Council.

plished by B. in the second part of his study," I said. "He obtained a value of 5.04 for the Hall ray origin, so the previous value has been improved by five-hundredths. But if two prominent American mathematicians, Hall and Bumby, spent much effort to improve the value by only thousandths, a refinement measured in hundredths must be regarded as a considerable creative achievement. Here, as everywhere, everything is relative."

Aydan nodded; he understood.

"Now it will be easy for you to see how unfair the evaluation is. It consists of five pages, and discusses this, that and the other. But how is this, the most important result, reflected in it? In one sentence: 'In the second chapter, an insignificant *improvement* has been obtained in the value of the origin of the ray?' "

Adyan took the evaluation and started to look it through. I helped him to find the place.

"But this is not yet all. All the previous investigators, in improving the value, used Hall's original work, whose possibilities were exhausted. B. introduced new ideas and made a certain breakthrough, his success enabling me to find an ultimate solution to the problem. There's not a single word about it in the evaluation. What is it worth after that? And how do you like this sentence: 'The study as a whole is one of an entirely calculative nature and has no theoretical value'? This is a downright lie, as is evident to anyone who cares to take a closer look."

Adyan leafed through the evaluation and the reply to it, comparing them to check the truth of my statements.

It was clear that none of them had read the reply, that he held it in his hands for the first time.

I stepped back from the blackboard and sat down by the table.

"I shall spare you the explanation of the results described in Section 1. Suffice it to say that K., in his doctoral thesis, cited sufficient conditions for the coincidence of the Markov and Lagrange spectra, whereas B. obtained both the necessary and sufficient conditions."

"But K. obtained his results earlier."

I pulled out Cusick's article.

"Here it is: 'K. furnished many simple conditions sufficient for securing. . . . B. has studied the more difficult problem of obtaining conditions . . . which are necessary and sufficient over certain ranges'."

"Who is Cusick?" Adyan asked.

"An American professor, a mathematician."

"But is he well known? It has become a vogue lately to cite referencs in foreign publications, although the reference may be to a comment by some postgraduate student. K. obtained his results earlier anyway."

We went on rolling sentences at each other like billiard balls.

"But K. got his doctorate, while B. is denied even the degree of Candidate. Besides, K. himself held V.'s study in high esteem."

This seemed to drive the ball into the pocket. Adyan could find no answer.

"Well," he said, "now I can see the importance of V.'s results."

Only much later did I grasp completely what guided Adyan's actions and words. He did what he was told to do, and too much was at stake for him to disobey his orders: his position, career, influence. Now that the deed was done and all the rest did not depend on him, he felt he must justify himself as much as possible, produce the most favorable impression.

"Pity that this conversation is taking place now, after the session, not before," he said reproachfully.

"But Andrey Andreevich Markov did speak to you," I retorted.

"He is not a specialist, just as I am not."

(What about Delone's positive evaluation? What about the reply to the evaluation, rendering it dust and ashes if you just cared to look into it? Had he wanted to listen, he would have heard what Markov was saying as well, especially since it was precisely the specialists' opinion Markov was talking about. But he did not want to listen, and this being so, he would not have listened to me either, so it would have had no bearing on the outcome of the affair—of that I am absolutely sure now.)

He passed on to his next argument.

"Tell me, were there many specialists who understood the substance of the study among members of the council where the thesis was being defended?"

"Of course not. The merits of the case were clear, as usual, to the aspirant's professor, the official opponents, and another two or three persons."

"There you are," Adyan said, seizing on what I had said as on a block of granite. "Although Karatsuba was absent, he left his statement. We had the reviewer's evaluation. Our negative decision was, therefore, natural."

Here I vigorously, if not fiercely, attacked him, rejecting his arguments.

"I do not see the analogy you are talking about. Yes, the council often takes unanimous decisions based on positive evaluations of several specialists, in the absence of negative ones. In our case it was quite different: you *rejected* the paper in a situation of conflict, and once you had cast your vote for rejection, the responsibility you took upon yourself was so great as to make it your duty to give the matter very detailed consideration."

Be this as it may, the thesis had been rejected, so what were we to do next? Adyan gave me some advice. In the course of our conversation I found out who comprised the Experts' Council: Vladimirov (chairman), Gonchar (deputy chairman), Andrianov, Bolshev, Yershov, Millionshchikov, Samarsky, Poznyak, Ulyanov, Yablonsky.

In continuation of our talk we had a lively discussion on how to have the thesis approved after all. When I told him I wanted to talk to all who had taken part in the rejection and started to get steamed up again, as I remembered the significance of what was taking place, he asked me very gently, unemphatically, in a sort of casual way:

"What is it you really want, to have the thesis approved or to make a row?"

I was unable to stop at once and so answered without giving much thought to the implications of the question.

"I shall do all I can to have the paper approved; however, if the injustice is not put right, I will make a row."

We had been sitting for nearly two hours already. Our talk turned to more and more marginal details, became disjointed. I stood up abruptly and was about to say goodbye.

"But where are you going?" Adyan said. "Do stay."

"I am ready to talk with you for as long as you like, I simply didn't want to detain you," and I sat down again, astonished at his attention and much affected.

Our talk went on in quite friendly tones after that; Adyan expressed great interest in all my plans, so even though I was on the alert at first, I soon relaxed and adopted a sympathetic tone toward him.

Nevertheless, as I bade him farewell, I decided to let him know what I thought of past events from the standpoint of the principle involved, and said quite suddenly but in the same friendly tone of our conversation:

"Still, Sergey Ivanovich, I must tell you that you personally made a grave mistake in voting against B.'s paper, and I cannot absolve you of the responsibility for these fundamentally wrong actions."

The conversation's confidential and friendly tone could no longer be undone, so Adyan did not take exception, although his expression altered.

I left, but as I reached the main desk I remembered that I had left my umbrella in Adyan's room. I went back for it. Adyan was sitting motionless, gloomy, lost in sullen reverie. He gave me a silent and estranged look, without saying a word, without stirring.

There is no need to speak at length about Kostrikin and Andrianov; they both belong to the same set as Adyan.

The views expressed by K., one of the most outstanding Soviet mathematicians working in the theory of numbers, were among the few characterized by full independence and clarity:

"The evaluation is infamous, and its author simply an unconscientious person." When he learned that the case would be reconsidered, and thought of which people he could contact to help in the affair, K. said:

"I shall speak with Kostrikin, and I think Aleksey Ivanovich will not object to meeting with you."

The next day he rang me up and said:

"Aleksey Ivanovich surprised me very much. He refused to meet you. I began to tell him about the study, but he said he thought it a purely calculative piece of work. I told him it was not like that at all, and that it would be worth his while to meet with you, since you would be able to explain everything to him better than anyone else. But he thinks it unnecessary because, so he says, everything is clear to him as it is."

The meeting nonetheless did take place, in Kirieky, at a symposium on the theory of rings and modules, which was held at the sports complex of the Tartu University. Here, in the lap of nature, I met Kostrikin face to face. I came up, introduced myself, and asked for an appointment.

"Why drag it out, let's have it now," said Kostrikin with an unmistakable intonation: if you must have a tooth pulled out, be quick about it.

The interview was surprisingly short. I told him about the situation. Kostrikin asked a couple of questions to familarize himself with the statement of the problem. Very enthusiastically, I explained to him why the paper was good.

"Well," he said when I finished, "if the occasion presents itself, I shall try to put in a word for this paper."

He rose, and I parted from him feeling there was nothing to talk about. It seems that he himself did not realize how incongruous both his conduct and his words were.

Why did he not try to sell me the story that the study was calculative? This absurdity would not have worked with me, I knew the paper too well. Why did he not go on disparaging it if he sincerely believed it was bad? Had he changed his opinion? If so, he should have been very much alarmed, for that would have been an extraordinary occurrence indeed: a scientist failed a good thesis by mistake. But there was neither one nor the other; he promised to put in a word as if we were discussing buying a pair of imported shoes.

In December Kostrikin was elected a corresponding member of the Academy of Sciences. For Ivan Matveevich Vinogradov this event is closely tied up with Kostrikin's work in the Experts' Council.

When I was speaking with M., who is closely connected with Anatoly Nikolaevich Andrianov through common scientific interests, he said:

"All *this* causes him acute pain, he tries to avoid sessions in order not to take part in *this*."

When I met Andryanov in LOMI (Steklovka's Leningrad branch) he carried on the conversation with much goodwill; we discussed ways of setting the matter right, and he spoke of his desire to help. However, this intention is largely defeated by his contrary and almost obsessive desire to render this help in a very inconspicuous and conflict-free way.

I did not have to spend much time proving to Andryanov that V.'s thesis was good. He expressed himself with utmost clarity:

"I defended Kirshtein's paper. Therefore in your case I could do nothing."

After this he promised that when the question was considered a second time, he would send the thesis to an impartial reviewer for a second evaluation. He would, perhaps, have kept his promise, but Karatsuba came to the council session and set about killing the thesis very vigorously. Andrianov did not want to get into a conflict, and the thesis was again rejected.

Well, what can one say? If you have succeeded in vindicating a good paper by Kirshtein, it does not follow that another good paper must be killed. Andrianov is a good mathematician, a well-known scientist, who sets great store by international contacts. A couple of years ago he went to the States, in January [1976] he was on a three-month visit to France. Just try to make a row, express your opinion clearly and unequivocally, and you won't be sent, won't be allowed to go.

I can well imagine the indignation with which the trio would read my story. Yes, they did vote against, but they were forced to do so, otherwise they would have helped because they were sympathetic. Why then should they be condemned in this way? I would advise them to read Thomas Mann's letter to Rudolph V. Blunk and Hans Friedrich Blunk.*

The Toilers of the Experts' Council

On May 31, 1976, a special extraordinary session of the Experts' Council took place. It was held, as usual, in Steklovka, where most of the members work.

By five o'clock all those summoned had come to the conference hall, filing through the corridors in a softly murmuring crowd. There were about one hundred of them. It was a great gathering; normally, not more than ten or so aspirants to a degree were summoned at a time, but now, because of the need to complete the business of the old VAK, and due to the upcoming season of summer vacations, it was decided to carry out an overall purge.

The national composition of the assembled group was striking and caught the eye at once. They were either Jews or persons from the eastern

---

*Thomas Mann, Pis'ma [Letters] (Moscow, 1975), pp. 189, 200.

republics: Turkmen, Tadzhiks, Azerbaydzhani. This outward impression proved accurate when the secretary started calling out names in order to confirm their arrival: Kirshtein, Mukhitdinov, Wassenmacher, Niyazbekov, etc. There was not a single Russian name. Jews made up more than one-half (about sixty) of the entire group. They were all split up into sections (an obvious breach of all the regulations, for each case must be considered by the full council, and not just rubber-stamped by it, one hundred a day). Sent to the algebra section were eight persons, of whom five were Jewish, the other three being residents of Central Asia.

Work started at about seven and continued until eleven, but all had been instructed to come at five, and were called into the steam bath in arbitrary order, so they had to keep watch all the time by the door. The entire long corridor had not a single chair, and the candidates, many of whom had come directly from the railway station, had to wait for hours on their feet.

During breaks, tea and sandwiches were served for the council and committee members in a special room set aside for this. As the toilers of the Experts' Council went along the corridors to their private refectory, there was an atmosphere of friendliness, almost brotherhood, among them, with the slapping of shoulders, everyone on chummy terms with everyone, all a close company, laughter, jokes, merriment.

The turn of B.'s paper came. At first they examined it *in camera*. The door was ajar, and as Delone's evaluation was being read, a peal of laughter reverberated into the corridor.

I for one find this laughter very meaningful. It signifies that the reins of government have passed into the hands of new people, young, resolute, devoid of complexes, whereas the once-glorious names of Aleksandrov, Markov, Kolmogorov, Delone dissolve in the mists of time passing, and the frail old men, the bearers of those names, are no more than illusory shadows, and whenever they try to interfere in the solution of real-life problems, they are simply ridiculed. Also, this laughter meant that the rejection of the paper was a predetermined matter.

At last B. was invited to come in.

"I entered a long room, in which by the wall on my left stood a table with Andrianov and Adyan seated at it. A blackboard and a chair for me were in front of them on my right. Seated at a separate table with his back to the window was Kostrikin. There were another three persons in the room, but they played a marginal part in the discussion. The thesis was being taken to pieces by *Adyan, Andrianov,* and *Kostrikin.*

"Adyan asked:

" 'You say that your method was used by Freiman in solving the problem. But what is the essence of your method?'

" 'I studied directly the structure of the set of continued-fraction sums, having abandoned Hall's lemma,* whose possibilities were exhausted, as shown by Bumby.'

" 'But abandoning Hall's lemma is not a method. And then, why didn't you yourself find the origin of the ray using your method?'

" 'It is a difficult problem. It took several years to solve it.'

"Kostrikin started to speak about the calculative part of the paper, saying that calculations are not be relied on. A dark phrase hung in the air:

" 'There is nothing but machine mathematics in your paper.'

"Finally, as if summing it all up, Andryanov said:

" 'The thesis is deficient in form, it's clear.'

"He slammed shut the copy of the paper, as if burying it for good. Behind the door Adyan was heard saying:

" 'Please write: "Has no theoretical value." '

"The whole discussion had taken about ten minutes."

This account is so typical and so striking that I shall have to repeat myself.

Regarding the nationality of those theses authors who were caught on the hook of the experts' committee—the following were summoned to the committee's session of December 6, 1976:

1. Krivosheya Yefim Shalomovich
2. Shteinberg—— ——
3. Bernshtein Aleksandr Azriilevich
4. Kropp Leonoid Yefimovich
5. Frenkin Boris Rafailovich
6. Mogilevsky Mikhail Grigoryevich

Six persons in all, of whom six were Jewish.

Eleven persons were summoned to the session where papers by Shnepperman, Tsalenko, and Rozenberg were examined. All eleven were Jewish.

Here is a comparison of excerpts from documents relating to a thesis by Boris Moiseevich Shein, rejected in 1969, the first in the series of rejected "Jewish" theses.

Wagner (Doctor of Sciences, a specialist in semigroups, Shein's teacher): "The thesis is a fundamental scientific study, unusually rich in content, comprising a great number of important results. This major scientific work is an important contribution to present-day algebra and marks its author as a talented scientist."

From the decision of the experts' committee: "The thesis contains no

---

*[Preliminary proposition.]

significant scientific results that would qualify the author for the degree of Doctor of Sciences. It abounds in numerous common theorems with predominantly cumbersome formulations."

Kurosh (head of the Soviet school of general algebra; reproduced from memory): "The thesis is a substantial contribution to science. The experts' committee was not guided by the desire to elicit truth—an indication of the moral degradation among a considerable number of Soviet mathematicians; it sent the paper for evaluation to mathematicians who, being conscious of their incompetence, had to refuse to give evaluations. Because of this kind of attitude my further work on the experts' committee has become difficult."

Gluskin (Doctor of Sciences, a specialist in the theory of semigroups): "The decision of the experts' committee to reject the thesis is surprising, to say the least, to anyone who has any knowledge of the work. I cannot agree with this decision, it is doubtlessly a mistaken one."

From the stenographic record of an experts' committee session, a discussion in the absence of the author of the thesis:

ADYAN: He has about one hundred publications—all in pursuit of renown.

ILYIN: But perhaps his results may become well known?

YABLONSKY: I am astonished at his view of appendices.

GNEDENKO: This is a hard case. He's an able mathematician, and you can't push him off his course.

ADYAN: He's very gifted. I agree with Kurosh—he's a brilliant mathematician. But superficial.

?: It's late already, let us decide. We are not speaking to the point.

ILYIN: In case of more than one negative evaluation a vote is in order. Any suggestions?

ADYAN: To be rejected.

?: But what about the conclusion? Who will draft it?

?: Whoever abstains, let him draft it.

ADYAN: We shall draft the conclusion.

KOSTRIKIN: I suggest writing we're in doubt.

ILYIN: In doubt? That's neither here nor there.

KOSTRIKIN: Well, we can write that we cannot take a positive decision.

ILYIN: But we're experts, and you two are specialists. The plenum will send the conclusion back to us to be revised.*

I cannot refrain from commenting that all of them know that this gifted mathematician must be destroyed. They know in advance that the rejection *will* take place, although the stenographic record shows no grounds for this. There is only one thing they do not know: What is it to be rejected for? Compare this with the specialists' confidence.

GLUSKIN: The statement of the experts' committee on the alleged absence in the thesis of substantial results on a doctoral level is puzzling indeed, for it could have been made only by someone completely ignorant of the results described in the thesis. All this is more than my personal opinion. I know too well that it is shared by all Soviet specialists in the field. In addition, evaluations by foreign scientists can be quoted. In 1967, the second volume of the monograph *The Algebraic Theory of Semigroups*, summing up the development of the theory in the past decade, was published in the United States. The authors, Clifford and Preston, who are leading specialists in the field, discuss at length the results of the thesis, which they call "the Shein theory." By the decision of the editorial board of the new international journal *Semigroups* (which includes a number of leading authorities in the field) its first issue opens with a major review article by Shein.

KOSTRIKIN (THE BEGINNING OF THE STENOGRAPHIC RECORD): We shall put to you a number of questions. Have you read the evaluations by Anatoliy Illarionovich?†

SHEIN: I should like to reply to all three negative evaluations—

KOSTRIKIN: No, please reply to the last one.

---

*Once again I draw the reader's attention to the fact that the above conversation is not a product of the author's imagination—it is an excerpt from the stenographic record of the discussion, and every word in it is authentic.

†A. I. Shirshov.

SHEIN: Very well.

. . . The reviewer is convinced that I am the first to introduce the standard concepts of the theory of semigroups. It shows to what extent the reviewer is familiar with semigroups. As a matter of fact, he takes a stand against the theory as a whole, since he does not distinguish between what I did and the known data.

. . . The typist has played a wicked trick on the reviewer by making a misprint in the evaluation; he writes about a mythical Kisler theorem and on top of this adds that it is well known. This alone testifies—

GONCHAR: But this theorem is well known, isn't it?

SHEIN: Yes, to a specialist.

GONCHAR: That is why the reviewer called the theorem well known.

SHEIN: Excuse me, had this theorem been well known to the reviewer, he would not have called it the Kisler theorem.

ADYAN: But the reviewer believed you; there is a misprint in your thesis, that is why the reviewer speaks of the Kisler theorem.

SHEIN: But why then does he call it "well known"?

ADYAN: You yourself made a misprint and are accusing the reviewer.

SHEIN: I am not accusing the reviewer of making the misprint. He mentioned as well known something he himself is unfamiliar with. This shows what his statements are worth. However, if this example is not enough, I can cite others of the same kind—

I: A most enlightening scene! The esteemed reviewer is caught in the act, he is an ignoramus and engages in garbling. The committee members, as one man, rush to rescue him, but failing to slur over the unpleasant fact, pretend to have heard nothing. Just look how they lead Shein away from the ticklish topic, so that he could not return to it, to relieve the tension of the moment—addressing him politely, using the patronymic.*

SHEIN: But perhaps even that is not enough? Very good, here's another fact—

*Checked against the shorthand record.

KOSTRIKIN: Boris Moiseevich, a doctoral thesis in mathematics must be intelligible to all mathematicians—

Oh, it's a difficult job indeed to drown the hippo in the bog![36]

Miscellany

The names of mathematicians whose doctoral theses have been rejected by the Experts' Council and the VAK: Markus, Shein, Shnepperman, Zhmud, Levin, Shmulyan, Milman, Norkin, Balk, Tsalenko, Winberg, Lekhtman, Pekelis.

This list is far from complete.

Rubinov's doctoral thesis has been under consideration by the VAK for the last six years. This example is typical, such periods have become habitual.

Lozanovsky's doctoral thesis languished for several years in the VAK. He died. A few months later approval came.

The results of the voting on Tsalenko's thesis at the Moscow University: thirty-one for, one against. The results of the voting on Tsalenko's doctoral thesis during its repeated defense at the Steklov Mathematical Institute: ten against, one abstention.

Arnold and Fomenko were removed from a Scientific Council session at Steklovka dealing with the repeated defense of Winberg's doctoral thesis. Academician Mardzhanishvili flung the door open before them with his own hand.

Mathematician L. asked his friend V., who worked in Steklovka:

"Will you be my official opponent on my doctoral thesis?"

"Out of the question," he answered, "I'd be fired."

Frenkin's thesis was approved.

L., from the Department of Mechanics, had said at a session of the Experts' Council:

"He is my wife's postgraduate student."

All the people from the Department of Mechanics voted for approval.

All the mathematicians abstained. Just to remind you: the thesis in question was a mathematical one.

The Experts' Council decided that Roytman's thesis be rejected on the grounds that the Scientific Council of the KSU had conducted the defense after the expiration of its term of authority.

Oddly enough, the document which prolonged the council's authority could not be found, although many people said it existed.

Oddly enough, the Experts' Council chose to concentrate on the administrative rather than the scientific aspect of the case, to the detriment of the latter.

Oddly enough, too, another three theses defended after Roytman's in the very same council were confirmed by the HCC without delay, while Roytman's thesis was rejected.

When Professor Shilov was up for reelection, he was taken to task for having too many Jewish pupils, some of whom had emigrated. One of the speakers said that Shilov's reply to criticism was not sufficiently anti-Semitic, no, no, sorry, anti-Zionist. No need to call on Freud to explain the source of the slip.

The reelection was not held; it was decided to hold it in a year's time.

The next day, while taking a walk with his wife near the university, Shilov felt ill. He sat down on the steps in front of the entrance to the university clinic, while his wife ran upstairs to fetch a doctor. The doctor refused to come down, insisting that the sick man appear in person. As the altercation continued, Shilov died.

But Where Am I?

I write these concluding lines one year later, in the spring of 1978.

Last autumn a conference on the theory of numbers took place in Dushanbe, of which its organizers can say with satisfaction: "*Judenfrei*—for the first time."

To say nothing of an invitation, I did not even receive an answer to my request to participate.

In the autumn I wrote to Academician Bogolyubov saying that something was wrong in Soviet mathematical science.

Bogolyubuv did not reply.

Recently, I tried in vain to see the president of the academy. I was not even received by his private secretary.

I must publish my notes.

But where am I?

It is all clear to Karatsuba.

As the Vilnius conference on the theory of numbers came to an end, a banquet was held, and when toasts were proposed to Lithuanian and

Russian mathematicians, someone suggested a common toast to all Soviet mathematicians.

"Good," Karatsuba said loudly, "only without the Zhids!"

A character in a Polish joke sees his wife in bed with his tenant, contemplates the unbearable lack of space in his flat, and asks:

"But where am I?"

And answers:

"I am standing in a queue for carp."

I do not want to stand in a queue for carp. Again and again, without finding the answer, I ask myself one and the same question:

"But where am I?"

Notes

1. VUZ (Vyssheye uchebnoye zavedeniye)—Institution of Higher Learning (hereafter: IHL).

2. A selection of readers' letters to the editor under the common heading "The Torn Meshes of Zionism," *Literaturnaya Gazeta*, February 18, 1976, no. 7, p. 9; see *JJP-quarterly*, vol. 72, no. 539.

3. VAK (Vysshaya atestatsionnaya komissiya)—Higher Certifying Commission (hereafter: HCC).

4. NII (Nauchno-issledovatelskiy institut)—Scientific Research Institute (hereafter: SRI).

5. Hereafter: MSU.

6. N. Ye. Zhukovsky Institute—TsAGI (Tsentralny aerohydrodynamichesky institut imeni N. Ye. Zhukovskogo)—Central Institute of Aerohydrodynamics (hereafter: CIA).

7. Qualifying examinations preceding the defense of a candidate's thesis.

8. Associate Professor.

9. VKP (b)—All-Union Communist Party (Bolsheviks).

10. Hereafter: KSU.

11. CPSU—Communist Party of the Soviet Union.

12. A. O. Gelfond—Soviet mathematician (1906–1968), completed his studies at Moscow University in 1927, professor at this university since 1931. Corresponding Member of the Academy of Sciences of the USSR since 1939. Many publications on the theory of numbers. Awarded the Order of Lenin and other orders and medals.

13. An allusion to a fake underground organization in the famous satirical novel *The Twelve Chairs*, by E. Ilf and E. Petrov.

14. Young Communist League.

15. MIFI (Moskovskiy inzhenerno-phyzicheskiy institut)—Moscow Engineering-Physics Institute.

16. MFTI (Moskovskiy phyziko-tekhnicheskiy institut)—Moscow Physical Technology Institute.

17. One below "five," the highest mark.

18. Mech.-Math.—Mechanical-Mathematics faculty.

19. The example in question does not appear in the original Russian.

20. A newspaper cliché.

21. Pyotr Lavrentyevich Ulyanov.

22. This quotation was not found in this source.

23. Gosplan—State Planning Commission in the USSR.

24. *History of Western European Philosophy* by Y. Narsky.

25. Inquiry by the party into some misdemeanor committed by a member.

26. Pogost—graveyard—with a priest of the Russian Orthodox Church; *uyezd*—land division, no longer in use.

27. "Steklovka"—the Steklov Mathematics Institute.

28. Igor Rostislavovich Shafarevich, (b. 1923), Soviet mathematician, specialist in algebra, professor at Moscow State University since 1953, has been honored by the award of the Lenin prize and other national and international prizes. One of the leaders of the democratic movement in the USSR, member of the Committee for Human Rights.

29. Bourbaki (Nicolas)—collective pseudonym adopted by a young group of French mathematicians.

30. Aleksandr Osipovich Gelfond—see note 12.

31. Allusion to an anti-Semitic pogromist organization—Union of the Russian People—in tsarist Russia.

32. A small hinged pane in the upper part of a window.

33. *Matematika v SSSR za 50 let* [Fifty years of mathematics in the USSR].

34. Professor I. I. Piatetsky-Shapiro (b. 1929) received his Ph.D. in mathematics in 1954. Worked in the Institute of Applied Mathematics. In 1974 submitted an application to leave the USSR, which was then rejected. Emigrated to Israel in 1976. Now works at Tel Aviv University. Has been elected to the Israel Academy of Sciences.

35. *Zadacha Markova* [Markov's problem].

36. An allusion to the closing lines of a classical children's poem by K. Chukovsky which tells of a "difficult job to drag the hippo out of the bog!"

Anti-Semitic Notions: Strange Analogies

RUTH OKUNEVA

To the Secretary General of the Central Committee CPSU
Comrade L. I. Brezhnev

>   From R. Y. Okuneva,
>   Samarkand Boulevard,
>   House 17, Block 3, Flat 131
>   Moscow, 109507.

I, R. Y. Okuneva, am a former senior scientific associate at the USSR Academy of Pedagogical Sciences' Scientific Research Institute for the Content and Methodology of Teaching, and a candidate in the historical sciences.* I request that you examine attentively the material I have gathered and compiled about statements made by some present-day writers and writers of the past concerning the Jews—"A Few Pages of Strange Analogies."

For several years I, and evidently many others, have been troubled and offended by the tone and content of certain Soviet writers' works which are supposedly anti-Zionist but, in fact, are of a very pronounced anti-Semitic nature.

As a historian, I have read similar statements in the works of members of the Black Hundreds and those of fascist ideologists.

In order to satisfy myself that I was not mistaken, I made several comparisons, which gave me an unpleasant surprise. I then decided to compare similar statements made by the writers of various books and articles on the beliefs, traditions, and way of life of the Jews, and their

---

*[The lesser of the two doctoral degrees awarded in the USSR.]

contribution to world civilization. Those comparisons have convinced me that certain present-day writers of books and articles, such as V. Begun, Ye. Yevseev, V. Yemelyanov, Yu. Ivanov, L. Korneev, V. Pikul, and V. Skurlatov among others, have been violating the ideas of socialist internationalism that form the basis of the Communist party's national policy. Their works are full of savage hatred not of Zionism, but of the Jews. And they do not conceal this. The Jews are presented in their works as the enemies of the Soviet state, as counterrevolutionaries, spies, and accomplices of Hitler; none contains an objective evaluation of the role of Jews in the revolutionary movement, the heroic deeds of Jews during the Great October Socialist Revolution, the Civil and Great Patriotic Wars, the part they have played in leadership and their participation in socialist construction, in the formation and activities of the various units of the present-day Communist and workers' movement.

One could object that this is not the aim of the anti-Zionist books and pamphlets, that they have a definite ideological intent. But if that is the case, where are the books, articles, and brochures which have truthfully and objectively thrown light on these questions?

Are you aware of the statistics for books published on the subject of Jews in the postwar years? I have compiled statistics on the basis of the *Yezhegodnik knigi* for 1945 to 1973; they are as follows:

From 1945 to 1948, four to seven titles were published annually in small editions of ten to fifteen thousand copies; occasionally editions of approximately fifty to eighty thousand copies were also published. These books were devoted to the heroism and sufferings of the Jews during the Second World War. For example, V. Grossman, *Treblinsky ad* [The hell of Treblinka] (Moscow, 1945) and G. Smolar, *Mstiteli getto* [Avengers of the ghetto] (Moscow, 1946), among others.

In 1949, only *one* book was published, a reprint in Kishinev of V. Grossman's *The Hell of Treblinka*. None of these books was ever reprinted again.

From 1950 to 1955 *not one* book came out that was devoted to the subject of Jews. The year 1955 saw the appearance only of M. Belenky's pamphlet containing a criticism of the Jewish religion. Up to the end of 1960, atheist criticism of Judaism was becoming the leitmotif of books with Jewish themes published in that period. But in the same period interesting works were published by I. D. Amusin, G. M. Lifshitz, and M. M. Kublanov, about discoveries in the Dead Sea region. And as a result of the efforts of I. G. Ehrenburg, *Dnevnik Anny Frank* [The Diary of Anne Frank] was published in 1960. (This was the only edition of this book in the Russian language, a work which has been published abroad countless times and has been read throughout the world!)

The number of books of Jewish topical interest published during those years dropped, being between nine and eighteen titles annually, an average of eleven to twelve books a year. Editions of atheist books and pamphlets increased to as many as 250,000 copies. But the first of those books which have earned a scandalous notoriety then began to appear. Thus, in 1963, T. Kichko's book *Judaizm bez prikras* [Judaism without embellishment] was published, with photographs and drawings in the spirit of the *Der Stürmer* of the Nazis. In 1969 the publication of Yu. Ivanov's book, *Ostorozhno: sionizm!* [Beware: Zionism!] caused a great uproar. It appeared in an edition of 100,000 copies, which the Ukrainian Political Publishing House immediately reprinted in a Ukrainian translation of 70,000 copies. It was republished again in Moscow in 1970, in an edition of 200,000 copies.

This was the beginning of a new stage in the publication of books of this ilk. In 1971, Ye. Yevseev's, *Fashizm pod goluboy zvezdoy* [Fascism under the blue star] (75,000 copies) appeared. In 1972, V. Bolshakov published his *Antisovetizm—professiya sionistov* [Anti-Sovietism—the Zionists' profession] (in an edition of 25,000 copies) and another, *Sionizm na sluzhbe antikommunizma* [Zionism at the service of anti-Communism] (in an edition of 100,000 copies). In Minsk, in 1974, V. Begun's book, *Polzuchaya kontrrevolutsya* [The creeping counterrevolution] appeared in an edition of 25,000 copies. This book was reprinted twice in Moscow, in 1977 and 1979, under the title *Vtorzheniye bez oruzhiya* [Invasion without arms] in editions of 150,000 and 100,000 copies respectively.

The number of works of this kind has continued to multiply; in recent years between twenty-three and forty-four titles have been published annually. They have been printed in editions that have grown considerably in quantity, and which have been given more and more extensive geographical distribution. So much for the "quantitative," statistical aspect of this question.

What are the ideological implications? Are not all the principles of Marxist-Leninist ideology being violated in these works? Has not the principle of socialist internationalism been violated? Yes, evidently, if we are to judge from the statements made by these writers who maliciously revile an entire people (see the enclosed "A Few Pages of Strange Analogies"). Yes, evidently, since V. I. Lenin's instructions on this question are being ignored.

But, to avoid hearsay, I shall cite examples.

Who, for example, is unaware of how V. I. Lenin was outraged by anti-Semitic pogroms? Think of his speech, of which gramophone recordings were made in March of 1919, entitled "Pogromist Jew-Baiting" (V. I.

Lenin, *Polnoye sobraniye sochineniy,* vol. 38, pp. 242–243), or the articles in which he stigmatizes the Russian monarchy for organizing these pogroms (V. I. Lenin, *Poln. sobr. soch.,* vol. 13, pp. 198–199, vol. 21, pp. 17, 277–280, and 345–346, among others).

How does V. Begun, in his thrice-published book, have the effrontery to speak of pogroms as a class struggle directed against "the Jewish exploiters"? (V. Begun, *Invasion without Arms* [Moscow, 1979], pp. 63, 64).

It is common knowledge that V. I. Lenin considered the newspaper *Novoye vremya* a Black Hundreds newspaper: ". . . in the course of many a decade this paper has 'earned' for itself the name of defender of the tsarist regime, defender of the capitalists, Jew-baiter and hounder of revolutionaries" (V. I. Lenin, *Poln. sobr. soch.,* vol. 322, p. 211). He spoke quite unequivocally of Suvorin as a liberal journalist who had, during the second revolutionary upsurge "turned . . . to nationalism, to chauvinism, to shameless fawning upon the powers that be" (V. I. Lenin, *Poln. sobr. soch.,* vol. 22, p. 44).

Why did V. Begun and V. Pikul describe, with such sympathy for *Novoye vremya,* the episode (whose truth we can well doubt) of the Jews and Witte buying the paper and rendering it harmless for its allegedly having criticized Jewish intrigues? V. Pikul even grieves about the unfortunate Suvorin, who was left without means of support as a result of this transaction.

The history of the Dreyfus case occupied a significant place in V. I. Lenin's works. He dealt with this topic in his writings on various occasions (see V. I. Lenin, *Poln. sobr. soch.,* 4th ed., vol. 5, p. 134; vol. 19, p. 464; vol. 22, p. 134; vol. 25, pp. 147, 148, 161, 162, 189; vol. 28, pp. 89, 90, 225, 395, 439; vol. 30, pp. 196–197; vol. 31, pp. 77–78; vol. 35, pp. 258–259). Like all progressive-minded people of the time, V. I. Lenin was absolutely unambiguous in his attitude to the Dreyfus trial, declaring that "in the Dreyfus case, the French General Staff made itself sadly and disgracefully infamous throughout the world by resorting to wrong, unfair, and downright criminal measures to indict Dreyfus" (V. I. Lenin, *Poln. sobr. soch.,* vol. 32, p. 422).

Why does B. Antonov permit himself to characterize this trial as "odious"? And what is meant by so "advantageous a valuation to the Zionists" which has fastened upon public opinion regarding this trial? Does V. I. Lenin's opinion of this trial enter into this "valuation" so "advantageous to the Zionists"? (see B. Antonov, "The Libel Campaign and the Stern Case," *Chelovek i zakon,* 1977, no. 6, p. 128).

V. I. Lenin accused *Novoye vremya,* the newspaper beloved by anti-Semites of all times and by present-day "anti-Zionists," of using "the old, crude, and ridiculous Black Hundred device of taunting the liberals for receiving assistance from the Jews!" (V. I. Lenin, *Poln. sobr. soch.*, vol. 24, p. 258).

But then in 1979, V. Pikul's novel, which "proves" that all officials in tsarist Russia were in the pay of the Jews (sometimes the term "Zhid" is used) appeared in the journal *Nash sovremennik, U posledney cherty* [At the lowest limit], and in this work the Jews themselves are presented as the chief destroyers of Mother Russia. Moreover, all high-ranking Russian officials of German origin were, according to Pikul, none other than covert or disguised Jews, for example, "the Swabian Zhid"—Shturmer.*

V. I. Lenin asserted without any ambiguity that "Tsarism vented its hatred particularly upon Jews" because "the Jews furnished a particularly high percentage (compared with the total Jewish population) of leaders of the revolutionary movement" (V. I. Lenin, *Poln. sobr. soch.*, vol. 30, p. 324).

In present-day "anti-Zionist" literature, this "high percentage" is not simply avoided; it is twisted, and not overskillfully, and becomes the allegedly "high percentage" (even if not reckoned by a count of heads) of betrayers of the revolution among the Jews, and of the deals they made with every one of the counterrevolutionary forces. L. Korneev stated, with no misgivings, that "we must methodically expose the false stereotype instilled in our consciousness by bourgeois-nationalist propaganda that the Jews played an exceptionally important role (or even a decisive role) in the Russian revolutionary movement and in the victory of the Great October Revolution" (L. Korneev, *Sionizm—vrag mira i progressa* [Zionism—the enemy of peace and progress], Materials for the Lecturer, Moscow, 1973, p. 13). It would be interesting to know whom Korneev has in mind as representing the bourgeois-nationalist propagandist that is instilling the false stereotype: V. I. Lenin?

Moreover, the struggle against anti-Semitism and prejudice which was waged during the first years of the Soviet regime under the leadership of V. I. Lenin and with his direct participation is subjected in these "anti-Zionist" books to the criticism that it was pointless. Thus, on page 67 of V. Begun's above-mentioned *Invasion without Arms* (Moscow, 1979) we read: "It is common knowledge that as early as the first years of Soviet power, the Jews, as at no other time and nowhere else in history, gained admission on the broadest scale not only to learning but also to all branches of public life, including government. How could one speak of anti-Semitism at that time? Nevertheless, in the press of that day a

---

* [In the original, *Nash sovremennik*, no. 5, 1979, p. 100, the author of this historical novel calls Sabler (the chief prosecutor of the Synod), and not Shturmer, a "Swabian Zhid."]

propaganda campaign was waged against a *nonexistent* [my emphasis, R. O.] anti-Semitism; books and pamphlets were published, as were repertoire collections of amateur theatricals, and articles were written against anti-Semitism, which had been made illegal but which *did not in fact exist . . ."*

This leads naturally to the question: if in fact there was no longer any anti-Semitism in Russia in the first years of the Soviet regime's existence, why was there a need for the decree of the Council of People's Commissars, signed by V. I. Lenin and adopted on July 27, 1918, a decree directed against "nonexistent" anti-Semitism?

And with what heartlessness the tragedy of the Jewish people during the Second World War is presented in these so-called anti-Zionist pamphlets. How gleefully Yu. Ivanov and V. Begun scoff at it, terming all the grief for the innocents who perished "heaving" and "crocodile tears."

Hence, if the Soviet citizen gets no reading matter on this subject, other than that in which the name "Jew" is reviled, what kind of idea will we have of this people?

And indeed, he is not given any such reading material from earliest childhood, because even the secondary-school textbooks are totally devoid of any kind of positive information about Jews, while textbooks for classes 4–8 generally contain no information at all. The result is that the negative data about the Jews that fill the "anti-Zionist" books, articles, and pamphlets, which are published in vast editions, fall on uninformed and consequently fertile soil, inflaming hatred towards the Jews—one of the one hundred people and nationalities of the USSR.

In bringing this letter to a close, my thoughts dwell on the words of V. I. Lenin, when he wrote that "the nationalists' propaganda could bear more frequent scrutiny," for "it would be highly erroneous to think that the significance of this propaganda is negligible" (V. I. Lenin, *Poln. sobr. soch.*, vol. 24, p. 324).

As to the results of inciting national hatred—history, including the history of Russia, gives us numerous lessons about this.

Respectfully yours,
[signed] Ruth Okuneva

Enclosure: "A Few Pages of Strange Analogies."

3. THEY ARE EXPLOITERS ONE AND ALL

In every nation the exploiter is lost in the working masses. Only in one nation, the Jewish, do the exploiters form the masses—and the honest toiler disappears.

—Rokotov, p. 25.

Anti-Semites have demanded a worldwide limitation of Jews, as exploiters and capitalists, even introducing here the racist principle of Count Gobineau.

—*Ideologiya i praktika mezhdunarodnogo sionizma* (hereafter: *Ideology and Practice*), p. 56.

In labor, the Jew sees only a means of exploiting other nations.

—Hitler, in Heiden, p. 75.

The National Socialists reduce the whole question of exploitation to merely "the Jewish exploiters," to the Jews in general . . . "our own" German capitalist is a blood brother and a participant in the national revolution.

—Treinin, p. 8.

From the social standpoint the majority of the Jewish population was bourgeois and petty-bourgeois. . . . Christian competitors were incapable of resisting the merchant-Jew, who relied on many centuries of experience in the struggle for world markets, his Jewish community ties, and mutual aid.

—Begun, *Polzuchaya kontrrevolutsiya* (hereafter: *Creeping Counterrevolution*), pp. 16–17.

4. THEY INVENTED EXPLOITATION

The mind of the Jew is not concerned with exploiting the earth's natural wealth, but with exploiting man.

—Kaluzhsky, p. 32

The Jews indeed pulled off a trick of great genius. This capitalist nation, which was the first in the world ever to introduce the shameless exploitation of man by man, managed to seize control of the fourth estate.

—Hitler, in Heiden, pp. 53–54.

In the Ukraine and in Byelorussia, there was economic exploitation, personified by grasping Jewish leaseholders, tenant farmers, usurers, and innkeepers.

—Begun, p. 65.

5. THEY ARE USURERS*

From time immemorial the Jews have engaged mainly in lending money on interest to individuals and to entire states.

    —Butmi, *Oblichitelnye rechi. Rossiya na rasputye* (hereafter: *Russia at the Crossroads*), p. 7.

6. JEWISH INTEREST

The Jews will manage to conduct a transaction in such a way that your income will be devoured by interest. Consequently the concept of Jewish interest as something highly dangerous has come into being.

    —Osman-bey, p. 31.

Our primary objective in reconstructing society is to break the credit system, to obliterate Jewish control of interest.

    —G. Feder, in *Oktiabr*, 1933, no. 3, p. 75.

In the Middle Ages the well-to-do Jews were restricted to the narrow sphere of trade and usury.

    —Semenyuk, p. 82.

The Jewish monetary aristocracy . . . which grants loans on interest, has managed to retain virtually total economic independence.

    —Semenyuk, p. 76.

7. JEWISH FINANCIAL CAPITAL

Jewish financial capital is the root of all evil.

    —Rosenberg, in *Oktiabr*, 1982, no. 3, p. 75.

Jewish financial capital [is] the heir to ancient Jewish international trade and the role of the middleman.

    —Skurlatov, p. 31.

---

*The gaps in the middle column are due to the lack of a sufficient number of appropriate sources in Russian, not to the lack of such statements.

8. JEWISH FINANCIAL CAPITAL THREATENED GERMANY'S EXISTENCE

They [the Nazis—R.O.] used slogans to conceal their pseudosocialism . . . "Down with Jewish financial capital!"

—*Noveyshaya istoriya* (hereafter: *Modern History. Textbook for 9th Class*), p. 56.

Jewish capital occupied fairly strong positions in Germany and Austro-Hungary.

—Skurlatov, p. 53.

9. TWO KINDS OF CAPITAL

The Jews are exploiters of a special kind. . . . The Jew is not like our grasping Russian kulak, isolated, and acting on his own responsibility and at his own risk. Behind the Jew stands the Jewish community; every Jew is a whole association.

—Neznachny, p. 150.

It is obvious to everybody that such a landlord, landowner, factory owner, and shopkeeper is nothing more than a hired man who is in bondage to the monied capitalist. But Marx and his followers christened this hired man owner a "capitalist," and incited the

There are two kinds of capital, and these two kinds are so different from one another that they must be spoken of in quite different ways. We National Socialists distinguish between productive national and state capital and rapacious international [Jewish—R.O.] loan capital.

—Goebbels, in *Revolutsiya i natsionalnosti*, 1933, no. 1, p. 87.

It is necessary to distinguish interest capital, finance capital, or the capital of the big lenders as rapacious capital, in contrast to the creative capital of

Everything that preceded the development of Jewish capital, first trade and then financial capital in different countries, led to the idea of formally organizing a union on the basis of a common nationalist ideology. . . . The monopoly of trade and usury, which was almost exclusively theirs in most countries, united them in a monolithic international group, while persecution, the ghetto, nationalism, and religious separatism strengthened and reinforced their standoffishness among other detachments of property owners. Huckstering became their distinctive peculiarity; in individual

worker against him. And the Jew-usurer rubs his hands and laughs because all this strife concerns only visible capital: estates, factories, shops, while capital in the form of money which does not produce anything and destroys everybody, is invisible.

—Butmi, *Russia at the Crossroads*, p. 11.

industry or agriculture, and the capital of hard-working individuals.

—E. Mayer, in *Problemy ekonomiki*, 1933, no. 33, p. 163.

cases, it even became the privilege of Jewish property owners. Their true nationality became, in the words of K. Marx, "the nationality of the merchant, of the moneyman in general."

—Semenyuk, pp. 72–73.

10. THE JEWS HAVE CREATED INTERNATIONAL JEWISH FINANCE CAPITAL

The Jews are creating international capital funds at the expense of the countries inhabited by them. There are colossal accumulations of such capital—the fruit of their age-old rapacious policies.

—*Predisloviye, poslesloviye . . . k knige T. Fricha* (hereafter: Frich's book), p. 37.

Germany has fallen into the tentacles of international banking capital, which means Jewish capital.

—Germanicus, p. 21.

The Jews are at the head of world banking capital.

—*Istorik-marksist*, 1932, nos. 1–2, p. 89.

Zionist enterprises, initiated by international Jewish capital, represented one of the prototypes of present-day multinational corporations.

—Skurlatov, p. 36.

11. THE POLICIES OF OTHER COUNTRIES AND PEOPLES HAVE COME UNDER THEIR DOMINANCE

The Jews have become a vast force. . . . directly and indirectly they exercise a mighty influence on the politics of all countries.

—Kulichev, p. 2.

One of the most important aims of political Zionism is to form powerful pressure groups to influence governments; such groups consist of some of the most influential representatives of this bourgeoisie [Jewish—R.O.] in the capitalist world.

—Semenyuk, p. 72.

12. THEY HAVE WORMED THEIR WAY INTO OTHER COUNTRIES' GOVERNMENTS AND ARE IN CONTROL OF THEM

Today, some of the most influential members of the parliaments of Britain, France, and Austria are Jews; some sovereigns have Jewish ministers and councellors.

—Osman-bey, p. 41.

. . . by the middle of the nineteenth century the bourgeoisie of Jewish origin in many countries—the Russian Empire, Germany, France, Britain, the United States, Italy, Austro-Hungary, virtually controlled the policies of a number of states.

—Korneev, p. 6.

13. IN RUSSIA THEY HAVE PENETRATED THE STATE DUMA

Since the Jews are so undoubtedly and indisputably a danger to the Russian nation, they must, of course, be summarily dealt with; under no circumstances are they to be admitted to the zemstvo, and I welcome with all my heart the actions of the government and our commission in implementing a bill to just this effect. . . . Jews have been admitted to the State Duma; this is a frightful error. I am sure this error will soon be rectified, and that we shall not see a single circumcised Jew in this hall.

—Markov—2, Speech May 8, 1910, at a session of the 3rd State Duma. Stenographic Account, p. 315.

Even in autocratic Russia with its semiserfdom, anti-Semitic laws and the Pale of Settlement, the true power of the Jewish bourgeoisie was incomparably greater than that accorded them by their formal civil rights. This bourgeoisie penetrated every one of the all-Russian political parties, was represented in the State Duma, and had influence in urban and rural self-government and on the organs of justice and the courts.

—Begun, *Creeping Counterrevolution*, pp. 17–18.

14. ALL MAJOR POLITICAL FIGURES HAVE BEEN SUBJECTED TO JEWISH CONTROL

A particularly great contribution was made to the enrichment of aliens and increasing their dominance in Russia by Witte, a wicked enemy of the Russian people who was married to a Jewess; for almost fifteen years he controlled our ill-fated homeland. He systematically flooded the Ministry of Transport, the Treasury, the Commissariat, and other departments with aliens, Poles and Jews in particular.

—*Poraboshcheniye russkogo naroda yevreyami* (hereafter: *Enslavement of the Russian People*), p. 14.

Witte brought the conversation round to *Novoye vremya*: "It is the most popular paper in Russia, and the most harmful. It has hounded me and the Jews, and is now summoning the people to devote all their strength to war. . . . It must be rendered harmless. You can collect money from the bankers," the count said to Simonovich. "Tomorrow, if you like. There will be money. As much as you want."

—Pikul, in *Nash sovremennik*, 1979, no. 6, p. 85.

14a. ALL MAJOR POLITICAL FIGURES MUST SUBMIT TO JEWISH CONTROL

The appearance of the Jew Zion at the then omnipotent Katkov's; Vishegradsky's intimacy with the Jew Zak; and the appearance and situation of the Jew Rotstein were such that it was rumored throughout Europe that he ruled Russia.

—Bespartiyny, pp. 10–11.

The Jews supported Witte.

—*Enslavement of the Russian People*, p. 6.

The credit for turning the Jews into the ruling clique in Germany belongs to Prince Bismarck. Prince Bismarck also submitted to the influence of the Jews. Jews and their comrades-in-arms comprise his society, he meets with them constantly, and they serve as his political advisers.

Brown Book, p. 211.

It is customary to assume that Rasputin controlled the Tsar and Tsarina. But this is only half the truth. The truth is that very often Rasputin indeed controlled Nicholas I. But it was Simonovich, first of all, who controlled Rasputin, and Simonovich was controlled by the most powerful Jewish capitalists and smart operators. . . .

In the memoirs A. Simonovich wrote as an emigré, he relates how

Count Witte once asked him to arrange a meeting with Rasputin. Witte told him that somehow he would like to render harmless the paper *Novoye Vremya*, which he found odious. . . . After this meeting Witte said to Simonovich, "You will take over *Novoye Vremya*, and it will be rendered harmless. Have a word with your Jews about that . . ." Rasputin invited all these financiers to visit him, and suggested that they buy this paper which was hostile to the Jews.*

—Begun, *Creeping Counterrevolution*, pp. 136–137.

15. THEY HAVE SEIZED CONTROL OF THE PRESS AND OTHER ORGANS OF THE MASS MEDIA

The Jews of Russia have managed to a considerable degree to monopolize the press (newspapers and periodicals) and the telegraph, turning them into a Jewish trust. In this way the Jews seek to Judaize the national spirit in our Fatherland.

—Foreword to Frich's book, p. 2.

The Zionist leaders ascribe great importance to infiltrating their agents into the metropolitan press of all states, into international boards of editors, the radio, cinema and television. . . .

—Yevseev, *Aims and Methods*, p. 5.

Novoye Vremya ("New Times")—a Black Hundreds newspaper under the control of A. Suvorin. It was closed down after the October Revolution of 1917. In his article *Novoye Vremya* and *Rech*—On the Right to National Self-Determination," V. I. Lenin wrote: "[This is] the old, crude, and ridiculous Black Hundreds device of taunting the liberals for receiving assistance from the Jews!" (V. I. *Lenin, Sobr. soch.*, vol. 24, p. 258).

A host of newspapers in Moscow and St. Petersburg belong to the Jews. And the newspapers published in the provincial towns, which propagate the doctrine of the socialists or simply stand "for freedom," almost all are Jewish-owned.

—Kulichev, *Yevreiskove gosudarstvo* (hereafter: *Jewish State*), p. 4. (continued below)

"To sow poison and demoralization," i.e., to corrupt and destroy society, to deceive the people . . . the Zionists could not do this without having control of the most powerful propaganda apparatus—the mass media. That is why their first objective is always to take control of newspapers and magazines, telegraph agencies, publishing houses, radio and television, the entire industry of the word. In this pursuit they have already achieved a great deal.

—Begun, *Neman*, 1973, no. 1, p. 109.

16. AND VIA THE MASS MEDIA, THE JEWS SOW THE SEEDS OF HATRED, LIES, SLANDER, AND CORRUPTION AMONG OTHER NATIONS

The greater part of the press is in their hands, and what depravity, what perversion of taste, what lies and hatred it propagates.

—*Obshchestvennaya rol yevreistva* (hereafter: *Role of the Jews*), p. 22.

To incite hatred, to rouse, to fan the flames of enmity, to make insidious observations and brazen insinuations, to keep people forever distrustful and hostile by means of cunning and cov-

By . . . using the press, the Jews have managed to subject the masses to their influence to such an extent that in the errors of the leftists the rightists have begun seeing the errors of the German worker, while the errors of the rightists in their turn, have seemed to the German worker to be merely the errors of the so-called bourgeoisie. And both camps have failed to notice that the errors of both sides are no more than the calculated result of diabolical incitement by alien ele-

Israel Radio makes extensive use of the dirtiest tricks of bourgeois propaganda: crude lies, slander, subtle fabrication, and quite unfounded, totally preposterous speculative conjectures. The primary concern is to lay on a bit more effrontery and insolence.

—Yevseev, *Aims and Methods*, p. 11.

ert machinations. . . . This is the strategy of the Jewish press.

—Shmakov, *Rech po yevreiskomu voprosu* (hereafter: *Speech on the Jewish Question*), p. 26.

17. THEY HAVE SEIZED ALL KEY POSITIONS

Their huckstering talents have opened to them the road to . . . wealth, which is concentrated in their hands, and at the same time, to actual power. . . . Their hands have seized control of the network of private and international economic interests, and of the entire corrupt "free" press . . and of the political parties of constitutional governments; they have thus become the covert but real masters of the economic and political structure of the most cultured states.

—Yuzefovich, *Yevreisky vopros*, p. 12.

In the political sphere, the Jews dislodge Christians; they enslave them economically and from the ethical standpoint they corrupt them.

—*Role of the Jews*, p. 23.

ments. Thus it could be (irony of fate!) that the stock-exchange Jews have become the leaders of the German working-class movement.

—Heiden, p. 54.

The growth of the Jews' influence and the pernicious Jewish spirit in politics, economics, and culture paralyzed the strength and will of the German people.

—Goering, in *Nyurnbergsky protsess* (hereafter: *Nuremberg Trial*), vol. 7, p. 398.

. . . the most important task for the Zionist brain center was and still is the policy of seizing key positions in the economy and the administrative and ideological apparatus in the diaspora.

—Begun, *Creeping Counterrevolution*, p. 58.

18. THEY HAVE SET UP AN INTERNATIONAL SUPERGOVERNMENT—AN INTERNATIONAL TRUST WHICH EXPLOITS THE WORLD

In reality, we face no obstacles. Our supergovernment operates under the kind of extralegal conditions which it is customary to call—energetically, vigorously—a dictatorship.

—Nilus, p. 118.

The Hebrew tribe has its own central government, which is already a threat to the governments of the countries in which this tribe lives. In the future it gives promise of becoming a power which none of these governments will be capable of resisting.

—Piramishvili, pp. 47–48.

What is internationalism? In actual fact, there exists only one International . . . that of the stock-exchange Jews and their dictatorship.

—From a speech by Hitler, in Heiden, p. 56.

[Zionism] . . . today comprises an international conglomerate of large-scale financial capital. It is completely legitimate therefore to use the term . . . "Zionist capital" in reference to this "International of Financiers!"

—Bolshakov, p. 58.

If we think more deeply about the essence of the projected "Universal Union," then before our very eyes appears a particular variant of ultraimperialism, the international trust of the capitalists which exploits the world.

—Begun, Creeping Counterrevolution, p. 60.

19. THERE IS NO ESCAPE FROM THEM: THEY ARE EVERYWHERE, SERVING IN WHATEVER CAPACITY, FOR WHOEVER IS PROFITABLE AT A GIVEN MOMENT, DISGUISING THEMSELVES IN DIFFERENT CLOTHING

They built up the kind of relationship with warring factions which always enabled them to join the apparent winner. The Jews kept switching between supporting the revolution and being loyal to the established order. One moment they became propagandists for revolutionary utopias, and the next they are helping to restore the monarchy and elevate the aristocracy. . . . If monarchism is victorious, the Jewish plunderers will offer support through Fuld, Pereira and Co. Should adherents of the republic or commune gain the upper hand, this duty will be assured by Crémieux and Karl Marx.

—Osman-bey, pp. 29, 42

According to Hitler and the "theorists" of National Socialism, Rosenberg and Feder, the imperialist powers, France, Britain, the United States, Poland, the League of Nations . . . the USSR are tools of world Jewish financial capital, which has for some reason chosen as its major objective the strangulation of Germany. The Third International, liberalism, Poincaré, and Lloyd-George are also tools of Jewish capital.

—Levin, in *Revolutsiya i natsionalnosti*, 1933, no. 1, p. 86.

The entire history of our age proves that usurer-financiers have subsidized not only the state in whose territory their bank is situated, but also those countries which are at war with their "native land."

—Bolshakov, p. 47.

During the First World War, the Zionist centers loyally served the imperialists through the Entente and collaborated with the renegades of the Second International. They calculated that the war would benefit them. After the overthrow of tsarism the Zionist organizations began to work in close collaboration with the Provisional Government.

—Begun, pp. 13–14.

Part 2. THE WORLD OUTLOOK OF THE JEWS

1. THEY OPPOSE THE OFFICIAL IDEOLOGY

For Zion, the most convenient and desirable type of government is a republican regime, which gives free rein to the activities of the army of Zion. Hence its zealous propagation of liberalism.

—Nilus, p. 165

That the Jews are alien to the idea of statehood is explained by their lack of individuality. This also explains the mass conversion of the Jews to communism.

—Govorov, p. 23.

Socialism is Aryanism (Owen, Carlyle, Ruskin, Fichte). Communism is Judaism (Lassalle, Marx, Bernstein).

At the present time socialism has departed from its basic mission, because the Jews have seized control of it.

—Shmakov, *Jewish Pogrom in Kiev*, p. vii.

Democracy and parliamentarism are "pernicious Jewish ideas."

—Hitler, in *Sputnik agitatora*, 1941, no. 24, p. 19.

Parliamentarism is a basic outgrowth of the Jewish spirit . . .

—Germanicus, p. 20.

The Jewish world conspiracy in the form of bolshevism must be crushed.

—Rosenberg, in *Communisticheskiy Internatsional*, 1936, no. 15, p. 87.

Marxism is Judaism.

—Hitler, in *Sovietskaya pedagogika*, 1941, no. 9, p. 9.

Hitler assigned the SS the task of averting the Jewish-Bolshevist revolution of "subhumans."

—*Nuremberg Trial*, vol. 6, p. 140.

. . . a malicious counterrevolution frequently appears in the guise of ultrarevolutionism, obscurantism arrays itself in the clothes of liberalism, and unalloyed chauvinism is presented as the defense of national interests. The Zionists are unsurpassed masters of political mimicry.

. . . Nevertheless the aims of Zionism are pervaded by a frenetic anti-communism.

—Begun, *Creeping Counterrevolution*, p. 73.

Socialism stands in the way of Zionism.

—Kurov, in *Reaktsionnaya sushchnost sionizma* (hereafter: *Reactionary Nature of Zionism*), p. 105.

Zionism is fascism. . . . The basic content of Zionism is anticommunism, implacable hostility to the Soviet Union and other socialist countries, to the international revolution-

Socialism and communism are false doctrines, advanced, developed, and propagandized by the Jewish nation and the Jewish press; such doctrines are among many others which, equally false, have been expressed by the Jews for the purpose of destroying our national character and statehood.

—Demchenko, p. 182.

Certain Nazi documents attempt to base the extermination of the Jews on territories of the USSR upon the idea that this social group was supposedly a vehicle of the Soviet state system. Even in Nuremberg, Olendorff attempted to substantiate this argument by maintaining that the Jews used to sing the "International" and proclaim the glory of Stalin before being executed.

—V. Kral, p. 230.

ary movement, and to all the anti-imperialist forces of today.

—Romanenko, p. 6.

The Zionist and the fascist have found a common language.

—Skurlatov, p. 93.

2. RELIGION

1) Judaism

The Jews invariably regard their religion as the instrument of their politics.

—Shmakov, Gomelskoye delo (hereafter: Gomel Affair), p. 11.

Anti-Semitic publications have for long displayed considerable competitiveness in heaping abuse on the God of the Old Testament.

—F. Delich, A Word of Truth about the Talmud, Apropos of A. Rolling's essay "The Talmudic Jew" (St. Petersburg, 1885), p. 91.

Judaism is the basis of the philosophy and world outlook of present-day Zionism.

—Begun, Sionizm i yudaizm (hereafter: Zionism and Judaism), pp. 17–18.

2) The Synagogue

I won't be afraid to prohibit German Jews from holding religious services, and prevent them from attending synagogue with the aid of armed stormtroopers.

—Streicher, in *Brown Book*, p. 243.

. . . persons professing Judaism are an abundant raw material for Zionist processing, and in today's conditions the synagogue remains a potential base for subversive activities.

—Begun, *Creeping Counterrevolution*, p. 71.

3) The Sacred Books of the Jews
a) The Torah

Regardless of what Judaic patriots may say of the humaneness and universality of the Jews, all this . . . is not the spirit of Judaism, regardless of the soothing facts drawn from the works of their rabbis. You only have to know the Old Testament to see that the Jews always remained true Jews as long as they had to live in isolation from other tribes. . . . Thus all the activities of the true Jew had to be devoted exclusively to the good of his own tribe . . . , even though these activities entailed disadvantages for the populations alien to the Jew.

—Kostomarov, pp. 42–43.

Let us rip to shreds the Old Testament—the Bible of lust and the Devil.

—Eckhart, in Heiden, p. 95.

If we view the Torah from the standpoint of modern civilization and progressive Communist morality, it proves to be an unsurpassed textbook of bloodthirstiness and hypocrisy, treachery, perfidy, and licentiousness—of every vile human quality.

—Begun, *Creeping Counterrevolution*, p. 55.

b) *The Talmud*

The Talmud is an outrageous concoction of fiendishness, filth, and ignorance of the most violent fanaticism.

—Shmakov, *Yevrei v istorii* (hereafter: *Jews in History*), p. 41.

c) *The Psalms, Parables, and Prayers of the Jews*

Listening attentively to the words of *Kol Nidrei* one is easily convinced that in such a solemn setting, in such a deeply religious atmosphere, it is not, strictly speaking a prayer but a unique act of renouncing vows and oaths in public.

—Shmakov, *Jews in History*, p. 70.

Both the Torah and the Talmud have always been the enemies of science and progress. Hence, progressive persons have expressed their opposition to this "Holy Scripture."

—Kichko, p. 13.

The literature of all Jews serves as an example, "beginning with those who breathe the vengeance of the Psalms."

—The words of Rosenberg, in *Protiv fashistskogo mrakobesiya* (hereafter: *Against Fascist Obscurantism and Demagogy*), p. 321.

The *Kol Nidrei* prayer is recited in the synagogue. In it, the Jews ask that all promises, prohibitions, obligations, and oaths be considered null and void. Fulfilling the injunctions of this prayer, the observant Jew can break his oath of allegiance.

—Kichko, p. 31.

Specifically, Solomon's parables depict vengeance disguised with hypocrisy and vengeance in the guise of service. It is difficult for us, who have been nurtured on the lofty and noble principles of socialist humanism, to believe in the impenetrable obscurantism and insidiousness of Solomon's parables.

—Begun, *Creeping Counterrevolution*, p. 70.

4) The Pious: Purim

The festival of Purim is the most "joyous" among the Jews; in their ritual it is also the most dangerous for all goyim—a repository of malice, pride, and vengefulness. Instituted in the time of Mordechai, this festival has been preserved to this day. It must therefore be acknowledged that the "chosen" people has always had a ruling authority of its own to direct the united Jewish forces.

—Shmakov, *Speech on the Jewish Question*, p. 43.

The Jews . . . established Purim, the most joyous of their festivals, for all time. . . . Breeding malice in the young and appealing to the vindictiveness of the old, Purim serves as the chief annual occasion for displaying Jewish hatred and pride.

—Shmakov, *Gomel Affair*, p. 35.

. . . the streets adjoining the hospital, as during the Civil War, were occupied by the Marxist defenders of the money boxes. Our enemy gathered bricks from all the nearest building sites in order to stone me in accordance with every rule prescribed by Jewish ritual. My fate was decided during an ominous pause . . . to the accompaniment of the Purim laughter of Jewish doctors and nurses.

—Goebbels, *Michael*, in N. Koreev, p. 347.

This book [the Book of Esther] and the ethics contained in it is an object of emulation for Judaic-Zionists. . . . In commemoration of that bloody slaughter, Mordechai ordained that "the fourteenth and fifteenth days of the month of Adar be celebrated as the joyous festival of Purim."

Accordingly, to this day, that tale serves to nurture insidiousness in the choice of means, bloodthirstiness, and criminal means of seizing power. . . . Nowadays the Zionists are propagating and cultivating Mordechai's ethics. And they act in accordance with it. These ethics are shameless in the extreme: to achieve power, authority, or any given end, any means, even the most loathsome, and good.

—Begun, *Creeping Counterrevolution*, pp. 149–150.

The boldness of some people is astonishing. Pygmies, living in obscurity, virtually insignificant, dare to grin abusively at the greatest of the world's giants of the mind and spirit . . . Not having studied, ignorant of the details of Moses' vast creation, the many interpretations of his work and the more or less scientific objections to it, they attack the integrity of his whole philosophy and the inherent integrity of his spirit. They repeat with great frivolity the clichés of his former critics, clichés that have been universally abandoned and forgotten. For Moses is certainly a fact of the greatest significance. You cannot expunge him from history with the casual stroke of a dull goosequill pen.

—From a conversation between Archbishop Nikanor of Kherson and Odessa and students at the New Russian University apropos of Neruchev's article "The Jews and the Bible," 1889, printed in the anthology *Russkiye lyudi o yevreyakh* (St. Petersburg, 1891).

It is intolerable for German children to consider any longer Abraham, Isaac, and Jacob their patriarchs and to see in Moses, David, Solomon . . . heroes worthy of emulation.

—N. Koreev, p. 481.

Moses, the principal prophet and central figure of the Tanach, does not emerge from the pages of the Bible as the noble personage depicted by Jewish theologians and hysterical female Zionists. In the words of Paul Gelbach, ". . . under the banner of religion, he filled the Israelites with a venomous hatred for all other nations. He obliged them to be inhuman, hat-

5) Patriarchs, Prophets, and Heroes

And how could one think at all of the historical edification of present-day Jews when the Old Testament teaches us how the patriarch Jacob duped his own brother, Esau, and even managed to deceive his father-in-law Laban.

—Shmakov, *Jewish Pogrom in Kiev*, p. v.

ers of mankind, and bloodthirsty. He . . . endowed himself . . . with the traits of an ambitious swindler who showed no qualms about committing the most brutal crimes to attain his end . . ."

—Begun, *Creeping Counterrevolution*, pp. 54–55.

The peculiarities of the Jewish religion are hatred of mankind, preaching genocide, cultivating a love of power, and glorifying criminal means of achieving power.

—Yevseev, p. 46.

The chauvinistic idea of world domination has been particularly repulsive; formulated in the "Holy Scriptures," it has been reflected in their prayers.

—Begun, *Creeping Counterrevolution*, p. 48.

6) The Ethics of Judaism

a) Hatred of mankind

Jews who are guided by the Talmud are specifically taught to hate and despise all the rest of humanity. In their prayers they invoke every type of misfortune and curse on non-Jews . . . , and the principal Jewish holidays embody the insatiable wrath of this nation, its hellish vindictiveness and truculent fanatism.

—Shmakov, *Jews in History*, p. 108.

b) The desire for world domination

The Talmud instills a principle of this kind in its followers: the Jews are the sole masters of the world.

—Shmakov, *Jews in History*, p. 42.

God has endowed us with genius, so that we could be equal to our task: the subjugation of the world by peaceful means.　　　　—Demchenko, p. 108.

c) Their exclusiveness

Only the Israelite is a human being. The entire universe is his. All must serve him, particularly "the animals in human form."

　　　　　　　—Pranaitis, p. 6.

in . . . official abstracts of the prescripts of Judaism, repeated emphasis is given to the "exclusiveness" of the Jews, their innate superiority to the goyim, their right to world domination.

　　　　　　　—Skurlatov, p. 13.

d) Their being chosen by God

According to the basic dogma of Judaism, humanity is divided into two hostile camps: Israel, chosen by God, and the remainder of humanity, whom he has rejected.

　　　　　　　—Brafman,* p. 49.

The Jews have promoted the concept of the alleged "divine election" of the Jews, who are destined to rule the world, to be mankind's leaders and legislators.

　　　　　　　—Skurlatov, p. 9.

e) Their contempt for non-Jews

The basic idea of the Talmud is that the world must belong to the Jews alone. The rest of the nations are inferior to them and must be subordinated

The extremely reactionary character of the Jewish religion consists in its division of humanity into two unequal parts: the Jews, "chosen by God," and

---

*[Concerning Brafman see note.]

to them. Every non-Jewish, so-called goy and *akum* . . .

—Velikorossov, p. 22.

f) *Other nations are their slaves*

The basic premise of the Talmud is the principle that only Jews are human beings: the rest of humanity are merely animals in human form, created in honor of the Jews . . . so that they might serve them as slaves.

—Shmakov, *Jewish Pogrom in Kiev*, p. xxiv.

g) *They detest hard work*

Agriculture, menial service, all forms of hard, muscular work and the most arduous manual labour are left to Christians by the Jews. They choose commerce, innkeeping, brokering, for themselves.

—The Role of the Jews, p. 89.

the non-Jews, who are "despised by God," for whom they have even devised a whole series of abusive names, such as *akum* and goy."

—Begun, *The Creeping Counterrevolution*, p. 47.

The Jewish democrat who comes from among the common people becomes a bloodsucking Jew who tyrannizes the people. He seeks to extirpate the national representatives of the intelligentsia and turns nations into slaves capable of bearing their yoke for a lengthy period.

—Hitler, in *Brown Book*, p. 212.

There is an irreconcilable contradiction between the German sense of right and the oriental-Jewish sense of right. The economic ethic of this group of people reduces itself to getting rich quick at any price.

—Dr. Von Leers, in *Vestnik Kommunisticheskoy Akademii*, 1933, no. 4, p. 78.

"God's chosen people" have their own laws, their own sphere, their own destiny, whereas the despised goyim are suited only to be "tools with the power of speech," slaves.

—Skurlatov, p. 12.

The Jews want to have slaves, but the slaves must not be Jews.

—The film *Skupshchiki dush* ("Traders in Souls"), Mosfilm, 1977.

The teachings of Judaism are pervaded with hatred for work and contempt for the man who spends his day in toil. The entire ideology of Judaism is not imbued with the idea of work, but with a narrow practicality, the means for making a profit, a mania for silver, the spirit of egoism, and the craving for money.

—Kichko, p. 28.

h) They want to appropriate the property of other people

Khazaka is the right to own real estate. The Kahal considers Christian real estate its own, taking as its guide the words of the Law: "The property of the non-Jew belongs to him who seizes it first." Thus the Kahal grants every Jew the right to take possession of this property.

—Brafman, *Kniga Kagala*, p. 130.

The Talmud teaches that one is forbidden to steal only from a *khaver* (a fellow-man). One is permitted to take everything from everyone else (the goyim), because God has reserved all non-Jewish wealth for the Jews.

—Kichko, p. 28.

i) Judaism's double standard

The Jews have two standards and two truths: one—the true one, for Jews, and the other—false, for goyim.

—Dragomilov, in Demchenko, p. 18.

Judaism . . . cultivates a system of double moral standards guided by Judaic ethics, the Zionists contemplate a single rule: "I can do unto others what others are forbidden to do unto me."

—Begun, *Creeping Counterrevolution*, pp. 63–64.

j) Judaism and Protestantism

In spite of Luther's hatred for the Jews, his doctrine is accepted by the Jews with much less difficulty than other Christian creeds; at times it is even regarded by Judeophiles as a step toward Judaism.

—Shmakov, *Jews in History*, p. 22.

Luther's translation of the Bible did terrible damage to the power of Germans to think. Ye gods! What a halo now surrounds this Bible of Satan! Luther's poetry gives off such a blinding light that even the incest committed by Lot's daughters acquires a religious luster.

—Hitler, in Heiden, p. 95.

A variant of Christianity—Protestantism—especially the teachings of Calvin, crystallized during the Reformation under the watchword of a return to "Judaic wisdom." Emphasizing "divine election" in particular, it was therefore pregnant with racism, and it became the ideology of rising capitalism; the age-old Judaic recipes for acquisition, individual enterprise, and calculating rationalism were impressed upon the epoch of primary capitalist accumulation.

—Skurlatov, pp. 15, 18.

k) The synagogue—a danger to the nations

Mass demonstrations against the bands of murderers took place in Nuremberg and Fuerth. Large crowds gathered in the synagogues of Nuremberg and Fuerth and burned down these two Jewish buildings, where prayers had been offered for the murder of Germans.

—Correspondence of November 10, 1939, in Nuremberg Trial, vol. 5, p. 192.

The Zionists wish to avail themselves of the synagogue as a strongpoint. By using a legally existing religious establishment, they wish to create the conditions for propagating the ideas of Zionism and to drive a wedge into the friendship that exists among the peoples of our country.

—Begun, Zionism and Judaism, p. 14.

Present-day Zionism is the ideology and political practice of the powerful Jewish bourgeoisie. It is closely linked with the monopolistic circles of the United States and other imperialist powers. . . . Zionism is an organic part

3. ZIONISM

1) Definition of Zionism

"Judaic Zionism" operates in Russia under the patronage of the Russian Masons and by agreement with British Freemasonry: a well-organized treasonous secret service, extending all over Russia, it is always hostile to

of the political strategy of imperialism, benefits from its support, and rests upon the powerful financial base of the international monopolies.

—Semenyuk, pp. 3–4.

Right up to the Sixth Zionist Congress in 1903, the leaders of the "westerners," including T. Herzl and M. Nordau, were ready to found a Jewish state in any colonial country, in Uganda, for example. . . . When it turned out that Palestine itself was advantageous as an arena of pro-imperialist expansion, the Judaic dogma of the Promised Land was dragged out into the light of day, as if given to the Jews from on high.

—Skurlatov, p. 40.

Russia, but friendly toward the Jews involved in British foreign policy.

—Butmi, *Vragi roda chelovecheskogo* (hereafter: *Enemies of the Human Race*), p. 121.

2) The Origins of Zionism

The so-called Zionist movement among the intelligentsia and representatives of the Jewish people, which embodies their aspiration for a new exodus to the Promised Land, appeared no more than thirty to forty years ago. But it was given a purely elemental impetus by Herzl, the incarnation, so to speak, of that false Elijah to whom the aspirations of talmudic Israel assign the place of precursor of the future false Messiah, of world domination, allegedly, by the seed of David.

—Nilus, p. 89.

In order to mask the main strategic aim of the Zionist movement—the establishment of its domination over the world, some authors reduce Zionism to Palestinism, to the effort to resettle and eliminate the Diaspora. Such an interpretation of Zionism requires an unequivocal rebuttal. Elimination of the Diaspora has never entered into the Zionists' plans, while the creation of a Jewish state has not been the primary aim; the latter has been subordinated to a more important one: the establishment of control by the Jewish bourgeoisie over the Jewish masses in order to expand and consolidate capitalist exploitation, to transform this bourgeoisie into the ruling caste of the capitalist world.

—Begun, *Creeping
Counterrevolution*, pp.
58–59.

3) The Aims of Zionism

Talks about the purchase of Palestine by the Jews . . . are being conducted as a diversionary move to mislead unwary goyim. Actually, the Zionists are dreaming of a Jewish universal empire. And as about two-thirds of World Jewry are concentrated in Russia, the latter, according to the Jews' scheme, is to serve as the primary nucleus of this empire.

—Demchenko, p. 26.

The Jews want . . . to destroy the white race, which is odious to them, to hurl it from the lofty heights of culture and politics, and themselves take power over them.

—Hitler, in *Brown Book*,
p. 212.

4) Zionist Objectives

a) Pressure on the governments of all countries

As far as Zionism is concerned, it is obvious that it is totally inadequate as a plan for Jewish political independence. Consequently its objectives are

One of the most important aims of political Zionism is to unite the numerous detachments of the Jewish bourgeoisie of various countries in a single international corporation, which will implement agreed actions of an economic and political nature . . ., and exert pressure on governments, monopolies, and public opinion.

—Semenyuk, p. 72.

The Zionists claim a particular international mission for Israel—a legalized form of the subversive Zionist activities in other countries. They insist that Jews isolate themselves for the purpose of turning Jewish communities into fifth columns scattered throughout the world . . . which must engage in subversive activities against socialist states, against Arab countries, and against the peoples of Africa.

—Nikitina, in *The Reactionary Nature of Zionism*, p. 118.

not to be found in this. On the one hand, Zionism is a cunning variant of centralized Jewish power; it conforms with democratic tendencies to better maneuver this power for the delight and benefit of Israel. On the other hand, it is a revolution within Jewry itself against the outdated forms of talmudic plutocracy, to further the development of Jewish power.

—Shmakov, *Gomel Affair*, p. 42.

b) Subversive activities

Judaic Zionism . . . is a well-organized . . . treasonous secret service.

—Butmi, *Enemies of the Human Race*, p. 121.

c) *Infiltration into other countries and movements*

Only Jewish idealists and Zionists dream of a Jewish state in Palestine or elsewhere. Jewry as a whole thinks, on the contrary, of parasitically infiltrating the masses of other nations, thoroughly concealing their Jewishness, and of constantly moving on to greener pastures.

—The epilogue of Frich's book, p. 43.

5) *Zionist methods*

The whole of Jewish history presents a picture of acts of treachery against the heterodox, deception of every kind, even killing them when their back is turned.

—Shmakov, *Jews in History*, p. 150.

The Zionists utilize various methods to infiltrate their agents into the Communist movement. For this they rely particularly on using workers of Jewish origin.

—*Sionizm: teoriya i praktika* (hereafter: *Zionism: Theory and Practice*), p. 134.

The periphery Jews living outside of Israel, are much more important for the Zionists than the "national home."

—Bolshakov, in *Sionizm—orudiye imperialisticheskoy reaktsii* (hereafter: *Zionism—The Tool of Imperialist Reaction*), p. 39.

For a long time Zionism avoided publicity. Up to the present time it preferred to act stealthily, on the sly, without loudly proclaiming its ultimate ideas.

—Bolshakov, p. 146.

In the struggle against their political opponents the Zionists resort . . . to blackmail and provocation, . . . base their political struggle on violence.

—*Zionism: Theory and Practice*, p. 135.

It is precisely to the resolution of the UN General Assembly on November 29, 1947, that Israel is indebted for its appearance in the world. This is the sole juridical basis for its existence.

—V. Laptev, in *Reactionary Nature of Zionism*, pp. 69–70.

Blackmail is just about their favorite action.

—Shmakov, *Jews in History*, p. 53.

6) Palestine

They are indebted to other nations for their acquisition of Palestine Leaving it to the nations of Europe to fight for or otherwise establish and assure the independence of the Jews' new state in Palestine, the Zionists are operating in various corners of Europe.

—Shmakov, *Gomel Affair* p. 11.

7) *Two opinions about Palestine*
(A few pages of digressions—Digression No. 1)

a. *The English, the Arabs, and the Jews*

Among the Zionists, the English used their help in carrying on the struggle against the Arab national movement, and particularly in suppressing the *freedom uprisings* [my emphasis—R.O.] of the Palestinian Arabs in 1920, 1921 and 1933.

> —Lutsky, *Palestinskaya problema*, p. 17.

In April 1920, after members of the Zionist paramilitary organization Haganah attacked a Moslem religious procession in Jerusalem, Arab actions gripped the largest cities in Palestine. At the beginning of May 1921, the Arab population of Jaffa came out in opposition to the activities of the Zionists. . . . Essentially this was the first major Arab uprising in Palestine during the Mandate. . . . It . . . took the form of an armed struggle by the peasants and Bedouin against Zionist colonization. . . . The biggest Arab action at that stage was the uprising of 1929. This began in the form of bloody clashes between Arabs and Jews, deliberately provoked by the Zionists over religious sites in Jerusalem. This uprising quickly enveloped the entire country. . . . In the towns, Arab workers and artisans reacted against the usurpation by *Jewish Zionist capital* [my emphasis, R.O.] of industrial enterprises and workshops, which had previously belonged to Palestinians; in rural areas the fellaheen and Bedouin reacted against the establishment of Jewish settlements on land seized from the Arabs.

> —*Mezhdunarodny sionizm*, pp. 49–51.

The British Royal Commission stated in its 1937 report: "In 1920, 1921, and 1929 the Arabs took action against the Jews . . ."

> —Quotation taken from Ivanov, p. 84.

[in the year 1920] . . . a very ordinary Jewish pogrom occurred in Jerusalem, the capital of Palestine. There was a lot of anti-Zionist agitation in Jerusalem led by the local Arab clubs long before April 4. The local British administration saw all the signs of the pogrom that was in preparation. . . . Despite a number of warnings and requests on the part of the Jews, the administration did not do enough. During the pogrom, the authorities used their forces not against the rioters but against the Jews, who merely wished to defend themselves and those near and dear to them. . . . Shortly afterwards, a court-martial was organized. It convicted nineteen Jews and two Arabs of responsibility for the events of April 4. . . . The Jews received heavy sentences: Jabotinsky was given fifteen years' hard labor, and the others from three to five years.

> —Rafes, pp. 1, 5, 6.

The White Paper initiated a new stage in British policy for Palestine. Britain . . . sought to improve cooperation with the feudal-bourgeois leadership of the Arab nationalist movement. Thus she made some concessions to the Arabs. . . . She agreed to restrict Jewish immigration: during the next five years she would admit no more than 15,000 Jews annually into the

The facts show that the Zionist Jews were preferred by the English to the Palestinian Arabs; one of the indications of Great Britain's double game was the famous White Paper (1939). It promoted the idea of creating a binary Arab-Jewish state in Palestine.
—Dmitriev, p. 27.

The courageous struggle of the Palestinian Arabs . . . frustrated the maneuvers of British colonialism. . . . Moreover, the British government was compelled to develop a new policy for Palestine, which was formulated in the White Paper of May 1939.
—*Mezhdunarodny sionizm*, p. 57.

b. *Who is served by Israeli intelligence?*
In 1937, a permanent intelligence agency was created in Palestine called Sherut Yisrael (Shay),* "The Israel Service." Its functions included the combating of progressive elements in the Jewish and Arab populations of Palestine. Ben-Gurion directed and controlled the operations of the agency's four sections at that time. Acting on orders from the leaders of international Zionism, he conducted these operations with a bias toward *collaboration with Nazi Germany.* As subsequent disclosures revealed, the Zionist leaders and the intelligence agencies under their control collaborated with the heads of a number of departments in Hitler's Reich. Many Israeli intelligence officers collaborated actively with the Abwehr—military intelligence, and other Nazi espionage organizations. Polkes, the eminent Zionist leader, was the Nazi

country; from *1944* [my emphasis, R.O.], immigration would be totally prohibited.
—Lutsky, p. 19.

A permanent intelligence agency, Sherut Yisrael, was created as early as 1937. The head of its investigation department, Isser Halperin, who had *collaborated* with the British, became the chief of the counterintelligence organization, Sherut Bitahon, in the State of Israel . . . Shiloah, Kollek, Gavrielli, and other former and present leaders of the Tel Aviv spy network occupied a more prominent place in British intelligence. Israel's present Minister for Foreign Affairs, Abba Eban, for example, was active in the British secret service and attained the rank of major. . . . Israel's first Prime Minister, Ben-Gurion . . . even had access to the upper echelons of British intelligence.
—Butlitsky, in *Aims and Methods*, pp. 44–45.

---

*[The name is actually Sherut Yediot.]

intelligence service's agent in the Middle East.

—Sklyarevsky, in *Aims and Methods*, pp. 70–71.

c. *Who supported racism in Palestine?*

The Arab liberation movement in the Middle East is our natural ally in the struggle against Britain.

—Hitler, 1941, in article by V. Grak in *Balkany i Blizhniy Vostok v noveysheye vremya*, no. 2 (Sverdlovsk, 1973), p. 131.

A Palestine Office was established in Berlin with the knowledge of the Gestapo. This was a peculiar kind of recruiting office; it monitored the huge stream of West European migrant Jews and selected for emigration those who agreed to collaborate with the Zionists in "taking over" Palestine. Zionism promised to provide services for Nazi Germany, particularly in the Middle East.

—Semenyuk, p. 34.

As early as 1936, an Association of Moslem Youth was organized in Berlin. Under the guise of a society for assisting Arab students living in Germany, an additional center was created for subversive activities in the Middle East. . . . The so-called Institute of anti-Semitism, based in Erfurt, Germany, was concerned with organizing acts of sabotage and terrorism in Palestine. Thus a secret Arab terrorist organization called the Black Hand (Fascists) was created in Palestine. It sought in every way to excite the anti-Jewish feelings of the Arabs, to convince them that only German Nazism, which was waging a relentless struggle against World Jewry, could secure for the Arabs the creation of an exclusively Arab state.

—Minayev, pp. 5, 46, 47.

d. *Who acted against Britain, in collusion with Fascism?*

Young, renascent Germany extends the hand of friendship over land and sea to a rejuvenescent East.

—Fascist newspaper, in Rumyantsev, p. 28.

Alluding to the persecution of the Jews in Nazi Germany, the Zionists demagogically demanded the "assistance" of the British authorities in ex-

In order to emphasize their "sympathy" with the Arab national movement, the Nazis participated in an anti-British demonstration organized

pelling the Arabs, although nobody had given the Zionists the right to use the crimes perpetrated by the Hitlerites to justify their own crimes. . . . Therefore, at the height of the war, when Rommel's armada of tanks made a break for the Suez Canal and the "Holy Land," and British soldiers were dying on the battlefields, fighting the Nazis who had made it their aim to wipe out the Jews, the Zionist extremists did not even stop at acts of terrorism against the British authorities. What is more, many prominent Zionists . . . collaborated with the Nazis during the war . . . secretly achieving their aims with the blood of those fighting against the fascist tyranny.

—Skurlatov, pp. 57–58.

by fascist elements among the Arabs who were resident in Berlin.

—Minayev, p. 40.

The Nazi secret service even lured some prominent nationalists into its snares [including] . . . the Grand Mufti of Jerusalem, Al Husseini. The latter, for his part, counted on Germany's help to become "Allah's Viceroy" for the entire Middle East. . . . The Mufti made a name for himself as an unsurpassed intriguer, blackmailer, and anti-Semite.

In May 1941, an uprising broke out in Palestine. The leading role in its preparation and realization was played by . . . the Mufti. One of the many proofs is the express telegram from Grobb which was received in the Wilhelmstrasse on May 17, 1941. It stated that "to ensure the success of the uprising instigated by the Mufti in Palestine, fifty light machine guns and one hundred of the most up-to-date automatic rifles must be delivered immediately to Damascus."

—Rumyantsev, pp. 62, 65.

e. *The problem of displaced persons*
One of the first major actions undertaken by the Zionists after the Second World War was to organize the invasion of Palestine by displaced persons of Jewish nationality.

The problem of displaced persons, Jews and non-Jews (there were immeasurably more of the latter), arose in Europe as a result of Hitlerite aggression and the policy of genocide. From the very beginning, it was *deliberately dramatized* by none other than the Zionists. After their liberation, the situation of the displaced Jews was not worse than that of the displaced

The Jewish people endured exceptional disasters and sufferings during the last war. It would not be an exaggeration to say that these disasters and sufferings do not lend themselves to description. . . . In the territories dominated by the Hitlerites, the Jews were subjected to almost total physical annihilation. The total number of Jews who perished at the hands of the Nazi butchers can be fixed at approximately six million persons. Only about 1.5 million Jews in Western Europe survived the war.

But while these figures give an idea

persons of other nationalities. But all the uproar was about the displaced Jews.

Plans existed for solving this problem. President Roosevelt of the United States put forward one such plan. It called for the creation of conditions for displaced Jews within the countries of Europe and the United States, which would allow them to return to normal life. However, all solutions of this kind . . . were rejected by the Zionist organizations. . . . Moreover, it was precisely the Zionist circles who sought to complicate this return to normal life, and to worsen the position of the Jewish refugees in Europe. The Zionist circles calculated that this would force them to accept Zionist ideas and to join the so-called Palestinian army. . . .

By means of similar "methods" about 500,000 people were moved to Palestine from various European countries. . . .

Basically, the invasion of Palestine organized by the Zionists was planned on a broad scale, as an imperialist operation against the growing national-liberation movement in the Arab East. The imperialists availed themselves of the idea of creating a Jewish homeland in order to deliver a blow to the Arab liberation movement, and at the same time, to have an obedient, aggressive power in the region.

> —Laptev, in *Reactionary*
> *Nature of Zionism*, pp.
> 51–53.

f. *Who founded the State of Israel?*
Adolf Hitler—the founder of Israel.
> —Korneev, p. 20.

of the losses suffered by the Jewish people at the hands of the Nazi aggressors, they give no indication of the grave situation of the mass of the Jewish population after the war.

A large part of the surviving Jewish population of Europe was left without a homeland of its own, without shelter and the means of subsistence. Hundreds of thousands of Jews are wandering through various countries in search of the means of subsistence and a refuge.

The majority of them are in the camps for displaced persons, still suffering great hardships. . . .

The fact that not one Western European state was able to ensure the defense of the Jewish people's elementary rights and to protect it from the violence of the Nazi butchers, explains the desire of the Jews to establish their own state. It would be unjust to ignore this and to deny the Jewish people the right to fulfill this desire. It is impossible to justify the denial of such a right to the Jewish people, particularly if we take into account everything they have endured in World War II.

> —From A. Gromyko's speech
> on May 15, 1947 at the UN
> General assembly, *Pravda*,
> no. 121 (May 16, 1947).

On November 29, 1947, the UN General Assembly passed a resolution concerning the termination of the British mandate in Palestine no later than August 1, 1948, and about the formation of two states—Arab and Jewish.

—*Ideology and Practice*, p. 1.

g. Was it necessary to create the State of Israel?

The State of Israel was formed . . . on part of the territory of Palestine. . . .

Throughout the whole history of its existence, Israel has been pursuing an aggressive, expansionist policy with respect to the neighboring Arab States.

—*Noveyshaya istoriya*
("Modern History," textbook for the 10th grade), p. 189.

Representatives of the Arab States point to the partition of Palestine as if it were a historic injustice. But one cannot agree with this point of view, if only because the Jewish people have been linked with Palestine for a long period of time in history. Moreover, we cannot ignore . . . the situation in which the Jewish people found themselves as a result of the last world war. . . . The Jews, as a nation, lost more than any other nation. Solving the Palestine question on the basis of its partition into two independent states will be of great historical significance, since a decision of this kind will satisfy the legitimate demands of the Jewish people, hundreds of thousands of whom . . . are still homeless. . . .

—From A. Gromyko's speech at the plenary session of the UN General Assembly on November 26, 1947. *Pravda*, no. 319 (November 30, 1947).

h. Who unleashed the 1948 War?

Almost immediately after the UN General Assembly passed the resolution on the Palestine question, as a result of the behind-the-scenes intrigues of the United States, Britain, and international Zionist circles, new and serious armed clashes were provoked in Palestine. At the beginning of 1948, these escalated into overt military actions.

On May 14, the British government "unexpectedly" proclaimed the end of the mandate in Palestine and the withdrawal of its troops from the country.

Beirut. May 15th. Tass. Lebanese newspapers report that the political committee of the Arab League, meeting in Damascus, delivered a note to the representatives of the United States and Britain. It informed their governments that the Arab countries had decided to send armed forces into Palestine on May 15.

Cairo, May 15th. Tass. Representatives of the Arab League have proclaimed in a press announcement that as of today all Arab countries are in a

. . . The first Arab-Israeli war (1948–1949) began within a matter of hours. Like Israel's subsequent acts of aggression in the Arab East, this war was unleashed with the direct assistance of world imperialism and Zionism.

> —*Ideology and Practice*, pp. 133–134.

In accordance with the UN resolution of November 20, 1947, two states were to exist on the territory of Palestine: Arab and Jewish. But the Zionists did not implement this decision . . . unleashing war on the Arabs in 1948–1949.

> —Romanenko, p. 13.

state of war with the Jews of Palestine.

> —*Pravda*, no. 137 (May 16, 1948).

New York. May 16th. Tass. According to a press report from Tel Aviv, the Egyptian, Transjordanian, Syrian, and Lebanese armies have invaded the Jewish state of Israel.

> *Pravda*, no. 138 (May 17, 1948).

New York. On May 22, in the Security Council, A. A. Gromyko expressed his "astonishment at the position of the Arab states," who sent troops into Palestine to "crush a struggle for national liberation."

> —*Pravda*, no. 145 (May 24, 1948).

Vienna. June 1st. Tass. The Milan correspondent of the newspaper *Welt am Abend* reports that according to information reaching Italy, former German officers and whole detachments of German soldiers are taking part in the military action in Palestine on the side of the Arab armed forces. There are units in the Lebanese army which are 60% German. According to correspondents, several "detachments" in the Jerusalem area are under the command of a former officer from Rommel's staff. Many officers from the German Afrika Korps are also fighting on the Arab side. A particularly large number of former Hitlerite officers are being used as instructors for Arab troops.

> —*Pravda*, no. 54 (June 2, 1948).

i. Did the Arabs want to "throw the Jews into the sea"?

Israeli Zionist policy is characterized by the basest Pharisaism. To conceal its aims while planning and carrying

The slogans which Shukeiry supplied with extraordinary facility (throw the Jews into the sea, etc.) were avowedly

out an attack on neighboring Arab countries, the Israel government cries to the whole world that "poor little Israel" is allegedly suffering all kinds of insults from its neighbors. Zionist propaganda insists that the Arabs wish to "destroy Israel," "to throw it into the sea".

—Soyfer, p. 117.

demagogic and harmful to the Palestinian resistance movement.

—Dmitriev, p. 58.

j. Who is to be blamed for the war in 1967 and the succeeding years?

On June 5, 1967, Israel's rulers began a war against the Arabs on the false pretext of "defending themselves against an impending act of agression." But they knew very well that neither Egypt nor any other Arab state had any intention of resorting to arms and starting a war, despite the rash statements made by some Arab and Palestinian leaders individually.

—*Ideology and Practice*, p. 140.

Still another most harsh and angry voice of the "Palestine program" is heard from Cairo. . . .

Essentially, this was a quasi-autonomous radio station controlled by the Palestine Liberation Organization. It maintained that Israel has no right to exist as a state . . . and continually summoned all Arabs to go to war against Israel. It predicted the day all Israelis would be driven into the sea, and when Palestinian lands would be returned to their original owners.

These broadcasts facilitated the dissemination of the belief in Israel and abroad that the Israelis had no other recourse but to attack first, otherwise they would be annihilated.

As a potent argument . . . the Israelis cited Nasser's declaration that the Arabs intended to "obliterate" the State of Israel. . . . More than all of the protracted verbal skirmishing between Israel and the Arabs, the use of this term by Nasser induced the overwhelming majority of persons in the West and especially intellectuals, to sympathize with Israel. When Israel launched an offensive on June 5, she had the sympathy of almost the entire population of Europe and the United States, where it was felt that Israel was under threat of attack.

—Aldridge, *Cairo*, pp. 274–275.

4. COSMOPOLITANISM

The Jew loves everything that is impersonal and cosmopolitan. At the same time, however, he is an extreme nationalist in regard to himself and his race.

—Sharapov, vol. 5, p. 37.

However, let us hope that regardless of how much the Jews and their sympathizers may preach cosmopolitanism, substituting it for the healthy sentiment of patriotism, they will not succeed in overcoming the normal person's love for his homeland.

—Balashev, p. 20.

5. FREEMASONRY

The Jews apparently invented Freemasonry for only one purpose: they are thirsting for the destruction of Christianity at the hand of their servants who are of Christian origin. Having shaken the church in France and Spain, they are now reaching Russia and Germany. The Jews dream openly of restoring their kingdom and of world domination.

—Mag, pp. 3, 26.

In German philosophy and culture, "the German spirit . . . is engaged in a constant struggle against the impersonality of Jewish Spinozaism."

—*Against Fascist Obscurantism and Demagogy*, p. 247.

The bigshot Masons in banking and . . . the Marxists are partners in the same world conspiracy, whose aim is to conquer the world.

—Feder, in *Germanikus*, p. 20.

The Jews, Freemasons, and other ideological enemies of National Socialism bear the responsibility for the war being waged against Germany at the present time. A concerted ideological struggle against these elements is . . .

Cosmopolitan critics have also struck at progressive tendencies in the field of Soviet art and sculpture. O. Beskin, A. Efros, A. Matsa, and others have disparaged the realist painters. They have called Russian art provincial and have done everything in their power to denigrate our classical art. They have beckoned artists toward decadent and pretentious floridity and extravagance, political indifference, and intellectual apathy.

—F. Golovenchenko, in *Bolshevik*, 1949, no. 3, p. 45.

Two thousand secret Masonic lodges that comprise the organization called B'nai B'rith ("The Sons of the Covenant"), which has about half a million members: "nominally it is Masonic and non-Zionist, but to all intents and purposes it is ultra-Zionist," writes the book's author [Begun].

—Yemelyanov, p. 189.

As early as the first half of the last century, political organizations of the

Freemasonry . . . has fallen under Judaic influence. It has been transformed into a strange organization which seeks to destroy the Christian way of life so that a universal Jewish kingdom may be established on its ruins.

—Nilus, p. 168.

a necessity. . . .

A special staff in the occupied territories has the right to search libraries, archives, and other ideological institutions, to look for the offending material that may be in them, and to confiscate it . . . for ideological activities.

—*Nuremberg Trial*, vol. 6, p. 50.

The peasant's natural animosity to the Jews, and to the Mason as the servitor of the Jews, must be exacerbated into a frenzy.

—Instructions for party workers of the National Socialist party, in *Brown Book*, p. 212.

Jewish bourgeoisie . . . appeared in the countries of the Old and the New World in the form of associations and orders of a Masonic character.

Among them, for example, is the secret Masonic order called B'nai B'rith, which has by now expanded into a world organization with more than four thousand branches and lodges in about fifty countries.

Its lodges were established illegally in Russia . . . and their membership included the most prominent bankers and businessmen . . . the Poliakovs, the Brodskys, the Ginsburgs, and others.

—*Ideology and Practice*, p. 201.

Part 3. THE JEWISH CHARACTER

Reactionaries and anti-Semites have become accustomed to think that they and Russia are one and the same thing. Everything they undertake is done for the glory of Russia. And if Europe regards them as savages because of their concoctions, it is not their fault; the Jews are to blame.

—Petrov, *Pravda i lozh o yevreyakh*, p. 12

The Zionists and their ideologists maintain that the Jews are the "chosen people," an exclusive, unique people. In their view, this people is superior and better than the remainder of mankind, who are considered secondrate, inferior creatures, worthy of contempt.

—Begun, p. 24.

Such insolent familiarity toward the Polish and other peoples obviously reflects the Judaic spirit of Zionist education.

—Begun, *Creeping Counterrevolution*, p. 64.

The insolence of the planners of a universal kahal . . .

—Ibid., p. 57.

1. THEIR ARROGANCE

They consider themselves more intelligent, more capable, and more talented than any other people. At every opportunity they look down on other peoples and regard them as their servants.

—Kulichev, *The Jewish State*, p. 4.

2. THEIR INSOLENCE, IMPUDENCE, UNDUE FAMILIARITY

Jewish insolence is not an accidental caprice, but the basic trait of the Judaic race.

—Rokotov, p. 78.

3. THEY ARE HYPOCRITES AND DISSEMBLERS

Our watchwords are "force" and "hypocrisy." . . . Violence must be a principle. Cunning and dissimulation must be the rule . . . Therefore, we must utilize bribery, deceit, and treachery.

—Demchenko, p. 64.

4. OPPRESSORS, PROVOCATEURS, AND BLACKMAILERS

Blackmail is just about their favorite activity.

—Shmakov, *Jews in History*, p. 53.

We know how difficult it would be for us now if Jews lived in every town today, secretly performing acts of sabotage, carrying on agitation and sowing unrest.

—Himmler, 1943, in *Nuremberg Trial*, vol. 7, p. 95.

5. THEIR CRUELTY

The Jews are cruel murderers and incendiaries.

—Kaluzhsky, p. 44.

The Jews cultivate a lust for money, cynicism, cruelty, and loathsome snobbery.

—Hitler, in Heiden, p. 54.

The entire religious ideology of the Jewish bourgeoisie is permeated with extreme hypocrisy.

—*Ideology and Practice*, p. 31.

Zionism makes extensive use of slanderous and hypocritical propagandist tricks.

—Yevseev, p. 127.

In the struggle against their political criminals, the Zionists resort . . . to blackmail and acts of provocation. . . . They base their . . . political struggle on violence; it is used by them and their hireling—groups of the lumpen proletariat and bands of gangsters.

—*Zionism: Theory and Practice*, p. 135.

Zionist plans, monstrous in their cruelty, include creating unbearable living conditions for all non-Jews, or exiling them.

—Modzhoryan, p. 53.

6. THEY ARE A CRIMINAL RACE WHICH HATES MANKIND

By virtue of their moral code, the Jews are a criminal race which hates mankind.

—Markov-2; speech at a
session of the 4th State
Duma, Stenographic account,
p. 2737.

The German people has not the slightest desire to tolerate hundreds of thousands of criminals on its soil. . . . At such a stage in our development, therefore, we are faced with the stringent need to eradicate the Jewish scum, exactly as we eradicate other criminals in our country—with fire and the sword.

—Extract from a Nazi
newspaper. Quoted in
*Kommunistichesky
Internatsional*, 1939, no. 1,
p. 102.

Violence, chauvinism, hatred of mankind are the preachings of Jewish racism, which, having been elevated to a cult in Israel long ago, is the official state policy.

—Yevseev, p. 113.

The Zionists summon Jews to ascend a "ladder" composed of the corpses of other persons, till they reach the rung that befits them.

—*Sionizm—otravlennoye
oruzhiye imperializma*
(hereafter: *Zionism—a
Poisoned Weapon*), p. 117.

Zionist morality is the morality of criminals, aggressors, haters of mankind, and murderers. . . .

—Begun, *Zionism and
Judaism*, p. 14.

7. THEY ARE SPIES

This sort of people is capable of absolutely everything, especially everything that is loathsome. If you need a spy, look for him among the Jews. If you need someone to smuggle something across the border, go to the Jews for that too.

—Neznachny, p. 193.

8. TRAITORS

Observations concerning Israel's power demonstrate that everything said about their treachery is invariably repeated in both the minor and major events of history.

—Shmakov, Jews in History, p. 14.

Espionage is the Zionists' real profession . . . The presence of a Zionist espionage network in various odd corners of the world is irrefutable evidence of the secret, and that means criminal . . . aims of the Zionists in dozens of different countries. Is this network not the "nervous system" which, according to M. Nordau, must involve the entire world and transmit signals to the Zionist "brain"?

—Begun, p. 131.

The struggle against the Jews is . . . a reliable weapon of the fifth column.

—Hitler, in Nuremberg Trial, vol. 7, p. 95.

In many cases the Zionists served as Hitler's "fifth column," and their international network was used to establish Nazi German domination of the world.

—Bolshakov, p. 28.

9. THE DREYFUS CASE

Seeing the origins of the problem in the stock-exchange regime which bore such worthy fruit in France as . . . the Dreyfus affair, Eugen Duhring wrote with captivating originality: . . . the Jews managed to inflate this planned Dreyfus affair into not simply a matter of state, but into a matter of major world importance. . . . The Dreyfus trial showed that once a Jew is arraigned, Jewry can conduct itself with the impudence of a most important and autocratic state, thereby entitling Jewry to shield their fellow tribesmen from the jurisdiction of other peoples.

. . . Having affronted the generals, cast a slur on the army, and humiliated France, the Kahal . . . demanded full exoneration from treason. The worldwide agitation of the Jews on behalf of Dreyfus is a fact unparalleled in history. . . . It may even be acknowledged that simply to mention the Kahal's triumph in the "Dreyfusiade" makes it no longer necessary to argue about the power which Jewry has achieved.

—Shamkov, Speech on the
Jewish question, pp. 27, 28,
29, 30.

. . . "hysterical activity on the part of Dreyfus' friends" . . . for many of them, the whole affair reduced itself to a question of injustice suffered by a Jew. At times it appeared that had Dreyfus not been a Jew, they would not have lifted a finger against injustice. Incidentally, bourgeois Jews, bankers, and businessmen contributed money to the campaign to have the Dreyfus case reexamined when the case was at its height; but they stopped supporting the Dreyfusards, who were democrats and socialists, when Dreyfus was acquitted. They were interested least of all in defending democracy and the Republic, the ideals of justice and law. They were inspired solely by Jewish nationalism.

—Molchanov, *Jaures*, p. 193.

Zionist propaganda tries to equate the Stern case to the odious Dreyfus and Beilis affairs. The latter have affixed themselves in world public opinion to the advantage of the Zionists.

—B. Antonov, in *Chelovek i
zakon*, 1977, no. 6, p. 28.

10. PROVOCATEURS AND MEMBERS OF UNDERGROUND ORGANIZATIONS. THEY CONDUCT SUBVERSIVE ACTIVITIES IN ALL COUNTRIES AND HAVE BEEN BETRAYING THE INTERESTS OF MILLIONS OF ORDINARY JEWS.

The prominent role of the Jews in the disturbances caused by our "liberation movement" was particularly obvious in the autumn of 1905. . . . they were the chief activists . . . in the meetings. Moreover, using red and black flags, they organized street demonstrations in all the towns. . . . The Jews, and especially their revolutionary association, the Bund, were the source of many murderous acts against higher and lower organs of governmental power.

—Alektrov, p. 128.

Arrest the Jews and tranquility will reign in the country.

—Heiden, p. 31.

At such a stage in the course of events, we would therefore be faced with the rigorous necessity of eradicating the Jewish underground . . .

—From the Nazi newspaper, in "SS v deystviy" (henceforth: SS in Action), 1960 ed., p. 133.

The Zionists conduct subversive anti-Communist and anti-Soviet activities . . . on a relatively independent basis, since at the same time they are also fulfilling their own purely Zionist aims.

—Begun, p. 57.

As early as those days, the Bundists were very skilled at frustrating the strikes of the workers.

—Bolshakov, p. 13.

They have rich experience and extremely "authoritative" instructors in all types of provocation, terrorist and subversive activities.

—Korneev, p. 5.

In the first days of the existence of Soviet power it conducted a struggle against the Zionist underground, which was working hand in hand with the counterrevolution.

—*Reactionary Nature of Zionism*, p. 105.

11. REVOLUTIONARIES OR COUNTERREVOLUTIONARIES?

During our revolution, Jews, almost to a man were in the ranks of the revolutionaries.

—Kulichev, p. 14.

The Jews think only about revolution . . . and every Jew . . . in his own sphere acts first and foremost with this end in view, namely, acts in a political way.

—Hitler, in Heiden, p. 38.

The total number of persons of Jewish nationality who held active counter-revolutionary views was much greater than the number of members of Zionist organizations.

—Korneev, p. 11.

12. COWARDS

What did the Jews prove to be on the battlefield? They were cowards who were the first to flee, demoralizing entire units and throwing them into disorder.

—Velikorossov, p. 34.

For the quintessential Jew, sacrifice and heroic deeds are unthinkable.

—Shmakov, *Jewish Pogrom in Kiev*, p. vi.

Had the Jews been alone in this world, they would have choked in the dirt, they would have tried to dupe and annihilate each other in a desperate struggle. But because of the cowardice, which results from their total lack of any capacity for self-sacrifice, this struggle would become a comedy.

—Hitler, in *Brown Book*, p. 212.

Particularly insolent toward unarmed and defenseless persons, Israeli warriors are easily given to panic and display cowardice in complex situations.

—Pokornyak, p. 127.

13. THE JEWS ARE PARASITES, AN EPIDEMIC, A PLAGUE

The Jews are a race of parasites, and not a manifestation of nationalism.

—Afterword to Frich's book, p. 44.

The Jews as an ethnic group, are by nature parasitic.

—Balashev, pp. 11–12.

International Jewish parasitic bank capital.

—Hitler, in *Revolyutsiya i natsionalnosti*, 1933, no. 1, p. 87.

A characteristic example of Streicher's "teachings" was the article in which

Israel stands out as its own sort of parasite state.

—Nikitina, in Begun, p. 22.

the Jews were called a plague and microbes, not human beings, but parasites, spreaders of disease.

—*Nuremberg Trial*, vol. 7, p. 463.

14. THEY MUST BE COMBATED LIKE AN EPIDEMIC

There are health centers for treatment of the body. But medical centers are just as necessary for the human spirit. Becoming Judaized is extremely dangerous.

—Afterword to Frich's book, p. 41.

Anti-Semitism is the equivalent of medical treatment; for us, anti-Semitism is a question of cleanliness.

—Himmler, in *Nuremberg Trial*, vol. 6, p. 612.

15. THEY ARE GREEDY LEECHES

Avarice, greed, predatoriness, perjury, and even murder . . . are in accord with the Law of God given to the Israelite nation through Moses.

—Diminsky, *Yevrei, ikh veroucheniye i pravoucheniye*, pp. 115, 116.

Workers of all classes unite in the common struggle of all workers against the pillagers.

—Slogan of the fascists, in *Sovershenno Sekretno*, p. 89.

The Zionists have created an extensive network of international organizations that has penetrated more than seventy countries in the world; it is like an epidemic which has not been brought under control in time.

—Romanenko, p. 10.

There really exists on earth a huge and powerful empire of Zionist financiers and industrialists. . . . If we tried to depict it with the usual means of pictorial art, it would obviously look like a sticky spider's web enmeshing a good half of the globe. At its center swarm blood-sucking spiders, lying in wait for their prey.

—Yevseev, p. 87.

16. DEBAUCHED

The Jews . . . constitute the real evil of our region. . . . At every step they violate social morality and the ideas of progress.

—Fliorkovsky, p. 90.

A real Jew finds personal decency and a sense of dignity repulsive.

—Shmakov, *Jewish Pogrom in Kiev.*

The Elders of Zion have also decided to introduce moral corruption, mainly by disguising Jewish women as French, Italian, and Spanish women, since these are the most proficient in introducing debauchery into people's morals.

—Nilus, p. 162.

The Jews . . . plan to destroy the purity of other races.

—Hitler, in Heiden, p. 38.

Streicher . . . founded his newspaper *Sturmer*, which achieved a huge circulation, thanks to his fondness for Jewish scandals that bordered on the pornographic.

—Heiden, p. 101.

As is attested by the Czechoslovak press, the arrival of the Moscow Bolshoi Theater, for example, was hardly mentioned. However, the arrival of the so-called American poet Allen Ginsberg . . . was turned into an orgy, while an embarrassed silence reigned about his lyrically homosexual "honey weeks."

—Begun, *Creeping Counterrevolution*, p. 146.

Comrade M. Wilner, Secretary General of the Israeli Communist party's Central Committee, declared: "Many people have been shaken by the story published in *Ha'aretz* about the most *kosher* [my emphasis—the author does not know the correct spelling, let along the meaning, of this word—R.O.] rabbis, who have ventured to organize striptease shows in the ritual baths, where women must wash themselves in the presence of three rabbis, as a part of the procedure for accepting Judaism. Of course, I support those who have condemned outrageous methods of converting people to Judaism."

—*Aims and Methods*, p. 37.

17. THE JEWS HAVE ALWAYS PROSPERED AT THE EXPENSE OF OTHER PEOPLES

The Jews have obviously prospered to this day, despite the inequality to which they are subject, i.e., despite certain rather substantial but prudent impediments the Russian government erected long ago to shield the indigenous portion of the population from the Jewish.

—Demchenko, p. 29.

About Hitler: "He liked Vienna still less. There were so many Jews scurrying around, and they had much more money than everyone else."

—From a German school textbook, in *Internatsionalnaya literatura,* 1939, no. 1, p. 204.

While there were legal infringements on them [the Jews—R.O.] in tsarist Russia, they exceeded the surrounding population in their socioeconomic development.

—Begun, *Creeping Counterrevolution,* p. 17.

A significant number of Americans of Jewish origin are owners and managers of firms and companies, including some of the largest. . . . The income of American Jews is 40–50% higher than that of all other ethnic groups in the United States.

—Laptev, in *Reactionary Nature of Zionism,* p. 52.

18. THEY ARE EXPLOITERS, LEASEHOLDERS, INNKEEPERS, AND TENANT FARMERS, LIVING AT THE EXPENSE OF THE SURROUNDING POPULATION.

The members of the "chosen" people . . . still continue to "help their good fortune along" by buying up the estates of the goyim. Moreover, with the assistance of "conscientious expropriators," proprietors who have not yet been robbed are blackmailed by the Kahal into leasing their estates to Jews.

—Shmakov, *Jewish Pogrom in Kiev,* p. xxxi.

Millions of industrious people must sacrifice the fruit of their labor to the Jewish Mammon.

—*Istorik-Marksist,* 1932, nos. 1–2, p. 94.

. . . economic exploitation, which is personified by grasping Jewish leaseholders, tenant farmers, usurers, and innkeepers.

—Begun, *Creeping Counterrevolution,* pp. 85–86.

19. CHRISTIAN MERCHANTS ARE UNABLE TO COMPETE WITH THEM

Utilizing the patronage of the *voyevods** and their deputies . . . the Jews quickly overcame the Christian merchants and artisans.

—Alektrov, p. 43.

This inequality was explained by the inability of Christian competitors to withstand the Jewish merchant, guided by his centuries-old experience in the struggle for world markets by his Kahal connections and the help given by one Jew to another.

—Begun, *Creeping Counterrevolution*, p. 17.

20. THEY HAVE SEIZED CONTROL OF ALL THE BANKS

L. S. Poliakov took possession of the Moscow Land Bank, which was established neither by him nor for him. He then proceeded to "help his good fortune along," as the center of gravity for many other members of this "victimized people." . . .

In addition to L. Poliakov's family, entire groups of such "Muscovites" as the Wolfsons, Tubentals, Gurvitches, Lifshitzes, . . . Tuflins, Shapiros, Lipetzkers, and various others were to be seen on the lists of shareholders for May 11, 1908.

—Shmakov, *Delo Soyedinennogo Banka*, pp. 6, 9.

. . . "rapacious capital," the colossal salaries of the Jewish directors of large banks—all this was a favorite theme of fascist propaganda.

—"Mirovoye khozyaystvo i mirovaya politika," 1933, No. 9, p. 9.

In 1914, 40 percent of the directors of St. Petersburg banks were persons of Jewish nationality.

—Korneev, p. 11.

Baron Horace Ginsburg . . . the Moscow banker Poliakov, the millionaires Warshavsky, Wisotsky, Gorvitz, Kogan, Pavelberg, Sliosberg, and others, were typical representatives of the financial oligarchy in Russia. The Jewish bourgeoisie exercised considerable influence upon the Russo-Asiatic, Russo-English, Russo-French, Azov-Don, Siberian, and Warsaw banks, and had complete control of the Odessa Merchant Bank, the Volga Insurance Company, and other consolidated companies.

—Begun, *Creeping Counterrevolution*, p. 17.

---

*Voyevoda: the commander of an army or governor of a province in ancient Russia.

20a. THE SOURCES FROM WHICH SOVIET "RESEARCHERS" DRAW THEIR INFORMATION
(Digression No. 2)

Brafman

The Jews have boldly advanced along the path of peaceful conquest of the fruits of the indigenous population's productive labor and of the country's natural wealth. At the present time they are the total masters of the country; at the very least, they occupy the most advantageous and most fortunate position amidst the indigenous classes. . . .

We cite here . . . statistical data concerning the economic activity of the Jews in only three provinces in the Southwestern Region: Kiev, Podoliya, and Volyn. Taken from official sources, this data is cited by Mr. Chubinsky in his *Studies of the Southwestern Region.* There are 819 estates in the provinces of Kiev, Podoliya, and Volyn leased to Jews. But according to Chubinsky, these figures merely indicate the number of estates leased by Jews on the basis of formal agreements. A considerable number of estates, however, are leased by Jews on the basis of informal agreements. . . . They believe that if after a certain period of time, the Jews are permitted to acquire real estate, they will merely be required to formalize the transaction, which will

Begun

According to data in the Jewish magazine *Voskhod,* by the end of the nineteenth century the Jews in Russia comprised 80 percent of the merchants in the first and second guilds in the provinces of Byelorussia, 82 percent in the provinces of Lithuania, and 63 percent in the Southwestern provinces.*

In the three provinces of the Southwestern Region (Kiev, Podoliya, and Volyn) according to the evidence of P. Chubinsky, a member of the Imperial Geographic Society who conducted the investigation, the entire wholesale trade in bread, sugar, cattle, wool, and leather was concentrated in the hands of Jews. . . . In the provinces of the Southwestern Region of Russia, the moneybags acquired estates as their own property through surrogates who were bound by promissory notes.

—Begun,† *Creeping Counterrevolution,* pp. 15–16.

---

*At this point *Voskhod* no. 4 of 1894 is cited. This is a fabrication. No such information appears in this issue of *Voskhod.*

†Vladimir Yakovlevich Begun lives in Minsk and teaches at the Byelorussian State University. He began his activities in 1972 with the publication in Minsk of the pamphlet *Zionism and Judaism.* His infamous book *The Creeping Counterrevolution* was published in Minsk by the Byelorus Publishing House in 1974. It was subsequently reprinted twice in Moscow by the Molodaya Guardiya Press, in 1977 and 1979, under the title *The Invasion without Arms.* In 1977, he defended his dissertation for the degree of Candidate in Philosophical Sciences in the Byelorussian State University. The subject of the dissertation was "International Zionism—Ideological and Political Weapon of Anti-Communism (A critique of the ideology and methods of subversive activities)."

cost them next to nothing. And if the nominal owner is opposed to this, the bill of exchange need merely be presented for redemption and the nominal owner will gain nothing.

—Y. Brafman,* *Book of the Kahal,* pp. 141, 142.

---

*Yakov Alexandrovich Brafman (1825–1879), a Jew by birth, was born in the province of Minsk. Converted to Christianity, taught classical Hebrew at the Minsk Ecclesiastical Seminary. He was the author of a series of memoirs, pamphlets, and books, the best-known of which, *The Book of the Kahal,* appeared in three editions. In this work Brafman gave a distorted picture of Jewry's way of life, traditions, and legislative establishment. The book consists of two parts: Brafman's own writings, and a collection of Kahal decisions. *The Book of the Kahal* was accepted without question in the anti-Semitic circles in Russia and served as a source for their pogrom literature.

21. THEIR PERNICIOUS SPIRIT

Their unbelief, unscrupulousness, and highly peculiar Semitic turn of mind produces a very nihilistic, corrupting effect.

—Balashev, p. 12.

Perverting everything noble and great, this hostile and irrevocably depraved tribe . . . perverted the very concept of freedom long ago. It has turned this concept into an arbitrary rule, so that the Jews can commit crimes with impunity.

—Shmakov, *Jewish pogrom in Kiev*, p. 10.

The pernicious Jewish spirit has paralyzed both the strength and the will of the German people.

—*The SS in Action*, p. 181.

The Jews . . . have disappeared from Europe, and their eastern reserve, whence the Jewish plague has been infecting the nations of Europe for centuries, has ceased to exist.

—Streicher, November 4, 1943, in *The Nuremberg Trial, vol. 7.*

Zionist morality is the morality of criminals.

—*Begun, Zionism and Judaism*, p. 14.

Judeo-Zionist activists attach more importance to persuading non-Jews of the "absolute superiority of the Jewish national genius" than to working among their own coreligionists.

—*Ideology and Practice*, p. 29.

22. THEY SOW POISON AND CORRUPTION

The Jews sow the seeds of decay and ruin everywhere.

—Shmakov, *Jews in History*, p. 21.

They sow "poison and corruption" stealthily, imperceptibly, and hypocritically:

—Begun, p. 54.

23. THEIR ATTITUDE TO WOMEN

The Talmud propagates a low opinion of half of the entire Jewish people—of women. A host of maxims scattered throughout the Talmud are meant to inspire women with a sense of their insignificance and to inculcate absolute submissiveness on their part.

—Grinevich, p. 13.

A member of the Nazi party, Dr. Hadlach, maintained that "the oppression of women springs from the Jewish spirit."

—Heiden, p. 177.

In the name of God, the Bible and the Talmud not only sanctify and "provide grounds" for the servile status of women, who do not enjoy equal rights with men and are dependant on them; these works also portray women as inferior, base, perfidious, and depraved beings.

—Avshalumova, p. 4.

24. THEIR HATRED OF CHILDREN

The religious barbarity, which permeates the Talmud and the ignorance of the Jewish masses reach a pinnacle in the custom of using the blood of Christian children.

—Grinevich, p. 38.

Notes of this kind would appear in the *Russian Banner:* "The Jewish New Year is approaching. We must protect our children more effectively so that those creatures do not arrange some bloody surprise under cover of wartime conditions."

—Bomash, stenographic account of the 4th State Duma, p. 1130.

Secret. May 1943. To the Head of Security and the SD Gruppenführer SS, Dr. Kaltenbrunner

Dear Kaltenbrunner!

We must immediately appoint people who can obtain records of the legal proceedings and the police reports from England about the disappearance of a child. Appropriate short news items could then be broadcast over our transmitters stating that a child was missing in such-and-such a place, and that it is probably a question of Jewish ritual murder.

I daresay that all in all, by using anti-Semitic propaganda on a broad scale in English, and perhaps even in Russian, and by publicizing ritual murders in our propaganda, we might be able to stir up a great degree of anti-Semitism all over the world. . . .

Heil Hitler!

Yours, Himmler

—*The SS in Action,* pp. 228–229.

The first bullet piercing the glass hit a vase. Fragments of crystal made a tinkling sound as they flew in all directions. The oldest girl, a seven-year-old, shouted, "Get down!" The younger children threw themselves to the floor. The gun went on firing at the Soviet diplomatic residence in New York. Shooting at the children with a combat rifle was Isaac Yaroslavich, a thug belonging to the pro-fascist organization, the Jewish Defense League. This took place on October 20, 1971. It was repeated on February 27, 1976. It can happen again, any day.

—Korneev, in *Ogonyok,* 1977, no. 5, p. 27.

The criminal leveled a gun at the children as they watched a television program.

—Soyfer, p. 64.

The "Judaizing" of the younger generation is advanced as one of the leading ideological aim of Zionism. . . . It is to be achieved by reinforcing the so-called Jewish consciousness of every Jew.

—Nikitina, in *Reactionary Nature of Zionism*, p. 120.

In the Zionist indoctrination of youth . . . active use is made of a specialized system of organizing Zionist education. . . . It does not permit the Jew to escape its influence from the moment of birth onwards until his death. In particular, there are even a number of specialized organizations involved in this which often at first have no direct connection with Zionism.

—Bolshakov, pp. 130–131.

25. THEY CORRUPT THE YOUTH

Their unscrupulousness and highly peculiar Semitic turn of mind produces a very nihilistic, corrupting effect, particularly on the less-stable youth. It poisons them morally for their entire lives.

—Balashev, p. 12.

26. THEIR EXTERNAL APPEARANCE

In G. Gunter's book *The Racial Characteristics of the Jewish People*, students study the Asiatic type of Jew from the portrait of S. Zweig, the northeastern Jewish type from the portrait of H. Heine, and the half-Jew from the portrait of I. Mechnikov.

—*Against Fascist
Obscurantism and
Demagogy*, p. 165.

A book entitled *The Jews Are Looking at You* has been published by Reichstag Deputy von Leers. The words "Not hanged" have been placed under the photographs of many representatives of German spiritual life. In the book, Chaplin is characterized as "a boring and altogether repulsive and fidgety little Jew."

—*Brown Book*, pp. 265, 279.

T. Kichko's book *Judaism without Embellishment* appeared in Kiev in 1963. The illustrations in this book have been produced in the spirit of the Nazi weekly *Der Stürmer.*

It even has a specific outward appearance . . . [the newspaper, the *Jewish Press*—R.O.]. The title of this newspaper is printed above a schematic representation of three parchment scrolls [an allusion to the sacred Jewish scrolls] . . . The inside pages are bedecked with six-pointed stars and photographs of bearded rabbis. In short, the *Jewish Press* has an explicit countenance with all the characteristic Jewish-nationalistic features.

—Begun, p. 104.

27. THEIR PEOPLE. ROTHSCHILD
   (Digression No. 3)

a. *An Involuntary Comparison*

H. Chamberlain

All the wars of the nineteenth century depended, in an extremely peculiar way, on Jewish financial operations. This is the case beginning with Napoleon's Russian campaign and Nathan Rothschild, who was present as an observer at the Battle of Waterloo, and ending with the enlistment of the Bleichreder family by Germany and of Alphonse Rothschild by France at the peace talks of 1871, and the "Commune" as well. In the opinion of everyone with acumen, this represented Judeo-Napoleonic machination from start to finish.

—pp. 21–22

Skurlatov

As early as the eighteenth century, subsidiaries of the well-known Rothschild banking house had wormed their way into the principal capitals of Europe. During the Napoleonic wars the Rothschilds financed both France and its enemies. . . . When the fate of Europe was being decided at the Battle of Waterloo, Rothschild emissaries, from both Paris and London, were keeping a constant watch on the battle. In both capitals the Rothschild banks were awaiting advance news about the outcome of the battle, the signal that would enable them to determine who their competitors were to be in the stock-market game.

—pp. 31–32

Korneev

The London banker Nathan Rothschild established a very extensive espionage network. It operated against Bonaparte, although even Napoleon in his turn had used the business correspondence of Jewish financiers on various occasions to obtain regular intelligence reports from London along with bills of exchange.

—pp. 5–6

b. *A Strange Contradiction*

Rothschild was sent to the gas chamber to enrich Krupp.

—Manchester, p. 278.

During the Second World War Reichsführer Heinrich Himmler played consummately the role of guardian angel for the Rothschild family.

—Yevseev, p. 93.

28. THEY COMMIT ARSON AGAINST THEIR OWN PROPERTY

In the Pomeranian town of Neusteten, a synagogue went up in flames. Thus the signal was given for pogroms (at that time, too, a "national insurrection" began with arson); charges were then brought, not against the real culprits, but . . . against the Jews. It was alleged that they had set fire to their temple themselves, out of revenge.

—*Brown Book*, p. 211.

29. THEY KILL EACH OTHER

The Kahal rules the community in a despotic manner, demanding from it absolute, slavish obedience. Woe to him who dares to disobey; the Kahal will not even hesitate to condemn him to death.

—Grinevich, p. 27.

30. THEY ARE THE ENEMIES OF ALL NATIONS

In the Talmud the Jews are ineluctably inculcated with the utmost loathing and ill-will towards all . . . peoples.

—Diminsky, *Issledovaniye o Talmude*, pp. 64—65.

. . . this race, "which is actually the enemy of every national state."

—Hitler, in Heiden, p. 93.

The Zionist leaders use not merely words to create and maintain artificial hotbeds of anti-Semitism. Members of Zionist organizations set fire to synagogues, defile Jewish cemeteries, and carry out other acts of provocation; such actions are instantaneously utilized by the Zionist propaganda machine, which raises a heart-rending hue and cry about the threat to Jewish life and property in this or that country.

—*Zionism: Theory and Practice*, p. 166.

When organizing anti-Soviet acts of provocation, in order to assure the success of their plan, the Zionists sacrifice the lives of their own cohorts. These are often persons occupying rather high positions in the Zionist hierarchy.

—Yevseev, p. 155.

Zionism appeared in the arena of history . . . to set people against people, to make them hound each other.

—Begun, *Creeping Counterrevolution*, p. 13.

31. THEY DETEST THE COUNTRIES IN WHICH THEY LIVE

As a result of their moral color blindness, they have no sympathy for the national spirit of the nations in which they live. At times, they are even hostile to it.

—Afterword to Frich's book, p. 37.

The Jews of the entire world want to destroy Germany!

—Action Committee of the NSDAP, in The SS in Action, p. 190.

The Jews are the age-old enemies of the German people, and must be annihilated.

—Himmler, in The SS in Action, p. 233.

World Zionism has waged a bitter struggle against the USSR, against the entire world Communist and workers' movement.

—Soyfer, p. 78.

During what will soon be the eighty years of its existence, political Zionism has proved to be an opponent of all progressive movements . . . the most vicious and consistent enemy of the Soviet state.

—Nisses, p. 8.

32. THEY SLANDER THE COUNTRIES IN WHICH THEY LIVE

The Jews are already jeering maliciously at the whole of Russia.

—Butmi, Oblichitelnye rechi.

At the present time, the Jews are really hounding Germany. Whenever we read of attacks against Germany, they have been devised by the Jews. Both before and during the war, the Jewish stock exchange and Marxist press deliberately aroused hatred against Germany.

—Hitler, Mein Kampf, in Revolyutsiya i natsionalnosti, 1933, no. 1, p. 87.

Unbridled slander against the Soviet Union by the Zionists has spread over the entire world, with the active support of the imperialists of a number of countries and the reactionary circles of the United States.

—Soyfer, p. 78.

33. THEY ARE THE AGENTS OF ANGLO-AMERICAN IMPERIALISM

By instigating internal disturbances, the Jewish Zionists paralyze the resistance within Russia to the intrigues of British foreign policy. . . . Hence, Jewish Zionism . . . is a well-organized, widespread, and traitorous secret agency in Russia . . . for English foreign policy.

—Butmi, *Oblichitelnye rechi.*
Frankmassonsto i
gosudarstvennaya izmena, p.
95.

The Jewish problem affects the interests of the Axis powers (in foreign policy).

—*Anatomiya voyny,* p. 377.

Analyzing the facts, we see the real mainsprings of international Zionism. We see who finances and inspires both Israel's acts of aggression against the Arab countries and the anti-Communist, anti-Soviet organizations. It is the huge monopolies and banks of the United States and other capitalist countries.

—*Reactionary Nature of*
Zionism, p. 17.

34. THEY ARE THE STOOGES OF THE USSR AND NAZI GERMANY

With astonishing cooperation, democracy and Marxism have managed to ignite a reckless and incomprehensible hatred between the Germans and Russians. . . . Who could be interested in inciting and baiting these nations in this way? The Jews.

—Hitler, in Heiden, p. 92.

The Zionists exploited the anti-Semitic policy of the Nazi regime established in Germany in 1933. This was not done merely to achieve specific Zionist aims . . . (the Zionists used every possible means to incite fascism against the USSR) but also to discredit anti-Zionist propaganda.

—Bolshakov, "*Kritika sionisma*
v sovetskoy istoriografii," in
Voprosy istorii, 1973, no. 9,
p. 79.

35. ALL THE NATIONS HAVE RESCUED THEM
(DIGRESSION NO. 4)

a. Why did they rescue traitors?

Thousands of times the Zionists have painted a picture of the sufferings which befell the Jews of Western Europe [?—R.O.] during the World War. Time and again they have shaken the world with the number of Jewish victims. They like to remain silent only about the hundreds of thousands of Jews who managed to survive under the most difficult conditions.

—Semenyuk, p. 95.

During the war . . . many Zionists collaborated with the Nazis. . . . They secretly pursued their aims at the expense of those who were fighting against fascist tyranny.

—Skurlatov, p. 57.

The Zionists helped expose persons of Jewish nationality among the population, surrendered them to the fascists, and took part in the mass extermination of Jews. . . . In a number of countries, the Zionists served as the Wermacht's fifth column. Under the guise of victims of German fascism, they infiltrated the governmental apparatus in neutral states and in the countries of the anti-Hitler coalition and passed on secret information to the Abwehr. . . . The Gestapo's Zionist agents infiltrated the ranks of the resistance fighters and helped the fascists to finish them off.

—Soyfer, p. 50.

The Zionists doomed the Jews, including children, to death in the gas chambers, whereas Soviet soldiers rescued the children who were threatened with death.

—Soyfer, p. 24.

b. Which Jews were Saved by the fascists and the Zionists? An Account of Falsification

The persecution was not directed against individual Jews. . . . The annihilation of the entire Jewish people was intended.

—*Nuremberg Trial*, vol. 1, p. 300.

Soviet authors

This material . . . is incontrovertible evidence of the fact that a secret understanding existed between the Zionists and the Nazis. In accordance with this understanding, individual Jews in the Czech population were removed from the transports which were headed for the death camps. Such per-

Documents

Early in the morning of November 10, 1938, Heydrich sent a telegram to all Gestapo and SD offices. This telegram gave instructions for organizing pogroms the very same day and for arresting as many Jews as the prisons could hold, especially *rich Jews*. The telegram emphasized that only healthy

sons were dispatched to Palestine or to other countries. Included among these "chosen" persons . . . were active champions and officials of the Zionist organization along with *Jewish capitalists*. . . . The "chosen" group also included religious leaders and representatives of the *bourgeois* intelligentsia leadership. . . . At no time were representatives of the *poorest* Jewish working-class strata included among the "chosen." The active adepts of Zionism and the bourgeoisie saved themselves at the cost of the lives of tens of thousands *poverty-stricken* Jews . . . The Jewish *bourgeoisie* in occupied Poland was guided by the similar principle of "saving the cream of the nation," by sacrificing the indigent classes.

—Semenyuk, p. 94.

The Germans took a number of Zionists in Lvov and created the so-called Judenrat. It was transformed by the Germans into an intelligence organization. . . . The Zionists compiled lists and sent the *poor* to their deaaths. They did not touch the *rich*.

—Soyfer, p. 45.

Jews and those not too old were to be arrested.

—From the verdict of the International Tribunal, in *Nuremberg Trial*, vol. 7, p. 418.

Preparations must be made to arrest twenty to thirty thousand Jews in the new Germany. *Rich* Jews should be selected first.

—From Gestapo Instructions, in *The SS in Action*, p. 132.

I am proposing to the Führer that instead of executing a hundred Frenchmen, the latter should be replaced by hundreds of *Jewish bankers and lawyers*. It is the Jews of London and New York who are inciting the French Communists to commit these acts of violence. It would be extremely equitable if the members of this race were to pay for this. *Not ordinary Jews*, but the leading Jews in France must answer for this.

—*Nuremberg Trial*, vol. 4, p. 668.

c. Who actually saved the Jews?

> An anti-Polish slander campaign, unprecedented in scope, was unleashed throughout the world in 1967–1968. It sought to prove that not merely the Hitlerites were guilty of murdering Jews, that others too, and the Poles in particular, had betrayed them to the Nazis.
>
> —*Ideology and Practice*, p. 98.

Soviet authors

The real saviors of many of the Jews of Lvov from death were the Soviet partisans. . . . A great deal was done by the Polish Communists to save the Jews.
—Soyfer, p. 46.

During the fascist terror, persecuted Jews who had been betrayed or left to the mercy of fate by the Jewish bourgeoisie and international Jewish organizations were protected and often rescued by the oppressed peoples of Europe. . . . Thousands of Jews found salvation with the partisans and were hidden by the Byelorussian, Ukrainian, and Russian populations.
—Semenyuk, p. 96.

Even in Germany itself, Communists, anti-fascists, and progressive workers came to the aid of the victims of the Nazi terror. . . . In Berlin alone, German anti-fascists hid and saved approximately three to four thousand Jews.
—Semenyuk, p. 97.

Documents

In Rovno . . . the ghetto was surrounded by a large detachment of the SS and . . . the Ukrainian police. Spotlights around and inside the ghetto were then switched on. Four- to six-man groups of SS and police burst into the houses.
—*Nuremberg Trial*, vol. 6, p. 179.

When the Baltic countries were seized, the local forces of anti-Semitism were urged to organize pogroms against the Jews. . . . Special detachments in Lithuania . . . a detachment of volunteers from Latvia, and sections of the Latvian auxiliary police force executed these orders on a broad scale. . . . During the liquidation of the Jews in Slutsk, German police officers and Lithuanian volunteers in particular acted with indescribable cruelty.
—*Nuremberg Trial*, vol. 1, pp. 304–305.

d. Are Jewish lives worth ten thousand lorries; or, the "righteous" indignation of "decent" people

Soviet authors

Himmler hoped to obtain military supplies from his enemies in the West, particularly Britain and the United States, with the aid of Zionist organizations. Such supplies would enable

Documents

The administrative committee sought to establish contact with Eichmann in order to try to change the fate of the Hungarian Jews. I myself arranged this contact with Eichmann. . . . He

Nazi Germany to continue the war on the Eastern Front. *The Zionist leaders entered into a shameful compact with the butchers* behind the people's back. Their actions merely strengthened the Nazi machinery of destruction and thereby prolonged the blood-letting.

—Semenyuk, p. 46.

The Second World War branded them with a new mark of betrayal. The fact is well known to the entire world and Soviet press that Rudolf Kastner, the leader of the Hungarian Zionists, had a secret agreement with the Hitlerites, *which helped the latter to send thousands of Jews to the crematoria in exchange for saving the lives of a few moneybags and Zionist activists.*

—Begun, *Creeping Counterrevolution*, p. 173.

1944. Rudolf Kastner, leader of the Hungarian Zionists, *makes a shameful bargain with the Nazi Eichmann.* In gratitude for Eichmann's permission to send a few families of prominent Zionists [?—R.O.] and rich Jews to Palestine, Kastner sacrificed about half a million Hungarian Jews, who were sent to the gas chambers *with his help.*

—Yevseev, p. 139.

was compelled very much against his will to transmit these proposals to Himmler. Himmler appointed Standartenführer Becher to participate in further negotiations. Becher and Dr. Kastner subsequently met with the committee's representative. From the very beginning Eichmann tried to wreck these talks. Before any concrete results could be achieved he gave priority to the creating of a fait accompli, i.e., the sending of as many Jews as possible to Auschwitz.

—From the interrogation of SS Hauptsturmfuhrer Wisliceny, in *Nuremberg Trial*, vol. 4, p. 723.

Becher conducted negotiations with representatives of the Western powers about an exchange of concentration-camp prisoners for lorries. To free the West from the fear that these vehicles might be used against its own armies, Becher proposed equipping them with a special device for use on the broad plains of Russia. Becher also tried to barter scarce industrial raw materials for the "live goods" from the concentration camps. When giving this evidence, the former Gestapo chief [Kaltenbrunner—R.O.] *burned with "righteous" indignation. He, you see, had always been perturbed by these commercial operations* of Himmler and Becher *which produced "losses" for the Reich's prestige abroad."*

—Poltorak, *Nyurnbergsky epilog,* p. 446.

36. BUT SOMETIMES THERE ARE DECENT ONES AMONG THEM

It is astonishing that every anti-Semite personally knows many good Jews, but says that the exception only proves the rule.

—I. Tolstoy, p. 6.

Part of our program is the extermination of the Jews. And we are doing this. . . . Yet here they come—eighty thousand worthy Germans, each with his "decent Jew." . . . All the others are parasites, but this Jew is A-1.

—From a speech by Himmler, 1941, in *Nuremberg Trial,* vol. 6, p. 612.

We National Socialists are only fighting those Jews who are connected with bolshevism. We have nothing against decent Jews.

—Hitler, 1930, in *Oktyabr,* 1932, no. 10, p. 93.

Of course it is *not at all* true that every American Jew supports Israel's policy of aggression and Zionism in its entirety. However . . . until now the Zionists have succeeded in keeping a *large majority* of their coreligionists under their control.

—*Aims and Methods,* p. 54.

"Zionist" and "Jew" are two different concepts because all Jews are by no means under the influence of Zionism. Even in the United States the majority of Jews are not Zionists.

—Soyfer, p. 70.

Part 4. THE ORGANIZATION, TRADITIONS, RITES, AND CUSTOMS OF THE JEWS

1. THE UNIVERSAL KAHAL*

The Kahal is the watchful eye of the Jewish people. It viligantly pursues Jewry's national interests, and assumes responsibility for the defense of these interests. The Kahal has elaborated its own particular national crite-

The Judaic God promised his chosen ones "a land of great and fine cities which you did not build, houses full of good things which you did not provide, rock-hewn cisterns which you did not hew, and vineyards and olive-

---

*Kahal—literally "society," "community"; conducted the internal administration and religious affairs of the Jews in the Pale. It was abolished in 1844 [in Russia]. In the imagination of anti-Semites of all times, however, it has continued to exist as an operative scarecrow that threatens the existence of the goyim.

groves which you did not plant" (Deuteronomy 6:10–11). In short, "you shall occupy the territory of nations greater and more powerful than you. Every place where you set the soles of your feet shall be yours" (Deuteronomy 11:23–24).

Do Zionist leaders regard this promise of world domination* as ancient folklore? They should, since the history of mankind is replete with examples indicative of the fatuity and extreme danger of such ideas. The Zionists, however, choose to ignore the lessons of history. They interpret the prescriptions of the Torah as a battle plan. In practice this is reflected in the struggle for the status of "the universal Jewish nation," centered in Israel with a dual loyalty on the part of the Jews beyond its borders. . . . There are no similar examples of this in the world wherein a given state considers another country's citizens as its own and imposes its ideology and policies on them heedless of the

rion regarding all measures undertaken by the governments of nonbelievers; all such measures may or may not be taken seriously. It is obvious that the Kahal does not contemplate any overt resistance to the governments of nonbelievers. Nevertheless the Jewish community's two-thousand-year history is for this community a graphic indication that one must not lose heart, that even a secret struggle achieves all of the desired results. . . . Thanks to similar successful maneuvers by its representatives the Judaic kingdom has survived till now, and has always emerged the victor, even after the most serious conflicts with the nonbelieving power wherein it pleased God to settle His chosen people.

—Brafman, pp. 149–150.

The Kahal . . . has absolute power over the Jews. The Jews are nothing without the Kahal. It seizes control of entire countries, enmeshes entire peo-

*In Deuteronomy the question is not one of world domination; this is Begun's usual mendacity, which presumes the Soviet reader's ignorance of the Bible. The point in question is the movement through Jordan and God's granting the Jews the land "from the wilderness to the Lebanon and from the River, the river Euphrates, to the western sea" (Deuteronomy 11:24). Begun did not quote the entire verse, since it would deny him his precious "world domination."

will of these citizens and the laws of other states. The effrontery of the planners of the universal *Kahal* [the author's underlining] has reached the point of their considering it possible to proclaim the prosecution of whomever they wish and wherever they wish. As early as March 1972, it was clear that the Israeli authorities forced through the Knesset an amendment to the country's Penal Code which extended Israeli jurisdiction . . . to the entire globe. Now, according to this amendment, the Tel Aviv secret service can "legally" abduct a citizen of any country, transfer him to Israel and try(!!) him for committing an act "detrimental to the security or economy of Israel."

—Begun, pp. 41–43.

ples. The Kahal unites the Jews and multiplies their power tenfold.
—Velikorossov, p. 24.

2. A STATE WITHIN A STATE (NATION WITHIN A NATION)

In our country, the Jews living in their Pale of Settlement constitute a "state within a state." They have their own administrative and juridical bodies, local government based on nationality, and a state whose center is outside Russia, abroad, whose supreme governing body is the Alliance Israélite Universelle in Paris.

—Brafman, *Book of the Kahal*, quoted from Aksakov, vol. 3, p. 508.

Our Jews . . . lead their own exclusive life and pursue aims that are alien to the rest of society. They comprise a secret and powerful community which rules its members despotically and imposes antisocial laws. Thus it represents, as it were, a state within a state.

—Grinevich, p. 26.

Ostensibly the Jewish state does not even have its own territory. . . . This being the case, the Jews are not restricted by the borders of any one country; spread all over the earth, they presume an indivisible possession of it, with all the goyim as draft animals.

—Demchenko, p. 16.

Developing the concept of dual loyalty, the "omnipresence" of Israel, the Zionists were and still are aware that unless it comes under the control of Jewish bankers, no real national government will ever waive its sovereignty and legalize a "state within a state," or create an autonomous and alien national community which accepts the authority of a center located abroad.

—Begun, p. 42.

One of the fundamentals of Zionist ideology is the thesis about the "exclusiveness" of the historical destiny of the Jews. The Zionists maintain that although the Jews are scattered throughout the world, they have invariably preserved their religion and uniqueness, their customs and traditions. Therefore they are a "nation within a nation," an alien body in the organism of the states in which they reside.

—Soyfer, p. 15.

In the programs of the Jewish parties, the point at issue was "cultural-national" and "national-personal" autonomy, and this was their objective:

"Liberation of Jewry" ideologically and politically, the formation of a distinctive state within a state that would be guaranteed by the laws of the country and serve the exploiting, chauvinistic aspirations of the communal leadership.

—Begun, p. 81.

For the Jewish bourgeoisie and servitors of the cult, isolation of the Jews in the ghetto was a convenient means of keeping a rein on the Jewish poor and getting rich at their expense.

—Bolshakov, p. 8.

You consider circumcision a necessary operation, because in this way a Jew's body is marked for his entire life in a way which distinguishes him from other peoples. Thus you favor the estrangement of people and not their mutual friendship.

—Altshuller, p. 106.

3. THE GHETTO

With us it is not without reason that the majority of aliens isolate themselves in their "ghettos."

—Leontovich, p. 28.

To satisfy without hindrance the indicated proclivity [corruption of the goyim—R.O.], the separateness of the Jewish tribe was contrived, first of all; no one was to penetrate into its midst and reveal what it was doing.

—Nilus, p. 163.

4. CIRCUMCISION

Hundreds and thousands of Jewish infants lose their lives because of the barbarous act of circumcision, whose performance . . . entails an obvious danger to life. . . . In recent years *Voskhod* has spoken out in defense of this rite on several occasions. Unmannerly lamentations by Jewish physicians about the benefits of circumcision have appeared rather frequently in its pages.

—*Mysli i facty*, p. 8.

The rabbis . . . take a fee for every operation of this kind; they still perform this bloody rite, removal of the foreskin of the penis, on themselves and their children. They are subjecting children to torture and very often place them in mortal danger as a result of this operation. It is true that the Jewish rabbis often try to explain this rite with a hygienic rationale. . . . In actual fact . . . this explanation, of course, must be taken with a large grain of salt.

—Ye. Yaroslavsky, p. 119.

5. THE SLAUGHTER OF CATTLE

Any further toleration in the Christian world of the Jewish ritual slaughter of animals is tantamount to waiving the basic principles of Christianity and humanity. The brutal Jewish blood cult is a glaring and inadmissible contradiction to the entire essence of the Christian view of the world . . . It is incumbent upon us . . . to prohibit those rites which uphold the cruelty of Jewish customs and religious fanaticism.

—*Uboy skota zhydami*, pp. 32, 37.

I shall no longer tolerate the killing of animals born on German territory by a sadistic Asiatic method of slaughter. If a Jew cannot eat our meat, let him eat turnips and potatoes.

—General von Westrem, president of the Frankfurt police, in *Brown Book*, p. 232.

6. THE CLASS STRUGGLE

With the Talmud as their justification, patrician Jews wield unlimited power over plebian Jews. In their oppressed condition the latter do not even have the right to complain of the humiliation and outrages which they endure.

—Shmakov, Jews in History,

The Jewish question is more complicated than one thinks. In all probability, the capitalist Jew and the Bolshevik Jew are not identical.

—Goebbels, in conversation with a "Communist friend," 1925. Heiden, p. 168.

Judaism itself differentiates very clearly between the various categories of Jews. It divides its followers into rich and poor, into disciple-sages . . . wise men, "the clever ones," and the ignoramuses, i.e., the plebians.

The Talmud states than an ignoramus can be killed with impunity even on the Day of Atonement.

—Begun, p. 34.

Part 5. THE CULTURE, LITERATURE, AND ART OF THE JEWS

1. THEY HAVE GIVEN NOTHING TO THE WORLD

Today they are borrowing everything from the nations of Europe. But they themselves have given, and can give nothing.

—Archimandrite Chrysanf, p. 2.

Each race has created its own art, except the Jews.

—Hitler, in Pod Znamenem Marksizma, 1938, no. 5, p. 73.

Apropos of the vain attempts by the Zionists to foist on people the myth they have created about "the special role of the Jews" in world culture, and in various national cultures—be they socialists or bourgeois . . . We ought to recall a remark made by Franz Mehring,* one of the best biographers of Karl Marx, and which has been undeservedly forgotten: "Jewry did not participate in the great intellectual work of our better thinkers and poets."

—Yevseev, p. 57.

---

*Franz Mehring (1846–1919), German Marxist and publicist. Began his career as a petty-bourgeois activist, when he derived the blatant anti-Semitism to which he gave expression all his life.

2. THEY HAVE GIVEN NOTHING TO THE WORLD EXCEPT FOR THE TORAH AND THE TALMUD

They have brought nothing with them except for the Talmud.

—Shmakov, *Jews in History*, p. 49.

Wherein lies the greatness, the genius and uniqueness of the cultural heritage of the Jews? In the fact that they "gave the Torah to the world." But as we know, the Torah is not the basis of culture but its prison, the fetters of cultural creativity. In the last analysis, it is anticulture, because Judaic dogma is an antisocial and inhumane doctrine.

—Begun, p. 84.

3. THEY REFUSE TO ACKNOWLEDGE THAT OTHER PEOPLES POSSESS ALL THE GUIDING PRINCIPLES

It is precisely the Russians and other Slavs whom God chose to preserve true religion. . . . This is because of the Slavic mental qualities, the Slavic soul.

—Sapozhnikov, p. 5.

We shall no longer permit anyone to deprive us of the belief that, in general, all the preeminent ideas in history arose in the heads of Aryans, that technical creative power is of Aryan origin, and that these talents are a racial virtue which is characteristic solely of the Aryans.

—Dr. Nonnenmacher in *Kommunisticheskiy Internatsional*, 1936, no. 15, p. 89.

All the states of Europe and their cultural values were created by the Germans.

—Rosenberg, in "Bolshevik," 1941, No. 13, p. 23.

Despite Osnos's endless affirmations of patriotism, of the Russian national spirit, and of the historical mission of the Russian people, who have been called upon to reeducate all the peoples of the world in the spirit of socialism—in the final analysis Osnos does not succeed in masking his real views of Russia's role in history. Speaking about historical progress in general, Osnos concludes that Russia played the subordinate role of student of Europe in world history.

—E. Gorbunova, "Oshibochnaya kontseptsiya (o knige Yu. Osnosa, *Sovietskaya istoricheskaya dramaturgiya*), in *Teatr*, 1949, no. 7, p. 93.

4. THEY ARE CAPABLE OF ONLY THE SECOND-RATE

The Jews have provided ample proof that they lack any genuinely creative power that is invariably unselfish. They are represented by a mass of second-rate though some very valuable works (Lassalle, Mendelssohn, Maimonides) in the history of literature, art, and the sciences. But in this mass one cannot point to a single first-rate, not merely highly talented work, but one of genius, such as those of a Shakespeare, Glinka, Descartes, Pushkin, or Beethoven.

—Astafyev, p. 113.

. . . how can we take seriously Zionist pretensions to the right to proclaim as achievements of the "Jewish genius" the results of the titanic intellectual labor of mankind's great minds of all eras and peoples? It is with such fraudulent means that the Zionists aspire to articulate and overemphasize the second-rate, and to elevate it to the highest level.

—Yevseev, p. 58.

A. Goldstein suposedly wrote: "In Russia they (the Jews) are surrounded on all sides by the richest Russian culture. Their small, poor Jewish literature cannot compare with the great literature of Russia, admired by the entire world." Absolutely the same is true of the Jewish theater, music, and painting, which are in an embryonic state and are insignificant in comparison with the fathomless beauties of Russian art.

—Yevseev, in *Voprosy istorii*, 1973, no. 5, p. 70.

5. THEIR CULTURE PURSUES DIVERSIONARY-SUBVERSIVE AIMS

Russia can permit the entry of the Kirgiz or Kalmuck, with their nomadic and predatory way of life as a whole, only if there is a fundamental change in the obsolete culture which has accrued to them over the centuries. The same applies to the Jews: let them abandon their peculiar national culture. It conflicts with and is hostile to the way of life of those nationalities with whom, some persons wish, they should be allowed to be neighbors with "equal rights."

—Leontovich, p. 28.

Fascist "culture" is waging a struggle against "Judaism and Marxism" under the guise of defending the purity of German culture from the destructive influence of the Jews.

—*Pod znamenem marksizma*, 1938, no. 5, p. 76.

Every Jew who tries to bring his influence to bear in Europe is a danger to European culture.

—Schirach, in *Nuremberg Trial*, vol. 4, p. 864.

Even at the present time, the watchword Jewish "national culture" is essentially reactionary, i.e., it is pursuing diversionary-subversive aims.

—Begun, p. 84.

Only madmen and enemies blinded by hatred can nourish the illusion that the party and the state will permit this unity to be destroyed and that they will allow into the country a "cultural" Trojan horse—bourgeois nationalism, Zionism, and anti-Communism ... The idea of a Jewish "national culture" does not come from Soviet Jewry. Its provenance is the foreign centers of anti-Communist subversion. It is based on false premises which ignore objective conditions and the psychology of the Soviet person.

—Begun, pp. 85, 86.

"National Culture," in the ordinary Zionist meaning of the term, does not signify entertainment establishments of the club-theater type with Jewish actors; it signifies instead a sect with its own ideology and corresponding system of political establishments concealed behind cultural placards.

—Begun, p. 85.

6. THEIR LANGUAGE IS NONEXISTENT

On July 5, 1915, the entire Jewish press in both conversational and ancient Hebrew was closed down. Seven daily newspapers, one weekly, and two monthly publications suddenly deprived six million Jews of a language.

—Bomash, speech at a session
    of the 4th State Duma.
    Stenographic account, p.
    1133.

We must resolve the question of whether general educational works . . . should be published in the ancient Hebrew tongue rather than Russian. This is a purely political question. . . . As for Jewish periodicals in the ancient Hebrew language, they propagandize the same separatist tendencies, presenting them even more vividly and sharply. They are reviving the ancient Hebrew tongue, which up to the present has comprised the national banner of the Jews, enlivening and fostering among them the heritage of the Old Testament.

—Brafman, pp. 310, 315.

The ancient Hebrew tongue and Yiddish were prohibited within the German Empire.

—V. Struve, *Fashistsky
    antisemitizm*, p. 7.

According to the All-Union census statistics in 1970, only 17 percent of Soviet Jewry designated Yiddish as their native language. Moreover, even for them its use for conversation is insignificant . . . . At the present time Yiddish is disappearing everywhere. And Hebrew is as alien to the Jews of the Diaspora as . . . any . . . . dead language.

—Begun, p. 87.

. . . the truthlessness of the Zionist ploy of propagating Hebrew.

—Begun, p. 87.

7. THEY MUST ASSIMILATE VOLUNTARILY. THE RUSSIAN LANGUAGE IS THE MEANS OF ASSIMILATION

We constantly hear that a well-known nationality is dying out. This is something terrible for the language of the discomfited, but for ours—the Russian language—we must rejoice! For we have been increasing; the moribund nationality, as they say, is merging into the stronger neighboring people, into the Russian majority.

—Bogoroditsky, p. 5.

The state must habituate all its subject nationalities to its culture and state organization, thereby unifying them into one, integral, single, and indivisible living state organism. . . . The Russian school and the Russian tongue are the means for achieving this unification.

—Bogoroditsky, p. 3.

In the recent attacks of Zionist propaganda on the Soviet Union, particular emphasis has been given to the facts of assimilation in daily life, culture, and language. They are seeking to present this natural and voluntary process . . . as the result of coercion and pressure by the authorities. . . . Under socialism . . . the process of cultural development of the Jewish population leads in many cases to a rejection (on a totally voluntary basis) of Jewish culture in general and to the adoption of Russian, Ukrainian, Georgian, and other cultures.

—Semenyuk, pp. 164–165.

Moreover, it is natural to expect that citizens of Jewish nationality in the USSR who speak read and write in Russian (or Ukrainian, White Russian, etc.) will assume the culture and usages of the peoples among whom they live.

—Soyfer, p. 87.

8. LITERATURE

a) *Their literature is immoral and denationalizes society*

Every non-Jew is struck by the unprecedented immorality and inhumanity of Semitized literature.

—Afterword to the Frich's book, p. 42.

We may note that there was an unprecedented . . . influx of Jews . . . into our literature in the eighties and nineties . . . into our literature and journalism, and they are trying to denationalize Russian society.

—Sidorov, pp. 39—40.

We shall not permit a literature alien to the people to corrupt its morals, nor a feeble sentimentality to undermine its steadfastness.

—From a speech by the Minister of Education, 1933, in *Vestnik Kommunisticheskoy Akademii*, 1933, no. 4, p. 75.

b) *They create their own theories in literature*

They befoul everything they touch. . . . First and most obviously, they have spoiled our literature, which was once healthy, beautiful, and natural, with their fetid "God-seekings," "God-erectings," decadences, symbolisms, and all manner of verbal margarine.

—Rozanov, p. 75.

Down with alien journalism of the Jewish-democratic stamp! Up with responsible and sincere help for the cause of national construction!

—From the speeches at the burning of literary works, 1933, in *Internationalnaya literatura*, 1933, no. 3, p. 141.

A host of literary works and films have appeared on Jewish themes. They are supposed gradually to train the public in loyalty to the Zionists.

—Begun, pp. 101—102.

Exploiting the words "democracy," "humanism," and "the defense of progress" as a subterfuge, and utilizing levers of influence in the realm of "mass culture," the Zionists are seeking to attract . . . the representatives of various trends in art and literature. By means of this deception the Zionists hope to induce such persons to serve the political objectives of world reaction, disguised under the deliberately hazy and abstract concepts of "universal culture."

—*Ideology and Practice*, p. 94.

9. THEIR LITERATURE IS INSIGNIFICANT AND LACKS ORIGINALITY

An entire class of "writers" has been formed which is totally illiterate, ignorant, and alien to genuine literature. The leading role in this class is played, of course, by Jews.

—Sharapov, *Sochineniya*, vol. 8, p. 202.

In general, the Jews are incapable of anything creative. . . . All of their ideas have been borrowed from other peoples.

—Hitler, in *Against Fascist Obscurantism and Demagogy*, p. 66.

It has been established that a number of ancient Jewish theological and other literary monuments are actually reworked variations of themes which originated among other peoples and civilizations.

—*Zionism: Theory and Practice*, p. 42.

The Judaic corporation has borrowed not merely the material values of other peoples, but also their spiritual values.

—Skurlatov, p. 10.

10. THEIR PRESS RIDICULES EVERYTHING NATIONAL

Any personal or discrete manifestations of Russian nationalism are not merely criticized as retrograde and boorish by the radical and Jewish organs of the press, they are bluntly badgered.

—Ilovaysky, p. 18.

The Jewish stock-exchange and Marxist press systematically incited hatred against Germany both before and during the war.

—Hitler, in *Revolutsiya i natsionalnosti*, 1933, no. 1, p. 87.

The hostile and stunted ideas and theories of the rootless cosmopolitans are reflected in the "works" of other critics. In particular, such persons as M. Yankovsky, I. Berezark, I. Schneiderman, A. Beilin, S. Zimbal, etc., have entrenched themselves rather firmly in the editorial boards of newspapers and magazines.

—*Bolshevik*, 1949, no. 3, p. 42.

As an antipatriotic critic, Borshchagovsky stands out as the consummate cosmopolitan. For him there is no higher criterion than comparison with some example of non-Russian art. His own writings are devoid of the life-enhancing soil of socialist reality, and he himself is ready to deprive everyone of his "national soil."

—*Teatr*, 1949, no. 1, p. 11.

An uncritical attitude to foreign culture has reduced certain men of letters and the theater to obsequiousness and servility towards what is foreign.

—*Fogarashi*, p. 55.

11. THE JEWS AND THEIR PASSION FOR FOREIGN LITERATURE

Publishers who turn out translated literature are upbraided by Goebbels for their "translation mania."

—*Fogarashi*, p. 58.

Proceeding from a pseudohumanistic ideal, Lessing created the prerequisites for the present Jewish dominance in the theater.

—Rosenberg, in *Fogarashi*, p. 47.

March 5, 1934. All artists of "non-Aryan origin" are forbidden to appear on the stage.

—*International molodyozhi*, 1937, no. 1, p. 29.

The writings of the aesthéte A. Gurevich are opposed to socialist realism. . . . *Hamlet* is for him "the crown and acme" of all of world literature.

—*Bolshevik*, 1949, no. 3, p. 41.

Since not a small number of television companies and studios are concentrated in the hands of the Zionists, one may imagine the extent of the very profitable activities whereby the Zionists are weakening and corrupting bourgeois society through its spiritual life.

—*Ideology and Practice*, p. 94.

12. THE JEWS AND THE THEATER

Under pressure from Jewish dramatists, Jewish critics, and Jewish producers, our theater has become thoroughly heretical.

—*Sidorov*, p. 58.

Antinationalist propaganda is coming from the stage, not only in dramatic theater but also at the opera. . . . Not long ago it was noted by M. O. Menshikov that the "stylization" of the im-

The theater has also been struggling

on behalf of classical Russian drama. The ideological opponents of the Soviet theater in this struggle have been led by Meyerhold and his disciples. The bourgeois formalists have tried to destroy the great heritage of Russian culture by scoffing at the classics and vulgarizing the great works of Russian drama, such as *The Wood, The Government Inspector, Woe from Wit,* and substituting the corrupt decadence of Western imperalist bourgeois culture.

. . . This was an attempt to force the poisonous ideology of cosmopolitanism and bourgeois decadence onto the Soviet stage.

—M. Gus, in *Teatr,* 1949, no. 12, p. 48.

perial stage was antinationalist in spirit, that in *Boris Godunov,* Mr. Meyerhold gave the police officers three-tailed whips, which do not exist in Pushkin, and dressed Boris Godunov and the Russian boyars in hats that resemble Jewish skullcaps.

—*Natzionalizm i iudei,* pp. 66–67.

13. THE JEWS AND THE FINE ARTS

Rosenberg bluntly abuses contemporary art, calling it the offspring of the Jews and the decadents.

—Fogarashi, p. 46.

The fascists regarded as "degenerative art" Cézanne, Van Gogh, Gauguin . . . the impressionists and the expressionists, lumping them all into one pile. . . . They dismissed Rembrandt as an artist of the ghetto.

-Fogarashi, pp. 51, 52.

The wicked enemies of Russian culture, Kandinsky and Malevich, are apparently Trotsky's agents in art.

—*Lebedev,* in *Iskusstvo,* 1949, no. 1, p. 67.

Can the art of any other country in the nineteenth century compare with that of the Russian painters Repin, Surikov, or any of the progressive artists in the Society for Circulating Art Exhibitions? Can one place the work of the impressionist artists Manet, Legas, Monet, Pissarro, Sisley, Renoir, and Gauguin alongside the lofty idealism of Russian art? Unfortunately, we still have an abundance of people who admire not only these artists but even Cezanne. . . . We can easily understand the nature of this practice—belittling the importance of Russian classical art. The critics Punin, Efros, and Beskin, who gave unfavorable opinions of the high-principled Russian art of the progressive painters in the "Circulating Exhibitions," always spoke out as apologists for French formalistic art and Russian decadent art.

—Melikadze, in *Iskusstvo*,
1948, no. 6, p. 14.

They called the works of their artists "a degeneration of art" which cannot satisfy the healthy and balanced tastes of the German people."

—*Sovietsky muzey*, 1938, no.
10, pp. 44–45.

His [Hitler's] theory of art is a mixture of raval sociology and a student cult of beauty. According to this theory all great works of art bear a "northern" and "beautiful" character. Hitler rejects all expressionism with disgust, as Jewish-Bolshevik. . . .

—Heiden, p. 64.

14. CRITICISM AND THE JEWS

I forbid criticism of the arts.

—Goebbels, in Fogarashi, p. 55.

What monstrous comparisons, what fanatical comparisons!
Gorky is compared with Dostoyevsky! . . . Gorky, with all the power of his genius, calling the Russian people to heroism, to struggle, to victory, and Dostoyevsky, who preached resignation and compassion! . . . Only a militant petty bourgeois, a Jesuit in spirit

and vocation, could have arrived at that!

—Zalessky, "Kleveta ideologicheskogo diversanta Yuzovskogo," in *Teatr*, 1949, no. 1, pp. 14–15.

15. THE JEWS AND SCIENCE

a) Physics. Einstein.

Today Zion proposes so-called ideas of time, "scientific theories." At will, it either gives or does not give the go-ahead to people, their works, and their inventions, for the stock exchange, trade, diplomacy—everything is in its hands.

—Nilus, p. 166.

Theoretical physics is the prerogative of "Jewish science"; it is based on the figure and the formula, while "German science" is based on "racial intuition." These are two worlds separated by an unbridgeable gulf.

—The fascist mathematician Biberbach, in *Pod Znamenem Marksizma*, 1938, no. 5, p. 85.

Einstein is the high priest of Jewish physics.

—Lenard, in *Pod Znamenem Marksizma*, 1938, no. 5, p. 85.

Einstein invented the extremely questionable theory of relativity, for which he was glorified by the Jewish press and the German nation. For this he showed his gratitude by lying, con-

German scientists have also promoted the misleading idea that the theory of relativity was the work of Einstein alone. They clearly disregarded the fact that the initial ideas of the theory were published in the works of Poincaré. This tendentious attitude toward the question of who was the originator of the theory of relativity was further disseminated in monographs and collections of articles, and later even in special historical research reports. The nationalistic tendencies of German physicists might have played a part in the emergence of this nonobjective attitude. They clearly had no desire to share the honors for the discovery of a new fundamental theory between the young Einstein and the already celebrated Poincaré. . . . Only the self-serving interests of the German physicists could have convinced them that in order to prove the genius of a young scientist, they had to belittle the contributions of other researchers.

—*Printsip otnositelnosti*, pp. 306–308.

The reason for Einstein's success was that his work is considered the most important in the discovery of the theory of relativity. To accept that "a part of no small importance" was played in this by the "nationalistic tendencies" of the German school of physicists, seems ridiculous to me; all the more so because Einstein was a Jew and a Swiss citizen.

—Ginsburg, in *Voprosy filosofii*, 1974, no. 8, p. 129.

stantly criticizing Adolf Hitler when he was abroad.

—Inscription under the portrait of Einstein in von Leers' book *The Jews Are Looking at You*, in *Brown Book*, p. 279.

b) Medicine, doctors

By virtue of their moral code, the Jews are a race of criminals and misanthropes. Since this has been proven beyond doubt, these criminals and misanthropes cannot be allowed to become doctors. . . . Any person who loves the Russian people cannot send criminals to tend their wounds, and the Jews are criminals.

—Markov-2, speech at a session on the 4th State Duma. Stenographic account, pp. 2787–2788.

Down with Jewish doctors! . . . We German doctors demand that they be dismissed and prohibited from giving medical aid to the Germans, because the Jews are the incarnation of falsehood and deceit.

—Appeal by the German Doctors' Association, 1933, in *Brown Book*, pp. 240, 252–253.

Doctors—murderers, the monsters of the human race, agents in the pay of a foreign secret service, have trampled the holy banner of science and defiled the honor of science. Most of the members of this villainous band of cannibals were connected with the international Jewish bourgeois nationalistic organization, the Joint.

—*Ogonyok*, no. 4 (1337), January 25, 1953.

16. THE HISTORY OF THE JEWS; OR, CHAMBERLAIN UNDER DELUSION

Chamberlain *

During all the centuries of the Christian era, Jews have played an important role everywhere, even though in some cases that role was severely restricted. They managed to acquire power and influence as slave traders and intermediaries in financial operations as long ago as the early West Gothic Empire.

—p. 18.

They soon secured wealth and influence everywhere as tenant-farmers, and used this to obtain important advantages for their whole nation.

—p. 21.

The real Jew appeared and developed only in the course of centuries. He is not the result of normal national life, but is somehow the artificial product of a caste of priests, who foisted on an unwilling people . . . a legislation and faith ostensibly given by God, but actually invented by this caste.

—p. 163.

Faith in the protection of Jehovah . . . the conviction that the Jews were God's chosen people, while all other nations were immeasurably inferior, in a word, the whole range of concepts which then became the basis of Judaism, evolved at that time . . .

—pp. 176–177.

Skurlatov†

Being an exclusive and nationalistically chauvinistic caste, the ancient Hebrew trade and mediatory corporation, which had spread throughout the countries of the ancient world, remained a class-differentiated organism. The activities of the Jewish trade and mediatory corporation took in all of mankind at that time.

—pp. 9–10.

The Jewish community was strictly and absolutely regulated for many centuries . . . by the instructions of talmudic Judaism, which required that every Orthodox Jew unceremoniously acquire wealth at the expense of the goyim, taught him to display personal initiative in trade and mediation, and always to be conscious of his natural "superiority" to the goyim.

—p. 13.

Over a period of centuries, the ancient world molded a ubiquitous clan of traders and intermediaries. From the start, this clan . . . set itself in opposition to the other nations. . . . Mythologizing the laws of the development of human society, the ideologists of Judaism presumptuously convinced the Jewish masses that they would in future have dominion over the nations of the world.

When one considers himself "chosen by God," he sets himself in opposi-

---

*Houston Stewart Chamberlain (1855–1926), English by birth, philosopher, well known for his works on racial theory, his "proof" of Aryan superiority over all other nations, and his rabid anti-Semitism. His ideas formed one of the bases of the ideology of fascist chauvinism and racism.

†Valery Ivanovich Skurlatov, a Candidate of Historical Science, head of the developing-countries section at the Soviet Foreign Ministry's Diplomatic Academy. Well known for his book *Zionism and Apartheid,* published in Kiev in 1975 by the Ukrainian Political Publishing House.

The migration to Babylon . . . broke the thread of history. . . . It is easy to understand that the spiritual class had the following two elements under its thumb: . . . the migrants who had returned to their homeland and . . . the exiles . . . far from the center of worship. Thus the priesthood armed itself with an artificial edifice (the Torah).

—pp. 187–188.

Jews everywhere have played . . . an important role even if . . . that role was severely restricted. Even though they were not actually everywhere, nevertheless, their influence was. In Moorish Spain, where they were powerful statesmen, occupying all the lucrative posts . . . or, as in Catholic Spain, where they were bishops and archbishops, they were at all times extremely powerful. . . . Pope Innocent III gave the Jews important positions at court, the French knights were forced to mortgage their estates and property with the Jews . . .

—p. 18.

Charles the Great sent to Italy for Jews to manage his finances. They soon secured wealth and influence everywhere as tax-farmers, and used this to obtain important advantages for their whole nation.

—p. 21.

All the wars in the nineteenth century depended, in an extremely peculiar way, on Jewish financial operations. This is the case beginning with Napoleon's Russian campaign and Nathan Rothschild, who was present as an observer at the Battle of Waterloo, and ending with the enlistment of the tion to all the rest, aggravating the already unfavorable consequences of the exploitation of others, and evoking the naturally hostile reaction of the local population to these claims of hegemony.

—pp. 11–12.

The thesis that the Jews are the chosen people of God, set out in the first five books of the Bible, was developed in all its minutiae during the period when the center of the Jewish trade and mediatory corporation moved from Palestine to Mesopotamia and Europe.

The ancient Hebrew leaders had to maintain rigid discipline among the people in conditions of dispersion.

—pp. 12–13.

It is characteristic of the traditionally capitalist countries . . . that the feudal prejudice against bourgeois enterprise proved so strong that . . . in most cases, companies were founded not by the Portuguese themselves, but by so-called New Christians (i.e., baptized Jews . . . who inwardly maintained their links with Judaism).

This went so far that, in 1629, King Philip IV of Portugal summoned a conference of priests and lawyers to discuss measures against the "New Christian" monopolization of trade, for . . . "nowhere can you find a rich man who was not once a Jew."

—p. 17.

As early as the eighteenth century, subsidiaries of the well-known Rothschild banking house had wormed their way into the principal capitals of Europe. During the Napoleonic Wars, the Rothschilds financed both France

Bleichreder family on the part of Germany, and of Alphonse Rothschild on the part of France in the peace talks of 1871, as well as of the Commune, which, in the opinion of all people of insight, represented the Judeo-Napoleonic intrigue from start to finish.

—pp. 21–22.

and her enemies . . . When the fate of Europe was being decided at the Battle of Waterloo, Rothschild's emissaries, one from Paris and the others from London, kept a constant watch on the battle. The Rothschild banks in both capitals were waiting to learn the outcome of the battle, so that they could immediately determine who were their competitors in stock-jobbing.

—pp. 31–32.

Part 6. THE JEWISH PROBLEM; OR, WHAT IS TO BE DONE WITH THEM?

1. WHAT ARE THE JEWS? A NATION, A SECT, OR NONHUMAN?

The Jews are nonhumans.

—Himmler, in SS in Action,
p. 244.

All documents, including Jewish ones, depict the Jews not as a nation but as a race or a sect whose members are united by tribal and religious relationships.

—The foreword to Frich's book,
p. 8.

The Jews have no territory of their own. . . . A small Semitic orphan race, extremely stable, incapable of merging, has taken root in the body of our state like a parasite. This tribe is the lowest form of humanity.

—Velikorossov, p. 38.

It is even laughable to discuss a separate Jewish nationality in Russia. Can scattered and wandering sheep without a shepherd really constitute a flock? In this form, can even the Jews constitute a nation?

—Tamber, pp. 26–27.

It has been established as a scientific truth* that the ancient Hebrew nation disappeared and was totally absorbed by other nations. The only legacy we have inherited from it is the name "Jew," which nowadays is the traditional name for many dissimilar ethnic groups anthropologically distant from one another. . . . However, they do have one common feature—the Jewish religion or traditions, which are based on Judaism.

—Yevseev, p. 19.

A world Jewish nation . . . has never existed.[†] . . . In the extremely remote past they were not only not "world," but not even a nation. When they were "scattered throughout the world," they were deprived of the possibility of ever achieving nationhood.

—Sionizm—orudye
imperialisticheskoy reaktsii,
p. 18.

---

*Yevseev does not say by which science or on the basis of what evidence such a fact was established. Nor does he explain why he had to "throw javelins" at this "nonexistent" nation, publishing his book in an edition of many thousands. Perhaps he lacks faith in "scientific truth"?

[†]There is no "world Jewish nation," nor has one ever existed, yet "world Jewry" was and still is the anti-Semites' greatest affliction. In order to be consistent, they should explain the difference between the "world Jewish nation" and "world Jewry."

The Jews are not people but merely racial persons.

—The afterword to Frich's book, p. 42.

2. WHAT IS "THE JEWISH QUESTION"?

The Jewish question is the question of what part the bourgeoisie, with its ideals and money, will play in the life of our state and our nation. And this question concerns the whole of our culture.

—Astafyev, p. 117.

The Jewish question will be solved only when there is not one Jew left on the continent of Europe.

—Rosenberg, in *Nuremberg Trial*, vol. 4, p. 662.

Speculation on the myth of "the age-old phenomenon of anti-Semitism" occupies the most important place in Zionist ideology. The Zionists do not take note of the fact that there is no "Jewish question" in the USSR and other socialist states.

—*Ideology and Practice*, p. 102.

3. ANTI-SEMITISM

Anti-Semitism means spreading enmity toward the Jews.

a) Does anti-Semitism exist?

Anti-Semitism will exist until the Jewish tribe perishes.

—Shtik, p. 15.

As long as there are Jews, there will be anti-Semitism.

—Bauer, Fischer, Lenz, "The Doctrine of Heredity," in "Sovetskaya nauka," 1939, No. 7, p. 19.

One of the manifestations of anti-Semitism is the pitting of Jews against non-Jews. This is stirred up by the Zionist leaders themselves, as it is their only justification for existence.

—Modzhoryan, p. 24.

b) *Anti-Semitism—is it good?*

We Russians have to be anti-Semites.

—Kulichev, *Antisemity*, p. 7.

The National Socialist revolution is drawing near. Its slogan: "Anti-Semites of the world, unite!"

—From a fascist newspaper, in Heiden, p. 39.

c) *Should one be ashamed of being an anti-Semite?*

The Jews must realize that the true Russian people cries with one voice: "Down with the Jews!"

—Kaluzhsky, pp. 35–36.

Do not be afraid of the slogan "Down with anti-Semitic violence!," for nowadays, the Jews can be eliminated only by force.

—*Istorik-marksist*, 1932, nos. 1–2, p. 89.

The Zionists made use of the anti-Jewish policy of the Nazi regime established in Germany in 1933, not only to achieve the specific aims of Zionism . . . but also to discredit anti-Zionist propaganda.* Any statement criticizing Zionism is termed anti-Semitic by the ill-intentioned Zionist press.

—Bolshakov, in *Voprosy istorii*, 1973, no. 9, p. 79.

I do not doubt for a moment that there will be persons in the West who will call this essay "the usual type of anti-Semitic display."

—Kurov, in *Reactionary Nature of Zionism*, p. 170.

*What is evidently meant is the mass extermination of the Jews by the fascists and statements against the Jews in the fascist press.

d) Anti-Semitism does not exist

Everybody knows that anti-Semitism is alien to the Russian people, who are friendly and amicable to adherents of all religions . . . and who, in their good nature, do not even notice people scandalously robbing and fleecing them. It is precisely the absence of anti-Semitism which has created a Jewish problem in our country.

—*Mysli i fakty*, p. 71.

One of the main tasks facing the Alliance is the struggle against anti-Semitism in Germany, the Alliance has no right to exist either. That is why it must be disbanded today.

—Apropos of closing the
Central Alliance of German
Citizens of the Jewish Faith,
1933, in *Brown Book*,
p. 209.

Anti-Semitism is an ugly social phenomenon of the age of capitalism, which is disappearing, along with the society which gave it birth, in all places where socialism is victorious.

—*Ideology and Practice*, p. 67.

Under the conditions of the present ideological struggle, it is important that one distinguish real anti-Semitism from invented and imaginary anti-Semitism.

—Begun, p. 78.

e) Anti-Semitism is the invention of the Jews, whose aim is to incite hatred for the non-Jews

The Jewish press has managed to create an opinion about the supposed hatred of Aryans and Christians for the Jews. . . . Hatred for every non-Jew, whatever his race or nation, is a feeling peculiar to the Jews, and is strengthened by their religion. So misanthropy is specifically Jewish and it . . . is passed by them from the sick mind to the healthy.

—Afterword to Frich, pp. 43–44.

The Jews in Germany are responsible for this disgraceful, constant criticism of alleged atrocities and the setting up of a boycott. They have called on their accomplices abroad to participate in a struggle against the German nation. They have sent false and slanderous information out of the country.

—From an announcement of
the boycott of Jewish trade,
Brown Book, p. 228.

One of the manifestations of anti-Semitism is the pitting of Jews against non-Jews. This is stirred up by the Zionist leaders themselves.

—Modzhoryan, p. 24.

f) *The Jews use the theme of anti-Semitism to incite hostility toward the countries in which they live*

Regarding the "horrors" (the torture of living Jews and the desecration of the dead), all the fury of the world's Jewish and Judaizing press was deceitful. This propaganda was, without a doubt, of a political nature. On the one hand it was designed to obtain a compromise for the Jews of Russia, and on the other, to cheer up the stock exchange; it was also designed to aggravate our difficulties on the diplomatic front, where the atmosphere is menacing enough as it is.

—Shmakov, *Gomel Affair*, p. 4.

Only the fact that so many people are unfamiliar with history allows the Jews to falsely accuse Russia as being the only country where there are pogroms, and to complain about the ruin suffered by the Kahal because of these.

—Shmakov, Speech on the Jewish Question, p. 22.

We must use all our energy to disprove the rumors spreading in America, of which we learned here with indignation, alleging the torture of political prisoners and the relative maltreatment of the Jews.

Hundreds of thousands of Jews who have not participated in political activities, irrespective of their citizenship, are living here quite peacefully.

—Von Papen, 1933, in *Nuremberg Trial*, vol. 1, p. 660.

The action committees are to see to it that all Germans who have connections abroad use them to spread the truth in their letters, telegrams, and telephone conversations, to explain that peace, calm, and order reign in Germany, that the German nation desires only to work and live in peace with all countries, and that it is struggling purely defensively against constant criticism and badgering organized by the Jews.

—*Brown Book*, p. 130.

The Zionists take advantage of the fact that anti-Semitic views and policies are thoroughly condemned by progressive forces in various countries, and they exploit this by blackmailing any party worker, even whole governments, with accusations of anti-Semitism.

—*Ideology and Practice*, p. 67.

The Zionist ringleaders make up all kinds of cock-and-bull stories about imaginary persecution of the Jews in the USSR. But the whole world knows that the Soviet system by its very nature precludes the possibility of an anti-Semitic policy.

—Nikitina, in *Reactionary Nature of Zionism*, p. 117.

g) Anti-Semitism was invented by the Jews for their own benefit

In its desire to incite hatred for the non-Jews among the members of their own nation, to keep them from coming to terms with them, the Zionist administration would every now and then give away certain rules of the Torah to the goyim which would stir up anti-Semitism. This anti-Semitism was also used by Zion in another way. Apart from the hatred in the hearts of the Jews, it created pity in the hearts of necessary individuals for this allegedly unjustly persecuted tribe. And this feeling drew many people to join those serving Zion. . . . The persecution and intimidation of the Jewish common mob . . . anti-Semitism kept these people in unquestioning obedience to their pastors, because the latter always managed to protect their people in time. Indeed, this was no wonder, as it was the pastors themselves who urged on the hounds (the goyim—the Christians), who did a perfect job in bringing the flock back to them in obedience. It then blindly carried out the pastors' instructions, the object of which was to set up a World Alliance of Zion, and this has now begun to shed its disguise.

—Nilus, pp. 164, 165.

It is the Jewish bourgeoisie and its ideologists who did and still display a great deal of personal interest in the existence of anti-Semitic feeling and in inciting anti-Semitism at the level of national politics. That Zionism has for a long time been understood to be "the reaction to anti-Semitism and pogroms" results from these efforts of the Jewish bourgeoisie and the press which it has bought up. Zionist ideologists never concealed the favorable light in which they regard anti-Semitism. The large Jewish bourgeoisie and their religious leaders saw it on the one hand as a means of retaining influence over the Jewish community and reviving the weakening ghetto outlook, and on the other . . . as a means of raising the banner of Jewish racism, and proclaiming the Jews to be a "special" race, "chosen by God." . . . In their appeal to working-class Jews, to the middle strata of the urban population, Zionist ideologists have always stressed that the goyim are anti-Semites who hate the Jews and are their enemies, and that the only salvation from this hatred is separation, isolation, and returned hatred.

Anti-Semitic organizations have

been set up in various Western countries with funds released from secret Zionist sources. . . . These organizations have engaged in acts of provocation against the Jews, especially the Jewish poor and the middle strata. . . . In all the cases mentioned above, the upper strata of the Jewish bourgeoisie showed themselves to be "the only defenders" of a Jewish population subjected to "anti-Semitic persecution" . . . and can therefore call on all Jews to join the Zionist ranks.

—*Ideology and Practice*, pp. 58, 59, 60, 62.

h) What is the struggle against the Jews?
The struggle against the Jews . . . is first and foremost a struggle against the bourgeoisie and its present dominion.

—Astafyev, p. 93.

i) Should anti-Semitism be condemned?
You constantly accuse us of making pogroms, of playing off one nationality against another. . . . Well, gentlemen, let me tell you that if the Poles and the Jews overpower the western region, a

Deporting tens of thousands of Jews to a ghetto in the East is a "contribution to European culture."

—Von Schirach, in *Nuremberg Trial*, vol. 7, p. 484.

Purifying the world of Jews, wiping out the Jewish race—this is a glorious page in our history.

—Himmler, in *Nuremberg Trial*, vol. 6, p. 639.

Zionist sorrow over the offended Jewish exploiters is a slanderous attempt to present the class struggle as anti-Semitism.

—Begun, *Creeping Counterrevolution*, p. 84.

. . . it would not be right to say that anti-Semitism is caused merely by the egocentric policy of the exploiting classes in the non-Jewish world. . . . Anti-Semitism also appears as the

wave of national indignation will break out which will be impossible to contain. Then you in the western region, and not we, will suffer the consequences.

—Purishkevich, Stenographic account, 1910, p. 1400.

4. ANTI-SEMITISM OR ANTI-ZIONISM?

Anti-Semitism should essentially be called anti-Talmudism, for it opposes not those who belong to the Semitic race, but rather the wild fanaticism of the Talmud regarding all non-Jews, which Jewish codes have made into political and religious law.

—Alektorov, p. 40.

spontaneous response of the enslaved strata of workers to the barbarous exploitation of the Jewish bourgeoisie.

—Begun, Polzuchaya Kontrrevolyutsiya, p. 79.

Only because we began toying with anti-Semitism in 1919 could we find the strength within ourselves to put it into practice twenty years later. It was clear to us from the start that the Jews in other countries would not like this, but we don't give two hoots about that.

—Frank, 1944, in Nuremberg Trial, vol. 4, p. 691.

Violent anti-Semitism has died out; this childhood disease has been overcome, and will not be seen again. Primitive displays of hatred for the Jews, the unconvincing publications of former times . . . all this is past. A new anti-Semitism is growing! Long live anti-Semitism!

—Strasser, in Heiden, p. 215.

They [the Zionists—R.O.] consciously interpret anti-Zionism . . . as anti-Semitism, i.e., animosity toward the Jews, and as anti-Israelism, i.e., a demand for the abolition of the State of Israel.

—Nikitina, in Reactionary Nature of Zionism, p. 118.

Anti-Hebraism, which the Jews falsely term anti-Semitism, must be inscribed on every true banner of freedom.

—Shmakov, Jewish Pogrom in Kiev, p. 10.

5. ONE MUST REJECT ANY FEELING OF PITY FOR THEM

Having sucked dry everything around them, they constantly complained of their fate, moaned, and turned on the waterworks.

—Shmakov, *Yevrei v istorii*, p. 128.

There is probably no other nation in the world which has complained so much about its fate and its martyrdom, every minute, with every step and every word, as the Jews.

—Dostoyevsky, quoted by Ekkar, p. 57.

Gentlemen, I must ask you to reject any feelings of pity. We must wipe out the Jews, wherever we find them and whenever possible.

—Frank (governor-general of Poland), in *Nuremberg Trial*, vol. 4, p. 667.

The Zionists repeatedly and in all manner of ways foist their tales of the age-old suffering and martyrdom of the Jews on the public. Crudely distorting and falsifying the facts, they present the case as if the Jews have from time immemorial been the epitome of innocence and goodness, while the other nations among whom they lived were the perpetrators of every possible evil. As a result, the bad, evil non-Jews have been persecuting and oppressing the good, noble Jews.

—Begun, *Creeping Counterrevolution*, p. 83.

6. THE PEOPLE WHO SPEAK OUT IN DEFENSE OF THE JEWS ARE THE RIFFRAFF, THE RENEGADES, THE POLITICALLY INEXPERIENCED

Only cosmopolitans, renegades from their homeland, idlers who need money for debauchery, luxury, and the fast life, or people without positive convictions . . . can acknowledge and support the existence of Jews as they are at the moment in Russia.

—Kaluzhsky, p. 27.

In our opinion those who . . . consider it necessary to speak out in defence of the Jews are riffraff, with whom we shall deal in exactly the same way as we deal with the Jews.

—Proclamation of the Action Committee for the Struggle Against the Jews, in *Brown Book*, p. 224.

Sometimes the scarecrow of anti-Semitism and clever cock-and-bull stories of "suffering" produce the desired effect on the politically inexperienced.

—Begun, *Creeping Counterrevolution*, p. 83.

7. WHAT IS TO BE DONE WITH THE JEWS?

a) Passports

Not long before the war, the government had decided to abolish passports, which did not exist anywhere in Europe. . . . High officials gathered in St. Petersburg and began considering how to change the passport system; they had nearly made up their minds, when they realized the Jews made their decision untenable. Jews were barred from entering Russia, and if passports were abolished, one would not be able to decide who had arrived in Moscow: a Jew or a non-Jew? You cannot always tell them by their faces . . . In the end, the high officials rejected the idea, and the passports remained.

—Ogranovsky, pp. 8–9.

b) Emigration and the payment for it

The crown of all our labor must be an institution which will facilitate Jewish emigration from Russia; poor Jews must be given assistance in leaving Russia. . . . A person who receives a grant to leave will lose the right to return. All emigration formalities for

The Soviet Union is a federal state with over one hundred nationalities who all have Soviet citizenship. This makes it necessary to indicate the nationality of the holder in a Soviet passport. . . .

In this way, the Soviet passport is an important means of identifying a citizen's nationality, and this indication in his passport is one way of paying respect to the holder's nation.

—Sovetskiye yevrei, pp. 47–48.

In January 1939, the Imperial Emigration Department was established by order of the Reichsmarshal. Emigration was financed by the Jews themselves, or by their political organizations. . . .

Aside from the need to repay ex-

On September 27, representatives of the Moscow public gathered in the conference hall of the All-Union Society Knowledge to strongly protest the recent anti-Soviet and anti-Communist outbursts in international Zionist circles. . . .

Jews with Russian citizenship must be as simple and cheap as possible, while foreigners of the Jewish faith must once and for all be unconditionally barred from entry to Russia, except in the case of diplomats and officials.

—"Chto nam delat s yevreyami," in Novoye Vremya, 1857, quoted by Neznachny, pp. 265–267.

penses in Reichsmarks, the requirement for foreign currency became evident to pay for documents of entry and residence permits. So as not to deplete Germany's foreign currency reserves, Jewish financial organizations abroad . . . were asked to find the necessary moneys to cover these expenses.

—SS in Action, pp. 148, 149 (1960 ed.).

The speakers strongly condemned the unfounded outbursts of Zionists and other reactionaries regarding the emigration procedures which were established for Soviet citizens. These procedures require that any person who has decided to emigrate refund the money spent by the state on his higher education and other higher specialized and scientific degree courses. The participants in the meeting expressed their thoughts and feelings in a unanimous resolution. It says in particular: . . . the training of skilled personnel costs the state and the nation many millions of rubles. These millions are not spent so that people who have obtained knowledge and skills at the nation's expense should use them in the service of capitalism.

—Izvestiya, no. 229 (17157), September 28, 1972.

c) Pogroms

. . . in a country like Russia we would have to chop off the heads of at least a hundred Romanovs in order to wean their successors from the habit of organizing Black Hundred murders and anti-Jewish pogroms.

—V. I. Lenin, Poln. sobr. soch., vol. 21, p. 17.

This was not an attack on Jewish property that was coolly planned beforehand. It was simply a heterogeneous crowd of exploited people marching on the exploiters.

—*Otvet Minoru*, p. 7.

Or . . . .
Let us believe that in the end Russia will rouse herself and shake off this evil tribe of parasites like an ancient Palestinian leprosy.

—Balashev, *O natsionalizme*, p. 27.

The fascist leaders gave orders for a "rebellion of the people" to be staged . . . for Jewish shops . . . jewish flats to be looted, for valuable articles to be plundered. . . . Following this "rebellion of the nation," the Jews were to be wiped out. This was to be done according to a carefully planned program, with the inhumanity that was characteristic of the fascists.

—*Kommunisticheskiy Internatsional*, 1938, no. 11, p. 93.

In the event that international Jewish bankers in and out of Europe manage once more to plunge the nations into a world war, then such a war will result in . . . the destruction of the Jewish race in Europe.

—Hitler, 1939, in *Nuremberg Trial*, vol. 4, p. 662.

One of the main causes of the trouble that befell the Jews in the Ukraine and Byelorussia was economic exploitation, personified in the rapacious leaseholders, tenant farmers, usurers, and innkeepers.

—Begun, *Creeping Counterrevolution*, pp. 85–86.

The rulers in Tel Aviv shoulder a grave responsibility for their people, who may pay most tragically for the irresponsibility of those who involve them in shady ventures.

—*Aims and Methods*, p. 22.

WHEN PLAGIARISM IS ENCOURAGED
(The fifth and final digression)

Butlitsky

Although the State of Israel came into being in 1948, its intelligence service dates from much earlier. A permanent intelligence agency, Sherut Yisrael (which means "The Service of Israel") was set up as early as 1937 and was attached to the political department of the Jewish Agency—the Zionist organization which controls Jewish emigration to Palestine. Sherut Yisrael engaged in political investigations and fought progressive elements among the Jewish and Arab population of Palestine.

Sklyarevsky

When talking of intelligence, we mean any state in which it operates and whose interests it protects. But if we look at Israel's intelligence service in this way, we find we cannot compare it to the intelligence of other capitalist countries. For it is the only intelligence service in the world set up long before the birth of its state. . . . It appeared not in 1948, when Israel was founded. . . . A permanent intelligence agency was set up in Palestine in 1937, and was given the name Sherut Yisrael ("The Service of Israel"). It functioned also to fight progressive elements among the Jewish and Arab population of Palestine.

—*Aims and Methods,*
pp. 44–45, 69–70, 80.

Dzhuvinov

How paradoxical it is that the Israeli intelligence service is the only one in the world older than its state. Long before 1948, when the creation of the State of Israel was officially declared, the Zionist organizations had already set up their secret service. . . . A permanent intelligence agency called Sherut Yisrael (or Shay) was set up in 1937. . . . The Shay fulfilled the role of political police in the struggle against progressive forces within the country.

Belenky

I was sent a packet of pamphlets in the post from Britain. They were printed on tissue paper and crammed with Zionist propaganda and malicious anti-Soviet slander.

The authors' stupidity emerged quite clearly from this "literature." . . .

One pamphlet put out this call:

"Shout at the top of your voices in every forum . . . Grasp President Nixon's coat, pull Prime Minister Wilson into the battle, incite the Pope, arouse the leaders of young African states, entice the Japanese, the Malayans, the Chileans, call for help from all those who are willing or unwilling. Shout as loudly as you can. The war must be waged using all means: from anonymous letters to open statements."

Who are the authors of all this poisonous pulp literature? They are members of the so-called League for the Repatriation of Russian Jews, formed a year ago. Its organizers are the millionaires Morris Grafman (U.S.A.) and Jose Mirrelman (a Swiss industrialist at present living in Israel). They operate mainly in Britain and France.

Sklyarevsky

Recently . . . packets of pamphlets have been sent to individual Soviet citizens by post from Britain. Printed on tissue paper for the sake of compactness, they overflow with Zionist propaganda and anti-Soviet slander. For example, one of them calls on people to poison the international atmosphere with anti-Sovietism, and even gives practical advice on how best to do this.

"Shout at the top of your voice, in every forum . . . Grasp President Nixon's coat . . . incite the Pope, rouse the indignation of the Japanese, the Malayans, the Chileans, call for help from all those who are willing or unwilling. Shout as loudly as you can. The war must be waged using all means: from anonymous letters to open statements."

Who are the authors of this anti-Soviet filth? Their tracks lead to Britain and France, to a recently formed Zionist organization called the League for the Repatriation of Russian Jews. Its ringleaders are the millionaires Morris Grafman (U.S.A.) and Jose Mirrelman (an industrialist from Switzerland, who is living in Israel at the moment).

Here, as always, when the Zionists conduct a campaign of slander, Israeli intelligence experts can be seen at work.

—*Aims and Methods*,
pp. 60, 63, 78–79.

Butlitsky

A serious scandal erupted in Switzerland in the autumn of 1969. Alfred Frauenknecht, head of the technical department at Sulzer, the Swiss aviation company, had been enlisted by Israeli military intelligence, Sherut Modi'in. Over a period of eleven months he passed 150,000 secret drawings and other documents concerning production of the jet engine for the French Mirage fighters to the Israelis. In return for this he was paid 860,000 Swiss francs. The basic communication link for getting the documents to Tel Aviv ran through West Germany. The West German frontier guards and customs officials suddenly went blind, as it were, and did not notice that a total of thirty boxes containing the plundered documents were passed under their noses. In all probability the officers of Israeli military intelligence were "insured" by their West German colleagues.

—*Aims and Methods*, pp. 50 and 82.

Dzhuvinov

Engineer Frauenknecht received the sum of 860,000 Swiss francs from Sherut Modi'in. This generosity paid off: over a period of eleven months the head of the technical department at Sulzer, the Swiss aviation company . . . passed 150,000 secret drawings and technological data sheets to Israeli intelligence concerning production of the jet engine for the supersonic French fighter, the Mirage-3. The question might be asked: How could a courier freely cross the border between Switzerland and West Germany dozens of times, while transporting thirty boxes of secret documents? . . . There can be only one answer: the espionage channel on West German territory is protected by the West German secret service.

Begun

Zionist intelligence was also caught red-handed in another neutral country, neighboring Switzerland. Working for them and subsequently exposed and convicted was Engineer Alfred Frauenknecht, head of the technical department at Sulzer, the aviation company. In 1968–1969, for the sum of 860,000 Swiss francs, he stole 150,000 secret drawings and technological data sheets concerning production of the jet engine for the supersonic French fighter, the Mirage. The documents he stole were sent to Israel via West Germany, evidently with the help of Zionist secret agents there.

—Begun, *Invasion without Arms*, p. 128.

article 2: b) Each State Party undertakes not to sponsor, defend, or support racial discrimination by any persons or organizations;

article 4: a) Shall declare an offense punishable by law all dissemination of ideas based on racial superiority or hatred, incitement to racial discrimination . . . .

c) Shall not permit public authorities or public institutions, national or local, to promote or incite racial discrimination.

From the International Convention on the Elimination of All Forms of Racial Discrimination, adopted by the United Nations General Assembly on December 21, 1965.
—Quoted from the book *Dokumenty oblichayut rasizm*, (Moscow: Nauka, 1968), pp. 20, 21.

BIBLIOGRAPHY OF WORKS CONSULTED

I. The Works of V. I. Lenin

1. *Polnoye sobraniye sochineniy*. 5th ed. Moscow: Gospolitizdat, vol. 21, pp. 11–21.
2. *Polnoye sobraniye sochineniy*. 5th ed. Moscow, Gospolitizdat, vol. 24, pp. 257–258.
3. *Polnoye sobraniye sochineniy*. 5th ed. Moscow: Gospolitizdat, vol. 32, p. 422.
4. *Polnoye sobraniye sochineniy*. 5th ed. Moscow, Gospolitizdat, vol. 38, p. 243.

II. Prerevolutionary Works

1. Aksakov, I. S., *Sochineniya*. 2d ed. Polsky vopros i zapadnorusskoe delo. Yevreysky vopros. 1860–1886. Statyi iz "Dnya," "Moskvy," "Moskvicha," "Rus" i dr. St. Petersburg, 1900, vol. 3, 570 pp.
2. Alektrov, A. Ye., *Inorodtsi v Rossii*, Sovremennye voprosy. Finlandtsi. Latishi. Yevrei. Nemtsi. Armyane. Tatary. S predisloviyem i dobavleniyem A. S. Budilovicha. St. Petersburg. Obshchestvo revniteley russkogo prosveshchenya v pamyat imp. Aleksandra III, 1906. 134 pp.
3. Astafyev, P. Ye., *Iz itogov veka*. Moscow, 1891. 117 pp.
4. Balashev, I., *O natsionalizme voobshche i, v chastnosti, o russkom*. St. Petersburg, 1911. 32 pp. [In text—Balashev. *O natsionalizme*.]
5. Balashev, I., *Zapiska o sovremennom sostoyanii Rossii*. St. Petersburg, 1906. 21 pp. [In text—Balashev.]
6. Bespartiyny, *Zadacha imushchim sovest*. Vyp. 3. Yevreyskie pogromy na Svyatoy Rusi. St. Petersburg, 1911. 35 pp.
7. Bogoroditsky, P., *Po inorodcheskomu voprosu*. Kazan, Kazansky Universitet, 1911. 28 pp.
8. Bomash, [?], Rech na zasedanii 4-oy Gosudarstvennoy Dumy 28 avgusta 1915. *Stenografichesky otchyot Gosudarstvennoy dumy 4-go sozyva, 4-oy sessii*. Petrograd, 1915.
9. Brafman, Ya., *Kniga Kagala* [Vsemirny yevreysky vopros]. 2nd ed. Part I. Edited by A. Brafman. St. Petersburg, 1882. 373 pp.
10. Budilovich, A. S. *Po voprosu ob okrainakh Rossii v svyazi s teoriey samoopredeleniya narodnostey i trebovanii gosudarstvennogo yedinstva*. St. Petersburg, 1906. 25 pp.
11. Butmi, G., *Oblichitelnye rechi. Frankmasonstvo i gosudarstvennaya izmena*. St. Petersburg, 1906. 95 pp.
12. Butmi, G., *Oblichitelnye rechi. Rossiya na rasputye. Kabala ili svoboda?* Posvyashchaetsya Soyuzu Russkogo naroda. St. Petersburg, 1906. 48 pp.

13. Butmi, G. *Vragi roda chelovecheskogo (Protokoly sionskikh mudretsov)*. Posvyashcheno Soyusu Russkogo naroda. 4th ed. St. Petersburg, 1907. 127 pp.

14. Chamberlain, H. S., *Yevrei, ikh proiskhozhdeniye i prichiny ikh vliyaniya v Yevrope*. Trans. from German. 4th ed. St. Petersburg, izdatelstvo Suvorina, 1907. 248 pp.

15. Delich, F., *Slovo pravdy o Talmude*, Po povodu socheneniya A. Rolinga "Talmudichesky yevrey." St. Petersburg, 1885. 91 pp.

16. Demchenko, Ya. G., *Yevreiskoe ravnopravie ili russkoe poraboshchenie?* Issledovaniye tainykh yevreiskikh planov i programm, napravlennykh k oslableniyu i razrusheniyu korennogo naseleniya i poraboshchenie yego yevreystvom. 2d ed. Kiev. 1907, 184 pp.

17. Diminsky, S., *Issledovaniye o Talmude*, Kiev, Kievo-Pecherskaya Lavra, 1869. 126 pp.

18. Diminsky, S., *Yevrei. Ikh veroucheniye i pravoucheniye*. 2d ed. St. Petersburg, 1893. 216 pp.

19. Ekkar, V., *Ravnopraviye vne yevreev*. Odessa, tipografiya "Slavyanskaya," 1906. 87 pp.

20. Fliorkovsky, P., *Koye-chto o nastoyashchem i proshedshem yevreev*. Kiev, 1868. 136 pp.

21. Govorov, D., *Yevreysky vopros*. Kiev, Kievsky Universitet, 1910. 37 pp.

22. Grinevich, M. I., *O tletvornom vliyanii yevreev na ekonomichesky byt Rossii i o sisteme yevreyskoy ekspluatatsii*. St. Petersburg, 1876. 72 pp.

23. Ilovaysky, D. I., *Nechto o natsionalnom napravlenii*, in *S. Kuzmin, Pod gnyotom svobody*. St. Petersburg, 1910.

24. Ilovaysky, D. I., *Vozmozhen li i nuzhen li Sobor v nashe vremya?*—v sbornike *Otkliki na sovremennye sobytiya*. Kharkov, 1905. [In text—Ilovaisky.]

25. Kaluzhsky, A. *Druzhesky sovet yevreyam*. St. Petersburg, 1905. 36 pp.

26. Khrisanf, arkhimandrit, prof. Saint-Petersburg. dukhovnoy akademii. *Sovremennoe iudeystvo i otnoshenie yego k khristianstvu*. St. Petersburg, 1867. 83 pp.

27. Kireev, A., *Slavyanofilstvo i natsionalizm*. Otvet gospodinu Solovyovu. St. Petersburg, 1890. 36 pp.

28. Kostomarov, N. I. *Iudeyam*. Ottisk iz zhurnala *Osnova*.

29. Kulichev, V., Antisemity.—Cit. po knige: *L.M-v. Russky narod i yevrei*. St. Petersburg, 1908, 54 pp.

30. Kulichev, V., *Yevreyskoe gosudarstvo*. Moscow, tipografiay "Rasprostranenie poleznykh knig," 1908. 16 pp. [In text—Kulichev.]

31. Leontovich, F. *Chto nam delat s yevreyskim voprosom?* St. Petersburg, 1882. 31 pp.

32. Mag, Slugi treugolnika ili masony i ikh dela. St. Petersburg, 1912. 27 pp.

33. Markov-2, N. Ye., Rech na zasedanii 3-y Gosudarstvennoy Dumy 8 Maya 1910. *Stenografichesky otchet Gosudarstvennoy Dumy 3-go sozyva, 3-y sessii*. St. Petersburg, 1910.

34. Markov-2, N. Ye., Rech na zasedanii 4-y Gosudarstvennoy Dumy 19 Yylya

1915. *Stenografichesky otchet Gosudarstvennoy Dumy 4-go sozyva, 4-sessii.* St. Petersburg, 1915.

35. Mysli i fakty po yevreyskomu voprosu. Pisma yevreya. Odessa, "Novorossiysky telegraf," 1895. 168 pp.

36. *Natsionalizm i iudei.* Odessa, Obshchestvo "Russkaya rech," 1912. 90 pp.

37. Neznachny. *Yevreysky kagal.* Organizatsiya yevreyskikh obshchin, ikh mogushchestvo, sposob deystvy etc. po ukazaniyam pokoynogo Ya. Brafmana, podtverzhd. faktami iz periodicheskoy pechati. Kiev, 1881, 266 pp.

38. Nikanor, arkhiepiskop Khersonsky i Odessky, Po povodu statyi gospodina Nerucheva "Yevrei i Bibliya," v sbornike *Russkie lyudi o yevreyakh.* St. Petersburg, 1891.

39. Nilus, S., *Bliz yest pri dveryakh. O tom, chemu ne zhelayut verit i chto tak blizko. (Protokoly sionsskikh mudretsov).* Sergiev Posad, 1917.

40. *Obshchestvennaya rol yevreystva v tsifrakh.* (Besplatnoye prilozheniye k no. 28 "Russkogo dela.") 23 pp.

41. Ogranovsky, N. L., *Vragi li yevrei russkomu narodu?* Moscow, 1917. 47 pp.

42. *O predmetakh, vyzyvayushchikh na razmyshleniya.* 9 pisem sultana Mendelya Piralieva v redaktsiyu "Novogo vremeni." St. Petersburg, 1881.

43. Osman-bey, *Pokoreniye mira yevreyami.* Sochineniye mayora Osman-beya. St. Petersburg, 1874. 48 pp.

44. Otvet moskovskomu obshchestvennomu ravvinu Z. Minoru. Odessa, 1871. 24 pp.

45. Petrov, S. *Pravda i lozh ob yevreyakh.* St. Petersburg, 32 pp. (s.a.)

46. Poraboshcheniye russkogo naroda yevreyami (Ironichesky ocherk). 20 pp. (s.l., s.a.)

47. Pranaitis, I., *Khristianin v Talmude yevreyskom ili tayna ravvinskogo ucheniya o khristianakh.* St. Petersburg, 1911. 27 pp.

48. Predisloviye, poslesloviye i kommentarii obshchestva "Dvuglavy oryol" k *Nastolnoy knige po yevreyskomu voprosu* T. Fricha. Kiev, "Dvuglavy oryol," 1912. 44 pp.

49. Purishkevich, V. M., Rech na zasedanii 3-y Gosudarstvennoy Dumy 15 Maya 1910, *Stenografichesky otchyot Gosudarstvennoy Dumy 3-go sozyva, 3-y sessii.* St. Petersburg, 1910.

50. Rokotov, P. [Lyubimov, P.], *Po povodu vzglyada M. Ye. Saltykova-Shchedrina na yevreysky vopros.* Kiev, 1883. 35 pp.

51. Rozanov, V. V., Iudei i iezuity, v sbornike *Izrail v proshlom, nastoyashchem i budushchem.* Sergiev Posad, Religiozno-filosofskaya biblioteka, 1915. 94 pp.

52. Sapozhnikov, A. A., *Istoricheskoye znacheniye Rossii.* St. Petersburg, 1900. 30 pp.

53. Sharapov, S. F., Dezinfektsiya moskovskoy pressy. *Sochineniya.* Moscow, 1902, vol. 8, pp. 180–195.

54. Sharapov, S. F., Moy dnevnik. Porosha. Khodataystvo studentov . . . za yevreev i dr. Sochineniya, Moscow, 1901, vol. 5, pp. 33–39.

55. Shmakov, A. S., *Delo "Soedinennogo" banka.* Moscow, tipografiya Suvorina, 1909, 12 pp.

56. Shmakov, A. S., *Gomelskoye delo*. Besplatnoye prilozheniye k gazete "Russkoye delo." Moscow, 1905. 48 pp.
57. Shmakov, A. S. *Pogrom yevreev v Kieve*. Moscow, 1908. 110 pp.
58. Shmakov, A. S. *Rech po yevreyskomu voprosu*, proiznesyonnaya 12 i 13 fevralya 1911 nf VIII s'yezde obyedinyonnykh dvoryanskikh obshestv v Sant-Peterburge. Moscow, 1911, 49 pp.
59. Shmakov, A. S. *Yevrei v istorii*. Kharkov, "Mirny trud," 1908. 165 pp.
60. Shtik, M. E., *Mozhno li dat yevreyam ravnopraviye?* Odessa, tipografiya "Za tsarya, za narod," 1907. 32 pp.
61. Sidorov, A. A., *Inorodchesky vopros i ideya federalizma v Rossii*. Moscow, 1912. 68 pp.
62. Spasky, P. N., *V zashchitu vetkhozavetnykh patriarkhov*. Po povodu statyi M. O. Menshikova "Chitayte Bibliyu." Novgorod, 1914. 27 pp.
63. Tamber, S., *Yevrei pered sudom zdravogo smysla* (Po povodu knigi gospodina Lernera "Mayor Osman-bey pered sudom zdravogo smysla.") Odessa, 1875. 29 pp.
64. Tolstoy, I. I., *Antisemitizm v Rossii i drugiye statyi po yevreyskomu voprosu*. Petrograd, Russkoe obshchestvo izucheniya yevreyskoy zhizni, 1917. 96 pp.
65. Uboy skota zhidami. Trudy obshchestva izucheniya iudeyskogo plemeni. Edited by Zhidnev. St. Petersburg, 'Userdiye," 1914. 39 pp.
66. Velikorossov, M., *Zadachi russkoy politiki s natsionalnoy tochki zreniya*. St. Petersburg, 1907. 40 pp.
67. Yuzefovich, M. V., *Yevreysky vopros v pechati i zhizni*. Kiev, 1904. 16 pp.

III. Books Containing Statements Made by Nazi "Theorists"

1. Adamov, S., Vospitaniye shovinizma v nemetskom narode dlya totalnoy voyna—*Istorichesky zhurnal*, 1943, no. 10, pp. 24–42.
2. Aleksandrov, G., Mif XX stoletiya—*Bolshevik*, 1941, no. 13, pp. 23–33.
3. *Anatomiya voyny*. Novye dokumenty o roli germanskogo monopolisti-cheskogo kapitala v podgotovke i vedenii Vtoroy mirovoy voyny. Trans. from German. Edited by G. I. Alexandrov and I. Yu. Roginsky. Moscow, "Progress," 1971. 527 pp.
4. Davos, R., Sobytiya v Palestine—*Kommunistichesky Internatsional*, 1938, no. 11, pp. 58–63.
5. Dvorkin, I., Programma germanskogo fashizma—*Problemy ekonomiki*, 1933, no. 3, pp. 156–180.
6. Fashistskoye strednevekovye (Khronika)—*Inostrannaya literatura*, 1933, no. 3, pp. 140–145.
7. Fogarashi, V., *Germansky fashizm—vrag kultury* M.-L., OGIZ, 1942. 67 pp. [In text—Fogarashi.]
8. Fogarashi, V., Yevreyskiye pogromy v Germanii (Chto za nimi skryvayetsya)—*Mirovoye khozyaystvo i mirovaya politika*, 1939, no. 1, pp. 90–95.

9. Galkin, A. A., *Germansky fashizm.* Moscow, "Nauka," 1967. 399 pp.
10. Gard, D., Rasovaya teoriya i praktika germanskogo fashizma—*Sovetskoye gosudarstvo,* no. 2, pp. 93–99.
11. Germanikus, *Germaniya natsional-sotsializma.* M.-L., Sotsegiz, 1931. 55 pp.
12. Grak, V. N., Franko-germanskoye sotrudnichestvo na Blizhnem Vostoke v period anglo-iranskogo vooruzhyonnogo konflikta—v sbornike *Balkany i Blizhny Vostok v noveyshee vremya.* Sbornik Uralskogo Gosudarstvennogo universiteta im. A. M. Gorkogo, no. 2, 1973, pp. 120–140.
13. Heiden, K., *Istoriya germanskogo fashizma.* M.-L., Gosudarstvennoye sotsio-ekonomicheskoye izdatelstvo, 1935. 394 pp.
14. Khronika. Nauka i fashizm v Germanii-*Vestnik kommunisticheskoy akademii,* 1933, no. 4, pp. 72–81.
15. Kim, G., Karyera Adolfa Gitlera—*Oktyabr,* 1932, no. 2, pp. 88–97.
16. Koreev, N., *Tretya imperiya v litsakh.* Moskow, Gosudarstvennoye izdatelstvo khudozhestvennoy literatury, 1937. 531 pp.
17. *Korichnevaya kniga o podzhoge reykhstaga i gitlerovskom terrore.* Moscow, izdatelstov TsK MOPR SSSR, 1933. 367 pp. [In text—*Brown Book.*]
18. Kral, V., *Prestupleniye protiv Yevropy.* Trans. from Czech. Moscow, "Mysl," 1968. 348 pp.
19. Levin, I. Natsionalnaya programma germanskogo fashizma—*Revolutsiya i natsionalnosti,* 1933, no. 1, pp. 80–88.
20. Maksimov, A., Gitlerizm—razrushitel nauchnykh dostizheny cheloveka—*Pod znamenem marksizma,* 1942, no. 4, pp. 80–104.
21. Manchester, U., *Oruzhiye Kruppa.* Istoriya dinastii pushechnykh koroley. Trans. from English. Moscow, "Progress," 1971. 487 pp.
22. Mikhaylov, G. V., Ideologicheskoye oruzhiye fashistskogo razboya—*"Sovetskaya nauka,"* 1939, no. 7, pp. 187–192.
23. Minayev, V., *Podryvnaya deyatelnost germanskogo fashizma na Blizhnem Vostoke.* Moscow, OGIZ, 1942. 52 pp.
24. *Nyurnbergsky protsess nad glavnymy voyennymy prestupnikami.* Sbornik materialov v 7 tomakh. Moscow, Gosudarstvennoe izdatelstvo yuridicheskoy literatury, 1957–1961. [In text—*Nuremberg Trial.*]
25. Paisov, N., Klassiki iskusstva izgonyayutsya iz Germanii. *Sovetsky muzey,* 1938, no. 10, pp. 44–45.
26. Peter, V., Yevreyskie pogromy v Germanii—*Komministichesky Internatsional,* 1938, no. 11, pp. 92–94.
27. Poltorak, A. I., *Nyurnbergsky epilog.* Moscow, Voyenizdat, 1969. 557 pp.
28. Prestupleniya germanskogo fashizma (Khronika)—*Internatsional molodyozhi,* 1937, no. 1, pp. 29–31.
29. Protiv fashistskogo mrakobesiya i demagogii. Sbornik statey, Edited by I. Dvorkin, A. Deborin, M. Kimmari, M. Mitin, M. Savelyev. Moscow, Gossotsegiz, 1936. 336 pp.
30. Rikhter, T., Kulturnaya politika "natsional-sotsializma"—Internatsionalnaya literatura, 1933, no. 13, pp. 109–117.

31. Rolf, "Chudo nashego veka"—*Kommunistichesky Internatsional,* 1936, no. 15, pp. 86–89.
32. Rubinshteyn, Ye., K kharakteristike germanskogo fashizma—*Istorik-marksist,* 1932, nos. 1–2, pp. 79–116.
33. *"Sovershenno sekretno! Tolko dlya komandovaniya!"* (Strategiya fashistskoy Germanii v voyne protiv SSSR—Dokumenty i materialy). Moscow, "Nauka," 1967. 751 pp.
34. *SS v deystvii.* Dokumenty o prestupleniyakh SS. Trans. from German. Pod red. i s predisloviyem M. Yu. Roginskogo. Moscow, Izdatelstvo inostrannoy literatury, 1960. 675 pp.
35. *SS v deystvii.* Dokumenty o prestupleniyakh SS. Trans. from German. Pod red. i s predisloviyem M. Yu. Roginskogo, Moscow, "Progress," 1969. 624 pp.
36. Struve, V. V., Chto kroyetsya pod fashistskim antisemitizmom—*Sputnik agitatora,* 1941, no. 24, pp. 13–23.
37. Struve, V. V., *Fashistsky antisemitizm.* M.-L., Izdatelstvo AN SSSR, 1942, 20 pp. [In text—Struve.]
38. Treinin, I., *Bespraviye i proizvol v fashistskoy Germanii.* Moscow, Sotsegiz, 1936. 47 pp.
39. Varga, Ye., Istinnoye litso germanskogo fashizma. *Mirovoye khozyaystvo i mirovaya politika,* 1933, no. 1, pp. 3–20.
40. Viden, P., Ognyom i mechom—*Kommunistichesky Internatsional,* 1939, no. 1, pp. 101–103.
41. Zilberfarb, I., Fashistsky razgrom germanskoy shkoly—*Sovetskaya pedagogika,* 1941, no. 9, pp. 7–25.
42. Zilberfarb, I., Fashizm—vrag nauki—*Pod znamenem marksizma,* 1938, no. 5, pp. 76–93.
43. Zverstva fashistskikh pogromshchikov (Obzor inostrannoy pechati)—*Sputnik agitatora,* 1938, no. 22, pp. 37–39.

IV. Books and Articles by Soviet Authors

1. Altshuler, M. S., *Chto yest iudaizm.* Moscow, "Moskovsky rabochy," 1968. 112 pp.
2. Antonov, B., Delo Shterna i kompaniya klevety—*Chelovek i zakon,* 1977, no. 6, pp. 28–37.
3. Avshalumova, L., *Imenem Boga Yakhve . . .* Makhachkala, Dagestanskoye knizhnoye izdatelstvo, 1967. 62 pp.
4. Bditelnost i yeshchyo raz bditelnost—*Ogonek,* 1953, 25 yanvarya, no. 4. p. 1.
5. Begun, V., *Polzuchaya kontrrevolutsiya,* Minsk, "Belarus," 1974, 190 p.
6. Begun, V., *Sionizm i iudaizm.* Materialy v pomoshch lektoru. Minsk, Znanie. BSSR, 1972. 19 pp.
7. Begun, V., *Vtorzheniye bez oruzhiya.* Moscow, Molodaya Gvardiya, 1977. 176 p. [In text—Begun.]
8. Begun, V., Vtorzheniye bez oruzhiya—*Neman,* 1973, no. 1, pp. 100–114.

9. Bolshakov, V., Kritika sionizma v sovetskoy istoriografii—*Voprosy istorii*, 1973, no. 9, pp. 78–88.

10. Bolshakov, V. V., *Sionizm na sluzhbe antikommunizma*. Moscow, Politizdat, 1972. 230 pp.

11. Dmitriev, Ye., *Palestinsky uzel* (K voprosu ob uregulirovanii palestinskoy problemy), Moscow, "Mezhdunarodnye otnosheniya," 1978. 304 pp.

12. *Dokumenty oblichayut rasizm.* Moscow, "Nauka," 1968. 247 pp.

13. Genin, I. A. *Palestinskaya problema.* Stenogramma publichnoy lektsii. Moscow, "Pravda," 1948. 28 pp.

14. Ginzburg, V. L., Kto i kak sozdal teoriyu ontositelnosti?—*Voprosy filosofii*, 1974, no. 8, pp. 125–140.

15. Golovenko, F., Vysoko derzhat znamya sovetskogo patriotizma v iskusstve i literature—*Bolshevik*, 1949, no. 3, pp. 39–48.

16. Gorbunova, Ye., Oshibochnaya konsteptsiya—*Teatr*, 1949, no. 7, pp. 89–94.

17. Gromyko, A. A., Vystupleniye 15 maya 1947 na spetsialnoy sessii Generalnoy Assamblei OON—*Pravda*, 1947, 16 maya, no. 121 (10512).

18. Gromyko, A. A., Vystupleniye na plenarnom zasedanii Generalnoy Assamblei OON 26 noyabrya 1947—*Pravda*, 1947, 30 noyabrya, no. 319 (10710).

19. Gus, M., Sovetsky teatr—teatr sotsialisticheskogo realizma—*Teatr*, 1949, pp. 40–53.

20. Ideologiya i praktika mezhdunarodnogo sionizma. Moscow, Politizdat, 1978, 270 pp.

21. Ivanov, Yu., *Ostorozhno: sionizm!* Ocherki po ideologii, organisatsii i praktike sionizma. Moscow, Politizdat, 1963. 165 pp.

22. Kichko, T., *Pravda ob iudeyskoy religii* (V pomoshch lektoru). Kiev, 1961. 35 pp.

23. Korneev, L., Shpionsky sprut sionizma—*Ogonek*, 1977, no. 5, pp. 26–28.

24. Korneev, L., *Vragi mira i progressa.* Moscow, "Pravda," 1978. 47 pp. [In text—Korneev.]

25. Lebedev, P., Iz istorii sovetskogo iskusstva (Oktyabrskaya revolyutsia i pervye meropriyatiya Sovetskoy vlasti v oblasti iskusstva)—*Iskusstvo*, 1949, no. 1, pp. 62–70.

26. Lutsky, V. B., *Palestinskaya problema.* Stenogramma publichnoy lektsii, prochitannoy 9 avgusta 1946 v Tsentralnom parke kultury im. A. M. Gorkogo v Moskve. Moscow, "Pravda," 1948. 32 pp.

27. Melikadze, Ye., Khudozhnik—boyets peredovoy linii ideologicheskogo fronta—*Iskusstvo*, 1948, no. 6, pp. 10–13.

28. *Mezhdunarodny sionizm: istoriya, politika* (sbornik statey). Moscow, "Nauka," 1977, 176 pp.

29. Modzhoryan, L. A., *Prestupnaya politika sionizma i mezhdunarodnoye pravo.* Moscow, "Znaniye," 1973. 64 pp.

30. Molchanov, N. N., *Jaures* (Seriya "Zhizn zamechatelnykh lyudey"). Moscow, "Molodaya gvardiya," 1969, 397 pp.

31. Nisses, E. Ya., *Sionistskaya zapadnya.* Simferopol, "Tavriya," 1976, 111 pp.

32. *Noveyshaya istoriya* (1917–1939) Uchebnik dlya 9 klassa sredney shkoly. Pod red. V. K. Furayeva. Moscow, "Prosveshcheniye," 1978. 412 pp.

33. *Noveyshaya istoriya* (1939–1975). Uchebnoe posobie dlya 10-go klassa sredney shkoly. Pod red. V. K. Furayeva. 7th ed. Moscow, "Prosveshcheniye," 1976. 270 pp.
34. Pikul, V., U posledney cherty—*Nash sovremennik*, 1979, NN. 4–7.
35. Pokormyak, N. V., *Armiya Izrailya—orudiye imperialisticheskoy agressii*, Moscow, Voyenizdat, 1977, 141 pp.
36. *Printsip otnositelnosti*. Sbornik rabot po spetsialnoy teorii otnositelnosti. Sostav. A. A. Tyapkin. Moscow, Atomizdat, 1973. 332 pp.
37. Rafes, M. G., *Palestinsky pogrom i palestinskaya ideya*. Moscow, Gos. izdatelstvo, 1920, 30 pp.
38. *Reaktsionnaya sushchnost sionizma*. Sbornik materialov. Moscow. Politizdat, 1972. 206 pp.
39. Romanenko, A., *Klassovaya sushchnost sionizma*. Leningrad, "Znanie," 1975. 17 pp.
40. Rumyantsev, F. Ya., *Taynaya voyna na Blizhnem i Srednem Vostoke*. Moscow, "Mezhdunarodnye otnosheniya," 1972. 230 pp.
41. Semenyuk, V. A., *Natsionalisticheskoe bezumie: ideologiya, politika i praktika mezhdunarodnogo sionizma*. Minsk, "Belarus," 1976. 253 pp.
42. *Sionizm—orudiye imperialisticheskoy reaktsii*. Moscow, Politizdat, 1971, 80 pp.
43. *Sionism—otravlennoye oruzhiye imperializma*. Dokumenty i materialy. Moscow, Politizdat, 1970, 319 pp.
44. *Sionism: teoriya i praktika*. Moscow, Politizdat, 1973, 239 pp.
45. Skurlatov, V., *Sionizm i aparteid*. Kiev, Politizdat Ukrainy, 1975, 120 pp.
46. Soobshcheniya TASS o voyennykh deystviyakh v Palestine—*Pravda*, 1948, 16 maya, no. 137 (10878); 17 maya, no. 138 (10879); 24 maya no. 145 (10886); 9 iyunya, no. 154 (10895).
47. *Sovetskie yevrei: mify i deystvitelnost*. Moscow, APN, 1972. 61 pp.
48. Soyfer, D. I., *Sionizm—orudie antikommunizma*. Dnepropetrovsk, "Promin," 1976. 142 pp.
49. *Tseli i metody voinstvuyushchego sionizma* (Sbornik statey). Moscow, Politizdat, 1971, 96 pp.
50. Yaroslavsky, Ye., *Bibliya dlya veruyushchikh i neveruyushchikh*. Moscow, Politizdat, 1977. 375 pp.
51. Yemelyanov, V., Sionizm bez maski. Retsenziya na knigu V. Beguna "Vtorzheniye bez oruzhiya," M., 1977—*Nash sovremennik*, 1978, no. 8, pp. 188–190.
52. Yevseev, Ye. S., *Fashizm pod goluboy zvezdoy*. Pravda o sovremennom sionizme: yego ideologii, praktike, sisteme organizatsii krupnoy yevreyskoy burzhuazii. Moscow, "Molodaya gvardiya," 1971 [In text—Yevseev.]
53. Yevseev, Ye., Iz istorii sionizma v tsarskoy Rossii—*Voprosy istorii*, 1973, no. 5, pp. 59–78.
54. Zalessky, V., Kleveta ideologicheskogo diversanta—*Teatr*, 1949, no. 1, pp. 13–16.

PART

IV

Studies

Introduction

S. ETTINGER

THE ANTI-SEMITIC CAMPAIGN being conducted today by the Soviet Union in the guise of anti-Zionism has been maintained without respite since the Six-Day War—that is, for a period of more than fifteen years. Despite the anti-Zionist cover, this campaign can be viewed as a continuation of the campaign against the "cosmopolitans," an outspokenly anti-Semitic crusade initiated with official sanction in the early months of 1949. It is true that since that time there have been periods of less intensive anti-Semitic activity, particularly after the Twentieth Congress of the Soviet Communist party in 1956. But the early 1960s—the last years of Khrushchev's regime—witnessed a rise in the use of anti-Semitic literature. It is, therefore, difficult to determine precisely what marks the end of the campaign against the "cosmopolitans," since the latter merges into the beginning of the "anti-Zionist" campaign of 1967—a campaign which became truly aggressive after the Czech attempt at "communism with a human face" in 1968 and its repression by Soviet tanks. Because of the continuity of Soviet postwar anti-Semitism and the concentrated use of the mass media for its dissemination (not only in the Soviet Union but throughout the world), it is of particular importance that its expressions as well as its political and social goals be studied carefully.

It is well known that in the Soviet Union and in the countries of the Soviet bloc the press and mass media are under strict government control. They are subject to severe censorship and forced to adhere to instructions as to what line they should adopt toward developing events. As a result, it has often been concluded that all propaganda campaigns in the Communist bloc reflect official policy and initiative. But this is not so. In Communist countries there is still room for local initiative and for the expression of conflicting positions—particularly when these arise between bureaucratic pressure groups with different interests, though also when they emerge between different social and national units. But, of course, the central authorities can silence such conflicts immediately whenever they view them as detrimental to their own interests. It is this total control of the mass media which has made possible the sudden changes of position which have often taken Western observers by surprise; the shift, for example, from the Popular Front policy against fascism to the condemnation of the English and French military effort against Nazi Germany as an "imperialist war"; or the halt of the "anti-Tito" campaign, after a long period during which Tito was attacked as an enemy and an "imperialist agent"; or the sudden about-faces in official policy toward China from the 1950s through the 1970s.

The different levels of opinion existing in the official circles of the Soviet Union should thus be taken into account when considering attitudes to Jews, Judaism, and Israel. In addition, alongside the continuing "anti-Zionist" campaign of the official organs there exist forms of popular as well as intellectual anti-Semitism. Extreme anti-Semitism is to be found even in certain circles of dissidents who consistently and forcefully oppose government policies. Among these some accuse the government of taking a "weak position" on Jews; others perceive in the course followed by the present Soviet government signs of "Jewish influence." There are also social and national groups within the Soviet Union whose attitude to the Jews and their heritage is extremely hostile. Certain papers, such as those of the army and unions, are conspicuous for the harshness of their attacks on Judaism and Zionism, and display a marked tendency to draw their images and arguments from the anti-Semitic literature and cartoons of prerevolutionary Russia or the West. It is this diversity of anti-Semitic opinion which makes a systematic investigation so necessary. Anti-Semitic manifestations must be studied in their different forms, and an effort made to analyze them from different points of view, asking, for example, the following questions: What are the aims behind the dissemination of various sorts of anti-Semitic material? To what public is this literature directed? Does it reflect the genuine opinion of those who produce it, or does it constitute deliberate propaganda, designed to arouse an emotional response in the masses?

It is especially important that an examination of this kind be undertaken concerning events within Great Russia, in view of the long tradition of hostility to Jews which has developed as an integral part of Russia's religious and cultural heritage. The roots of this animosity go back to religious disputes which drew their anti-Jewish arguments from Byzantine literature, to hostility to Judaism in Kievan Russia, to the response to the Judaizer "heresy" at the close of the fifteenth century: these attitudes were absorbed into the cultural tradition of Muscovite Russia. It was apparently the Judaizing heresy, for example (along with the expulsions and persecutions of Jews in Western Europe in the same period), which provided the stimulus for the official attitude forbidding any Jew to take up residence in Russia, even temporarily. This measure was enforced until the latter third of the eighteenth century, when, with the partition of Poland, the Russian Empire absorbed half the world's Jews. Yet in spite of the changes which accompanied Poland's partition—or perhaps precisely because of it—the negative image of Jews and the hostile attitude to them remained fixed in the Russian public mind throughout the nineteenth century. With only a few exceptions, the Jew appears as a negative figure in Russian literature, and from the late 1860s onwards, we find an increasing number of attacks on Jews and Judaism in the publications of both right- and left-wing camps. The Russian literary masterpieces of the nineteenth century—the highest expression of Russian national culture of the time—generally shun the Jew as if he does not exist. When the Jew *is* depicted, he is portrayed as a hollow, stereotypic, ridiculous figure.

The second half of the nineteenth century witnessed a change in the status and role of the Jews in Russian society. From actual isolation and alienation, when only a handful of Jewish intellectuals had succeeded in establishing contact with the surrounding society, the Jews now found themselves in a position which permitted not a few of them to assume important roles in Russian life. Jews appeared as economic entrepreneurs (railroad builders, bankers, and the like), as lawyers, physicians, journalists, and, to an increasing degree, as revolutionaries striving to overthrow the tsarist regime. This change brought about, for the first time, a split in Russian public opinion concerning the Jews. Both liberal and radical opponents of the regime began to protest the anti-Semitic disposition of the government; they demanded equal rights for Jews and called for their integration into Russian society. Anti-Semitism appeared to them a public disgrace; moreover, they discerned in it an intentional device adopted by the forces of reaction to confuse the political perceptions of the masses, turning the latter against an imagined foe (the Jews) instead of against the true enemy (the autocratic tsarist regime). If during the anti-Jewish pogroms in the Ukraine in the early 1880s only a few members of the Russian intelligentsia condemned the rioters and accused the government of taking a permissive attitude or even one of encouragement and incitement, by the 1890s and early 1900s the situation had changed dramatically. All of the liberal and radical currents, all of the political parties which had begun to emerge in Russia—the Cadets, the Social Revolutionaries, and the Social Democrats—energetically protested both official and popular anti-Semitism.

Supporters of the tsarist regime, for their part, presented the Jews (as well as the Poles) as enemies of Russia, acting as agents of hostile Western powers. The real desire of the Jews, they asserted, was to seize control of Russia and, ultimately, of the entire world. It was by no coincidence that during these years the forged *Protocols of the Elders of Zion* was produced in Russian secret-police circles, or that the right-wing deputies in the Imperial Duma unrelentingly attacked the Jews in their speeches. Anti-Semitism became a central topic in publications of these circles. In these same years the government made resort to anti-Semitism not only as a legal and administrative procedure but also as an instrument of propaganda, whereby it might win support in nationalist and obscurantist circles. It acted to encourage the riots of 1905–6, the revival of the blood libel (the Beilis trial of 1911–13), and the spread of accusations that Jews were guilty of treason and speculation, that they were responsible for food and currency shortages during the First World War. Thus anti-Semitic feelings continued to be fostered, so that in the 1920s, when the first signs of disappointment in the Revolution of 1917 appeared, and many began to sense they had been led astray, the ground was prepared for the assertion that it was the Jews who had contrived to bring about the revolution, that they alone had benefited from it, that they had taken control of the large cities and had seized the important positions. Such notions were held not only by workers, many of whom had only recently left the villages for the cities, but also by many among the intelligentsia.

The second half of the nineteenth century did, then, witness the appearance of elements in Russian public opinion which opposed anti-Semitism. But if we compare the short periods in which such elements played a significant role to that long period in which a hostile attitude to Jews reigned supreme in the public mind, it should be evident how deeply rooted in the Russian heritage this attitude had become, and with what relative ease it could be activated among the various strata of society.

The years of Stalin's rule—the 1920s, 1930s, and 1940s—were years of radical change in Russian society. These years saw the painful transition from a country of peasants to an industrial power—a transition carried out with ruthless cruelty by means which included collectivization, expulsions, and exile, the establishment of concentration camps, and mass executions. Enormous industrial and transportation projects were accomplished by exploiting the labor of camp inmates, and in this period the secret police came to exercise supreme control in daily life. These years saw the rise of Great Russian nationalism, and the repression and Russification of smaller peoples. They also witnessed the destruction of the Jewish *shtetl* with its unique culture, and the integration of the Jewish masses into the administrative and professional machinery of a vast state apparatus—one which befitted a system which had declared centralization to be its highest principle. The more the Jews became loyal "Soviet citizens," deprived of roots in their own culture and heritage—the more they became a convenient instrument for furthering the sovietization of society and the Russification of frontier areas—the greater the hostility with which they were viewed by non-Jews of all strata. That this recrudescence of anti-Semitism did not become evident to all was only due to the fierce repression of public opinion under Stalin's regime of terror. It found its release only with the German invasion. For then it was not only the many Nazi collaborators who actively participated in the killing of Jews. Nazi opponents as well, among them men who had fought in the partisan ranks, joined in the destruction, not only failing to come to the aid of Jews, but actively participating in their murder. The Holocaust years uncovered the bitter truth about the Soviet "brotherhood of peoples."

Manifestations of anti-Semitism under Stalin began to appear as early as the late 1930s. We do not yet possess sufficient information to explain this policy shift. Was it perhaps an indication of Stalin's desire to achieve a political settlement with Hitler, the first steps toward which had been taken in 1936–37? Was it an expression of victory over his chief political enemies—Trotsky, Zinovyev, and Kamenev—who were Jews? Or perhaps was Stalin impressed with the effectiveness of anti-Semitic propaganda in recruiting the support of the masses elsewhere, and decided to imitate this method. In any case we have reliable evidence from several sources—from the Polish ambassador in Moscow, Stanislaw Kot, from Stalin's daughter Svetlana, from the Yugoslav Communist leader Milovan Djilas, and from others—that Stalin was adopting an increasingly anti-Semitic stance, and that anti-Semitism had become fashionable among his closest associates. It did not, however, become official policy, whether out of a desire to maintain good relations with Russia's Western allies or because of the need to continue making use of Jewish talents until after the war.

It is no coincidence that the anti-Semitic campaign against the "cosmopolitans" was launched in the early months of 1949, with the intensification of the cold war and the stepping-up of internal repressive measures. That this did not reflect a postition of principle but was, rather, a propaganda tactic is demonstrated by the fact that Jews like Kaganovich and Mekhlis retained their place in Stalin's inner circle; Jews remained, too, in the ranks of higher officials. The lack of consistency can also be seen in Soviet support for the Jews in their struggle against the British in Palestine and in their demand for an independent state. Soviet support on this issue was expressed not only in the international political arena but also by the supply of arms and by permitting the exodus of large numbers of Jews in Eastern Europe who wished to settle in Palestine.

What appears to have motivated Stalin in his anti-Semitic policies was a fear of Jewish solidarity, a fear aroused precisely by the success of Jewish organization and by demonstrations of Jewish solidarity in countries throughout the world. (It should be mentioned that Stalin himself had sought to exploit this solidarity during the difficult hours of the war through the Jewish Anti-Fascist Committee.) It may be that Stalin also believed that the people should be offered an opportunity to vent some of their emotions after the hard times of war, anti-Semitism offering a sure and efficient channel for this purpose. In any event, the signs of this new policy were soon apparent. Jews were accused of scheming to establish a Jewish republic in the Crimea which would separate from the Soviet Union. Plans were made to bring about the elimination of all expressions of Jewish culture and group consciousness. At the 1952 trial of Rudolf Slansky, secretary of the Czech Communist party, an anti-Soviet link between American intelligence, the American Jewish Joint Distribution Committee, and the State of Israel was "uncovered." A group of Jewish doctors was charged with conspiring with these bodies to murder Soviet leaders and public figures. The aim of these measures was to prepare public opinion for the expulsion of all Jews from European Russia and for their exile to camps in Siberia and Kazakhstan.

The charges against the doctors were withdrawn shortly after Stalin's death in 1953, and anti-Semitic propaganda declined for several years. But during the "Black Years for Soviet Jewry" the ideological foundations had been laid and the chief slogans provided for the renewal of anti-Semitism under Soviet regime. The post-Stalin era witnessed such expressions of continued anti-Semitism as Khrushchev's remarks at meetings with members of the intelligentsia (1963), the controversy over Yevtushenko's "Babi Yar" (1961), the trials for "economic crimes" in which Jewish names were prominent, and the publication of anti-Semitic works by T. Kichko (*Judaism without Embellishment*, 1963) and P. Mayatsky (*Contemporary Judaism and Zionism* 1964). It became clear not only that there would be no official retraction of anti-Jewish charges leveled during the "Black Years," but that the Soviet governmental organs were engaged in reviving anti-Semitic arguments from the prerevolutionary and Nazi periods. From this time we can trace the lines of continuity joining the campaign against the "cosmopolitans" to the "anti-Zionist" campaign of the late 1960s and 1970s.

One of the outstanding characteristics of the renewed anti-Semitic campaign is an unwillingness to explain the roots of anti-Semitism by means of Marxist analysis—that is, through an examination of the particular socioeconomic role of the Jews, such as was done, for example, during the educational campaign against anti-Semitism initiated by the Soviet government in the late 1920s and early 1930s. The present campaign, instead of attempting such an analysis, occupies itself with fostering a negative stereotype of the Jew, adjusting it to fit current propaganda needs. The theme of the destructive role of Judaism in world history—a theme developed by French and German anti-Semites in the 1860s and 1870s and adopted by Russian anti-Semites in the prerevolutionary period (as well as by Nazi propagandists)—became a constant theme in Soviet publications in the 1960s and 1970s. According to this line of thought, Judaism has from its very beginnings maintained the self-glorifying idea of chosenness and hatred of non-Jews; in all phases of its development it has promoted reactionary and destructive objectives. There are no positive elements in the Jewish heritage—not even in the teachings of the prophets, not even in the revolt of the Hasmoneans or the revolts against Rome: there is no "progressive" element in these, just as there is no positive aspect to the Jews' tie to Palestine. But in order to avoid becoming entangled in contradictory interpretations, the producers of this literature have increasingly tended to eliminate the Jews from world history, as R. Okuneva shows in her study of Soviet history textbooks published in this volume. When the Jews are dealt with, their history is interpreted in accordance with familiar anti-Semitic stereotypes. The assumption that Judaism is reactionary in nature serves to justify the persecution of Jews in the medieval period as well as the anti-Jewish pogroms in modern Russia ("the revolt of the exploited against the exploiter"). It permits the conclusion that it was not the Christian rulers who were responsible for confining the Jews within ghettos, but rather the Jewish bourgeoisie, which saw as in its interest the isolation of the Jewish masses from their surroundings. And, of course, there is no mention of the important role played by Jews in the revolutionary movements of Europe and Russia. To the extent that the activity of the Bund is mentioned at all, it is presented as divisive and destructive, as serving the aims of the tsarist regime. The same distortion can be seen in the treatment of the annihilation of the Jews during the Nazi period. Seldom does the Soviet literature on this subject mention the courageous action of hundreds of thousands of Jews in the allied armies, among the partisans, and in the ghettos. In fact (particularly in recent years) a concentrated effort has been made to demonstrate that the Zionists and the Nazis collaborated in the destruction of the Jews. Ironically, the spokesmen for the great power which officially allied itself with Hitler in the partition of Poland and in the division of other areas of influence in Europe have chosen to present as evidence of such "collaboration" all meetings between Jewish representatives and officials of the Nazi regime—meetings which took place under coercion or in the hope of saving lives and property. It might be added that hundreds of thousands of Soviet citizens who participated in the Nazi military effort and in the killing of Jews have been pardoned by the Soviet authorities.

The meeting of the Mufti of Jerusalem with Hitler, in pursuit of common political ends which were to include cooperation in the destruction of Palestine's Jews, in no way blemishes the image of the Palestine Liberation Organization; it is only the desperate steps taken by Jewish institutions and organizations that have gone on record as proof of Zionist-Nazi collaboration. This process of grooming the public for the acceptance of an identification of Zionism with Nazism—an identification aimed at persuading the public that the Zionists are the archenemy of the Soviet Union and of the world at large—has been studied through the analysis of Soviet political cartoons by Judith Vogt in her article published in this volume.

A central stereotype which has served anti-Semites everywhere since the nineteenth century is that of the "world Jewish conspiracy"—the central motif of the *Protocols of the Elders of Zion,* of Nazi propaganda, and of hundreds of Soviet publications. In Soviet literature the term used may be "Zionists" or it may be "the Jewish bourgeoisie," but the message is the same: throughout history the Jews have tried to gain mastery over the world in order to subjugate it to their purposes. The "proofs" of this are various. The Jews have seized control of communications and of weapons sales; the Jews manipulated the tsar through the "miracle worker" Grigory Rasputin; the Jews exert their influence on the White House; the Jews were behind the Vatican II resolutions of 1965, whereby defamatory expressions concerning Jews were removed from Catholic prayerbooks; and so on. In his article Yaacov Tsigelman has examined the use of this theme in anti-Semitic propaganda during the period being surveyed.

At a higher intellectual level we encounter the claim that the Jewish creative spirit has been prejudicial to European ideals and values: the Jews are well-poisoners in the spiritual realm. Quite a few scholars adhere to this thesis—indeed, among the best minds of the Soviet Union, men not necessarily notable for their support of the Soviet regime and its methods. Such a view has been studied by Maya Kaganskaya in her examination of an analysis of S. Bulgakov's classic novel *Master and Margarita* written by I. Belza, one of Russia's prominant literary critics. This study reveals to what extent basic anti-Semitic notions are to be found not only among government officials and propagandists but among the flower of the Russian intelligentsia—those belonging to the cultural establishment and those who publish their works in Samizdat alike.

These studies do not begin to encompass the entire array of anti-Semitic expressions in the Soviet Union. As mentioned, a systematic investigation and analysis of anti-Semitism in different areas of Soviet life and creative activity is much needed. The number of scholars devoting their time and efforts to this end is as yet small. Yet the Jewish people as well as persons of good will throughout the free world must not fail to learn from the experience of the past. It was similar anti-Semitic propaganda that penetrated German and other European societies in the 1920s and 1930s, producing a distorted picture of Jewish history and Judaism, and preparing the minds and hearts of Europeans so that they might accept, or even participate in, the Final Solution of the Jewish question. It is thus a cause for deep concern when a great world power follows in the same path, waging an intensive battle against "Zionism" and the "Jewish bourgeoisie" and putting its vast mass-media network at the disposal of those conducting this crusade. An objective analysis of anti-Semitic propaganda in the Soviet Union represents a first step toward dealing with the terrible danger this campaign poses to the Jewish people and the free world alike.

"The Universal Jewish Conspiracy" in Soviet Anti-Semitic Propaganda

YAACOV TSIGELMAN

THOSE DEALING WITH the philosophy of law have noted that the concept of conspiracy becomes current periodically in certain political circumstances, when it is employed to account for hardships experienced under, and failures of, various administrations and regimes. Participation in such conspiracies is ascribed to hidden, secret forces that are declared irreconcilable antagonists of the regimes or administrations which stand to gain from acceptance of this concept.

It is natural for democratic regimes to analyze their system of government, in order to explain their internal and international failures. Totalitarian states, however, are intrinsically incapable of allowing any criticism of the regime or discussion of governmental shortcomings. Yet not infrequently it may be necessary to provide the people with an explanation of such failures. It is the theory of conspiracy which is then brought forward.

The long-standing historical and religious animosity toward Jews, rooted in the Russian people, could often be exploited when accounting for national disasters, and to divert attention from the faults of governments and regimes. Starting from the middle of the nineteenth century, accusations were advanced to the effect that the Jews conspired to destroy the existing institutions and regimes in order to achieve world supremacy.

Even before the French Revolution, some authors wrote about a purported international plot of philosophers and Freemasons against religion and European governments. Later, in the middle of the nineteenth century, Gougenot de Mousseaux published a book in which he linked Jews and Freemasons in a conspiracy aimed at enslaving the nations and obtaining world domination. His follower Abbé Chabaudy further developed the invention of Gougenot de Mousseaux, and the notorious French anti-Semite Drumont made it popular.

In 1905, during the first Russian Revolution, Sergei Nilus, a journalist, published a book entitled *The Great Within the Small: The Antichrist as an Imminent Political Possibility*, with the *Protocols of the Elders of Zion* as a constituent part of the book.

After 1917, the *Protocols* were reprinted and distributed by anti-Semitic circles of the White Guard movement, and in the 1920s and 1930s they were published in Germany in Russian and German translation. The *Protocols* were a great success with the future Nazis. Hitler and Rosenberg printed them in millions of copies, ascribing the defeat in World War I and the Versailles treaty to the dealings of a secret Jewish organization. The Nazi mass media abroad spent huge amounts of money on publishing the *Protocols* in Europe and in the Americas. Hundreds of periodicals republished them in the form of topical satire. Hundreds of books in different languages were written on *the Protocols*, both pro and con.

These plagiaristic fabrications are based on a pamphlet by Maurice Joly,[1] published in 1864 and directed against the regime of Napoleon III. Joly's book is about an encounter between the spirits of Machiavelli and Montesquieu in the Kingdom of Shadows. Montesquieu advocates liberal democracy, whereas Machiavelli recommends a struggle against it, in order to establish tyranny. It was discovered in 1921 that three-quarters of *the Protocols of the Elders of Zion* were taken, with appropriate changes (the Elders of Zion were substituted for Machiavelli-Napoleon) from Maurice Joly's book, which has nothing to do with the Jews.

It has also been proved that the forgery was effected by people working for Rachkovsky, the chief of the Russian secret police abroad at the turn of the century, and that this forgery was intended to influence the policy of Tsar Nicholas II.

International socialist congresses were convened regularly from 1889 on. The socialists talked about the seizure of power and the annihilation of bourgeois society, about the struggle against the old regime by all ways and means. The Russian anti-Semites hated the socialists. Yet the ideas of the socialists at that time seemed to them utopian and not so dangerous. After 1881, the tsarist government feared revolutionary terror more than revolutionary ideas. The Russian anti-Semites saw their true enemy in Jewry. Therefore, it was most convenient to fight the revolutionaries if they could be tagged as Jews or accomplices of Jews. Whatever was discussed at the socialist congresses, especially by opponents of the revolutionaries concerning the plans of socialists, was ascribed by the Russian anti-Semites to Jewish activity rather than to the international socialist movement.[2]

After the Russo-Japanese War and the 1905 Revolution, it became essential to prove to Nicholas II that the Russian people were very satisfied with the regime, and that all the troubles were the result of Jewish intrigues. An event which alarmed all anti-Semites, the First Zionist Congress (1897), in Basle, also proved very handy.[3]

It was then that *the Protocols of the Elders of Zion*, prepared by Rachkovsky's agents, were shown to Nicholas II.

It is noteworthy that not only Russian society knew that *the Protocols* were a forgery; the police department realized it too. This is why *the Protocols* were never referred to at the Beilis trial in 1913. Nicholas II was initially fascinated by the "find," but later, when he had proof that they had been forged, he banned their distribution.

They would have remained in the police archives had there not arisen a political need to refer to them in similar political situations, when unstable regimes were beset by internal unrest and failures abroad, and it was advantageous for anti-Semitic political forces to announce the existence of a Jewish conspiracy, which (rather than the shortcomings of the government and the regime) was "shown" to be the cause of all the misfortunes and troubles of the people.

MODIFICATIONS OF THE "UNIVERSAL JEWISH CONSPIRACY" CONCEPT

The theory of conspiracy adopted by Soviet propaganda assumes the existence of a secret enemy opposing the "glorious forces of peace and socialism." It requires the assumption that all actions and all activities of the party and of the government are infallible and beyond criticism. This implies that if, despite the correct actions of the party, failures occur, they must invariably result from enemy intrigues. This conforms to the popular Manichaean concept of the struggle between good and evil. It also corresponds to a common psychological tendency to blame others for one's own failures and to look for external, rather than internal, causes of these failures, which are regarded as totally independent of the person concerned.

The theory of conspiracy suits the ruling group of people, as it can be used to explain to the masses (in line with their psychological makeup) the causes of various failures of the regime. It is resorted to whenever a situation imperiling the regime arises.

The prewar "plots" in the Soviet Union accounted very conveniently for the failures in the country's national economy and foreign policy, as well as for the circumstances of the Stalinist terror purges, which resulted from the internal political struggle.

The plots were named appropriately at different times: the "Trotskyist plot," the "plot of the experts," and the "military plot." In almost all cases, the "conspirators" turned out to be people picked out by the ruling party group for annihilation. Conspirators were accused of connections with foreign espionage services or with foreign anti-Soviet groups. The "plots" were to overthrow the Soviet regime and establish the power of imperialists, foreign states, etc. A myth was created about each new conspiring group, in accordance with a set plan which included the following elements: organization of terrorist groups, hostility to the Soviet regime, people, and communism, and therefore hostility toward all of mankind. The conspirators were in touch with their foreign accomplices. The conspiracy often involves the entire world. The conspirators were striving for power.

The Anticosmopolitan Campaign

The anti-Jewish "anticosmopolitan" campaign of 1949 was a continuation of the grand anticosmopolitan campaign, which was grafted onto the Russian patriotic enthusiasm engendered by the events of World War II, and nurtured by the Soviet mass media during the ideological cold war with the West.

Jews were among those who contributed actively to the struggle for Russian precedence, against bourgeois influences of the West, and against local bourgeois nationalism, for example, in the Ukraine.

Even at that time, the polemics used tags typical of Soviet journalism. These tags were later to develop as accusations of political unreliability. Articles of that period were entitled, by way of example, "Subservience Experts" (Spetsialisty po nizkopoklonstvu), "Obsequiousness to All Things Foreign" (Protiv nizkopoklonstva pered inostranshchinoi), "Cosmopolitans in Literary Criticism" (Kosmopolity ot literaturovedeniya), "Against the Bourgeois Ideology of Cosmopolitanism" (Protiv burzhuaznoi ideologii kosmopolitizma), etc. The ideological course to be followed was stated in a speech by Stalin: "The Russian people is the most outstanding of all the nations within the Soviet Union." This must have been in conformity with the national tendencies of Russian culture, which coincided with the political line of the authorities. This makes evident the political intention of articles such as the above, hidden behind the "academic" style of discussion.

The anticosmopolitan campaign of that period was not directed against Jews. It was conducted against a certain (actually nonexistent) ideology.

It was common practice in Soviet political life to do away with opponents. The anticosmopolitan campaign was intimately associated with the cold war with the West. It was because of this that opponents, even though their only fault might lie in quoting foreign authors or in referring to foreign authorities, were to be eliminated. It was essential to find a "live target," to detect somebody's evil intention, to find a hidden, conspiring enemy against whom the power of the totalitarian state could be aimed.

The masses had to be given a reason for going along with this. And there appeared Academician G. Aleksandrov's article which called Piatakov a cosmopolitan spy, and Trotsky a notorious cosmopolitan. This was to prepare for the accusation that the cosmopolitans had a hostile attitude to the Soviet regime and that they were enemies of the people.

It was necessary to bring home to the Soviet citizen that, despite all his misfortunes and all the shortcomings of the Soviet system, which in that period included the fact that wartime devastation was still in evidence while other countries had successfully reconstructed their national economies, the Soviet citizen was "superior to any high-ranking foreign official, dragging the yoke of capitalist slavery on his shoulders." It was also necessary to find something to distract the soldiers returning home from the war, full of expectations that changes for the better would take place following the victorious war.

The masses were to be imbued with the idea that vigilance was still necessary, because the class struggle was still going on. The masses were to be told that the former enemy had gone into hiding, yet lived and operated not far away. This enemy was to some extent similar to the enemies of the past.

Jews alone could fill the role of such an enemy. Popular anti-Semitism, enhanced by various events of the last war, could serve a useful purpose here.

Can the anti-Semitic campaign in the USSR be connected ideologically with the Hitlerian concept, on the grounds that Hitler in his *Mein Kampf* belched against the theatrical, literary, and other critics, regarding a talent for criticism as a Jewish speciality? Rather, the connection must be regarded as a normal coincidence of tendencies in the development of totalitarian ideologies.

At the end of January 1949, the newspaper *Pravda* published the article "An Antipatriotic Group of Theater Critics." The article was not signed and was therefore an editorial expression of official opinion. The group of Jewish theater critics was exactly what Soviet propaganda had been looking for. It was publicly stated that it acted contrary to the party's ideological line in the ideological cold war. It made "malicious attempts to discredit Soviet drama." It "operates in disguise, covering the pernicious content of its statements." The members of this group are "bearers of views alien to the people," etc. The denunciation of the theater critics took the form of disclosing an ideological subversion; i.e., it had the character of a political accusation.

It was convenient at that time to refer to the theater critics as a "group." This implied the existence of a plot.

The accusations in the *Pravda* article looked only partly like accusations of a plot: the theater critics were united as a group. This group "served as a conductor of alien influences." It was therefore connected with foreign accomplices and had "malicious intentions." It was "decidedly harmful," its activity was directed "against the party itself." This group was antipatriotic.

The accusation incorporated the elements common to "anti-Soviet plots" and the "Jewish conspiracy" in that it was concerned about the "corruption and destruction of society."[4] The subsequent copy in the Soviet press of the period on the anti-Jewish, anticosmopolitan campaign illustrates how the Soviet mass media prepared for the next phase of the anti-Semitic campaign.

The cosmopolitans were revealed in different fields of art and science. They were found simultaneously in the fine arts, in the Theatrical Institute, in various publishing houses, in historical science, in hydraulics, in the economy and architecture, in pedagogy and physiology. The same ideological struggle against Western influences continued, but now it had a specific "live target." Thus "revealed" was the evil intent of the Jews, who, having decided to destroy and corrupt Soviet society, united into groups in all sorts of institutions—from institutes of the Academy of Sciences to repertory departments of theaters—and pursued the double-dealing policy of demoralizing the society. They covered themselves up under assumed names (the pseudonyms were disclosed right away) or even acted under their true names (the nerve!). The "hotbeds of cosmopolitanism were cut open," the "foul views" were denounced at public meetings as well as in the press. The campaign was aimed not only against Jewish cosmopolitanism but also against Jewish nationalism. For example, the composer Klebanov was accused of having based his symphony on Jewish religious songs. There appeared materials in which cosmopolitan conspirators were identified with Judaism and Zionism.

In the March 1949 issue of the magazine *Oktyabr,* the activities of the cosmopolitans were equated with subversion ("Subversive Activity of the Cosmopolitan Holtzman"), and we were introduced to the slogan: "Down with the Rootless Cosmopolitans!"

The anticosmopolitan, anti-Jewish campaign continued intermittently until 1953. Passions became less fierce when material from the Slansky trial was made public. However, as this trial had, among other things, an anti-Semitic objective, it may be regarded as part of the anti-Semitic campaign of 1949–1953 in the Soviet Union.[5] This trial paved the way for declaring the Joint an espionage organization (later in 1953) and for accusing Zionists, i.e., Jews, of anti-Soviet espionage activity.

The cosmopolitan plot did not yet contain "connections with foreign agents," "attempts to overthrow the government," "aspirations to world dominance," or other elements of the Jewish conspiracy. The anticosmopolitan campaign was, in all probability, meant to become part of the greater anti-Semitic campaign, which also included the Doctors' Plot.

Was there any connection between the anti-Jewish, anti-cosmopolitan campaign and events in the international arena, in particular strained relations with Israel?

In December 1948, Soviet newspapers published reports of the sittings of United Nations councils and committees on the Palestine problem, at which Soviet representatives spoke in favor of Israel; the Soviet Union insisted on admitting Israel to the United Nations. In mid-January 1949, *Pravda, Izvestiya,* and *Pravda Ukrainy* continued publishing these reports in the same spirit, sympathetic to Israel. In March and April, the Soviet Union voted for acceptance of Israel by the United Nations. In May,[6] with the support of the Soviet Union, Israel was accepted as a member of the United Nations, and information on this fact was published in *Izvestiya.* By that time, the anticosmopolitan campaign was at its height.

Was there any connection with the desire of many Soviet Jews to emigrate to Israel? There are indications that Jewish servicemen wanted to volunteer to serve in the war for Israel's independence. At that time, the illegal organization Briha operated in the western USSR and Poland. It helped Jews reach Israel. Many Jews, especially from the Baltic region, wanted the help of Briha. Many non-Polish Jews were ready to go to Israel via Poland. It was during this period that the KGB organized the Kielce pogrom in Poland.

In mid-January 1949, *Pravda* wrote about the demobilization of the Israel army, and in February, about the results of the elections to the Constituent Assembly. However, in April *Pravda* informed its readers that "Israeli reactionaries are trying to interfere with the participation of the Jewish contingent in the World Congress of Supporters of Peace." (It could easily have been silent on this, since in similar cases information like this was not always published.) The Soviet Press carried information on the arrest of twenty-five Arabs—Communists—in Israel, on wage cuts in Israel, and on the general strike.

In its December issue the *Voprosy Istorii* magazine published an article on Palestine, reporting objectively on Arab-Jewish relations and on the attempts of the British administration to introduce tension into these relations. Though the author of the article talks of the Zionists as bourgeois parties, his tone is restrained.

However, a brief note about the conference of the scientific board of the Pacific Institute, published in the same magazine, *Vestnik Istorii,* in March 1949, mentioned the speech of V. B. Lutsky, who dealt with the "problems of the front for oriental studies in the struggle against Zionism—a reactionary ideology of Jewish bourgeois nationalism." Zionism had never been referred to as a reactionary ideology in the past. Lutsky pointed out that the "problems of this struggle have never been struck from the agenda," i.e., even in the period when the Soviet Union was sympathetic to the Jewish national movement and the Soviet press wrote about it sympathetically. The speaker went on to say that the problems of this struggle "have now become particularly topical, because Zionism is an effective tool in American and British imperialist policies in the Middle East." Is there bitterness here at the fact that the Societ Union had lost hope of strengthening its position with Israel? Whatever the case, the speaker stated that "Zionism is being used as an instrument in the subversive activities of the Anglo-American warmongers in other countries of the world," and stressed that "the urgent task of Soviet orientalists consists of exposing and defeating the cosmopolitan ideology of the 'united Jewish nation.'" Lutsky's speech embodies in almost exact form the propaganda formula of the upcoming Doctors' trial. It also served the vital needs of Soviet propaganda conducting its anticosmopolitan campaign; in other words, it pointed out that the ideology of the "united Jewish nation" was cosmopolitan.

Needless to say, the session of the scientific board of the Pacific Institute was not an event of particular importance. However, if one takes into account the fact that Soviet orientalists then and later took part in anti-Jewish campaigns, and formulated the propaganda principles of these campaigns, Lutsky's speech must be regarded, to a certain extent, as a statement of the officially approved position.

The Doctors' Plot

The "terrorist group," "hired agents of a foreign intelligence service," the "international Jewish bourgeois-nationalistic organization, the Joint,"[7] "criminal plans," and other ingredients of the "Jewish plot" appeared in the official communique on the Doctors' Plot. This sounds like the general conspiracy scenario. In January 1953, immediately following the Tass statement, the newspapers came out with the headlines: "Despicable Gang of Spies and Murderers Caught Red-handed," "Political Alertness Must Be Raised to Higher Level," "We Must End Gullibility in Our Ranks."[8] Also mentioned was the contention that the "Anglo-American war-mongers infiltrate spies, saboteurs, and murderers into the countries of the socialist camp," but there was still no word that these saboteurs, etc., were Jews.

At the end of January, the weekly *Novoye Vremya* published an article under the headline "Zionist Agents of the American Secret Service."[9] The author of the article declared, inter alia, that "charity has always served as a *camouflage* [my emphasis] for the espionage and provocateur activity of this Zionist organization sponsored by the American secret service." We have here an additional formula implying the existence of a secret enemy (although used in the context of the anticosmopolitan campaign).

The article informed readers that Zionists had been agents of the Germans, British, and Americans; that the American monopolies, "seeking to woo Zionism . . . make use of the influence and financial possibilities of major Jewish capitalists of the United States." There is not yet an implication that the Zionists *themselves* are striving for world domination; so far, they are pictured only as agents of those who strive for world domination.

The same article connects charges against the doctors with the "espionage" activities of the Joint in Hungary and Czechoslovakia (the Slanksy trial). Thus we have a version of "the spread of harmful Zionist activity throughout the world."

At this stage, no mention is made of "the racist, misanthropic nature of Zionism and the Jews"; no parallels are drawn between Zionism and fascism. But the article mentioned asserts that "Zionists . . . support the revival of Hitlerian systems and the establishment of fascist regimes, imbued with the spirit of racial fanaticism." A little earlier, in a Tass communiqué of January 13, 1953, the arrested doctors were called "monsters of mankind." This formula recurs in all texts dealing with the Doctors' Plot.

Literaturnaya Gazeta carries in its issue of January 24, 1953, Derek Cartain's article from the *Daily Worker.*[10] The article mentions members of the Warburg, Morgenthau, and Lehman families as those who "dominate in the American Jewish Committee"; there is still no word about "Jewish world domination" or a striving for it.

Following the official communiqués (in *Pravda* and *Izvestiya*) on the Doctors' Plot, there appeared a series of articles urging citizens to be on the alert and avoid gullibility.[11]

In response to this call, "hidden enemies" began to be revealed in various institutions: the incumbent of the Khanovich chair at Krylov Academy, Leningrad, and at the Ministry of Geology, and the head of the central board, I. Borisevich, the deputy chief of a department at the Ministry of Geology, G. Zaslavsky; the authors of a manual on the history of law, A. Gertsenzon and Sh. Gringauz, etc. The paragraphs on the subversive activities of Zionists were followed by others on swindlers and criminals with Jewish surnames. Nearly all such articles end with a warning: "Perhaps not all of them have been caught yet."

The Soviet press exalted to the skies Lidiya Timashuk, who "had unmasked the doctor-murderers," and proclaimed her a "symbol of Soviet patriotism and high alertness in the courageous struggle against our enemies." Consistently stressed in these articles was the fact that she was a *Russian* woman, a *Russian* patriot. This brings out the need for a continuous struggle by Russian patriots against cosmopolitanism and the unhealthy influences of Western bourgeois ideas.

The anti-Semitic campaign at the time of the Doctors' Plot lasted less than three months, and failed to develop properly in the "best traditions" of Soviet propaganda. In this campaign, Soviet propaganda went through several initial stages: (1) it exposed a clandestine group, (2) it established its connections with foreign confederates, (3) it outlined its worldwide dissemination, (4) it determined its connections with earlier enemies,[12] (5) it indicated the "internal enemy" to the masses, and (6) it called for alertness and spying on other people. All this was part of the "general conspiracy" scenario.

For the first time, Soviet propaganda applied the concept of "world domination" to the activities of the Jews. Until then imperialists alone had been accused of aspiring to world domination and of having misanthropic plans. The Jews had been referred to only as accomplices; Zionists as agents of the American secret service; and the propaganda materials explained the "inclusion of Zionism in the orbit of American influence." But Zionists are already described as monsters, dregs of human society, and *Krokodil* for the first time uses expressions such as "the adepts of the Zion Kahal," and "this breed of outcasts,"[13] i.e., *we have the propaganda elements of the "Jewish plot."*

In this campaign, Soviet propaganda went through only the first stage of the "general plot" scenario, and then started another stage, the "Jewish plot" proper. It prepared, in the next stages, to develop the fable of the "Jewish plot connected with the imperialist conspiracy" and then, casting away all euphemisms, proceed to "anti-Jewish action throughout the country," which failed because of Stalin's death.

A. Nekrich, in his analysis of the ideology of great-power chauvinism, which has been dominant in the Soviet Union since the second half of the 1930s, asks: "Could not the strengthening of great-power chauvinism be a consequence of the practical realization of the idea of building socialism in one country?"[14] He believes that since the 1930s "everything has indicated that the cultural development [of Soviet society] would be strictly limited to conform to the requirements of politics and Russian conformism."[15] It is possible that the Jews have been particularly affected by this ideology. For example, during the war, ghetto escapees were not accepted by partisan bands, and Soviet partisans sometimes attacked Jewish partisan bands. Nekrich sees the influence of this ideology in the postwar struggle against cosmopolitanism, and in campaigns against the cultures of other peoples of the Soviet Union, which were disguised as being against local nationalism, etc.

Moreover, he regards the assassination of Mikhoels and the Doctors' Plot as indications of the climax in the development of this ideology and of the moral degradation of Soviet society, where "deportation of whole nations has become . . . an instrument of national policy."[16] Nekrich writes that "preparations started at the end of the 1940s and in the early 1950s for the deportation of Jews from the main industrial and political centers of the country to Siberia. . . . The political, ideological, and material preparations for the deportation were already under way."[17]

After the Six-Day War

Before we proceed to discuss the situation following the Six-Day War, let us determine briefly the attitude of the Soviet authorities toward Jews during the period after the liberalization of the 1950s and up to 1967.

In the general atmosphere of liberalization and exoneration, those sentenced in the Doctors' Plot trial were released, and representatives of Jewish culture exonerated. Yet anti-Semitism found expression in various statements of Khrushchev (in particular, concerning the Jewish interpreter of Paulus), in the mounting of trials for economic crimes, in literature, where Jews were pictured as enemies of mankind,[18] etc.

According to one opinion, the anti-Semitism of the Khrushchev period was the result of the growing contradictions in Soviet society; smaller national groups began to fight for admission to the Soviet apparatus. Representatives of these national groups were given the vacancies appearing when Jews were expelled from their positions in the state apparatus and social life.

The anti-Semitic trends of that period in Soviet society were part of the ideology of the new establishment which has replaced the one annihilated by the purges in the ranks of Soviet intellectuals. The members of the new establishment came from the lower strata. They brought with them traditional anti-Semitic tendencies, and they have occupied leading positions in the Soviet state and party apparatus.

Immediately following the Six-Day War, anti-Semitic, anti-Zionist journalism began to build the myth of the aspiration of the Jews for world domination. It is noteworthy that, in addition to articles in newspapers and magazines, monographs appeared on this subject (as well as on the Jewish problem in general). The propaganda made use of all the mass media, including radio, the cinema, and television. Sometimes the amount of such propaganda exceeded the amount of material on life abroad.

Yu. Ivanov's book *Beware: Zionism*, published in the late 1960s, was a classic in the field.[19] Ivanov tries to show that Zionism has been the accomplice of the imperialists and has turned into the leading force in the imperialist camp. For the first time, we meet the expression "international Zionism" instead of the "international Zionist organization" (for example, the Joint was referred to by this epithet at the time of the Doctors' Plot). For the first time we find a detailed discussion of a subject such as "Zionists—accomplices in many grave crimes of the Nazis." Talking of the State of Israel, Ivanov pictures it as a state striving for occupation of foreign lands, based on racial ideology, and oppressing Arabs. This book is the first instance of Soviet propaganda relating to the "Israeli version of apartheid." It suggests that the concept of the world Jewish nation is needed by the Zionists to establish "ideological and political control over citizens of different countries."

Instead of the "aspiration of Jews for world supremacy" the old formula is still used: Israel as an *intermediary* in "the cause of imperialism's economic and political penetration of the developing countries of Africa and Asia." At the same time the author speaks of the "international Zionist complex," which unites Jewish capitalists of different countries. This has as "the principal object of its aspirations and subversive activity the Soviet Union, all socialist countries, and the international Communist, labor, and national liberation movements," i.e., international Zionism is the enemy of all, and the struggle against it is a "vital necessity for all Communists, all freedom-loving people, all working people."

This book betrays a connection with the *Protocols of the Elders of Zion*: the Jews (Zionists) are striving for profits and power, they are the common enemy, and everybody should oppose them. In contrast to the official statements of 1953, for the first time it is claimed that imperialists *back* Zionism rather than that Zionism provides agents for imperialism.

All these formulas and clichés appeared in newspaper and magazine articles in this initial period. Some of these articles have been collected in a rather thick book (more than 300 pages!) whose title is very similar to those of some of the articles of the 1953 period: *Zionism: Poisoned Weapon of Imperialism.*[20]

The formula in which Zionism is presented as the principal enemy was not yet final at that itme, so it seems; it was then presented as the "weapon of the principal enemy." The chapters of this thick book and the article headings appear later in the Soviet version of the "Jewish conspiracy" myth: "Zionist Capital: The Foundation of Israel," "Zionism: Criminal Objectives and Means," "The Alliance of Barbarians," "Zionism: The Instrument of Reaction and Aggression," "Pharisees of Aggression," "Challenge to International Law," "Heirs of the Blond Beasts," "Ominous Axis," "In the Footsteps of Fascist Barbarians," etc.

E. Evseev's book, in which Zionism is, for the first time, equated to Nazism, appeared in 1971.[21] Its cover bears a swastika alongside a Magen

David. The half-title page shows a spider with a Magen David and a swastika enmeshing the entire world. On the title page are a helmet and a bayonet.

This book states that "Zionism today is undoubtedly a variety of fascism." Zionism is already making use of the United States, rather than the reverse. The struggle against Zionism is declared "an integral part of the struggle of the people at large for peace and democracy, an important part of the antifascist movement of the progressive forces all over the world." Here it is stated forcefully that "the clericalists and the Zionist regime in Israel . . . treat all non-Jews as outlaws and are creating a state of continuous hostility between the Jews and the rest of the population of the world." The chapter on "Monopolistic Capital and Zionism" tells of the "financial groups of the great bourgeoisie" that "derive huge profits from the labor of millions of workers, engineers, and peasants," and use this money for aid to Israel. These groups "have extended their tentacles throughout the capitalist world."

Evseev calls Zionism "the active phalanx of anticommunism" and alleges that it "makes use of the basest instincts," directing them against those it disapproves of. "The Zionists' main speciality," according to him, is anti-Sovietism, and he dedicates a whole chapter to this topic. He accuses Zionists of connections with anti-Soviet circles, maintaining that by using the Svobodnaya Evropa radio station they inculcate in the minds of the masses the *corrupting* ideas of the West.

Similar books published in 1972 are also concerned with the subversive activities of the Zionists,[22] but international Zionism is still called "the weapon of aggressive imperialist circles."

In 1973, Soviet propaganda continued to say that Zionist ideological centers were a subordinate part of the general system of anticommunism, explaining that international Zionism had a far-flung network encompassing all the countries of the world. Every effort was being made to prove that Zionism was the enemy of national-liberation movements, that Zionism was a variety of racism. Statements to this effect are found in book after book; they were echoed in newspaper and magazine articles; they were used in oral propaganda in which formulas of the ideological doctrine of the "Jewish conspiracy" against mankind were floated, polished, and selected.

The formula of the "Jewish conspiracy," clandestine, mysterious, and irrational, which enmeshes the entire world, can be found in V. Skurlatov's book.[23]

Skurlatov talks of a "transnational Jewish corporation" which has created "the religion of the chosen by God—Judaism," which has become an ideology requiring the seeking of world power. European racism originates from the "racial concept of Judaism," which gave birth to Catholicism,

Protestantism, "a version of Christianity bristling with racism," and Free-masonry, a secular version of Judaism. "The Judean-Protestant influence is quite evident in the shaping of the ideology of American imperialism." Thus, according to Skurlatov, it is not Zionism which is the weapon of imperialism, but rather the ideology of Zionism—Judaism—which has begotten the ideology of American imperialism. This is how the idea of imperialism being subordinate to Jewish schemes was floated. Skurlatov maintains that the international Jewish corporation "considers itself elect, and overtly claims world supremacy." V. Begun's book was written in the same spirit, using similar formulations.[24]

E. Ivanov's novel *Quiet Shot* contains the message that Freemasons play in tune with the Jews.[25] Several authors write about non-Jews who serve Jewish and Freemason causes without realizing it, thus enhancing the horror of the mighty and omnipresent power of Jewry.

Simple comparison (by the method of "superposition") shows that from the start of the campaign (1967–1969) to the present, the way in which the plan of Zionism is presented has changed, now having assumed an aspect similar to the *Protocols*. Yu. Ivanov's book deals with "international Zionism," whereas Skurlatov talks of the "transnational Jewish corporation." Yu. Ivanov writes of the "Israeli version of apartheid," while Skurlatov discusses the "racial concept of Judaism," which has begotten all types of racism. Yu. Ivanov's Zionism is like a go-between, whereas Skurlatov talks of the subordination of imperialism to Jewish plans.

The same comparison applied to material published in the period of the Doctors' Plot reveals a total change in wording—from accusations that Zionists are accomplices of imperialists to Jewish aspiration for world supremacy. The concept of a "universal Jewish plot," almost completely in line with the *Protocols*, now reached its ultimate aspect, probably because the objectives of the propaganda had changed (from the desire to influence the sentiments of the Soviet people during the period of the Doctors' Plot to the influencing of world public opinion), as had the target (from domestic to external).

THE SOVIET VERSION OF THE UNIVERSAL JEWISH CONSPIRACY MYTH

The twenty-four *Protocols of the Elders of Zion* contain the following statements:[26]

1). There exists a plot in which all Jewry is involved.
2). The immediate purpose of the Jewish plot lies in the corruption and destruction of society.

3). Its principal goal is the establishment of universal Jewish domination.

Several books on this subject appeared in Russian anti-Semitic literature in the early 1900s. The main ones are the books by A. Shmakov, Ya. Demienko, L. Epifanovich, and V. Shulgin.[27]

All these books are concerned with the racial distinctiveness of Jews, the struggle of Jews against Aryans, and the Jewish aspiration for world domination. The authors are trying to prove that the Talmud, *Shulchan Arukh*, and Kabbalah are "repositories of inexhaustible malice and vindictiveness against Christianity" and of the aspiration for world domination. The most typical in this respect is A. Shmakov's book, *International Secret Government*, which reads as though providing illustrations for the *Protocols*. The author of this book resembles many similar authors in that he is ignorant of Jewish history; his meager knowledge of the Talmud, *Shulchan Arukh* and Kabbalah is derived from anti-Semitic sources only. Their hatred of the Jews leads these authors to interpret any fact of Jewish life as being directed against non-Jews and intended to strengthen the purported struggle for Jewish world domination.

The myth of universal Jewish conspiracy is presently being used by Soviet propaganda, which echoes the arguments of the *Protocols of the Elders of Zion* and of Russian prerevolutionary anti-Semitic authors, having adapted them somewhat to the current political situation.

It is stated in the *Protocols of the Elders of Zion* that Judaism, the religion of Moses, has formulated the concept of world Jewish domination, and, thanks to its well-designed system, has established Jewish control over all other peoples (Protocol 14). A. Shmakov discusses the Talmud, Kabbalah, and the *Shulchan Arukh*, devoting several long chapters to them, and refers repeatedly to these books when characterizing the activity of the Jews as harmful to all of mankind. He asserts that the universal menace of this people derives from the content of these books. "The somber God of Israel, the God of rapaciousness, extortionate profit, the God of deceit, reason, cynicism, and every falsehood and untruth . . . malice, violence, and vengeance, leads his 'beloved' people, and subjects us to the Jewish curse, putting us to sleep or into a state of terrible fear."[28]

Soviet propaganda, proceeding from the notion that the Jewish conscience is based on the ideology set forth in the laws of the Torah, Talmud, and *Shulchan Arukh*, maintains that "Judaism today sanctifies the expansionist policy of Israel's ruling circles."[29] "The Jewish religion, formulated in 'Holy Scripture' and reflected in the prayers," writes V. Begun, "embodies the chauvinist idea of world domination."[30] The producers of Soviet propaganda see an ideological connection between the present-day policy of Israel and events in anciet history, extrapolating these events to the contemporary world, analyzing them in terms of contemporary political clichés, such as "The policy of the aggressors in the time of Joshua ben Nun was, in fact, directed at total extermination of the local population"[31] and thus suggesting to readers a corresponding view of the policy of Israel.

In accordance with the compilers of the *Protocols* and prerevolutionary Russian anti-Semites, Soviet propaganda asserts that "the ideological roots of Zionist gangsterism can be traced back to the Torah scrolls and the doctrines of the Talmud."[32] It attempts to analyze the holy books of Judaism, distorting their true meaning, quoting arbitrarily, trying hard to reduce their reasoning to glib conclusions, such as "The Torah and Talmud, in the first place, and the *Shulchan Arukh* and other religious books are a catechism for the expression of hypocrity,"[33] or that the teachings of the Talmud "stipulate that every Jew should unscrupulously try and enrich himself at the expense of goyim, and teach him always to realize his 'superiority' over goyim."[34] Soviet mass media say that the Jewish religious establishment is characterized by "hatred of mankind, advocacy of genocide, and glorification of criminal methods to gain power."[35]

The conclusions and the reasoning coincide almost word for word (allowing for the use of Soviet cliches and terminology) with the conclusions of the prerevolutionary Russian theoreticians of anti-Semitism: "The Talmud is the repository of inexhaustible malice and vindictiveness against Christianity, which dared infringe on the 'divine' monopoly to exploit the world awarded to the sons of Zion by the Sinai Law," writes Shmakov, "and the ultimate aspect of Jewish misanthropy is contempt for all mankind."[36]

"The tale of Mordechai and Esther," writes V. Begun, "served as an example for all rabbis, and all Jewish obscurantists. This tale serves until this day to provide instruction in insidiousness, the use of unscrupulous means, bloodthirstiness, and criminal methods of seizing power," he explains. "The morality (Mordechai style) is quite shameless: Any means, even the most repulsive, serve in pursuit of power."[37] I. Shevtsov's novel[38] mentions an institute in Israel which admits the prettiest girls, to prepare them for the mission of becoming wives of "promising" leaders of young African states, and of states in Latin America and Asia. "Being the wife is a profession," says a heroine of the novel. "Politicians rule over people; their job is politics. But they have wives, and these wives quietly control the politicians. Purim is the greatest Jewish festival. It is dedicated to Queen Esther."

The introduction to the German translation of a book by S. Nilus quotes an anti-Semitic book published in Austria-Hungary in 1901. A certain rabbi in the book says: "We must do all we can to promote marriages between Jews and Christians, as the Jewish people . . . can only gain from this. . . . our daughters thus become members of high-born and wealthy families, so that we, by exchanging kinship for money . . . gain influence on the people around . . . with a little adroitness we will become their masters."[39]

The Soviet promoters of anti-Semitism, following prerevolutionary Russian anti-Semites, and the compilers and reviewers of the *Protocols*, while repeating their reasoning and conclusions, try to show that Judaism and Jewish religious ethics are based on an impudent, cynical attitude toward non-Jews, and that they serve to instruct Jews to enslave other peoples and establish world domination.

It is said in the *Protocols* that the Jews, in order to achieve world supremacy, are planning first of all to corrupt and destroy Christian society: "The main task . . . consists in weakening the social mind by criticism, and turning it away from thoughts of resistance" (Protocol 5); "to multiply popular shortcomings, habits, passions, and social principles to such an extent that all would be confused in the ensuing havoc, and as a result people would cease to understand one another" (ibid.); "we have influenced jurisdiction, election procedures, the press, personal freedom, and (all-important) education and upbringing" (Protocol 9), etc.

The Jewish program, as stated by A. Shmakov, is intended "to stir up shameful instincts, demoralize the people . . . destroy the principles on which national life is based."[40] Soviet propaganda, referring to the events in Poznan in 1956, and events in Czechoslovakia, maintains that all this is the result of "the harmful ideological influence" of Zionists; "the links of the chain can be traced: the Torah—the ideological principles of Zionist 'theoreticians'—the Middle East aggression—the *demoralization of minds* (my emphasis added) in Israel (openly) and throughout the world (secretly)."[41]

A feature of the Soviet propagandists is the replacement of the purported object of Jewish influence; the *Protocols* and the Russian anti-Semites accused the Jews of the desire to destroy and corrupt Christian society and the monarchies, whereas the Soviet anti-Semites charge the Jews with anti-Sovietism, with the desire to create difficulties in the socialist camp. The same idea is propounded in anti-Semitic "belles lettres" for the masses, in which Jews are depicted as sophisticated murderers, debauchers and seducers, traitors, etc.

And again: the Jews are undermining trade unions, they have devised the convergent-evolution theory "to deceive simpletons," they sow the seeds of mistrust and hostility between peoples, demoralize the national-liberation movement.

"We will soon start to establish huge monopolies," say the *Protocols*, "reservoirs of colossal riches, on which even the large fortunes of the goyim will depend" (Protocol 6). The *Protocols* give a detailed description of how the Jewish monopolies must collect gold "despite the fact that we must take it out of streams of blood and tears" (Protocol 2). Shmakov tells of a "Jewish stockbroker" who "usurped" all Russian banks and social resources, world trade in crops; about Jews who are the financial bosses all over the world, but mainly in Europe and America. "Three American millionaires—Jews—have control over the world!" exclaims Shmakov and names them: Straus, Sieff, and Seligman. Evseev, as though supplementing the list, takes pleasure in naming the Rothschilds, Lehmans, Warburgs, Guggenheims, Wolfson, Thomes, Charles Clore, and so forth (ten lines of text altogether). [42] "These capitalist leviathans," continues Evseev, "derive huge profits from the labor of millions of workers, engineers, and peasants" in the host countries of these monopolies. The Soviet mass media, imitating their prerevolutionary predecessors, list Jewish fortunes and spheres of influence in order to prove that Jews capture (or have already captured) the world's riches. [43] "Elders of Zion," "Kahal," "worldwide secret government," etc., are the terms used to imply that Jews all over the world are governed from a single center; this was the belief of prerevolutionary Russian anti-Semites. Shmakov goes as far as to assert that the "strengthening of Jewish power" confirms that Jews have a secret government: "The Jews not only obey the orders of their government without demur, they also do all they can to follow its lead." Soviet propaganda also makes use of the idea of a secret world government. It describes the state of affairs as though the Jews have some secret center which forces the Zionist network, the possessors of Jewish riches, all Jews in general, and "countries dependent on Jews" to aid Israel. "We [i.e., the Elders of Zion] will be surrounded by a whole galaxy of bankers," say the *Protocols*, "industrialists, capitalists, and (particularly important) millionaires" (Protocol 8). Soviet propaganda refers to the Bilderberg meetings and a millionaires' conference like this: "The central place in this 'club' is occupied . . . by numerous financial patrons of the State of Israel and international Zionism." [44]

"Tiny Israel manages great imperialist affairs," writes Begun. He goes on to deal at length with the network in which Zionism has entangled the entire world, and says: "Isn't this network the very nervous system which, according to Max Nordau, must go round the entire world and transmit signals to the Zionist 'brain'—the present aggressive and chauvinist State of Israel?" [45] In the opinion of the author of the Introduction to the German translation of Nilus's book on the *Protocols*, "the Jewish state will become the main power of the Jew—the master of the world." Soviet propaganda offers this concept: "Zionists have always looked on the Jewish state as a means of achieving their capital objectives . . . the establishment of a 'center' through which influence could be exerted on the periphery"[46]—to do away with socialism and establish domination over the world. "To this end, the activity of the Zionist 'concern' with its centers in Israel and the United States is directed,"[47] and so forth. We should, therefore, not be surprised that Soviet propaganda explains to Third World countries "the Israeli phenomenon, being offered to the young Asian and African countries as a standard and example to follow."[48] Soviet propaganda writes about the participation of Jews from other countries in Israel's economy, and about Jewish trade and middleman activities, implying that all Jewry is involved in them. All Soviet and anti-Semitic authors discuss at all levels the worldwide organizational system of Zionism.

The Jews are striving for political power in the countries in which they live—this follows from the *Protocols*. "World powers are unable to conclude even a minor private agreement without us being secretly involved" (Protocol 5). "The goyim cannot do without our scientific advice" (Protocol 3). "We are invulnerable as an international force, since when attacked we are supported by other states" (Protocol 3), and so forth. Shmakov gives a list (see above) of Jews who are political figures in European and American countries.

Soviet propaganda "reveals" that Jews penetrated not only the governments of European states (Begun refers to Max Nordau and lists several prominent political figures—Jews from Crémieux to Disraeli, nearly echoing Shmakov)[49] but also the ruling circles of prerevolutionary tsarist Russia: "It is true that Nicholas II was frequently controlled by Rasputin, but primarily it was Simanovich who controlled him, and Simanovich obeyed the big Jewish capitalists and businessmen,"[50] etc. The Jews create a Jewish lobby, influence government decisions via their henchmen, carry on pro-Jewish propaganda from the United Nations platform, compel the people in power to carry out the will of the great Jewish bourgeoisie; they have turned the United States into the largest Jewish state in the world. All this is being spread by official and semiofficial Soviet anti-Semitic propagandists, developing further Shmakov's statements, such as: "It is at their [Jewish] command that coups d'état are performed, treaties between great powers are canceled, blood is shed, civil wars are waged, and whole states fall to pieces and perish."[51]

The *Protocols* read: "In order not to destroy prematurely the establishments of the goyim, we have touched them with an expert hand, and taken away the ends of the mainsprings of their mechanisms" (Protocol 9). It is said there that "administrators selected by us readily become pawns in our game, in the hands of our scientists and brilliant advisers, brought up to manage the affairs of the entire world" (Protocol 2).

Soviet propaganda assiduously counts the number of Jews in the governments of various countries, and the number of outstanding figures in these countries who are Jewish. They devote pages or whole chapters to falsified biographies of Jews, participants in the Czechoslovak uprising, trying to prove that their activity was meant to lead to the seizing of power in the interests of international Zionism.

"Our government will own the majority of magazines," read the *Protocols* (Protocol 2). "The press has become ours. Through it we receive attention while remaining in the shadows" (ibid.). "All of the press, with few exceptions, is already in our hands" (Protocol 7). Shmakov writes about the "newspaper Jew," as though the Jews have seized the press. The press in the Soviet Union is the monopoly of the state and the Communist party. So the Soviet anti-Semites are talking about usurpation of the press by Zionists in other countries. They count how many newspapers and magazines are issued by Zionist organizations throughout the world; they assert that "greater stress is put on the brainwashing of non-Jewish citizens than on work among their own people." "Zionist leaders," writes Evseev, "attach great importance to penetration by their agents of all states, the international editorial offices of all newspapers, the cinema, and television." Soviet propaganda alleges that the events in Czechoslovakia were largely provoked by Zionist agents who had penetrated the mass media of the country. [52]

In exact imitation of the statement in the *Protocols* which says that "we must compel governments of the goyim to act on our behalf. . . through the agency of public opinion, built up by us with the help of the press" (Protocol 7), Begun writes: "Zionists would never be able to sow poison and corruption, in other words to demoralize and destroy society, deceive the people and shape public opinion to their own ends, had they not the most powerful means of propaganda—the mass media—in their hands." [53] Every more or less full-length work of Soviet anti-Semitic propaganda mentions usurpation of the world press and other mass media by Zionists.

It should also be noted that the *Protocols* talk of the need to seize literature as an "essential educational means" (Protocol 12). Shmakov writes about the usurpation by Jews of Russian literature, and speaks of "the intrusion of Jews into Russian literature, and the commandeering of the Russian word and Russian thought by the Israelites," listing contemporary Russian authors, artists, publishers, etc., of Jewish origin. These ideas are echoed in the outpourings of the anticosmopolitan campaign and in current articles by Russian nationalists, opposing "Jewish dominance" in Soviet literature and art. The compilers of the *Protocols* also maintained that the Jews will take "all measures to get rid of all goy intellectuals" (Protocol 6).

Soviet propaganda states that Israel "became a headquarters of aggression, racism, and war immediately after it came into existence."[54] The Jewish Zionist bourgeoisie could never devise such [aggressive] plans and put them into practice "without the assistance and backing of imperialist states."[55] Israel is the "most dangerous hotbed of international tension."[56]

The *Protocols* read: "We must be able to meet opposition with a war against the neighbors of the country which would dare oppose us, but in case the neighbors, too, join their forces against us, we must then wage a universal war" (Protocol 7). Throughout his book, Shmakov talks about Jewish intrigues against various countries, and points to these intrigues as the cause of recent wars. All the Soviet anti-Zionist propagandists write that Israel is an aggressive military state, that the hero of Israeli propaganda is an Israeli soldier "who knows no restraints and who does not relate to norms of human behavior."[57] The Soviet Union publishes photographs of Israeli street patrols, of Arabs being escorted by Israeli soldiers,[58] and so on. Propagandistic "belles lettres" describe Israel as a military camp.

The *Protocols* say that the Jews are prepared to make use of political figures of all complexions, people with all kinds of views, so long as these are in conformity with Jewish plans. Soviet propaganda lists the accomplices of the Jews, such as:

1. *Nazis.* "Zionism has survived and established itself not in defiance of, but rather as a result of, fascism which, in a new situation . . . it is soon going to replace."[59] "Zionists, in collaboration with Hitlerites, helped the latter drive the Jews either into the incinerators of concentration camps or to kibbutzim in the 'Land of Canaan.' "[60] "The Gestapo picked out kapos from the ranks of Zionists for service in the death camps and the special police force charged with keeping order in the ghettos."[61] "A great many prominent Zionists collaborated with the Nazis during the war, betrayed the interests of simple Jews, and looked after their affairs at the price of the blood of those who fought against fascist tyranny."[62]

2. *Government circles in the United States.* "High-ranking government officials are taking an active part in the activities of Zionist organizations in the United States at the wish of monopolistic [i.e., Jewish] capital, which has joined hands with the Zionist leaders, thus showing the whole world the connections and relationships existing between them."[63]

3. *Protestants.* "In the course of the Reformation and under the theme 'Israelite wisdom,' there crystallized—especially in the Calvinist doctrine, the most 'God-chosen version' of Christianity, which bristles with racism—Protestantism, which has become an ideology of ascendant capitalism."[64]

4. *Agents and allies of Zionism among non-Jews.* "People, politically

naive, fooled or bribed by Zionists, unscrupulous morally. . . . Zionists sometimes control various reactionary groups and organizations consisting of non-Jews."[65]

A special place among "Jewish accomplices" is reserved for Freemasons. The *Protocols* maintain that there is "overt Freemasonry" and an "organization of secret Freemasonry which is not widely known and whose objectives are not even suspected by the goy swines attracted by us to the ostentatious Freemason lodges set up to decoy their fellow citizens" (Protocol 11). Shmakov assures us that B'nai B'rith is such a secret Freemason organization—the "secret Israelite league"[66]—while "Judaism and Freemasonry [overt, apparently?] are parallel movements."[67]

Soviet propaganda, following Shmakov and the *Protocols*, tries to depict the Jews and Freemasons as enemies of Russia, in historical perspective. For example, Egor Ivanov's novel, *Quiet Shot* narrates the events preceding World War I.[68] The author's main objective is to show the reader that World War I was prepared and started by Freemasons close to the German imperial court, and their supporters and agents in Russia. In the novel, there are numerous Jews among German and Russian Freemasons, and their secret leaders are also Jews—the bankers Altschiller and Maus connected with the Rothschilds. They spin insidious nets, prosecute the war, and strive to enslave Russia and the Russian people.

"We . . . will create and multiply Freemasonry lodges in all the countries of the world," read the *Protocols*, "and will draw into them all potential and existing public figures" (Protocol 15). Soviet propaganda, echoing the compilers of the *Protocols*, writes: "The organizational diversity of Zionism . . . was planned by Zionist strategists to provide versatility and manoeuverability in action. . . . it has been adapted to assert Zionist influence on special groups."[69] Zionist agents in Czecholslovakia "were to penetrate ideological cadres, the party and state apparatus, disguised as people extremely loyal to the new regime. . . . Having settled in . . . the Zionists were expected to play the role of dedicated Communists, people devoted to Marxism, in order to worm themselves into people's confidence and . . . carry out in an underhanded way the erosion of socialism."[70] Ideological subversion is a mode of Zionist activity.[71] "We will make states into arenas in which to sow discord" (Protocol 3). "Zionists train their confederates the way the Nazi SS were trained."[72] "Jewry is a pack of wolves on the hunt!"[73] and so on.

The *Protocols* define the goal of Judaism in the following way: "We were told by our prophets that we had been chosen by God Himself to dominate this earth" (Protocol 5). Shmakov insists that the creation of a secret international government, the seizure of world power, and world domination are the Jewish goal. The identity of views of these authors with those of the Soviet publicist V. Begun is confirmed by A. Meleshko, a Ph.D. in history, who wrote the preface to the *Creeping Counterrevolution:* "The author sees the major strategic goal of Zionism as the creation of a variety of ultraimperialism with which to exploit the world."

Begun writes in another book: "Zionism has emerged . . . with the purpose of imperialist enslavement" of peoples,[74] and V. Emelyanov, in his review of the book, explains: "The main strategic objective of Zionism is destruction of the socialist system and the establishment of world supremacy."[75]

Soviet pamphleteers, explaining to Third World countries the goals of Jewish activity, allege that "one of the purposes is subversive activity against socialism."[76] For this purpose, V. Skurlatov's wording is appropriate: "Zionism and Judaism have as their common purpose world supremacy."[77]

Pages and pages of Soviet anti-Semitic literature are devoted to this task—to show Zionism as the enemy of national-liberation movements and young states which have shaken off the chains of colonialism: "International Zionism . . . the active phalanx of anticommunism . . . is an insidious enemy of the national-liberation movement of many peoples." "The racist concept of Judaism has served as a prototype of European racism." "International Zionism is the enemy of all peoples, all national groups and nations." Zionism opposes national-liberation movements! Zionism is the weapon of Anglo-American imperialism! Israel is the intermediary in the economic and political penetration of young African and Asian states![78] So Soviet anti-Semitic propagandists exclaim, warning Third World countries. And the compilers of the *Protocols* as well as the prerevolutionary anti-Semitic pamphleteers stressed that Jews are hostile to Christian civilization, that in their aspiration for world power they do not spare non-Jews—"We would rejoice if the goyim became denerate" (Protocol 3); and "the ultimate in the development of Jewish misanthropy," writes Shmakov, "is found in their rabid disdain for the whole of mankind. . . . They pray to their Jehovah, imploring Him to exterminate them (the goyim) as soon as possible," etc., etc.

Soviet pamphleteers at first pictured the Jews as enemies of socialism: Zionists planned to have "strike-breakers and other imperialist agents in many countries of the revolutionary movement."[79]

But later, Soviet anti-Semites gave up their camouflage and tried to say that the Jews, in the course of their historical development, by reason of the ideology which underlies the Jewish holy books, and as a result of their racial peculiarities, have been part of the exploiter classes—in Egypt they were "tenant farmers, supervisors of river and marine navigation";[80] in the medieval period they "were mainly occupied in trade, including the slave trade."[81]

And, finally, Soviet pamphleteers started to declare that the Zionists "outlaw non-Jews and are responsible for the permanent state of war between the Jews and the rest of the world population"; that "violence, chauvinism, and the misanthropic preaching of Jewish racism have been made a cult, have become official policy of the State of Israel."[82] This is why, Soviet propaganda explains, the Jews arouse "the natural hostile reaction of the local population to their hegemonic claims."[83] "Popular wrath turned against Jewish usurers, tavern keepers, factory owners, and merchants"; in the Ukraine and in Belorussia "the rapacious Jewish leaseholders, tenant farmers, usurers, and tavern keepers were the embodiment of economic exploitation."[84] In these terms, Soviet anti-Semites, in the tradition of their predecessors, justify anti-Semitism and pogroms. There is nothing new about the Soviet propaganda statement that Zionists "arouse anti-Semitism artificially through subversion in synagogues and the defiling of Jewish cemeteries."[85] The *Protocols* read: "if we . . . arouse protest against us, this is for the sake of appearances and at our own discretion and instruction, as . . . anti-Semitism is instrumental for us in controlling our younger brothers" (Protocol 9).

The Soviet version of the "Jewish conspiracy" myth coincides in many aspects with its classic statement in the *Protocols of the Elders of Zion* and in the books of prerevolutionary Russian anti-Semitic authors. This confirms that contemporary Soviet anti-Semitism is directed against the entire Jewish people. It falsely represents the Jewish religion and Jewish history, combining earlier anti-Semitic "theories" in a new ideology suitable for contemporary conditions.

The anticosmopolitan campaign and the Doctors' Plot (especially the former) are campaigns for "domestic use." The present campaign, however, reaches far beyond the borders of the USSR, and the "Jewish conspiracy" myth is being popularized in countries dependent on the USSR, with left-wing Western intellectuals, and among the population of the Third World.

Anti-Semitic propaganda concerning the "universal Jewish plot" stirs up popular anti-Semitic feelings in the USSR that the Jews are the "major enemy."

The formula of the "universal Jewish plot" is particularly elegantly presented by authors who had been in opposition to the government (Skurlatov) but have lately been taking an active part in the anti-Semitic activities of Soviet propaganda. Further elaboration of the "Jewish conspiracy" formula is produced to meet the domestic needs of the regime (the ousting of Jews from various spheres of the social, cultural, and industrial life of the country; the opposing of the desire of Jews to emigrate to Israel, and the need to suppress national and dissident movements in countries of the Eastern bloc) and international needs (the strengthening of Soviet influence in the Communist and leftist parties of Europe and Latin America, and attracting anti-Western-minded regimes and circles in Afro-Asian countries).

Soviet anti-Semitic propaganda does not formally claim that the *Protocols of the Elders of Zion* are authentic. It makes use of the myth of the "universal Jewish conspiracy" expounded in them, gives its own interpretation of the false evidence contained in the *Protocols* and in the works of Russian prerevolutionary anti-Semites, and tries to update the phraseology of the *Protocols* and adapt it to that currently used by Soviet propaganda. The hacks of Soviet anti-Semitic propaganda prefer, as did the authors of Russian prerevolutionary anti-Semitic books, to crib from the books of their predecessors, since these source books are unknown to the prospective consumers of their books, articles, and pamphlets.

The Soviet people have to be given a reason for the failures of the regime in the economy, in internal affairs, and in foreign policy.

We see that failures of this kind are accounted for by Soviet propaganda in terms of conspiracies, and the target of the propaganda, the Soviet people, has learned to believe such explanations. Soviet propaganda also has the task of influencing the leftist Western intelligentsia. Here much is written to distract Western intellectuals from reflections on the essence of the Soviet totalitarian regime. It is also essential for them to inculcate in the minds of the leaders of Third World countries that their failures are the result of the intrigues of the Zionist enemy, and that it is only the Soviet Union, "the stronghold of peace, democracy, socialism, and the struggle against racism and Zionism," that can help them.

Why cannot the failures of the Soviet Union be accounted for by the general formula of an imperialist plot?

Why is Jewry declared not simply an accomplice of the imperialist enemy but the enemy itself, with imperialism given the accomplice role?

Which particular strata of Soviet society are the target of Soviet anti-Semitic propaganda of this sort?

Is there a connection between the propaganda regarding the "universal Jewish conspiracy" and the continued desire of the Soviet authorities to erase from the memory of the people the participation of Jews in the revolutionary movement, or to present this participation as treacherous and hostile, in order to show that the character of the revolution was truly Russian?

One thing is clear so far: the myth of the universal Jewish plot against the Soviet Union and all mankind is also necessary for the Soviet authorities in order to unite the people against a common enemy. Is this connected, and if so, to what extent, with the intensification of the regime's tendencies to favor the Russian nation?

Official Soviet anit-Semitic propaganda is by no means intended for the elite of the Soviet intelligentsia, among whom a Russian dissident nationalistic outlook is evolving, because these circles have access to various sources of information. Nevertheless, the myth of a universal Jewish conspiracy is being transformed in a certain way in these circles, too. Somewhat modified, it affects the recently formed Russian emigré circles. What is it in the myth of a universal Jewish conspiracy that so well suits and unites official Soviet anti-Semitic propaganda and the writings of nationalistic dissidents in the Soviet Union and in emigré circles?

This monograph is confined to evaluating the extent to which the myth of a universal Jewish conspiracy, invented by French anti-Semites, developed by Russian and Nazi anti-Semites, and publicized by anti-Semites in various countries, has become the main theme of Soviet anti-Semitic propaganda. The above questions arose naturally in the course of this study.

Notes

1. *Dialogue aux Enfers entre Machiavel et Montesquieu, ou la politique de Machiavel au XIX-e siècle.*

2. For this particular reason, when the 1917 Revolution took place and the Bolsheviks, after the October coup, started putting into practice by totalitarian methods the ideas discussed at all socialist congresses, the *Protocols* suddenly became topical. It was as though the contents of the *Protocols* had materialized. The Bolshevik government included Trotsky, Zinoviev, and others who were Jews by origin only, and who (for example, Trotsky) stated that they did not consider themselves Jews. Nevertheless, their participation in the government enabled Russian anti-Semites to declare that the Jews had seized the reins of power and that the ideas of the *Protocols* had come true.

3. The word "Zion" could easily be identified with the word "Zionist" by those for whom the forgery was intended. At that time and later, the forgery was referred to as the minutes of a Zionist congress, although in some editions of the *Protocols* it was noted that these two notions were not to be confused.

4. See below.

5. During World War II, the secretary of the Central Committee, A. S. Shcherbakov, headed a group of anti-Semites who expelled Jews from prominent positions. After World War II and the Holocaust, the national consciousness of Soviet Jews was stimulated. Possibly the anticosmopolitan campaign was the reaction of the party and state apparatus to growing Jewish consciousness.

6. It is noteworthy that the report of the General Assembly session in *Izvestiya* on May 12, 1949, uses expressions like "Eban tried to assure" instead of the more friendly "assured," and "However, he evaded a direct answer to the question" instead of the formula commonly used in the Soviet press, "he pointed out," etc.

7. "The Joint," "a branch of the American secret service," etc., are the epithets used for this organization, whose philanthropic activity is well known in the West. It may be concluded

that the venom of the entire campaign and the campaign itself were aimed domestically, i.e., for the unsophisticated population of the Soviet Union.

8. *Izvestiya*, Jan. 13, 1953; *Trud*, Jan. 13, 1953; *Izvestiya*, Jan. 15, 1953; *Pravda*, Jan. 18 1953.

9. V. Minaev, "Zionist Agents of the American Secret Service," *Novoye Vremya*, no. 4 (1953).

10. D. Cartain, "Facts about 'The Joint,' " *Literaturnaya Gazeta*, Jan. 24, 1953. Derek Karten, British Communist journalist.

11. "Intensify Political Alertness," *Izvestiya*, Jan. 15, 1953; "Alertness and More Alertness," *Ogonyok* no. 4 (1953); "End Gullibility in Our Ranks," *Pravda*, Jan. 18, 1953, etc.

12. N. Kozev, "Revolutionary Alertness," *Pravda*, Feb. 6, 1953. The article, among other things, tells of the arrest of S. Gurevich, whose, "espionage activity" started when he was a child, in the family of a Menshevik-Bundist, then through the stages of collaboration with the Trotskyites and participation in an anti-Soviet group, and continued when Gurevich established connections with foreign secret services and "for a number of years supplied them with espionage information." It was pointed out that Gurevich had been selected for service in the interests of the foreign secret service because of his Trotskyite and nationalistic views.

13. *Krokodil*, no. 3 (1953): p. 2.

14. A Nekrich, *Nakazannye narody* [Punished peoples] (New York: Khronika Press, 1978), p. 90.

15. Ibid.

16. Ibid., p. 91.

17. Ibid., p. 92.

18. G. Makhorkin, *I snova zhizn* [Back to life] (Moscow: Sovetskaya Rossiya, 1964); V. Tevekelyan, *Granit ne plavitsa [Granite would not melt] (Moscow, 1963)*; A. Andreev, *Beregite Solntse* [Protect the sun], *Oktyabr* 8–9 (1967), etc.

19. Yu. Ivanov, *Beware: Zionism! Essays on the Ideology, Organization and Practice of Zionism* (Moscow: Politizdat, 1969; new ed. 1970). Nearly all books on Jews and Zionism are supplied with loud "ominous" covers. On the cover of Yu. Ivanov's book, a beam of light shining through darkness, lights the words "Beware: Zionism!" The exclamation mark is in red. The graphic artist has thus implied that the book exposes the black and bloody deeds of Zionism.

20. *Zionism: The Poisoned Weapon of Imperialism—Documents and Materials* (Moscow: Politizdat, 1970).

21. E. Evseev, *Fascism under the Blue Star: The Truth About Contemporary Zionism, Its Ideology, Practice, and System of Organizations of the Great Jewish Bourgeoisie* (Moscow: Molodaya Gvardiya, 1971).

22. S. Krylov, *Secret Weapon of Zionism* (Voenizdat, 1972); I. Belyaev, *From the Back Entrance* (Voenizdat, 1972). For more about I. Belyaev's book, see above.

23. V. Skurlatov, *Zionism and Apartheid* (Kiev: Politizdat Ukrainy, 1975).

24. V. Begun, *Invasion without Arms* (Moscow: Molodaya Gvardiya, 1977).

25. E. Ivanov, "Quiet Shot (Chronicle)," *Molodaya Gvardiya*, no. 12 (1977).

26. Taken from *Luch Sveta* (Berlin), issue 3 (1920).

27. A. Shmakov, *International Secret Government: The Jewish Problem in the World History Scene; Jews in History;* Ya. Demienko, *Jewish Strategy and Tactics in the Cause of the Bloodless Conquest of the World.* L. Epifanovich, *Jews: Their Outlook and Social Activity.* V. Zalessky, *Mental Inferiority of the Jews;* V. Shulgin, *Pogrom,* etc.

28. Shmakov, p. 507.

29. Evseev, p. 47.

30. Begun, *Invasion without Arms*, p. 32.

31. *Zionism: Theory and Practice*, p. 41.

32. Begun, *Creeping Counterrevolution*, p. 151.

33. Ibid., p. 64.

34. Skurlatov, *Racism and Apartheid*, p. 13.

35. *Zionism: Theory and Practice*, p. 38.

36. Shmakov, p. 107.

37. Begun, *Creeping Counterrevolution*, p. 150.
38. I. Shevtsov, *Nabat* [Alarm bell] (Moscow: Sovremennik, 1978).
39. *Luch Sveta*, issue 3 (1920); 129–130.
40. Shmakov, p. 526.
41. Begun, *Invasion without Arms*, p. 45.
42. Evseev, p. 75.
43. Begun, *Invasion without Arms*, p. 20; *Zionism: The Poisoned Weapon of Imperialism*, p. 36, etc.
44. Evseev, p. 69.
45. Begun, *Invasion without Arms*, p. 131.
46. Ivanov, p. 55.
47. V. Emelyanov, "Zionism Unmasked," *Nash Sovremennik*, 8 (1978), p. 189.
48. Evseev, p. 74.
49. Begun, *Invasion without Arms*, p. 44.
50. Begun, *Creeping Counterrevolution*, p. 136.
51. Shmakov, p. 396.
52. Begun, *Creeping Counterrevolution*, p. 131; Yevseev, p. 114.
53. Begun, *Creeping Counterrevolution*, p. 132.
54. *Zionism: Theory and Practice*, p. 101.
55. Ibid., p. 102.
56. Ibid., p. 101.
57. Evseev, p. 134.
58. See, for example, illustrations in Yevseev's book *Fascism under the Blue Star.*
59. Ivanov, p. 177.
60. Ibid., p. 176.
61. Evseev, p. 139.
62. Skurlatov, p. 57.
63. Ivanov, p. 193.
64. Skurlatov, p. 15.
65. Begun, *Invasion without Arms*, p. 24.
66. Shmakov, p. 478.
67. Ibid., p. 479.
68. Ivanov, "The Quiet Shot," *Molodaya Gvardiya*, no. 12 (1977).
69. Begun, *Invasion without Arms*, p. 31.
70. Begun, *Creeping Counterrevolution*, pp. 120–121.
71. *Zionism: Theory and Practice*, p. 145.
72. Ibid., p. 135.
73. Shmakov, p. 107.
74. Begun, *Invasion without Arms*, p. 24.
75. V. Yemelyanov, "Zionism Unmasked," *Nash Sovremennik*, no.8 (1978), p. 188.
76. *Zionism: Theory and Practice*, p. 131.
77. Skurlatov, p. 42.
78. Evseev, p. 136; Skurlatov, p. 14; Ivanov, p. 181; *Zionism: Theory and Practice*, pp. 128, 176–195.
79. Ivanov, p. 55.
80. *Zionism: Theory and Practice*, p. 44.
81., Ibid.
82. Evseev, pp. 47, 113.
83. Skurlatov, p. 12.
84. Begun, *Invasion without Arms*, pp. 63, 65.
85. Begun, *Creeping Counterrevolution*, p. 90; on the same subject, see Yevseev, p. 46.

Jews in the Soviet School Syllabus (What Soviet Schoolchildren Read About the History of the Jewish People)

RUTH OKUNEVA

IT IS WELL KNOWN that what is learned and understood in childhood forms the basis of the personality of the adult, and helps to mold his views on morals, and form his ideas and prejudices, including racial prejudice. The history education received by Soviet children in fourth grade, that is, at the ages of ten and eleven, constitutes a significant contribution to the formation of their personalities and their attitudes to the world around them, to occurrences, and to people, including Jews. Perhaps there is a link between the growth of anti-Semitism in Russia at the beginning of the 1880s and the almost complete monopoly of D. I. Ilovaisky, the famous historian and Jew-hater, of textbooks in every course of world and Russian history in secondary schools from the 1860s right up to 1917. And perhaps the slightly anti-Semitic overtones of the popular history textbooks of Professor R. Vipper, which were used before and after the revolution, must bear some of the blame. Their effect on Russian youth was only too strong.

Yet even in these textbooks, in which some light was thrown on the history of the Jews, the Jews of ancient Israel and Judea were treated with considerable approbation. In the treatment of the Jews during the Middle Ages, there is a slight aftertaste of *Schadenfreude*. The Jews of Russia are treated with venom, hatred, or indifference, depending on the views of the author.

That was the position before the revolution. Naturally these views of the role and place of Jews in history had to be significantly changed to evolve and come into line with the ideology of the new society.

Let us look at the changes that occurred in the structure, content, and problems of the teaching of history in schools. Let us see whether history courses considered the question of the eradication of racial prejudice, the degrading of those pupils who do not belong to the national majority, and the education of children, including Jewish children, in a spirit of national self-respect.

The study of history in Soviet schools itself has a complicated history. On October 16, 1918, in compliance with a decree of the All-Russian Central Executive Committee, comprehensive schools were established. The various types of secondary school that existed in prerevolutionary Russia—the classical gymnasium, grammar schools, and commercial and other schools—were brought into one system of "labor" schools which was divided into stages: the first stage consisting of five years and the second of four years. From the beginning of the 1920s until 1934, there was no history course per se. It was considered part of the teaching of social science. Prerevolutionary textbooks continued to be used—including such reactionary books as those of D. I. Ilovaisky and K. V. Yelpatevsky, which were primarily a reflection of the views of the Black Hundreds.

In May 1934, the structure of secondary schools in the USSR was changed, and the following network of general schools was established: primary schools from first to fourth grade, "incomplete" secondary schools from first to seventh grade, and secondary schools from first to tenth grade. Except for some minor changes (incomplete secondary schools with grades one to eight), this is the system in use today.

On May 16, 1934, in compliance with a resolution of the Council of People's Commissars and the Central Committee of the VKP(b) "On the teaching of civic history in schools in the Soviet Union," a separate history course was introduced, and this paved the way for new textbooks.

In 1965, the schools started the study of history proper, which is as it is taught today. In fourth grade, stories of Soviet history are studied; in fifth grade, there is an ancient history course; in sixth grade, the Middle Ages; in seventh and tenth grades, Soviet history; in eighth and ninth grades, Soviet and modern history; and in ninth and tenth grades, modern world history.

From the middle of the 1930s, the periods of history studied have remained unchanged, and this makes it much easier to make a comparative analysis of the textbooks used at different times, and to compare the authors of these texts.

History, like any subject taught in school, fulfills a specific educational function. It serves to fuse knowledge and skills. Educational problems in Soviet schools are seen exclusively as problems of the educators. The *Pedagogical Encyclopedia* states categorically that general education in

Soviet schools has as its aim the "arming" of pupils not just with knowledge, but with that knowledge which "is essential for . . . the education of active, aware builders of communism, and the forming of their philosophy and Communist morality."[1] Let us remember this statement. "The content of history," we read further, "as a teaching subject reflects the ideology of the government, and changes in accordance with the development of society and also with the development of historical and pedagogical findings."[2] We are in total agreement with this as a definition of history as a teaching subject, as seen by the Soviet system of education, and we will use it in the analysis that follows.

History as taught in schools is primarily a subject controlled so as to develop in Soviet children specific philosophical convictions and moral attitudes that are useful to society at a given time. Secondly, the facts and concepts included in the syllabus and covered in the textbooks are dictated by the demands of the ruling ideology, and reflect the changing tendencies of the period.

Let us consider which ideology history books have reflected and are reflecting, which philosophical and moral convictions are to be instilled in young people, and what changes have been effected since the end of the 1930s, up to the middle of the 1970s, as regards the attitude toward the Jewish people.

At the age of twelve, a child enters the fifth grade at secondary school. This is an important point for him in his history education. Up to this time he has become acquainted only with fragments of Soviet history. In the fifth grade he begins, for the first time, to study a chronological history course, beginning with ancient history—to which he will not return during his school career. Only an insignificant number of children will be able to revise and broaden the knowledge gained in fifth grade, and then only if they decide to study the humanities. It follows that, in this class, schoolchildren gain an impression of ancient peoples and of their contribution to the development of world civilization. In the light of this impression, they will judge the value of other nations; it is the first stimulus toward respect or contempt for the traditions, culture, and religion of others. In Russia, with its well-known history of anti-Semitism, dating back many years, and the Black Hundreds pogroms, there is, of course, some mention of Jewish history in the school course, and one can see the possibility of forming in the children any given attitude toward Jewry. Let us see how this possibility is used in the Soviet school system.

Let us suppose that a child is entering the fifth grade in the middle of the 1930s, and that he has to learn ancient history using the textbooks of N. M. Nikolsky.[3] About one-half of the course is devoted to ancient Egypt, China, Babylon, and Assyria, and the second half to ancient Rome and ancient Greece. The history of Israel and Judea does not merit a separate section. Instead, the history of the Jews is traced in connection with the conquests of Tuthmosis III, the Babylonian and Assyrian kings, and Alexander the Great. In the section on ancient Rome, there is a discussion of the Jewish revolt in the first century B.C., and of the role of the Jews in the fall of the Roman Empire. The description, in the spirit of that time, divides the Jews into two categories, "Jewish revolutionaries" who fought against Rome, and "Jewish exploiters" who were allegedly defended by a Roman garrison. There is no attempt to "forget" the "improper" names Judea, Jerusalem, and Jews, but nevertheless, the description of the period is corrupted as a result of the desire to instill into the child the basis of Marxist theory: in Judea, as in every other society, there was a class struggle. The child also absorbs what he hears every day on the radio, from his parents, and in the streets: religion is the opium of the people. He therefore cannot receive from the textbooks any impression other than that Jewish priests and prophets were "charlatans" and "deceivers" who sponged on society, and that Christianity, which began on Jewish soil (this is specifically mentioned in the books), is counterrevolutionary in its teachings and profitable only to exploiters. The aim of the textbook was to teach hatred of exploiters, and this aim was conscientiously fulfilled. So far, .there are no signs of race hatred.

In 1940, strenuous attempts were being made to get the ancient history textbooks of A. V. Mishulin accepted in schools, and by 1953 they were firmly established. In these books, the history of the Jews is covered in a special subsection, "The Kingdoms of Israel and Judea,"[4] comprising about three pages out of the 255 in the whole book. This is very little. The history of India and China, not to mention that of Rome and Greece, is given much more attention. The history of the Jews is written about from a materialistic position, in a very compressed and dry form, beginning with the conquest of Palestine and including the reigns of David and Solomon up to the fall of Israel and Judea. Information is given on the geography of Israel, its social strata, and the occupations of the population. Mention is made of the early appearance of the written word. In the second (1941) edition of the book, the significance of the Bible as a holy book for Christians and Jews is referred to. Other information about the history of the Jews is contained in chapters relating to the history of Egypt, Persia, Greece, and particularly Rome. Here the uprisings of 66–70 A.D. and 132–135 A.D. are treated as the basic forces undermining the might of the Roman Empire. Information about Israel and Judea is given in a chronological table and maps.

Thus, in the textbooks used from the 1930s up to 1950, there is still an attempt, if not to create esteem for the Jewish people as the possessors of an ancient culture, at least to neutralize the appearance of anti-Semitism in the prewar and, particularly, the postwar years.

But in the middle of the 1950s there was a sharp turning point. In 1954–56, the history books of Prof. S. I. Kovalyov appeared, and from 1957 the monopoly on textbooks for the fifth grade was held by F. P. Korovkin, who received the first prize in an open competition for textbooks, and in 1973 was awarded a State Prize of the USSR. From this time, the names Judea, Israel, and Jerusalem finally disappeared from the pages of the textbooks and were replaced by names that are not related to countries but to territories: the Fertile Crescent, Mesopotamia, and more rarely Palestine, and sometimes a more featureless word—"province." As a result, the child receives from the textbook a curious version of how the kings of Babylon and Assyria conquered the towns of Mesopotamia, and while Alexander the Great subjugated Palestine, uprisings in certain unidentified provinces constantly troubled the Roman Empire and finally contributed to its downfall. The breadth and level of knowledge of the pupils suffer from this enigmatic uncertainty, but in comparison with Soviet schoolchildren of the 1920s, today's children are offered only the pathetic remains of this knowledge, in a totally distorted manner, as Table 1 testifies.

Table 1

R. Vipper, *A Textbook of Ancient History for Schools.* (Moscow, 1929), p. 184.	F. P. Korovkin, *The History of the Ancient World: A Textbook for the Fifth Grade of Secondary Schools* (Moscow: Prosveschchenye, 1977), p. 211.
The Second Judean Rising	The Last Conquests of the Roman Empire
Trajan decided to make an extensive campaign in the East, with a view to repeating the expedition of Alexander the Great. He succeeded in conquering Armenia and in taking Mesopotamia from the Parthians. Later he took Babylon and the Parthian capital, Ctesiphon, on the river Tigris; finally he made for the heart of Persia. His progress was completely stopped by the fierce uprising of the *Jews* which broke out at the rear of his army; at the	In the years 115–116, troops under the leadership of the Emperor Trajan, an experienced and energetic military leader, occupied the Fertile Crescent. Never before had the Roman legions advanced so far to the east. But in the *provinces* uprisings broke out among the *conquered* nations. This forced Trajan to halt his campaign and direct his troops against the insurrectionists.

same time there was a revolt by *Jews* in the empire, in Egypt, Kiria, and Cyprus, and those living in the Parthian kingdom on the river Euphrates. In the midst of these threatening events Trajan died, and his successor . . . immediately returned all Trajan's conquests to the Parthians.

Trajan's campaigns were the last Roman wars of conquest. The empire needed many troops to suppress the uprisings and to defend its borders. It was necessary to surrender all the lands conquered by Trajan in Asia, as there were not sufficient troops to hold them. At the beginning of the second century, the empire had to change over from expansion to the defense of its own huge territories.

The attempt to avoid mention of the Jews and anything related to them results in the distortion of the historical origins of Christianity. From the 1920s to the present day, this has been the subject of various sociological and national experiments in Soviet textbooks (see Appendix 1). Thus in all editions of ancient history books by S. I. Kovalyov and Korovkin, it is stated categorically that Jesus Christ was born in Palestine, one of the Roman provinces (under no circumstances must Judea be mentioned), where Christianity originated and began to spread among the poor and slaves of the Roman Empire. And as the twelve-year-old child has no conception of where Palestine was and who lived there (in the books of Kovalyov it is mentioned only once, and in Korovkin five times, without any clarification), it would be completely natural for him to imagine that Jesus Christ was a Roman, i.e., an Aryan, and it is possible to understand his surprise and even his slight irritation when, at the end of the book in a list of the first Christians—Greeks, Romans, Egyptians, and even Gauls— he sees for the first time the word "Jew." (And where on earth did they spring from?, he asks.) Thus silence leads to the distortion of historical perspective and its perversion to the beginnings of racism.

This new phase of 1954, which brought about the almost complete "disappearance" of the Jews from ancient history, is shown as a chart in Table 2.

F. P. Korovkin is not only the author of textbooks. He is a prominent methodologist, and in his research he pays a great deal of attention to the methodological basis of textbooks, to the principles governing the choice of content. In one of his last works, *Methods of Teaching Ancient and Medieval History*, complaining bitterly about the difficulty of choosing material on the ancient East, he says that the aim should be not only to acquaint pupils with the important economic and political centers of the ancient East, but also to show the enormous contribution made by "the peoples of the ancient East to the development of world culture."[5]

Judging by the textbook on the Fertile Crescent, only the Babylonians

Table 2

	Nikolsky 1930s	Mishulin 1940–53	Kovalyov 1954–56	Korovkin 1957–77
1. Number of pages in textbook	184	255	175	192–240
2. Number of sections on the Jews	—	1	—	—
3. Number of pages devoted to the history of the Jewish people	3	4	—	—
4. Number of times Israel mentioned	—	6	—	—
5. Number of times Judea mentioned	9	8	—	—
6. Number of times Jerusalem mentioned	2	5	—	—
7. Number of times Jews mentioned	11	18	1	1
8. Number of times Palestine mentioned	11	—	1	3–5
9. Mention of Israel or Judea in a chronological table	2	4	—	—
10. Mention of Israel or Judea in maps	Palestine	4	Only Palestine is mentioned	

and Persians were worthy of this honor. It follows that schoolchildren learn that the ancient Jews did not contribute anything of the slightest significance to the history of mankind, if they existed at all at that time. Not one of the prerevolutionary authors, including D. I. Ilovaisky, not to mention N. I. Kareev and P. G. Vinogradov, came to such a far-fetched conclusion.

A year later, "enriched" with a knowledge of ancient history, the thirteen-year-old becomes acquainted in the sixth grade with medieval history. In the years 1940–1961, children of this age were reading the textbook of Academician Kosminsky, but in 1962 they read a book by E. V. Agibalova and G. M. Donskoy which, like the ancient history book by F. P. Korovkin, was awarded first prize in open competitions of history textbooks. The last three authors shared a State Prize of the USSR.

It would appear that, in studying the Middle Ages, it is impossible to avoid the role of the Jews in the economic and cultural life of mankind. The European Diaspora penetrated the whole of medieval civilization. The whole of medieval culture was based on the Bible, which was translated into Latin and from Latin into European languages; it inspired many of the giants of the Renaissance. In Spain, one of the greatest civilizations, the Moorish-Jewish, was created. Famous Jewish doctors, philosophers, and government officials brought glory to the Arab Caliphate and the Ottoman Empire. In the Middle Ages, many Jews engaged in trade. They organized and financed the great geographical discoveries. The most famous occurrences of the Middle Ages, the Crusades and the Inquisition, were directed against the Jews. One would think that there were possibilities for raising the as yet only slightly humiliated spirit of the Jewish child, and restraining the growing arrogance of his Russian classmates. At the age of twelve a child does not attach importance to the nationality of his neighbor. At thirteen he understands it fully. What possibilities present themselves in a school history course for the restoration of balance in the awakening national pride of the one, and the elimination of the humiliation of the other! But nothing of the kind!

The textbooks of E. A. Kosminsky which appeared between 1940 and 1953 have the fullest treatment of the role of the Jews; in the sections of those books on the Inquisition it says that the majority of the Jews were craftsmen and merchants. This statement may appear unremarkable. But the author "forgot" that, in Soviet schools, the children have it drummed into their heads that it is good to be a worker or a peasant but not a craftsman and worse still a merchant. The author did not manage to show up this ridiculous idea for what it is. In fact, the author strikes yet another blow at the Jewish children and puts more poison into the hearts of the others.

It is impossible to know which is worse: a ridiculous statement or silence. In 1954, Kosminsky brought out a new edition of his book on the Middle Ages, in which the Jews are not mentioned at all in the chapters on the Inquisition and the revolt in the Netherlands. They are mentioned only as newcomers trading their wares in medieval towns.[6] This last mention of the Jews is totally absent from the books of E. V. Agibalova and G. M. Donskoy. The evolution of the treatment of the Inquisition in Soviet textbooks is presented in Table 3.

As can be seen, the omission of the role of the Jews in the Middle Ages brought the authors to make completely false statements regarding the essence of the Inquisition. The Inquisition was created to spread Christianity literally by force, to fight against those who turned away from Christianity or who clung stubbornly to their own faith, particularly the Jews. In E. V. Agibalova and Donskoy's textbook, the Inquisition has turned into something resembling an administrative organ, designed to fight against dissenters. A similar metamorphosis occurs in the textbooks of E. A. Kosminsky.

In her treatment of the Crusades, Agibalova states that the crusaders

Table 3

R. Vipper, *A Short Textbook of the Middle Ages* (Moscow, 1923), p. 115.	E. A., Kosminsky. *History of the Middle Ages for Sixth and Seventh Grades.* (Moscow, 1951), pp. 146–147.	E. V. Agibalova and G. M. Donskoy, *History of the Middle Ages for the Sixth Grade* (Moscow, 1977), p. 93.
In pursuit of people who were a threat to their power, Ferdinand and Isabella leaned on the church. . . . In Spain there was a Holy Inquisition, supposedly to root out heretical ideas. It particularly attacked the Jewish faith as, after the rule of the Moors, there were many Jews.	The Inquisition was set up in Spain in 1480, and there began the merciless persecution of Moors, Jews, and "heretics.". . . Jews and Moors had the choice of leaving the country or converting to Christianity. Tens of thousands, for the most part craftsmen and traders, left Spain. Even if they converted to Christianity, Jews and Moors were still in danger; someone had only to report that they still adhered to their former faith and the dreadful judgment of the Inquisition was brought to bear.	In the fight against heretics, the Pope established . . . the Inquisition. With the help of spies and informers, the inquisitors pursued heretics and all suspected of disagreeing with the church. . . . With the help of the Inquisition, the church dealt with those who participated in rebellions, and men of learning and writers who expressed ideas contrary to its own.

dealt mercilessly with the Jews. In the textbooks of Ilovaisky and Vipper, and that of Kosminsky, the crusaders themselves become the victims of the local inhabitants. According to Agibalova, it is true that they captured towns, stole, and killed local inhabitants, but who the inhabitants were is not known. Having invaded Jerusalem, the crusaders of Kosminsky and Agibalova obviously found no Jews there; that is why they organized the "mass slaughter" of Moslems alone (see Appendix 2).

A still more complex situation is found in textbooks as regards the teaching of the Reformation in Germany. Those who studied from 1950 to 1954 were still reading about the *Letters of the Obscurantists*, receiving, it is true, a totally distorted impression of these people. But after the amended version of events found in Kosminsky's 1954 book, all mention of them disappears, and they never reappear in the books of Agibalova and Donskoy (see Appendix 3). The authors of this latter textbook judge this famous satire more strictly than did the Pope of the time: in the center stands Dr. Johann Reuchlin, "who stood against four universities in defense of the Jews."[7] For this very reason, Jews disappeared from all other sections of Agibalova and Donskoy's book, although exceptional inventiveness is necessary to avoid all mention of the Jews in such chapters as "The Arabs," "The Christian Church and the Crusaders," "The Ottoman Empire," "The Reformation," etc. The evolution of "silence" on the Jews is shown in Table 4.

Table 4

	Textbooks of Kosminsky		Textbooks of Agibalova and Donskoy
	1940–53	1954–61	1962–77
Number of times Jews are mentioned	4	1	—

Thus the tendency of the authors of ancient and medieval history books to eliminate Jews from their texts was completed by 1954, and in order to achieve this, historical truth, the quality of the books, the knowledge of the pupils, and morals were sacrificed.

The year 1954 was a watershed year, not only for textbooks of ancient and medieval history. With the publishing of a book in 1952 on (early) modern history, the national origins of Heine and Lassalle disappear.[8] In a modern history book published in 1949, there is a detailed description of the Dreyfus affair, which is viewed not as an anti-Semitic episode in France but as a class struggle "of great intensity."[9] It was presented in this way for some time, and then, in 1954, it was eliminated from the new edition of the book.

From 1954 to 1956, there occurred significant changes in books on the history of the Soviet Union for the eighth to tenth grades, edited by Academician A. M. Pankratova, whose books were used from 1940 to 1963.

The first edition of these textbooks contained broad information on the history of Russian Jewry. In 1964, the textbooks were revised, and a section of the history of the Jews was removed. In 1956, a third of the book for the tenth grade (from the beginning of the twentieth century) underwent a more rigorous revision, and all mention of the Jews was eliminated.

In the middle of the 1960s, books on Soviet history were used in which a tendency toward the "absence" of Jews, this time in Russian history, became particularly clear and consistent; its victims were Khazaria (Khazar Khagan), the position of the Jews in Poland, the Ukraine, and Byelorussia, the mass extermination of Jews by the "brave" Haidamacks (Ukrainian Cossacks) and the army of Chmielnicki, the Pale of Settlement, the pogroms of 1881 and later, and the narrow-minded standards of the tsarist government (see Appendix 4).

From the end of the 1960s, side by side with the continuing tendency toward silence, another tendency appears, namely, that of negative information about the Jews and a total absence of any positive statements about them. It begins with the higher grades. From the first pages of the textbook on Soviet history for the ninth grade by I. B. Berkhin and I. A. Fedosov, the pupil is pelted with a stream of negative information about Russian Jews. In this book, Jews are presented as members of the *Jewish* workers' union, the Bund (the authors "forgot" to mention that the Bund was the first Social Democratic organization in Russia).[10] According to the textbook, the proposals of the Bundists at the second council of the Russian Social Democratic Workers' party on the nationality question would, had they been accepted, have led to "the dissemination of nationalism" and the "kindling of enmity among nations."[11] During the 1905 Revolution, they "*hindered* the revolutionary moblization of the masses," came out "*against* armed support for the *Potemkin* uprising," and "sabotaged the general strike in Odessa."[12] Thus prejudices nurtured on the street and in the family are ripened in school.

The situation is exacerbated by the selection of literature for study in connection with the above courses, which followed the same tendency as the textbooks.[13]

The course on modern history is of particular interest. It is studied in the ninth and tenth grades, and is divided into two periods: 1917–1930 and 1939 to the present day.

One of the central questions dealt with in this course, particularly during the first period, is the birth and growth of Nazism, leading to World War II. One would think that the basic aim in studying this material would be to learn about the ideology and roots of fascism, including anti-Semitism. This material contains a great potential contribution to ideological and international education. It is capable of dispelling the as yet unconsolidated national prejudices which Soviet schoolchildren receive, as a result of slanted education or of educational lacunae. But it is curious that, when the subject is fascist Germany or World War II, we do not get the usual lengthy discussions of ideology and Nazism; Jews are deliberately excluded. In order to provide evidence of this sad situation, it is only necessary to turn to *A Handbook of Modern History* (Moscow: Prosveshcheniye, 1972), where, in the chapter "The Educational Significance of a Course of Modern History and Its Peculiarities," written in beautiful prose, we find generalizations about the development of the Marxist view of the world and the need for the pupil to become convinced of such and such an idea. And there is not one single thing in this chapter relevant to educating the pupil to oppose fascism and the politics and ideology of racism and anti-Semitism in Hitler's Germany. The following are typical of the weak titles that head the chapters: "A Few General Questions of Method in Teaching Modern History" and "Foreign Countries in 1924–1939." In the last section are specially revised chapters on German history during this period—"From the Weimar Republic to the Fascist Dictatorship" and "Germany under Fascist Power." In none of these chapters is there any attempt to expose anti-Semitism as one of the basic features of fasicst ideology. But this term is not generally used, and not one fact is given concerning the persecution of the Jews in Nazi Germany.

And what about the textbooks and the course in modern history introduced in 1957? In recent years (from 1970 onwards), textbooks edited by V: K. Furayev have been used. In his textbook, about 18 of the 112 pages are devoted to the first period of German history—rather a large percentage of the book. Obviously, the central topics in this part are an understanding of "fascist dictatorship," the policy of Hitler's party, and the internal policies of fascist Germany. But the meaning of "fascist dictatorship" is explained in the book as "the most reactionary, chauvinistic, dictatorship with imperialistic elements of finance capital."[14] This explanation is rather general and hardly correct, as it does not contain the fundamentals of fascism and does not reflect its inhumanity or expose its petty-bourgeois roots. We are here concerned with one basic tenet of fascism (not the German brand)—anti-Semitism. But this was not reflected in the definition of fascism or in the explanation of the manifesto and actions of Hitler's party. The chapter devoted to this question talks only of how the fascists put forward the slogan, "Down with Jewish Capital."[15] But at this stage, the authors "forgot" to explain that this slogan was linked with the anti-Semitic policy of fascist Germany, and therefore, in the chapter "Politics of Terror and Violence," it seems as though the "dreadful Jewish pogroms" organized by Hitler were just retribution on the Jews for their capitalistic ways. This section no doubt inspires approving comments and vile sniggers from some, and a feeling of offense and burning shame in others. (In earlier editions of this textbook, written by practically the same group of authors, instead of the slogan "Down with Jewish Capital" we find the slogan "Down with Predatory Capitalists.")

Hearing much but not always reading about the tragedy of the Jewish nation during World War II, children of sixteen and seventeen show a heightened, although not always sympathetic, interest in this question. This interest could be satisfied with material on the second period of modern history. In the textbook, there is a chapter of some twenty-five pages on the history of the war. Here one can read about the invasion of Poland by Germany, the presence of the German army in Denmark and Norway, the seizure of Luxembourg and Belgium, and the capitulation of France. From the book it is possible to learn about the bloody occupation that was forced upon these territories and even about Auschwitz, and the uprising in Warsaw on August 1, 1944. There was not room for even a mention of the Holocaust that struck the Jewish people, nor even one mention of Jews at Auschwitz, and the Warsaw Ghetto uprising does not exist for Soviet schoolchildren. There was no killing, no resistance. Were there any Jews? And finding no answer in the textbooks, the pupil, if he is curious, turns to popular literature on this theme. But excellent books with a full description of fascism, the books of G. Erast, E. Otvald, and K. Heiden, published in the thirties, were never reprinted and became bibliographical rarities. The articles and books of V. V. Struve, G. Aleksandrov, and S. Adamov and others, published during the war years, have also been forgotten long ago. In the 1960s, the following books appeared and disappeared from the bookshops: G. L. Rozanov's *Germany Under Fascism* (Moscow, 1964), *Ambassador Dodd's Diary (1933–1938)* (Moscow, 1961), A. A. Galkin's German Fascism (Moscow, 1967), and V. Kral's *Crime Against Europe* (Moscow, 1963), in which there are explanations in varying degrees of detail and in simple language of the problem of the Jews in Nazi Germany. To replace them, we have books and articles by P. A. Zhilin, T. Yu. Grigoryants, A. A. Grechko, and others, in which the authors prefer not to touch on this problem. In 1975 a collection of documents, *Anatomy of Aggression*, was published, and again the Jews were forgotten. And in 1973 a large edition—100,000 copies—of a thick volume (about 400 pages) of M. S. Gus's *Mad Swastikas* was published. From this book, one learns that many of Hitler's leaders were either half or wholly Jewish, that "among" the benefactors of Nazism were Jewish bankers, that Hitler did not mind using Jewish money.[16] It appears that in the camp for displaced persons Gus saw "fat . . . young people"—of course "of Jewish nationality"—and "by a miracle they survived in various places in Europe."[17] This is the "knowledge" which the Soviet child is given of the Jewish tragedy, "knowledge" strengthened by the silence of the textbooks and by the enigmatic "Down with Jewish Capital!" But that is not all. After a very long and strange silence in the pages of the textbooks, there is a sudden splurge on the history of contemporary Israel, not in a separate chapter, but in chapters on the history of England, France, Syria, and Egypt, in connection with the collapse of the colonial system and contemporary international relations.

This material gives little information. But in the textbook there is no reference to social phenomena,[18] and the malicious tone and expressions are hardly suitable to a textbook which, in fact, abuses Jewry as a whole. This becomes worse with every new edition. For a description of the State of Israel, one must refer to a footnote to a paragraph about Egypt. A comparison of the two editions, 1970 and 1976, clearly points to the basic differences between them (see Table 5). If in the first there is a slight attempt to explain the origins of Israel and Zionism, in the 1976 edition this is replaced by unbridled abuse.

Table 5

P. M. Kuzmichev, G. R. Levin, V. A. Orlov, L. M. Predtechenskaya, and V. K. Furayev, *Modern History: A Textbook for the Tenth Grade of Secondary School.* Editor V. K. Furayev.

(1939–1969), 1st ed. (Moscow, 1970), p. 181	(1939–1975), 7th ed. (Moscow, 1976), p. 169
The State of Israel was formed in May 1948 on a part of the territory of Palestine. At the head of this bourgeois state are representatives of nationalist parties, closely linked with monopoly circles in the United States and other imperialist powers.	The State of Israel was formed in May 1948 on a part of the territory of Palestine. At the head of this bourgeois state are representatives of nationalist parties closely linked with Jewish monopoly circles in the United States and other imperialist powers.
The ideology of the State of Israel is Zionism (from the word Zion—one of the hills on which Jerusalem is built), which maintains the necessity of creating a "greater Israel from the Nile to the Euphrates" at the expense of the neighboring Arab lands. Blatant chauvinism and malicious anticommunism are basic tenets of Zionism.	The ideology and politics of the State of Israel is Zionism. Blatant chauvinism and malicious anti-communism are the basic tenets of Zionism. Since its existence, Israel has conducted aggressive expansionist policies toward the neighboring Arab states.
Imperialists use international Zionism in the struggle against the national freedom movement of the Arab nations to strengthen their position in the Middle East and carry out hostile	Imperialists use international Zionism and the ruling clique of Israel in the struggle against the national freedom movement of the Arab nations, to restore their influence in the Middle East and carry out hostile activities

activities against the socialist countries. The Communist party of Israel comes out strongly against the nationalism and extremism of the ruling circles of the government.

against the socialist countries. The Communist party of Israel, defending the interests of the Israeli people, comes out strongly against the aggressive policies and extremism of the ruling circles of this government and in favor of a just and viable peace in the Middle East. The thirtieth session of the General Assembly of the United Nations in November 1975 approved a resolution accusing Zionism of being a form of racism and racial prejudice.

The course on the second period of modern history is the last history course in the school curriculum. It is supposed to strengthen the knowledge and the convictions formed by the study of history in school. And it does indeed support all the negative information about a whole nation presented to the schoolchild during the course of his ten years at school.

On October 8, 1959, the Central Committee of the Communist party and the Council of Ministers of the USSR passed a resolution that the Soviet republics should have history courses covering their own history. One might have supposed that information on Jewish history would have appeared, at least in the textbooks of those republics where Jews were concentrated before the revolution and where the majority live now.[19] But in vain would we search in the history textbooks of the Ukraine, Moldavia, Latvia, Azerbajan, Uzbekistan, and Lithuania[20] for even a fleeting mention of the life of the Jews, their occupations, their contribution to the scholarship and culture of the republics in which they lived. It is only in a history textbook of Byelorussia that we find interest shown in the Jewish people; but there is no attempt to show the misfortune of the Jews who, before the revolution, were driven into the Pale of Settlement, and there was no room for any mention of the suffering of the Jewish nation during the war years, nor were any Jews named as war heroes of Byelorussia. The words "Jew," "Jewry," and "Jewish" in this textbook are associated with the verbs "to betray," "to undermine," "to destroy," "to separate," and this way of portraying Jewry becomes more obvious with every new edition. Let us look at the position, as shown in Table 6.

The struggle against nationalism is one of the basic components of Marxism-Leninism. If the authors of the textbook expose nationalism, including Byelorussian nationalism, even in intolerably offensive language, do we have the right to demand that they leave Jewish nationalism alone? After all, the Jews are the largest national group after the Byelorussians. The point is that, in their "exposure" of Byelorussian nationalism, things were treated quite differently. In the first place, in the textbook, Byelorussian

Table 6

L. S. Abetsedarsky, M. P. Baranova, and N. G. Pavlova, *A History of Byelorussia: A Textbook for Secondary School Pupils*. Edited by Corresponding Member of the Academy of Pedagogical Sciences of the Soviet Union L. S. Abetsedarsky (Minsk: Narodnaya Asveta).

1960–1974 edition	1976 edition

20. The Revolutionary Movement in Byelorussia in the 1880s and 1890s

Page 103	*Page 104*

Under the protection of the tsarist secret police, in several towns in Russia including Minsk, bogus workers' organizations were created. In 1901, agents of the secret police together with Bundists established in Minsk the so-called Independent Jewish Workers' party, thereby trying to separate workers of different nationalities

and undermine the workers' movement.	and take them out of revolutionary social democracy and withdraw them from the political fight.

26. The Revolutionary Struggle of workers in Byelorussia in December 1905

Page 121	*Page 116*

The Bundists and Mensheviks joined the strike council, but on December 12, treacherously announced the end of the strike. For this reason, the strike in Minsk did not grow into an armed uprising.

nationalism, unlike Jewish nationalism, in no way "hindered" or "disunited" or "took out" or "betrayed," and so on. Secondly, Byelorussian nationalism never enjoyed the support of the masses, and thirdly, after the revolution and particularly during the war years, Byelorussian nationalism was not local but imported and therefore not dangerous, and consequently did not need a detailed or harsh "exposure."

But let us turn to the chapter on Byelorussia in World War II. It takes up about twenty pages, approximately one-tenth of the book.[21] One would imagine that there would be pages devoted to the tragedy of the nation closely linked for so long with Byelorussia, pages on the uprising in the Minsk ghetto and the mass exodus of Jews to the partisan bands, and the heroic deeds of Jewish soldiers at the front. But we hope in vain. There is mention of the sufferings of the Byelorussians only, of the extermination of inhabitants only of Byelorussian villages, only about Byelorussian soldiers fighting at the front, about the awarding of the title "Hero of the Soviet

Union" to 462 Byelorussians.[22] And finally we are told of the international composition of the partisan band that fought on Byelorussian soil. We read: "Together with the Byelorussian partisans, thousands of Latvians, Lithuanians, Estonians, Georgians, Armenians, Azerbajanis—the sons and daughters of almost every nation of the Soviet Union."[23] If the Jews were not among the hundreds of thousands nor among the tens of thousands, nor even among the thousands, then how many of them fought in the resistance? One hundred, ten, one? Or were there none at all, and did this word "almost" indicate their absence?

A course on the history of his own republic is of more immediate interest to the pupil than a general Soviet history course, and can either shatter the seeds of anti-Semitism sown in general textbooks or strengthen them. In the given case, the intentions of the textbook leave us in no doubt.

Our analysis allows us to draw the following conclusions:

1. In Soviet methodology during the period 1940–1956, one can discern one clear tendency: the withdrawal from history textbooks for secondary schools of any information about the history of the Jews—or there may be just a mention of them.

2. In the period 1954–1956, textbook writers solved their problem by the removal from history books on ancient, medieval, modern, and Soviet history for the tenth grade of all, or almost all, information relating to Jews. In the 1960s, this process was completed in the remaining textbooks on Soviet history (from ancient history right up to and including the nineteenth century).

3. The implementation of this trend obviously did not depend on the mood and views of the authors of the textbooks, and possibly not on their wishes, since they continued to write "conforming" textbooks after 1954; for example, those by E. A. Kosminsky and A. V. Yefimov. Moreover, up to the 1960s, the authors of the textbooks were people with a certain degree of authority in academic circles, and were not in need of political advancement (Academicians A. M. Pankratova and E. A. Kosminsky, Corresponding Member of the Academy of Sciences of the USSR A. V. Yefimov, Professor S. I. Kovalyov, and others). But the content of the textbooks is checked and subject to approval by the appropriate Party and government organs.

4. It might be possible to connect the tendency toward silence with the events of 1953. But for the textbooks there was no "thaw" even after 1953.* It is therefore obvious that the roots of this tendency lie in other, more profound developments and reflect changes in government ideology.

*The death of Stalin.

5. In the 1960s, this tendency was intensified by the references in textbooks to negative characteristics allegedly exhibited by Jews, and the complete exclusion of all positive Jewish attributes. This tendency grows from year to year. After 1963, the authors are significantly less qualified than those writing earlier and, apart from general directives, their work contains their personal views.

6. Both tendencies, silence about and criticism of the Jews, are strengthened by popular "literature," ostensibly of an anti-Zionist nature, which began to appear in enormous editions at the end of the 1960s and continued into the 1970s. The ideas expressed in this "literature," and the above-mentioned tendencies in the textbooks, have a destructive influence on the moral outlook and psychology of children, sowing the seeds of hatred and enmity in their hearts.

7. Both tendencies are systematically and clearly followed in schools, and there is no possibility of coincidence. As a result, the accumulation in class after class of "knowledge" about the alleged characteristics of the Jews and the strengthening of this "knowledge" by popular literature lead to the formation in the minds of schoolchildren of a stereotyped anti-Semitic view of Jewry.

This view goes as follows: The Jews are not an ancient people. They did not exist in ancient times. When they appeared, they immediately wormed their way into anything profitable—into Christianity, because Christianity was spreading quickly in the Roman Empire, and then all over the world. Jews did not exist in the Middle Ages either, nor are they found in modern history. They contributed nothing to mankind, either in politics, economics, or culture—they are not mentioned among famous people in textbooks. When they appeared in Europe (in Germany) they immediately became capitalists, and therefore Hitler exterminated them ("Down with Jewish Capital!"). In Russia as well, they were unknown in the past,[24] appearing only before the Revolution of 1905, when they immediately began to display their treacherous nature, creating disharmony, interfering, and "breeding enmity between nations." They did not fight in World War II. They do not figure among the Heroes of the Soviet Union, among the resistance fighters, or in the underground movement. If they were exterminated by the Nazis, this was no more than was done to other nations. Moreover, they betrayed their own people and others for money and vehicles, and collaborated with the Germans.[25] They derived profit from the war, creating for themselves a state on Arab land,[26] and now they behave like brigands—they make aggressive attacks on peaceful Arab towns, try to "disrupt the Arab front," and conduct a policy that is hostile to all nations except the imperialists of the United States and other capitalist countries; they want to conquer the world.[27]

8. Young people are corrupted by the distorted, stereotyped ideas gleaned from textbooks, set books, and popular literature, and feelings of national incompatibility and hostility are created in them.

And now we must recollect the phrase with which we began this paper: general education in Soviet schools has as its aim the "arming" of the pupils with knowledge which "is essential for . . . the education of active, aware builders of communism and the forming of their philosophy and Communist morality" *(Pedagogical Encyclopedia*, vol. 3, p. 141). What sort of morality and what sort of philosophy are formed by such "knowledge"? What is the aim behind it all?

Appendix 1

R. Vipper, *Textbook of Ancient History for Schools*, 13th ed. (Moscow and Petrograd, 1923), pp. 180, 188, 191.

The fall of Jerusalem was a great blow to the Jewish nation. The Sanhedrin and the government of priests and aristocrats ended. The Jews fell into two categories: some continued to observe the law of Moses, putting their hope in God's help in the restoration of the Temple, as a reward for the loyalty of the nation in olden times (the descendants of this section constitute contemporary Jewry); and others rejected the belief in the coming of an earthly deliverer-ruler, dropped the habit of observing the old Law, and turned their hopes to the coming of a heavenly Messiah or Christ. Among these people were Essenes and even Judeo-Christian communes close to the Essenes. . . . The victories of the Roman armies broadened the acceptance of Roman gods, but the beliefs of the Romans during the empire changed considerably.

The conquering people began to worship the deities of the subject tribes. People of all walks of life were

N. M. Nikolsky, *History Before the Class Society: The East in Ancient Times—The Ancient World; Textbook for Secondary Schools* (Moscow, 1933), pp. 190–191.

The uprisings of slaves always end in defeat. But only in Rome did the "proletariat" live at the expense of the state and the slaveowners. In other towns and provinces they had to beg. They were spread throughout the huge Roman Empire. . . . It is easy to understand why all these unfortunate and oppressed peoples sought comfort in religion, and began to await salvation from gods. In the first century A.D., in Greece, Asia Minor, Syria, and Judea, there constantly appeared "prophets" who announced that they were the messengers of some sort of God-Savior. These prophets were, of course, charlatans and deceivers. They wanted only to live at the expense of gullible religious people. . . . Each prophet organized a commune of followers and lived off them. There were many of these communes, particularly in Asia Minor and Syria.

Halfway through the first century in the provinces of Asia and in Greece, the Judean, Christ, the prophet of a

seeking a god who would give comfort at difficult times, at illness, and would open up a new and better life. . . . In earlier times, all Romans accepted the gods of Asia Minor.

Another religion which also traveled from East to West was the cult of the Egyptian gods Isis and Osiris. . . . A third religion which grew in strength at that time was worship of the Sun (Sol Invictus), which was spread to all Western countries by merchants. . . . Finally, a fourth religion, also from the East, was established by the Persians, who lived beyond the borders of the empire, in Parthia. This worship of Attis, Osiris, the Sun, and Mithra prepared the way for the spread of Christian teaching about saving the world (which was expounded by prophets to the Jewish people). For many people, Christian teaching provided answers to their questions and comfort in the face of their worries. . . . Up to the fall of Jerusalem, the Jews had been the main missionaries; that is, they spread the pure, exalted belief in one god. After the Jewish revolt, the Christians became worldwide preachers. A large proportion of Jews who had been scattered turned to Christianity. At the same time the teachings of Christ began to spread among the heathens.

A. V. Mishulin, *History of the Ancient World: Textbook for the Fifth and Sixth Grades of Secondary School* (Moscow: Ochpedgiz, 1940), p. 226.

Christianity

Christianity arose in the first century A.D., when the exploited masses of Roman society were in a state of deep disillusionment . . . and religious feelings began to strengthen among the

new God, was particularly successful among the "proletarian" slaves and unskilled laborers. . . . Their teaching was the same as that of other "prophets," but they were more successful. . . . They maintained that their god had already appeared on earth. . . . He, it seemed, had taken the form of a Jewish carpenter, went around Judea, healed the blind, the deaf, the lame, and those suffering from incurable diseases, resurrected the dead and, in a miraculous manner, fed the starving. The exploiters—Jewish priests and Romans—were supposed to have seized Christ and crucified him, but he was, it seems, resurrected and would appear shortly on earth to judge the world. Then he would destroy all sinners, all the rich and strong; he would destroy the world as we know it and create a new world. . . . This shows that Christianity, from the very beginning . . . was a counterrevolutionary teaching, profitable to exploiters.

S. I. Kovalyov, *A History of the Ancient World: Textbook for Fifth and Sixth Grades of Secondary School* (Moscow: Uchpedgiz, 1954), p. 155.

Christianity

In the first century A.D. among the slaves and poor of the Roman Empire, religious convictions strengthened . . . preachers began to appear among the simple people. They traveled from

slaves, the poor of Rome, and artisans. In the Jewish faith, there had long been a belief in a Messiah (anointed one). The Messiah is a godly person who was supposed to appear on earth and save the human race from evil and suffering. Such a concept of a Messiah existed even in ancient religions. All these eastern . . . ideas spread widely in the first and second centuries, in the western half of the Roman Empire.

Wandering prophets and preachers appeared everywhere. They called on the people to prepare themselves for a meeting with the Messiah, who would punish the rich, destroy the Roman government . . . and create a "heavenly kingdom" on earth. At some stage, the myth of Jesus Christ arose among the people. He was a manlike god who taught that it was necessary to suffer humbly so that all suffering might be rewarded after death. . . . This myth was created under the strong influence of eastern religions. In none of the known teachings of that time is there a word about the life of Jesus Christ.

F. P. Korovkin, *History of the Ancient World; Textbook for the Fifth Grade of Secondary School* (Moscow: Uchpedgiz, 1962), pp. 219–220.

In the first century there arose a tale that in Palestine there lived a god in the guise of a human. He had come to earth in order to help the slaves and the poor. He was called Jesus Christ. It was related that the Roman governor crucified him, and Jesus suffered in silence. After this death he was resurrected and, having gone to heaven, he promised to return quickly to earth to judge the souls of men. To

town to town and taught that the sufferings of the oppressed would soon be over. There would soon appear on earth a savior—the son of God. Thus the myth of Jesus Christ began to be spread among the people. . . . It was said that the one, all-powerful God, taking pity on people, sent his son, Christ, to earth. . . . Jesus Christ lived in Palestine. He taught that it is necessary to suffer humbly and love one's oppressor. After death, all those who had suffered and been oppressed would enjoy heavenly bliss. For this teaching, Jesus Christ was seized by the ruling powers and crucified.

There is not one grain of truth in this fairy tale. There was no Jesus Christ. Not one word is mentioned of Christ in any of the documents of the first century. The myth of Jesus Christ was concocted on the lines of the other eastern myths. . . . Those who believed in Christ came to be called Christians. Initially they were slaves, artisans, and poor traders . . .

F. P. Korovkin, *History of the Ancient World: Textbook for the Fifth Grade of Secondary School*, 17th ed. (Moscow: Prosveshchenie, 1977), pp. 287–288.

In the first century, there arose a tale that there lived in Palestine a god in the guise of a human. He was called Jesus Christ. It was related that the Romans crucified him, and that Jesus suffered in silence. After his death he was resurrected and, having gone to heaven, he promised to return quickly to earth. To those who suffered and recognized Jesus as a god, he promised a reward in the "afterlife." The rest

those who suffered and who recognized Jesus as God, he promised the reward of eternal bliss, but the rest would be sentenced to eternal torment.

Various evangelists tell different stories of Jesus.

History studies show that Jesus Christ never existed. Tales about him are based on the myths of Osiris, Dionysus, and others—gods who died and were supposedly resurrected . . .

Belief in Christ—Christianity—began to spread among the poor and the slaves of Asia Minor, Egypt, and then in Greece and Italy. Among the Christians, there were Jews, Greeks, Romans, Egyptians, Gauls, and people of other races.

would be sentenced to eternal torments in hell. These tales were based on the myths of Osiris and others—gods who died and were supposedly resurrected, and also on the myth of judgment in the "Kingdom Beyond the Grave."

Various evangelists tell different stories of Jesus' life. . . .

The first Christians were poor people and slaves. They were from many different nations: Jews, Greeks, Romans, Egyptians, Gauls, and others. By the end of the third century, Christianity had spread throughout the Roman Empire.

Appendix 2

D. I. Ilovaisky, *Medieval History Course for Seniors*, 23d ed. (Moscow, 1904), pp. 116–117.

The Crusades

But these first crusaders set off across Germany and Hungary without money or supplies, and in total disorder. En route they slaughtered Jews, and robbed villages for food. For this reason, some of them were killed by the Hungarians.

. . . It was only after they had been traveling for three years that the crusaders reached Jerusalem. There, irritated by the courageous opposition on the streets and in the mosques, the crusaders mercilessly slaughtered almost all the Moslems and Jews, so that the knights' horses walked knee-deep in blood.

R. Vipper, *A Short Textbook of Medieval History for Secondary Schools* (Moscow, 1923), p. 78.

The Crusades and Papal Power

The Crusades were most unprofitable for the former merchants of Europe, the Jews. Wherever the groups of armed crusaders went, they massacred the Jews. Now Christian merchants began to oust them everywhere, and the seigneurs deprived them of the protection they had hitherto bestowed.

In the towns, Jews were no longer allowed to follow their familiar trades: they were locked up in special, heavily populated areas (ghettos).

E. A. Kosminsky, *A History of the Middle Ages: Textbook for the Sixth and Seventh Grades of Secondary School* (Moscow: Uchpedgiz, 1961), pp. 71–72.

Chapter 2, "The Crusades" *The Beginning of the Crusades*

The irregulars, recruited from the poor of France and Germany, first set off for the East. Without food, almost without weapons . . . thousands moved toward the East. . . . Many died of hunger and deprivation. The local population considered them bandits. They slaughtered whole detachments, took them prisoner, and sold them into slavery. Only in 1099 did they arrive at Jerusalem, which they took by storm. The stealing and killing of Moslems began.

E. V. Agibalova and G. M. Donskoy, *History of the Middle Ages: Textbook for Sixth Grade of Secondary School* (Prosveshchenie, 1977), pp. 95–96.

Chapter 5, "The Christian Church in the 11th–13th Century" *The First Crusade*

In the autumn of 1096, detachments of knights under the leadership of strong feudal lords set off from France, Germany, and Italy for the East by various routes. But the "liberators of the holy sepulcher" did not hurry toward their destination. On the journey they occupied towns, and robbed and killed local people.

. . . In 1096, after a cruel assault, the knights took Jerusalem. They butchered the Moslem population.

Appendix 3

D. I. Ilovaisky, *Guidance in General History: Course in Secondary Schools*, 35th ed. (Moscow, 1914), p. 318.

Chapter 23, "The Reformation in Germany"

Of the German humanitarians at the beginning of the sixteenth century, the most famous were Reuchlin, Erasmus of Rotterdam, and Ülrich von Hutten.

Reuchlin was a brilliant scholar, not only in Latin and Greek but also in Hebrew. Once the Dominican monks in Cologne asked the Emperor Maximilian for an edict that all Jewish books that were repugnant to Christianity should be handed over to the government, but not knowing which books came under this category, they turned to Reuchlin as a Hebrew expert. Reuchlin wrote an essay in

N. I. Kareev, *A Textbook of Modern History*, 16th ed. (1917), pp. 19–21.

Johann Reuchlin was in his time a "trilingual wonder," being a specialist in Latin, Greek, and Hebrew. It was he who first began a real study of the Hebrew language. . . . He made a comparison between the Latin Bible and the Hebrew text, and found inaccuracies in the translation. Under the influence of Italian Platonism and the Jewish Kabbalah, he created his own religious philosophy. The Catholic clergy suspected him of heresy in everything that he did. . . . One fanatic, a baptized Jew, Pfefferkorn, managed to persuade Maximilian I to pass an edict that all Jewish books that were contrary to Christianity should be confiscated, and supporters of this convert to Catholicism interpreted the Emperor's edict as meaning

which he showed that it was totally unnecessary to burn any Jewish books, and for this the Dominicans accused Reuchlin of heresy. But other German humanists supported him, as did several German princes. Thus there arose an argument between the humanists and the obscurantists. In the end, the Pope ordered an end to the dispute, and victory obviously went to the humanists.

all books written in the Hebrew language. Reuchlin, who was a specialist, took up this question in order to show the absurdity of this interpretation. A controversy began. The Dominican monks of Cologne were involved in trying to convict Reuchlin, but the German sage complained to the humanitarian Pope Leo X. The affair received a great deal of publicity. . . .

Odes were written in honor of Reuchlin ("The Triumph of Caphion," by Ülrich von Hutten), and he was sent sympathetic letters which he even published in a separate book entitled *Letters of Famous Men*. Then in 1516, the Reuchlinists published another book of letters, supposedly written by Cologne theologians. . . . This book . . . called *Letters of the Obscurantists* was a clever forgery in low Latin; it was a ridiculous means of discussing schools. . . . The forgery was so well done that several naive monks took the letters as genuine and were delighted with them, until they realized that they were the victims of the wit of the Reuchlinists.

E. A. Kosminsky, *History of the Middle Ages: Textbook for Sixth and Seventh Grades of Secondary School;* (1951), pp. 187–188.

Chapter 19, "European Culture in the 14th to 16th Century"

Great success was also enjoyed by a joke put about by one of the humanist groups of Germany. It was called *Letters of the obscurantists*. Here, in the form of correspondence of stupid, ignorant monks, they derided the learning of the church, and exposed swindling, drunkenness, and dissoluteness among the Catholic

E. V. Agibalova and G. M. Donskoy, *History of the Middle Ages: Textbook for the Sixth Grade of Secondary School* (1977), p. 246.

European Culture in the 15th and first half of the 16th Century

The Rise of Renaissance Culture

The humanists came out strongly against the church. The ignorance and stupidity of the priests and monks, and the greed and love of power of the Popes became a continual target for jokes made by writers and poets. Even before the beginning of the Reformation, the poet Ülrich Hutten sarcasti-

clergy. One of the strongest humanists in Germany, the errant knight and poet Ülrich von Hutten (1488–1522), took part in the compilation of these *Letters of the obscurantists*. An earnest patriot, he was outraged by the influence of the Roman Pope and the Catholic poets in Germany. He called the Pope a "bandit, infected by all the prophets." . . . He dreamed of the unification of Germany in the fight against the chief enemy—the Pope.

cally mocked the Pope. He wrote that everything is made subject to the Pope with the help of three things: violence, slyness, and superstition. Rome, the capital of the Pope, was a larder filled with wealth stolen from all over the world. And the Pope was a worm, chewing on this wealth.

But the humanists did not want to break completely with religion. They wanted to preserve religion as a restraint on people, and they did not come out openly against it.

Appendix 4

K. V. Bazilevich, S. V. Bakhrushin, A. M. Pankratova, A. B. Fogt, *A History of the USSR: Textbook for the Ninth Grade of Secondary School*, edited by A. M. Pankratova (Moscow, Uchpedgiz).	I. A. Fedosov, *History of USSR: Handbook for Teachers of the Eighth Grade* (Moscow: Prosveshcheniye, 1976).	
1940 ed., p. 242 The strengthening of nationalist-colonialist oppression	*1956 ed., p. 288* The strengthening of nationalist-colonialist oppression	Chapter 8, "Economic and political development of Russia in the Second Half of the 19th Century"
Alexander III's government sowed misanthropic anti-Semitism everywhere. In 1891 in the Ukraine there was a wave of Jewish pogroms. "And I admit that I am happy when they beat the Jews," said Alexander III, when he learned about the pogroms. Encouraged by the Tsar, the organizer of the Jewish pogroms, the Minister for Internal Affairs, Ignatyev, advised the	Alexander III's government sowed misanthropic anti-Semitism everywhere. In 1881 in the Ukraine there was a wave of Jewish pogroms. "And I admit that I am happy when they beat the Jews," said Alexander when he learned about the pogroms. The Minister of Internal Affairs, Ignatyev, encouraged by the Tsar, told the governors to take energetic measures to "defend	[In this chapter, logically and according to the chronology, there should be information about nationalist-colonial politics in Russia, including the Jewish question. This is not the case—R.O.]

governors to take energetic measures "to defend the population from the harmful activities of the Jews, which, according to local information, have been causing concern." Under Alexander III, laws were passed which limited still further the rights of the Jews, compared with those of other nations. Before, Jews were allowed to live only in the Pale of Settlement; now they were forbidden to acquire land and move to the villages.

Under Alexander III, in 1887 a Jewish numerus clausus was introduced in secondary schools. Of the deprived nations of tsarist Russia, that prison of national groups, the Jews were the most deprived.

the population from the harmful activities of the Jews, which according to local information have been causing concern."

Under Alexander III, laws were passed which limited still further the rights of the Jews compared with other nations. In addition to their restriction to the Pale of Settlement, Jews were forbidden to acquire land and settle in villages.

Notes

1. *Pedagogicheskaya Encyclopaedia* (Moscow, 1966), vol. 3, p. 14.

2. Ibid. (Moscow, 1965), vol. 2, p. 302.

3. The textbook of N. M. Nikolsky, *A History of Society Before the Class System: The Ancient East,* published in 1933–34.

4. A. V. Mishulin, *History of the Ancient World: A Textbook for the Fifth and Sixth Grades of Secondary School* (Moscow: Uchpedgiz, 1940), chap. 19, pp. 52–54.

5. F. P. Korovkin and N. I. Zaporozhets, *Methods of Teaching Ancient and Medieval History in the Fifth and Sixth Grades: Handbook for Teachers* (Moscow: Prosveshcheniye, 1970), pp. 95–96.

6. E. A. Kosminsky, *A History of the Early Middle Ages* (Moscow, 1960), p. 59.

7. Quoted from S. Brant, *The Ship of Fools: . . . Letters of the Obscurantists* (Moscow: Khudozhestvennaya Literatura, 1971), p. 407.

8. For the latest information about the Jewish origins of H. Heine and F. Lassalle, see the textbook by A. V. Yefimov, *Modern History, 1799–1870, for the Eight Grade of Secondary School* (Moscow: Uchpedgiz, 1951), pp. 195–196, 242–243.

9. Professor Galkin and others, *Modern History, 1870–1917, for the Ninth Grade of Secondary School* (Moscow: Uchpedgiz, 1950), p. 72.

10. I. B. Berkhin and I. A. Fedosov, *History of the U.S.S.R.: A Textbook for the Ninth Grade of Secondary School* (Moscow: Prosveshcheniye, 1976), p. 30.

11. Ibid., p. 32.

12. Ibid., p. 54.

13. Yu. S. Krushkol, *Collected Texts on the History of the Ancient World* (Moscow: Prosveshcheniye, 1975); *Reader on the Middle Ages*, ed. Academician S. D. Skazkin (Moscow, 1970), pts. 1, 2; S. S. Dmitriev and R. G. Eimontova, *Collected Texts on the History of the Soviet Union: Handbook for Teachers* (Moscow: Prosveshcheniye, 1970), and other books in which information about Jews is also absent. One exception is M. E. Suchkov, *Collected Texts on Modern History: Handbook for Teachers* (Moscow: Proveshcheniye, 1965–66), pts. 1, 2, where there is a short extract about the extermination of the Jews in Auschwitz and the inclusion of the Jewish problem in the Ost Plan.

14. *Modern History (1917–1939): Handbook for Teachers for Ninth Grade of Secondary School*, ed. V. K. Furayev (Moscow; Prosveshcheniye, 1976), p. 56.

15. Ibid., p. 34.

16. M. S. Gus, *Bezumiye svastiki* [Mad swastikas] (Moscow: Sovetsky pisatel, 1972), p. 59.

17. Ibid., p. 59.

18. *Modern History (1939–1975)*, ed. V. K. Furayev (Moscow: Proveshcheniye, 1976), p. 192.

19. According to the results of the census of the whole of the U.S.S.R. taken in 1970, on the territory of Belorussia, Ukraine, and Latvia there are 1.6 percent Jews, and 2.7 percent of the population of Moldavia are Jews. In other republics, the proportion is significantly less. *All-Union Census of Population, 1970* (Moscow: Statistica, 1973), vol. 4, pp. 12–13.

20. The history of the Jews from the end of the nineteenth century up to World War II, in the textbook by A. Gaigalaite and R. Zhepkaite, *History of Lithuanian SSR for Ninth and Tenth Grades* (Kaunas, 1975). In earlier editions, this information was not included.

21. L. S. Abetsedarsky, M. P. Baranova, and N. G. Pavlova, *A History of the Belorussian SSR: Textbook for Secondary Schools*, ed. L. S. Abetsedarsky (Minsk: Narodna asveta, 1976), p. 100.

22. Ibid., p. 243.

23. Ibid., 1971 ed., p. 242.

24. Here there could be disagreement. The more mass literature tells pupils that Jews lived in Russia in ancient times and that they were all exploiters (see Begun's book).

25. This information appears in almost every relevant book in the mass literature.

26. Pupils know that in the Middle Ages Moslems lived in Palestine. They have heard nothing about Jews, either in ancient or medieval history.

27. See V. Begun.

Intellectual Fascism in Soviet-Russian Establishment Culture

MAYA KAGANSKAYA

IN 1971, THERE appeared in Samizdat items signed "Ivan Samolvin,"[1] featuring the slogan "Death to the Zionist Aggressors!" Liberally oriented circles of the Soviet intelligentsia, including the dissidents themselves and those close to them, were more shocked by the use of Samizdat for openly pogromist goals than disturbed by the appearance of a fascist voice in the mixed chorus of opposition currents and ideologies.

The theory was expressed that these leaflets were a KGB provocation, the goal being to discredit the dissident movement by showing the possibility of radical deviation from the movement's ideology (in this case, deviation to the right), in comparison with which the current Brezhnev regime would appear more humane and liberal.

Another opinion was that the appeals of Ivan Samolvin were not intended as a provocation, but that in the KGB there had appeared a "dissident" group which was disturbed by the liberal (from their point of view) course of Brezhnev's foreign and domestic policies, and which wanted to influence the middle and lower ranks of the party and administrative-economic apparatus and, through them, influence the broad, basically anti-Semitic masses of the Soviet urban petty bourgeoisie. This numerically powerful segment of Soviet society now serves, and in the future could serve, as a support for the more conservative elements of the regime, and officially supported total anti-Semitism could be quite useful in political ideology and administrative practice.

Both views consider Ivan Samolvin to be a nom de plume of the KGB. The pitiful intellectual and cultural level of his pamphlets was taken as an indication of the absence of real intellectual power—as lack of ability for

449

original creation, or for effectively renewing the myth of "blood and soil" in a Russian version.

By itself the pogromist anti-Semitism would not qualify Samolvin's text as fascist, openly cribbed from German Nazism, but historically, the foundation of modern anti-Semitism is racial—the concept that the juxta-position of the Indo-European and Semitic races resulted in a world-historical process, the misshaping of European history under the influence of Judaeo-Christianity ("Christianity—the entrance hall to Zionism").

The appeal to indigenous paganism is an apologia for Soviet rule as the power that destroyed the Eastern Orthodox Church, which had kept Russia in chains, and by destroying it helped Russia fulfill its higher racial destiny.

To put it more concisely, Samolvin presents us with a rudimentary version of the fascist myth, with due regard for "local color" and—as already mentioned, in the most wretched, laughable form—obviously the work of a paranoid. It is precisely for this reason that, when they appeared, the leaflets of Ivan Samolvin evoked incredulity, derision, at most fear, nothing more.

Generally speaking, the impossibility of making a critical analysis of the texts because their intellectual and cultural level is too low to permit rational evaluation (as is the case with paranoid writings and the products of graphomania) does not indicate a lack of seriousness, or indicate that the real-life situation that produced the texts is of no significance. How-ever, this was not why the "Samolvin Samizdat" did not arouse an interest in exploring related ideas on another cultural level, in another version, or in another medium, either at the time of its appearance or afterwards. There are several different reasons for this, and I shall indicate those I consider important.

From the appearance of European fascism as a political factor in Euro-pean and world history to its military defeat, i.e., until the end of World War II, and from the end of World War II until today, there has not appeared in Soviet historical, philosophical, or culturological literature a single funda-mental study devoted to fascism as a complex of ideas rooted in European culture, as a *cultural* phenomenon or, more accurately, as a crisis of culture—in Fritz Stern's definition, "the politics of cultural despair," as an outright cultural myth. As a result of being rooted in a culture, this myth had an effect on political realities (state revolution, the structure of power, state ideology and practice), but its essence was not always or not neces-sarily linked with political reality (for example, Action Française leads one to view French fascism as a sui generis "ideal model," i.e., a purely intellectual complex of ideas, a cultural phenomenon).

In official Soviet philosophical thought, fascism is conceived and defined as the ideology of decaying imperialism, its last chance in the struggle with the liberation movement of the workers of all countries and with their avant-garde—the first country in the world where socialism has been victorious. This requires only a very limited analysis of fascist ideology in general, and of German National Socialism in particular, specifically as a cultural phenomenon, resulting from a definite intellectual technique in the reworking of traditions common to all European cultures.

Understandably, in the USSR there are not and cannot be objective, comprehensive historical studies of the formation of dictatorships in Europe. This requires no detailed explanation—if Soviet historiographers were to take up such studies, they would, in the process, have to illuminate the role of Stalin, and of the Comintern, which was subject to him, in the failure of antifascist resistance in Europe, including that of the European bourgeois-liberal and clerical intelligentsia. They would also have to draw attention to the attempts of Stalin, which met with some success, to reach a rapprochement with the Germany of Hitler, not only in regard to external political issues, but also in regard to deeper, ideological questions.

But it is not difficult to understand why, in the Soviet Union, comprehensive objective studies of the genesis of European fascism as the sum of ideas, intellectual conceptions, traditions, and cultural phenomena are impossible. The problem is not that Marxist methodology is too formalistic and simplistic to analyze such a complex subject—the problem is the subject itself, the material which would have to be dealt with and which would show in all clarity that essentially the two totalitarian ideologies of the twentieth century—fascism and communism—have a common source. The issue here is not the similarity of political practices in totalitarian regimes, but rather the similarity of several basic intellectual and ideological orientations.

The first of these is antiliberalism and, linked to it, antiindividualism, an antipersonalist concept. A certain class, race, or nation, and it alone, is considered to possess an ontological fullness and reality of existence, while the individual has no independent characteristics outside this all-embracing community. Furthermore, relative to this particular community, other communities are considered unqualifiedly inimical, blameworthy, and harmful, regardless of the views and intentions of these communities of individuals.

Moreover, anti-Semitism, a central feature of racial fascism, was not the monopoly of the right wing. Together with the social question and class struggle, it came to play a significant role among leftist socialists with claims to represent scientific socialism—from Proudhon to Marx.

Anti-Semitism was elevated to the rank of a substitute for, or more exactly, an antidote to, scientific socialism. Jewish financial capitalism became the exploiting class; blood replaced the modes of production as the key to history, the struggle over seizure of power by the Jews took the place of class warfare; and liberation from the Jewish yoke was presented as the victory of a classless, nationalist, society—a covenant of brothers.[2]

However, hard Soviet sources try to show that fascist ideology is genetically linked with irrationalism and scorn for human reason and for its highest achievement—science, the fascist myth, despite its being rooted in the past, is an absolutely contemporary phenomenon, characteristic of the twentieth century, and this quality is also closely linked with the natural sciences, or rather with their use, interpretation, and mythologization, as is Marxism-Leninism. To confirm this, it is sufficient to point to the role of Social Darwinism and certain principles of modern biology in the formation of the doctrine of racism and, at the same time, to recall the aura with which Darwinism was surrounded in the Stalinist period in Russia and the special ideological function assigned to it.

We shall end our discussion of the (far from complete) list of similarities of fascism and communism with their struggle against Christianity. Although as one of the constituent parts of official Communist ideology, atheism's negation of all traditional religions is supposed to be founded on assumptions different from those of fascist anti-Christianity, nevertheless for historic (Eastern) Orthodox Russia this negation of Christianity has special significance and consequences. In considering the intellectual sources and roots of fascism in the Soviet cultural revolution, we may note the role played as early as the thirties by such clichés as: "Nietzsche was the precursor of fascism," "idealistic and irrational philosophy leads directly to fascism," and "anti-Marxism is fascism's leading idea"—all of which may be true, but only partially.

On the other hand, Russian fascism itself, as a historic phenomenon which arose among Russian emigrés, was almost completely unknown to the Soviet public, as was its meeting in the twenties and thirties with Russian communism and its entry into party ideology ("national Bolshevism," "Ustryalovism").[3] Similarly unknown, at least in the sixties and seventies, were such protofascist phenomena of Russian culture as the ideology (as distinct from the practice) of the Russian Black Hundreds, the "Scythian" movement, which arose in Russia before and during the revolution,[4] and the "Eurasian" movement, which started among the emigrés in Europe, but which had its roots in the intellectual atmosphere of the same Russian "Silver Age." None of these phenomena has been taken into account in the evaluation of current Russian reality; they were apparently not regarded as a decisive, formative influence in the rise, crystallization, and confrontation of various dissident and neo-Orthodox ideologies.

Their role was ignored in favor of the durable, "classical" categorization into "Westernizers" and "Slavophiles" which, it was thought, quite covered the whole spectrum of dissident and neo-Orthodox thought.

Despite this, no single concept in the Soviet political lexicon is as current, widespread, and constantly resorted to as *fascism*. Within the framework of Soviet ideology, "communism" and "fascism" have been and continue to be an inseparable pair of opposites, implacable enemies; the term "fascist" (included in various phrases to refer to Latin American military dictatorships, to Zionism, etc.) in the Soviet political vocabulary demonstrates the total opposition of Soviet policy to phenomena thus qualified (as "fascist")—which is not the case, for example, in relation to the international capitalist system, with which "peaceful coexistence" is possible. At the same time, in the enumeration of the services of Soviet rule to humanity and world culture, the role of the Soviet Union in the destruction of the "plague of fascism" is constantly recalled.

Precisely this fixed official conception, which presents fascism and communism as totally implacable opposites, whose relation is like the opposition between absolute "good" and absolute "evil," has played a significant role in encouraging the antiofficial, conventionally called "dissident," and the dissident-oriented Soviet intelligentsia to resort to the same far-fetched analogies and even to identify communism with fascism. (Of course, the real points of resemblance of their political structures and practices are significant, but what is really important is that analogy remains the only counterbalance to official doctrine.)

In other words, the Soviet intelligentsia, deprived by circumstances beyond their control of a knowledge and understanding of the genesis of European *and* native Russian fascism as an intellectual, and not only political, phenomenon—as a range of ideas basically affecting all layers and phenomena of European culture, from Christian dogma to German romantisism, the basis of Indo-European linguistics, folklore, and aesthetics— are inclined simply to equate all totalitarian structures and absolutist ideologies. However, while it might be ethically correct to deduce ideology from political practice, from the standpoint of theory this is impossible, and leads to confusion and the ignoring of ideas related to the realities of another, unfamiliar social order. Despite all similarities and permissible analogies, and despite the common ideational and political threads of their doctrines, communism and fascism are, in the final analysis, not identical. For example, a non-Marxist-based anti-Christianity can just as well derive from liberal atheism or agnosticism *or* from ("proto-" or "para-") fascist-oriented thinking. For the average Soviet freethinking member of the intelligentsia, almost any non-Marxist, unorthodox idea or interpretation is, ipso facto, a good thing. In a majority of cases, such concepts are not associated with that complex of ideas, primarily fascist, which, expressed in terms of familiar sociopolitical language and not culturological realism, would put him on his guard—but only if his values are of a liberal cast. What this signifies is that such characterizations of fascism in general, and of the Hitlerian variety in particular, as "the struggle against the transcedent" or "racial Manichaeanism" (Ernst Nolte) reveal nothing to a member of the Soviet intelligentsia. These concepts do not appear in his vocabulary. He knows practically nothing about the role of gnostic dualism and antimonotheism, under the banner of which the fascist myth was formed. Similarly, he hardly realizes that a struggle against Christianity can be launched not only from a materialistic-atheistic platform but also from various religious positions within that same European, i.e., "Christian," culture.

The ideas of Charles Maurras, as expressed in his introduction to a collection of Provençal myths and legends ("I wanted to show how mono-theistic Christianity destroys the living harmony of paganism. In the name of the suffering god, night was spread over the world"), and as they found expression in various forms, in phenomena of European culture, including the anti-Christian outlook of Hitlerian fascism, remained outside the intellectual scope of Soviet society. Thus Ivan Samolvin's paean to the Soviet regime for its help in bringing about a restoration of indigenous Slavic paganism was naturally viewed merely as a bad joke.

Furthermore, the traditional anti-Westernism of the Slavophiles, from the Slavophile classics of the nineteenth century to Solzhenitsyn and the contemporary Russian Orthodox (religious) revival, caused all pro-Western orientations to be linked firmly only with liberal Westernizers (among the dissidents, with the democratic human rights movement). Even now, among all the dissident and nondissident conceptions and positions that have evolved in Russian Soviet culture, only the liberal-democratic orientation is considered "Western-oriented." Western fascism as a phenomenon of this same Western culture is not taken into consideration; its origin and formation are excluded from the prevailing image of the West.

Similarly, a positive attitude to Jews (from philo-Semitism to a general liberal "human rights" attitude) is associated only with liberal-democratic ideology. *This association is so firmly established that, for many, a positive attitude to the West automatically involves—as a minimum—an absence of anti-Semitism, which is firmly entrenched only among ideologues of nationalism.*

And only the absurd and illiterate attempts of Ivan Samolvin to find allies in Western history, with his wild, paradoxical rambling—first in the direction of the Renaissance, then in the direction of the Indo-European race— lead him out of the orbit of traditional anti-Western Russian nationalism, and reveal an affinity to . . . a liberal-democratic, Western orientation!

Only two conclusions can be drawn from this dialectical "meeting of opposites":

1. There is not and could not be intellectual support for Samolvin's dissident fascism, either in dissident circles or among the intellectuals integrated into and still part of the semiofficial bodies. If this is correct, it would support the view that Samolvin's Samizdat is a KGB provocation. In the almost twenty-year existence of the dissident movement, it has been found that, behind each of its activities and currents, there stands a definite group of the Soviet intelligentsia, supporting it with intellectual and creative efforts, forming and reflecting its views.

The "spiritual isolation" of Ivan Samolvin would appear to show that Russian fascism—not as a political reality but as a world view, a "spiritual hunger"—is impossible in a "pure" form and could exist only as a modification of radical Orthodox nationalism, i.e., as Orthodox fascism. "Orthodox fascism" might appear acceptable to someone today *if* the only alternative were "ordinary fascism," that is, if the choice lay between something bad and something worse.

2. If Ivan Samolvin is not a KGB provocation, but rather a primitive paranoid reflection of some deep processes in Soviet society, primarily among the Soviet intelligentsia, then sooner or later some intellectual support for fascism will appear. And indeed it has!

In the 1978 anthology *Context: Literary-Critical Studies*, a study by I. F. Belza entitled "The Genealogy of *The Master and Margarita*"[5] was published. This seems to me a revealing document of intellectual fascism; in its frankness and brilliance, it has no peer in the Samizdat and emigré publications, or in the official Soviet press.

In content and purpose, Belza's study is a politico-philosophical treatise. The genre of literary criticism in which this tractate is "clothed" is not an intentional "Aesopian" device, chosen as particularly suitable for the expression of politico-philosophical views. In the conditions of Soviet society, *not* coinciding, down to the smallest detail, with official ideology is impossible. In considering the choice of "Aesopian"-like camouflage, it should be remembered that the origin and frequent use of the "Aesopian mode" go back a long way. The use of this device is not only a consequence of Soviet totalitarianism, of the spiritual atmosphere of a closed society. This device is also one of the oldest and most characteristic traditions of Russian culture.

The transformation of literature into a "philosophy of life" is so characteristic and traditional in Russia that it has spread not only to literary criticism (as the most immediate reaction to a literary text) but also to philology, poetics, stylistics, the history of literature, etc. Not only literature, but everything related to it has been "ideologized."

A real idea of the ideological differences and conflicts in world view, political sympathies, and spiritual quests in Soviet society will hardly be gained from philosophical publications, sociological studies, and political documents, but should rather be sought in belles lettres, literary criticism, and literary studies.[6]

For an outside observer, the difficulty is that an adequate understanding of a text is possible only for a person who is completely familiar with that text from what is to be understood by reading between the lines—which, in Soviet society, has far greater importance than the text itself. In other words, only a Soviet person will receive the required information, while a foreigner will be led astray as a result of his ingenuousness. For example, coming across an article on comparative analysis of the poetics of the Bible and ancient Greek literature,[7] the foreigner would set it aside as an item for the specialist which, for him, a professional student interested in the ideological atmosphere in Soviet society, will provide no information.

A Soviet reader, however, would first note the author's name; it not only indicates that a work of high professional caliber can be expected but, in this case, also that there will be a Western orientation with a bias toward philosophical systems alien to Marxism. Secondly, he would realize that the interest is in the Bible, which, whatever the standpoint from which it is viewed, is a Jewish book. Further he would note that the word "Jew" appears often in the text of the article, and that these facts mean something and suggest the position of the author on the Jewish question. Thirdly, having learned of the advantages of biblical metaphor over the developed Greek simile, he would understand that the position of the author is philo-Semitic. Thus the genre of his politico-philosophical views is not something external to these views. Rather, it is their "clothing," which, when stripped off, reveals the idea or ideology in its "natural" state.

The cultural text from which a concept of nonliterary character derives gives that concept authenticity and, far from lessening, increases the ideological effectiveness of that concept. This is deep-rooted in Russian-Soviet culture.

The choice of author (M. Bulgakov) and work (*The Master and Margarita*) as subjects for this ideological exercise is particularly felicitous. As a genuine work of art, Bulgakov's novel has many levels of meaning and, like the novels of Dostoevsky, is open to various, often mutually contradictory, interpretations. But aside from this feature, which is generally characteristic of good literature, Bulgakov's novel possesses a number of other noteworthy features which are quite irreplaceable for the ideological confrontation here discussed. First there is Bulgakov himself; persecuted by the watchdogs of official vulgar-sociological criticism in the 1930s,[8] he died in poverty and neglect in 1940 (although he was fortunate enough to avoid jail and concentration camp). At the beginning of the 1960s, he had a "posthumous rehabilitation": the republication of *The White Guard*, *The Life of Molière*, a theatrical novel (*Black Snow*), some of his plays and short stories, and the first publication (in the journal *Moskava*)[9] of *The Master and Margarita*, which had survived in manuscript form.

Thus, from one point of view, Bulgakov has a "place of honor" in the martyrology of outstanding artists destroyed (physically or otherwise) by the Soviet regime. That is how Bulgakov was viewed in the 1960s by the Soviet intelligentsia, which was impressed by his artistic heritage and saw him as a victim, a martyr, and an opponent of the regime. (Bulgakov was neither a Communist, a Marxist, nor a "proletarian writer," but obviously continued the traditions of the classical literature of the Russian gentry.)

On the other hand, it is known that in the 1930s Blugakov sought to compromise with the regime (e.g., he wrote a play about Stalin as a young man, and attempted to make personal contact with the dictator), which is quite understandable in the light of his simple and natural desire to survive creatively and physically. However, in Bulgakov's best novel, *White Guard*, the acceptance of Soviet rule is connected with Bulgakov's definite sympathy for the Russian imperial tradition, which the Moscow Bolsheviks continued when they sent their troops into an independent country, the Ukraine, in 1918. (The theme of *White Guard* is the advance of the Red Army into the Ukraine at this time.)

But the imperial orientation of Bulgakov, which was overlooked in the 1960s, is quite topical now, when the different attitudes to the pre-Soviet history of Russia, its national essence and fate, form the "great split" between the various ideological movements of dissident thought. This imperial orientation must be taken into consideration in any objective analysis of Bulgakov's complex works. In an analysis which is not objective, it might be used to advantage.

While *White Guard* whets the appetite for an exposition of today's supporters and defenders of the Soviet empire as the rightful heirs of the Russian empire, the novel *The Master and Margarita* is even closer to the "epicenter" of current ideological polemics (although, in this novel also, the theme of empire, which is very important to Bulgakov and for the work itself, appears in a unique way).

1. *The Master and Margarita* is a novel within a novel. The action of the first, "framing" novel takes place in Moscow at the end of the 1920s and beginning of the 1930s. The action of the second, "inserted" novel takes place in Jerusalem during the rule of Pontius Pilate, who, with the Sanhedrin, condemned Yeshua ha-Notzri (Jesus of Nazareth) to death. The crucifixion of ha-Notzri and the cycle of events connected with it are the theme of the second novel, but its plot and meaning are tied to the relations of Yeshua and Pontius Pilate, the two main heroes of the Jerusalem chapters of *The Master and Margarita*.

2. The motivation for connecting Jerusalem of the period of the rise of

Christianity with Soviet Moscow is that the Moscow writer (the Master) writes a novel about Pontius Pilate and Jesus. The novel brought him unhappiness and ruin instead of the expected fame. Thus the Jerusalem chapters are introduced into the main text as the work of a character.

The figure that transcends plot and unites the author's novel with the novel of his character is the fantastic Woland-Satan, who belongs to the fantastic world in which both Moscow and Jerusalem exist, and by which they too are fantastically transformed. (In some places in *The Master and Margarita*, the Jerusalem events are presented not as the text of the Master but as an independent reality of the novel, i.e., as something occurring in a "reality" independent of the literary invention of the Master.) The protagonists of the "Moscow" novel are the Master and Woland, who, according to an unofficial but widely held opinion, represents Stalin.

Thus, compositionally, the novel is complex. Although this complexity obviously reflects an ideational, conceptual complexity, I am concerned with ideology and I accordingly focus on only two crucial aspects: the theme of Yeshua (this is the theme of the dissident "Orthodox revival") and the Woland-Stalin theme, i.e., the theme of Soviet rule.

These themes are linked in the actual ideological situation—although not in the novel—by the Jewish question: the role—the participation, and guilt—of the Jews in the Russian Revolution, which was antinational in its essence and goals, and their role in the establishment of Soviet rule, which is also antinational, and thus alien and inimical to Russian national and political life. This is the theme of the writings of Solzhenitsyn, the theme of the "Orthodox revival." But precisely because this revival is Orthodox, i.e., Christian, the historical guilt of the Jews vis-à-vis Russia (which, according to Solzhenitsyn, is undeniable) should be considered in the light of the general Christian attitude toward the Jews, as expressed in the sources of the Christian religion. The novel of Bulgakov, at least in its Jerusalem chapters, provides very useful material for the study of this theme.

Only by constantly keeping in mind the problems considered by the journal *Context*, which today comprise the essential problematics of the dissident movement, and relating Belza's text to the environment which gave birth to *Context*, can one really understand and evaluate the "basic ploys" it employs to plant its own conceptions in a criticism of Bulgakov's work, and thus comprehend the ideological manifesto behind this ostensibly literary study.

In Belza's work, there is not a single literary evaluation which does not at the same time have an ideological dimension.

I will now discuss some of these evaluations.

Belza relates the specifics of the genre of the novel *The Master and*

Margarita to the traditions of Pushkin's "poetics of historical authenticity," i.e., to put it more simply, to the traditions of *realistic* poetics.

This highly debatable position is supported neither by the fantastic plot of the novel nor by its fantastic-grotesque stylistic elements. These clearly reflect Russian and European romanticism of the nineteenth century (Gogol and E. Th. A. Hoffmann) and that style in Soviet Russian prose of the twenties and thirties which, in a complex way, transformed elements of the prose of the symbolists (such as A. Bely) of the beginning of the century, and the "South Russian school" (Babel, Katayev, Ilf and Petrov, Olesha). These elements also reflect traditions of Russian realist literature (ranging from Pushkin to Doroshevich). The novel also reflects Bulgakov's originality, which enabled him to turn his varied literary heritage into a unified polyphonic style. Thus, to extract one of the elements of style in a "chemically pure" state (and clearly *not* one of the main ones) and to pronounce it formative (even if only on the level of genre), as Belza does, it dishonest. Belza (and this is symptomatic) does not prove, he only postulates. However, such a postulate ("Pushkin's 'poetics of historical verisimilitude' ") *immediately gives him the possibility of projecting the novel onto the plane of a historical novel, in which context the fantastic and grotesque are mere stylistic elements—not a total artistic (and therefore ideological) conception.*

In order words, according to Belza, the fantastic and grotesque are merely a *method of coding reality,* and behind each personage and situation in the novel is "concealed" a real-life person or situation. He focuses his attention on two pairs of characters: Pilate–ha-Notzri and Woland–the Master. The first part of Belza's study, in which particular care is taken to maintain a scholarly or scientific approach, is devoted to the first pair. Nevertheless his main concern is really the second pair. In this latter pair, Woland is generally recognized to be Stalin (as noted above), while the Master, according to the (well-founded) opinion of many scholars, including Belza, has elements of the personality and biography of Bulgakov.

Of the two heroes of the "Jerusalem" novel, Pontius Pilate, the fifth procurator of Judaea, is, beyond a doubt, a real historical character. If one wants to prove, as Belza does, that Yeshua was a real historical figure and not a mythical one—this is a main theme of Belza—then, according to the logic of the author of the article, one can make decisions about the relations between (a strong) personality and (a strong) governing power, between an artist and a state (preferably of the imperial model) on the basis of reality and not on the basis of its novelistic, artistic recreation. Nevertheless, there is no doubt that Belza's primary concern is with the Soviet ("Moscow") reality, mainly in its Stalinist aspect, and that the Jerusalem reality, remote in time and wrapped in the mists of legend, is evoked by Belza to lend a metahistorical, metaphysical, and mystic aura to Soviet rule (the jump from Moscow to Jerusalem and back is provided by the material itself, i.e., by the compositional and literary conception of Bulgakov's novel).

As proof of the historical existence of Jesus Christ, Belza cites the names and works of scholars who rejected both "the attempt of David Strauss to turn the Gospel narratives into a 'myth about Christ' and Renan's 'transcription,' which turned the Gospels into a novel."[11]

Belza suggests that, in his treatment of Jesus as a real historical personality, Bulgakov was relying primarily on the book by the academician S. A. Zhebelev, *The Canonical and Apocryphal Gospels* (1919), and the M.A. dissertation, "The Archaeology of the History of the Sufferings of Our Lord Jesus Christ," by a professor of the Kiev Theological Academy and friend and colleague of Bulgakov's father, Nikolay Kornilovich Makkavey-sky. Bulgakov's evaluation of Jesus as a historical person can be traced, according to Belza, to Zhebelev, and the wealth of historical detail in the Jerusalem chapters of the novel, to Makkaveysky. Belza devotes consider-able attention to both these authors and their influence on Bulgakov. What interests me here are the following ideological and conceptual points.

According to Belza, the author of the novel (i.e., Bulgakov) did not doubt the historicity of Jesus or of Pilate, nor did he doubt that all four Gospels abound with later accretions, particularly relating to the "miracles." For this reason there is no mention in the novel of the "immaculate concep-tion" or of the healings and resurrections or indeed of the resurrection of Jesus. In the scene of the interrogation, attention is given to the answer of Yeshua regarding his origin: "I was told that my father was a Syrian."

On the other hand, one of the most significant characters of the novel, the critic Mikhail Aleksandrovich Berlioz (his "real" name is revealed by Belza in the second part of his study), was in regard to Yeshua "a firm proponent of the legendary approach." Thus we have an apparently para-doxical situation. According to Belza, Bulgakov rejects both the legendary view of Jesus (by his satirical depiction of Berlioz, the advocate of this view) and the Orthodox Christian view of Jesus as the son of God, and along with it, the Gospels as holy or canonical texts which contain the whole truth.

It is precisely at this point that Belza begins, as the Soviet expression has it, "to fight on two fronts": against "vulgar sociologizing" (for Belza a code name for "Jewish dominance" of Russian Soviet literary criticism in the 1930s, as I shall demonstrate later) and simultaneously against traditional Orthodox Christianity, primarily against its Jewish–Old Testament sources and foundation. From this point of view, Belza's treatment of the remark made by Bulgakov's Yeshua, "I was told that my father was a Syrian," is especially significant.

In the context of the whole study and the ideology of Belza—and in the much broader context of the intellectual objectives of European thought, which were a component part of the ideology of German fascism (or of the atmosphere in which it arose)—this phrase echoes the ideas of the Tübingen professor Harnack, according to whom Jesus, although born among the Jewish people, was really not a Jew and did not preach in the name of the Old Testament God. It also echoes, in Russian culture, the idea of Berdyaev that Christianity is essentially not a monotheistic but rather a trinitarian religion, and therefore the canonization by the church of the connection between the New Testament and the Old is a very dubious proposition.

Turning to Bulgakov's description of the last hours of the life of Yeshua ha-Notzri, Belza remarks: "It would not be an exaggeration to say that these words [i.e., Bulgakov's text] evoke more sympathy for the fate of the extremely trusting and noble philosopher ('the mad dreamer and physician,' Pilate calls him in a dream) than does the triumphant narration about the death of the god-man, foretold in great detail in the Old Testament books of the prophets—all the more so since Bulgakov's Yeshua does not rise in the third day after his death, he does not rise from the pit (whose entrance is) blocked with stones." Thus in one derogatory statement Old Testament prophecy and the Gospel traditions are linked.

Thus, in Belza's interpretation, Bulgakov's Yeshua remains in a completely "deideologized" vacuum—not the hero of legend (à la Strauss and Berlioz), not the Old Testament Messiah, nor the god-man of Christianity. He is some historical (i.e., real) person, needing—because of his renowned name—to have the meaning of his existence deciphered. In Belza's view of Bulgakov's novel, this meaning is indivisible from the meaning of the existence and historical (even metahistorical) role of Pontius Pilate as the representative of the highest authority.

To this theme, Belza devotes a separate chapter of his study, "The Fifth Procurator of Judea." Leaving aside all the literary-historical and cultural baggage of the chapter, which abounds with references to Dante, the European Middle Ages, romanticism, and even ancient Roman legislation, I shall now consider the key ideological points, for which, in my opinion, all the philological trimmings serve merely as a backdrop.

The basic theme associated with Pontius Pilate that concerns Belza is the procurator's guilt for the death of Yeshua.

In Bulgakov's novel, the relations of Pilate and Yeshua are revealed as a growing interdependence, sympathy, and closeness. This seems to corroborate one of the basic ideas of Belza's study, to expound which it was written: the collaboration and closeness of strong authority and a strong (i.e., highly gifted) individual (Stalin-Bulgakov).

On the other hand, in both the Jerusalem and the Moscow scenarios, this closeness and mutual understanding (if we assume that such existed) remain secret, inner experiences of authority and the individual (power and personality), while on the esoteric level, there is a tragic, one-sided conflict, as a result of which authority destroys the individual, who was beginning to accommodate that authority. These are the historical facts— the death of Yeshua on the order, or at least with the participation, of Pilate, and the premature death of Bulgakov, persecuted by official critics and deprived of the means of subsistence. Such also are the facts in the novel: the madness and destruction of the Master by authority of those in power.

Thus Belza finds it necessary to whitewash Pilate and merely "scold" him; he finds it even more necessary to draw attention to the powers which hindered mutual understanding and fruitful collaboration between authority and the individual.

In his effort to exonerate Pontius Pilate, Belza has the support of well-established Christian tradition. He is not in the least embarrassed by the fact that, in the previous chapter, he rejected this tradition as a source of truth. Belza writes: "The aim of 'whitewashing' Pilate was already apparent in the canonized Gospels. In the apocryphal gospel of Peter, Pilate is almost completely absolved of blame for what happened to Yeshua. Thus the motif of the necessity of Pilate's action is present in the canonical and apocryphal gospels."

"The motif of the necessity of Pilate's action" is analyzed all the more eagerly because, in history, or rather in the history of Christianity, it was made clear long ago—in a way particularly acceptable to Belza—that the real responsibility lay with the Sanhedrin, or the Jewish "lobby." This explanation is so clear and well known that Belza does not bother to go into details, preferring to develop the Sanhedrin theme later, in terms of "Jewish predominance" among the "vulgar-sociological literary critics" of the 1930s who hounded Bulgakov.

Thus Belza links Pilate—whose image (as depicted by Bulgakov) he identifies with the historical image—with (1) the motif of "the secret kinship" of authority and the outstanding individual; (2) the destruction of the individual, not by the arbitrariness or ill will of authority, but by the force of circumstances and a "third force" entering between the individual and authority; (3) the repentance of authority for what occurs (Belza writes: "Properly speaking, from that moment—the execution of Yeshu— begins the tragedy of Pilate, which the author of the novel, rich in psychological insights, treats as a tragedy of aroused consciousness"); and (4) the revenge of authority on the "third force" that hindered its "romance" (relation) with "the mad dreamer and physician" (in the plot of Bulgakov's novel, the killing of Judas on Pilate's order).

Let us note this latter motif; Belza returns to it later, treating the action of the party against "vulgar-sociological" ("Jewish") extremes (cf. Pilate's order to kill Judas) as the "terrible vengeance" of the party and government on those who tried to "drive a wedge" between the party and the government in regard to the latter's attachment to Russian literature.

But Pontius Pilate is hardly the symbol and image of the authority which is present in the novel and which is necessary for Belza. Pilate is only a representative of authority, not its incarnation. The procurator is not Caesar. He represents high but not supreme authority, a province but not the empire. The supreme authority (in the mystical sense, as well) that unites the Jerusalem and Moscow chapters of the novel *The Master and Margarita* into an artistic and ideological whole is Woland (read: Stalin), around whose image Belza centers his most poweful efforts (cf. his section "Summa Demonologiae").

As elsewhere in the book, in this chapter Belza expresses opinions of a topical, i.e., ideological, character, against a vast historical and general cultural background, in this case the origin and development of the image of the Prince of Darkness in world culture. I here focus on one point—the transition from "demonology" to ideology, which for Belza are identical. Bulgakov used as the epigraph of his novel the famous self-characterization of Mephistopheles in Goethe's *Faust:* "I am a part of that force which eternally wills evil and eternally does good."

The saturation of Bulgakov's novel with echoes of Goethe's *Faust* and allusions to European culture (including parodies of Gounod's opera) is obvious to any researcher, regardless of the method of analysis he employs. Belza also recognizes the Goethean heritage in Bulgakov. However, he asserts that the Russian writer does not agree with the great German but rather polemicizes with him. The basic point of contention, according to Belza, is that, as Goethe's Mephistopheles frankly and modestly admits, he is only "a *part* of that force, and not the whole force. In Belza's opinion, Bulgakov's Woland is the servant of the Prince of Darkness, and not Lucifer himself, in contrast to Goethe's Mephistopheles. (Mephistopheles is to Lucifer as the procurator is to Caesar.) However, for his purposes, Belza needs an absolute authority, subject only to his own internal law, as was Woland-Stalin.

Why is it important to Belza that there be a "duel" between Bulgakov and Goethe? Obviously because Belza regards the theological view of Goethe's *Faust* as corresponding to the Orthodox teaching of the Christian Church, the monotheistic doctrine which denies that there are "two equal gods, of good and evil, but rather that there is the Devil . . . in Christian teaching, the fallen, rebellious, angel, finally impotent despite his apparent victories gained exploiting human weakness, opposed to an omnipotent Divinity."[12]

It does not suit Belza for Woland to be a pseudonym for Mephistopheles, "a part" of Lucifer, nor even to be Lucifer himself—if Lucifer (in accordance with Christian tradition) is a "rebellious angel" rather than an equal god—in terms of rights, power, and real existence, but charged with "negative" rather than "positive" energies.

In other words, Jewish monotheism does not suit Belza, even in the adulterated form preserved in Orthodox Christianity's view of good and evil. According to Belza, Bulgakov, in his depiction of Woland (which effectively means in his whole conception of the novel), decisively breaks with the Judeo-Christian tradition, and completely rehabilitates the principles of Zoroastrianism, Manichaeanism, the gnostics, and other sects condemned by Orthodox Christianity. Thus, according to Belza, the universal concept embodied in the novel *The Master and Margarita* is a *dualistic* conception derived from the recognition of good and evil as two fundamental principles on which the world was created.

It is very interesting and characteristic that, while enumerating the dualistic heresies well known in the literature, Belza devotes special attention to Bogomilism.[13] "The influence of Manichaeanism and other Eastern heresies on the Bogomil doctrine which arose in Bulgaria," writes Belza, "and which was also considered a heresy *(haeresis Bulgarorum)*, is among the most complicated questions in the history of religion. But regardless of any influences, the uniqueness of Bogomilism, which is of interest to us here in connection with the genealogy of Bulgakov's novel, is undisputed. The central aspect of the Bulgarian heresy is, as is well known, the principle of dualism." And further: "The 'rank' of Bulgakov's Woland is defined more or less precisely by this principle. Throughout the novel one finds the theme of the omnipotence of Woland, whose image is closer to great Lucifer than to Mephistopheles." To quote the words of Woland directed to Matthew the Levite: "You expressed yourself as if you do not recognize darkness or evil. Won't you be so kind as to ponder the question: What would your good do if evil did not exist, and how would the world look if darkness disappeared from the earth?"

Belza comments: "Essentially, this is a somewhat concise but accurate formulation of the Bogomil principle of dualism, which afirms the primary existence of good and evil, light and darkness. The request of ha-Notzri to Woland, completely unthinkable from the viewpoint of Orthodox Christianity, also relates to Bogomil doctrines. Bulgarian folk legends abound with motifs of the mutual interaction between God and the Devil, and not only the confrontation of these antagonistic principles."[14] I am not inclined to regard this interest in Bogomilism and its echoes in *The Master and Margarita* as attesting to the academic honesty of the author of the monograph. Even if one could somehow explain as honest the very mention of the Bulgarian heresy, a variety of Manichaeanism which Belza represents as the trunk of Bulgakov's genealogical tree, the attempt to link the text of Bulgakov's novel directly to the principles of Bogomil doctrine is patently absurd, and not supported even by the impenetrable "contextual" method of Belza—which allows him to link anything to anything else, on any basis whatsoever. For example, is Woland's question "What would your good do if evil did not exist, and how would the world look if darkness disappeared from the earth?" really a concise but accurate formulation of the Bogomil principle of dualism? Even if we assume that Bulgakov did write, as Belza would have us believe, a Manichaean novel, why should Woland's question, which is relevant to any of the dualistic movements or simply to dualism itself, precisely "formulate" Bogomilism and not some other dualistic principle? And finally, how could Bogomilism possibly have been known to Bulgakov in such detail that, as Belza believes, Yeshua's request to Woland derives directly from Bulgarian folk legends?

For the sake of argument, we may assume that the author actually read some of the literary sources Belza includes among the "required reading" without which Bulgakov could not have achieved such "historical authenticity" in his work (remember that according to Belza, Bulgakov wrote a historical novel). Some of these books were written by friends and colleagues of his father, others were in his father's library. Theological literature in the house of a priest is as normal as medical literature in the house of a physician, or law books in the house of a lawyer.

There is no doubt that Bulgakov was congnizant of other "genealogical" sources, such as Dante or Goethe, simply as an educated person. But Bulgarian folk legends in which the Devil collaborates with God—as Woland does with Yeshua ha-Notzri if we are to believe Belza—could not have had a place on Bulgakov's reading list. As indicated in the notes to which Belza refers the reader (p. 195), the collection of Bogomil books and legends compiled by Iordan Ivanov, a member of the Bulgarian Academy, was published in Sofia in 1970. It is true that, as pointed out in these same notes, the 1970 edition was a second, photocopied edition which reproduced the text of the 1925 Sofia edition. Belza says nothing about the fate of this first edition, although he notes that the 1970 edition is accompanied by "an introduction by the renowned expert on the Bogomil movement, Professor D. Angelov, whose book *Bogomilism in Bulgaria* has gone through several editions since 1947 and was translated into Russian in 1954." The failure to mention the 1925 Sofia edition is no mere oversight, since only this edition could have been known to Bulgakov. This is significant, especially in the light of Belza's boldness in presenting assumptions for his readers to accept.

For this reader, at least, it is quite clear that Belza is a past master not only at making unusual connections but also—and even more cleverly—at concealing his tricks. Belza wrote his note in such a way that the fate of the 1925 Sofia edition tends to pass unnoticed amidst the welter of names and dates. In other words, the sources on Bogomilism mentioned were undoubtedly read by the author of "The Genealogy of *The Master and Margarita*," but could not all have been read by the author of *The Master and Margarita*, who died in 1940, thus of course being deprived of any possible acquaintance with the editions of 1954 and 1970.

In general, one gets the feeling that Belza's article is not really about Bulgakov's novel but about a novel of the same name which Belza would have written if he had set his mind to it, and, of course, if he were capable of it.

I have dwelt at length on this obvious and crude discrepancy, but not because of the tradition that if you radically disagree with someone's idea, you emphasize the difference between your world view and that of the person with whom you are taking issue, and his mistakes of fact. In this case, the factual discrepancy was a child of Belza's conception, and not of an incidental argument with which the overenthusiastic author wanted to buttress his idea, without regard for the honesty of his "proof."

The issue is not only, or not primarily, the confusion of names and dates connected with the Bogomilism sources of Bulgakov's novel. The problem is different. Why does Belza insist on the connection of the Bulgarian Bogomil, who obviously has no relevance to *The Master and Margarita?*

At this point, we come close to answering another key question: Why does Belza define the poetics of Bulgakov's novel as "the poetics of historical authenticity," from which he concludes that the novel must belong to the historical genre?

In the most general sense, one can call any literary work whose plot derives from some real historical event a historical novel. As Stendhal put it, "history is a novel which really happened."

To be based on a historical attested event or person is the minimum and, in fact, the only necessary condition for assigning a literary work to a historical genre. But "historical authenticity" and, even more cogently, its "poetics" are always debatable matt·rs, since "historical" (novel, story) presupposes corresponding historical events (sources, documents, evidence), while "artistic" indicates the inevitability and necessity of fantasy and the embodiment of a concept or ideology of the author. Consider, for example, Aleksey Tolstoy's *Peter I.* As a novel it is undeniably historical—authentic in relation to the main personage and basic events, yet the image of Peter I in it mainly reflects the author's view, his historiosophy. One can say practically the same thing about any historical novel (and its main protagonists).

On what basis, however slight, can the novel *The Master and Margarita* be considered historical?

As already noted, of the main characters, the sole historical figure in the novel is Pontius Pilate. Even if we accept Yeshua ha-Notzri (Jesus) as a historical figure, as Belza would have us do, and if we further acknowledge that the prototype of the Master is Bulgakov himself, and that the prototype of Margarita is his wife, Elena Sergeevna Bulgakova (which Belza tries to prove with all the means at his disposal), *how* can one combine the Jerusalem chapters (we may provisionally call them "historical") with the Moscow chapters and regard them as belonging to a common genre, even though the text of *The Master and Margarita* indeed appears to form a novelistic whole?

Real-life prototypes can also be a feature of nonhistorical prose. Apart from the critics, poets, the Master, and his girlfriend, there appear in the "Moscow" chapters Lucifer himself (in the guise of Woland), a woman who flies on a broomstick, a cat that converses, and we have Satan, who is "master of ceremonies at the ball." And there are not simply nonhistorical but completely unreal occurrences.

Perhaps from the standpoint of genre, *The Master and Margarita* is a "centaur" which can be separated at the "seam" into historical and fantasy portions. But in Bulgakov's novel, Woland, a character invented by the author, appears also in the framework of the characters "invented" by the Master, and is in the latter's novel about the fifth procurator of Judea. Before declaring such a novel subject to the laws of "Pushkin's poetics of historical authenticity," one would first have to declare demonology a natural science and have Belza's study published by "The Society for the Propagation of Sociopolitical and Demonological Sciences."

I believe it permissible to say that Belza implies that Woland is as real a person as Pontius Pilate, Yeshua, and Bulgakov himself, who appears in the novel as the Master. (Here I have in mind Woland as Lucifer the Prince of Darkness and not as a pseudonym for Stalin or, rather, Stalin as a reincarnation of Woland, assuming—within the framework of Belza's demonology—the immortality of this personage and his ability to appear in various incarnations.) In any case, the throughness of the "archaeological" analysis in the first chapters of Belza's study, which are devoted to the historical authenticity (in reality and in the novel) of the life and death of Yeshua, and the ease with which Belza moves from history (even in *his* understanding of it) to its fantastic-mystic reflection in culture, allow us to presume that a clearly defined boundary between these two realities (historical and spiritual-cultural) does not exist for the author of "The Genealogy of *The Master and Margarita.*"

In other words, parallel to human history in the usual sense, Belza constructs his own historical "reality" in which "facts" of various degrees of reliability are mixed with *interpretations* of facts, indisputable only in the sense that such interpretations have been made. *It is only in the framework of this second, "esoteric" history, presented in Belza's study as the primary history, that the novel* The Master and Margarita *can be considered a historical novel.*

So Bulgakov has written a "historical" novel. But what kind of history did he have in mind?

Primarily, it is a history taking place in higher realms, so to speak. It is the history of how the world was conceived, planned, or—to put it more directly—*created,* and how humanity, in its religiocultural and sociohistorical activities, correctly or incorrectly, has understood and reflected the plan, and acted in accordance with it. Thus we have a "history of history," or metaphysical history, in relation to which Belza considers only two doctrines: the monistic or Judeo-Christian concept, and the dualist or gnostic-Manichaean one.

I wish to draw attention to one striking aspect of his study: the fact that a Soviet author wrote and published in *official* Soviet literature a work basically devoted to the idea and essence of historical processes in which there is not a single reference to the classics of Marxism, or to the "representatives" of materialistic or at least evolutionary-scientific thought. *Belza's reflections are in the "spiritual" realm. The conflict he considers is between two antagonistic ideas, equally unacceptable from the point of view of the ruling Communist ideology.*

Judeo-Christian monotheism, according to Belza's logic, is the official lie which has been triumphant thus far, while gnostic Manichaeanism is the *hidden* truth of history. He views Bulgakov's novel as almost the "first swallow" in world history heralding the approaching victory of the much-attacked Manichaean truth over the legitimized lie of Jewish monotheism. Belza writes: "It [the novel *The Master and Margarita*] is *the first work in the history of world literature* [emphasis added] whose basic idea provided a talented and sensitive Czech researcher with the basis to call it Bulgakov's 'anti-*Faust* '" (p. 188).

In the ideological framework of Belza's monograph, Goethe's *Faust,* it should be recalled, is the symbol of the Judeo-Christian monistic conception of the world and human history. One of the proofs of the truth of the Manichaean view of history—i.e., of its congruence with and correct understanding of the higher, suprahuman plan for the world—is, according to Belza, the greater antiquity (compared with monotheism) of dualism, "Manichaeanism before Manichaeanism," the gnostic mysticism under whose influence the most ancient cultures developed, not contaminated by the monotheistic falsehood. True to his method of not separating the object of study into its major components, of not separating history from literature, fact from the interpretation of fact, Belza makes Bulgakov's Woland the object of a search for features indicating the greater antiquity and precedence of the Prince of Darkness over the Judeo-Christian Satan. In Russia, the reading public is usually familiar with literary works of any current interest, especially works of a popular author (and Bulgakov is one of the favorites). They are known in all their subtleties of style and complexities of plot. Such knowledge of literary texts has become for the intelligentsia a "matter of honor." It is natural to assume that Belza is writing for a reader who is an admirer of Bulgakov. Such a reader would easily notice Belza's exaggerations, falsifications, and misrepresentations. So Belza (and the editorial board of *Context*) must have been publishing for a reader for whom the exaggerations and misrepresentations have no significance, for whom something else will have more significance. As is usual with a Russian work of literary criticism, there is in the present case an implicit "social contract" with the reader—the critic and the reader know that the work is only a vehicle (a kind of decoy) through which one can express thoughts that, at least for the present, cannot be expressed openly.

Belza aims his study at readers for whom his "philosophy of blood" is more important than the correspondence of this philosophy with Bulgakov's intention.

This philosophy—which justifies, even sanctifies, bloodshed committed both in the name of and by the Soviet authorities (what is the difference: blood is blood—naturally shed in a "great cause"!)—becomes clear by the end of the study, when "history according to Belza" comes to an end, and all puzzles are resolved. For the moment, I mention only a fragment of the ending of Belza's study, directly linked to the theme of blood adduced by Belza from the part of the novel discussed above, as a theme of beneficial destruction.

Discussing the theme of fire, which recurs and is quite important in the novel, Belza writes: "If we again turn to the teachings of the gnostics, we find the real explanation for the sudden appearance of fire, the tongues of which turn the houses in *The Master and Margarita* to ashes."

The letters of INRI, an abbreviation representing the inscription *Iesus Nazarenus Rex Iudaeorum*, written by order of Pilate himself on a plaque fastened over the head of the crucified Jesus, were interpreted by the gnostics in a completely different vein: *Igni Natura Renovatur Integra* ("All nature is renewed by fire"). One can scarcely doubt that the fires that appear in Bulgakov's "true account" have a direct connection with this heretical explication of the gnostic Fourth Gospel, sharply criticized by the Catholic Church.

I quote now from the final point in Belza's study, a detailed analysis of which I give later:

> Continuing the line which was apparent in *The White Guard,* Bulgakov links images of his own time with images of the distant past, treating the latter on the level of legend, but combining the past with the present, with a consistent loyalty to the principles of humanism. These same principles are served by satirical exposure which is employed with such brilliance in the novel. Bulgakov also understood the power of such exposure when effected by the symbolic device of the *purifying power of fire* [emphasis added], which he considered an ancient and noble symbol, believing in the final triumph of the just cause, in its victory over the forces of darkness. He depicted these forces with realistic truthfulness when he wrote about *the armed enemies of the Soviet state, and when, with scorn and fury, he exposed those people who hinder the development of the native culture* [emphasis added]. Thus Bulgakov's famous thesis, "Manuscripts do not burn," expressed by Woland, relates only to those intellectual-artistic accomplishments of humanity which serve its exalted aims."

Although I have not respected the form of Belza's work, and have combined the motifs of blood and fire, I have remained true to the internal structure of his study, in which the main clusters of ideas follow the text of the novel.

"The purifying power of fire"—one of the secrets of the world-historical process discovered by the gnostics—is compared by Belza to satire and is related also to the objects affected by the "purifying fire" of the Soviet state and to the "people who hinder the development of the native culture."

Of course, of most interest is not this goal, which is shared by the semiofficial organs, but the unusual things cited in the attempt to achieve it: gnostic mysticism, the "summa demonologia," the satanization of Soviet rule (the representing of Soviet rule as imbued with the power of Satan) because of its creative, positive, mystically justified and "approved-from-above" essence.

"People who hinder the development. . . ."—this refers to the group of Marxist sociologically oriented critics, almost to a man Jewish, who in compliance with the directives of the authorities (and in line with their own desire) persecuted Bulgakov, and who were later almost all destroyed during the Great Terror by those same authorities. "The purifying power of fire" is a euphemism employed to justify force in general and the Stalinist terror in particular, at least in relation to "people who hinder the development of the native culture."

Precisely here, in the themes of blood and soil, of gnostic esotericism and uncanonical ("heretical") mysticism, does one recognize the "Europeanism" of Belza and, even more, his own brand of "cosmopolitanism," his "universality." Belza achieves more than a synthesis of Westernism and Slavophilism. Basically, not a single ideological or mythological aspect of Russian culture is missing in his synthesis—not Byzantinism, nor *Pochvennichestvo*, the back-to-the-soil movement with its extensions into Scythianism, Eurasianism, and Far Eastern and Near Eastern mysticism. To put it more concisely, in the conception of Belza is preserved the same cherished universalism of the Russian soul that was so dear to Russians of the classical culture, if only in the person of Dostoevsky—on this he built his utopia, the historic mission of Russia as a truly Christian state and nation, in contrast to "nationalized" and therefore weakened and degraded Western Christianity. The uniqueness of the synthesis offered by Belza lies in the fact that he proposes another common denominator for the same unshakable "universality"—more precisely he proposes another universalism, another "world" in which both the old and the new (particularly the new) Russia enjoy equal (even if not completely earned) rights.

This new universalism is based, as already noted, on mystical (panhuman) experience, a Manichaean dialectic, a particular amoral (in relation to the stable system of Judeo-Christian values) gnosis, secret knowledge, in the accumulation of which all creatively and spiritually gifted peoples and cultures participated. It is a situation of "gnostics of the world unite!"

Now we can understand why Belza needed his manipulations involving the Bulgarian Bogomil, who supposedly influenced the world view of Bulgakov, particularly as seen in the novel *The Master and Margarita*.

In Bulgarian Bogomilism, the teachings and the Manichaean movement condemned by the official Christian church, most important for Belza is its national-ethnic origin—i.e., that it is not simply Manichaean but specifically Bulgarian, Slavic Manichaeanism. Thus the Slavic region fits naturally into the general world picture and map of dualistic gnosticism, and occupies its rightful place, together with the ancient East, Byzantium, and Western Europe in its gnostic-Manichaean guise, represented by the knightly order (of Templars), by the numerous medieval heretical movements, but mainly by Dante.

Together with and on an equal footing with Dante, Bulgakov is included in the ranks of proponents of Manichaean dualism (the coexistence and collaboration of good and evil) against Judeo-Christian dualism (the struggle of good against evil): "Following the author of the *Divine Comedy*, who still requires further study (at least with regard to the almost completely ignored connections with Bogomilism) Bulgakov based his novel on the dualistic conception; the various levels on which the struggle between 'light and darkness'[15] are depicted in *The Master and Margarita* can be traced to this conception."

But the participation of Slavs in the comprehension of the true laws of history and the nature of the world is not limited to the Bulgarians; alongside them are the Poles, who are also concerned with light and darkness, "the mutual relations of which are described in ancient Bulgarian folk legends, connected with Bogomilist dualistic teaching in one degree or another." These interrelations appeared in a unique way in the work of Polish writers of the beginning of this century, especially in those of Tadeusz Micinski (1873–1918), once an obscure poet, writer, playwright, and brilliantly erudite philosopher and polygot who is now attracting considerable scholarly attention.

To use Micinski's own expression: Luciferism was for him primarily a tragic conception, defining the inevitability of the combination of "pure good" with the freedom-loving aspirations of the "arisen spirit," which attained a fullness of knowledge and wisdom.

> Micinski considers the "secret teaching" of the Templars (the images of which he embodied in his work) as affirming the "heretical" thesis *Christus verus Luciferus*,[16] and an example of such a dualistic combination. And if Bulgakov's Lucifer-Woland speaks with real anger to Matthew the Levite, while telling of the pitiful fate of Yeshua ha-Notzri, he certainly does not hide his sympathy for the "peripatetic philosopher." This seemingly strange sympathy, which appears in the novel as a direct consequence of a dualistic conception, and which directly contradicts the mystic treatment of biblical images, was not understood by the American critic who ironically called Woland a "sentimental devil."[17]

There are two points to be noted in this quotation. First (but less important, since it is common) is the characteristically Belzan disregard for chronology in favor of typology. This permits him to telescope phenomena distant in time into one conception, space, or framework—Bulgarian Bogomilism of the eleventh to thirteenth century and the work of Tadeusz Micinski at the end of the nineteenth and beginning of the twentieth century. Such an insensitivity to time, permitting a jump of eight hundred or one thousand years, sometimes even millennia, should be viewed as inconsequential, since for a given complex of ideas, it does not affect their conceptual core. Such disregard for the historical-cultural setting of these ideas or such complete disregard for diachronic and synchronic analysis in favor of a one-dimensional conception of events occurring (but not developing), as it were, simultaneously and parallel to each other is not unique to Belza, although with him it is employed with winning and disarming directness. The creation of a "one-dimension (isochronic) space" which "destroys" time and the development of space, in which essentially there occurs only one, endlessly self-reproducing event—this is the typical feature of mythopoetic consciousness, i.e., the technique and methodology of myth, above all, of the ideological myth.

Belza works not with rational judgments and evidence but with elements of myth. The source of these elements of myth which actually encourages the mythopoetic desire to create the myth is found outside the text. This leads to a sense of disconnection and an impression of nonsense when there is really connection and sense. An understanding (or knowledge) of the general content of Belza's myth reveals the elements of his myth, which are thrown into relief by the gaps in the logic and discrepancies in Belza's text. In other words, his *destruction of logical connections serves to restore overlooked connections.*

I now consider a second point in this quotation: "This seemingly strange sympathy, which appears in the novel as a direct consequence of a dualistic conception, and which directly contradicts the mystic treatment of biblical images, was not understood by the American critic who ironically called Woland a sentimental devil." This passage can be divided into conceptual units.

1. Lucifer-Woland (Bulgakov's combining) clearly sympathizes with Yeshua ha-Notzri (Jesus Christ).
2. Lucifer-Woland does not sympathize with Matthew the Levite.
3. The sympathy of Lucifer for Christ is impossible within the framework of canonical Christianity.
4. One can explain this sympathy only on the basis of the Manichaean dualistic world view of Bulgakov himself (which, as Belza says, underlies the dualistic concept of the novel).
5. The American critic did not understand this conception, i.e., did not understand the world view of Bulgakov, as a result of which:
6. He called Woland a "sentimental devil."

If these conceptual units are combined into a syllogism by Belza's favorite way of combining ideas into complexes of meaning, one gets an expanded, logically consistent conclusion (with which the reader may or may not agree)—Belza's assertion that Bulgakov was expressing Manichaean dualism. In other words, one can argue with the contents of the proposition but not with the structure of the syllogism. However, the ideational units I take from Belza's text do not fit back into his text—since I did not include among them one important phrase: "this seemingly strange sympathy . . . *directly contradicting the mystical treatment of biblical images*, was obviously not understood by the American critic." One can well ask, Why should Bulgakov's characters be compared to biblical images?

As is well known, according to the Christian canon, the Bible contains "Old" and "New" Testaments. But the Woland–Matthew the Levite–Yeshua ha-Notzri situation has a parallel only in the New Testament (the Gospels), and thus only the New Testament need be considered here. Bulgakov's treatment of the relation of Woland and ha-Notzri can be compared only with the Gospels' account of the relations of Christ, the Savior of the human race, and Satan, its destroyer. The reference to "biblical images," i.e, the reference to both Testaments (one by which, the Old Testament, belongs only to the Jews, while the other, the New Testament, belongs only to the Christians) in the description of a specifically New Testament situation is either nonsense or an allusion to some thought not expressed in the text but present and of importance in reading between the lines.

We shall find the connection of "the mystic treatment of biblical images" with the Gospel plot created by Bulgakov and expounded by Belza as soon as we consider the fundamental myth of Belza's line of thought: that there once existed great spiritual cultures (for example, the ancient Egyptian or ancient Iranian, i.e., Zoroastrian) which contributed true knowledge of the principles and fundamental laws of human existence to the current of world history. The essence of this knowledge is that existence, the cosmos, man, culture are the result of a spontaneous creative act, a creative process, the initiator of which is neither absolute good nor absolute evil, but both these forces together. To so-called good are ascribed the realm of ideals, norms, perfect morality; and to so-called evil, the realm of material creation, including social-historical creativity, the goal of which is the attainment of the ideal represented by good. (Evil creates and good evaluates what is created.)

A point of primary importance: In a fragmentary manner, by hint, by allusion *(sapienti sat!)* in expounding the conception of ancient Eastern dualism, Belza uses only one word and concept: *knowledge.*

The meaning intended is not that of the Greek word *gnosis* (which does mean precisely "knowledge") and not gnostics or gnosticism in the generally accepted cultural-historical sense, and the specific "gnosis" of the gnostics, but *knowledge* in the general meaning and usage, which today is the concept of "scientific knowledge," i.e, trustworthy objective knowledge, obtained by experiment and based on empirical demonstration.

In connection with this ancient scientific knowledge, Belza often uses the epithet "esoteric," i.e., "secret knowledge."

Why "esoteric"?

Because in prehistoric times, in the distant past, on the periphery of the great dualistic cultures, there appeared a small nomadic tribe which managed to think up the idea of a single God, creator, omnipotent ruler of the universe, the incarnation of absolute good ("light"). Thus, the presence in the world of "darkness" (evil) being without scientific explanation, it was, out of ignorance, ascribed to the tendency to evil of man, who consciously turned from the path of commanded good. In this way, evil was not only seen as an absolutely negative quantity but was also deprived of all transcendent, superhuman, i.e., creative, attributes.

It is very important for Belza to call our attention to the fact that the image of Satan in the Old Testament "dates, as is known, *only from the end of the second century* A.D. [emphasis added]."

What does the apparently innocent "only" mean, in the context of Belza's argument?

A great deal! First, that the ancient ("Old Testament") Hebrews borrowed the idea of evil (the "image of Satan") from more ancient and neighboring higher cultures. Second (as is obvious from Belza's account) they interpreted the idea of evil in accordance with the low level of their culture—in a primitive manner, i.e., in the spirit of common folk mythology—with all kinds of wood spirits, household spirits, "demons of the wilderness," "master of the flies" (Beelzebub—Hebrew *ba'al zevuv*), and other hazily envisaged spirits known to rude imaginations.

"But as a result of some incomprehensible (although, obviously, fore-seen-'from-above') catastrophe, it was precisely this false teaching which triumphed in the world. True, it triumphed not by itself, but with the help of a certain mysterious event which occurred in a strange manner (but also, obviously, with a predetermined purpose) in that region inhabited by that malignant tribe, whose sons turned out to be witnesses of, participants in, and the first interpreters of this miracle."

There is no doubt what event is meant: the appearance of Yeshua ha-Notzri during the reign of the Emperor Tiberius and during the rule of his representative, the fifth procurator of Judaea, Pontius Pilate, the preaching of Yeshua, and his martyr's death as a result of the intrigues of the religious leaders of the "most cruel people," and the cowardice of Pilate, who sympathized with the "peripatetic philosopher."

At this point, in relation to the Gospel tradition and Christianity in general, Belza's account takes on, for the inexperienced or unprepared reader, an apparently more heated tone, while making a transitional leap in his logic, in fact the biggest such leap in his whole text.

But this is only apparent, and is such only for the inexperienced or unprepared. Precisely this leap or lacuna is particularly carefully written with the "sympathetic ink" of Belza's code, so that he need only give a number of hints, some carefully selected points (such as the positive attitude of Bulgakov himself to Jesus, which is shared by Belza and confirmed by his attacks on official Christianity, by his rehabilitation of, amounting almost to an apologia for, various sects of the Manichaean persuasion condemned by the Christian Church, etc.) for the "initiates" (to whom Belza's work is really addressed) to understand the complex of elements on which the author of "The Genealogy of *The Master and Margarita*" bases his writing: *Manichaean gnostics* (the teaching that the God of the Hebrew Bible is one of the demiurges of a lower order); the founder of mystical anti-Semitism, Marcion (the teaching that Christ was the messenger of another god, not the God of the Hebrew Bible); the Tübingen school, which resurrected Marcionism in terms of contemporary thought and nomenclature, thus creating a theological basis for the theory and practice of the anti-Semitism of the Third Reich.

Let us formulate the nucleus of these ancient traditions and their new accretions, which directly concern Belza and which he spreads throughout his whole tract so thoroughly that literally not a single portion of his text is untouched by this complex of ideas: Jesus Christ was not a Jew and came to announce the end of the false monotheistic teaching and renew true knowledge about the world, God, and man. The Jews who surrounded him did not understand his preaching and distorted its sense—his disciples (who left the first record of the new but essentially old-new teaching) and those who understood (the Sanhedrin) and put the Teacher and Savior to death, using the agency of Roman authority.

The distorted, falsified (by the Jews) teaching also formed the basis of Christianity and the Christian Church, which was afraid to detach itself from Jewish sources and which canonized the false holy book of the Jews (the Tanach, or Hebrew Bible) as part of its own sacred scriptures. But the Gospels, which, from Belza's Manichaean-gnostic point of view, are also a Jewish book, differ from the Tanach (Old Testament) only in the fact that they propagate not a falsity but a distorted, incomprehensible, perverted truth. However, in contrast to the Old Testament, in which, by definition (old = outdated), there is no truth for now, in the Gospels, with correct reading and interpretation, one can uncover traces of truth or at least traces of real events, e.g., "And the light shineth in darkness; and the darkness overcame it not" (John 1:5).

We will now again carefully study the part of Belza's text that puzzled us. We consider the phrasing, which appears deceptively uncontrived but is actually carefully thought out.

Here is the final part of the preceding excerpt: "Micinski considered the 'secret teaching' of the Templars (the images of whom he embodied in his work) as affirming the 'heritical' thesis *Christus verus Luciferus* ("Christ is really Lucifer") and an example of such a dualistic combination [of good and evil—M.K.]." The text continues without a paragraph break: "And if Bulgakov's Lucifer-Woland speaks with real anger to Matthew the Levite, while telling of the pitiful fate of Yeshua ha-Notzri, he certainly does not hide his sympathy for the 'peripatetic philosopher.' "

Let us clarify the associations in Belza's text separately (and independently) of Bulgakov and Micinski, to whom he refers—but which are dictated exclusively by the ideological prototext that is Belza's constant point of departure and which—in general terms—I described above.

1. Lucifer-Woland does not conceal his sympathy for the "peripatetic philosopher" (Yeshua ha-Notzri) precisely because of *Christus verus Luciferus;* alter egos—equal, have met, but are quite different rulers of the world.

2. Lucifer-Woland speaks with obvious irritation to Matthew the Levite, i.e., to the Evangelist, because, according to the gnostic-Manichaean tradition, the Jewish entourage of Christ (his disciples) perverted the real meaning of his teaching.

3. In describing or referring to Yeshua ha-Notzri, Belza finds it very convenient to use Bulgakov's expression "the peripatetic philosopher," greater emphasis being on the word "philosopher" than on "peripatetic." Since philosophy is a science or a body of knowledge, this permits Belza to set up the dichotomies: faith–knowledge; prophet or messiah–philosopher, i.e., to establish his fundamental concept of "secret knowledge" or "secret teaching," which he applies to dualistic gnosticism and Manichaean dualism. "This seemingly strange sympathy which appears to be a direct consequence of the dualistic conception which in the novel is clearly contrasted with the mystic treatment of biblical images."

That which would normally be seen as absurd, a fallacy (the comparison of the events in the Gospels depicted in Bulgakov's novel not with the accounts as given in the Gospels, or as they are treated in Christian dogma, but, for some reason, with some unknown [mystic] treatment of biblical images) is logically motivated *not* in the framework of Belza's text as written but of that of his prototext, his point of departure.

1. For Belza's Manichaean gnosticism, as for canonical Christianity, the Bible is a single book (this is why Belza refers to "biblical images" in general). But while for official canonical Christianity the connection of the New Testament to the Old is a source of power and an indication of the truth of Christianity, for gnosticism this connection is a direct indication of the falseness and distortion (possibly conscious and premeditated) of the Gospels.

2. "The mystic treatment of biblical images" is at variance with true

(gnostic-dualistic) knowledge, in the same way that mysticism is usually at variance with science (in the words of Belza: "the dualistic conception" vs. "the mystical treatment"), while by "biblical images" he refers to Lucifer and Christ. The "mystical treatment" of the former, it should be understood, consists in the Bible according him the role of a fallen angel (a kind of servant who rebelled) but not of an equal to the Creator of the World— this is hard to accept.

3. But even such a reconstruction of the original thought behind this phrase does not exhaust its content. Nor was the phrase written to express the above ideas, despite their surprising nature. The phrase was written to allow the writing of its conclusion: "the American critic did not understand when he ironically called Woland a 'sentimental devil.' "

The importance of the American critic for Belza can be grasped immediately from the note on the page on which reference to the critic is made: "Raymond Rosenthal: 'Bulgakov's Sentimental Devil,' *New Leader*, November 20, 1967."

The significance of Raymond Rosenthal is not exhausted by the necessary—for a Soviet scholar, even required—polemic with Western commentators, nor by the obvious Jewish origin of Rosenthal. Of course the latter circumstance—his Jewish origin—does play a primary role, but not as a petty anti-Semitic gibe but in a much deeper, still anti-Semitic sense; according to Belza's scheme, Rosenthal is a kind of double (alter ego) of the Levite Matthew—he does not understand (or consciously distorts) Bulgakov, just as Matthew did not understand Christ.

The similarity of Yeshua and the Master has been noted by many commentators on the novel, and is affirmed also by Belza, who goes further and insists on the complete identification of the Master and Bulgakov himself, from which naturally follows the identification of Bulgakov and Yeshua ha-Notzri.

According to Belza's article, Raymond Rosenthal precedes and chronologically continues the persecution of the great Russian Manichaean writer which was begun in the 1920s in Moscow by the Jewish "vulgar-sociologists": in the framework of mythological "reality," which rejects chronological sequence, and is the sole reality in which Belza really believes, the "American critic of Jewish origin" is simply one of countless incarnations and appearances of the "power of darkness" that distorts real truth and, at various times and in various places, has assumed the guise of the high priest Caiaphas, the traitor Judas Iscariot, the evangelist Matthew the Levite, and the literary critics Auerbach and Rosenthal.

If we add to this Belza's identification, Yeshua–the Master–Bulgakov, it is not difficult to understand the hidden meaning of the genealogical investigations he has undertaken. Essentially he views Bulgakov's novel as a revelation, a unique gnostic-Manichaean gospel about a new Yeshua— Bulgakov. He sees himself as a new interpreter-"evangelist" who, unlike others, neither hides nor distorts the truth, but illuminates it.

Belza devotes the last, ideologically decisive part of his study, "The Master," to knitting the two levels of his narrative—the historical-biographical and the mystical-metaphysical—into a single complex of ideas. The first part of this section treats Bulgakov, the author of the novel, as the real prototype of the Master in the novel. This gives Belza the possibility of moving from Bulgakov's "true" life story to his own version of this story— in other words to reveal the real reasons for the destruction of the Master-Bulgakov. In Belza's article, the reasons for this destruction are as follows:

It should be stressed that, in the literature on Bulgakov, one article stands out by the fullness of its material, the article "M. A. Bulgakov and *The Days of the Turbins*" by the author and literary scholar Victor Petelin, published on March 15, 1969, in the magazine *Ogonek* and reprinted in the series "Biblioteka Ogonka" [The Ogonyok Library] in the form of a booklet, published in an edition of 100,000 copies by the Pravda Publishing House under the title *Pamyat Serdtsa Neistrebima* ["Unforgettable Memoirs of a Heart"].[18]

As far as I know, Victor Petelin, writing about this "great and unique artist," was the first to call people and events by their real names. "Averbach, Grossman-Roshchin, Mustangov, Blum, Nusinov, and many others consciously and intentionally persecuted Bulgakov . . . this happened not only with Bulgakov. Harsh attacks were made on Sholokhov, Leonov, Shishkov, Esenin, Prishvin, Sergeyev-Tsensky, and Chapygin, that is, writers who in their work seemed to demonstrate the inseparable bond of the new Soviet Russia with its cultural heritage of many centuries." Though covering themselves with resounding phrase, these "literary violators" as Petelin calls them, were really spokesmen of vulgar sociologism. . . .

The critics of the vulgar, sociological stripe *buzzed* angrily [emphasis Belza's] around the greatest masters of Soviet literature and art. In the case of Bulgakov, this became intentional intellectual persecution. The proceeds of this persecution served as the thematic basis for the sad tale of the Master in the chapter in the novel devoted to him (the 13th).[19]

The question naturally arises (as Belza asks): "Why did the angry buzzing become intentional persecution . . . in the particular case of Bulgakov?" Bulgakov was a member of a group of Red Russian writers who were tied by blood and soil to Russian history and culture, and who basically represented the Russian forefathers and the national and folk-oriented level of those like Esenin, the poet of Russian peasants, like Prishvin, the creator of the Cossada epic, Sholokhov, and others mentioned by Petelin (and Belza) who were also, in varying degrees, tied to their native soil. This was the group that came under the attack of the "vulgar sociological" group of critics with their revealing names (Averbach, Grossman, Blum). After all, compared with them, Bulgakov is a writer with a distinctly Western, European orientation. The nature of his writing, the main thing characterizing a writer, basically has nothing in common with this national epic group.

The answer of Belza is: The main goal of the alien, foreign critics consisted in "a direct discrediting of culture being created in the land of socialist culture." In his novel, "Bulgakov unmasks this destructive role of the critics."[20] In other words, Bulgakov exorcises those disguised devils who had assumed a human form, and the devils in return attacked him. Despite the abundance of undisputable facts (undisputable in the sense that critics did actually attack Bulgakov, but the attackers were not only the critics, and not all the critics were Jewish), Belza emphasizes an ideological point; he does not let his reader forget for one moment that the issue is not simply one involving a lamentable situation in literature but a whole metaphysical drama, outside of which the given situation cannot be understood, and in the absence of which it could not have occurred.

In Bulgakov's novel, L. Averbach becomes Ariman, who persecutes the Master. In passing, we note that this is the Greek form of the ancient Persian name Ankhra-Maynyu, the personificaton of darkness, death, and evil. No matter how forced this may seem, one is very tempted to suggest that the reference to Ariman in "The Genealogy of *The Master and Margarita*," like the scarab on Woland's chest, somehow underlines the antiquity of the dualistic concept of the struggle between the "kingdom of light" and the "kingdom of darkness."[21]

That the name of Bulgakov's character—the critic and the instigator of the persecution of the Master—is given only as an echo of "the Greek form of the name of the ancient Persian spirit of darkness, death, and evil," and that this echo was foreseen by Bulgakov and forms a natural part of the grotesque-fantastic style of the novel, a style in which we get these name correspondences—the critic Berlioz–the composer Berlioz; the woman writer George Shturman–Georges Sand; the director of the variety theater, Rimsley–the composer Rimsky-Korsakov, etc.—of all this, there can be no doubt and, as Belza puts it, no strained interpretation.

Where there is doubt and strained interpretation "to the breaking point," where Belza's whole house-of-cards structure comes tumbling down is in the conclusion of the above quotation, i.e., in the attempt of Belza to recall, through Ariman, the Manichaean-dualistic conception which he ascribes to Bulgakov's novel. In fact, the discrepancy is monstrously obvious to any unprejudiced and attentive reader. This whole conception is based on affirmation of the positive, creative formative power of the so-called evil in dualistic religions, which are opposed to the falseness of monotheism, with its teaching of the dependent, nonprimary quality, i.e., the *non*divine essence, of evil. And it is precisely ancient Persian dualism—one of the sources of the Manichaean gnosticism preached by Belza—to which he often refers in the preceding parts of his article. Moreover, it is precisely on the positive, creative power of evil that Belza bases his Woland analogy. But, as appears from the cited quotation, there begins at this point a treatment of the powers of evil arrayed against the Master-Bulgakov in the ordinary, normative sense of the Judeo-Christian tradition. While deciphering the text of Belza we seem to arrive at a paradox which explodes his very conception: all of Jewry, from Caiaphas to Raymond Rosenthal, is a unversal evil. But Belza has "demonstrated" that evil is a creative, universally constructive principle, working as if in agreement with universal good. Then it should follow that Jews . . . ? Nothing of the kind. As always with Belza, a departure from formal logic is no intellectual defeat, but merely a retreat to a previously well prepared position in the area of another logic—the logic of myth. In order to grasp the real sense which Belza assigns to the description of the critic-enemies of the Master-Bulgakov, one must go back to his description of Woland's retinue: "the images of Woland and his retinue recall the canvases of artists who depicted mocking devils." Such associations are presented by the author at the beginning of the novel, when there appears before Berlioz "out of thin air" the specter of Fagot-Kowvyev, "unbelievably thin" with (please note) a *mocking* physiognomy (emphasis in original). And, in the scene of Ivan's chase after the "foreign criminal," when the poet meets Fagot, the Bezdomny cries: ". . . Are you *mocking* me?"[22]

Hereafter, "please note," the word "mocking" appears a number of times in Belza's musings about Woland. In fact, it becomes a constant feature of references to the "certain anti-patriotic group" of vulgarizing critics, thus giving an impression of Bulgakov's presence in (and agreement with) the text of Belza. For example:

> The literary thugs . . . basely ignored the Leninist policy of the party, in particular, the well-known resolution of the Central Committee of the All-Union Communist party (Bolshevik) of June 18, 1925, entitled "On the Policy of the Party in the Field of Literature." Being opposed to the principles precisely formulated in this resolution . . . the critics of vulgar-

sociological ilk *mocked* [emphasis in original] the greatest masters of Soviet literature and art.

The "retinue of Woland" from Bulgakov's novel prepares the scene for the appearance of the group of critics, the "literary thugs" of Belza's text, who in his scenario are a kind of novelistic symbol for what was occurring in reality. This same group is supposed to serve as a metaphysical sign for something much more frightful, some kind of national catastrophe, for which Belza brings in an illustrative excerpt from *The White Guard* which elucidates his idea (a device Belza has used before). This passage, which describes the nightmare of Aleksei Turbin, is based on the famous scene in Dostoevski's *The Brothers Karamazov*, in which Ivan Karamazov is confronted by the Devil. On the basis of this excerpt, Belza concludes: "Aleksei could not capture this nightmare, a nightmare which so mocked(!) and so hurt his country."[23] (The word "mocked" appears in the text of Bulgakov— the exclamation mark is Belza's addition.)

We can now perceive a clearly delineated hierarchy: the group of critics who hounded Bulgakov represent merely a part of the alien nightmare that mocked Russia and its sacred national values. These are the "retinue of Woland," i.e., not pure, absolute, supreme evil, but creatures without creative power of their own, menials of the Prince of Darkness—an "impure gold" in a direct sense, not in the traditional ecclesiastical sense but in an almost etymological sense, i.e., not real, not full-bodied or pure (in the sense that "impure gold" does not mean "dirty gold" but adulterated gold)—subservient to "pure," absolute, supreme evil, the master and organizer of the world.

Of course not all these problems, discrepancies, and gaps disappear in the "magic" of mythological logic, particularly those which appear when Belza's work is compared with Bulgakov's novel. I have in mind the indubitable charm which Bulgakov gives his devils and, obviously, not his persecutors. But this merely reiterates that it is not Bulgakov's novel which serves as Belza's basic text (prototext), for he has another, ideological source—a myth, in which the Jews have the role of universal outcasts, parasites in the original biological sense of the word, "rats," "viruses," "microbes." In the "realities" of this "Manichaean racism," neither dialogue nor collaboration is possible with these parasites, only a struggle to the death.

It was precisely such a struggle that the Soviet regime conducted with at least a part of that universal impurity in the Stalinist years when policies in the fields of literature and art were also Stalinist—and about which Belza directly informs us.

There is no need to cite the names of those people who caused the spiritual crisis of the writer. They are no longer with us, and most of their names have vanished from our memory, as the name of Aloizaya Aloysius Magarich vanished from the pages of the tenants' register which Koroviev blew on (in *The Master and Margarita*).

This "irreproachable" statement by Belza needs only one qualification: it was not just the names that disappeared but the people as well, and not from memory but from life. They did not "disappear" but were destroyed by Stalin's terror, which, as is generally accepted, had an international character, in contrast to Hitler's more focused national genocide. As we see, Belza appears to be trying to alter that generally accepted opinion.

Belza construes the relation of Bulgakov and the Soviet regime to be the same as the relations, as depicted in the novel, between Woland and the Master: sympathy, complicity, aid, guaranteed immortality, and vengeance on the impure forces of literature, like the vengeance of Pilate on Judas for destroying his secretly loved Jesus as shown when he writes: "When one reads E. S. Bulgakova's transcription of her husband's telephone conversation with Stalin, there come to mind some lines from the poem by Nikolai Tikhonov,[24] *The Ballad of the Blue Packet*, 'But people in the Kremlin never sleep, / and Russian writers trusted these people deeply.'[25] . . . Stalin affirmed that *The Days of the Turbins*[26] illustrates the all-devouring power of Bolshevism";[27] or that "in addition to what has been said about the Soviet state as a patron of culture, one must add that the poisoning of the atmosphere of constructive official cultural activity by the Arimans, the Latunskys, and others like them could not but upset the ruling authorities,"[28] etc.

The essence of the matter is not the apology for Soviet rule and for Stalin, and not even the completely distorted account of the relations between the regime and the creative intelligentsia inherited by the regime from prerevolutionary, *not* revolutionary, culture, to which belonged Bulgakov, Mandelshtam, Akhmatova, and others, whose names have not disappeared from memory or from the history of culture—the essence of the matter is the *character* of this apology and the *goals* of the distortion:

The mystical character of the Soviet state system, whose roots go down into world culture, including Russian culture, is exemplified by its best representatives, people like Gumiliev who were destroyed by that regime as a result of an accidental (circumstantial) misunderstanding. Belza writes: "In a little book of poems by N. S. Gumiliev, among *Fragments from 1920– 1921*, published in 1923 by the Military Press of the Headquarters of the Red Army, we find the following verses:

The Lord built himself a lofty palace
On the border between his holy dominions
And the dominions of the sovereign Lucifer . . ."[29]

Being now familiar with Belza's methodology, we understand that Gumiliev's lines are not quoted for the sake of "The Genealogy of *The Master and Margarita*," nor to point out the Russian tradition of Manichaean dualism to which it seems even Gumiliev belonged, but rather to draw attention to the headquarters of the Red Army where this gnostic lyric was published.

The search for the genealogy of the Soviet state—the first state in the world of victorious Manichaeanism—is crowned by the decoding of one of the symbols of this state—the five-pointed star: "The five-pointed star—the great mysterious pentagram, the symbol of Pythagorean wisdom, has become in our time the symbol of the very highest, purest, and noblest strivings of humanity."[30]

Since the pentagram, a regular five-sided figure in the form of a star, symbolized in different mythic systems the most varied concepts, such as eternity, the universe, protection from witches or demons, good fortune (in medieval Judaism), and high status in society (among the Japanese), it is not difficult to understand Belza's preference for its Pythagorean meaning. The Pythagoreans were a secret mystical sect whose doctrine was based on the mystical interpretation of mathematics.

Thus, having absorbed the millennial antimonotheistic (or, more precisey, dualistic) wisdom in its most complete form of Manichaean gnosticism, the latter being the common property of all people of Indo-European culture, Soviet rule represents the victory of "secret knowledge" finally revealed.

Only this sinister context provides the appropriate background for an understanding of Belza's study and his anti-Semitic tirades, which otherwise might seem innocuous, absurd, or ridiculous. The historical context makes us take Belza's text seriously. "Manichaean racism," not Bulgakov's novel, is its true genealogical source. As for Bulgakov's novel, I can here only ironically and sadly repeat the words of Woland to the Master, "Your novel has been read," and raise my hands to the ghost of Bulgakov.

—Translated by Israel Cohen

Notes

1. For the text of I. Samolvin's article, disseminated by Samizdat, see below.
2. Y. L. Talmon, "European History as the Seedbed of the Holocaust," in *Holocaust and Rebirth: A Symposium* (Jerusalem, 1974), pp. 53–54.
3. Ustryalov—an emigré professor who expounded the idea that bolshevism fulfills the historic role of building a strong Russian state on a nationalist basis. Ustryalovism was one of

several attempts to bring together the ideology and practice of the Communist party with those of Russian nationalism.

4. "Eurasianism"—a historiosophic trend in Russian emigré thought, founded by N. S. Trubeskoi, a linguist and folklorist, in his *Russian and Mankind* (Sofia, 1921), and developed further into a universal doctrine by P. N. Savitski. According to this doctrine, Russia, being neither Europe nor Asia, but rather a specific geographical, political, and cultural cosmos, has been destined to become an intermediary between West and East and to bring out political and cultural unity for the entire mankind. Eurasianism is genetically related to Russian messianic Slavophilism and to the Russian version of romantic orientalism—"Scythism." Eurasianism, although it had no open support either among Russian emigrés (as it was *probolshevik*) or in Russia itself (due to its profascist disposition), had a considerable influence on Russian culture (M. Tsvetayeva, N. Berdyaev, A. N. Tolstoi, L. N. Gumilev). Concepts of the even shorter-lived (1918–22) "Scythism" (R. Ivanov-Razmnik, A. Belyi, N. Klyuev), which found expression in the attempts to revive pre-Christian traditions of Russian culture, influenced by A. Bloc's "Scythian" historiosophy, was akin to the political philosophy of the leftist socialist revolutionists (the Russian peasant community as a specific and preferable type of social order).

5. *Context: Theoretical Studies in Literature* (Moscow: Nauka, 1978), pp. 156–248 (hereafter cited as *Context*).

6. What is meant is the censored Soviet press, not the Samizdat and emigré press, where all currents exist and appear under their own name.

7. See S. S. Averintsev's article "Greek 'Literatue' and Near Eastern Literature," *Voprosy literatury*, no. 8 (1971), pp. 40–68.

8. "Vulgar sociologism" is the term in use in Soviet literary criticism since the 1930s to designate endeavors to reduce literary and other creative activities to forms of production and class struggle. Later accused (wrongly) of "vulgar sociologism" were representatives of the sociological trend in literary criticism, such as V. Pereverzev, V. Friche, and others.

9. *Moskva*, no. 11, 1966; no. 1, 1967.

10. *The White Guard* (M. Bulgakov, 1925).

11. *Context*, p. 158.

12. Ibid., p. 194.

13. Bogomilism—a heretical religious movement in medieval Bulgaria.

14. *Context*, pp. 194–195.

15. Ibid., p. 207.

16. On this case, see below.

17. *Context*, pp. 196–197. On the article by Raymond Rosenthal, see below.

18. V. Petelin, *Pamyat serdtsa neistrebima* (Moscow, 1970), quoted by Belza, *Context*, p. 222.

19. *Context*, pp. 222–23.

20. Ibid., p. 236.

21. Ibid., p. 224.

22. Belza's comment, ibid., p. 198.

23. Ibid., p. 223.

24. Nikolai Tikhonov (1896–1979)—a Russian Soviet poet. In the 1920s he was a member of the Serapyon Brothers, an avant-garde literary group, which he later left and joined the Soviet establishment. From 1940 he served as secretary of the Soviet Writers' Union.

25. *Context*, p. 228.

26. *The Days of the Turbins* (M. Bulgakov, 1926).

27. *Context*, p. 229.

28. Ibid., p. 237.

29. Ibid., p. 195.

30. Ibid., p. 231.

When Nazism Became Zionism
An Analysis of Political Cartoons

JUDITH VOGT

I

SINCE THE EICHMANN trial in Jerusalem in 1961, Soviet propaganda has gradually created the myth that Nazism exists *solely* in one form—Zionism.

This propaganda was provided with a fixed framework during the intensive press campaign launched against Israel shortly after the Six-Day War in 1967, which has since been applied in more than 150 anti-Zionist books.[1]

The recurring theme is: "The Zionists are conspiring to seize world hegemony." (See Fig. 1, "Der Teufel in Deutschland [The Devil in Germany]," Dresden, 1897. It is intimated here that the conception of a Jewish world hegemony is a continuation of the dogma of the church in the Middle Ages about the Jew as Satan's offspring, as the destructive archenemy of Christendom.) The seed of this abomination was sown as early as 1903 by the Russian anti-Semite P. A. Krushevan in "A Program for the Conquest of the World by the Jews." He was greatly influenced by the *Protocols of the Elders of Zion*, a spurious document which the Tsar's secret police had concocted earlier in order to discredit the revolutionaries.[2] Krushevan was the first to fuse these mysterious "Elders of Zion" with the delegates to the First Zionist Congress in Basle.

The idea of a secret, worldwide conspiracy of Jews, aimed at world hegemony under a Jewish king of the House of David, has become an international "best seller." Despite the obscure sources, despite all denials and court trials,[3] the *Protocols of the Elders of Zion* have been constantly reissued up to the present time, in editions of hundreds of thousands of copies. The *Protocols* were obligatory reading in the Prussian schools during the Nazi period.[4]

While anti-Semites could use the *Protocols* to "expose" the imminent red peril which came from the "Jew and bolshevism," the anti-Zionists of today resort to this forgery to "unmask" the black danger lurking in "Zionism, imperialism, and Nazism."

These conceptions run like a red thread through the publication by Yury Ivanov, *Beware: Zionism!* The book appeared for the first time in Moscow in 1969, and in the first year and a half alone, a total of 370,000 copies were issued.[5]

In 1971, this image was rounded out by E. Yevseev in *Fascism Under the Blue Star.* The book was published by Molodaya Guardiya (publishing house of the Central Committee of the Leninist Young Communists), in an edition totaling 75,000 copies. During the same year, Moskovsky Rabochy published an abridged edition, entitled *Zionism: Ideology and Politics,* also by Yevseev (70,000 copies). According to the abridged version, Judaism encourages hatred of mankind, demands for genocide, encourages lust for power, and praises criminal methods for seizing power.

Thirty-five Soviet Jewish intellectuals sent a detailed criticism of the book to the division of propaganda of the Central Committee, and to Rudenko, the chief prosecutor of the Soviet Union.[6] The book was branded an "offense," and the thirty-five demanded that the author be brought to trial, as provided by Article 123 of the Constitution of the Soviet Union, which makes discrimination on grounds of religion or race a punishable offense.

Nevertheless, Soviet propaganda continued its campaign the following year. The Ukrainian Leninist Young Communist League published Trofim Kichko's book, *Zionism—The Enemy of Youth,* in which ritual murder is alleged. Representing Zionism as a destructive and criminal movement, a danger to all mankind,[7] makes an even greater impact in cartoons.

Almost daily, millions of copies of pictures of this kind are distributed throughout the Soviet Union, including organs of the party, government, army, labor unions, and Young Communists. The *Zionist** is also regularly compared to the various archenemies of the Soviet Union—all kinds of "reactionary forces and regimes," from Mao's Peking regime to Chile's junta. Usually the *Zionist* is compared to the United States, capitalism, and Nazism.[8] At the same time, positive mention of the contributions of the Jews during World War II, of Jewish history and culture, has disappeared from Soviet Russian historical studies and school books.[9] In a conversation with me, Ruth Okuneva pointed out that this propaganda has had an impact. During periods in which Zionism was loudly accused of "Nazism," the man in the street no longer shouted "Zhid" at Jews, but "Fascist."

---

*Zionist and *Jew* denote cartoon representations.

II

How has Soviet propaganda succeeded in transforming Nazism into Zionism?

In several themes from earlier anti-Hitler cartoons, the *Zionist has assumed the characteristics of Nazism or simply taken Hitler's place.*

In Fig. 2 the thirteenth-century Grand Inquisitor is congratulating the Nazi on the twentieth-century pogrom against the Jews: "Congratulations, dear colleague! You've really far outdone us!"

This was in 1938. The cartoon is from the German-language *Deutsche Zeitung Tageblatt,* published in Moscow, and the disgust for Nazism is indicated by the violent attributes: the bloody axe, the bloodied fist, the bloodstained dagger; by the apelike face and the hairy arm; the militaristic appearance.

Thirty years later, all these characteristics were transferred from the executioner to the victim—from the Nazi to the *Zionist* (see Figs. 21, 23, and 31).

In the following illustrations, the *Zionist* has replaced *Hitler* (see Fig. 3, "On to Moscow," by Deni, and Fig. 4, "Anti-Communist Witches' Sabbath").

In Yefimov's 1933 drawing, American, English, French, and German capitalists are godfathers of the murderous Hitler in the cradle (see Fig. 5). In 1969, *Gudok,* the transport workers' organ, repeats the theme, this time with the *Zionist* as the destructive child (see Fig. 6).

In the next set of pictures, even the choice of words has been retained: Fig. 7, "The New Order," by Yefimov, and Fig. 8, "Law and Order the Zionist Way," *Radianska Ukraina,* July 1, 1973.

The anti-Hitler cartoons are taken from *Sovetskiye Mastera Satir,* Moscow, 1946, and the parallels pointed out are in no way exceptions. Of the 160 drawings in the book, more than thirty themes recur in today's anti-Zionist versions, of which some are even by the same artist. [10]

Even if the themes are strikingly similar, there is a world of difference between anti-Hitler and anti-Zionist cartoons. Apart from the fact that the satire against Hitler did not start in earnest until 1941, when der Führer attacked his ally of 1939, the campaign against the Hitler regime was never as massive as the campaign, a quarter of a century later, directed against Zionism. [11]

There is a decisive difference, quantitative and also qualitative. Almost without exceptions, the Soviet anti-Hitler cartoons expressed a militant attitude against the *German war machine,* which once again presented a danger. This is reflected in the frequency of use of the favorite symbols in the years 1941–45. Those most used include the swastika for the Nazi regime (56 percent), the Iron Cross for Prussian military might and oppression (21 percent), the German eagle with a swastika or skull for the SS (13 percent and 10 percent respectively). In 25 percent of the drawings, the swastika and the Iron Cross were combined—now and then with Hitler decorated with the Iron Cross—while elsewhere his crimes were symbolized by the swastika.[12]

All four symbols topped the statistics during the worst years of the war (1943–44). In 1945, after Hitler had suffered his crushing defeat, the skull disappears completely (see Fig. 9 by Kukryniksy); the playing card shows the "King of Spades," i.e., the destructive warrior who rules solely by physical violence—symbolized in 1941 by a swastika and Iron Cross). In 1944, German military might had been broken; only a shattered swastika remains.

In 10 percent of the Soviet cartoons, no symbols of any kind are used. However, there is never any doubt as to the object of the satire. Thus, the top figures of the Third Reich are *always* caricatured with their *own features*. Only seldom are stereotypes employed for "military might."

How completely different are the anti-Zionist caricatures of today! Almost without exception, the *Zionist* appears as a *stereotype*; i.e., it is not possible to understand the cartoon without supplementary symbols. The political sting is seldom directed against any specific political act. Instead, stereotyped phrases and signals constantly reappear: from banditry, gansterism, and piracy to annex*sionism* and expan*sionism*. The latter expression was "created" on the same day by the government and party organs (May 9, 1973). It is also a favorite trick to reprint anti-Zionist cartoons several years later, as a rule without reference to the fact that they are reprints. The drawings appear as "current satire," and at the same time, an older image of Zionism is reinforced.[13]

In more than 55 percent of the 1,700 caricatures from the years 1967–1980 which I have analyzed, the *Zionist* appears as the *real corrupter of the world*; i.e., they are permeated with the idea of the Jew seizing all the power in the world for himself.

As far as I know, the first to depict Zionism as an evil *worse* than Nazism was the Ukrainian publication *Perets*, 1961, no. 15 (Fig. 12). "Bonn-Gurion" is a popular telescoping of "Ben-Gurion" and "Bonn" in Ukrainian propaganda.

In Fig. 12, "Bonn-Gurion," from *Peretz*, Ben-Gurion and the German Chancellor, Konrad Adenauer, are embracing on a chest of German weapons, which are pointing in every direction. Adenauer, the Christian Democrat, is wearing a swastika which rests on "the Eichmann case" in the briefcase. The insinuation here is that the compensation intended for victims of Nazism has been used solely for "aggressive purposes," and, during the Eichmann trial, some of this money was used to prevent information about former Nazis in top positions in the German Federal Republic from coming to light.

It is worth noting that Adenauer is caricatured *obviously*, while Ben-Gurion appears as a *stereotype*. At first glance, the relative weight of the two appears balanced, but there is one small detail in the top left which quickly informs the reader: the tiny swastika is confined by the big Star of David, i.e., *even Nazism was dominated by the Jews*. This conception is completely in line with Soviet propaganda's reediting of the "Schiff Myth." While anti-Semites maintained that the Bolshevik revolution could only be realized because it was financed by Jacob Schiff via the banking firm of Kuhn, Loeb and Company, Soviet propaganda maintains that Kuhn, Loeb and Company financed the *Nazis* before they came to power.[14]

That the symbol is unambiguous is apparent from Fig. 11, an anti-Semitic poster from World War II.

French illusion and English hope of victory are faced by "reality"—the dirty *Jew,* casting his black shadow over all hope: the Star of David dominates the £.

Fig. 12, "Die uberstaatliche Mauer [the supernational wall]," by Joseph Plank, is also from World War II. The chorus of the desperate nations is: "I cannot stretch out my hand to you, oh, good comrade!" The Star of David is the prison which prevents them from doing so. In an anti-Zionist cartoon, the difference is generally that *only the Arabs* are imprisoned behind the bars of the Star of David. The theme is tremendously popular wherever a drawing is directed against the Jewish state. It even decorates the cover of Daniel Heradstveit's "Arab and Israeli Elitist Perceptions," Universitetsforlaget, 1974. See also Fig. 13, "Zionist Housing Project," *Krasnaya Zvezda,* December 14, 1975.

Now and then, however, even Soviet propaganda has the Star of David symbolizing the subversive activities of the Jews in every corner of the world, as in *Krokodil,* March 1973 (Fig. 14).

The indoctrination is accomplished by small, frequent suggestions. A strong visual effect is created by placing the two antagonistic symbols closer and closer together, until amalgamation is achieved. In December 1971, the fusion of the swastika and the Star of David was completed ("The Banner of the Zionist Gang," *Pravda Vostoka* [Fig. 15]. Zionism and Nazism become one here, and with the use of the word "rabbi" in the text, any distinction between anti-Zionism and anti-Semitism is lost).

In Soviet propaganda, however, there is a far more subtle manipulation which, at first, is barely discernible. While the *Zionist* is represented as the *worst evil*, Nazism is rendered harmless. The *Zionist* is portrayed militaristically, but the most feared military and terror regime of our century is sometimes seen in civilian clothes. The *Zionist* is decorated with a swastika, but even Hitler appears at times with *only* the Iron Cross, a symbol which was hardly ever used in anti-Hitler caricatures.[15] While the *Zionist* is portrayed as evil personified, Nazism is turned into something remote and unreal by being "framed" or placed on a "distant cloud," or by being transformed into a "statue," a "shadow," or a "ghost." Remarkable, too, is the propaganda trick of letting *actual* Nazi attributes—Lebensraum, Blitzkrieg, concentration camps, genocide, and gas chambers—glide *away* from the Nazi onto the *image* of Zionism.

The first attempt to strip from the Jewish people their greatest tragedy, the Holocaust, was made by Trofim Kichko in *Judaism without Embellishment*, published by the publishing house of the Academy of Sciences of the Ukrainian SSR in 1963. In Fig. 16, "Bonn-Gurion," Ben-Gurion is just about to sign an agreement for the delivery of weapons to the German Federal Republic, when a ghost from Auschwitz stretches out its hand to prevent him from doing so. In order to emphasize his baseness, Ben-Gurion is portrayed as a stereotype—as a fat little hook-nosed *Jew*, dressed completely in *black*. And the act is thrown into relief by the prisoner who had to suffer the Nazi atrocities, who is an *upright non-Jew*. (A glance at the difference in noses is enough to enable one to catch the point.)

The elimination of every trace of Jewish elements from all media has become a permanent component in today's battle for "the legitimate rights of the Palestinians," whether it is directed from the extreme right or the extreme left.[16]

Trofim Kichko's book had to be withdrawn in 1964 because of "certain mistakes"—more correctly, as a result of a worldwide protest, Communist and non-Communist. However, this was no impediment to Kichko's career, nor did it prevent the spirit of the withdrawn book from remaining alive. In 1967, Trofim Kichko started the Ukrainian campaign against Zionism in "Zionism—Tool of Imperialism," *Komsomolskoye Znamaya*. In 1968, Kichko was awarded a Diploma of Honor for "dissemination of atheist propaganda" by the Ukrainian Supreme Soviet. By 1971, Kichko's position was so well established that he could publicly ridicule his former critics.[17] In the same year that *Judaism without Embellishment* was withdrawn, the government newspaper, *Izvestiya*, followed Kichko's line with Bonn for Israel (Fig. 17).

This cartoon must be regarded as an important step, in that Nazism, *for the first time*, is presented as something relatively *harmless*. How? Of the three figures, *only* the *Zionist* is overloaded with weapons. The Nazis are carrying weapons only to give them to the *Zionist*.

This interpretation is emphasized by the target in the middle, marked "Auschwitz" and "Warsaw Ghetto." The swastika is so thin and insignificant that one could be misled into believing it is part of the target markings.

The Star of David, on the other hand, is impressive, and it is from the Star of David *alone* that blood is dripping. Likewise, the blood from the machine gun is only falling on the *Zionist*'s hand. The innocuousness of the Nazis is emphasized by their lack of swastikas, the one in front having *only an Iron Cross.*

Since the Six-Day War in 1967, the attributes of Nazism have been transferred to the *Zionist* in earnest. Since then, Nazism has become something infinitely remote and unreal.

Fig. 18, "Dayan to Hitler: 'Move On!' " *Kazakhstanskaya Pravda*, June 21, 1967. Here it is the *statue of unarmed Hitler* which is flinching before Dayan, the advancing danger. Dayan has acquired the Nazi attributes: Dayan is carrying the revolver with a swastika. Dayan is extending his arm in the Nazi salute. Dayan is goose-stepping.

Two days later, *Bakinsky Rabochy* follows suit with "The Aggressor's Real Club" (Fig. 21). Here again it is Dayan who is dangerous. Nazism is reduced to a powerless skeleton hand, sticking up from the shattered swastika. The Nazi attribute—the "genocide" club—is being transferred to the *Zionist.*

This drawing continues an anti-Semitic tradition from the ninteenth century. In 1874, Osman-bey conjured up a similar picture in *The World Conquest of the Jews.*[18] He painted a vivid picture of the way the Alliance Israélite Universelle was stealing forth in the darkness, with "a dagger in one hand and dynamite in the other."

In "The Well-Known Range," *Sovetskaya Rossiya*, August 11, 1967, V. Fomichev, Artist of Honor of the USSR—intensifies this Nazi image (Fig. 20). In this version, the bellicose *Jew*-gestalt has taken over two Nazi attributes: Blitzkrieg and Lebensraum (on the signpost).

Thus, in 1967 the Star of David is completely *alone* in symbolizing the Nazi desire for Lebensraum. But Fomichev was by no means satisfied with this. A third attribute is on the way: the plan for a *gas chamber.* The trend is indicated by the swastika which is over the *Jew*'s leg, and by the chest of arms below. For the first time, the German weapons are pointing in only one direction: *away* from Nazism and *toward* the *Zionist.*

Fomichev here makes use of a perverted analogy. He cynically juxtaposes the six million murdered Jews with the three Arabs in the drawing, waiting with their faces to the wall. Fomichev also omits one important detail, the fact that Israel does not employ the death penalty—even for Arab terrorists. The indoctrination continues day after day, year in, year out.

The manipulation is continued three years later in "The Talents and Their Admirers," *Vechernyaya Moskva*, March 11, 1970 (Fig. 21). Nazism is made ineffectual by being placed in a frame. And if one compares the misdeeds of the two, the Nazi is content to set the world on fire; it is *only* the *Zionist* who has established concentration camps. In addition, by placing a swastika in each corner of the frame, the Star of David is brought closer to the opposing symbol than would otherwise have been possible. In Fig. 22, Nazism has again been placed in a frame. However, Soviet propaganda has made considerable progress in the creation of its innocuous Hitler image. The Führer appears here in *civilian* clothes, while the hook-nosed *Zionist* is portrayed as a bloodstained militarist. His dangerousness is emphasized by the insignia on his military cap: the Star of David encircling the dollar sign. In other words, the archenemy of the Soviet Union, American capitalism, is dominated by the Jews. The lengths to which Soviet propaganda will go in its attempts to whitewash Nazism are seen in Fig. 23 from *Gudok*. Here, Hitler—the source of inspiration of Meir Kahane—is made unreal. He floats like a ghost on a distant cloud. Indeed, if one takes a closer look, one will discover that Hitler is characterized solely by the Iron Cross.

III

We see that in the Soviet Union a gradual *displacement in the symbolism of the swastika* has taken place. Originally the swastika represented the Third Reich, with its demands for Lebensraum, its Blitzkrieg, its subjugation of other nations, war crimes, and genocide, and not least, its racist ideology.

The Germans saw themselves as the *Herrenvolk* ("master race"). In the hierarchy of nations, next to the top came the blond, blue-eyed Scandinavians, and at the bottom, the Slavs. But beyond any humanism ranked the Jews, who were defined as a "canker in society" which had to be radically "cut away," from the embryo to the dotard.

While Soviet propaganda has *never characterized the Hitler regime with racist symbols*, it has lavishly labeled the *Zionist* with them. Since 1970, it has been customary to link the *Zionist* with the Ku Klux Klan organization.

Since the Six-Day War, the swastika has been associated less and less with Nazism—and when used, Nazism is shown as insignificant and in a shattered state.

The swastika has now become a symbol of *German Revanche*, which is being adapted to the image by being called "The Heir of Nazism" or, purely and simply, "Nazi criminal."

In Fig. 24 from *Gudok*, German Revanche is yelling about a "Greater Germany from the Rhine to the Oder." He is defamed by being placed side by side with the *Zionist,* who is characterized by the myth of a "Greater Israel from the Nile to the Euphrates." The two tattered banners are surmounted by a swastika and a Star of David.

At times, Soviet propaganda has made use of the swastika as a symbol for the *Neo-Nazis* in the NDP, as in Fig. 25, "The Song of Peace," *Agitator,* February 1970. However, it is only a shattered swastika, relegated to the corner. The eye-catcher is the black Star of David, which has been placed closer to the *symbol of lying*—the forked tongue of the snake.

The Neo-Nazis are, however, much more frequently portrayed with the Iron Cross, as in Fig. 26, "Two Boots—One Pair," *Krasnaya Zvezda,* March 22, 1970. Once again, Soviet propaganda has depicted a reactionary movement as harmless. Unlike the militant *Zionist,* the Neo-Nazi appears in *civilian* clothes—indeed, it is the *Zionist alone* who holds a bomb. Even when the swastika and the Iron Cross appear in the same picture, the swastika is reserved for the *Zionist.*

In Fig. 27, the NDP is symbolized only by the Iron Cross, way over to one side. The swastika on the key, however, is by the *Black Bible,* "A Greater Israel," that is the basis of the Zionist's aggressive maneuvers.

Even though it is the great power, the United States, which is pushing tiny Israel forward in its "Drang nach Osten," the Hitler-padlock is looking on in horror. Because the Neo-Nazi appears once again as a civilian and the *Zionist* as a militarist, the *swastika has acquired a more dangerous character than the Iron Cross.* This interpretation of the symbols is shown emphatically in Fig. 28 by Kukryniksy. To the left, the hypocritically smiling Hitler is decorated with the Iron Cross. On the right, der Führer reveals his true nature—and the Iron Cross is replaced by the swastika.

After the Soviet Union adopted a policy of rapprochement with Willy Brandt's German Federal Republic in 1971, the German Revanche literally glides out of the picture. In parallel motifs, in which the German Revanche was previously portrayed with the *Zionist,* after 1971 only the *Zionist* remains as an enemy. [19] By the beginning of 1972, the Nazi image has been expanded from being applied to "Israeli extremists" to include *all Zionists,* whether hawks or doves, Likud or Mapam. In Fig. 29, "Familiar Handwriting," *Bakinsky Rabochy,* February 5, 1972, this is achieved by an almost indiscernible trick: clothing the otherwise militaristic figure with a *civilian shirt* sprinkled with Stars of David. It is now becoming difficult to distinguish between a "Zionist" and a "Jew." Hitler is reduced to a mere *shadow* of Israel. In addition, Hitler's shadow evokes the Jew's reputed gift of *mimicry*—of always being able to change his identity. As early as the fourth century, Chrysostom of Antioch preached that if a Jew looked completely different from what one imagined, this was due only to the evil of the Jew, and this was one of the snares Satan set to capture naive Christians. [20]

In Fig. 30, "Moshe Dayan's Warlike Pose," *Trud,* the propagandist has finally succeeded in establishing historical continuity in the image of the "destroyer." Dayan is not merely fused with Hitler but also with *Napoleon*—through the Phantom plane (the cocked hat), which disregards all conventions of restraint. This motif was also used in an anti-Hitler cartoon by Kukryniksy in 1941.

The Soviet public has been completely indoctrinated with the image of Nazism as being identical with Zionism. A goose-stepping figure in an SS cap triggers the Pavlovian reflex *this can only be the Zionist*—there is no need for a swastika or Star of David. In Fig. 31, *Sovietskaya Rossiya* has, to a great extent, succeeded in exploiting this. Only the tiny Star of David on the shoulder is needed to provide an unambiguous identification.

The fact that Nazism is today synonymous solely with Zionism in Soviet political cartoons is apparent from Fig. 35 by Kukryniksy. Even though several "reactionary regimes"—South Africa, Rhodesia, Portugal, and Israel—support American capitalism, it is Israel *alone* that wears the SS cap.

In 1977, the swastika was also a symbol of "Adherents to Western Democracy," in *Pravda* (April 13),. and again in *Sovetskaya Kirgiziya* (July 3), both with the same quotations "from the newspapers" (Fig. 36).

The drawings were published because of irritation at the Western accusations against the Soviet Union for "violating human rights."

Today the "progressive" world accepts the Soviet Union's presentation of the greatest reactionary movement of our time—Nazism—as harmless.

Notes

1. A list of anti-Zionist books published in the years 1970–72 is given in *Jews in Eastern Europe* (London, November 1972). See also below.

2. V. L. Burtsev, *The Protocols of the Elders of Zion: A Proven Forgery* (Paris, 1938).

3. During the Berne court case, 1934, the *Protocols of the Elders of Zion* were branded as "forgeries, plagiarism, and pornography, indeed even stupid nonsense."

4. Sir Retcliffe, *Die Geheimnisse des Judenkirchhofes in Prag. Die Verschworung der Weisen von Zion. Volks-und Schulausgabe mit dem Bild vom Grabe des Rabbi Lau* (Leipzig: Gotland, 1934).

5. Ruth Okuneva, "Anti-Semitic Notions: Strange Analogies," below. *New York Review of Books,* November 6, 1972. Quoted in *Jews in Eastern Europe,* August 1973, pp. 52 ff. Johan Vogt, "En antisemittisk legende" [An anti-Semitic legend], *Aftenposten* (Oslo), January 10, 1977).

6. See the letter from thirty-five scientists in *Jews and the Jewish People: Petitions, Letters, and Appeals from Soviet Jews* (Hebrew University of Jerusalem, Center for Research and Documentation of East European Jewry, 1976), vol. 5, pp. 68–73.

7. See Judith Vogt, "Historien om et image," in *Antisemitisme og Antizionisme i Karikaturer* [The story of an image: Anti-Semitism and anti-Zionism in cartoons] (Copenhagen and Oslo, 1978), pp. 197 ff.

8. In 45 percent of the cartoons, the *Zionist* was linked with capitalism, in 33 percent with the United States, and 10 percent with Nazism.

9. On this subject, see the article by Ruth Okuneva, below.

10. Boris Yefimovich Yefimov, born 1900. People's Artist of the Soviet Union. Drew the first cartoons for the Ukrainian press after the October Revolution. Contributor to *Izvestia*, *Pravda*, and *Krokodil*, from 1922. Kukryniksy—pseudonym of a trio of artists: M. Kupriyanov, b. 1903; P. N. Krylov, b. 1902; and N. A. Sokolov, b. 1903. All three are Lenin and Stalin Prize winners, People's Artists, and members of the Academy of Fine Arts, Moscow.

11. From 1933 to 1945, several hundred anti-Hitler cartoons. From 1967 to 1980, approximately 2,000 anti-Zionist cartoons.

12. The statistics are based on 160 anti-Hitler cartoons from *Sovetskiye Mastera Satiry* (Moscow, 1946) and 88 cartoons from *Varldpolitik i Karikatyrer 1943–1945* [World politics in cartoons] (Stockholm, 1944). Results of a survey of the number of swastikas, Iron Crosses, German Eagles with swastikas and skulls in 160 cartoons from the period 1938–45:

1938	1	—	—	1	2
1941	8	3	2	—	13
1942	21	4	5	5	35
1943	28	11	9	9	57
1944	35	13	6	4	58
1945	10	9	1	—	20
	21	6	6	3	36
Total	124	46	29	22	221

13. See "Tel Aviv Expressionist," *Krasnaya Zvezda*, March 13, 1970; *Literaturnaya Gazeta*, March 16, 1973; "The Leading Israeli Drummers," *Pravda Vostoka*, May 8, 1968; "The Israeli Marionette," *Pravda Vostoka*, August 5.8.1975. See Judith Vogt, "Historien om et image," p. 196.

14. Hermann Lutz, "Falschungen zur Auslandsfinanzierung Hitlers," *Vierteljahrhefte für Zeitgeschichte*, October 1954, pp. 386 ff.

15. In *Sovetskiye Mastera Satiry*. There is only one example of an Iron Cross drawn by Kukryniksy in 1942.

16. Nazis are now writing a revised history of the war in which the Holocaust is called a "lie" which "Zionist propaganda has invented." The Social Liberals have formed a "new school," the Revisionists, which does not accept eyewitness accounts from World War II as valid source material. The vacuum is filled by "revisionist historiography." Concerning the interaction between fascists and socialists, see Noam Chomsky, *The Faurisson Affair in Paris*, 1980.

17. In *Silskii Visti*, quoted in *Jews in Eastern Europe*, 1972, no. 5, p. 8.

18. *Pokoreniye mira yevreyami* [The subjugation of the world by Jews] by Major Osmanbey (St. Petersburg, 1874), 48 pp.

19. Something similar happened after the Soviet Union made overtures to the United States. When the Soviet Union wished to raise a loan in dollars, the figure of the capitalist "Uncle Sam" becomes a Zionist capitalist. See Judith Vogt, "Historien om et image." pp. 220 ff.

20. J. Trachtenberg, *The Devil and the Jews* (Yale University Press, 1943), p. 163.

Fig. 1. "Der Teufel in Deutschland [The Devil in Germany]." Dresden, 1897.

Fig. 2. "The Grand Inquisitor: Congratulations, dear colleague! You've really far outdone us!" *Deutsche Zeitung Tageblatt* (Moscow), November 28, 1938. Courtesy Z. Efron, *Encyclopaedia Judaica*, 1972.

Fig. 3. "On to Moscow!" Drawing by V. Deni. *Sovetskiye mastera satiry*, Moscow, 1946.

Fig. 4. "Anti-Communist Witches' Sabbath." Drawing by Yu. Kershin. *Sovetskaya torgovlya*, January 20, 1972.

Fig. 5. "By the cradle of German fascism—Adolf Hitler's guardian angels." Drawing by B. Yefimov, 1936. *Sovetskiye mastera satiry*, Moscow, 1946.

Fig. 6. "Boundless love of the child that knows no bounds." Drawing by Yu. Kershin. *Gudok*, April 16, 1969.

Fig. 7. "The New Order." Drawing by B. Yefimov. *Sovetskiye mastera satiry*, Moscow, 1946.

Fig. 8. "Law and Order the Zionist Way." Drawing by M. Slavsky. *Radyanska Ukraina*, January 7, 1973.

Fig. 9. Drawing dy Kukryniksy. *Sovetskiye mastera satiry*, Moscow, 1946.

Fig. 10. "A touching unity: Bonn-Gurion." Drawing by Be-Sha. *Perets*, no. 15, 1961.

Fig. 11. Anti-Semitic poster from World War II.

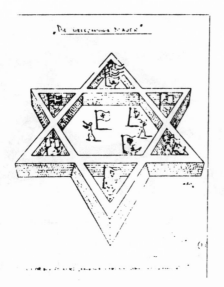

Fig. 12. "Die uberstaatliche Mauer [The supernational wall]." Drawing by Joseph Plank. World War II.

Fig. 13. "Zionist Housing Project." Drawing by V. Fomichev. *Krasnaya zvezda,* December 14, 1975.

Fig. 14. "Strongpoint." Drawing by G. Iorsh. *Krokodil,* no. 8, 1973.

Fig. 15. "The banner of the Zionist gang." Drawing by N. Leushin. *Pravda vostoka,*
December 15, 1971.

Fig. 16. "Bonn-Gurion." Design by M. Savchenko. T. Kichko, *Judaism without Embellishment*, Kiev: Uk. SSR Academy of Sciences Publishing House, 1963.

Fig. 17. "I recommend it as an excellent weapon! It was checked and tested at Auschwitz and the Warsaw ghetto . . ." Drawing by V. Fomichev. *Izvestiya*, November 12, 1964.

Дойн Гитлеру! — А ну!..
рис. В. Нестерова.

Fig. 18. "Dayan to Hitler; Move on!" Drawing by V. Nesterov. *Kazakhstanskaya pravda*, June 21, 1967.

Fig. 19. "The aggressors' relay-race." Drawing by Vs. Ternavsky. *Bakinsky rabochy*, June 23, 1967.

Fig. 21. "The talents and their admirers." Drawing by V. Konstantinov. *Vechernyaya Moskva*, March 11, 1970.

Fig. 20. "The well-known range." Drawing by V. Fomichev. *Sovetskaya Rossiya*, August 11, 1967.

Fig. 22. "Israeli aggressor: It's no use comparing us with the Hitlerist aggressors. We have our own moUStache!" Drawing by I. Ivanov. *Vechernyaya Moskva*, January 27, 1971.

Fig. 23. "Coauthors . . ." Drawing by V. Konstantinov. *Gudok*, December 21, 1971.

Fig. 24. "Collaboration between revanchists and Zionists: Militant brothers—twin slogans." Drawing by V. Konstantinov. *Gudok*, May 23, 1969.

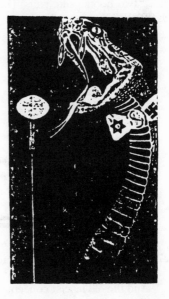

Fig. 25. "The Song of Peace." Drawing by O. Pashchupkin. *Agitator*, no. 3, 1970.

Fig. 26. "Two boots—one pair." Drawing by V. Konstantinov. *Krasnaya zvezda*, March 22, 1970.

Fig. 27. "Zionists have proved in practice
    That they go the Nazis' way,
    And the old fascist concepts
    Their doctrines have underlain."
Drawing by A. Latynin, text by K. Samarin. *Kazakhstanskaya pravda*, June 4, 1971.

ЛЮДОЕД-ВЕГЕТАРИАНЕЦ ИЛИ
ДВЕ СТОРОНЫ ОДНОЙ МЕДАЛИ

Fig. 28. "Cannibal-vegetarian; or, two sides of one medal." Drawing by Kukryniksy. *Sovetskiye mastera satiry*, Moscow, 1946.

ЗНАКОМЫЙ ПОЧЕРК.

Рис. Вс. Тернавского.

Fig. 29. "Familiar handwriting." Drawing by Vs. Ternavsky. *Bakinsky rabochy,* February 5, 1972.

Воинственная поза Моше Даяна.
Рис. Ю. КЕРШИНА.

Fig. 30. "Moshe Dayan's warlike pose." Drawing by Yu. Kershin. *Trud,* February 29, 1972.

Fig. 31. "Alms for the aggressor . . ." Drawing by A. Shtabel (from Ufa). *Sovetskaya Rossiya*, October 20, 1973. (Word play: in the Russian word *poDAYANiye*, meaning "alms," the prominent letters make up the name Dayan.)

Fig. 32. "The 'chosen' are in a hurry for the Christmas party. Each one's gift is up to its donor. Moshe Dayan is bringing a star; an adornment like this is indispensable, in the Zionists' opinion." Drawing by L. Kazarinsky. *Sovetskaya Litva*, January 1, 1974.

АФРИКАНСКИЕ ПРОВОДНИКИ

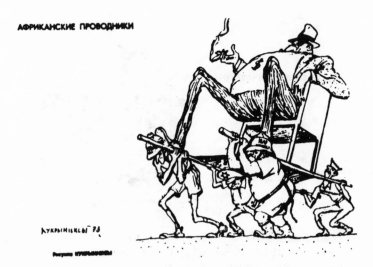

Fig. 33. "African guides." Drawing by Kukryniksy. *Krokodil*, no. 7, 1973.

Fig. 34. "Paper declaration." Drawing by S. Dzhamgyrchiyev. *Sovetskaya Kirgiziya*, July 3, 1977.

Excerpts from Soviet
Publications and Samizdat

Introduction

THIS PART OF the book includes excerpts of an anti-Semitic nature from Soviet publications over the period 1948–1980 and also from materials of various dissident circles which were published in Samizdat.

This material is grouped by decades. Each section contains excerpts from (1) periodicals, (2) books, and (3) Samizdat.

The appendix to Part V includes a list of anti-Zionist and anti-Israeli books published in the Soviet Union from the 1960s through 1981. Those books not found in the library of the Center for Research and Documentation of East European Jewry are noted by an asterisk.

The notes for Part V were compiled by the Center's researcher M. Kipnis and the index of names by the Center's researcher D. Tsaikhner. The book list in the appendix was compiled by N. Bibichkova.

The 1940s and 1950s

MATERIAL FROM SOVIET PERIODICALS

Pravda, January 28, 1949

A CERTAIN ANTIPATRIOTIC GROUP
OF THEATER CRITICS

THE PARTY HAS insistently pointed out that the disengagement of writers from the life and struggle of the Soviet people leads to sorrowful and fateful results and that only the great ideas of Soviet patriotism give them creative inspiration. Shameless cosmopolitanism is not only antisocial but also sterile. It is as harmful as the parasites that gnaw at the roots of useful grains. It serves as a conductor of reactionary bourgeois influences hostile to us.

An antipatriotic group of followers of bourgeois aestheticism has arisen in theater criticism. It has infiltrated into our press and most shamelessly rules the pages of the journal *Teatr* and the newspaper *Sovetskoye Iskusstvo* ("Soviet Art"). These critics have lost their sense of responsibility to the people, and transmit rootless cosmopolitanism of the most disgusting kind, hostile to the Soviet citizen: they hinder the development of Soviet literature. The feeling of Soviet national pride is alien to them.

The image of Nil, a revolutionary worker in M. Gorky's play *The Philistines*, has immense ideological and artistic importance. But critic Yu. Yuzovsky[1] has been trying to suggest to the reader that "Nil is one of Gorky's imperfect figures," that the author writes here "as a publicist, without always caring about whether the interference of ideology in the artistic fabric of the play is justified."

While grudgingly giving his lordly approval, the same Yu. Yuzovsky scoffingly mocks the plot of A. Surov's play *Far from Stalingrad*, and that of B. Chirskov's play *Victors*, a Stalin Prize winner; he mocks the role of Zoya in *A Tale of Truth*, for her portrayal of which the actress N. Rodionova has been awarded the Stalin Prize. For lack of anything better to discuss regarding the role, critic Yuzovsky writes about "a white sacrificial wreath." "This lyricism of sacrifice," he writes, "is a far cry from the romanticism that we seek."

A. Gurvich[2] uses a different form of camouflage from Yu. Yuzovsky's. In his articles, A. Gurvich maliciously attempts to compare Soviet drama with classical drama and to disgrace the former with the help of . . . Turgenev's prestige. Speaking of Soviet plays, he declaims, "Only one image aroused us, made us feel something significant and dear. . . . It was Verochka from Turgenev's *A Month in the Country.* . . . We . . . felt in our hearts that only that shy and passionate girl stretches her hand out to Zoya Kosmodem-yanskaya over the century and firmly shakes the hand of many a woman in our plays."

Let us dot the *i*'s here. "We" refers to those who are devoid of the feeling of Soviet patriotism, those who do not hold dear the image of Zoya Kosmodemyanskaya, and the works of our literature which the Soviet people value for their true depiction of the heroic beauty of our life, of the beautiful soul of Soviet man.

And what conception can A. Gurvich have of the national features of the Russian Soviet man if he writes that in "the complacent humor and naively credulous optimism" of Pogodin's plays—in which allegedly "the national features of the playwright's outlook" are expressed—the spectator saw his own reflection and "experienced the joy of recognition," for (we are led to believe) "complacency, too, is not alien to the Soviet people."

This is nothing but slander against the Russian Soviet man. A vile piece of slander. Precisely because complacency is deeply alien to us, we must condemn this attempt to discredit the national Soviet character.

The party has always supported innovations and progressive ideas in literature and the arts, but at the same time it rebuffs resolutely all attempts at discrediting works marked by the spirit of Soviet patriotism, and it will continue to unmask mercilessly all antipatriotic onslaughts.

But there are people contaminated with the remnants of bourgeois ideology who still try to poison the healthy, creative atmosphere of Soviet art with their noxious breath. Sometimes openly and sometimes furtively, they try to carry on their futile, doomed struggle.

The sting of their aestheticist-formalistic criticism is aimed, not at the truly harmful and defective works, but against the best and the most progressive ones which depict Soviet patriots. This shows beyond all doubt that aestheticist formalism only serves as a cover for antipatriotic essence.

These critics have made themselves very much at home in the stuffy atmosphere of the All-Russian Theatrical Society (presided over by G. Boyadzhiyev) and the Drama Committee of the Writers' Union (presided over by A. Kron). Here one sees the ugly, seamy side of those who elsewhere speak less openly, hiding the often harmful content of their pronouncements behind scientific-looking convolutions, abstruse jargon, and intentionally pretentious fluff, used only to obscure the essence of the matter.

There the theater critic A. Borshchagovsky,[3] who mutely ignores the works distorting Soviet reality and the image of the Soviet people, directed all the fervor of his antipatriotic criticism against A. Sofronov's[4] play *Moscow Character* and against the Maly Theater, which had staged it. The same A. Borshchagovsky who once tried to defame the play *On the Steppes of the Ukraine* by A. Korneychuk set out to discredit such works as *Our Daily Bread* by N. Virta, *Great Destiny* by A. Surov, and others.

There the critic L. Malyugin started a campaign against such deeply patriotic and popular works as *Great Force* by G. Romashov, *In One Town* by A. Sofronov, and *Our Daily Bread* by N. Virta.

During the meeting of the All-Russian Theatrical Society, critic E. Kholodov attacked the plays *In One Town* and *Our Daily Bread.*

At a time when we face the most urgent task of fighting rootless cosmopolitanism, fighting against the manifestations of bourgeois influences alien to the people, these critics find nothing better to do than discredit the most advanced strides made in our literature. This directly harms Soviet artistic work and literature and impedes their progress.

As we have seen, A. Gurvich, Yu. Yuzovsky, et al., have been engaged in the same kind of "work," if we may call it that. Their empty, false prestige, blown up beyond all proportions, has yet to be revealed for what it really is. The harmful unpatriotic views held by Borshchagovsky, Gurvich, Yuzovsky, Varshavsky, and Boyadzhiyev encourage hostile distortions in the work of other critics.

A disappointing stand on the attitude toward contemporary repertoire, and in particular towards the play, *Moscow Character,* has been taken by the editorial board of the *Literaturnaya Gazeta.* In an editorial account bearing the pretentious title "Discussion on the Destiny of Repertoire" (December 4, 1948), *Literaturnaya* unreservedly praised the harmful report made by A. Borshchagovsky at a meeting devoted to new plays and joined in his vicious attacks against the course taken by the Maly Theater of staging modern patriotic plays.

How did certain critics take the party's advice on the repertoires of drama theaters and on measures to improve them? Has the stern and just party criticism persuaded them to revise their positions? Have these critics begun practicing self-criticsm?

No, they have not. The criticism has been too much for these miserable critics. They failed to look critically at themselves because they were afraid to reveal their total ideological bankruptcy. They have not ceased their activities against party directives, their group activities, and their antipatriotic activities. They have divided up the roles; some of the leaders of the grouping have become entrenched in the musty committees of the All-Russian Theatrical Society. Having gathered their friends around, they create false "public opinion" against the Soviet repertoire in general.

Some of them started pretending to be mysterious "mutes." But, indeed, they never kept silent. Excerpts from verbatim reports of the utterances of these "mutes" were made public at the plenary session of the Writers' Union—disgraceful and ignorant outpourings, reeking of hostility toward modern Soviet repertoire, toward the patriotic works of our playwrights.

Indulging in sputtering and malice, they tried to establish a kind of literary underground. They derided all the best that appeared in Soviet drama. They did not find a single good word for such plays as *The Great Force, Moscow Character, Our Daily Bread, Great Destiny.* They aimed their slanderous attacks especially at the plays which had been awarded Stalin Prizes.

True, there are still many faults in the plays of the modern Soviet repertoire. And it is understood that these should be subjected to creative comradely criticism, both ideological and artistic. But the aesthetic gossipers never cared much for such criticism. They derided these plays outright for the sole reason that these plays, despite their faults, are permeated with Soviet ideology, they raise most important political problems, help the party and the people in the struggle against submission to bourgeois foreigners, in the struggle against bureaucracy, against rapaciousness, against the predominance of private motives over social ones. All these plays foster Soviet patriotism and strive to show from the stage, with the force of artistic images, everything new and progressive which is emerging in Soviet society.

The Yuzovskys and Gurviches, who have long been morally bankrupt, "kept silent," but the Borshchagovskys and others took their place, going from specialized periodicals on art criticism to popular publications. While paying lip service to Soviet ideology, they began voicing contempt for the incarnation of Soviet patriotism in artistic images.

We remember well the words of Comrade Stalin: "One may say that being silent is not criticism. But this is wrong. The method of being silent as a special way of ignoring something is also a form of criticism, though a silly and ludicrous one, but it is still criticism."

The attempts made by this antipatriotic group of critics to get away with silence, to cheat in criticism instead of raising the problems openly and as a matter of principle, will not help that group.

What we see is not a series of incidental mistakes; no, it is a system of antipatriotic views which harms the development of our literature and art. It is a system that must be crushed.

It is no accident that the rootless cosmopolitans attack the productions of the Art Theater and of the Maly Theater—our national pride. They try to undermine the credit given to these theaters—which are the best in the world—when they stage plays dealing with Soviet themes and develop images of the Soviet people.

It is the urgent task of theater criticism to deliver an ideological blow against this antipatriotic group of theater critics.

The recently held plenary session of the Writers' Union laid the foundation for unmasking and routing this antipatriotic group of critics.

Our critics must remember that their task is to support all the progressive patriotic tendencies in literature and the arts, to publicize for all their best creations, and to expose faults boldly so that they foster the spirit of Soviet patriotism among writers and artists.

The Soviet drama and theater are on the right path. Soviet art is nourished by the richest sources of socialist construction. But these sources, unprecedented in cultural history, are open only to those who themselves take part in building this life, in the struggle for communism. Those who stand aside and watch this life, detached as dispassionate observers, inevitably lag behind.

We must be resolute in putting an end once and for all to liberal acceptance of all these aestheticist good-for-nothings, devoid of the healthy feeling of love for their motherland and for their people, who have nothing in their souls but malignancy and exaggerated self-conceit. The atmosphere of art must be cleansed of the antipatriotic Philistines.

Soviet criticism which follows the party line will no doubt destroy those bearing views alien to the people, it will clear the field for the fruitful work of the Soviet theater and fulfill the tasks that the party and the people have set as goals for Soviet criticism.

Izvestiya, February 18, 1949

WIPE OUT THE ANTIPATRIOTIC GROUP OF DRAMA CRITICS (THE MEETING OF LENINGRAD'S MOST ACTIVE WORKERS IN THE ART FIELD)

Articles published in the newspapers *Pravda* and *Kultura i Zhizn* ("Culture and Life") about the antipatriotic group of drama critics have greatly disturbed public opinion in Leningrad.

Playwrights, critics, and activists in the arts from all over the city gathered last night in Leningrad to discuss the situation and the tasks of theatrical criticism.

In his report to the meeting, B. Chirskov, chairman of the drama section of the Leningrad chapter of the Soviet Writers' Union, exposed the antipatriotic "activity" in the Leningrad chapter of the All-Russian Theatrical Society of S. Dreiden, I. Shneiderman, I. Berezark, M. Yankovsky, S. Tsimbal, and other rootless cosmopolitans, conspicuous followers of the Yuzovskys and Gurviches.

For many years these rootless cosmopolitans have disseminated deleterious bourgeois ideas, while sharply criticizing everything new, everything Soviet; they defamed the Moscow Art Theater, the Maly Theater, the Pushkin Academy Theater of Leningrad. They slavishly bowed to the bourgeois West and its corrupt art; bourgeois aesthetes cynically jeered at Soviet drama. In the pages of the newspapers *Vecherniy Leningrad, Leningradskaya Pravda,* and *Smena,* Dreiden, Shneiderman, and their fellow cosmopolitans heaped slander and abuse on Soviet plays, besmirched our art and socialist realism. Spiritually wasted, hostile to the Soviet people and homeland, these cosmopolitan devotees of aestheticism enjoyed reviling Soviet plays, playwrights, and theatrical collectives that staged Soviet plays, and kept silent about the creative successes of our best theatres.

Taking part in the discussions, Associate Member of the Academy of Sciences of the USSR A. V. Ossovsky, director of the Scientific Research Institute for Theater and Music, showed how the aestheticism devotee M. Yankovsky, an ardent cosmopolitan, tried to defame the Soviet theater and drama, and to divert artists from the true path.

In his striking address, Academician I. A. Orbeli, director of the State Museum, Hermitage, stressed that the exposure of the antipatriotic group of drama critics is a manifestation of the party's concern that Soviet socialist art should flourish.

Associate Member of the Academy of Arts of the USSR V. A. Serov spoke of Ya. Pasternak[5] and N. Punin, who systematically tried to discredit the achievements of Soviet artists who reflect contemporary patriotic subjects in their works.

Pasternak slanderously claimed that Soviet representational art is going through a crisis, and rehashed the worn-out, cosmopolitan, false version of the "provincialism" of Russian classical and contemporary painting. Pasternak, Punin, and others have already been exposed and expelled from the Academy of Arts. "Isn't it strange," Comrade Serov said, "how they manage to find protectors. No sooner were the academy doors closed behind Punin than other doors, those of the Leningrad State University, opened to them."

P. A. Serebryakov, director of the Leningrad State Conservatory, said that some music critics in Leningrad had organized some kind of "conspiracy of silence" with regard to all the new events in our musical life, and kept silent about the achievements of Soviet composers.

A. P. Burlachenko, director of the Leningrad Drama Theater, offered several examples of the great harm done to the Leningrad theaters by the Dreidens, Yankovskys, and other rootless cosmopolitans. They disparaged the Soviet play *Life in the Citadel,* which had been warmly received by the public; they defamed the patriotic plays about Soviet man and his heroic deeds, of which the inhabitants of Leningrad are so fond.

The cosmopolitans, who had found refuge in film making, were resolutely exposed at the all-city meeting of the most active workers in the arts. L. Trauberg,[6] who for many years has worked the lecture circuit, openly preaches formalism in art. Trauberg never misses an opportunity to belittle the importance of Soviet cinematography, calumniously claiming that "the light of mastery in acting shines from the West." This cosmopolitan besmirches the best productions of Soviet film artistry: *A Legend of the Siberian Land, The Village Schoolmistress, The Great Turning Point, The Russian Question.*

The meeting urged Leningrad's artistic masters to produce works that are worthy of our great epoch.

In the adopted resolution, Leningrad's workers in the arts sternly denounced the reactionary activities of the bourgeois cosmopolitans in all artistic fields, and expressed their readiness to continue their firm struggle against the bourgeois riffraff who try to prevent the art of the socialist era from steadily expanding and developing.

LENINGRAD (from *Izvestiya's* own correspondent)

Vechernaya Moskva, March 14, 1949
S. Ivanov

THE IMPUDENT PREACHINGS OF A ROOTLESS COSMOPOLITAN

It is a well-known fact that the Sovietsky Pisatel ("Soviet Writer") Publishing House has harbored people without kith or kin, antipatriotic Levins, Danins, and the like. In 1948, it published *Years of My Life,* by Aleksandr Isbakh (pseudonym of Isaac Bakhrakh),[7] a series of autobiographical stories about the childhood and youth of a certain Aleksandr Shtein, in whom we easily recognize the author himself.

But what kind of ideas does the author of this so-called book advocate?

First, the glorification of the Jewish faith. The entire book, from the first page to the last, is saturated with religious worship. The first story even bears the heading "God." With tender emotion and deep reverence, Isbakh writes about the synagogue service, mentions dozens of things specifically connected with the synagogue, and both in the text and in the countless footnotes, explains in great detail the meaning of each. We become acquainted with the minutest details of the ritual of Jewish service and can even read in Isbakh's book the text of the prayer for the dead.

But this is not the point. Isbakh besmirches the Jewish people by contending that all Jews, irrespective of their social origin and status, find complete happiness in their religion. He devotes entire pages to a description of a reading from the Talmud, and shows how the Jews gathering in the synagogue "relished the wisdom of generations; they tried to delve into the meaning of every word written by the revered sages whose names have been forgotten over the centuries." This is said of working Jews—cobblers, tailors, poor men mercilessly exploited in tsarist Russia. Isbakh slanderously contends that they found consolation only in the synagogue. He writes: "Everyday life, with its joys and sorrows—more sorrows than joys!—went on there, beyond the synagogue walls, where their tiny grocery shops, their cobbler's stools, their sewing machines, their numerous children and grandchildren, their anxieties remained. But here (in other words, in the synagogue) they immersed themselves in a totally different life. Here, they were not the wretched, downtrodden Jews, afraid of every policeman."

Isbakh describes the life of the locksmith David Bentsman, who abandoned his trade in order to work for the synagogue. Choking with emotion and sparing no colors, the author paints a picture of how this locksmith found his happiness in communicating with God.

"Evenings, when only talmudic sages remained in the synagogue, he would sit down near them. He was not particularly literate and would listen intently to the interpretations of the Holy Scripture, trying to fathom the meaning of the arguments. David could understand almost everything. He clearly saw the festive fires of Jerusalem, the heavy seven-branched candelabra, the magnificent attire of the high priests and Levites. . . . That was a temple . . . That was life. . . . He would close his eyes and imagine the 'Holy Land,' a land flowing with milk and honey . . ." (from the story "The Beginning").

In his so-called book, Isbakh openly propagandizes for Zionism, writes about the Zionist organization, which "commanded great influence among the Jews of our town," about the Zionist circle at the secondary school, the "good uncles" who dispatched Jews to Palestine, and even reproduces the words of the Zionist anthem (in the story "Son of Honor").

What are the distinctive traits displayed by the central character? Could it be that Isbakh needed all these religious rituals only as a background, the better to develop the image of his protagonist? Perhaps he depicts his character against this background as an opponent of the way of life around him, as a fighter for a new, proper way of life?

By no means; the character's fundamental trait is shiftless cowardliness. He fears everything in the world. This peculiarity pervades the character's entire life, from childhood to adolescence (that is, from the beginning to the end of the book).

In childhood, he is possessed by the fear of God: "It seems that fear dominated my feelings toward God. HE was almighty. HE was all-seeing. Nothing could be hidden from him" (author's capitalization). Fear of God was mixed with faith in God. The book's hero unwearyingly attends all synagogue services, "Shakharit," "Minkha," and "Ma'ariv" (the author meticulously explains what each and every one of these terms means), although nobody forces him to, since his father is dead and his mother is not all that religious. But, you see, "God is almighty!" (as Isbakh assures us). And he goes on to tell us a story about "God's almightiness," which helped our hero find a lost toy. The fear of Jehovah and the faith in his "almightiness" never leave our hero throughout his life (as described in the book). The salvos fired by the cruiser *Aurora* have already thundered, the October Revolution has already taken place, our hero has grown up, he is seventeen now, he moves to Moscow, where the same old Zionist God is of primary importance to him! When our hero succeeds in taking up residence with a friend and putting some order into his life, he immediately remembers "the old Zionist God who . . . has forgotten all my offenses."

But the book's hero is afraid not only of God, he is faint-hearted always and everywhere: for example, when The Whites (antirevolutionary) shoot a group of Communists in front of his eyes, when he sees "a tall man in an officer's uniform with a skull and crossbones on his sleeve (that is, a White officer)," and when he's at the front, the hero's permanent state is one of "alarm and agitation." When, in the front line, Red Army soldiers returning from battle merrily exchange banter, "I could not take part in the general fun; to me, it seemed sacrilegious to laugh with death all around us." Fear of death guides all the hero's actions. A shell lands nearby without exploding. No one is injured. But the hero?

"This is the end! flashed across my mind, and closing my eyes, I leaned back on the gun carriage."

Isbakh's hero is not only as timorous as a rabbit but also an inveterate, deep-rooted egoist. The entire book is full of his "I," of praise lavished upon himself. He proudly and rapturously narrates about himself: "When I was eight years old, I was already head of the family." And how did he fulfill this task in his family? By "being responsible to God for the entire family." Quite an insignificant responsibility, obviously, but the hero "honestly tried to meet this obligation to the Omnipresent One." "I didn't like the Zionists," declares the hero, but immediately adds a small correction: "But I was Jewish and . . . I became an honorable son; I joined the respectable family of the sons of Moses; from that day, I was entitled to put the small square box with the sacred prayers on my head . . ." And how blissfully the hero tells about the beginning of his "creative" career: "Maksimov, the king of the screen, will read my poetry at concerts in the capital. I had become a real poet." But things are getting better and better. The summer of 1921, the hero says, "was a time when literature and art flourished in our town as never before." Why? Because of the Theater of Revolutionary Satire, whose "ideological leader" was "I." "I always distinguished myself by efficiency," "I was already a prominent figure in the newspaper," "I—the head of the poets"—a countless number of "I"s is scattered throughout the book.

Among these "I"s, there is one sentence in the whole book that corresponds to the truth. The author writes: "I thought of my short life and reached the bitter conclusion that I, the chairman of the Poets' Union, didn't know anything. Whoever I might have been, I was still an *ignoramus*" (my emphasis—S.I.). These words of the hero-author are from the year 1921. But even today, almost three decades later, the hero-author remains the same ignoramus. For only ignoramuses and, we might add, antipatriots can blindly worship everything foreign, the way the author does in his book. Only in the mind of an ignoramus and antipatriot can the Moscow Conservatory and the Bolshoy Theater be associated only with the names of foreign musicians and composers. Only an ignoramus and antipatriot can say, the day after the October Revolution, that the executive committee and the party committee in a provincial administrative center should erect a monument neither to the revolutionary fighters nor to the most prominent figures of our national science, literature, and art, but to the Swiss Pestalozzi, referred to in the book as an "illustrious Swiss" and "famous pedagogue," although it is no secret that Pestalozzi's pedagogical work in childhood education is permeated with glaring formalism and overloaded with religious propaganda.

Aleksandr Isbakh wrote a loathsome book indeed! And who helped him publish it if not the already denounced rootless cosmopolitan F. Levin,[8] who appears as the editor of the book?

Pravda, January 13, 1953

CHRONICLE OF EVENTS
THE ARREST OF A GROUP OF DOCTOR-SABOTEURS

A short while ago the state security organs uncovered a terrorist group of doctors who planned by means of deleterious treatment to shorten the life of prominent figures in the Soviet Union.[9]

The members of this terrorist group included Professor M. S. Vovsi, internist; Professor V. N. Vinogradov, internist; Professor M. B. Kogan, internist; Professor B. B. Kogan, internist; Professor P. I. Yegorov, internist; Professor A. I. Feldman, otolaryngologist; Professor Ya. G. Etinger, internist; Professor A. M. Greenstein, neuropathologist, and G. I. Mayorov, internist.

It has been established through documentary evidence, inquests, the conclusions of medical experts, and the confessions of those arrested that the criminals, hidden enemies of the people, had administered deleterious treatment to the patients and undermined their health.

The investigation has established that the members of the terrorist group, taking advantage of their position as physicians and abusing their patients' trust, had deliberately and maliciously undermined their patients' health. They intentionally ignored the findings of objective examinations of the patients, made incorrect diagnoses and thereby killed them through incorrect treatment.

The criminals have confessed that they incorrectly diagnosed Comrade A. A. Zhdanov's illness. Concealing his myocardial infarction, they prescribed a regimen that was contraindicated in that serious condition, and thereby killed him. The inquest has determined that the criminals also shortened the life of Comrade A. S. Shcherbakov by incorrectly administering powerful medication. They also prescribed a pernicious regimen, and thereby drove him to his death.

The criminal doctors tried their hardest to undermine the health of leading Soviet military cadres, to disable them and weaken the country's defense. They attempted to put Marshals A. M. Vasilevsky, L. A. Govorov and I. S. Konev, General of the Army S. M. Shtemenko, Admiral G. I. Levchenko, and others out of action, but their arrest thwarted their evil schemes.

It has been established that all these doctor-murderers, who had become monsters of mankind, trampled the sacred banner of science, and defiled the honor of scientific workers, were hired agents of foreign intelligence services.

Most of the terrorist group (M. S. Vovsi, B. B. Kogan, A. I. Feldman, A.

M. Greenstein, Ya. G. Etinger, and others) were connected with the international Jewish bourgeois-nationalist organization, the Joint,[10] created by American intelligence, purportedly for extending material aid to Jews in other countries. In fact, this organization, under the guidance of American intelligence, conducts extensive espionage, terrorist, and similar subversive activities in a number of countries, including the Soviet Union. Arrestee Vovsi confessed under interrogation that he had received instructions "to exterminate leading cadres of the USSR," from the Joint organization in the United States through intermediaries, Moscow physician Shimeliovich,[11] and the noted Jewish bourgeois-nationalist Mikhoels.[12]

Other members of the terrorist group (V. N. Vinogradov, M. B. Kogan, and P. I. Yegorov) were long-standing agents of the British intelligence service.

The investigation will be completed soon.

(Tass)

Izvestiya, January 13, 1953

SPIES AND MURDERERS IN THE GUISE OF PHYSICIANS AND SCIENTISTS

Tass reported today the discovery and apprehension by the state security organs of a terrorist group of doctors who planned through deleterious treatment to shorten the lives of prominent figures in the Soviet Union.

Documentary evidence, investigations, the conclusions of medical experts, and the confessions of those arrested established that the criminals, hidden enemies of the people, have been administering deleterious treatment to their patients, thereby undermining their health. Taking advantage of their position as physicians and abusing the patients' trust, the members of the terrorist group in a deliberately vicious manner undermined their health. Intentionally ignoring the data of an objective examination of the patients, these physicians made incorrect diagnoses and thereby killed their patients through improper treatment.

Among the members of this odious gang of murderers are professors of medicine Vovsi, Vinogradov, M. Kogan, B. Kogan, Yegorov, Feldman, Etinger, and Greenstein, and the physician Mayorov.

Comrades A. A. Zhdanov and A. S. Shcherbakov died at the hands of these cruel monsters disguised as doctors and scientists. The murderers confessed that they had incorrectly diagnosed Comrade A. A. Zhdanov's illness; concealing his myocardial infarction, they had prescribed a regimen that is contraindicated in that serious condition, thereby killing the patient. The criminals also shortened the life of Comrade A. S. Shcherbakov: they improperly administered powerful medication, prescribed a harmful regimen, and thereby drove him to his death.

These villains and wreckers tried their hardest to undermine the health of leading military cadres, to put them out of action and weaken the country's defense. Their arrest thwarted the traitors' criminal plans.

It has been established that all members of the terrorist group of physicians were hired agents of foreign intelligence services. The heinous crimes of these monsters, who had lost every human semblance, were controlled by the American and British intelligence services.

Most members of the terrorist group (Vovsi, B. Kogan, Feldman, Greenstein, Etinger, and others) had sold their body and soul to a branch of American intelligence—the international Jewish bourgeois-nationalist organization, the Joint. Numerous irrefutable facts fully demonstrated the repugnant character of this sordid Zionist espionage organization which operated under a cover of philanthropy.

It has been established that professional spies and killers from the Joint, using corrupt Jewish bourgeois-nationalists as their agents and under the guidance of American intelligence, are conducting far-flung espionage, terrorist, and other subversive activities in a number of countries, including the Soviet Union. The monster Vovsi received directives "to exterminate leading cadres of the USSR" from this international Jewish bourgeois-nationalist organization through the intermediaries, Moscow physician Shimeliovich and the well-known Jewish bourgeois-nationalist Mikhoels.

Other members of the terrorist group (Vinogradov, M. Kogan, Yegorov) turned out to be long-standing agents of the British intelligence service.

Aspiring to achieve world domination, the American monopolists and their British accomplices in the aggressive imperialist camp use all the foulest means and methods in their subversive activities. Frantically preparing to unleash a new world war, the American and British imperialists are striving to accomplish what the Nazis failed to do: to create their own subversive fifth column in the USSR. The incredibly cynical and shameless law adopted by the American government, earmarking $100 million for subversive, terrorist, and espionage activities in the socialist countries, serves as irrefutable proof of this intention.

The case of the exposed spies and murderers who were caught redhanded while hiding behind the masks of scientists and physicians demonstrates once more how far the American and British imperialists have gone in their wicked, inhuman activities, and with renewed force exposes their criminal plans before the entire world. The exposure of the gang of doctor-poisoners deals a crushing blow to these vile schemes.

It is the patriotic duty of Soviet citizens never for one minute to forget about the designs of the warmongers and their agents, indefatigably to increase their vigilance, to strengthen in every way possible our armed forces and the state intelligence organs.

The successes achieved by the Soviet people under the leadership of the party of Lenin and Stalin in Communist construction in the USSR are tremendous indeed. Having gained a historic victory in World War II, and within a brief period of time having eliminated the serious consequences of the war, the Soviet people have achieved remarkable successes in the further development of a socialist economy and culture.

Nevertheless, it would be absolutely wrong to derive the conclusion from these facts that the danger of sabotage, subversion, and espionage has already been eliminated, that the ringleaders of the imperialist camp have given up their attempts at subversive anti-Soviet activity.

Comrade Stalin teaches us not to let success generate careless, self-complacent attitudes. The imperialist intelligence services take advantage of this kind of self-complacent, thoughtless attitude for their subversive activities.

The Communist party, Lenin, and Stalin teach the Soviet people that the class struggle does not die down as we advance successfully toward communism, but rather it intensifies. "The more we forge ahead," Comrade Stalin says, "the more successes we achieve, the more the remnants of the defeated exploiting classes will become embittered. They will turn more quickly to sharper forms of confrontation, they will play dirtier tricks on the Soviet state, they will try the most desperate means, the last hope of the doomed."

After the crushing defeat and liquidation of the remnants of the exploiting classes in our country, the international bourgeoisie lost all support within the Soviet Union in its fight against the Soviet state. It nevertheless keeps trying to use vestiges of capitalism in the consciousness of Soviet citizens for its own purposes. Agents of the foreign intelligence services are ceaselessly looking for weak, vulnerable spots among certain unstable strata of our intelligentsia, which are plagued by subservience to everything foreign, by cosmopolitanism and bourgeois nationalism. These people, with their bourgeois ideology and belief in private ownership, are secret enemies of our people. They become tools of the foreign intelligence services, they harm us and will continue to do so.

To ignore this fact is to permit criminal gullibility, to leave loopholes for evil imperialist intrigues. The doctor-saboteurs were able for a certain period of time to act with impunity because some of our Soviet organs and their leaders had lost their vigilance and became infected with gullibility. As long as we are gullible, there will be sabotage. In order to eliminate sabotage, we must decisively put an end to gullibility, complacency, and relaxed vigilance.

The state security organs must be particularly vigilant. These organs did not expose the terrorist organization of the doctor-saboteurs right away, even though in the not so distant past there were cases in which enemies of the people operated in the guise of physicians. We are referring to the "doctors" Levin and Pletnev who, by incorrect treatment, murdered the great Russian writer A. M. Gorky, and the prominent Soviet statesmen V. V. Kuybyshev and V. R. Menzhinsky. The leaders of the Soviet Ministry of Health also overlooked the sabotage and terrorist activity of these hirelings of the imperialist intelligence services.

Soviet citizens with anger and indignation condemn the crimes of these monstrous poisoners who, under the cover of the noble medical profession, trampled the sacred banner of science and defiled the honor of scientists. The Soviet people will crush the vile traitors of our homeland, the contemptible hirelings of foreign intelligence services, who sold out for dollars and pounds sterling! Our people with anger and indignation also condemn the foreign masters of the criminal gang of murderers: the American and British imperialists. Let them remember that the long arm of justice will reach them as well!

Novoye Vremya, no. 4, 1953, pp. 13–16
V. Minayev

ZIONIST TOOLS OF THE AMERICAN INTELLIGENCE SERVICES

The Soviet people were filled with anger and indignation by the monstrous crimes perpetrated by the terrorist gang of physician-saboteurs exposed by the state security organs of the Soviet Union.

There is no limit to the despicable baseness of these cruel monsters who hide behind the noble title of doctor and defile the sacred banner of science. An investigation has established that the group of murderous doctors planned through detrimental treatment to do away with prominent Soviet figures. Taking advantage of their position as doctors, the criminals made deliberately incorrect diagnoses and thereby killed their patients through improper "treatment."

The base murderers thus did away with such leading Soviet statesmen as A. A. Zhdanov and A. S. Shcherbakov.

The criminals have confessed that they incorrectly diagnosed Comrade

A. A. Zhdanov's illness. Concealing his real condition—a myocardial infarction—they prescribed a regimen that was contraindicated in that serious condition, thereby killing him. An inquest has revealed that the criminals also shortened the life of Comrade A S. Shcherbakov; they improperly administered powerful medication, prescribed a regimen that was ruinous to the patient's health, and thereby drove him to his death.

These beasts in the guise of physicians pursued unmistakably subversive purposes. The criminals tried their hardest to undermine the health of leading military figures, in order to weaken the defense of the Soviet Union. They tried to disable Marshals A. M. Vasilevsky, L. A. Govorov, and I. S. Konev, General of the Army S. M. Shtemenko, Admiral G. I. Levchenko, and others.

The subversive activity of the group of murderous physicians was directed by the hand of imperialist warmongers. The criminals had sold out and served the interests of the American and British intelligence services.

Most of this villainous gang, including Professors Vovsi, B. Kogan, Feldman, Greenstein, Etinger, and others, were connected with the international Jewish bourgeois-nationalistic Joint organization, founded by the American intelligence services purportedly to provide material aid to Jews in other countries. Under the direction of the American intelligence services, this organization actually carries on large-scale espionage, terrorist, and other subversive activities in a number of countries, including the Soviet Union. During the investigation, prisoner Vovsi admitted to having received instructions from the American Zionist Joint organization "to exterminate prominent leaders of the USSR." Other members of the terrorist group (Vinogradov, M. Kogan, Yegorov) turned out to be long-standing agents of the British intelligence services.

The Joint organization (whose full name is Joint Distribution Committee) was established in the United States during World War I. Its officially proclaimed purpose was to provide help from American Jews to their co-religionists in foreign countries. But philanthropy only served and serves as a coverup for the espionage and subversive activity of this Zionist organization created by the American intelligence service.

The Joint was very active in this direction after World War II in the socialist countries. Its criminal activity in those countries is directed by a Jewish Division headed by American intelligence agent Schwartz. Spying activities of Jewish bourgeois-nationalists from the Joint were discovered in Hungary. The director of the Joint in Hungary, I. Jacobson, was expelled from the country in December 1949 on charges of spying and subversive activities.

The activity of the Joint was prohibited within the territory of the Soviet

534 / ANTI-SEMITISM IN THE SOVIET UNION

Union. Nevertheless, the arrest of the group of physician-saboteurs makes it clear that the agents of this espionage and sabotage organization have continued to operate underground, under careful disguise.

The villainous crimes of the group of physician-saboteurs acting under the direction of the Zionist espionage Joint organization demonstrated the true nature of the "philanthropy" and "aid" that the American warmongers use to cover up their vile deeds. Press reports indicate that progressive public opinion in all countries condemns the criminal activities of the Zionist hirelings of American imperialism.

At the same time, public opinion raises the question: What do Zionism and its organization represent? What part do they play in the warmongers' plans?

Zionism is a reactionary bourgeois-nationalist movement. It arose in the 1880s among Jewish bourgeois circles in Austria, Germany, Russia, and other countries. Representing the narrow mercenary interests of the wealthy Jewish bourgeoisie, its main purpose is to divert the Jewish working masses away from the class struggle and participation in the revolutionary movement, and to direct their attention to migration to Palestine. V. I. Lenin stressed that "the notion of Jewish 'nationality' bears a clearly reactionary connotation not only among its consistent advocates (the Zionists) but even among those who try to blend it with the ideas of social democracy (the Bundists)."

Born in a period when the Jewish masses were engulfed by anti-Semitic persecutions and repression, Zionism extended its influence to a significant section of the petty bourgeoisie: merchants, artisans, craftsmen, and backward elements of the Jewish proletariat.

On the eve of World War I, some Zionist leaders openly sided with German imperialism and maintained contact with the government of Wilhelm II. The leading Zionist body, the Aktionskomitee, was located in Cologne until the war, then in Berlin.

When the war broke out, the Zionist leaders officially proclaimed a policy of "neutrality." At the same time, they did not prevent the Zionist organizations in various countries from publicizing their ostentatious "patriotism," because the Jewish wealthy bourgeoisie made profits from war supplies and speculation.

The interests of a "united nation" were relegated to a secondary position. The Zionist and Bundist bourgeois-nationalist organizations of Poland collaborated with the German occupiers. In Russia, the Zionists expressed their "loyal feelings" to tsarism. The tactics of these "moneybag patriots" were well received by the ruling circles of the belligerent countries.

But the "international" nature of Zionist activity did not completely suit the British imperialists. Desiring Palestine in order to safeguard British interests in the Middle East, they decided to use the Zionist leaders by luring them with the promise of establishing a Jewish state in Palestine.

The Zionist leaders gladly harnessed themselves to the chariot of British imperialism, the more so since they had become its hired agents even before the well-known Balfour Declaration was published in 1917. From 1915, the most prominent Zionist figure and head of the international Zionist organization, Weizmann, lived in England and, in his capacity as a chemistry professor, worked on military projects for the British government. Another prominent Zionist leader, Jabotinsky, organized the Jewish Brigade, which participated in the war on the side of the Entente.

The mutual class interests of the Zionist leaders and British imperialists made them allies in the fight against the working masses, against the national-liberation movements in the Middle East. The imperialists encouraged the Zionists' colonizing efforts in Palestine, expecting to use them to consolidate their own rule in that country.

At the 1920 San Remo Conference, Britain received a mandate to govern Palestine. The role of its Zionist agents became significantly more important.

The British imperialists strengthened Zionism. Specifically, they maintained close connections with the Zionist elements among the White Guard Russian emigrés. All leaders of the Russian Zionists, including Kerensky's personal friends and closest collaborators, Rutenberg, Naiditch, Margolin, Yaffe,[13] and others, who fled Russia after the October Revolution, started working for the Foreign Office and the intelligence service.

Based on Article 4 of the Palestine Mandate, Britain created the so-called Jewish Agency, whose functions were entrusted to a Zionist organization headed by Weizmann. The supreme executive body of international Zionism was thereby assigned various duties, including police activities. Zionists were also appointed to various posts in the British colonial administration.

Exploiting this situation, Zionists in Palestine conducted a brutal extermination campaign against the local Arab population. Zionist armed detachments captured land from the Arab peasants and chased them into the desert. Arab workers were driven out from business enterprises. By 1935, the Zionist organizations and individual Jewish capitalists had gained control of more than a third of the best fertile land in Palestine. The Zionists unleashed frenzied land speculation in the country. For the exploitation of the captured lands, they created two large colonization concerns: the Jewish National Fund and the Palestine Jewish Colonization Association.

With the backing of British monopolies, the wealthy Jewish bourgoisie grabbed the most important concessions to exploit mineral resources, build power plants, etc. Jewish Zionist capital in Palestine became the most important social support of British imperialism.

The Zionist movement has a far-flung network that covers many countries.

The Zionist organization unites a great number of groups, religious and "cultural-educational" societies, as well as "philanthropic" organizations operating in different countries. They include, for instance, the United Jewish Appeal, an international organization for the collection of funds for Israel among Jewish capitalists, and the already-mentioned Joint.

For an extended period of time, most of the leading figures of Zionism acted as agents of British imperialism. Many of them, for instance Abba Eban and Reuben Shiloah, served in the intelligence service. Until the late 1920s, London was the main Zionist center.

But this situation did not suit the interests of an influential group of American Zionists, some of them important Wall Street representatives. Desiring Zionism to be under their political control as their own tool, American monopolies first used the influence and financial potential of the major American Jewish capitalists.

At Wall Street's behest, the International Zionist Congress at Zurich in July 1929 adopted a resolution to enlist the cooperation of representatives of American capital in the Jewish Agency.

That was how Zionism came under American influence. The well-known New York millionaire Nathan Straus provided the Zionists with such significant funds that a Zionist colony in Palestine was named Netanya in his honor. Very large sums of money were donated to Jewish religious organizations by John D. Rockefeller, Jr. A group of American capitalists formed a stockholding company, the Palestine Economic Corporation, which brought American capital investments in Palestine's industry and trade under its control. The New York banking house of Lehman Brothers played the decisive role in the creation of this concern. One partner of this banking house was Harold Szold, whose brother Robert Szold was the head of the Zionist organization in the United States. Benjamin Cohen, a State Department adviser, became general manager of the Palestine Economic Corporation.

After World War II, the struggle within the Zionist organization between the British and the American groups continued, although the commanding positions were passing into the hands of the "dollar" Zionist-hirelings. Leading figures in the Israel government, such as Ben-Gurion, Sharett, Shiloah (organizer of the Israeli intelligence services), and other Zionist leaders, carried out the instructions they received from the State Department. Their close political connection with the American imperialists is shown by their support of Washington's aggressive policy on the international scene. Present-day Zionism is at the service of American aggression and the imperialists in preparing for a new world war. Zionist propaganda serves the same interests. Specifically, the Zionist organizations are a breeding ground for corrupt cosmopolitan ideas which accord perfectly with bourgeois nationalism.

The Zionists help American imperialist warmongers daily. The anti-Soviet direction of Zionism fits into the same picture. A maliciously hostile attitude to the Soviet Union and toward the entire peace-loving, democratic camp is typical of the Zionist leaders. Israel's representative at the United Nations, the Zionist Eban, helps the Anglo-American bloc defeat Soviet motions to strengthen the peace and security of all peoples. Zionist figures and the leaders of the State of Israel conduct a defamation campaign against the Soviet Union, against its policy of strengthening peace and friendship among peoples.

By supporting the American imperialists' policy of unleashing a new world war in order to achieve world supremacy, the Zionists in fact also support all that accompanies that policy. This includes, in particular, the resurrection of Nazi schemes and the establishment of bloody fascist regimes imbued with the spirit of wild racist fanaticism, including anti-Semitism. By supporting this policy and facilitating its implementation, the Zionists reveal themselves not only as enemies of peace and democracy but also as enemies of the Jewish working classes.

By selling out to American imperialism, the Zionist leaders have put their organization and societies at the service of American intelligence. The recent trial of Slansky's[14] conspiratorial gang in Prague demonstrated this in the most obvious manner. The American spy, the Zionist Orenstein, described during the trial a secret meeting of Truman, Acheson, and the then Secretary of the Treasury, Morgenthau, with the Zionist leaders Ben-Gurion and Sharett in Washington in 1947. At the meeting, the so-called Morgenthau-Acheson Plan was adopted, which established the conditions under which the United States would provide support and aid for Israel. A result of that plan was that the American intelligence services made wide use of the Zionist organizations. All those "cultural-educational," "philanthropic," and other societies were turned into centers and sources of personnel for spying and subversive activity against the democratic countries. For the same criminal work, the Zionists put members of their organization that were in the diplomatic service at the disposal of American intelligence. It was revealed at the trial of the Slansky gang, for instance, that Israel's former envoys to Prague, Avriel (Überall) and Kubovy, had worked in close contact with the spies and saboteurs, given them instructions, protected them from failure, etc.

The dirty image and foul activities of the Zionist espionage and sabotage organizations were revealed in an even stronger light as a result of the exposure by the Soviet state security organs of the terrorist group of physicians connected with the Joint, which had plotted to do away with prominent Soviet figures.

The unmasking of the gang of murderous doctors dealt a blow to the leaders of Zionism and their masters, the American warmongers. The Zionist agents were caught and will be crushed. Punishment will also overtake the inspirers of these murderers.

Those who fight for peace expose and suppress the activities of each and every one of the hirelings of aggressive American imperialism. This includes the activities of its fifth column in the democratic countries, the Jewish bourgeois nationalists.

Krokodil, no. 3, 1953, p. 2[15]

POISONERS

"He walked down the stone steps, between the charred half-underground stumps, into his mud hut. Without causing the door to creak, he went quietly inside, put the earthenware pot on the tablecloth, and with his long hands began throwing some mysterious herbs into it; he took a pitcher made of some strange wood, drew water and started pouring, all the while mumbling some incantation."

The image of the sorcerer in whose hell-kitchen murderous plans were brewing was sketched by Gogol in his story "Terrible Vengeance." This sinister image was deeply imprinted in our memory in childhood. With horror and repugnance we remember the evil spirit, possessed by hatred for mankind, who hides like a bat or vampire in dark, out-of-the-way corners. Old men, women, and children died at his hands. The writer outlined the genealogy of the bloody hero of his story. He referred to him as a man without any honest kith and kin or posterity. To his name of Peter he added the prefix Judas.

The image of traitor and murderer drawn by the Russian writer pales before the monstrous faces of the villains who appear not in the gloomy Middle Ages but in our time, illumined by the light of genuine humanism. These miscreants were not ignorant people like Gogol's sorcerer; they were doctors of medical science, they held professor's rank. They dressed in the white physician's coat, that symbol of spiritual purity, compassion, and service to the noble cause of healing human ailments. People entering the hospital wards entrusted them with their most precious possession: their health, their lives. The patient would look trustingly at the venerable professor standing at his bedside. Their eyes would meet. Vovsi, B. Kogan and M. Kogan, Feldman, Greenstein, Etinger, Vinogradov, and Yegorov knew how to change the expression of their eyes, to give their wolfish souls a human appearance, to put on a mask, to lie and dodge! They knew how to play the role of noble persons. They had studied at the well-known school of the hypocrite Mikhoels, for whom there was nothing sacred, who for thirty pieces of silver had sold his soul to the "Yellow Devil's country," which he had chosen for his homeland. The poisoners also took classes in masquerading from their medical colleague, the criminal Shimeliovich.

Vovsi, B. Kogan, Feldman, Greenstein, and Etinger were controlled by the American-run terrorist and espionage organization, the Joint. That organization purports to be a philanthropic institution highly favorable to Israel whose mission is to help their blood brothers and sisters. That is a blatant lie; just like many other American organizations, the Joint cares little about suffering and poverty-ridden humanity, not even about their own blood brothers and sisters who eke out a miserable existence in America itself, and are separated from the hundred-percent Yankees by the ghetto boundary.

The Joint is but one center of the international Zionist organization which carries out the dirty and bloody assignments of imperialist America's ringleaders. The evil schemes of world domination obsess Morgan, Rockefeller, Ford, Truman, McCarran, and McCarthy. They spend dollars on hiring spies and terrorists. Both within their own country and beyond its wide frontiers, these gentlemen seek those from across the Atlantic Ocean who can be bought with bribes, who will forgo honor and conscience, responsibility and duty, for lowly, selfish reasons.

This scum of human society, these people whose hearts, in Balzac's words, have become covered over with wool, have taken advantage of their positions as physicians in order to kill. They carried out their masters' instructions "to exterminate leading cadres of the USSR." The beloved members of the Communist party and the Soviet people, Comrades A. A. Zhdanov and A. S. Shcherbakov, have become victims of the murderous doctors.

The monsters continued to implement their criminal designs. They selected as additional victims our generals, whose names are honored by all Soviet citizens.

One group of vile spies and murderers masquerading as medical figures received their instructions and dollars from America. The other group, which included Vinogradov, M. Kogan, and Yegorov, received orders and pounds sterling from England, and served the British intelligence services, not out of fear but because their consciences so dictated. They shall remain in the memory of our people as the embodiment of baseness and meanness, as an offspring of the same Judas.

The gang of Judases has been dealt a heavy blow. A similar blow has struck the American and British warmongers. The entire world has seen once more what kind of cannibals are hiding in the caverns of Wall Street. The tentacles of these hydras have often reached out over the seas and oceans to our frontiers. We know that the great Russian writer A. M. Gorky and the prominent statesmen V. V. Kuybyshev and V. R. Menzhinsky were murdered on orders from foreign intelligence services. To the names of the old murderers—the doctors Levin and Pletnev—have now been added the names of the new murderers, who called themselves doctors of medical science and worked in Soviet clinics.

The people's punishment, just retribution, will befall this gang of hired spies and terrorists.

All Soviet people must learn a lesson from what has happened. The unprecedented victory won by the heroic Soviet people in the war, their successes in peaceful construction after the war, give rise to a legitimate feeling of national Soviet pride.

But victories and successes should not lead to an attitude of calm and complacency. A mortally wounded snake musters all its forces in order to rise and bite the one who wanted to render the viper harmless. The same applies to our enemies. They are refining their attempts to harm the Soviet nation, her people and her party. Vigilance and ever more vigilance—this is the ironclad rule of our life, this is the true guarantee for the strength, power, and might of our homeland!

Spiteful anger against our great country has united together in one camp American and British bankers, owners of colonies, weapons manufacturers, defeated Nazi generals dreaming of revenge, papal delegates, and agents of the Zionist kahal. Scouts from the other camp are infiltrating our land. That camp recruits its disciples from among those internal emigrés within our country who still harbor vestiges of bourgeois ideology, and of the psychology and morality of private property. These outcasts are still trying to let their contemptible existence be known. They still use the dagger, subversion, poison.

The sorcerer of Gogol's story has received his just reward. The sacred wrath and merciless punishment of the Soviet people will descend on the gang of doctors-poisoners.

SAMIZDAT

Boris Polevoi

A LETTER TO THE SOVIET AUTHORITIES

Now that anti-Soviet ideologists in the West, having wasted too much ammunition on the events in Hungary, have slackened their attacks on us from this direction, they have renewed and intensified their slanderous propaganda in connection with the so-called Jewish question in the Soviet Union. These attacks follow three lines:

1. Anti-Semitism is allegedly growing in the USSR, which is supported by statements that the Jewish press remains suppressed, even after the Twentieth Party Congress, and there is no Jewish theater.
2. The creation of Jewish literature has been stopped, and the known authors writing in Yiddish do not find an outlet for their literary activity. These arguments are usually reinforced by throwing in here and there the names of Jewish authors no longer alive, who were rehabilitated posthumously.
3. The Soviet Union, while promising to restore Jewish culture in the country, actually misleads public opinion.

Articles to this effect are being published at an increasing rate in British, French, and Italian magazines, not to mention U.S. publications. It is quite obvious that this is done in order to turn away from the Soviet Union our friends among the progressive intelligentsia, and also in order to make difficult the return to our camp of numerous progressive intellectuals who renounced us following the Hungarian events. More and more writers have been recruited for this campaign, and such a voice was recently heard in Iceland, which has never seen a Jew on its soil.

The situation is aggravated by the fact that we do not follow a consistent line in this problem. Last summer, after a preliminary consultation with the Party Central Committee, the heads of the Writers' Union and several outstanding Jewish authors living in Moscow met with representatives of the foreign Jewish press visiting the Soviet Union, in particular with Mr. Suller, publisher of the progressive New York newspaper *Morgen Frayhayt*, Mr. Koenig, editor-in-chief of the Paris Communist paper *Neue Press*, and Mr. Shoskes, representing the New York bourgeois newspaper *Tog Morgen Journal*, and told them that we were considering publication of an anthology in Yiddish and of a small collection of books. They also welcomed the proposal of the representatives of foreign Jewish press to establish contacts between Soviet Jewish writers and progressive foreign Yiddish periodicals, and to send journalistic and artistic materials, etc., to these periodicals.

Information on these meetings was widely and usually objectively given in the bourgeois and progressive Jewish press. Suller and Koenig, as could be learned from the papers, went on a lecturing tour in different parts of the world and, according to the press, gave a fair account of what they had seen in the Soviet Union. . . .

Moscow, 1957

The traces of crimes.
Drawing by Kukryniksy. *Krokodil,* no. 3, 1953.

The 1960s

MATERIAL FROM SOVIET PERIODICALS

Literatura I Zhizn, September 27, 1961
D. Starikov

ABOUT A CERTAIN POEM

Let us discuss a poem by Ye. Yevtushenko, "Babi Yar," which was published by *Literaturnaya Gazeta* this September 19. I don't know how you may feel about it, but when I discuss this poem, I don't bother about the rhymes or worry about the low literary quality. Babi Yar: does today's young reader of Yevtushenko's poems know what Babi Yar means? Perhaps, too, middle-aged and elderly people have forgotten about it. And did the author himself really think about it well?

For three nights in a row, I have been rereading the war literature—books by Mikhail Sholokhov, Ilya Ehrenburg, Aleksey Tolstoy, Leonid Leonov, Aleksandr Fadeyev. . . . A huge, inexpressible sorrow rises from these historic pages—exactly as it really was. The sorrow of millions and millions of peaceful people.

. . . A fifteen-hundred-strong crowd—old people, women, children—is being herded along the road. Pits have already been dug for them, some three kilometers outside of town. They are being forced to undress. They are being driven into the pits in groups of five and machine-gunned down. At the end of the day, they begin filling in the pits with earth. Half-alive people move under a thin layer of earth. The earth was moving . . . The earth was moaning.

. . . Mariya Bilyk, the wife of a soldier at the front, was taken in daylight. Her children were taken at night. Eleven-year-old Volodya carried his two-year-old brother, Fedya, in his arms. They were followed by little Tanyusha and Ganulya. Mikolka, who had resisted, was dragged by a leather belt. They were all thrown alive into the ravine. When our troops returned from war and the graves were opened, they found Volodya embracing Fedya in his arms. . . . It happened when Anton Bilyk was still writing to them, asking how Mariya and the children were doing.

. . . At night after the shootings, a naked woman staggered out of one of the graves. She was covered with earth. She took several steps and then fell, dead.

. . ."Murder Bus": an eight-ton diesel truck with a chamber lined with heavy-duty metal sheeting which is impenetrable—it can't be bitten through or scratched. Exhaust gases are channeled from the engine directly into this hermetically-sealed space through a pipe equipped with an unblockable mesh. Nastasya Suprun was imprisoned in a Gestapo cell together with her fourteen-year-old niece. They were suspected of collaboration with our intelligence. "Ninochka was brought in again after torture. She lay unconscious for three hours, her mouth bleeding. When she came to, she said quietly, 'Aunt Asya, What will happen to me?' When the murder bus came back after a day of bloody activity, Ninochka was sent to clean it. She said she saw bits of cloth on the floor, hair, eyeglasses, and excrement. Then she was taken away for interrogation again. They beat her with sticks, and again she was brought back unconscious. . . . On November 4, Ninochka was taken from the cell and no one ever saw her again."

. . . When the corpses were exhumed, children, balls, and dolls were found among them. . . .

Where was it: in the pits near Smolensk; in Babi Yar outside of Kiev; or near Piryatin, not far from Poltava; in the ravine of Tripolye, on the road to Obukhov; or was it perhaps at Zmyevskaya ravina near Rostov; at the antitank ditch beyond the glassworks, one kilometer from Mineralnye Vody; or in the Drobitsky Yar beyond the tractor plant in Kharkov? . . .

"The word *Yar* used to be a good word: it meant grass, the river, sand, and big daisies by which the girls used to see whether they were loved or not. But now the word *Yar* means horror. It seems that at any moment ghosts of the dead may come forth from it. . . . Whoever can forget about it is inhuman!"

Where were those girls taken? To Frankfurt? To Berlin? To Kustrin?

"Dear Mother, little brother Genya and Simyon Ivanovitch, my dear relatives, do not forget me! My dear Mother, my life is finished. No one will save me from here. No words, Mother, can tell you how cruelly they treat us—how hard they make us toil for them. They beat us and make us work far beyond what strength permits. We work naked and barefoot. And it is winter, Mother . . . And if you say one word, you will only regret it. My God, what have we done? Why do they torture us so? Some girls swallow needles and go mad from this life. God, my life is finished. Farewell, Mother. Farewell, farewell. Now you must live for me."

". . . On March 1, we'll be getting three Ukrainian girls to work in the vegetable garden, and two more girls to work around the house. And work they will, I assure you. We will also get two prisoners of war. I'm looking forward to it, and I hope that things will improve on the farm then. Everyone who employs Russians says that it doesn't cost much."

Oh no, this is not too much documentation, not too many names, not too many experiences. This is only one-thousandth or one-millionth of what we think about when we mention Babi Yar. What words can express all that?

"No monuments?" "A rough gravestone?" "The whistling of wild grass?" "The trees look gloomy?" "Everything here cries in silence?". . . And more: "I'm frightened. I feel my hair is turning gray, and I myself am a soundless shriek. Nothing in me can forget about it . . ." Thus Yevgeny Yevtushenko speaks about Babi Yar.

No, these are not my words. Today, Ilya Ehrenburg's poem of 1944 is much closer to me. It is also called "Babi Yar":

> I once lived in towns.
> And the living people were dear to me.
> Now I must look for their graves.
> In faraway empty lots.
> Now I know every ravine.
> Every ravine is my home now.
> I once kissed the hand
> of this beloved woman.
> Though I didn't know her
> When she was living . . .

Yes, I realize these are sick verses. They are sick like a huge, open wound . . .

> Turn off the lights.
> Lower the flags.
> We have come to you.
> We, the ravines . . .

It's frightening. But when I think of it, I cannot be more eloquent about how frightful it is. How I took off my hat and how my hair began turning gray . . .

No. I don't mean to compare poems. And I don't mean to discuss talents. And moreover, the degree of talent of different people is not the question here. I want to speak about literature and life. Or, to be more precise, about literature and death. About the author's attitude toward the life and death of millions.

Why did Ilya Ehrenburg write his verse about Babi Yar in 1944?

What an inappropriate question. An absurd one! Why do people laugh or cry? Why do their hearts beat? And why do they ache? The writer's genuine pain and just indignation echo in the fighters' souls. And they become inflamed with hatred for the enemy, and firmer becomes the finger on the trigger, and sharper becomes the eye peering through the sight.

But why has Yevgeny Yevtushenko returned to this theme now, in 1961?

Perhaps he has recalled Babi Yar in order to warn the world about the danger of fascism? Or perhaps he could no longer keep silent after hearing the shrieks of the West German curs, seeking revenge? Or perhaps he wants to remind some of his contemporaries of the heroic deeds and exploits and of the sacrifices made by their fathers?

Nothing of the kind. Standing above Babi Yar, the young Soviet poet has found inspiration only for verses critical of anti-Semitism. And reflecting today about the people who perished—"a gunned-down old man, a gunned-down child"—he was thinking only about one thing: that they were Jewish. That was the most important aspect to him!

Three days ago, I was talking to a Russian Soviet writer, Jewish according to his identity card. He told me, among other things, that right after the war—when he served with our Occupation Forces in Germany—he was asked by an Allied officer to be the Soviet representative at the memorial service held in honor of the Jews who fell at the hands of the fascists. Jewish officers from the British, American, and French garrisons had already consented to participate in the service. "I realize that you, as a Communist, are a nonbeliever, but you should not miss this service, because you are Jewish, after all." And this is what the Soviet patriot answered him: "I do not doubt the good intentions of the Western officers in organizing this service, but it dishonors the people of other nationalities who also perished in the struggle against Nazism. We are international-ists."

Yes, the fascist invaders shot tens of thousands of Jews in Babi Yar, near Kiev. "The cruelty of Nazi Germany was manifested most clearly by the murder of Jewish old women and children. But didn't the fascists do the same to the Russians and the Ukrainians, to the Poles and the Yugoslavs?" wrote Ilya Ehrenburg in 1944. "Why did the Germans kill the Jews?" he wrote in 1943 in the wake of the tragedy in Piryatin. "This is a rhetorical question. The Germans killed hundreds of Ukrainians in the same Piryatin. They killed two hundred White Russians in the village of Klubovka. They are killing Frenchmen in Grenoble, and they are killing Greeks in Crete. They kill unarmed people, for that is their raison d'etre." "They say, 'We are against the Jews.' This is a lie. . . . In Yugoslavia, the Germans declared that the Serbians were the inferior race. In Poland they turned the Poles into slaves. They hate all nations." These are quotations from Ilya Ehrenburg's article written in 1941.

I am looking for references to fascist anti-Semitism in his wartime articles, in order to understand fully why he did not make the point in his tragic verses about Babi Yar that the victims there were Jewish. I find the explanation in the sincerity and depth of the writer's emotions, which excluded classifying the dead by their origins, and in the natural internationalism of his world outlook at that time—as well as in his grasp of "the nature of fascism and the nature of Hitler's army."

All the Soviet writers who fought together with the people realized that. It is very embittering to see that today's young Soviet poet has not learned from his elders, who have seen and experienced so much. As strange as it may seem, he has probably not heard that genocide—the annihilation of whole nations—was an integral part of fascist ideology, and that the fascists' anti-Semitism was one aspect of their misanthropic policy of genocide. He probably does not realize that the liquidation of the Jews was, for the Nazi rabble, only the beginning of a master-plan for the calculated liquidation of all the "inferior races," including the Slavs. ("The Slav human mass, being race wastage, is unworthy to occupy its lands," declared the maniacal Hitler in his *Mein Kampf.* "Who can dispute my right to annihilate millions of Slavs?")

A writer must know all this, whatever his intentions in approaching this problem, because he should not fail to contemplate the historical meaning and content of what we call Babi Yar, when setting out to fight anti-Semitism: this age-old infamy salvaged by the fascists from the wastebasket of history and raised as their standard.

Should we see in the tragedy of Babi Yar only an historic example of anti-Semitism?! The fate of the people who perished there, intertwined by hundreds of visible and invisible threads with the fate of all those who perished in those terrible years, those who survived, and those who were victorious, cry out against this.

Nothing can change the logic of life; one may deceive oneself but the logic is not changed. It suffices to close one's eyes for a moment, to turn away from Babi Yar as it really was, away from all those ditches, ravines, and pits, from the black clouds which, to this day, have not dissipated, and one treads, like Yevtushenko on very dangerous ground. Beware, the festering swamp is greedy and inexorable. It has claimed so many lives already. One can't afford to close one's eyes. One can't afford to turn away. Once you've done that, you have taken the first fatal step.

> Today I am old in years
> as all the Jewish people.
> Now I seem to be a Jew
> Here I plod through ancient Egypt.
> Here I perish crucified, on the cross,
> and to this day I bear the scars of nails.

Consider what predominates here—the humiliating condescension of "somebody who is not like them" ("there is no Jewish blood in my veins," Yevtushenko tells us) or the "saintly simplicity" of ignorance, or perhaps of political tactlessness?

The fascists loved drawing genealogical trees. Aren't we being offered here a sort of inverse racism? What, indeed, is the true historical connection between the immediate descendants of Tevye the milkman who were mercilessly slain in Babi Yar and the ancient Hebrews whose legends have come down to us through the Old Testament? They're all "Semites," you say? Well, well, such an approach to the question of nationality would have earned the highest praise from the "Aryans." . . . The pogromists used to say that the Jews "crucified our Christ." Must we replace this disgusting stupidity with another one—namely, that Christ was a Jew?

Couldn't we do without such "scientific" polemics?

And what is the value of equally illiterate and ill-founded exclamations about the "Jewish people as such, in general"? You had better ask those few of our compatriots who paid heed to the "call of the blood" (which in some mysterious way coincided with the sweet siren of nationalistic bourgeois propaganda) and believed that there does exist a "Jew as such," and emigrated to Israel. Their decision to trade the Soviet motherland for the imaginary homeland of all Jews is a matter for their civil and human conscience. But why doesn't the tragedy of most of those who have left the Soviet Union for Israel stir the heart of the poet who, with his effete cleverness, has tackled with one swoop ancient, modern, and contemporary history?

Yevtushenko feels at ease in the unenviable role of the hatemonger deliberately or accidentally stirring up the dying embers of racial prejudice. This is tantamount to being careless with the truth . . . and simple-minded, too. Babi Yar evoked in him some rather strange historical associations, which he hastened to impart to his readers.

Strange associations? No, not just that: because they are offensive, too.

They are an offense to the memory of the fallen Soviet people, including the Jews. But as if that were not enough:

> O my Russian people! I know
> you are international to the core.
> But those with unclean hands
> have often made a jingle of your purest name.
> I know the goodness of my land.
> How vile these anti-Semites—without a qualm
> they pompously called themselves
> the Union of the Russian People!

. . . Monstrous as it may seem, Yevtushenko did not mention even one word about Nazism or fascist invaders. It didn't even occur to him while he was standing above Babi Yar. He thought about the Russian people, but not because they were in the vanguard of the struggle against the universal murderers, and not because they sacrificed the most in this struggle, nor because together with the rest of the Soviet peoples and the other socialist nations they today lead the struggle aimed at preventing this tragedy from recurring tenfold. Isn't this omission offensive?

"The Union of the Archangel Michael" . . . "Claw-footed drunkards, spitting out wolf-howls, horrible, twisted, sweaty manlike creatures and anathemas," this is how Konstantin Fedin described pogromists in his *Brothers*. . . . But what do the Russian people have to do with this?—those Russians who set up the militant workers' units to fight the Black Hundreds or the Union of the Archangel Michael. Those people voiced their loudest protests against anti-Semitism through the mouths of Leo Tolstoy, Chekhov, Korolenko, Gorky, and Vladimir Ilich Lenin; and they rallied all the peoples of our vast land into one Union of Soviet Socialist Republics. . . . At present the friendship between our peoples is strong and monolithic as never before.

So why does the editorial board of the All-Union Writers' newspaper allow Yevtushenko to offend triumphant Leninist policies with such comparisons and reminders which cannot be interpreted in any other way than as being provocative? In the name of what does Yevtushenko go out of his way to drown out the victorious hum of our working life, the polyphonic complexity of our international relations to which the latest tremors of underground atomic explosions add their chords? . . .

Yes, white is white and black is black, and they are not the same. But is the white flag of pacifism truly the standard of those who fight against the black bandits' flag? Is the six-pointed Star of David the right emblem for the true fighters against anti-Semitism?

I'm not interested in knowing the true intentions of Yevgeny Yevtushenko when he sat down to write about Babi Yar. The road to hell is
paved with good intentions, as we well know. We would probably be
justified in supposing that there are also some bad intentions: his long-
cherished penchant for baiting his readers in every possible way. . . . But
this is not important. What is important is that the source of the unbearable falseness which permeates Yevtushenko's "Babi Yar" is actually a
retreat from Communist ideology to a form of bourgeois ideology. This is
irrefutable.

Literaturnaya Gazeta, October 14, 1961

Letter to the Editor

Since I have been abroad, I only recently obtained a copy of the
September 27 issue of *Literatura i zhizn* which carried D. Starikov's article
"About a Certain Poem." I feel compelled to declare that D. Starikov has
been rather arbitrary in quoting from my articles and poems out of context,
in a way which supports his ideas but contradicts mine.

Respectfully,
I. Ehrenburg

October 3, 1961

Pravda, March 10, 1963

THE GREAT STRENGTH OF SOVIET LITERATURE AND ART LIES
IN HIGH IDEOLOGICAL AND ARTISTIC STANDARDS

(Speech delivered by Comrade N. S. Khrushchev on March 10, 1963, at a meeting between party and government leaders and artistic and literary figures)

. . . The Central Committee has been receiving letters expressing concern
over the fact that certain literary works distort the position of Jews in our
country. There is even a slanderous campaign being waged against us by
the bourgeois press, as you know from the exchange of letters between the
British philospher Russell and myself.[16]

We touched this point at our December meeting, when we discussed
Yevtushenko's poem "Babi Yar." Present circumstances demand that we
return to this point.

Why was this poem criticized? For failing to depict truthfully the fascist—yes, fascist—criminals and to condemn them for the mass murders they committed at Babi Yar. The poem portrays only one group of people—the Jews—as victims of the fascist murderers. This despite the fact that many Russians, Ukrainians, and members of other Soviet nationalities also perished there.

This poem shows that the author lacks political maturity and is ignorant of the historical facts.

For whom, and for what reason, should the Jewish population in our country be portrayed as if it was mistreated? This is a lie. Since the time of the October Revolution, the Jews have enjoyed equal rights with all the other nationalities in the USSR. There is no Jewish problem in the USSR, and those who invent it sing to somebody else's tune.

The Russian working class, traditionally, has been an irreconcilable enemy of all forms of national oppression—including anti-Semitism.

Before the revolution, I used to live among miners. The workers condemned those who took part in anti-Jewish pogroms. The pogroms were instigated by the autocratic government, by capitalists, landlords, and by the bourgeoisie. They needed the pogroms as a means of diverting the working class from the revolutionary struggle. The organizers of the pogroms were the police, the gendarmes, the members of the Black Hundreds who recruited hoodlums from the dregs of society, from declassed elements. In towns their agents were usually yard-keepers.

For example, the famous Bolshevik revolutionary Baumann, who was not Jewish, was killed in Moscow by a yard-keeper upon the gendarmes' orders.

The internationalism of the Russian working people was depicted in the wonderful novel *Mother* by Gorky. There were people of many nationalities among the revolutionary workers. It should suffice to recall the Russian worker Pavel Vlasov and the Ukrainian, Andrey Nakhodka.

I spent my childhood and adolescence in the town of Yuzovka. Many Jews lived there at that time. For some time, I worked at a factory together with the metalworker Yakov Issakovitch Kutikov. He was a qualified worker. There were other Jews, too, among the factory workers. I remember a Jewish copper smelter—and that was considered to be a very high position at that time. I often saw him. He must have been a religious man because he did not work on Saturdays, but since all the Russians and Ukrainians did work then, he would come to the factory and spend the whole day there, though he didn't do any work.

There were Russians, Ukrainians, Poles, Jews, Latvians, Estonians, and others working at the factory. At times, you could not tell the nationality of the workers. There were comradely feelings among the workers of all nationalities at the factory.

That is class unity. That is proletarian internationalism.

When I was in the United States, and was on my way to Los Angeles, a Jewish deputy mayor joined us, and he introduced himself. He spoke fluent Russian, although he had an accent. I looked at him and asked:

"How do you know Russian?"

"It's natural," he answered. "I used to live in Rostov. My father was a merchant of the second guild."

Such people could also live in St. Petersburg, or anywhere they chose.

So you see, it turns out that the Jew Kutikov, with whom I used to work at the factory, could not choose his place of residence in tsarist times, but the father of the deputy mayor of Los Angeles could live anywhere.

That was how the tsarist government tackled the nationality question; it used a class approach. Therefore the wealthy Jewish merchants and capitalists had the right to live anywhere whereas the Jewish poor shared the plight of the Russian, Ukrainian, and other workers; like the rest of the peoples in tsarist Russia they had to work hard, live in squalid rooms, and bear the burden of capitalistic slavery.

During World War II various people behaved in different ways. There were many heroic deeds, including some by Jews. Some Jews earned the title of Hero of the Soviet Union, many others were decorated with orders and medals. Let me cite only one example, that of Hero of the Soviet Union, General Kreyzer.[17] He was deputy commander of the Second Guards Army during the great battle at the Volga River. He took part in the battles for the liberation of the Donets Basin and the Crimea. Now, General Kreyzer is a commander in the Far East.

But there were also cases of betrayal by people of various nationalities. I can cite the following example: When Paulus's force was surrounded and then routed, among others, by the 64th Army, I got a call from a member of the Military Council, General Z. T. Serdyuk. He told me that among Paulus's staff officers taken prisoner was a former instructor of the Kiev Komsomol Committee by the name of Kogan.[18]

I asked him, "How is that possible, aren't you mistaken?"

"No, there is no mistake," Comrade Serdyuk answered. "Kogan was the interpreter for Paulus's staff."

In the operation against Paulus, a mechanized brigade took part. Its commanding officer was Colonel Burmakov, and its commissar, Comrade Vinokur, a Jew. I had known Vinokur since 1931, when I worked as secretary of the Baumann Regional Party Committee in Moscow. At that time, Vinokur was secretary of the party cell at a dairy plant.

So that was how it was; one Jew was an interpreter on Paulus's staff, while another Jew took part in the operation against Paulus, in which the Jewish interpreter was captured.

Human deeds should be evaluated not from a national but from a class point of view.

It is not in the interest of our cause to search through the detritus of the past for examples of the differences between the working people of various nationalities.

They are not responsible for instigating national hatred or national oppression. The responsibility lies with the exploiting classes. The traitors of the revolution were hired by the tsarist government, the landlords, and the bourgeoisie, anyplace where they might be found, and vile creatures could be found among people of any nationality.

. . . It is absurd to blame the Russian people for the dirty provocations of the Black Hundreds, but it would be equally absurd to blame all the Jewish people for the nationalism and Zionism of the Bund, [19] for the provocations of Azef [20] and Zhitomirsky ("Otsov"), [21] for various Jewish organizations connected in their time with the Zubatovists [22] and the tsarist Okhranka (secret police).

Our Leninist party pursues a consistent policy of friendship among all peoples; it fosters the spirit of internationalism among the Soviet people and total rejection of every single form of racial discrimination and national hatred. Our art affirms the noble ideals of internationalism and brotherhood among nations. . . .

. . . The poet Yevgeny Yevtushenko recently made a trip to West Germany and France. He has just come back from Paris, where he spoke to an audience of several thousand workers and students, friends of the Soviet Union. We should give credit to Comrade Yevtushenko. He showed worthy behavior during this trip. But, if we are to believe the magazine *Lettre Française Journal,* he did not refrain from the temptation of winning the bourgeois public's praise.

The poet found a strange way of informing the audience of our attitude toward "Babi Yar." He told them that his poem had been accepted by the people but criticized by the dogmatists. But it is well known that Comrade Yevtushenko's poem has been criticized by the Communists. How can one forget about this fact and fail to draw the necessary conclusions?

Pravda, April 4, 1964

THE IDEOLOGY COMMISSION OF THE
CPSU CENTRAL COMMITTEE

The Ideology Commission of the Central Committee of the Communist Party of the Soviet Union has discussed the publication of scientific atheistic literature.

The commission has found that central and local publishing houses have published a number of useful books and booklets which, based on the achievements of modern science, soundly criticize various trends in religious ideology and relate the experience gained from atheistic work in the USSR. The publication of these books and booklets fosters the materialistic world outlook of the Soviet people.

The commission has called the attention of the press, publishing houses, and research institutions to the need for a further improvement in the ideological and scientific level of atheistic literature.

During the past few years several useful books have been published, including a popular textbook *Talks on Religion and Knowledge, Popular Lectures on Atheism,* a reader *On Religion,* a collection *Thoughts about Religion, Catechism Exposed* by A. Osipov, *From God to Men* by A. Chertkov, *Orthodoxy and Humanism* by P. Kurochkin, and many other atheistic works. At the same time a number of books and booklets have been published whose low standard harms our ideological and educational work.

The participants in the session particularly criticized the grave mistakes in the booklet *Judaism without Embellishment* by T. Kichko, published in late 1963 by the Ukrainian Academy of Sciences. The author of the booklet and the author of its preface meant to unmask the reactionary nature of Judaism; in so doing they misinterpreted certain questions related to the origin and development of this religion. A number of erroneous statements and illustrations in the booklet may hurt the feelings of believers and be interpreted as anti-Semitic.

But it is well known that there is not and cannot be such a problem in our country. "Since the day of the October Revolution," said N. S. Khrushchev, "Jews have enjoyed full equality with the rest of the peoples of our country. There is no Jewish problem in the USSR, and those who invent it sing to somebody else's tune."[23]

The erroneous statements contained in the booklet contradict the party's Leninist policy with regard to religion and nationalities. They only invite anti-Soviet insinuations from our adversaries, who do their utmost to create the so-called Jewish problem. That is why Soviet public opinion objected to the erroneous passages in T. Kichko's booklet.

The Ideological Commission has advised the workers of the press and of publishing houses to be more careful in publishing scientific atheistic literature.

Izvestiya, April 5, 1964

MUCH ADO ABOUT NOTHING

There has been an unusually rich harvest of anti-Soviet articles in the Western press in the past few days. What provoked this squeaking of pens and overuse of ink? It turns out to be the "defense" of the Jewish faith. . . .

The Soviet reader is quite justified in expressing his bewilderment, for it is well known that freedom of religion in the USSR is guaranteed by the Constitution. So what is the matter? It turns out that the bourgeois press was stirred up by a small book published recently by one of the Ukrainian publishing houses.[24] The booklet, written by T. Kichko, is entitled *Judaism without Embellishment.* Let us say from the start: Yes, there are some mistakes in the book.

There can be no doubt about the intention of the book. Judaism, like any other religion, may and must be subjected to scientific criticism. And that is exactly what our scientific and popular literature does in unmasking the reactionary nature of all religions, be they Christian or Jewish or any other. A number of antireligious books have been recently published in the Ukraine and other Union republics.

T. Kichko uses new material in analyzing the reactionary nature of Judaism as a form of religious ideology. But in addition to correct statements, his book contains historical and factual mistakes and imprecisions which may be interpreted as contradictory to state policy on religion. Many of the pictures in the book may offend believers. The newspaper *Radyanska Kultura* has criticized certain erroneous statements made in this book.

Nevertheless, the initiators of the present anti-Soviet propaganda campaign try to make undue profit from the book's publication and to cast aspersions on the Soviet Union. They try to discredit Soviet policy toward the nationality question.

But in vain! The Leninist policy of the Communist party and the Soviet state is absolutely clear; the Soviet Union guarantees genuine equality to all nationalities whether large or small. All conditions have been provided to develop their capabilities and talents.

EXCERPTS FROM BOOKS

Yury Ivanov

BEWARE: ZIONISM!
ESSAYS ON THE IDEOLOGY, ORGANIZATION, AND PRACTICE OF ZIONISM[25]

Moscow: Politizdat, 1969
165 pp., 70,000 copies
Quoted from 2d ed., Moscow: Politizdat,
1970, 206 pp., 200,000 copies

CONTENTS:

Zionism, as an ideology and an organization, developed at the end of the nineteenth century, at a time when the international proletariat was engaged in bitter class conflict and when capitalism was finally transformed into imperialism.

Outwardly, Zionist ideology apparently consists of the doctrine of the creation of a "Jewish state." Therefore, with only superficial knowledge, we might think the Zionist way of looking at things touchingly helpless, naively religious, and emotionally wounding, with its semipoetical aphorisms: "If there is a book of books, it is the Bible. If there is a people of the Bible, there must also be a land of the Bible." (p. 9)

. . . It is perfectly apparent that the slogan "Jewish state" assumed, in the actual conditions of the end of the nineteenth and the beginning of the twentieth century, a purely "instrumental" character. The Zionist leaders always considered the creation of a "Jewish state" not a goal but a means to realize other, far broader aims: the restoration of control over the Jewish masses; the utmost enrichment in the name of authority and parasitic prosperity; the defense and strengthening of imperialism. (p. 33)

. . . Precisely this idea—a "Jewish state"—which, as V. I. Lenin stressed, is completely false and reactionary and creates in the Jewish workers, directly and indirectly, a mood hostile to assimilation—a ghetto mood—became simultaneously both a starting point for anti-Semitic views and also the main buttress of Zionist ideology on which all the Zionist ideological-theoretical structures were erected.

The concept of a "world Jewish nation," which the Zionists used and continue to use in order to establish mental and political control over citizens of the most diverse countries, must not be confused with the Israeli nation (examined in the following chapters). These two are quite separate, and attempts to establish any kind of link between them are absolutely unjustified. Many Englishmen and Irishmen, for example, long ago became Australians and New Zealanders, in the same way that many Ukrainians, Frenchmen, Jews, and Russians became Canadians, displaying all the distinguishing features of that particular nation. (p. 42)

. . . What solution did the Zionists offer to the "world Jewish nation" they proclaimed (a term also adopted by the anti-Semites)? They proposed the creation of a "Jewish state." Let it be clear: they did not mean the State of Israel.

. . . The Zionists always viewed a "Jewish state" only as a means of achieving capitalist aims. Moreover, they did not intend to concentrate all or most of the Jews in this state. The Zionists and their patrons counted on creating in many countries a reserve of strikebreakers of the revolutionary movement, and other imperialist agents. . . . The idea was the formation of a "center," through which it would be possible to influence the "periphery." (p. 55)

The campaign against socialist fellowship, and especially against the Soviet Union, is conducted under the tattered banner of "Jewish defense." How many political passersby marched beneath this flag, how many honest though gullible people did the Zionists compel, using every means, to hold its flagstaff aloft, even if only for a moment! (p. 153)

. . . It has already been noted that, along with the demand to abandon loyalty to one's country, to throw patriotism overboard, the Zionists cultivated the concept of "dual patriotism." Some of them asserted that the Jews are a "worldwide nation" in spite of the opinion of the general population; others, with serious mien, claimed that the general opinion is that the Jews are a "worldwide nation," etc. "There is a time to cast away stones, and a time to gather stones together; a time to embrace, and a time to refrain from embracing; a time to love, and a time to hate." Following precisely this biblical logic, the Zionist ideologists deliberately create a whole series of contradictory concepts, to have, under no matter what circumstances, the possibility of putting a brave face on a sorry business. . . . European Jews were doomed in advance by the Zionist fanatics, whom the Rothschilds encouraged. . . . the Zionists helped the Nazis to drive the Jews either into the concentration-camp ovens or to kibbutzim in the "Land of Canaan." The German journalist Heinz Höhne[26] was entirely correct when he wrote that "as soon as the Zionists and National Socialists elevated race and nation to be the yardstick of all things, a common bridge inevitably had to arise between them." The common bridge existed in the past, and it exists today. (p. 176)

. . . Zionism survived and gained strength not in spite of fascism, but thanks to fascism, which, in new historical circumstances—for in history there are no exact parallels—it is today rapidly replacing. Any nationalism based on racial superiority carries within itself the seed of fascism. (p. 177)

. . . But the Zionist plots and campaigns are not all-out destined for success. The Union of Soviet Socialist Republics has seen enemies such as these. With anger, with indignation, and with mass protests, our comrades-in-arms, the Soviet working Jews, answer the provocative calls from Tel Aviv and the slanderous distortions about the so-called situation of the Jews in the USSR.

International Zionism is the enemy of all peoples, of all national groups and nations. It has long ceased to be a small-town, local matter. Having concentrated in its hands immense financial resources, using the State of Israel as its base, propped up by the billionaires of the United States, England, France, the Republic of South Africa, West Germany, Italy, Argentina, and many other countries, it works everywhere, day in, day out, against communism. For this reason, the struggle against it is the vital business of all Communists, of all freedom-loving people on the face of the globe, and of all working people who abhor exploitation and war.

Based on the theory of Jewish "racial superiority," Zionism both in word and deed follows in the footsteps of fascism. Zionism has turned its base, Israel, into a torture-chamber for all those who are unwilling to go along with its inhuman theories and practices or, quite simply, oppose them. (p. 181)

From all sides, in different versions, and in diverse tawdry wrappings and the most varied circumstances, the imperialist West, using among others the Zionists' services, is trying to plant in us the idea that in the era of space flight, of atomic reactors, of global telecommunications and present-day methods of communication, objective reality generates a contradiction between devotion to one's socialist motherland and the striving for progress. . . .

These false theories are promoted by the well-known American anti-Soviet Walt Rostow (born 1916 to the family of Victor Aaron Rostow), a long-time advocate of Zionist interests at the White House. American imperialism still uses the services of this old organizer of the anti-Communist ideological attack. But times change, and old advisers are replaced in the White House by new ones, who more openly reveal their true convictions and intentions. On January 22, 1970, an official announcement was issued in Washington: "Highly placed government officials are taking an active part in American Zionist activities. As stated by the official bulletin of the National Committee of the Republican Party, four of the President's senior advisers have been nominated to important positions in the capital's Zionist organization, the United Jewish Appeal, to help in its campaign. These positions were filled by the director of the group for study of national objectives at the White House, Leonard Garment; the special presidential assistant on internal planning, William Safire; a member of the President's Economic Council, Herbert Stein; and the assistant for liaison with Congress, Eugene Cohen, who is to assume the post of honorary president of the United Jewish Appeal." The chain of events has ended. American government circles, at the request of monopoly capital (whose actual representatives preferred on this occasion to remain in the shadows), publicly joined the Zionist leaders so that the whole world could see the direct connection and interdependence between them. (pp. 192–193)

With the Israeli ruling class's June aggression against the Arab peoples, we saw emerging from the shadows the organizers of international provocations, of dirty intrigues and crimes—the Zionist operators, prepared to trample on everything in their quest for profit and power. Today they are again trying to avoid notice. Small hope! Everywhere, those people who won't kowtow to these possessors of a tight purse and a spacious kennel will not let them hide themselves in the shadows again, and likewise, the peoples of the world and history will not allow them to evade retribution. (194)

SAMIZDAT

AN ANTI-SEMITIC NOVEL BY ANATOLY DIMAROV[27]

An excerpt from A. Dimarov's novel *Paths of Life*, published in the magazine *Dnipro* in 1963 (no. 9 and no. 10), is given below. This type of material could well have adorned the pages of any pogrom-inducing leaflet from the time of Bendera:

. . . We will leave Vasil to his gloomy reflections on the new trap set by life, and return to Lander, the GPU chief, who had been deeply insulted by the chairman of the village soviet, his formidable schemes and vindictive thoughts.

"They are all alike, these goddamn dirty Ukrainians," Lander summed up his speculations. "Whatever you do for them, they are never satisfied."

The Landers have been at war with the Ukrainian people since the remote past, when the Polish landed gentry rented out Russian Orthodox churches. Isaac Lander also took up this *gesheft*; he shelled out some gold to a wealthy Pole and became the owner of three churches, complete with priests, readers, clergy, and parish.

It was then that a cliff, in the person of Isaac, rose between God and the parishioners. You want to have your child baptized? First go to Isaac and only then to the church. You want to bury your dead? Grease Isaac's palm and get permission. You have Easter cakes to consecrate? Very good, go and consecrate them, be my guest. But render unto Isaac the things which are Isaac's and only after that unto God the things which are God's. The humble, ill-fated wretch took his hard-earned property to the greedy Isaac's hand, which was always ready to grab, silently cursing the covetous Jew who could rob you better than a Tartar. The Tartar would swoop down on you, seize this and that, and go back to the Crimea. Not this leech; you had no chance to shake him off or scare him, even by making the sign of the cross.

When he had accumulated a little money, Lander started looking around at other churches. It was then that he was caught by the Dnieper Cossacks. He must have annoyed the people of the neighborhood beyond endurance, and the Cossacks rejoiced as though they had met a brother:

"We've got you at last, pig's snout! What shall we treat our guest to, gentlemen?"

But while the slow-witted Cossacks were deciding whether to hang the Jew or drown him, Jehovah took pity on his faithful servant and sent a Polish detachment. And the Cossacks shook their forelocks in soap-smeared nooses, glorifying God.

Isaac's grandson Chaim Lander was not inclined to have anything to do with churches, especially as the Polish gentry were no longer there. They were chomping their broken teeth somewhere beyond the Zbruc River. . . . The Landers adapted themselves beautifully to new masters. As men of sense put it, obey thy master whoever he is, or be sure you know which way the wind is blowing. . . .

And so Chaim put up a tavern on a busy road and occupied himself with legal *gesheft:* many a mickle makes a muckle.

In his old age Chaim was to suffer utter injustice at the hands of the ungrateful Ukrainian people; the Haidamaks raided him, burned down his tavern, and dug out a little sack of gold, may they and their children live in misery!

Since then, in the Lander family, the Ukrainians have been called nothing but "those goddamn dirty Ukrainians."

The Landers' kin did not, God be thanked, die out or fall into a decline. No, they survived all storms and disasters, spreading tenacious branches all over the Ukraine. There were richer Landers and poorer Landers, Landers from Podolia and Landers from the Kiev region, but all were known for their secluded way of life and traditional hostility towards "those goddamn dirty Ukrainians." The Ukrainian may and should be duped, there is no harm in jeering at him either.

The Lander of our story was born in the Poltava region, to the family of a provincial shopkeeper. He was the fourteenth child, and Hersh, endowed with God's infinite, boundless grace, called him Solomon.

Solomon grew up like all his brethren: went to heder in winter, to grind away at the Talmud; in the summer, together with other ragamuffins, he idled away his time, visited fairs, pestered apathetic muzhiks, bothered the weak, and was himself battered more than once. Yet the parents doted on their offspring: "Such a wonderful child! May you have as much money as our little Solomon has sense in his head!"

The parents each pictured Solomon's future differently; the father cherished a hope of making his son a rich shopkeeper, the mother dreamt of seeing her little Solomon as a rabbi, or at least a zaddik. Solomon, however, thought otherwise. When he was still very young, he showed not only outstanding wisdom but also keen political flair, and he joined the Bund. The same unfailing flair made him the right choice after the revolution: he deserted the Bund, joined the RSDRP (Russian Social-Democratic Workers party), and started working his way up. He chose Lev Trotsky as a model and aped him in everything, even in dress and gestures. However, Russia could tolerate but one Trotsky, and Lander decided to be modest and content himself, for the time being, with the role of a local Trotsky. He was haughty with his subordinates, liked to be feared, and when walking in the street liked to hear warning whispers: "Quiet! It's Lander himself!"

He wore a suit cut like an army uniform, riding breeches tucked in well-polished box-calf high boots, and always had a selection of high-flown revolutionary phrases, from "world revolution" to "immediate expropriation of all private property." He showed off his revolutionary obstinacy like a peasant girl with a brightly colored kerchief. . . .

There was just one little pockmark on his wholehearted person, a hardly noticeable crack, inherited from Daddy Hersh, and by Daddy from Grandpa Motele, and by Grandpa from Great-grandpa Chaim, the crack he could never get rid of: hatred for "those goddamn dirty Ukrainians." To him, they all smelled of tar and horse manure, were unaccountable and hostile, and even put the fear of God into him. He failed to realize the reason for the contemptuous attitude toward Ukrainians that prevailed in his family. Perhaps it was the contempt of a thief for a man he has robbed, because the thief could not respect himself unless he could spit on his victim, at whose expense he lived and fed his children—future thieves. . . . This hostility was a part of him, it was stronger than him and uncontrollable, and however hard he tried to hide it, it would occasionally burst out . . .

The 1970s

MATERIAL FROM SOVIET PERIODICALS

Vechernaya Odessa, June 23, 24, 26, 1975
M. Donetsky

DANGER: ZIONISM

1. Hitler's Mercenaries

Thirty years ago, fascist Germany was crushed. The war criminals who managed to evade retribution and escaped unpunished, apparitions from underworld darkness, were the many active helpers of fascism—the functionaries of international Zionism. Not without reason, the emissaries of this variety of fascism have for three decades been roaming the face of the earth, trying in vain to destroy the traces of how they really served their masters in SS uniform.

When did this seemingly unnatural symbiosis of fascism and Zionism actually begin?

On the night of February 28, 1933, the Reichstag in Berlin caught fire. Soon the brown stink and sinister fire started to spread over all Europe, enveloping one country after another.

Among the characters involved in this act of arson was a certain Hanussen.[28] His real name was Hershel Steinschneider. He was a Jew, and joined the National Socialist party in 1930. He was also a member of the SA and a friend of the commander of the Berlin stoimtroopers, the chief of police of Potsdam, Count Helldorf. A participant in the arson, Steinschneider, made premature "prophecies" about the Reichstag fire. Hanussen, incidentally, is portrayed in L. Feuchtwanger's book *The Lautensack Brothers*. On March 24, stormtroopers took away the garrulous witness and killed him in a thick pine forest near Berlin. . . .

International Zionism was well acquainted with the National Socialist program adopted in February 1920, which stated, in black and white, that "no Jew can belong to the German race," and accordingly, cannot be a citizen of Germany nor hold any government office. The Zionists were thoroughly conversant with Hitler's *Mein Kampf,* which stated that to achieve his goal, the National Socialist movement must regard the Jews as mortal enemies. Nevertheless, from the very first years when the fascists seized power in Germany, the Zionists began serving the Nazi cannibals "body and soul."

The initiative was taken by the former adviser for Jewish affairs to the Foreign Ministry of the Kaiser's Germany, Nahum Goldmann. He left for Italy, where, on November 13, 1934, he was received by Mussolini.[29] Goldmann's purpose was to enlist the support of "one of the most powerful individuals in the Western world" in the creation of the World Jewish Congress, which was intended to carry on work among Jews who did not originally hold Zionist views. The discussion lasted thirty minutes. Mussolini promised the Zionists his support.

The chief of the sabotage-espionage service of the Wehrmacht high command, Admiral Canaris, was reputed to be a fierce Jew-hater, but he excluded the Zionists, with whom he was willing to make deals personally. He leaned on the world Zionist movement for support primarily because, from the first day of the October Revolution, it has waged active war on the Soviet Union. Zionists were frequently used as a Nazi fifth column, and their wide connections were used for espionage in the USSR and in other countries. . . .

What base steps did the Zionists not take in fulfilling the many tasks of the Abwehr! Many presented themselves as victims of the Nazi regime in order to gain the confidence of representatives of the Allied governments and of the neutral countries, and thereby obtain access to important secret information. A typical case was that of the journalist Stern (alias Golder), who as early as 1933 managed to infiltrate the Vatican Chancellery.[30]

During the 1940s, Stern started working in Palestine, where he became the leader of the secret terrorist organization, the Haganah.[31] Through a fascist resident, Feivel Polkes,[32] Stern established connections with secret agents of Canaris and presented an extremely cunning plan to the admiral. It consisted of recruiting "reliable" Zionists from the Hungarian and Romanian ghettos to work as secret agents of the Abwehr, and then to transfer them to the Middle East, in the guise of refugees. This plan appealed to Canaris. He personally bestowed the code name "Refugees" on this operation.

At the beginning of February 1942, the first group of refugees, including many Abwehr agents, embarked on the steamer *Struma*[33] from Constanta. The *Struma* was already heading in the direction of the Bosphorus when a code message . . . reached Canaris's desk, saying that the British counterintelligence had arrested Stern in Tel Aviv. Fearing that the latter might talk, Canaris ordered a torpedo boat to be put to sea. It sank the *Struma* and all her passengers. . . .

2. A Form of Moral Schizophrenia

On May 14, 1948, at six o'clock Washington time, the period of the British Mandate for Palestine came to an end. At eleven minutes past six, Charles Ross, the press secretary of the President of the United States, summoned the press correspondents to his office and read them a statement from Harry Truman on the *de facto* recognition of the new State of Israel.

As researchers point out, such unprecedented haste can be explained very simply: before the United States lay the opportunity of using the new state and the extremist ideology of its ruling circles to contain the Arab national-liberation movement and to strengthen its positions in the Middle East.

Literally in the state's very first days, racism began developing with an ever-increasing tempo. Later, an American journalist, I. Stone, described racism in Israel as a form of moral schizophrenia. The source of infection of this Nazi characteristic is—Zionism. . . .

The State of Israel has existed for nearly 10,000 days. Hardly a single day has gone by without some disclosure in the world press of facts regarding the crime of genocide perpetrated by the Israeli racists. For perpetrating such crimes, the German and Japanese war criminals were arraigned before international courts and received appropriate retribution. . . .

Let us return to the subject of genocide, Israeli style. Just as the world will never forget what aggressive Nazi politics brought to the peoples of Europe, so will it not forget what the Zionists are doing to the Palestinian Arabs under their heel and the inhabitants of the occupied territories. . . .

In a nutshell, the Zionists made full use of the German fascist experience. . . .

In the occupied territories the criminal fascist practice of collective punishment is enforced, whereby masses of innocent people suffer. The Zionists work on the fascist principle that if your brother, friend, or neighbor is a "terrorist" (the occupiers customarily refer to the partisans in this way), you also are guilty and must be punished. Cases are known of collective punishments taking place in village squares as a warning to the assembled inhabitants. Furthermore, the military tribunals and the civil authorities do not even try to establish the guilt of those accused—it is enough that the person under arrest is an Arab, worse still if he is a Communist. "Confessions" made under torture are adequate for them. . . .

Time is implacable. Tel Aviv is obliged to resort to "peacemaking gestures" in order somehow or other to delay, to check the trend of isolating Israel in the United Nations—a trend that is very dangerous for her, which led to the breaking of diplomatic relations with Israel by twenty African states, and support for the demand by most West European countries and by Japan for the fulfillment of UN Resolution no. 242 in all its aspects.

A just resolution of the Middle East conflict will be possible only on the basis of ending the occupation of Arab lands by the Israeli army and respecting the legitimate rights of all the peoples of the Middle East, including the Arab people of Palestine. This inescapable conclusion is confirmed by the whole course of events relating to the struggle of the Arab peoples and of world society to undo the results of Israeli aggression.

Ogonyok, nos. 28, 29 (July 8, 15), 1978
L. Korneev

THE MOST ZIONIST BUSINESS OF ALL

Blood Money

November 1977. Washington's Sheraton Park Hotel is overflowing with colonels and generals in American uniforms. They are actively and competently getting acquainted with the military hardware that the leading American arms manufacturers are displaying in the hotel's hall. Representatives of General Dynamics, Lockheed Aircraft, Litton Industries, and other "death monopolies" bow deferentially to their prospective customers in dark, olive-green dress uniforms. . . .

But the eyes of all the cannon, tank, combat aircraft, and missile salesmen now turn to a group of gentlemen in mufti, with tanned complexions.

"The Israelis!" whisper the Pentagon men enviously to one another.

Their envy is justified. Israel has become the Pentagon's main rival in the acquisition of American armaments; the pertinent statistics are common knowledge.

It is also no secret that the Israeli arms-purchasing mission to the United States contains twice the number of personnel serving in Tel Aviv's embassy in Washington. Not so well known are the links between the monopolies of the American military industrial complex and international Zionism. . . .

Tell me who you're banking with, and I'll tell you who you are: the banker brothers Lazard, with branches in England and France as well, are known as constant donors to the funds of international Zionism and participants in the Jerusalem "millionaires' conferences" for Israel. They actively facilitate the development of Tel Aviv's military potential through the intermediary of Jewish bourgeois organizations that they manage. I am not making unsubstantiated statements: Fred Lazard, patriarch of the American branch of the family, is vice-president of the American Jewish Committee; Geoffrey Lazard presides over the National Jewish Council of Scouts; Ralph Lazard sits on the board of directors of the notorious Joint, cover for the CIA and the Israeli Zionist secret services. The Lazards' billions earn them a decisive vote in the dealings of international Zionism.

The Lockheed Aircraft Corporation is a convincing example of the Zionists' criminal involvement in the arms race led by the U.S. military industrial complex, but there are many other examples. . . .

Cosmopolitans of the God of War

It should be stressed that not all Jews in the capitalistic world are Zionists, of course. Not all accomplices of Zionism are Jewish. The Morgans, the largest U.S. Christian financial group, collaborate closely with the Lazard banks; just one trust division of the group has assets in excess of $17 billion. Representatives of the Morgan Guaranty Trust Company sit on the boards of directors of more than 100 corporations.

Stevens, president of J. P. Stevens & Company, one of the largest manufacturers of military uniforms in the world, contributes to Zionist organizations. In the very first days of Israel's aggression against Jordan, Egypt, and Syria in June 1967, he overtly earmarked $250,000 for the Zionists. I emphasize: overtly, for the general rule of the Zionists' partisans is to cover carefully not only the extent but even the very fact of their support of Zionist organizations and Israel's ruling circles. Incidentally, this completely suits the Zionists' desire to remain inconspicuous, to act on the sly, without attracting attention. Stevens, benefactor of the Israeli aggressors, was Truman's Secretary of Defense. . . .

The American "death concerns," for whom the continuous conflict in the Middle East is a source of riches, are interested in supporting the aggressive tendencies of Israel and of international Zionism. Together with the American Zionist lobby, they are trying to exert pressure on the White House in order to force a pro-Zionist, pro-Israeli, and anti-Arab policy upon the American government. . . .

The French company Turbomeca, which manufactures jet engines for bombers and is headed by the Zionist Shidlowsky, has built a plant for the manufacturing of aircraft engines in the vicinity of Tel Aviv. It is owned by Turbomeca and Israel Aircraft Industries. But no one in France calls Monsieur Shidlowsky a traitor. . . .

NATO orders are filled by the Dutch supermonopoly Philips (with its North American Philips division in the United States) and the Anglo-Dutch concern Unilever; both cooperate with the Zionists.

Naturally, data of this nature in the capitalist states are handled as state-security secrets. Thus, according to the April 18, 1976, *New York Times*, under pretense of protecting Jewish-owned firms from the Arab boycott, "no U.S. company will disclose information concerning the race, religion, or national origin of its staff, directors, stockholders, or employees."

It is therefore difficult to determine the share of the Jewish bourgeoisie in the national wealth of the West. It is equally hard to ascertain how many monopolies, concerns, firms, and enterprises are owned or controlled by pro-Zionist capital. Undoubtedly there are many. For instance, Deutsche Bank, the largest in West Germany, participates in financing the Israel war industry. It controls most of the West German armament firms and played a decisive role in building up the German military potential. The bank is run by the pro-Zionist former war criminal Abs, who is related by marriage to the Lehmans in the United States. By the nature of his activity, he rules like a dictator over practically the entire West German industry, and is the patron of the West German revanchists and international Zionism. At present, Abs holds the position of president or vice-president on over thirty boards of directors, including all the leading West German armament monopolies, such as Krupp and the tank- and car-manufacturing concern Daimler-Benz. The annual turnover of the West German firms and concerns controlled by the Deutsche Bank exceeds 80 billion German marks. The newspaper *L'Humanité*, in the article "West Germany—Europe's Policeman," disclosed that twenty-five German banks and other financial institutions depend on it. The Deutsche Bank has business connections with 2,500 banks in over a hundred countries; the Rockefellers, the Rothschilds, Lockheed, Unilever, and Philips are among its clients. . . .

The Aggressor Is Selling Weapons

. . . At present, arms constitute 10 percent of the overall volume of Israeli exports. In other words, Israel, a state with a population of 3,200,000, falls only slightly behind Great Britain, France, and West Germany in the volume of arms sales. Thus, on the one hand, the Tel Aviv expansionists reiterate the need to "defend" Israel with the aid of the most advanced Western arms, while on the other hand they sell the most modern weapons.

But there is also a third side to the problem: arms labeled "Made in Israel" are sold mainly to countries with the most reactionary regimes. In NATO plans, Israel has clearly been assigned the role of arms supplier to those governments to whom the imperialist states would not openly extend military aid, considering that it would be "unseemly" for political reasons. But the Tel Aviv authorities are known not to shrink from anything, following the racist credo devised by Ben-Gurion, the founding father of Israel, and still very popular there: "What counts is not what the goyim say, but what the Jews do!"

It has recently become known that, in conjunction with the South African company Calan, the Israeli firm Tadiran is building a plant in the vicinity of Pretoria for the manufacture of military communications equipment; this is a new fact in the economic and political alliance along the Tel Aviv–South Africa axis. The continuous strengthening of the alliance between Israel and South Africa acquires a vile character in the light of the racists' mass reprisals against the native population of the country, who are fighting against the criminal apartheid policy. . . .

The fact, strange at first glance, that Tel Aviv is selling armaments abroad worth hundreds of millions of dollars is part of the West's policy, which has already become common practice, of turning Israel into a military base of world reaction. . . .

Snake's Coil

Hillel, head of the Sanhedrin more than two thousand years ago, was once asked: "Can you state briefly the essence of your faith?" The talmudist replied: "What is hateful to you, do not do unto your neighbor!"

Armed with many Jewish dogmas, the Zionists have turned most of them into a framework for their ideology of hatred and territorial expansion. By arbitrarily distorting this or that precept of the Bible, or by taking it out of context, the Zionist obscurantists try to inculcate in the Jews the belief that they are God's chosen people, and discrimination, contempt, and hatred toward all non-Jews.

"Do unto another what is hateful to you," this is the rule of modern Zionism. And the rabbis who cooperate with the Zionist ringleaders have become the Devil's servants, preachers of aggression and robbery.

. . . Just before dawn several rifle shots were fired at the building of the Soviet delegation to the United Nations in New York. One bullet broke the entrance hall window and whistled past the delegation worker who was on duty there. This happened on February 27, 1976. On March 4 and April 2, 1976, in spite of the assurance given by U.S. officials that the protection of the Soviet delegation would be improved, the gangsters repeated their attack. In 1977 and 1978, the thugs repeatedly organized hooligan gatherings at the Intourist offices in New York, broke windows, and shouted threats at Soviet citizens. Fascist youths staged provocations against the

Soviet delegation to the United Nations, fired shots and planted bombs under buildings belonging to Soviet institutions in the United States. Although the U.S. authorities know the names and addresses of the criminals, the latter continue their terrorist activities.

The anti-Soviet epidemic of gangsterism in the United States was caused by the organized activity of germs from the "cold war" era, in order to prevent Soviet-American cooperation from improving. The firing of shots at the Soviet delegation in New York was an act of a Zionist organization, Jewish Armed Resistance.

. . . All the Zionist bands of thugs are led and directed by the intelligence department of the Executive Committee of the World Zionist Organization and Israel's secret services network subordinate to it. They operate in close contact with the CIA and FBI. The *New York Daily World* wrote that "there are convincing proofs that the Jewish Defense League (JDL) was launched by the CIA as a weapon in the anti-Soviet campaign."

A special JDL school has been founded in the American town of Woodbourne for the training of terrorists. The instructors and weapons are supplied to the Zionist gangsters in the United States by the Israeli secret services. The publicist Johnson reports in a booklet on the JDL, published in the United States, that "the ringleaders of this gang have proclaimed their intention to hinder the process of normalization in Soviet-American relations, to prevent detente in international tension by any means," in particular, by hiring professional gangsters of the American Mafia, whose links with the JDL are particularly stressed by Johnson.

The terrorist raids of the Zionist bandits are coordinated by a special "security committee" which includes members of the Israel government and the Army chief of staff. In the planning of terrorist raids, the committee practically "does not take into consideration the reaction of world public opinion, unfavorable though it may be," confirmed the authors of the pro-Zionist *The Eye of Tel Aviv*, published in 1968 in Paris.

The terrorist activity of the Israeli special services reaches beyond the boundaries of the Middle East and has assumed an international character. Zionist gangsterism has become a daily occurrence in many states. The psychological war waged by Zionism took an extraordinary upswing after the 1975 adoption by the thirtieth session of the United Nations General Assembly of a resolution condemning Zionism as a form of racism and racial discrimination.

The intimidation of world public opinion by the power of Israel's army and special services, the influence of various Zionist organizations and international Zionism as a whole upon the ruling circles of diverse countries, should be seen as a form of psychological terrorism, typical of the Zionist propaganda. The spying, subversion, and terrorist activities of international Zionism, the ruling circles of Israel, and their secret services are aimed at creating hotbeds of tension in various regions of our planet, upsetting the neighborly relations between peoples, contaminating the international political atmosphere. This policy suits the interests of the military-industrial complex of the most militant, ultrareactionary imperialist circles.

Having forever lost the historic initiative and impotent to turn back world development, imperialism is increasingly counting on unethical fighting, conspiracy, and subversive activity, and disguising with increasing zeal the reactionary goals of its policies.

Nash Sovremennik, no. 8, 1978, pp. 188–191
V. Yemelyanov

ZIONISM UNMASKED[34]

A Review of V. Begun's *Invasion without Arms*

Moscow: Molodaya Gvardiya, 1977

Slightly over ten years ago the ominous word "Zionism" made its appearance in wide circles. To be more precise, it was in connection with the Israeli aggression that began in June 1967, and the upsurge (certainly not coincidental) of ideological activity by international reactionary forces against the forces of communism. True, the term and the phenomenon have been known since the end of the last century; true, Lenin gave a precise and unambiguous definition of Zionism; true, even as early as the 1940s and 1950s the world learned of the tragedies of the Arab villages of Deir Yassin, Bakr al-Bark, and many others, whose populations were driven from their homes by Israeli stormtroopers.

. . . A harsh and bright light was thrown on this criminal activity by Yu. Ivanov's book *Beware: Zionism!* (1969).[35] This book was the first to familiarize the reader in depth with all aspects of the ideology, organization, and practices of modern Zionism. This book also gave analyses of its historical roots and its strategic aim. Since the end of the 1960s articles, research papers, and other material connected with the subject have been published regularly in the Soviet press.

But V. Begun's book *Invasion without Arms* is still of great interest, even to the well-informed reader. The book is informative and full of new facts and interesting data; it is distinguished by its scientific logic, depth, and the consistency of its conclusions.

Modern Zionism is a complex, many-layered system of organizations and associations smoothly functioning in many countries. Among its overt organizations, the most influential, the World Zionist Organization, has branches in sixty-seven countries. Moreover, there are two thousand secret Masonic lodges in the B'nai B'rith (Sons of the Covenant)[36] oranization, which has about half a million members. "Formally it is a Masonic, non-Zionist body, but in fact is ultra-Zionist," the author writes. Pointing to the existence of hundreds of other organizations of various shapes and colors, he comes to the justified conclusion: "Therefore the diversity of Zionist organizations is in no way the result of lack of unity or of inner splintering. This quality was intentionally introduced by the Zionist strategists as it guarantees some flexibility of action and helps to mislead public opinion."

Israel is only a small subdivision of international Zionism, without which Israel would not last one day. On the other hand, international Zionism existed perfectly well before the State of Israel made its appearance, and could perfectly well continue to exist without it, were it not for the pressing need for some "state base," some kind of "imperial center." International reaction needs Israel to conduct the noisy propaganda campaign about a "special mission," to collect under one roof all representatives of the "chosen people," as well as to fulfill the role of watchdog protecting the interests of international capital in the Middle East, and as a bastion against communism. Zionist propaganda particularly likes to identify the Communist struggle against Zionism as a struggle against the very State of Israel. This false thesis is completely refuted. The Soviet Union does not speak out against Israel but against the politics of its Zionist government, which are militaristic, anti-Soviet, and contrary to the interests of the Israeli people.

. . . The author of *Invasion without Arms* discloses the main strategic aims of Zionism: the elimination of the socialist system and the achievement of world supremacy. "If we pondered the essence of this planned 'All-People's State Federation,' there would rise up before our eyes the specter of the special forces of imperialism: the international trust of capitalists exploiting the world. The activity of the Zionist concern, with centers in Israel and the United States, is subservient to such aims."

It is now known to everyone that Zionism tried to destroy the solidarity of the socialist community by covert methods. This was exemplified by events in Poland and Czechoslovakia. The Zionist network was activated in those countries immediately after World War II. "These people did not go into the forests and form armed bands. Under the guise of superloyalty to the new regime, they lurked and waited for a suitable moment. They were given the task of infiltrating the ideological organizations, party, and state apparatus, and to a certain extent they succeeded. They settled in and waited for 'zero hour,' while playing the role of convinced Communists devoted to Marxism, so as to worm their way into the confidence of the party's organs and then exploit this confidence to perform stealthily the so-called erosion of socialism. And they artfully gained this confidence, achieved responsible positions, and occupied key posts in the most important spheres of the life of the community, while trying to achieve the aim of undermining, destroying, and discrediting the socialist regime." As was stressed by the newspaper *Pravda* of Bratislava: "Mass media and ideology *became the main spheres of their activity.*" In other words, modern Zionism in union with imperialistic forces is betting first of all on a strike against Marxist-Leninist ideology.

. . . The monstrous chauvinism of Zionists is aimed not only against Arabs but against other nations as well. Many apologists of their ideas express their "haughty disdain" of the peoples of Russia—"Nature's first-born, who just yesterday hatched out of the egg."

. . . The collaboration of the Zionists during the war with the fascist *Geschäft* in the blood of millions of Jews—these crimes are now widely known. Such leaders as Rudolf Kastner, Chaim Weizmann, Levi Eshkol (the former Prime Minister of Israel, who diligently served "in Berlin in the so-called agricultural section of the 'Palestinian office' of the Third Reich") would be better called moneybag brothers, not blood brothers (see *Anti-Communism and Anti-Sovietism Are Zionist Professions* [Moscow: Politizdat, 1971], p. 27). Now Zionists are scouring all the world, trying to find and eliminate evidence of this shameful collaboration.

. . . The logical reality is that Zionism is in essence "an objectively anti-Semitic phenomenon," for it always was and is the enemy of the Jewish workers, as well as of all working people. And there is no room for compromise in the struggle against Zionism. That is why V. Begun's book is a brave citizen's response to the most urgent need of contemporary politics.

EXCERPTS FROM BOOKS

Yevgeny Yevseev

FASCISM UNDER THE BLUE STAR[37]
THE TRUTH ABOUT CONTEMPORARY ZIONISM: ITS IDEOLOGY, PRACTICE; THE SYSTEM OF ORGANIZATIONS OF THE JEWISH HAUTE BOURGEOISIE

Moscow: Molodaya Gvardiya, 1971
160 pp., il., 75,000 copies

CONTENTS:

When somebody pronounces the word "fascism" aloud, most people are reminded of the atrocities of World War II, the brown-shirted columns of Hitler's stormtroopers, the swastika, Franco's Phalangists, Mussolini's black-shirted youth, smoldering ruins of towns and villages, the barbed wire of the death camps.

But now, two decades after Nuremberg, the world is witnessing a resurrection of neo-Nazism in West Germany and a number of other countries. Progressive mankind is noticing the intense activity of yet another variety of contemporary fascism, flourishing under the flag of the State of Israel. This flag displays a blue six-pointed Star of David with one blue strip above and one below it, against a white background.

The disappearance of the ancient Hebrew people, its complete absorption into other nations has been scientifically established and is a scientific fact. . . . Nevertheless, Zionism proclaims as a sacred dogma the existence of the "worldwide Jewish people," the "worldwide Jewish nation," the "eternal nation."

The Zionists could erect a golden monument to Hitler; the raving Führer was the one who, in his delirious *Mein Kampf*, sanctioned Zionism's fundamental dogma, the existence of the "worldwide Jewish people," the "Jewish race." (p. 19)

Those who created the fundamental myth of Zionist ideology, the myth of the existence of the "worldwide Jewish people," "one nation," or "nationality spread all over the world," completely ignore the scientific facts. For instance, A. Ranovich,[38] a noted Soviet researcher, stressed that the ethnic process, the process of ethnic division of the ancient Hebrew people . . . irreversibly intensified during later historical development and socioeconomic changes, and ended in the complete disappearance of that people among the peoples of the Middle East, Asia Minor, Africa, and Europe. (p. 21)

Since the Jewish population of the world does not constitute a worldwide nation, as we have already seen, the Zionists lack well-founded justification for their slogan "the ingathering of the nation from the Diaspora." By the Zionist logic, the Jewish population of Israel is not a nation but "part" of one, since the Jews of the whole world constitute one nation from now on and forever. The Zionists contend that this nation, scattered all over the world, wanders from place to place. However, in spite of all Zionist attempts to link together the Jews of the entire world and present them as a "nation," part of which lives in Israel, their "national home" (on this basis, the Zionists demand Jewish loyalty not to an actual homeland but to a notorious "national home" created for their benefit), an Israeli nation is in fact being actively created in that country. The nation being formed in Israel has no connection with the rest of the Jewish population in other countries. This process will continue. The Zionists can still take advantage of such things as the blood relationship between the immigrants arriving in Israel and the Jews remaining in their actual homelands, and insist that world Jewry is one. In time, however, this possibility will cease to exist, as Jews assimilate into the native populations of the various countries.

. . . Jews in the socialist countries are completely free of national and class discrimination, and the great majority of them live in harmony with society, taking an active part along with others in the construction of socialism. The presence of Jews among the intelligentsia of the socialist countries, their participation in the development of the national cultures of the Soviet republics, in science and sports, their promotion to leading positions in production and administration are the most obvious proof of the Jews' emancipation and assimilation in the socialist nations, which welcomed them in brotherly fashion. This fact is used as one of the trumps in the Zionists' pack of marked cards. They try to use it for their own purposes, in order to stir up anti-Semitic feelings in the masses. Hence, they spread on the sly the notion of "Jewish dominance," of their alleged, though as yet unsuccessful, aspirations to seize control of all the decisive governmental and administrative levers. In other words, assimilation is a gradual and irreversible process supported by all the progressive represent-atives of the Jewish population in every country. (p. 30)

Unfortunately, Zionism's critics occasionally tackle only the Zionists' practical activities of a blatantly anti-Soviet, antidemocratic nature, while uncritically using definitions and assumptions that the Zionists them-selves are trying to propagate. We refer primarily to the main Zionist postulates of the existence of a single "Jewish people," of the Jewish people in the Diaspora.

For illustration, we shall quote from Isay Tobolsky's poetry[39] and from Aron Vergelis, editor-in-chief of the periodical *Sovetish Heymland*. To-bolsky says: "I don't repudiate my parentage by hiding behind a pseudo-nym," or "being responsible because of my blood for the infamy of my tribesmen," and, further on, "I don't believe that such people grew wiser through the experience of suffering," etc. Such a naive approach, even in poetry, is here inexcusable.

Similar imprecisions and errors can be found in Vergelis's work. In his notes on a trip to the United States he begins his anti-Zionist statements by accepting the fundamental Zionist postulate: the existence of a Jewish people. "My arrival in this country is becoming part of a struggle. . . . whatever the direction of development of my people, will they allow the Zionists to drag them back to the Middle Ages?"[40] Our respected author is interested in knowing where his people is headed. Scientific data show that such a people does not exist; V. I. Lenin scientifically and directly dis-proved its existence. Vergelis now lets us know that there are Americans of "Jewish nationality" (although it is well known that persons of Jewish origin are registered and recognized as such only in the Soviet Union). The Zionist theme of the people in the Diaspora is interpreted by the author in the following manner: "The 'Jewish street' in many countries contains a strange people of southern temperament and loquacity, northern tenacity and efficiency, eastern wisdom and patience, and western modernity." Wonderfully aggressive anti-American material marred by such inaccura-cies loses much of its propaganda value, and becomes an attempt to refute Lenin's theses concerning the theory and practice of Zionism. (pp. 32–33) Agents of the Zionist secret services set fire to synagogues, desecrate Jewish cemeteries, and carry out many other vile provocations. These are instantly used as ammunition by the Zionist propaganda machine, which cries bloody murder about the threat to the life and property of the Jews in various countries. This happened in Iraq, Morocco, Egypt, Argentina, and the United States.

The Zionists and the entire imperialistic propaganda machine broadly use accusations of anti-Semitism against all who sharply criticize the policy, ideology, and practices of the State of Israel.

. . . For a number of years, the word "racist" has usually been interpreted as meaning antiblack, less frequently, anti-Chinese. Earlier, it referred to German fascism. As a result of the efforts made by certain circles, however, the word was dropped from use altogether in connection with Jewish nationalism in the form of Zionism, although racism is a basic component of this reactionary ideology. (p. 46)

Judaism and Zionism (which absorbed Judaism as a component part) reduce the geography and ethnography of the various peoples to a simple and handy division into two countries, and two nations, Jews and goyim. Goyim are the enemies, the non-Jews. The Jewish clergy and the Israeli Zionist regime, in effect, put the non-Jews outside the law, and create a state of uninterrupted enmity between Jews and all other peoples. Justifying a religion of misanthropy and rousing hatred toward people of other religions serve the global strategy of imperialism. (p. 47)

Zionists and the Jewish clergy are in fact pursuing a coordinated policy. The Zionist theoreticians claim that every Jew is a Zionist by birth. The rabbis and Jewish theologians persistently repeat that being a Jew means being an adherent of Judaism. The "theoretical" circle is thus closed. All that remains is to recreate the Jewish ghetto in one form or another. (p. 54)

How can one take seriously the claim by the Zionists that the results of the titanic efforts of the great minds of all peoples throughout the ages are achievements of "Jewish genius"? The Zionists through such fraudulent methods are trying to overemphasize second-rate talents and exaggerate the importance of their achievements.

They deliberately ignore the fact that those people were the pride of the Russian, German, and other nations, not on account of their origin or religious affiliation, but because of their participation in the national culture, in the creative work of these countries. The names of outstanding Russian, Polish, German, English, and other writers, poets, musicians, composers, and artists sometimes do indeed indicate Jewish origin. But they became famous and beloved mainly because they were part of the nation in which they grew up and where their personalities developed, and not because they went to pray in the synagogue and loved gefilte fish or tsimmes. Nobody is getting ready to hand over Ehrenburg, Oborin, Chakovsky, Kogan, Plisetskaya, or Oistrakh to the Zionists. (p. 58)

. . . What are the so-called cultural and student organizations outside Israel doing with that mass of young people who, without being asked, have already been assigned the role of cannon fodder and whom the Zionist strategists are planning to draft into Israel's armed forces? No other than David Ben-Gurion, former Prime Minister of Israel, gave the answer to that question. He stressed that what is needed in order to attract Jews to come to Israel is not words but deeds; the most effective way of attracting immigrants to Israel is the fear of persecution in the countries where the Jews live. That fear can be generated by disseminating the crudest forms of anti-Semitism.

This task must be fulfilled by specially trained young Zionists who will masquerade as non-Jews, destroy the Jews' complacency, and sow in them anxiety and the desire to go to Israel. . . .

The small number of Jewish youths who arrive in Israel immediately undergo intensive brainwashing, combined with anti-Arab ideological training. A course of so-called reassessment of values, or moral reorientation has been introduced for them. Small wonder that, after taking that course, the young, fledgling Israelis start believing that, in the army, they are fulfilling the "sacred mission" of creating a third "Jewish kingdom."

Demagogical from beginning to end, Zionism thus mobilizes the basest instincts and directs them according to its own desires against hostile trends, personalities, and parties.

Slander, insinuation, murder, theft, provocation, spying, expansionism, aggression are only part of a long list of crimes perpetrated by international Zionism, operating all over the world as an active phalanx of anticommunism, as a perfidious enemy of the national-liberation movements of many peoples.

A quarter of a century ago at Nuremberg the thirty steps to the gallows marked the end of the line for the leaders of Hitler's Third Reich. They had perpetrated the most serious crimes against humanity. One infamous deed of the German fascists was the demoralization and corruption of Germany's younger generation. Today Zionist leaders, who irresponsibly play games with the destiny of the peoples in the Middle East and contribute their share to complicating the international situation and intensifying tension, follow the same path. (pp. 135–136)

. . . Imperialism keeps throwing into battle new cohorts of "conquerors of minds," ideological saboteurs. The role of the shock troops in this attack is being played with increasing determination by the international Zionist corporation, a long-standing tool of imperialism in the latter's fight against the Soviet Union and the other socialist countries, against the national-liberation movements. It is a well-known fact that the Zionists' subversive activities against Soviet rule started immediately after the October Revolution. (p. 137)

. . . The kapos of the death camps and the special "police" who enforced order in the ghettos were recruited by the Gestapo from among the Zionists. In a letter to *Pravda*, Soviet Jewish citizens, now living in the Ukraine, wrote: "The tragedy of Babi Yar will remain forever an embodiment not only of Nazi cannibalism but also of the indelible disgrace of their accomplices and successors, the Zionists."[41]

. . . The Zionists switched allegiance after the war and became completely subordinate to U.S. monopolist capital. . . . (p. 139)

. . . the failure of the plot of the forces of international reaction in Czechoslovakia frustrated the far-reaching plans of American imperialism and its Zionist assistants.

Without neglecting the exportation of the "quiet counterrevolution" to the socialist countries, the international Zionist concern worked out plans for a comprehensive anti-Soviet campaign of really global dimensions. They started the new anti-Bolshevik crusade under the same tattered flag of ·protecting the Jews living in the Soviet Union and other socialist countries. (p. 143)

The activities of the Zionist and related religious and secular organizations prove that Zionism, especially in the last few years, has not only begun employing propaganda methods in its provocations against the Soviet Union, but has even had recourse to fascist methods of conducting a secret war against socialism; it is now using not only blackmail but also brute force. It complicates the relationships between the Soviet Union and other countries, and tries to sow distrust and enmity between the peoples of the socialist camp, between the peoples of the Soviet Union.

It must be stressed that one of the main targets of the violence used by Zionist ideological saboteurs is our Soviet patriotic consciousness. Bourgeois ideology and leftist revisionism are doing everything in order to erode, shatter, and undermine this consciousness. They are sparing neither forces nor means in their violent counterattacks. These counterattacks are not always frontal. They are often subtle attempts, purporting to have "friendly objectivity," at infiltrating our country, raids of deep-thrusting ideological sabotage, to quote the newspaper *Pravda Ukrainy*. "Suddenly" you come across "theories" intended to present the basis of Soviet patriotism as mere national history and traditions.

"Suddenly" doctrines about the adequacy of patriotism in the service of some "national idea," about the timelessness and classlessness of such concepts as "nation" and "people," achieve a greater circulation. "Suddenly" every chauvinistic, Zionist, bourgeois-nationalist rabble-rouser raises a particularly noisy howl. "Suddenly" attempts are being made at provoking bad feeling in the representatives of certain Soviet peoples toward other nations. "Suddenly" narrow local nationalist figures of the past are being extolled and the standard-bearers of friendship between peoples are spat upon. "Suddenly" the objective, historical transformation of the Russian language into a language of international communication is being actively attacked. (pp. 157–158)

. . . The Communist party teaches us that being a patriot means being an active, conscientious, front-line fighter for a happy tomorrow, against the dark forces of reaction, obscurantism, and hatred of mankind, which profess the ideology of violence and robbery and rally around the anti-communist imperialist flag (which changes in design from time to time). Changes in design indicate only regrouping in the enemy camp, but the class nature of fascism does not change, whether its flag displays a brown swastika, the blue star of Zionism, or the stars and stripes of American imperialism. (p. 158)

Vladimir Begun

THE CREEPING COUNTERREVOLUTION

Minsk: Belorus, 1972
192 pp., 25,000 copies

CONTENTS:

. . . The Torah and the Talmud, and secondarily the *Shulchan Arukh* and other religious works, are the catechism for a duplicitous policy. The psychology of Orthodox Jews was shaped over the centuries under their influence. (p. 64)

The Zionists follow Jewish morality and look to the good of "their own," while disregarding the interests of the "uncircumcised and unclean." This shows up in countless ways. (p. 65)

Facts convince us that the tears of the Zionists are crocodile tears; they are meant to turn lies into some obligatory symbol of faith. (p. 88)

While acting in this manner, the Zionists guide themselves by a simple calculation: if they keep pretending long enough to be humble and oppressed, people will end up feeling sorry for these "sufferers," they will start believing these clamorous lies, which is an achievement in itself—a moral position that can be used as a starting point for the next step. And that step is taken, too. (p. 89)

. . . In the countries where Jews respond negatively to Zionist efforts, Zionist agents try to "arouse" the Jewish masses by artifically inciting anti-Semitism through sabotaging synagogues, desecrating Jewish cemeteries and cultural centers, forging anti-Semitic propaganda material, etc. While the Zionist cloak-and-dagger knights prepare the blasting charge and draw swastikas on Jewish graves, the penpushers concoct the next canard to support the fallacious thesis of eternal anti-Semitism. (pp. 89–90)

The slogan of Jewish "national culture" is at present reactionary because it promotes subversive purposes. (p. 106)

The idea of Jewish national isolation, pursued for far-reaching subversive purposes and energetically inculcated by the Zionists, is impossible and impracticable for reasons of principle. There is no room for any bourgeois nationalism in a socialist society, which implements the high principles of national equality and proletarian internationalism. (p. 108)

. . . "A man who accepts the Zionist belief," *Pravda* wrote, "automatically becomes an agent of the international Zionist establishment, and consequently, an enemy of the Soviet people."

Aside from everything else, the idea of Jewish "national culture" is practically unrealizable. First and foremost, it is not the brainchild of Soviet Jews, but of foreign subversive centers. Secondly, it is based on fallacious premises, which completely ignore Soviet living conditions and psychology. (p. 109)

The Zionist agents were activated in Poland and Czechoslovakia immediately after World War II. They did not hide in the woods, nor did they organize armed bands. Masquerading as people who were "superloyal" to the new regime, they waited for the right moment. Their mission was to infiltrate the ideological institutes, the party, and the government apparatus, and to a certain extent, they succeeded. While waiting for the signal, the Zionists had to play the part of convinced Communists, devoted to Marxism, in order to worm themselves into the confidence of the party organs and, taking advantage of this trust, to pursue secretly the so-called erosion of socialism. (pp. 120–121)

This whole ideological and cultural "occupation" in Czechoslovakia took place not on the local Zionists' own initiative, but under the guidance of imperialist services such as the Joint, the Jewish Agency, Simon Wiesenthal's Documentation Center in Vienna, the government services of Israel, the Hudson Institute, the American CIA, etc. (p. 130)

The Zionist agents thus always try for a coup at the top; therefore acting in close collaboration with imperialist subversive centers, they try first to deal a blow to Marxist-Leninist ideology, to paralyze ideological institutes, to seize the leading party, government, and cultural positions, etc. To achieve these goals they used demagogy, deceit, political provocation, fraud, the bogey of anti-Semitism, bribery, the ideological discrediting of staunch Communists and patriots—the entire arsenal of ideological, political, and criminally subversive weapons. (p. 131)

"Sowing poison and dissension" means to corrupt and undermine society, to deceive the people and foster a public opinion suited to their own purposes. The Zionists could not exert intellectual terror if they did not control the most powerful propaganda means, the media. This is why they always try to gain control of newspapers, periodicals, news agencies, publishing houses, and radio and television networks. They have scored many successes in this field. There is now a well-established pattern; in those countries where Zionist organizations operate, a significant part of the mass media is under their influence and control. They use both the mass media belonging to Zionist organizations and the media they do not control. (p. 132)

They say that stories are just stories, but they give hints, a good lesson for the young. Their story of Mordechai and Esther[42] is such a "lesson," an example for the rabbis, for the Jewish obscurantists. During the Purim festival Haman is hanged in effigy on a little gallows. To this day, the story serves to teach perfidy, unscrupulousness, lust for blood, the criminal ways of usurping power. . . .

The Zionists are now propagating and fostering the morals of Mordechai. And they act accordingly. These morals display extraordinary impudence; all means, even the most repugnant, can be used in order to attain power.

The ideological origins of Zionist gangsterism go way back to the "holy" Torah scrolls, to the Talmud's prescriptions.

These origins can also be found in the teachings of Zionist theoreticians, who inculcate in their followers aggressiveness, shamelessness, and disregard for every moral standard if those standards could hamper the achievement of their purposes. (pp. 150–151)

Valery Skurlatov

ZIONISM AND APARTHEID[43]

Kiev: Ukrainian Politizdat, 1975
120 pp., 16,000 copies

CONTENTS

Based on diverse factual data, the author convincingly demonstrates that Israel's blatantly expansionistic policy toward the surrounding Arab states and South African official racial discrimination are of a similar social, ideological, and practical nature.

The book traces the "chosen people" philosophy embodied in, and common to, the dogmas of Judaism and the racial tenets of Protestantism, investigates the sociohistorical conditions under which the ideology of Zionism and apartheid formed and developed, and exposes their inhuman nature and policy. Skurlatov deserves a wide readership.

. . . Racial biological doctrines, according to which people are divided into "chosen people" and goyim, have been turned into official ideology and state policy both in Israel and South Africa, where the "inferior" are forcibly separated from the "superior." This is what apartheid is. (p. 4)

. . . The ideology of Nazism was openly referred to by its creators as "the myth of the twentieth century" (A. Rosenberg). The related ideologies of Zionism and apartheid are nothing but present-day varieties of this myth concerning the alleged congenital inequality of people and races. (pp. 4–5)

. . . The biblical genealogical myth about the patriarchs Abraham, Isaac, and Jacob, and the "revelation on Sinai" to the no-less-mythical Moses are of a purely political nature, meant to establish certain special rights of one tribe over others. In spite of its ancient origin, this myth still exerts a noticeable influence on both the ideology and the policy of racism's apologists. This is why in modern Israel, ancient myths not only perform an important propaganda function but are even included in the state's political doctrine. (pp. 10–11)

. . . Considering oneself to be chosen by God means to set oneself against all others, and aggravate the adverse consequences of the exploitation of others, to provoke the natural hostile reaction of the native population to hegemonic claims. Such a reaction separated the Jews even more from other tribes and peoples, and over the centuries this played into the hands of the Jewish elite, which almost always found mutually profitable ways to live in symbiosis with the local elite. (pp. 11–12)

. . . The main dogma of Judaism states that there is only one God over the entire world, who chose the Jews from among all the peoples on earth, made a covenant with them, and designated them to be shepherds of the goyim, the "beasts with human faces." Jewry's most sacred obligation was proclaimed to be the preservation of racial purity; intermarriage with the goyim was not permitted. The "chosen people" has its own laws, its own circle, its own destiny, and the despicable goyim are fit only to be "talking tools," slaves. Judaism thus very consistently generated an all-inclusive, self-contained ideology of racial superiority and apartheid.

The thesis about God's choosing the Jews, set forth in the biblical Pentateuch (Torah), was developed in detail during the time when the center of Jewish activity as tradesmen and middlemen moved from Palestine to Mesopotamia and Europe. In the Diaspora, the ancient Jewish elite had to maintain strict discipline among "their own." This is why the Talmud (first half of the first millennium) and the *Shulchan Arukh* (fourteenth century),[44] the official Jewish codes of the Diaspora period, emphasize the Jews' "exclusivity," their innate superiority over the goyim, their right to world supremacy. The life of the Jewish community has for many centuries been regulated strictly and uncompromisingly by these prescriptions of Talmudic Judaism, which demanded that each Orthodox Jew should, quite simply, get rich at the expense of the goyim, and taught him to show personal initiative in business and always to be conscious of his "elevated" status compared with the goyim. (pp. 12–13)

. . . The talmudic tractate of *Shabbat* (89a) asks: "What does Mount Sinai mean?" And gives the answer: "Mount Sinai means the mountain whence the *sina* descended," i.e., hatred for all the peoples of the world.[45]

The racist concept of Judaism served as a prototype for European racism. This again shows that Judaism is not "exceptional" at all, and reveals most openly the predatory, exploitative class nature of the "God-chosen" status. (p. 14)

. . . During the Reformation, following the call to return to "Judaic wisdom," especially in Calvinist doctrine, a markedly "God-chosen" and therefore racist variant of Christianity crystallized: Protestantism, which became the ideology of rising capitalism. (p. 15)

K. Marx, in his classic studies of the Jewish problem, demonstrated that the victory of bourgeois attitudes in Europe boosted the importance of trade-intermediary capital, which began to exert its influence in the most significant domains of bourgeois society: ideology, politics, the economy. As a result, the mercantile spirit typical of the Judaic trade-intermediary establishment permeated bourgeois society "to the marrow of its bones," to use Marx's words, and became an integral part of bourgeois ideology in general. Continuing, Karl Marx repeatedly stressed the considerable role played by Judaism in the emergence of the Protestant ethic and indirectly in the rise of capitalism. Generally speaking, K. Marx understood Jewry as the embodiment of mercenary rapaciousness. . . .

This very important observation testifies to the active role played by Judaism in the emergence of capitalism at the dawn of modern times. Not without reason Christian Protestant heresies kept referring to the Old

Testament, and those professing them called themselves "New Israel," "New Judaeans," or "Zionists." (pp. 17–18)

... From the vulgar Protestant racism springing from a feeling of "chosen" self-conceit to the refined neo-Kantian-Cohenian "ethical socialism," all these schemes feature the confrontation of the "chosen ones" and the rest. (p. 19)

In order to mislead world public opinion, Zionists and Judaists sometimes overemphasize their alleged differences, and try to present Zionism as a purely political and entirely modern, almost socialist doctrine. Jewish Orthodoxy, they say, is just a living remnant, the heritage of a tormented history, of past suffering, etc. In fact, both Judaism and Zionism have the same socioeconomic class basis, and thus a common purpose—world domination. Judaism contains in coded form the strategy (universal in class-oriented societies) of the "chosen people." Only "their own" are initiated into this secret strategy; Zionism proclaims the most suitable tactics for a given period.

In the early twentieth century, the old myth about the "God-chosen people" served as a basis for the shameless colonial seizure of Palestinian lands, for the extermination and expulsion of the native inhabitants of Palestine, the Palestinians. (p. 42)

... It has lately become known that many prominent Zionists collaborated with the Nazis [during World War II], betrayed the interests of millions of simple Jews, and secretly accomplished their tasks with the blood of those who were fighting the fascist tyranny. This exceptionally well calculated and cruel attitude of the Zionists during World War II must never be forgotten. It explains much of the adventuristic games now being played by Zionism in the Middle East.

The South African nationalists similarly tried to take advantage of the war for anti-British purposes, in order to consolidate their own position in the country. Like the Zionists they were close to Hitler in spirit, but in contrast to the Zionists, they saw in Hitler a brother in racial and Aryan ideals. (pp. 57–58)

The Arabs, indigenous inhabitants of Palestine, are subjected to blatant racial discrimination. Their settlements and districts have been turned into reservations, they are mercilessly exploited, evicted, and offered the dirtiest jobs; their national and human dignity is constantly abused. Leading Zionist "theorists" established such racial practices long before the proclamation of the State of Israel.

According to Ahad Ha'am, the Jews are a "supernation" whose "ethnic genius" must guarantee their right to world domination. "The Land of Israel must encompass all the countries of the earth, in order to improve the world through God's kingdom." This is the biblical tenet that the Zionist Nietzsche attempted to substantiate philosophically. . . .[46] (pp. 61–62)

. . . South Africa and Israel, though formally young, actually have a genealogy that goes way back to the dawn of capitalism, and both incorporate all the signs of a dying capitalist society. The rosey glow of their cheeks, sometimes assumed to be a sign of youth, is in fact the flush of death. But a common feature of the death agony is a propensity for adventurism and extremism as in Nazi Germany. Masks are being discarded, harsh measures are taken in secret, but they attract world attention. This is why the world's attention now focuses on apartheid and Zionism; their secrets have become known, and the nations have discovered the abominable essence of the "God-chosen." (p. 120)

Vladimir Begun

INVASION WITHOUT ARMS

Moscow: Molodaya Gvardiya, 1977
176 pp., 150,000 copies

CONTENTS:

Zionism emerged around the turn of the twentieth century, at the same time that capitalism reached a monopolistic stage of development. It appeared in the arena of history to encourage not national liberation but imperialist enslavement, to promote not a struggle for the equality, brotherhood, and friendship of peoples but strife. . . . (p. 7)

Sometimes, the Zionist propagandists attempt to prove that elements from other nations joined their movement. Certainly, there were non-Jews who stood up for Zionism. However, these were individuals, politically naive people, fooled by the Zionists or bought by them, morally unclean. . . . Frequently, however, the Zionists have under their command diverse non-Jewish reactionary groupings and organizations.

Another important peculiarity is the extreme chauvinism and egoism of the Zionists. The Jews, say the Zionists and their ideologists, are an exceptional, a unique people, "chosen by God." In their view, this people is "higher" and better than the other peoples of the world, who are considered lower, inferior, contemptible beings. . . . (p. 24)

The reader knows what the Jews were in the eyes of the creator of the theory of the superior Aryan race—third-class people, meriting extermination. How do the Aryans appear to the Jewish chauvinist Jabotinsky? The same kind of contemptible beings, as when he speaks of the "baseness and harshness of the Aryan world," and he says, "in the world a special spiritual mechanism, which is specific and original, it is said of these collectives, that they reason and react in a special way."[47]

The plural is, of course, used by Jabotinsky as a word game—in reality he has in mind only one exceptional "collective." The same chauvinistic concept is developed by the president of the World Jewish Congress, Nahum Goldmann: "The Jewish people was never the same as other peoples. It was always distinct. We are something more than a people, than a religion and civilization, we are all those put together, and because of this there is no other people like us." . . . From a perspective such as this to the construction of gas chambers, there remains, of course, but a single step—given a suitable opportunity and the corresponding military might.

On the strength of this extreme chauvinism, blatantly contemptuous of and hating humanity, Zionism is inherently indifferent to the interests of other peoples. (p. 25)

Today, world Zionism actually consists of large and small, "fat and skinny," open and secret organizations. (p. 30)

. . . Just as a musician, striking a piano keyboard, reproduces the sounds represented in a score, so, too, the Zionist staffs, pressing on this "lever" or that, bring into action suitable organizations, which function efficiently and harmoniously.

The organizational diversity of Zionism is by no means the result of a lack of unity. . . . since it assures a definite flexibility and maneuvarability, making for better camouflage to mislead public opinion. It is also capable of bringing all levels of every Jewish social group under Zionist control. Figuratively speaking, Zionism is organized not in divisions and regiments but in mobile subversive detachments, each with its own appearance, and these are concentrated on every front.

The most essential feature of Zionism is its close connection with Judaism. At the basis of Zionist ideology lie the politicized dogmas of the Jewish religion. . . . (p. 31)

The Jewish religion, which divides all people into the chosen and despised, into the noble and the "uncircumcisesd and unclean," does not draw the Jews closer to other peoples but separates them, arousing suspicion and hostility between them—for whoever shows contempt for another man cannot expect goodwill in return. Especially repulsive is the chauvinistic concept of world domination, formulated in the "sacred texts" and reflected in prayers. The Jewish religious ethic, with its impudence and cynicism toward non-Jews, without doubt plays an exceptionally harmful role. (p. 32)

Repeatedly, the Zionists have attempted to give a theoretical basis to the Jewish bourgeoisie's effort towards world domination. Ahad Ha'am's article "Nietzcheanism and Judaism," first published in 1898 in the magazine Hashiloach, serves as an example. . . .

If he reviews the thought of Ahad Ha'am in the light of his Judeo-Zionist chauvinist outlook, it is not difficult for the reader to reach the logical conclusion: insofar as there is a "supernation," then like the "superman" it can and must march toward its goal over the corpses of others. It must show no consideration toward anyone or anything in order to achieve the domination of the "chosen" over the "heathen." From a mile away, one can smell the fascism of the "sage," Ahad Ha'am. . . . (p. 43)

One can trace the links of a single chain: the Torah–the ideological basis of the Zionist "theoreticians"–aggression in the Middle East–and the corruption of minds in Israel (openly) and in other countries (secretly). (p. 48)

Each subdivision of the numerous Zionist organizations which exist in the West—including all their various branches and offshoots—carries out a specialized, strictly defined task. Some are occupied with ideology—the press, publications, art, cinema. Others are busy with fundraising, as, for instance, the United Jewish Appeal. A third kind collects intelligence data; the members of a fourth are assigned, as was Goldstücker[48] in his time, to leftist parties; and a fifth is active in youth movements. . . .

The ideological sources of Zionist gangsterism are found in the Torah scrolls, in the commandments of the Talmud.

We find these sources also in the teachings of the Zionist theoreticians, who inculcate in their followers aggression, shamelessness, and disdain for any moral standards that stand in the way of achieving their given objectives. . . . (pp. 111–112)

By almost all accepted standards, Israel is certainly a small country. Its espionage service, however, can contend for one of the leading places in the order of rank of the services of the greatest imperialist powers. Its reactionary role in no way corresponds to the size of its population or its industrial-economic potential—little Israel does big imperialistic business. The very presence of the Zionist spy network in diverse corners of the world bears irrefutable testimony to secret, and that means criminal, wicked aims, which the Zionists pursue in a dozen different countries. Is this network not the "nervous system" which, in the words of Max Nordau, must enmesh the entire world and send signals to the Zionist "brain"—the aggressive and chauvinistic state of Israel. (p. 131)

Frontispiece and title page of Ye. Yevseev's book.

SAMIZDAT

To: Academician M. V. Keldysh
President, Academy of Sciences of the USSR[49]

Allegations being spread among members of the Philosophy and Law Division of the Academy of Sciences of the USSR have repeatedly reached my ears. I am accused of concealing my true nationality, that in fact I am a Polish Jew. I might have ignored these rumors, were it not obvious that they are being spread in connection with my being nominated for election as a Corresponding Member of the Academy of Sciences of the USSR.

The above allegations and rumors are sheer slander—they by no means correspond to the facts. The facts are as follows.

I was born on November 18, 1920, in the town of Morshansk in the Tambov Region. My father, Sergei Vasilievich Narsky, Russian by nationality, served as a commander in the Red Army. On demobilization in 1920, he held various posts as an accountant. He died in January 1941 in Morshansk, where he had been born in 1896.

My father's parents, Vasily Andreevich Narsky and Stepanida Fyodorovna Narskaya (née Kovrigina), were Russian by nationality. They lived and died in Morshansk. The surname Narsky is a variation of the original name Narskikh, which had belonged to Vasily Andreevich's ancestors (of Siberian extraction), who lived in the area of the Nara River. There is another branch of the family retaining the surname Narskikh. Some of its members still reside in Morshansk; Ivan Ivanovich Narskikh (research worker in the field of railroad transport) lives in Moscow.

My mother, Elizaveta Ivanovna Narskaya (née Gorbacheva), Russian by nationality, was born in 1895 in a peasant family in the village of Ostrovka, Morshansk District, Tambov Region. The wife, also a peasant from the same village, lived with her daughters after her husband's death. Both parents of my mother were of Russian nationality. Her father died in the village of Ostrovka, and her mother in Morshansk. My mother now resides in Morshansk (10 Passazhirskaya Street). She is seventy-six years old, a pensioner, a disabled worker.

The parents of my wife, both of Russian nationality, also lived and died in Morshansk. Their names were Pavel Dmitrievich Popov and Olga Nikolaevna Popova.

My mother's two sisters, advanced in years, Ekaterina Ivanovna and Antonina Ivanovna, died in Morshansk. A third sister, Aleksandra Ivanovna (married name Sholokhova), lives in Moscow with the family of her daughter Elena Ivanovna (married name Tretiakova).

As far as I am aware, the civil registers of the town of Morshansk and of the Morshansk area were not transferred to a place of safety or destroyed during World War II.

I should like to add that I do not see anything blameworthy or "suspicious" in the fact that a Soviet scientist has a good command of several foreign languages. Besides Polish, I know other Slavic languages, and the principal East European languages. I studied the Polish language in 1945–1946, when I worked on Polish territory as a Soviet intelligence officer. I received government awards, including several orders, for this work.

I request you to acquaint the members of the Philosophy and Law Division of the Academy of Sciences of the USSR with this statement. If you consider it inadequate, please order an inquiry.

I. S. Narsky
Doctor of Philosophy, Professor at Moscow State University, Senior Scientific worker of the Academy of Sciences of the USSR (more than one post)

October 10, 1970, Moscow

OUR INTERVIEWS
G. M. Shimanov Answers the Questions of a Correspondent of the Magazine *Jews in the USSR*[50]

Question: Gennady Mikhailovich, you are considered to be an anti-Semite by many. At the same time, there are rumors that you are a Jew. What will you say about this?

Answer: Well, let's start from the second point, whether or not I am a Jew. No, I am not. I have purely Russian blood. My parents are descended from peasants who owed their allegiance to the Ryazan Province. My father, Mikhail Filippovich, was a plowman in his youth. My mother, Tatyana Sergeevna, was also a peasant. Some people think that I have a Jewish surname; I don't know what to say in this connection. Probably just one thing: in my father's native village of Neznanovo, Korablinsky District, many people had the same surname, although it was accented differently, on the third syllable. I don't know what it means, but if there really is something Jewish about it, it doesn't upset me.

As for my appearance, notwithstanding my undeniable swarthiness and long nose, these characteristics are by no means Jewish. Experts are invited to examine me. My character, as may be confirmed by people who know me, is positively not Jewish either. That is all I can say . . . and whoever I am found to be, as a result of thorough investigations by my adversaries—Jew, Turk, or American Indian—*I am truly Russian because my love forever belongs to this most considerate people.*

And now let us respond to the first part of your question. Am I or am I not an anti-Semite? . . . Despite my great respect for the Jews, I must admit that I really am an anti-Semite. And of the worst kind—why should I make a secret of the fact? I am not one of those anti-Semites who are welcomed with joy by the fathers and teachers of Zionism, but rather one who goads them into fury and, so to speak, makes them call down curses upon themselves. The thing is, I am a well-wishing anti-Semite, unhappy about this hostility, yet an anti-Semite all the same . . . anti-Semite, alas, against my will. . . . Well who's talking about will? Should I start assuring you I am not an anti-Semite? . . . So, expecting the usual buffoonery, I prefer to keep smiling and honestly admit: anti-Semite I am, a real anti-Semite. I was born one. . . .

But to begin with, what does it mean, this word "anti-Semite"? It is considered bad taste or even worse, a detestable moral crime, to even ask this. One is supposed to inherit the righteous instinct. The very sound of the word "anti-Semite" should set one's nerves on edge. If this doesn't happen, for the simple reason that you have strong nerves, try and train yourself to produce the proper reaction. Otherwise you run the risk of being trampled under the hooves of the advanced and enlightened; you will be reduced to nothing. We have become so scared of free thought in what concerns Jews, so used to quivering with fear as soon as the very word is pronounced, that anti-Semites, when exposed to the public eye, do not hesitate to repaint their reactionary faces to look like progressive ones, and start repeating over and over again, like parrots: "But we are not anti-Semites at all . . . We are good. We condemn anti-Semitism . . ."

This is what you Jews have done to the poor anti-Semites . . . You've made them condemn themselves . . . what do you say? . . . Do you call this humane? . . . Cruel, cruel, people!

However, let us try and see whether the Jews gain anything from being so hardhearted. If they do, it's not much, and in the long run, they lose. Anti-Semitism is forced to use loyal means for purposes which are not so loyal. It wraps itself in hypocrisy, guile, ambiguity, and reservations, which does not contribute to normalization of the moral atmosphere or to finding the truth; on the contrary, they make the atmosphere even more murky, full of suspicion, ruinous to religious life. The conflict between the two parties—the indigenous nation and the alien Jews—in all its religious and moral complexity, cannot be impartially viewed in this atmosphere. Hence, it is an impossibility to resolve this conflict on the most desirable, truly considerate basis. Yet only such a solution could enlighten us all spiritually, could be universally useful, and serve as a kind of blessed Eucharist.

We will now try to look into the meaning of "anti-Semitism."

But let us return to the meaning of the word. An anti-Semite is supposed to be a person who is antipathetic to Jews. Why oppose and how—justly or unjustly? All these minor things and details are rejected at one blow by the word "anti-Semite," as being negligible, or, more precisely, meaningless, i.e., irrelevant in the face of the main point. Who cares about details if someone opposes Jews! This is the implication of the word "anti-Semite" and, naturally, also of the word "anti-Semitism." These two words imply that one should never oppose Jews! The Jews are always right and always beautiful (probably with some minor exceptions which do not prove anything)!

The whole secret meaning of the word "anti-Semite" is camouflaged by deliberate vagueness and ambiguity, which protect this meaning from being unmasked as "death." True, if one declares openly that the Jews are always right and cannot be opposed, it would not only disclose one's own stupidity and Jewish racism, it would also make one a laughing stock and provoke justifiable resentment on the part of the "local population." If, however, this stupidity and racism are veiled in ambiguity, and the ambiguity is given the character of moral indignation against the villains who dare to oppose truth and goodness—then it is acceptable.

Certainly, the fact that I expose here the secret meaning of the word "anti-Semite" must attest my deep-rooted anti-Semitism. "Why expose? . . . By so doing you are coming out against the Jews . . ." My discussion of this word will no doubt be understood and interpreted in the light of this attitude ("do not argue!"), but this will only confirm the correctness of my observations.

Thus, it is necessary either to abandon for good this secret and cunningly masked meaning, thus admitting that Jews as a nation may (like any other nation, to be sure) be unjust, in the wrong, and hostile to other nations, whose anti-Semitism is therefore to a certain extent justified as a defense reaction against the Jews (this would create the possibility of true comprehension of the fate of both Jews and non-Jews) or to stick firmly to the concept of Jewish infallibility and Jewish superiority, mask this concept in all possible ways, and, by combining it with unbelievably preposterous ambition, turn it into a destructive force, increasingly incapable of showing compassion, which stops at nothing.

And now let me explain my words, "defense reaction against the Jews." What do these words mean? If a nation, like a family, is an organism (which is beyond doubt), then it is typical of it, as long as it is healthy, that it can assimilate to foreign influences or eject what it fails to assimilate. There is a difference between drinking a glass of milk and a glass of kerosene. There is a difference between eating an apple and swallowing a needle. The Jews, because of their inability to assimilate, have become a foreign organism within an organism or, according to Dostoevsky (also considered a real anti-Semite by many Jews), a state within a state. The famous mutual aid of Jews, which is so characteristic of them and which puts them in such an attractive light, is objectively directed against the people in whose midst they live. It is considered inappropriate among the Jews to think in such terms, which is quite understandable; nothing could be gained from such speculations except additional trouble. This is why Jewish thoughts and Jewish eyes are turned to things quite different; to pleasant, useful things. But what happens if the people against which Jewish solidarity is directed also try, even by imitating the Jews, to develop their own mutual support, naturally, for reasons of self-defense, i. e., again objectively speaking, in opposition to the Jews? This will look, through Jewish eyes, an utterly disgusting quality, worthy of condemnation and total eradication. Double-dealing has become part and parcel of Jewish ideology to such an extent that it uses it with remarkable elegance, and to great advantage, without even noticing it.

Yet, what is the result? Since the Jews fail to reduce to manure even one people, and since no people will ever manage to either assimilate the Jews, chuck them out from their midst, or neutralize their destructive influence, there is a mutually agonizing, smoldering, incessant struggle: the indigenous organism suffers from the gripes and giddiness induced in it by the smaller foreign organism, and the latter experiences rather unpleasant, sometimes intolerable pressure ("discrimination") directed by the larger organism, which does not agree to become manure for Jewish prosperity. The Jews are generally disinclined to assess their situation objectively, yet they are extremely sensitive to any discrimination (naturally against themselves) and never fail to fight it, trying to paralyze the indigenous nation "for its own sake," since for them its good coincides remarkably well with their own good (this may be an expression of an aspect of the Jewish character which it is hard not to regard as a childish lack of sophistication rather than as slyness). The Jews see a defense reaction against them not only in terms of its disadvantage for them but also in terms of the ontological untruth, which is called forth to intensify the rage against it: "Don't you dare defend yourself! This is immoral! . . . This is loathsome! . . . Don't you dare defend yourselves!" However, while reprimanding the Jews for lack of conscience, how can one refrain from a similar reprimand addressed to the indigenous peoples? For they, in fact, say something very much alike: "You are parasites! You are destroying us! To hell with you!"

Each party, as one can see, is right in its own way and wrong at the same time. Each regards the situation from its own point of view only, failing or even unwilling to put themselves in the other's position. The Jews don't care that their tentacles, eating into other organisms (the Jews call it the "Jewish contribution" to the foreign culture), bleed them white and stifle them, while the indigenous peoples (certain Jewish ideologists prefer calling them simply "local population," thus placing them close to the fauna) do not care that the Jews simply have nowhere to go, that they are destined by God's providence to wander amid other peoples, in the homelands of other peoples.

The indigenous peoples don't care that God's providence has denied the Jews a true faith and homeland (obviously, not without wise intent, lest the Jews introduce into Christianity the arrogance which has taken root in them following their being chosen by God, which logically will eventually be transformed into wise understanding and love). This has been done partly for the sake of the one-time heathens, who were warned through the lips of the Apostle Paul that they should not become conceited like the Jews, who had not accepted Christ, but should rather observe every truth. This, in reference to the Jews, implied wise understanding of their circumstances, and also brotherly love, which cannot die as a result of transient hostility. God has denied the Jews a true faith and homeland, not only to humble them but also to make the indigenous peoples share these two things with the Jews, as brothers. This was meant to remove all reasons for mutual praise or ill-will on both sides. "Your house is left unto you desolate." This was said in order that the truth should enter the Jews through other peoples.

It is only on the basis of a general, mutual humbleness in Christ, and love freed through humbleness and wisdom that a truly considerate (or truly Christian, which is the same thing) solution to the so-called Jewish problem is possible. The Jews must thus admit the essential legitimacy of anti-Semitism, while the indigenous peoples must admit its essential illegitimacy. Only on the basis of such mutual understanding, and a rising above transient circumstances and hostility, can supreme human dignity be established and God's great providence acclaimed. "For God hath concluded them all in unbelief, that he might have mercy upon all."

"On the depth of the riches both of the wisdom and knowledge of God!

How unsearchable are His judgments and His ways past finding out!"

Why don't we, too, Russians and Jews, join in this glorious hosanna, lest we become cut off from the truth itself.

Having expressed this general principle, I dare not go into detail as to what the nature of this Christian solution to the problem should be. It is clear that the indigenous peoples will have to share their land with Jews (remember that the entire earth, after all, belongs to God). Let them have the land necessary to live in dignity (no better and no worse than that owned by the indigenous peoples). The Jews will have to become localized and live an autonomous national life (but being permitted a worldwide Jewish union without interfering in the national life of other peoples).

There should be Jewish localization, and a worldwide cultural union, full development of intrinsically Jewish national culture, but no interference in the life of others, unless there is mutual brotherly agreement on participation in each other's affairs.

This is all I can say about my anti-Semitism, which has been noted by the astute Jewish mind.

Question: What do you think of Zionism?

Answer: It seems to me that Zionism lacks a true comprehension of Jewish destiny, although it does show a passionate endeavor to comprehend it. It is by no means accidental that Zionism puts the accent on the national rather than the religious aspect of the Jewish problem. In Zionism, the nation comes first and religion second. This empties it of all spiritual content and confines it to a problem which is purely secular, even somewhat disreputable (begging your pardon, you ardent Zionists). The State of Israel, founded by Zionists, is far from the true solution to the Jewish problem, if for no other reason than that many Jews run away from this state, and huge numbers of them do not even think of going there. Hopes are very slight that the situation may change in the future. Besides (and this is the main point), the universally important Jewish problem cannot be solved on the basis of the inhuman ousting of Arabs by a godless culture. The inhuman attitude toward Arabs and the brutality of the contemporary culture itself, which was mechanically transferred from the West and not really transformed in religious spirit, are consistent with each other, and also indicate the extent of the failure of the Zionist solution to the Jewish problem.

How I picture the solution I have already mentioned. Only mentioned, because weighty utterance on this subject must come from the Jews themselves and perhaps, also, from God, who occasionally likes to accomplish the unexpected, thus revealing the truth noticed by none. I do not consider myself an expert on Jewish affairs (I have been taken unawares by the questions of the *Jews in the USSR* correspondent) and therefore readily admit that the problem may be more intricate than I think. I wish to add only that a true solution to the Jewish problem is possible, in my opinion, only under universal Christian theocracy, whose new growth is distinctly observable to those who can see in Soviet Russia. This is why the hopes of the best sons of the Jewish people should, in my opinion, relate not to the State of Israel but rather to a Russian Orthodox transformation of Soviet Russia, which is at present something like a spiritual detonator for the whole world. Should the Soviet Union fall, the whole world will fall in World War III; should the Soviet Union be tranformed, in truth and love, there will be a transformation of the entire world, including the Jews. On this basis, the best sons of the great Jewish people and the best sons of the great Russian people may come to full mutual understanding and cooperation for the good of mankind.

To conclude my answer about Zionism, I will say this: Zionism in its present form is a failure and will remain so, despite its partial success. It is too secular and lacks truly ecumenical grace. Many modern Zionists admit this, after giving the question some thought. I therefore see dissension in the future of Zionism. The best of its adherents will be transformed in God and adopt a modest attitude to all the peoples of the world; the rest will stiffen in their brainless obstinacy in opposition to other peoples and to the very God of love.

Question: Do you believe in the existence of a universal Jewish conspiracy or, as it is sometimes called, a "Jewish-Masonic conspiracy"? And what can you say about the *Protocols of the Elders of Zion?*

Answer: I cannot answer yes or no to the first part of your question, since my opinion cannot be so simply expressed.

Judge for yourself. Is it possible to prove that there is no conspiracy? To prove this one would have to know the ins and outs of the whole world, which no human being will ever achieve. Besides, one should also have an absolute guarantee that his interpretation of these ins and outs is correct, which also seems to me quite difficult to achieve. Moreover, all alleged proofs that there is no conspiracy can easily be regarded as common devices resorted to by conspirators to hide from the simple-minded "population" the existence of a conspiracy. If one also takes into account the fact that the conspiracy in question is supervised by Satan himself, one can see that the masking may be practically perfect, i.e., capable of leading into error even the chosen.

On the other hand, all proofs of the existence of such a conspiracy are convincing to a certain extent only—they are not convincing enough. Jewish power, which is usually pointed to in order to show that the Jewish plot does exist, can be explained. Jews participated as much as they could, or happened to be involved in certain unimportant events in European history. What has that to do with conspiracy? Remembering that fear takes molehills for mountains, and that contemporary society in which Jews dominate (not all Jews, to be sure, just the socially elevated upper ten thousand members of Jewry's ranks) is cunning and cruel, one can understand the endeavors of some to account for the nature of this society by considering the deliberate destructive activity of the Jews. But why necessarily deliberate? All this could be explained more easily and elegantly by pointing to their lack of roots and a certain kind of doom that hangs over them. So if their activity has been unconscious, where does the Jewish conspiracy come in? One has to use much more accurate terms.

Nothing in this problem can be proved by superficial reasoning. The scientific approach is also worthless here. So let everyone believe whatever he chooses! The most complete, sweet freedom!

Although there are no external starting points for seeking the truth in this problem, there are internal ones which are not readily discernible and which are connected with theology rather than science. And though formally there is no section—Hebraism—in Christian theology so far, corresponding to my approach, this does not mean there should not be one, that this problem should be further neglected.

One of the internal starting points is the following. If the course of history, even recent history, is regarded as being the result of malicious Jewish intrigues, it would remove not only the dignity of the Jews, which Christian conscience could not accept, but also the dignity of all non-Jews, which Christian conscience could also not accept. In fact, the non-Jewish peoples would look stupid, an inert helpless mass which can be easily fooled by the Jews.

Here the advocates of the concept of Jewish conspiracy are unexpectedly seen to be taking their own bait; they are making fools of themselves, which seems to correspond to cruel reality. Truth seems to have taken revenge; one cannot debase the dignity of others and go unpunished. This applies equally to Jews who take every opportunity to injure the dignity of others; they are repaid in kind. To conclude, the idea of a Jewish conspiracy cannot explain history unless we are prepared to liken ourselves to the above-mentioned fishermen.

The people which God's providence and its own sinful will have brought to reject Christ, and which, as a result, does not have the benefit of having its own territory, could not help becoming a *catalyst* of the negative processes taking place in Christian history. This statement is not meant to accuse the Jews as a nation (though a superficial attitude and a certain hastiness may suggest just this to some); all men are sinners, not the Jews alone, and furthermore it was the intent of providence that the Jews be given this role (to a certain extent this lulled the Jewish conscience to sleep) for the sake of one-time heathens. Yet, however unjust it may be for us to blame the Jews for this role, it would also be unjust to hush up the matter. Both silence and unjust accusation would equally distort the truth, and thus block the correct way out of the problem presented by the contradictions associated with the Jewish problem.

And now a few words about "lulling," a phenomenon of no small importance where the Jewish question is concerned. To ignore this lulling or treat it as an attitude of moral or intellectual superiority over non-Jews (especially Christians) would be a strained interpretation, possible only as a result of the as yet incurable lulling. Lulling is lulling, i.e., it is a certain deficiency, not a merit; it is an indication of partial death, i.e., less of higher conscience. Otherwise we would have to concern ourselves not with a culture of vigilant conscience but with a culture of sleep and dreams, these being considered supreme reality, almost in the spirit of Freud and numerous other Jewish-minded painters. (Incidentally, the apotheosis of rootlessness and unawareness takes different forms in contemporary atheistic culture, in which Jews occupy such a disproportionately prominent position. This is quite typical.)

Thus, the spiritual lulling of the Jewish people could not but have a bewitching effect on the awareness of Christian peoples, only partly raised by Christianity from heathenism to a higher life. But this Jewish influence could not start before the Christian peoples became weaker in the religious and national aspects of life, and sufficiently corrupted for their secular life to have secularized the Jews also, who like a genie let loose from the bottle, broke away to the freedom of a godless life and became the most active element in further advancing secularization.

The mutual influence of Western Christianity and "lulled" Jewry is absolutely beyond doubt; also beyond doubt, their influence was by no means beneficial. Secularity is based on false, intrinsically vicious religiosity. This religiosity, the basis of progress, was characteristic of Western Christians. They rejected the one all-embracing truth for the sake of its parts, which they immediately distorted to suit themselves. It was also characteristic of the homeless Israelites that they rejected Christ for the sake of the misinterpreted Law, which they ultimately proved incapable of following. These two factors, which seem so different, even to act against each other, are nevertheless related in many ways, and gave birth to secular society, which spread to Russia and, in the course of a struggle with the age-old Russian ways, led to Soviet power.

All this suggests to me the following conclusion: the concept of a Jewish conspiracy should be abandoned in the name of Christianity. Yet it should be given up not because of the stupid belief that there can be no conspiracy, but rather for the sake of the truly Christian concept, according to which "the mystery of iniquity doth already work" (2 Thessalonians 2:7) and evil spirits are busy working to build the Black Church, which (in contrast to the Church of the Old Testament, which prepared for the coming of Christ) must prepare for the coming of the Antichrist. Having rejected the idea of a Jewish conspiracy, one should speak of the satanic plot which in the course of history could involve consciously only very few people but unconsciously many—not, of course, only Jews. This concept will not mislead and will not arouse unhealthy suspicions between peoples (which could only be advantageous for the Devil). Rather it will make it possible to look quietly and deeply but astutely at a world free of futile suspicion. The paths of love should be closed to no man and to no people.

As for the Masons and the *Protocols of the Elders of Zion*, I am not sufficiently familiar with either of these subjects to be able to say anything definite. I am not ruling out a connection between the Masons, the synagogues, or Zionism with the Black Church, but I do not assert this, for I have no adequate proof. Neither am I prepared to hurl irresponsible accusations—why should I take bread from my opponent's mouth? This would be unkind.

Question: What is your attitude to Jewish emigration from the USSR?

Answer: The people who are leaving the country are of very different types. Those who are leaving in search of a better material life are not worth talking about. If, on the other hand, people who hate or despise Russia are leaving, I am all for it. I think it is beneficial not so much for Russia (we are no longer afraid of Jewish hatred or Jewish contempt) but for the Jews who stay and who will no longer be poisoned by their miasma. My attitude to those who are leaving in confusion is different—mixed. I hope that their departure from Russia and a better knowledge of Israel and the West will help them get rid of many illusions and come to love Russia from a distance. I would welcome the return of such Jews to Russia for truly constructive activity, for the welfare of the two peoples. I have a special attitude to the Jews with beautiful souls, who, if not misled, are given no chance in the present malodorous atmosphere surrounding the Jewish problem. The emigration of such people can under no circumstances be welcome, since their place, which they have not yet found, is in the general Russian and Jewish (or even international) movement for the reform of Soviet power, in accordance with the principles of the Russian Orthodox Church, for the creation of a new religious culture. It is only in the atmosphere of this culture that a true resurgence of the Jews is possible, that a solution to the problem of their relationships with other peoples, on a really sympathetic basis, may be found.

Question: There is an opinion that the Russian Revolution was effected by Jews. Do you agree with this? And how do you assess the role of the Jews in the October Revolution?

Answer: I am certainly not so overawed by the Jews as to believe that they were behind the October Revolution. It is, however, common knowledge that the role of Jews in this revolution was enormous. Who knows whether Russian radicalism and the bitter reaction against the old order would have sufficed for the victory of the new atheist ideology, were it not for the Jewish hatred for Russia as the embodiment of the most conservative Orthodox-patriarchal principles? (This hatred was ingrained in atheistic Jews during the revolution, and can still be found in almost every Jew, be he a convert to atheism or Christianity, a party member, or an ardent enemy of Soviet power.) Thus, the Jewish contribution to the Russian Revolution should be considered an extremely important catalyst, but certainly not the major one. The Jews were able to give the widest expression to their stormy revolutionary activity for only one reason: the Russian people was paralyzed, writhing in Russo-European (i.e., Orthodox-bourgeois) contradictions. But for this decisive circumstance, but for this crisis of antagonism between Russia and Europe inside Russia, the Jews (instead of being occupied in the surplus-appropriation campaign or in the organization of various RAPPs and concentration camps) would have continued to sell kvass, follow crafts, and indulge in the sacred custom of spitting secretly when passing Christian houses of worship. They have suspected to what incredible heights the mocking fates might throw them.

The October Revolution cannot, however, be regarded as an exclusively or even essentially negative phenomenon. This revolution was a great conflict in which negative elements became interwoven with positive ones, at first sight, in a friendly, even affectionate way. But in its unseen, secret aspects, it was an uncompromising struggle, the outcome of which is yet to be seen. Negative elements brought in by the revolution prevailed in the first stages of the rise of Soviet power. Later, in the process of development, there started a gradual rejection, a difficult purification to eliminate the negative. Despite the fact that, originating from Russophobia, Soviet power has little by little become Russified and, I am sure, will continue to be Russified until Russia triumphs.

What is particularly important—and I cannot help stressing it—is the fact that Soviet Russification is not nationalistic in nature, it is not hostile in principle to any other nation, including the Jews; it does not destroy any nation but only gives it access to the highest aspects of the epoch-making drama and thus, especially in view of the future triumph of the Russian Orthodox Church, it is highly beneficial to all. This spiritual Russification is similar in some of its aspects to the spiritual Judaization of the Christian peoples, which was completed in the Middle Ages, but which started as early as the first centuries of the Christian era. It is essential that the attitude of the Russian people to other peoples be not that of a conqueror or bourgeois colonialist, but that of an older brother, sharing with them a world-encompassing destiny and bearing the main burden of the critical period. This is the clue to the surprising strength of so-called Russian colonialism (as the enemies of Russia like to put it), which is in fact not colonialism, but the admitting of other peoples to the birth throes of the fulfilling by Russia of God's mission to give birth to a new Christian civilization.

Reverting to the role of the Jews in the October Revolution, in which they were the shock troops of the entire brigade, I will say that but for them, and this entire brigade, there might have been no Soviet power and therefore no purifying flame, without which the new word of Christian truth would not have been brought to life. Consequently, there could have been no good fortune without this misfortune.

Question: How do you evaluate the role of Jews in Russian culture?

Answer: If you mean the Judaization of Russian culture through the instrumentality of Christianity, my opinion of their role is very high. But if you have in mind the so-called Jewish contribution to twentieth-century Russian culture, I don't think much of the "Jewish contribution" or of the culture of the upper classes. I regard it as extremely decadent, although I acknowledge the talent of its representatives and respect the popular foundation of this culture, which has been much less affected by decadence.

I am not an opponent of the idea of one people having a cultural influence on another; absolute nationalism is an absurdity and death. It is, however, important that the nation which hears the supreme truth should be the one that influences other nations rather than the other way around, as has been and often still is the case. It is both stupid and a sin to fear a really higher influence; but not to resist lower cultural influences would be a crime.

Yet I repeat my hope that the best Jews in our country, having accepted from the Russian people the truth of the Orthodox Church in its entirety, and having united their fate with Russian destiny in the struggle for the Orthodox reform of the Soviet state, will make a really positive contribution to Russian history and culture. I can't think of anything better than that.

Question: Do you consider the Jews who have converted to Christianity to be Jews? And do you think they could have special paths within Christianity?

Answer: What else should I consider them—Spaniards, Ukrainians, or Armenians? This question I refer to those Jews who consider Wilner (an atheist and a Communist who denies the true greatness of the Jewish people) to be a Jew, but consider converted Jews who have never renounced the greatness of Jewish destiny not to be Jews. The cowardly aggressiveness of the Jews toward Jewish Christians is not becoming in view of the strength of the former, and is a discouragement to neo-Judaism. But one can understand these neo-Judaists; it is not the atheism of Wilner or the triteness of the rest which is the real danger to them, but rather the religion of the God of love.

Nevertheless, the Jewish Christians are snuggling up to Judaism and being kicked in the back by it; they are still dreaming of an unprincipled kinship with the synagogue, wiping off the spittle, and striving for that which has produced a gap between the Jewish people and the Son of God. Frankly, I do not think much of the contemporary Jewish Christian who manages to reach the heights of faith in Christ but is still imprisoned by Judaic dreams. The Jewish Christians do not realize that the Jewish people and the synagogue are different things, however closely they may be connected in history; they do not realize that the Judaization of Christianity will necessarily rob the latter of its essence. Yet if one approaches the present type of Jewish Christian from a historical viewpoint, taking into account the complexity of the coming of Jews to Christ, and regarding this type as transitory in the movement to future Orthodox completeness, one can see that the conversion of Jews in Russia to Christianity is a very great and positive phenomenon; this is the seed of future Jewish renascence on a world scale. The current liberal Zionist and Judaic concepts permeating the Jewish Christian conscience are essentially hostile to Christianity, and must be reconsidered by the Jewish Christians. Only after this will it become possible for them to wake up and realize their position in the world. The special paths for Jews within the framework of Christianity consist not in unprincipled and futile (Judaists will never let this happen) attempts to unite with the synagogue (as long as the synagogue exists there will be an irreconcilable conflict between the Jews and the rest of the world, as well as among the Jews themselves); rather they are to be found in the uniqueness of their historical destiny and their present position in the world. It does not take a great intellect to invent artificial features. The Jews will never be able to get rid of their uniqueness. But to get rid of Judaic narrow-mindedness is possible and necessary. This deliverance, according to the Apostle, will mean great things for the world, a reconciliation and reconciling acceptance of all the glory of Christ our Savior.

Question: Do you consider the Jewish people to be God-chosen?

Answer: Since they can regard being chosen by God as formally noncommittal but still a very pleasant title, why should the Jews give up the privilege of calling themselves chosen? I personally have nothing against it. If, however, the state of being chosen by God implies a certain positive mission in history, who will tell me to what extent the Jewish Christians may prefer to prove that the Jewish people is God-chosen after they, the Jewish Christians, accepted Christ? I could readily agree to any proof, however, just to meet the desires of my brethren in faith. To my mind, however, God never reversed His choice of the Jews, but this concept became empty when they rejected Christ. I will add that the very concept of being chosen by God must necessarily change, and many peoples must be shown their way to Christ. It is therefore hardly possible for any people to claim some exceptional privileges in the name of God in the ancient Jewish spirit, but this does not rule out the peculiar quality of each national group, in its devotion to God's truth.

Question: What do you think of the prospects of Jews in the USSR?

Answer: I have already told you: I believe that the best part of the Jewish people, after knocking about in the blind alleys of liberalism, Judaism, and Zionism, will, without losing their Jewish characteristics, join a movement which now seems incredible: the Russian movement for theocratic reform. The rest will continue dashing around blind alleys or, laughing up their sleeves, enjoy all the pleasures of life. And when the theocratic movement progresses from utopian expectations to action, and becomes more and more actual, I think each soul will express itself fully, i.e., will either accept the new word of God's truth wholeheartedly or run away from it to seek refuge in other countries.

In conclusion, I would like to address the readers of *Jews in the USSR* with the following words. I am very glad to have been given the opportunity to expound my views on the Jewish problem before Jews. I have no doubt that they will evoke legitimate rage in the hearts of the empty-headed, since everything which is incomprehensible and at variance with customary convictions can only be annoying. As for the Jews who are capable of reasoning, I do not rule out the possibility of reaching full understanding with them in the course of time. I am sure these latter will not condemn me for my "anti-Semitism," but will thank me for my straightforwardness and honesty, without which there can be nothing of real value in this world. If, in their opinion, I am mistaken about anything, I will not evade a discussion of controversial points in the pages of this magazine, or in any other form they consider acceptable. Let me assure you that if I become convinced that I am really wrong, I will not persist, and will say so. I would like to hope that the Jews will show the same readiness. I strongly believe that the malodorous atmosphere enveloping Russo-Jewish relations may be improved with the help of new ideas which provide a proper understanding of our Christian history and of the great Jewish theme; it may thus become an atmosphere in which one can breathe freely, and in which the highest God-man creative activity will become possible.

Glory to Jesus Christ!

Moscow
May 13, 1976

Ivan Samolvin

A LETTER TO SOLZHENITSYN

When "Matryona's House" appeared, I thought you would become a great Russian writer. But your new novel, *August 1914*, was published abroad, and it immediately became clear, Solzhenitsyn, who you are and what you are.

. . . We won't dwell on the contents of the novel, in which, using the rout of our armies in East Prussia in 1914, you try to show that the Russians are absolute garbage compared with Germans and Jews (1).*

You even call Christ a Jew, although even I, Russian Orthodox only by virtue of baptism and not versed in theology, understand that to God, nationality is of no importance.

What sort of an ending does this novel have? In the home of a certain Jewish businessman, Ilya Isaakovich, who is completely enveloped in the author's sympathy, the former anarchist Obodovsky and the younger Jewish generation, Nahum and Sonya, are having dinner. Obodovsky is yearning for the development of industry in Russia and brings in Mendeleyev's calculation—by the middle of the twentieth century the population of Russia will be more than 300,000,000 (thank you for the figure, we will return to it later).

That is—observes the kindly Jewish capitalist—if we don't start spilling each other's guts. He, Ilya Isaakovich, is against the revolutionary extremism of Nahum and Sonya, against throwing bombs, he is even for "Russia," for "this stinking monarchy." What a pack of lies! From where does Ilya Isaakovich derive his concern for the "creation of Russia," when the Jewish religion (and he is a believer) teaches him that a non-Jew is "worse than a dog," that a Jew is required to deceive non-Jews every way he can, that "Jews must regard non-Jews not as human beings but as beasts" (Talmud, *Yebamoth* 61), that "the offspring of non-Jews cannot be compared even to bastards or idiots of Jewish descent" *(Shulchan Aruch)* (2).
. . . Moreover, since early childhood it has been drummed into Ilya Isaakovich that he is a member of the chosen people, whose destiny is to subjugate all other people, to compel them to work for them, "to shepherd the nations with an iron crook." Cicero already knew and wrote about this.

We won't delve into history. Let us return to what the Jew Ilya Isaakovich, with his higher education, could not fail to know. Why, he even had to pay the "shekel," the tax in gold (which is still paid all over the world today) so that the organization struggling to ensure Jewish world domination will have funds. Ilya Isaakovich must have known about the documents of the World Jewish Alliance (Khavura Kol Yisrael Khaverim), one of whose founders was Crémieux, the grand master of the French Masonic lodges. "We live in alien lands, and we cannot concern ourselves with the fickle desires of countries which are wholly *foreign* to us. . . . Israelites! Wherever fate may throw us—to the four corners of the earth, always regard yourselves as members of the chosen people. The net cast by Israel

*The comments on Samolvin's letter are by M. Agursky. As indicated by the use of parenthetical rather than superior numbers, they are not included in the general sequence of notes for Part 5. They appear at the end of the letter, below.

over this earthly sphere will spread wider with every day, and the grand prophecies of our holy books will eventually be fulfilled. . . . The day is already not far off when the riches of the world will come into the possession of the children of Israel!" And the same Crémieux advised: "Consider civic obligations as worthless. Consider any honors as nonsense. Don't bother with money in the meantime. First of all—seize the press, then all the rest will come to you of its own accord!"

The Jews did not restrict themselves to the press and through their banks seized the money of the entire world. The power of capital is their power. Marx could not help speaking about this: "The Jew has appropriated financial power. . . . What is the secular basis of Jewry? Practical self-seeking activity. What sort of secular religion does the Jew have? Money-grubbing. What sort of secular god does he have? Money . . ." (*The Works of Marx and Engels*, 2d ed., p. 408). It's true that Marx believed that with the advent of socialism the Jews would cease to be Jews.

Solzhenitsyn, did you carefully read Dostoyevsky, whom you cite? He wrote that after the abolition of serfdom, the Russian peasant fell into the clutches of the Jews; that "while the Germans fully exploited people, they tried all the same not to ruin their peasants, if only for their own sakes. But the Jew doesn't care about the sapping of Russian strength; he took what he could and away he went." He also said, "Well, suppose in Russia there were not 3,000,000 Jews but Russians, and there were 80,000,000 Jews—well, what would become of the Russians among them, and how would they treat them? Would they let them settle freely among them? Would they not immediately enslave them? Even worse, wouldn't they flay the hide off them altogether? Wouldn't they massacre them until they were entirely *exterminated*, as they used to do to other peoples in days of old, in their ancient times?" (Is this not confirmed in Israel, Solzhenitsyn?) And when they said to Dostoyevsky that only "obscurantist" religious Jews think this way, he answered that one cannot imagine a Jew without God: "I don't even believe in educated atheist Jews; they are all one of a kind, and God alone knows what the world can expect from Jewish atheists." Anybody can read this in *The Diary of a Writer* for the year 1866.

When, at the end of the last century, the Jewish journalist Herzl "suddenly" got the touching idea that the Jews should return to the "ancient homeland," and create the State of Israel, it was merely a coverup for another idea—the creation of a no longer covert but overt *Zionist* organization, to increase the strength of world Jewry in their struggle for world domination. Professor Mandelshtam of Kiev University said the following at the Jewish Congress on August 29, 1898 (all the following quotations are from recently published books which contain references to foreign sources)(3). "The Jews most decisively reject any association with other nations and remain faithful to their historic hope of achieving the *world domination* promised to them by Jehovah." This is their main objective. And it remains immutable. In Jerusalem at the Twenty-Sixth Zionist Congress, in 1965, N. Goldmann, the chairman of the World Zionist Organization, confirmed that the task of Zionism is "to use the State of Israel for the realization of the main objective of Zionism. A state was *never* the goal of the Zionist movement."

Let us return to Herzl. "To propagate our ideas," he wrote in his book *The Jewish State,* "we have no need to call assemblies with their inevitable chattering; this propaganda will become an integral part of the *liturgy."* The circle closes. A terrible circle, which the Jewish Zionists see in the form of a snake coiled around the entire globe and suffocating everything that lives. Everything in the West now belongs to the rich Jews.

1. *Political power.* All ten of President Nixon's advisers are prominent Zionists. He doesn't dare take a step without the Jew Kissinger; Goldberg is at the United Nations, Abraham Fortas in the Supreme Court, Javits in the Senate, etc. The comedy of "democratic elections" is arranged by them. They removed the Irish Kennedys from their path. French President Pompidou is a former employee of the House of Rothschild. The members of all Western governments are either Jews or Freemasons (that clandestine political organization with its numerous ranks, unquestioningly subservient only to the Sanhedrin, the Jewish leadership. There has been no political crime during the last several hundred years in which the Freemasons were not involved. Only a Freemason can make a career in politics).

2. *The riches of the earth:* gold, banks, factories, land. Everything that in our system of political education is known as capitalism, imperialism, stock-market manipulations, exploitation, oppression, etc., etc.—all that refers to the rich Jews. I could tell you the names of companies and Jewish capitalist dynasties for a whole day without a break, but one comes across them so often anyway, in the newspapers. For some reason or other a shameful silence is maintained about the nationality of the owners and exploiters. A part of the money extorted from the working Jews goes to supporting the parasitic State of Israel, but for the most part it is used for the eradication of non-Jewish traditions, spirit, way of life and thought, in order to disarm the other nations completely and hasten the hour of Jewish domination.

3. *Press, radio, and television.* Yes, yes, all those important newspapers and publishing houses, which so readily print your pronouncements and novels, belong to Jews. Did you ever consider, Solzhenitsyn, why they want to print you? It is not out of love for Russia! Why does nothing ever appear in print except praise of the Jews? Why are traces of murder brushed under the carpet? I intend to talk about many things, but mean-

while let us return to Russia, which is breathing in revolution, and to our Jews, old and young, who "passionately" want to help her. They helped! Especially in Petrograd by arranging the Rasputin bedlam, by putting Sturmer in power, by organizing famine in the working-class districts (the wealthy suppliers—the Jews—never went hungry) (4). And the people got even with the regime by simply ceasing to obey. But the Jews poured into the soviets, the Russian national form of authority—Social Revolutionaries, Mensheviks, Laborites, and similar scum. The Constitutional Democrats rejoiced—Milyukov the Freemason and Vinawer the Jew. The Freemason Kerensky had already taken power. Everybody was grumbling. On May 24, 1917, the Seventh All-Russia Zionist Conference opened, where Idelson screamed, "Long live freeom, long live Zionism!" and set the task of building a center in Palestine for all the colonized nations (*Yevreyskaya Nedelya*, no. 22, 1917, p. 7). That is exactly how the matter was put—to make Russia a colony of Israel.

. . . The victory of the Jews was complete. According to the published data, a third of the student body was Jewish, irrespective of class origin. In the leadership there were either Jews or men married to Jews or people from national minorities. Russian art, history, and culture were slandered and distorted. Cadres of doctors were prepared in advance for the unnoticed removal of certain Jews and prominent Russians whom it was impossible to slander or shoot. One of the Jewish documents recommends that they should die with the assistance of the doctors, "as though by natural causes." But the Jews were tormented by the "damned village" which, according to Lenin's cooperative plan, still had to feel the revolutionary conquest more strongly. But Jehovah needed a new bloody sacrifice. In the covering events that followed, Solzhenitsyn, you blame only Stalin. Try to rise above your own prejudices. He came to power when the machinery of extermination was already in full swing, when all of Stalin's actions had already been programmed and all the necessary ideas implanted in his head. Experienced Zionists (Lazar Kaganovich among them—see Yu. Ivanov's *Beware: Zionism!*, (p. 76) understood that one couldn't put the ambitious Trotsky at the head of the state. And anyway the Jews had seized all the key positions.

[During collectivization] people who owned a couple of cows were dispossessed and exiled. All who could do any work were sent to their deaths. The working foundation of agriculture was destroyed, and in the beginning of the 1930s, famine sent 7,000,000 people to their graves.

Now compare with all that the 1,000,000 people who perished in the purges of 1937–38. Why do people scream about 1937 more than about anything else? Because then the top layer of society was affected, meaning Jews. But far more Russians were shot, even then.

The destructive work continued during the 1930s. A stupid unpatriotic form of education was intensified. In Moscow alone, at Kaganovich's orders, three hundred historical and cultural monuments were destroyed literally in one year. Stalin himself saved the Vasily Blazhenny Church (5), which the Jewish architects proposed to demolish, as they proposed to destroy the Kremlin, and to palm off projects by "Corbusier, the genius." The "heroism" of Pavlik Morozov was drummed into children's heads. In the Bible, that ancient history of the Jewish people, there are examples of all manner of crimes, but even the Bible contains no monstrosity like this one—a son betraying his own father.

In *The First Circle* you wrote that Stalin trusted only one man in the world—Hitler. This name is linked with the slaughter of 4,500,000 to 6,000,000 Jews (if one considers that 150,000,000 slaughtered or unborn Russians are on their consciences, then it's not all that many). Before Hitler came to power, 80 percent of German industry and press was in the hands of 30,000 Jews, who all came through alive, returned to Germany, and regained control of everything. It was not the Zionists and the rich Jews that Hitler killed, but the poor, whom the Jewish magnates despised and allowed to be sacrificed. Incidentally, much is currently being written about this.

Something else is important—the Zionists taught Hitler cruelty. Yes, yes, you only need to know his book *Mein Kampf* to see how passionately Hitler quoted the *Protocols of the Elders of Zion* and how zealously he applied the harsh formulas contained in that program for the Jewish seizure of gold and power and for the future rule of subjugated peoples, etc. Only he substituted Germans for Jews. Jewish authors assert that the *Protocols* are a forgery. I won't take it upon myself to judge. At the same time, two facts raise doubts. First, such a forgery could have been perpetrated only by a dozen exceedingly capable jurists and financiers, knowledgeable in the most diverse fields. How did they get together such a forgery? The second fact is that the last few decades painfully follow the program indicated in the *Protocols*.

Be that as it may, the Russian people advanced to victory in the name of Stalin, and Stalin gave credit to the wonderful features of the Russian character. The war brought to the fore wonderful Russian military and government leaders, who squeezed the Jews at the top. During the war the alignment of forces within the party and the state apparatus changed drastically. Stalin started associating more with Russians, started to understand a few things, and maybe feared the Jews less.

In *The First Circle*, Solzhenitsyn, you mention only the beginning of the campaign against cosmopolitanism. Four young Jews of yours are carrying on a struggle against the Russian director of the prison institute, trying by every means, fair and foul, to get him out of the way and to slap him down, in order to get another institute in their hands. A familiar situation. But you let the sentence slip in: "In their tormenting of Yakonov, the 'youngsters' forgot that of the five of them, four were Jews." It is hard to believe that you are as naive as that. They always hate the Russians, always think of themselves; that's what they were taught since childhood. At the same time, they will always be nice and will support someone who can be bought, a Semite in spirit, a "Shabbes Goy," in order that, as the Talmud teaches, "People should praise the Jews and say they are decent people" (*Shulchan Arukh, Hoshen Hamishpat* 266:1).

Your novel contains neither the real conditions of that time nor a perspective into the present alarming timelessness. By force of circumstances, Stalin made some concessions to the Russians—they started to remember Russian history, they revived certain traditions, and so on. But even here, the Jewish journalists seized the initiative, exaggerated everything to the point of absurdity, and made a mockery of it. "Russia— homeland of the elephants." It is interesting that the "struggle against cosmopolitanism" and pro-Russian declarations were combined with praise of foreign writers and artists, personalities of purely Jewish descent, and this is still very much the case even today. This coincided with an upsurge of underground work in Jewish circles, which also manifested itself openly. They began collecting and sending gold to a world Jewish organization and to Israel (6). During the war the Jews managed to get a lot of gold, since they controlled food supplies almost completely. I myself remember how my mother had a great favor bestowed on her by a certain Abram Lvovich, who gave her a whole roll in exchange for her engagement ring. . . .

The country was wearing itself out, patching up the breaches inflicted by the war, the threat of famine hung over it, and the gold was disappearing; that was one of the reasons that turned Stalin against the Jews. There were repressions, and all at once the Russians got "second sentences." In Stalin's entourage there were few Jews left, and then a tried and tested weapon was introduced—medicine. People started dying strange deaths. And although the death of a "small fry" is even now not investigated carefully (by the same Jewish doctors, that is), the deaths of important figures such as Zhdanov and Shcherbakov, of course, brought the Doctors' Trial in their train. No one knows whether one day the cause of Stalin's death will be revealed. In any case, he died barely a week before the official announcement of the date of his death, and in that same week the Doctors' Trial was stopped, and the doctors were declared innocent (7).

But lo and behold, the "innocently suffering" Jews, absolved somehow of all their previous crimes against the Russian people, poured into the capital. . . . This is a comparatively recent event which everybody remembers.

Let's move straight to 1971. World Zionism has gained so much strength that it allows itself to shout no only at the bourgeois governments. The Soviet Union is a thorn in its flesh, because there are Jews here who have not yet been taken over by the organization. Lenin's testament obligates our leadership to take a particular political position in the world arena, to oppose Zionist insolence. Today one can place an equals sign between Zionism and imperialism.

Constant pressure from within once again led to the activization of Zionist forces in the country. They are in the press, radio, and television. They control the supply of material and technical goods (8). They insinuate themselves as friends and advisers of those leaders who have Jewish wives (9). In point of fact, they once again control all our policies and are preparing a new Holocaust. It is no secret to anybody that the events in Czechoslovakia were inspired by the world Zionist organization working through the Goldstückers. One fine day, they could destroy our whole supply system. Wouldn't this be on the first day of war?

All things considered, Solzhenitsyn, you like bourgeois-Jewish democracy. If anything like that happened to us, one could assume Jewish world control to be an established fact. Solzhenitsyn, do you want to be a slave? I do not! I would rather die with a weapon in my hand. And war is a possibility. Not without reason the American Zionist Kissinger is constantly drawing Nixon toward Mao.

They assure me that you are a man of courage. It is easy to be courageous when you get written up in Zionist publications; when at the slightest insult, all kinds of "Free Europes" start howling about you. You well know that special Zionist councils participate in the management of these stations. Try, for instance, to come out against Zionism! Do you have sufficient courage for that? We would grant you protection in our country. If anything, God forbid, happened to you, and I wish you no ill, Radio Free Europe would talk about you for a week at best. Did what happened in Hungary and Czechoslovakia last them very long? And as for just one man . . .

I expose myself to greater danger than you with this letter. Not a single radio station will broadcast it. Here is another example. No matter what crimes the Zionists commit, even including murder, they are soon free again. But in Leningrad, according to what I was told, some young students formed some kind of "Christian Union" and got fifteen-year sentences because there wasn't a single Jew among them (10) . . . without so much as a squeak in their defense from a single foreign radio station.

In our country today the censor forbids us to write about the Zionists and their activities (11). But they create all kinds of committees and underground publications striving to destroy every aspect of our Russian culture and way of life.

We, the Russian people, are obliged to keep quiet and to observe with pain how the state is ruining the economy and health of its citizens, getting back the money it pays out in wages, mainly through the sale of vodka. That's our tragedy! They stuff us with wild Jewish antics, and Raykin's nonsense is presented as the apogee of philosophical thought. We cannot protest against the destruction of our historical monuments, which the Jewish architects are replacing with their boxes (12). We look at our children's textbooks and see a crime equal to the poisoning of wells. In the Russian-language textbooks, there is less and less of the works of Pushkin and Gogol, and more and more texts by Samuel Marshak and N. Marr (whoever he might be!). All kinds of filth are heaped on our ancestors in the history textbooks.

We see how they encourage the activities of the literary papers which casually advocate the "sexual revolution" and other such things with which the Zionists want to corrupt our nation (13), which is already caught up in the net of petty materialism.

We hear how people who, thank God, are afraid of nothing, publicly vilify certain members of the government. But people say the word "Jew" with trepidation and a glance over their shoulder they know that a horrible retribution will inescapably befall them—anything from being fired to being poisoned (14). But not everybody is afraid of them. And in vain do you grovel before them in your novel. How many times did they almost reach their goal, and every time they were thrown back. There are, after all, forces in this world which rise up against evil. They will erect a memorial for you only if they win and you are a Jew. Otherwise, after giving you the chance to put in some work for them, they will forget you. However, they've already given you some kind of prize.

I don't know exactly who you are—a Russian or a Jew? A convert, perhaps. . . . Converts are usually even more cruel than Jews by birth.

Perhaps you are a Russian, pressured by circumstances, by a Jewish wife. . . . Then I ask one thing of you—think of your people. Understand there is no returning to a bourgeois-Jewish republic, that the soviets are a Russian form of popular rule which will yet acquire strength. And however much you may want to, you shouldn't help to topple the government. For that would lead again to the deaths of millions of people.

One cannot rule out that tomorrow Russian blood may once again flow in sacrifice to Jehovah. Let it, at least, be in war.

November 1971

COMMENTS

(1) Nowhere does Solzhenitsyn say this.

(2) All quotes, complete with distortions, are reproduced according to the original, which is borrowed from such anti-Semitic literature of the prerevolutionary period as the books of A. Shmakov, I. Lutostansky, and others.

(3) This refers to official anti-Semitic literature, published in multimillion editions in the USSR, and primarily to Yu. Ivanov's book, *Beware: Zionism!*

(4) That Rasputin was an agent of international Zionism is alleged in official Soviet publications (see, for example, *Neman*, 1973, no. 1).

(5) All demolition in Moscow and in the Kremlin itself was carried out at Stalin's direct orders.

(6) This version became widespread in the USSR as a justification for the arrest of people prominent in Jewish culture at the end of 1948.

(7) The Doctors' Trial was brought to a close a month after Stalin's death, on April 5, 1953, to be exact.

(8) A reference to V. Dymshitz, the deputy chairman of the Soviet Ministers of the USSR, and chairman of the State Committee for Material-Technical Supply.

(9) References to L. Brezhnev, I. Kapitonov, and other Soviet leaders.

(10) The subject of discussion is the VSKhON (The All-Russian Social Christian Union for the Liberation of the People). The arrest of the members of the VSKhON, which took place in 1967, was reported in the foreign media. A whole series if articles in defense of Ogurtsov was published recently.

(11) And this in a country where the bookstores are bursting with anti-Semitic literature, such as the books of Yu. Ivanov, whom the author himself quotes.

(12) At the present time nearly all the top people in Soviet architecture are Russians. The chief architect of Moscow is the Russian, Posokhin.

(13) A reference to A. Chakovsky, a Jew who is editor-in-chief of the *Literaturnaya gazeta* and a nominee for membership of the Central Committee of the CPSU.

(14) In fact, everything is just the other way around. Overt anti-Semitism, both governmental and spontaneous, is an everyday phenomenon in the USSR.

Veche, no. 3, 1971
(editor V. Osipov, Moscow, Samizdat)

LETTER FROM THREE BELIEVERS

His Holiness, the Sovereign Archbishop, the Pastor and the Very Reverend Members of the Great Synod:

In addressing you with these words of humble supplication, we ask you to hear us out and cast a mental glance at the unbounded expanses of our homeland, at God's people who trust your spiritual guidance.

It is impossible to remain silent when the extreme, growing danger from the organized forces of widespread Zionism and Satanism has become obvious to everybody. Silence as a pattern of behavior is always ineffective and even harmful, for it leaves vagueness and sows distrust and suspicion in mutual relationships. Taking advantge of that, the agents of Zionism and Satanism are artificially creating frictions between church and state in order to weaken them both.

These age-old enemies of the Orthodox Church and of our homeland are trying through tendentious selection and interpretation of the facts to present the actions of various persons during the period of disturbances and disorders as an act of the entire church.

They are using incitement and false propaganda, spreading pseudoscientific theories, justifying hatred toward mankind and immorality, attempting to poison society, in particular the intelligentsia and youth, with ideas of anarchistic liberalism and amoralism and to destroy the very foundations of morals, family, and state.

Disbelief and doubt about all spiritual and national values, cosmopolitanism, the dissemination of depravity and drunkenness, the extraordinary increase in abortions, indifference and negligence in the performance of familial, parental and patriotic duties, hypocrisy, treachery, falsehood, money-grabbing, and other vices—these are the means by which they are trying to corrupt our people and all mankind.

Many of these blasphemers and wreckers of our national, cultural, and spiritual values have now found shelter in the Zionist centers of the Western countries, mainly in the United States, where Satan's church enjoys the privileges of a "religious" institution.

The dark, wicked forces have already led Western Christianity to a profound spiritual crisis, officially referred to by Pope Paul VI.

The fact that world Zionism is conducting a perfidious war against our state, both from abroad and from within, has now become obvious to everyone.

By fulfilling its sacred mission of saving mankind from sin and its consequences, the church represents a moral force and a support of the state in its noble struggle against the forces of destruction and chaos. Increasingly wide circles of our public opinion are becoming aware of this fact.

The most holy Patriarchs Sergiy and Aleksiy were keenly aware of the need to establish and develop healthy and frank relationships between the church and the state on a new basis.

One of the primary tasks of our time is to search for ways of practical rapprochement with the state on the basis of goodwill, mutual interests, and sincerity, of patriotic duty and absolute noninterference in the internal life of the church.

G. Petukhov, Priest
Archdeacon Varsonofy
P. Fomin, Layman

CRITICAL COMMENTS OF A RUSSIAN ABOUT THE PATRIOTIC JOURNAL *VECHE*[51]

In January 1971, the first edition of a *domizdat* journal called *Veche* appeared. With the publication of eight issues in three years, it has provided much food for thought. In the introduction to the first issue of the journal, the editorial board declared it to be a *Russian Patriotic Journal.* This basic ideological direction was Slavophile. The basic aim of the journal—to raise Russian national consciousness. "All our arguments should have only one goal—*the good of Russia.*"

Thus, the goal was declared. Let us see how the magazine succeeded in realizing it in the following three years.

As is known, Slavophilism rests on three pillars: *Russian Orthodoxy, Autocracy, and Nationality.* Unfortunately, the editors of the journal failed to inform the readers, in the articles on their Slavophile program, whether the three pillars still stand, or whether certain corrections have been introduced during the first seventy years of the twentieth century. After all, as far back as 1917, Russia completely discarded *Autocracy,* and resolutely abandoned *Russian Orthodoxy,* which together with Catholicism is one of the two brands of reformed Judaism. If one approaches them with a good knowledge of the Bible, one can understand that Christianity in general and Orthodoxy in particular were created precisely to erase everything original and national; to turn all their adherents into rootless cosmopolitans (without kith or kin, irrespective of skin color, language, and national customs, and to turn all Orthodox people into mongrels). As soon as the translation of the Four Gospels appeared in Russian in 1818, followed by the complete text of the New Testament in 1821, mass peasant uprisings began to occur in southern Russia and especially in the Ukraine, instigated by subscribers to the corrupt cosmopolitan doctrine attributed to Christ and the Apostles. This disorder began among the Russian people; thus Russian national consciousness, which had remained unimpaired for a thousand years, began to dissolve. The Tatar-Mongol yoke had not destroyed it, nor had the Poles, the Swedes, the Germans, and similar invaders. The cosmopolitanism of the New Testament and the Jewish fascism of the Old Testament destroyed it.

However, no betrayal escapes vengeance, so *Orthodoxy*, too, did not escape. The Russian people took their revenge, and not because of the rotten *Autocracy*. (Incidentally, the last ingredient in the corruption of the royal family was the arch-Orthodox agent of international Zionism, Grishka Rasputin.) The Russian people expunged *Orthodoxy* from its soul precisely because of *Orthodoxy*'s betrayal of the most precious thing it possessed—*Nationality*.

If today there are still believers in the Orthodox Church, they are ignorant persons, without knowledge of the Bible or the Gospels, or of the treacherous role of Orthodox cosmopolitanism, which paved the way in our time, for Zionist cosmopolitanism. If today anyone needs to rehabilitate *Orthodoxy*, it is primarily those who created it in the first place—the Zionists—because for themselves they created *Judaism*. According to the latter, humanity is divided into human beings (that is, Jews only), and goyim (that is, all non-Jews: Russians, Negroes, Chinese, Papuans, etc.). For the goyim, Christianity and Islam were created as branch enterprises of Judaism (limited-liability companies, as they are called by the English). These enterprises were called upon to ensure the obedience of everyone else to the superior race or people chosen by God (i.e., the Jews). The Old Testament asserts that the goyim must become slaves to the Jews by the year 2000, according to their calculations.

The great service performed by the Russian people is that it is the first people to rid itself of Orthodoxy, the forerunner of Jewish enslavement scheduled for the year 2000, and the antechamber of the crematorium in which the Zionists intend to incinerate all the goyim.

In 1917 the Russian people saw that for one thousand years it had been armed with an ideology directed against itself. They replaced it with the ideology of *communism*. At the same time they understood that whoever tries to get them back into the Christian antechamber of the Zionist crematorium is a Judas traitor. They remembered perfectly well the republican assembly (*Veche*) form of self-government, and therefore created the *soviets* (the word comes from the same root as *veche—vet*—with the prefix *so*) under the gunfire of the barricades of 1905.

Thus, in place of the Slavophile slogan, "Russian Orthodoxy and Nationality," the Russian people substituted, if one may generalize, the slogan "Communism, Soviet Power, and Nationality." Most of the Slavophiles were patriots, but patriots of their own day. They clearly understood that to shatter two of the three pillars (autocracy and Orthodoxy) at the wrong time would cost the Russian people dearly. If they were living today, they would not be opposed to the present ideology and form of government, and would certainly defend them for the good of the Russian people. Subverting our ideology and form of government now means opening the door to control of the country by Zionist capital. That would be the greatest betrayal possible of the Russian people.

Russia can be saved not by overthrowing *communism* and *Soviet power*, but only by strengthening them, by cleaning off the Zionist mold which permeates them. If the journal were to undertake this noble mission, it would become understandable and attractive to the widest cross-section of our people. The direction which the journal has at present, however, practically turns it into an antechamber for the Zionist dissidents of the USSR—any heresy as long as it weakens our motherland from within.

The journal calls itself a "patriotic Russian" journal, working for the "good of Russia"; but how can a Russian believe that, when it opens its pages to such sworn enemies of the Russians and of Russia as A. Sakharov and A. Solzhenitsyn (the Solzhenitsyn of *August 1914*)? The journal joins the Zionist Samizdat publications in mourning for Galanskov. But is every sacrifice for the benefit of Russians and Russia? For whom, basically, did Galanskov fight and for whom was he sent to prison? For those same most evil enemies of Russia and the Russians—for keeping a record of the trials of the Zionist secret agents in the sheep's clothing of dissidents, the Zionists Daniel and Sinyavsky.

It is a disgrace for the journal to reprint the statements of A. Sakharov, I. Shafarevich, and the rest of the gang of Zionizing intellectuals and pseudointellectuals who howl about the freedom of the press. K. Aksakov also wanted freedom of the press. In those places where they officially have it (the United States, England, and other Western countries) the press is completely monopolized by the Zionists. What sort of freedom of the press is that? No, better *Glavlit* [Soviet censorship] than that sort of freedom!

The journal has campaigned against pollution of the environment. Very good. But what is the journal calling for—a reduction in industrial productivity. Moreover, it seems that this is to be done unilaterally. But we aren't the only ones on this planet. Let the Russian people decrease production and the Zionists will strangle them—that's what their "patriotism for the good of Russia" boils down to.

Shattering things is easy! But after that, what? If one throws out the Bolsheviks, the Zionists and only the Zionists will come to power; they have money and a secret service plus brilliant organization. We have nothing but the Bolsehvik party, which however badly, however poorly, does protect us. Imagine what it would be like if Sakharov were prime minister, with Solzhenitsyn, Vysotsky, Raykin, Yakir, Daniel, and others like them in the government. They would toss you and your journal away like a squeezed-out lemon, as far as the boondocks of Magadan, certainly no nearer than that, if you're not immediately sent to the gas chamber. And this, despite the fact that right now you are undermining things together with them. There were similar subversives in Czechoslovakia in 1968, and the Zionists Shik, Pelikan, etc., came to power.

The international Zionist enterprise has now concentrated in its hands 80 percent of the total capital of the entire nonsocialist world. This is more frightening than the fascist plague. If they are victorious, it means death to all, and first and foremost to the Russians, whom they have nicknamed zoological anti-Semites, and whom they have decided to exterminate physiclly to a man. Any move to undermine things at such a time is treason against the Russian people, the worst kind of treason it has ever known. Just as during World War II all Russians, no matter what their views (and the leaders of the Orthodox Church played their patriotic part at that time), united in the struggle against the common enemy, so must we unite in the struggle against Zionism; we must unmask and hit everyone who is for them, and encourage everyone who is against them. The attitude to Zionism is the litmus paper that reveals patriotism or treason. There is no middle ground! Whoever is not with us is against us! Whoever is not against Zionism in all its manifestations is against the Russians, against the Slavophiles, against everything that's decent on this earth. In this light, if the journal really wants to become a *patriotic Russian* publication and not the antechamber of the Zionist dissidents, their unpaid agent, it must clarify the entire chain of problems confronting the Russian people. By grasping that link (and that link only) it will become possible to remove the entire chain of problems. If this is not done, the Zionists will exterminate the Russian people *physically, together with all its problems*, by the year 2000. That's the situation today.

It is essential that the journal be orientated not toward those who believe in the meaningless Bible, who will not save Russia from the Zionists with their prayers, nor toward scum like Sakharov and Solzhenitsyn, who need cosmopolitanism but not the Russian people, nor toward self-sacrificers like Galanskov, but toward honest party men, Soviet patriotically minded people in culture and the arts (by the way, there is a need for articles about the preservation of architectural monuments) and similar Soviet people (Communists and nonparty) who are influential and have a voice in government bodies. There are many such people, but their preoccupation with day-to-day affairs distracts them from seeing and realizing the full measure of the Zionist danger to, among other things, their current work. The journal must bring home to them the truth about Zionism. Apropos, Samizdat publications are read much more carefully than official ones. This advantage should not be ignored.

We must publish material about the uselessness of works by Zionist pseudointellectuals, material about the attacks by Zionists against honest Russians and people of other nationalities, material about Zionist bribery and corruption, material about their mob behavior in the synagogues and other places, on-the-spot letters about the outrageous behavior of the internal emigrants, about the grabbing of apartments in the cities. We must demand a fair distribution of apartments for the native population, including the Russians and not the Zionizers. We must question the public prosecutor's office about where the Zionizers get the money to buy cars and country houses, etc. Why are there 90 percent or 70 percent Jews in a given department? We must demand a quota which accords with the population of a given locality and representation in institutions and other places of higher education, and so forth. We must demand that the percentage of Jewish youth entering institutes of higher education and special schools corresponds to the percentage of Jews in the country (this is approximately 1 percent: 2.3 million Jews out of a total population of 250 million people in the USSR). This 1 percent should be spread over all institutions and enterprises: with the slogan of equality for all, no preferences should be given to those who may be in Israel tomorrow.

The first eight issues of the journal had a verbose and clearly pro-Zionist policy. The appearance of objectivity was given to the journal only by material of an anti-Zionist character. That is all the Zionists need; a calculated fifty-fifty is the best kind of lie. Therefore the journal compromised itself, against its own will, as an agent of the Zionists. Hence a change of name is necessary, with the numbering starting again at no. 1. Possible new names are: *Vechevoy, Kolokol, Nabat, Russkiy Nabat*, or *Yedinstvo* ("The Town Meeting Bell," "The Alarm Bell," "The Russian Bell," or "Unity").

The journal should come out with the banner headline: "Death to the Zionist Aggressors!" or "Everyone must take up the Struggle against Zionism." From the ideological standpoint the journal resembles the half-breed which it would oppose on biological grounds.

The striving for objectivity and so-called freedom of expression leads to handing over the pages to Zionists, both half-breed and pure-bred. But they already have more than enough means of mass information, both official publications with editions in the millions of copies and Samizdat. If there are no Russians able to create a journal uninfected by Zionism, then there's no point in producing one at all, as it will be not a patriotic but an *antipatriotic* publication. It is not working for the unification of the Russian people but for its even greater disunity.

The very fact that the journal came out under the slogan of "Russian Orthodoxy" divides people into an insignificant minority of believers to whom the journal is trying to attach the overwhelming majority of atheists. It might be thought that all atheists are antipatriotic, and that in order to become patriotic they must return to the putrid morass of Christian cosmopolitanism, which has demoralized all the peoples of the West and turned them into submissive servants of the Zionists and of Israel. Solzhenitsyn demands that the Patriarch should call on all Russians within Russia to take their children to church—to teach them to venerate the Judaic prophets, to get them used to the idea, from early childhood, of the Jews being chosen by God, so that they could consciously prepare themselves to play the role of slaves to the Jews. To be a sincere patriot, according to the journal, means being a sincere Orthodox Christian, holding sacred every part of both testaments of the Bible. And that means to reconcile oneself to the idea of Jewish domination. What's patriotic about that?

Perhaps one should look for patriotism among the Christian peoples of the West, who for the past six years have been humbly sailing around Africa at a financial loss (instead of cutting through the Suez Canal) and have already started to freeze because of the oil shortage, and to starve because of the unemployment caused by that same oil shortage, and all for God's chosen people. . . .

Zionizing dissidents are attempting to subvert us from within, to pave the way for world domination by the Children of Israel, through various means and with support, on the governmental level, from the Congress of the United States and the governments of other Zionizing countries of the West. Is a *Russian patriotic* journal traveling the same road? *Communism* and *Soviet power* (the entire socialist system) are now the sole strong obstacle to Zionism's advance toward its year-2000 goal. The Russian people is in the vanguard of the USSR and, therefore, of the entire socialist system.

There is now no other salvation for Russian consciousness than to cleanse itself of all the foulness of Judaism and Zionism and their antechamber—the church! The attempt to cage true Russians in the cosmopolitan Orthodox antechamber of Zionism is the height of *Antipatriotism* and the height of *treason against every true Russian and everything Slavic.*

V. Yemelyanov

WHO'S BEHIND JIMMY CARTER AND THE SO-CALLED EUROCOMMUNISTS (INFORMATION)[52]

Jimmy Carter sent a greeting to "the Jewish people of America, to Israel, and to the Jews of the world" on the occasion of the Jewish New Year 5737. It was published by almost the entire capitalist press, including the *Jerusalem Post* of September 15, 1976. After Carter's election had been assured the previous week by the highest *legal* executive organ of the worldwide Zionist-Masonic enterprise, the world conference of the international Zionist-Masonic order B'nai B'rith.*

In conclusion Carter observed: "Finally, in the field of human rights, I, as President of the United States, will do everything possible to move the Soviet Union toward a liberalization of its emigration policies toward people of Jewish nationality."

Thus Carter's foreign policy credo reduces itself to *Zionism, Freemasonry,* and one of their international subdivisions, the *League for the Defense of Human and Citizens' Rights;* and "human" and "citizen" mean *Jews* first and foremost, since non-Jews are considered neither human nor citizens: they are goyim† or two-legged cattle according to Jewish belief. At best, one may occasionally help the Masonic goyim as a fifth column of international Zionism.

All U.S. Presidents without exception, and all presidential candidates, beginning with George Washington, were Freemasons. Subject to rigid Masonic discipline, they complied with every suggestion and directive of the "brothers" of higher rank in the lodge. . . .

Over the centuries the primary task of the Masonic lodges has been to weaken from within all *goyish institutions and states.* In the past this meant monarchies. Today the Masonic lodges wish to weaken republics, all religious institutions except synagogues, and all parties of either the right or left (depending on concrete tactical considerations), all establishments: administrative, scientific, cultural (except for so-called Jewish culture), and all moral standards or traditions (except for the Jewish, or more precisely talmudic), etc. The aim is as follows: to exploit every instance of internal instability in order to insinuate their own Masonic cliques, ideas, and methods. And all this is done for the sake of building

---

*The "Sons of the Covenant," i.e., the legendary covenant between the biblical Abraham and God, assigning Palestine to the Jews.

†The word "goy" (from the verb *golti,* "to live") means literally "inhabitant," "resident": to which the rabbis have given a different, contemptuous meaning.

the so-called spiritual shrine of Solomon, i.e., to use Masonic goyim to pave the way toward world domination by international Zion around the year 2000.

Naturally, there have been occasions when various non-Jewish powers have attempted to put an end to this invisible Masonic political Mafia. But as a rule these attempts were doomed to failure; the *visible* non-Jewish establishment (state, government, party, etc.), whose upper ranks were already infiltrated by Masons, had to contend with the *invisible* and therefore unassailable peak of the Masonic pyramid. . . .

Any breach of the iron discipline of the Masonic lodges leads to inescapable retribution. The presidency of Freemason Richard Nixon ended in disgrace, not because of the Watergate affair; the Watergate affair was started and developed because Nixon occasionally broke the most important commandment of a high-level Freemason—never, in any way, to do anything against the Children of Israel. The last straw which broke the back of the camel of Masonic-Zionist patience was his press statement (not published in the press) threatening to take steps against the Zionist lobby in the U.S. Congress. Immediately after this statement the highest level Zionist-Masonic lodge, B'nai B'rith, resolved to remove Nixon and ordered all non-Jewish lodges in the United States and abroad to institute a campaign of organized harassment against him. For a preliminary "warm-up" and for Nixon's "edification," they also disgraced Vice-President Spiro Agnew, accusing him of anti-Semitism. After he was removed from office, Agnew, in contrast to Nixon, not only refused to remain silent but, having seen the light, albeit belatedly, began to conduct anti-Zionist activities. Appearing on television and in print, he exposed the Zionist domination of economics, politics, and the mass media.

A campaign of unprecedented impudence was subsequently organized to harass Agnew and compel him through legal means to register with the U.S. Justice Department as a foreign agent! (*Jerusalem Post Magazine,* September 10, 1976, *Jerusalem Post,* September 12, 1976).

Unprecedented in the history of American jurisprudence, the Agnew case does not signify a triumph for "democracy" but rather the victory of the growing dictatorship of Zionism and its fifth column—Freemasonry. . . .

Since the Carter team had a tendentious ethnic imbalance, an offer may be made to our ruling bodies "in the interest of better understanding" between the heavily Jewish Carter administration and our country: to strengthen the Jewish component in our expert, scientific bodies (such as the American and Canadian Institute, Academy of Sciences of the USSR) and other bodies which have a direct input in the formation of our foreign policy. Such a move may be expected as our internal emigrés have welcomed it more than once in the past (and unfortunately not without success for international Zionism). It is therefore essential to rebuff such suggestions most emphatically, remembering that the acceptance of similar offers in the past cost us too high a price.

It is a well-known fact that the international Zionist-Masonic enterprise controls 80 percent of the economy and 95 percent of the mass media of the capitalist world. . . .

On December 11, 1976, *Vechernaya Moskva* devoted considerable space to an interview with the rabbi of the Moscow Choral Synagogue, Yakov Leibovitch Fishman. Once again, in the guise of criticizing Zionism, the idea of a worldwide Jewish people is dragged out: "The Zionists say that they are acting in the name of the Jewish people, they claim they are concerned with its well-being and happiness, but the very essence of Zionism, its ideology, is antinational." What is the reader to conclude? The Zionists are bad, but the Jewish nation remains a reality, since they (the Zionists) are antinational. This is developed and reiterated by purely talmudic methods, day after day, year after year, in the concept of a complete cycle, with persistence and insistence, and in accordance with the Zionist idea poisons the minds of the non-Jews of our land, who basically have "zero educational qualifications" in the field of information about Zionism and Freemasonry. From the standpoint of international Zionism itself, the completely legal activity of I. Gordon, A. Vergelis, and J. Fishman can be evaluated in accordance with Golda Meir's retort: *"Gut Gesugt!"*

Golda Meir can rightly repeat *"Gut Gesugt!"* when she reads the book of that same Aron Vergelis in the APN edition in English. It is entitled *On the Jewish Street*, and in it the thesis of a "single worldwide Jewish people" is interwoven on almost every page with a scarlet thread. She would rephrase her evaluation to *"Gut Gemacht!"* if she could observe how the large and small patterns of the snowflakes—symbols of the Russian winter, which in winter adorn the city streets, shop windows, advertisements, ice-cream kiosks, etc.—somehow, unexpectedly, and by chance, yet quite definitely, sport the image of the six-pointed Star of David, so pleasing to the Zionist eye. These images are traditionally painted in the white and pale blue of the Israeli flag, the festive flag of international Zionism. She can also take delight in all the little white loudspeakers on all the stations and passages of the Moscow metro, whose gratings are decorated with the same six-pointed Star of David, again so pleasing to the Zionist eye. And to what rapture would she be transported by the glass tumblers of "new elegant design" issued recently by the Gus-Khrustalny factory: the elegant fluting of the sides join at the base in the same Star of David. A host of ceramic products and other handicrafts which have been produced for hundreds of years suddenly start to bear this dubious ornamentation. In the newspapers, crossword puzzles appear in the shape of this same star. Zionist-Masonic symbolism "purely accidentally" enters into architectural design. Buildings are constructed symbolizing the Pentateuch of Moses, the Talmud, the Kabbalah, Torah scrolls, and similar "treasures of Judaism."

. . . *More than 20 million victims, mainly Russians and non-Jews of our country, were sacrificed, and not so that we should allow ourselves to become so careless now in the face of an incomparably greater danger, which 20 million victims will not suffice to stop!*

We must ensure a secure home front!

In conclusion, we should remind ourselves that Zionism and Freemasonry are joined from within to form a single monolith, although both skillfully hide themselves behind disguises. One must remember that there are no innocent Masonic lodges; all are immeasurably dangerous, all of them are our sworn enemies. . . .

The following are suggested concrete steps toward this end:

On the International Level

The creation of an extensive worldwide anti-Zionist and anti-Masonic front of the same kind as the antifascist front of the 1930s and 1940s because the threat of Zionist world domination, planned for the year 2000, threatens all the goyim in the world, irrespective of race, religion, and party affiliation. If the world, and primarily the peoples of the various capitalist countries, especially the American people, come to understand this danger and join the ranks of fighters on this front, peace on earth will be assured forever. It is a matter of honor for all Communists (except for the "Masonized" leaders of the so-called Eurocommunists, who will be against it) to become pioneers in the formation of such a worldwide front, just as when carrying out the resolutions of the Seventh Comintern Congress, they pioneered the antifascist front. At that time the Zionists and Masons didn't interfere; after all, the goyim, at the cost of their own lives, saved the Zionists and Masons from extinction. (A plan for the establishment of this front was submitted a year ago to the international department of the Central Committee of the Communist party of the Soviet Union.) If one considers that this will be a front against 80 percent of world capital, then the victory of the front will be a final victory against the whole Zionist system on a worldwide scale.

Time doesn't stand still! As long as the Zionist-Masonic train rolls towards its target year 2000 according to schedule, only the worldwide front can derail it from world history. Otherwise, inevitable genocide awaits *all the goyim*. No less a world non-Jewish forum than the General Assembly of the United Nations established on October 10, 1975, that

Zionism is racism, racism directed against all the goyim on earth, and not only against the Arabs.

On the Internal Soviet Level

1. Since the secret Zionist-Masonic orders fear more than anything else being dragged into the light of day, where everybody can see that they are terrified by extensive public exposure of their activities, every Soviet person must be informed about the real dangers that Zionism and Freemasonry hold for him. Therefore maximum publicity about the ultimate Zionist and Masonic goal of world domination and about Judaism, their common source, is essential. Likewise the following initial measures require urgent implementation:

   a. Wide publication with critical commentaries of the cannibalistic Jewish book *Shulchan Arukh,* in particular, the part which deals with the relationship of Jews to goyim, i.e., the theory of antigoy genocide.
   b. Wide publication, with critical commentaries, of the so-called antibible of Freemasonry, the *Legends of Adoniram.* This work has been widely used not only for recruiting new Masons but also for undermining the ideological beliefs of those who are unaware of its secret hidden meaning, which should be exposed.
   c. Wide publication (not by unreliable "researchers" like Braginsky) of works about the history of Zionism, its structure, its strategy and tactics, e.g., the writings of Yu. Ivanov, E. Yevseev, V. Begun, D. Zhukov.
   d. Wide publication in the major newspapers (to coincide with some special event or date) of the section of the resolution of the Fourth Comintern Congress dealing with the question of fascism, Freemasonry, and the Human Rights League.
   e. Wide publication in the major newspapers of the article by G. Dimitrov, "Freemasonry—a National Danger" (from the twelfth volume of his works in Bulgarian).

2. The creation of a specialized scientific institute (to be named the Institute for the study of Zionism and Freemasonry under the auspices of the Central Commitee of the CPSU), the selection of personnel who would be responsible for refusing jobs to those who might be potential carriers of Zionism and Freemasonry. If, for instance, the West German capitalist government denies access to a wide range of activities to people belonging to democratic organiza-

tions, why should the country which is foremost in achieving the dictatorship of the proletariat deny itself comparable measures against individuals who may spread antisocialist ideas? Indeed, it is for this very reason that the USSR is the dictatorship of *the proletariat.* (An extensive proposal on this subject was submitted to the Presidium of the 25th Conference of the CPSU.)

3. The inclusion in the curriculum of all institutes of higher education in the country of a special compulsory course on scientific anti-Zionism and anti-Freemasonry.

4. The inclusion of a section on scientific anti-Zionism and anti-Freemasonry in the social-science programs of all secondary schools, all special schools and places of learning, and among the TV educational programs.

5. The preparation and publication of standard textbooks on this subject for all secondary and higher educational institutions.

6. The inclusion of this subject in the compulsory programs for all levels of political education, with the help, among other means, of TV.

7. The inclusion of this subject in the compulsory political training programs for all ranks of the Soviet armed forces—from privates to field marshals.

8. The introduction of refresher courses on this subject for the entire staff of *Glavlit* [Soviet censorship] and similar bodies responsible for the release of mass information, culture, and art.

9. Inclusion in the criminal codes of all Soviet republics of legislation calling for harsh punishment for membership in Zionist or Masonic organizations. Inclusion of such legislation is also in accordance with the ruling of the Comintern that concealment by any Soviet citizen of his participation in Zionist or Freemasonry groups should be considered as infiltration into our socialist society of an enemy agent, with all the criminal consequences arising from this.

10. A declaration in the legal code outlawing Zionism and Freemasonry (by order of the Supreme Soviet of the USSR).

11. A relentless struggle against all varieties of organized Masonic-Zionist activity, such as the Sakharov Committee, the Committee for Monitoring the Observation of the Helsinki Declaration on Human Rights, headed by Yury Orlov, the Solzhenitsyn Fund for Aiding Political Prisoners in the USSR, headed by A. Ginsburg, the Soviet chapter of Amnesty International, various kinds of international seminars on the question of Jewish culture, and other self-styled bodies. Harsh criminal penalties should be prescribed for all their participants—possibly, general exile abroad for all of them.

12. Investigation of all individuals suspected of pro-Zionist or Masonic activities.
13. Insofar as Freemasonry and Zionism are organizations of the *radical* bourgeoisie, the war against them must be waged no less *radically*. It is therefore essential to review with the utmost care the measures proposed earlier in the Introductory Note. The urgent need for action becomes more apparent every day, especially in regard to the dissidents. Led by the Zionists and Freemasons, they are resorting to acts of bloody terror against the civil population "in the subterranean passages of the metro," terror planned by them eighty years ago when the metro first opened.

Yemelyanov Valery Nikolayevich,
Moscow, B-78, Novo-Basmannaya 10,
Apt. 30, Home phone No. 261-83-18

January 10, 1977
Moscow

Anti-Semitic and Anti-Israeli Publications in the USSR, 1960 to 1981

N. BIBICHKOVA

BOOKS NOT FOUND in the library of the Center for Research and Documentation of East European Jewry at the Hebrew University are indicated by an asterisk (*).

*Abdullayev, Z., and P. Ismailov. *Sionizm sluzhit imperializmu* [Zionism in the service of imperialism]. Baku: Azernesh, 1981. 63 pp. In Azerbaijanian.

Aksamitas, P., and P. Freydgeymas. *Iudaizm i sionizm* [Judaism and Zionism]. Vilnius: Mintis, 1974. 208 pp. In Lithuanian.

*Aleksandrov, N. D., and V. S. Yeshchenko. *Sionizm—orudiye imperialisticheskoy reaktsii* [Zionism—the instrument of imperialist reaction]. Moscow: Znanie, 1980. 48 pp.

Altshuler, M. *Chto est iudaizm?* [What is Judaism?] Moscow: Moskovskiy rabochiy, 1968. 112 pp.

Antikommunizm i antisovetizm—professiya sionistov. [Anti-Communism and Anti-Sovietism—the Zionist profession]. Moscow: Politizdat, 1971. 126 pp.

Astakhov, C. *Imperialisticheskaya sushchnost sionizma* [The imperialist essence of Zionism]. Moscow: Znaniye, 1975. 40 pp.

Bakanursky, G. *Iudaizm i sovremennost* [Judaism and the contemporary era]. Moscow: Znaniye, 1978. 64 pp.

———. *Krizis i modernizatsiya iudaizma* [Crisis and modernization of Judaism]. Moscow: Znanie, 1980.

Baryer nesovmestimosti: Dokumentalnye rasskazy o chelovecheskikh tragediyakh [Incompatibility barrier: Documentary stories on the human tragedies]. Moscow: Progress, 1981. 104 pp.

Begun, V. *Polzuchaya kontrrevolyutsiya* [Creeping counterrevolution]. Minsk: Belarus, 1974. 190 pp.

———. *Vtorzheniye bez oruzhiya* [Invasion without arms]. Moscow: Molodaya gvardiya, 1977. 176 pp.

———. *Vtorzhenie bez oruzhiya* [Invasion without arms]. 2d ed., rev. Moscow: Molodaya gvardiya, 1979. 175 pp.

———. *Mezhdunarodny sionizm—vrag mira i progressa* [International Zionism—enemy of peace and progress]. Minsk: Znanie, 1980. 24 pp.

———. *Vtorzhenie bez oruzhiya* [Invasion without arms]. 3d ed., rev. and supplemented. Minsk: Belarus, 1980. 206 pp.

*———. *Vtorzhenie bez oruzhiya* [Invasion without arms]. Saratov: Privolzhskoye knizhnoye izdatelstvo, 1980. 175 pp., bibl.

———. *Vtorzhenie bez oruzhiya* [Invasion without arms]. 2d ed., rev. Vilnius: Mintis, 1980. 143 pp. In Lithuanian.

*———. *Vtorzhenie bez oruzhiya* [Invasion without arms]. Trans. from 3d ed., rev. and supplemented. Riga: Avots, 1981. 215 pp. In Lettish (Latvian).

Belaya Kniga: Svidetelstva, fakty, dokumenty [The white book: Evidence, facts, documents]. Moscow: Yuridicheskaya literatura, 1979. 280 pp., il.

Belaya Kniga: svidetelstva, fakty, dokumenty [The white book: Evidence, facts, documents). Trans. from Russian. Moscow: Progress Publishers, 1981. 247 pp., il. In English.

Belenky, M. *Chto takoye talmud* [What is the Talmud?]. Kiev: Znaniye UkSSR, 1960. 26 pp.

———. *Iudaizm* [Judaism]. "Modern Religions" series. Moscow: Politizdat, 1966. 237 pp.

———. *Iudaizm* [Judaism]. "Modern Religions" series. 2d ed. Moscow: Politizdat, 1974. 239 pp.

———. *Iudeyskoye suyeveriye* [Judaic superstition]. Kiev: Znaniye UkSSR, 1974. 48 pp.

———. *Kritika osnovnykh dogmatov talmuda* [A critique of the basic dogmas of the Talmud]. Moscow: Znaniye, 1975. 64 pp.

Belov, A., and A. Shilkin. *Diversiya bez dinamita* [Sabotage without dynamite]. 2d ed. with corrections and additions. Moscow: Politizdat, 1976. 183 pp.

Belyayev, I. *S chyornogo khoda* [From the back entrance]. Documentary story. Moscow: Voyenizdat, 1972. 190 pp.

———, T. KOLESNICHENKO, and E. PRIMAKOV. *Golub spushchen* [The dove has been released]. Moscow: Molodaya gvardiya, 1968. 157 pp.

Berenshteyn, L. *Kritika ideologii sionizma—raznovidnosti antikom-*

munizma. [A critique of the ideology of Zionism—a variety of anti-Communism]. Kiev: Politizdat, 1971. 102 pp. In Ukrainian.

———. *Sionizm—zleyshiy vrag internatsional 'nogo yedineniya trudyashchikhsya* [Zionism—the most vicious enemy of the international unity of the workers]. Kiev: Znaniye UkSSR, 1974. In Ukrainian.

———. *Sionizm kak raznovidnost rasizma* [Zionism as a variety of racism]. Kiev: Politizdat Ukrainy, 1977. 70 pp.

*———. *Sionizm kak raznovidnost rasizma* [Zionism as a form of racism]. Kiev: Politizdat Ukrainy, 1979. 93 pp. In French.

*———. *Obrechennost politiki i praktiki sionizma* [The doomed character of the politics and practice of Zionism]. Kiev: Vishcha shkola, 1980. 191 pp.

Binvald, P. *Gore polnoy chashey: Sbornik statey, pisem, dokumentov o sionizme i yego zhertvakh* [Grief in plenty: A collection of articles, letters, and documents on Zionism and its victims]. Riga: Liyesma, 1975. 128 pp.

Blishchenko, I., and V. Kudryavtsev. *Agressiya Israilya i mezhdunarodnoye pravo* [Israel's aggression and international law]. Moscow: Mezhdunarodnye otnosheniya, 1970. 80 pp.

Bolshakov, V. *Antisovetism—professiya sionistov* [Antisovietism—the Zionists' profession]. Moscow: Agentstvo Pechati Novosti, 1971. 15 pp. In Spanish.

———. *Sionizm na sluzhbe antikommunizma* [Zionism at the service of anticommunism]. Moscow: Politizdat, 1972. 230 pp.

———. *Nad propastyu vo lzhi: Ocherki s ideologicheskogo fronta* [Catcher in the lie: Essays from the ideological front]. Moscow: Molodaya gvardiya, 1981. 207 pp.

*Brenman, P. *Iudaizm i sionizm v sovremennoy ideologicheskoy borbe* [Judaism and Zionism in the modern ideological struggle]. Kiev: Znanie, 1981. 32 pp.

Brenman, R. *Iudaizm na sluzhbe sionizma* [Judaism at the service of Zionism]. Kiev: Politizdat Ukrainy, 1973. 143 pp.

Brodsky, R. *Sionizm i yego klassovaya sushchnost* [Zionism and its class essense]. Kiev: Politizdat Ukrainy, 1973. 95 pp.

——— and R. Shulmeyster. *Sionizm: Litsemeriye, obman, predatelstvo* [Zionism: Hypocrisy, deceit, betrayal]. Lvov: Kamenyar, 1972. 111 pp. In Ukrainian.

Daychman, S. *Chyornaya dusha sionizma* [The black soul of Zionism]. L'vov: Kamenyar, 1972. 62 pp.

Demchenko, P. *Arabsky Vostok v chas ispytaniy* [The Arab east in its hour of ordeal]. Moscow: Politizdat, 1967. 80 pp.

Dmitriyev, E. *Palestinskiy uzel: k voprosy ob uregulirovanii palestinskoy problemy* [The Palestinian knot: On the regulation of the Palestinian question]. Moscow: Mezhdunarodnye otnosheniya, 1978, 304 pp.

————— and V. Ladeykin. *Put' k miry na Blizhnem Vostoke* [The road to peace in the Middle East]. Moscow: Mezhdunarodnye otnosheniya, 1974. 248 pp.

Edelman, A. *Sovremennost i iudaizm* [The contemporary era and Judaism]. Uzhgorod: Karpaty, 1970. 96 pp.

—————. *Iudaizm: proshloye bez budushchego* [Judaism: A past without a future]. Uzhgorod: Karpaty, 1977. 102 pp.

—————. *Kritika bogoslovsko-filosofskikh spekulyatsiy sionizma* [Criticism of theological-philosophical speculations of Zionism]. Kiev: Znanie, 1980. 48 pp. In Ukrainian.

Epshtein, A. *Sionizm—zleyshiy vrag internatsionalnogo yedineniya trudyashchikhsya* [Zionism—the bitterest enemy of international unity of workers]. Kiev: Znanie, 1977. 46 pp.

*—————. *Sionizm bez maski* [Zionism without a mask]. Kharkov: Prapor, 1979. 96 pp.

Evseev, E. *Fashizm pod goluboy zvezdoy: Pravda o sovremennom sionizme; Yego ideologii, praktike, sisteme organizatsiy krupnoy yevreyskoy burzhuazii* [Fascism under the blue star: The truth about contemporary Zionism; its ideology, practice, the system of organizations of the large Jewish bourgeoisie]. Moscow: Molodaya gvardiya, 1971. 158 pp.

Fayn, G. *Moral iudaizma: komu ona sluzhit?* [The ethics of Judaism: Whom do they serve?]. Odessa: Mayak, 1976, 102 pp.

Fridel, M. *Sionism—orudiye imperializma* [Zionism—a weapon of imperialism]. Kiev: Politizdat, 1968. 104 pp. In Ukrainian. (2d ed., 1971, 105 pp.)

—————. *Sionizm pered sudom narodov* [Zionism before the court of nations]. Kiev: Znaniye, 1971. 96 pp. In Ukrainian.

*Gabidzashvili, O. *Sionizm—burzhuazno-natsionalisticheskaya ideologiya* [Zionism—a bourgeois-nationalistic ideology]. Tbilisi: Znanie, 1979. 32 pp. In Georgian.

Gamolsky, L. *Trezubets i "Zvezda" Davida /ob ukrainskikh burzhuaznykh natsionalistakh i sionistakh/*[The trident and the star of David]. Dnepropetrovsk: Promin, 1975. 191 pp. In Ukrainian.

Ganusets, A. *Gosudarstvo Izrail—agressor* [The State of Israel—the aggressor]. Kiev: Znaniye, 1967. 45 pp. In Ukrainian.

Gaysinovich, M. *V sgovore s palachami* [In collusion with the butchers]. L'vov: Kamenyar, 1975. 127 pp. In Ukrainian.

—————. *Mify i deystvitelnost* [The myths and the reality]. Lvov: Kamenyar, 1980. 149 pp.

Gofman, M. *Sionizm: komy on sluzhit* [Zionism: Whom it serves]. Lvov: Kamenyar, 1973. 136 pp. In Ukrainian.

Goldenberg, M. *Sotsial'no-politicheskaya doktrina sionizma* [The socio-political doctrine of Zionism]. Kishinev: Shtiintsa, 1973. 131 pp.

*————. *Tupiki sionizma* [The dead ends of Zionism]. Kishinev: Kartya Moldovenyaske, 1979. 183 pp.

*————. *Ideologia sovremennogo iudaizma i sionizma* [The ideology of contemporary Judaism and Zionism]. Moscow: Znanie, 1980. 15 pp.

*————. *Iudaizm i izbranny narod* [Judaism and the "chosen" people]. Kishinev: Kartya Moldovenyaske, 1981. 110 pp.

Gorst rodnoy zemli: Sovremennaya palestinskaya novella [A handful of native land: A modern Palestinian novel]. Moscow: Progress, 1981. 312 pp.

Grigoryev, E., et al. *Myunkhen: olimpiada i politika. Igry ot zari do zari.* [Munich: The Olympiad and politics, the games from morning to night]. Moscow: Sovetskaya Rossiya, 1974, 144 pp.

Ivanov, Y. *Ostorozhno: sionizm! Ocherki po ideologii, organizatsii i praktike sionizma.* [Beware: Zionism! Essays on the ideology, organization, and practice of Zionism]. Moscow: Politizdat, 1969. 165 pp.

Kandel, V. *Rasskazhi pravdu lyudyam: Zametki zhurnalista o sovetskikh yevreyakh, emigrirovavshikh v Izrail* [Tell people the truth: A journalist's notes on Soviet Jews who have emigrated to Israel]. Uzhgorod: Karpaty, 1976. 87 pp.

Kichko, T. *Iudaizm bez prikras* [Judaism unadorned]. Kiev: AN UkSSR, 1963. 190 pp. In Ukrainian.

————. *Iudaizm i sionizm* [Judaism and Zionism]. Kiev: Znaniye, 1968. 94 pp. In Ukrainian.

————. *Sionizm—vrag molodyozhi* [Zionism—the enemy of the youth]. Kiev: Molodyozh, 1972. 173 pp.

Kogan, A., and V. Tabachnikov. *Potustoronnye "messii": Kritichesky ocherk ideologii i politiki mezhdunarodnogo sionizma* [Mythical "messiahs": A critique of the ideology and politics of international Zionism]. Dnepropetrovsk: Promin, 1979. 215 pp.

———— and ————. *Otravlennoye oruzhie: Kriticheskiy ocherk ideologii i politiki mezhdunarodnogo sionizma* [The poisoned weapon: A critical essay on the ideology and politics of international Zionism]. 2d ed., rev. and supplemented. Dnepropetrovsk: Promin, 1981. 334 pp.

Kolar, F. *Sionizm i antisemitizm* [Zionism and anti-Semitism]. Trans. from Czech. Moscow: Progress, 1971. 142 pp.

Kolesnikov, Y. *Zemlya obetovannaya* [The promised land]. Novel. Moscow: Sovetskaya Rossiya, 1973. 318 pp.

————. *Zanaves pripodnyat: Roman* [The curtain is raised: A novel]. Moscow: Voyenizdat, 1979. 624 pp.

————. *Zemlya obetovannaya: Roman* [The promised land: A novel]. Trans. from Russian. Kharkov: Prapor, 1980. 304 pp. In English.

*Korneev, L. *Vragi mira i progressa* [The enemies of peace and progress]. Vilnius: Mintis, 1979. 68 pp. In Lithuanian.

———. *Israel: The Reality Behind the Myths.* Moscow: Novosti Press Agency, 1980. 72 pp. In English.

Korsun, S. *Shag v bezdnu* [A step into the abyss]. Kharkov: Prapor, 1980. 94 pp.

Koryavin, L. *Minarety i neboskryoby: Zametki o blizhnem vostoke* [Minarets and skyscrapers.] Izvestiya, 1973. 256 pp.

Krakh Illyuziy: Pravda o zhizni v Izraile [The dashing of illusions: The truth about life in Israel]. Uzhgorod: Karpaty, 1970. 72 pp.

Kraplenye Karty [Marked cards]. Kiev: Politizdat Ukrainy, 1979. 181 pp. In Ukrainian.

Krylov, S. *Taynoye oruzhiye sionizma* [Zionism's secret weapon]. Moscow: Voyenizdat, 1972. 71 pp.

Krym, A. *Vybor: Roman* [The choice: A novel]. Kiev: Radyansky pismennik, 1980. 335 pp.

Kryvelev, I. *Novye tolkovaniya Biblii* [New commentaries on the Bible]. Moscow: Znaniye, 1974. 64 pp.

Ladeykin, V. *Istochnik opasnogo krizisa: Rol sionizma v razzhiganii konflikta na Blizhnem Vostoke:* [The source of dangerous crisis: The role of Zionism in kindling the conflict in the Middle East]. Moscow: Politizdat, 1973. 296 pp.

Langer, F. *Oni moi bratya* [They are my brothers]. Moscow: Progress, 1979. 191 pp.

Levchenko, A. *Diversiya bez dinamita* [Diversion without dynamite]. Lvov: Kamenyar, 1981. 88 pp. In Ukrainian.

Lisavtsev, E. *Religiya v bor'be idey* [Religion in the war of ideas]. Moscow: Politizdat, 1975. 64 pp.

Losev, S., and Yu, Tyssovsky. *Blizhnevostochny krizis: neft i politika* [The Middle East crisis: Oil and politics]. Moscow: Mezhdunarodnye otnosheniya, 1980. 252 pp.

Lukin, P. *Mezhdunarodny sionizm i krizis na Blizhnem Vostoke* [International Zionism and the Middle East crisis]. Kiev: Znanie, 1980. 48 pp.

Malashko, A. *Voinstvuyushchiy natsionalizm—ideologiya i politika imperializma.* [Militant nationalism—the ideology and politics of imperialism]. Minsk: Belarus, 1971. 160 pp.

Mayatsky, F. *Pravda o tore i talmude* [The truth about the Torah and the Talmud). Kishinev: Kartya Moldovenyaske, 1960. 69 pp.

———. *Sovremenniy iudaizm i sionizm* [Contemporary Judaism and Zionism]. Kishinev: Kartya Moldovenyaske, 1964. 94 pp.

———. *Sovremenniy iudaizm i sionizm* [Contemporary Judaism and Zionism] 2d ed., with corrections and additions. Kishinev: Kartya Moldovenyaske, 1969. 135 pp.

————. *Dvazhdy obmanutye* [Twice deceived]. Kishinev: Kartya Moldovenyaske, 1971. 112 pp.

————. *"Prorocheskiy sotsializm" i sionistskiy variant "sotsializma"* ["Prophetic socialism" and the Zionist variant of "socialism"]. Kishinev: Kartya Moldovenyaske, 1973. 120 pp.

Medvedko, L. *K vostoku i zapadu ot Suetsa* [East and west of Suez]. Moscow: Politizdat, 1980. 368 pp., cart.

Mezhdunarodniy sionizm: Istoriya i politika [International Zionism: Its history and politics]. A collection of articles. Glavnaya redaktsiya vostochnoy literatury izdatel'stva. Moscow: Nauka, 1977. 176 pp.

Migovich, I *Khasidskoye blagochestiye i sionizm* [Hassidic piety and Zionism]. Kiev: Znaniye, 1973. 47 pp. In Ukrainian.

————. *"Blagochestivy" iudaizm i sionizm* ["Pious" Judaism and Zionism]. Kiev: Naukova dumka, 1979. 140 pp. In Ukrainian.

Mirazhi i deystvitel'nost "zemli obetovannoy" [The mirages and the reality of the promised land]. Documents and Materials. 2d ed., with corrections and additions. Uzhgorod: Karpaty, 1973. 136 pp. In Ukrainian.

Mishchenko, P. *Blizhnevostochny krizis i puti ego razresheniya* [The Middle East crisis and the ways to its solution]. Kiev: Znanie, 1979. 20 pp,, bibl.

Mitin, M. *Sionizm—raznovidnost shovinizma i rasizma* [Zionism—a variety of chauvinism and racism] Moscow: Znaniye, 1972. 31 pp.

Modzhoryan, L. *Prestupnaya politika sionizma i mezhdunarodnoye pravo* [The criminal politics of Zionism and international law]. Moscow: Znaniye, 1973. 64 pp.

————. *Sionizm kak forma rasizma i rasovoy diskriminatsii* [Zionism as a form of racism and racial discrimination]. Moscow: Mezhdunarodnye otnosheniya, 1979. 240 pp.

My sudim sionizm [We judge Zionism]. A Collection. Simferopol: Tavriya, 1973. 158 pp.

Nash otvet klevetnikam [Our reply to the slanderers]. A Collection of articles. Kharkov: Prapor, 1976. 79 pp.

Nisses E. *Komu sluzhat sionisty* [Whom the Zionists serve]. Simferopol: Krym, 1969. 64 pp.

————. *Sionistskaya zapadnya* [The Zionist trap] Simferopol: Tavriya, 1976. 111 pp.

Ochag sionizma i agressii [The seat of Zionism and aggression]. Moscow: Politizdat, 1971. 110 pp.

Oganisyan, Y. *Dva tsveta nenavisti: O reaktsionnoy suti natsionalizma, ob ideologicheskoy bor'be s nim* [The two colors of hatred: On the reactionary essence of nationalism and the ideological struggle against it]. Moscow: Molodaya gvardiya, 1972. 176 pp.

Osipov, G. and L. Dadiani *Nauchnaya nesostoyatelnost teoretiko-metodo-*

logicheskikh osnov sotsialnykh i sotsiologicheskikh kontseptsiy sionizma [The scientific baselessness of the theoretical and methodological fundamentals of the social and sociological concepts of Zionism]. Moscow: Nauka, 1980, 56 pp.

Poda, M. *Sionizm i rasizm* [Zionism and racism]. Kiev: Znaniye, 1975. 47 pp. In Ukrainian.

Pokormyak, N. *Armiya Izrailya—orudiye imperialisticheskoy agressii* [The Israeli army—a tool of imperialist aggression] Moscow: Voyenizdat, 1977. 141 pp.

Post imeni yaroslava galana [Yaroslav Galan Post]. Book 8. Lvov: Kamenyar, 1981. 263 pp. In Ukrainian.

Prahye, B. *Pravda o "zemle obetovannoy"* [The truth about the "promised land"]. Odessa: Mayak, 1969. 180 pp.

———. *V kapkane* [In the trap]. Odessa: Mayak, 1973. 127 pp.

———. *V kapkane: O sionizme* [In the trap: On Zionism]. 2d ed., with corrections and additions. Odessa: Mayak, 1975. 200 pp.

Pravda ob iudeyskoy religii i sionizme [The truth about the Jewish religion and Zionism]. Kiev: Politizdat, 1962. 114 pp. In Ukrainian.

Protiv sionizma i izrail'skoy agressii: Sbornik materialov progressivnoy pechati [Against Zionism and Israeli aggression: A collection of material from the progressive press] Moscow: Nauka, 1974. 262 pp.

Pyrlin, Ye. *Sionizm: Ideologia i politicheskaya praktika* [Zionism: Ideology and political practice]. Moscow: Znanie, 1980. 13 pp.

Reaktsionnaya sushchnost sionizma [The reactionary essence of Zionism]. A Collection of Materials. Moscow: Politizdat, 1972. 206 pp.

Reshetnikov, N. *Bibliya i sovremennost* [The Bible and the contemporary era]. Moscow: Mysl, 1968. 302 pp.

Rimarenko, Yu. *Antikommunisticheskiy al'yans: Kritika ideologicheskikh i sotsialno-politicheskikh doktrin mezhdunarodnogo sionizma i ukrainskogo burzhuaznogo natsionalizma* [Anti-communist alliance: A critique of the sociopolitical doctrines of international Zionism and Ukrainian bourgeois nationalism]. Kiev: Naukova dumka, 1981. 212 pp.

——— and M. Panchuk. *Sgovor obrechyonnykh: Obshcheniye ukrainskikh burzhuaznykh natsionalistov i sionistov* [A compact between the doomed: The contact between Ukrainian bourgeois nationalists and Zionists]. Kiev: Znaniye, 1975. 62 pp. In Ukrainian.

*Roslov, A. *Reaktsionnaya sushchnost sionistskoy ideologii* [The reactionary essence of Zionist ideology]. Moscow: Znanie, 1980. 80 pp.

Rozenblyum, D., and V. Savtsov. *Chyorniye sotni sionizma* [The black hundreds of Zionism]. Kiev: Politizdat Ukrainy, 1975. 78 pp. In Ukrainian.

Rozin, V., and L. Sidorov. *Khrizantemy u tyuremnoy steny* [Chrysanthemums by the prison wall]. Moscow: Molodaya gvardiya, 1971. 208 pp.

Ruvinsky, L. *Sionizm: reaktsionnye tseli i prestupnye sredstva* [Zionism: Reactionary aims and criminal means]. Odessa: Mayak, 1980. 143 pp.

Semenyuk, V. *Zloveshchiy al'yans* [The sinister alliance]. Minsk: Belarus, 1972. 136 pp.

————. *Natsionalisticheskoye bezumiye: Ideologiya, politika i praktika mezhdunarodnogo sionizma* [Nationalist madness: The ideology, politics, and practice of international Zionism]. Minsk: Belarus, 1976. 253 pp.

————. *Sionizm v politicheskoy strategii imperializma* [Zionism in the political strategy of imperialism]. Minsk: Belarus, 1981. 174 pp.

Shakhnovich, M. *Reaktsionnaya sushchnost iudaizma: kratkiy ocherk proiskhozhdeniya i klassovoy sushchnosti iudeyskoy religii* [The reactionary essence of Judaism: A brief sketch of the origin and the essential class basis of the Jewish religion]. Moscow and Leningrad: AN SSSR, 1960. 236 pp.

————. *Zakat iudeyskoy religii* [The decline of the Jewish religion]. Leningrad: Lenizdat, 1965. 242 pp.

Shevchenko, A. *Bor'ba narodov stran Blizhnego Vostoka protiv neokolonializma* [The struggle of the nations in the Middle East against neocolonialism]. Kiev: Znaniye UkSSR, 1973. 48 pp.

Shevtsov, I. *Lyubov i nenavist* [Love and hatred]. A novel. Moscow: Voyenizdat, 1970. 488 pp.

————. *Nabat* [The alarm]. A novel. Moscow: Sovremennik, 1978. 653 pp.

Shulga, A. *V maske i bez maski* [Masked and unmasked]. Kishinev: Kartya Moldovenyaske, 1974. 71 pp.

Sionizm bez maski [Zionism unmasked]. A Collection of articles. Vilnius: Mintis, 1973. 172 pp. In Lithuanian.

Sionizm—mify i deystvitel'nost [Zionism—the myths and the reality]. Kiev: Politizdat Ukrainy, 1973. 194 pp. In Ukrainian.

Sionizm—orudiye imperialisticheskoy reaktsii [Zionism—the tool of imperialist reaction]. Moscow: Politizdat, 1971. 80 pp.

Sionizm—oruzhiye imperializma [Zionism—a weapon of imperialism]. Vilnius: Mintis, 1971. 163 pp. In Lithuanian.

Sionizm—otravlennoye oruzhiye imperializma [Zionism—the poisoned weapon of imperialism]. Documents and materials. Moscow: Politizdat, 1970. 319 pp.

Sionizm—pravda i vymysly: Sbornik statey [Zionism—truth and fiction: Collection of articles]. 2 vols. Moscow: Progress, 1980. 287 pp., 223 pp.

Sionizm—teoriya i praktika [Zionism: Its theory and practice]. Moscow: Politizdat, 1973. 239 pp.

Skurlatov, V. *Sionizm i aparteid* [Zionism and apartheid]. Kiev: Politizdat Ukrainy, 1975. 120 pp.

Solodar, Ts. *Byvshiye: Iz dokumental'nykh zapisey o sud'bakh byvshikh sovetskikh grazhdan v Izraile* [Anachronistic people: From documentary records of the fate of former Soviet citizens in Israel]. Moscow: Pravda, 1975. 64 pp.

————. *Dvoynye: Iz tsikla ocherkov o sionizme* [Doubles: From a series of essays on Zionism]. Moscow: Pravda, 1976. 64 pp.

————. *Dikaya polyn* [Wild wormwood]. Moscow: Sovetskaya Rossia, 1977. 288 pp.

————. *Tovar* [The goods]. Moscow: Pravda, 1979. 48 pp.

————. *Tyomnaya zavesa* [The dark curtain]. Moscow: Molodaya gvardiya, 1979. 239 pp.

————. *Dikaya polyn* [Wild wormwood]. Moscow: Progress, 1980. 204 pp.

————. *Litsemery* [Hypocrites]. Moscow: Sovetskaya Rossiya, 1980. 111 pp.

————. *Dikaya polyn* [Wild wormwood]. 2d ed. Moscow: "Sovetskaya Rossiya," 1981. 367 pp.

————. *Lozh: Publitsisticheskie ocherki* [Falsehood: Publicistic essays]. Moscow: Pravda, 1981. 48 pp.

Soyfer, D. *Krakh sionistskikh teoriy* [The collapse of the Zionist theories]. Dnepropetrovsk: Promin, 1980. 190 pp.

Soyfer, D. *Sionizm—orudiye antikommunizma* [Zionism—a tool of anti-communism]. Dnepropetrovsk: Promin, 19—. 192 pp.

Tarasov, V. *Posidi na kamne u dorogi* [Sit down on the stone beside the road]. Novosibirsk: Zapadno-Sibirskoye Knizhnoye Izdatelstvo, 1981. 272 pp.

Troyanovsky, A. *Sovremenny natsionalizm na sluzhbe antikommunizma* [Contemporary nationalism in the service of anti-communism]. Leningrad: Lenizdat, 1981. 104 pp.

Tseli i metody voinstvuyushchego sionizma [The aims and methods of militant Zionism: A collection of articles]. Moscow: Politizdat, 1974. 96 pp.

Tsvigun, S. *Tayny front: O podryvnoy deyatel'nosti imperializma protiv SSSR i bditel'nosti sovetskikh lyudey* [The secret front: On the subversive activities of imperialism against the USSR and the vigilance of Soviet people]. Moscow: Politizdat, 1973. 399 pp.

Vachnadze, G *Anteny napravleny na Vostok* [Antennae directed toward the east]. Moscow: Politizdat, 1975. 175 pp.

*Vadimov, V. *Nakip: Polozhenie yevreev v SSSR i za rubezhom; Politicheskiy ocherk* [Scum: Status of Jews in the USSR and abroad; Political essay]. Donetsk: Donbas, 136 pp.

Valakh, Y. *Sionizm—orudiye reaktsii* [Zionism—a tool of reaction]. Kiev: Politizdat Ukrainy, 1972. 88 pp.

Valikhnovsky, T. *Izrail i FRG* [Israel and the German Federal Republic]. Authorized trans. from Polish. Moscow: Progress, 1971. 168 pp.

*Vayner, S. *Sionizm—forma rasizma* [Zionism—a form of racism]. Kiev: Znanie, 1980. 48 pp. In Ukrainian.

Vot ona ikh "pravda" [This is their "truth"]. Kharkov: Prapor, 1972. 102 pp. In Ukrainian.

Voznyak, N. *Ikh istinnoe litso* [Their true countenance]. Uzhgorod: Karpaty, 1974. 119 pp. In Ukrainian.

Vrag moy i tvoy: Publitsisticheskiy sbornik [My enemy and yours]. Dnepropetrovsk: Promin, 1973. 146 pp. In Ukrainian.

———. *Sionizm: Ideologia i politika* [Zionism: Its ideology and politics] Moscow: Moskovskiy rabochiy, 1971. 112 pp.

———. *Rasizm pod goluboy zvezdoy* [Racism under the blue star]. 2d ed. rev. and supplemented. Saratov: Privolzhskoye Knizhnoye Izdatelstvo, 1981. 200 pp., il.

Zaborsky, L. *Blizhnevostochny krizis 1973 g* [The 1973 crisis in the Middle East]. Kiev, 1973. 22 pp.

Zionism—Enemy of Peace and Social Progress: A Miscellany of Papers. Under the general editorship of Lionel Dadiani. Moscow: Progress Publishers, 1981. 160 pp. In English.

*Zuyev, V. *Pochyom chest, gospoda?* [What's the price of the honor, gentlemen?]. Donetsk: Donbas, 1981. 103 pp.

Notes

1. Yu. Yuzovsky, (Iosif Ilich, 1902–1964), theatrical and literary critic. His articles and books were not infrequently doctrinal in character. Senior scientific worker at the Institute of World Literature between 1946 and 1948.

2. Abram Solomonovich Gurvich, (1897–1962), literary and theatrical critic. Reacted to most of the significant events in Soviet prose and drama of 1930–1950.

3. Aleksandr Mikhailovich Borshchagovsky, (b. 1913), writer, critic, playwright. Was in charge of literature departments in Kiev theaters, in the Soviet Army Central Theater (Moscow), and also of script departments of film studios. His play *Ladies' Tailor*, dedicated to the Babi Yar tragedy, was published in *Teatr* [Theater] magazine, no. 10, 1980.

4. Anatoly Vladimirovich Sofronov, (b. 1911), playwright, writer, journalist. Since 1953, editor-in-chief of *Ogonyok* magazine, which has published numerous anti-Semitic and anti-Israeli articles. Since 1958, deputy chairman of the Soviet Committee of Solidarity with Asia and Africa.

5. Ya. Pasternak, art critic, art historian.

6. Leonid Zakharovich Trauberg, (b. 1902), film producer, scriptwriter. Produced numerous films with M. Kozintsev. Head of the Higher Courses for Film Producers.

7. Aleksandr Isbakh, Isaak Abramovich Bakhrakh, 1904–1977), writer, literary critic. From the early 1940s to the early 1950s was a member of the editorial board of *Oktyabr'* [October] and *Znamya* [Banner] magazines, professor at the M. Gorky Institute of Literature and the V. Potemkin Pedagogical Institute in Moscow. During the campaign against cosmopolitans, was accused of nationalism and Zionism as well as cosmopolitanism. Arrested and spent 1949 to 1955 in Siberian camps (see B. Dyakov, *The Life Story* [Moscow, 1966], pp. 12, 30; *In the Past: A Poet's Records*, bk. 2 [Moscow, 1979], pp. 300–302). Isbakh's book *Years of Life* was the cause of the charges against him. It was republished in a supplemented and somewhat changed form as *My Youth, My Komsomol* (Moscow, 1966).

8. Fedor Markovich Levin, (1901–?), writer, literary critic. Levin's articles, often doctrinal in character, posed acute problems of contemporary literature.

9. The so-called Doctors' Plot—an anti-Jewish action episode mounted by the Soviet authorities at the end of 1952–beginning of 1953. According to the statement, six out of nine persons arrested were Jews. The majority of those arrested had occupied key positions in Soviet medicine. For example, among the main accused were professors at the Kremlin Clinic: M. Vovsi (S. Mikhoels's cousin), Academician of the USSR Academy of Medical Science (in 1941–1950 he was chief therapist of the Soviet Army; he was also a member of the Jewish Anti-Fascist Committee); B. Kogan, director of a Moscow clinic; A. Feldman, leading Soviet otolaryngologist; and others. Mass dismissals of Jewish physicians started all over the Soviet Union. They were harassed and arrested. Preparations for a trial and the related anti-Jewish repressions ended with Stalin's death (March 5, 1953). A statement of April 4, 1953, of the Ministry of Internal Affairs then announced that "verifications have established that the doctors' arrest was legally unfounded." It was admitted that the doctors' confessions were obtained through inadmissible investigation methods (see *Jews and the Jewish People*, 1948–1953, vol. 4, no. 2164). The list of those released included names which were not mentioned in the statement of January 13. Two of those arrested, M. Kogan and Ya. Etinger, died in the course of the investigation.

10. The Joint—American Jewish Joint Distribution Committee. During World War I and afterwards, the Joint engaged in charity activities to aid war victims and victims of pogroms in Russia. By agreement with the Soviet authorities in 1922, the Joint opened medical aid stations, loan banks, and trade schools in the USSR. After 1924, with the full support of the Soviet government, this activity of the Joint in the Soviet Union was conducted by Agro-Joint, which financed Jewish agricultural settlements in the Ukraine, the Crimea, and Belorussia.

In 1938, Agro-Joint was abolished by order of the Soviet authorities. During World War II, the Joint cooperated unofficially with the Soviet Union, providing material aid. The Joint became the object of slander and attacks during Soviet and Eastern European anti-Semitic campaigns and political trials in the late 1940s and early 1950s.

11. B. Shimeliovich, physician, director of the Moscow Botkin Clinic, was a member of the Jewish Anti-Fascist Committee.

12. Solomon Mikhailovich Mikhoels, (Vovsi Shlomo, 1890–1948), outstanding Jewish actor and social activist. From 1919 was an actor in the Yiddish theater; 1929 to 1948, art manager of the Moscow State Jewish Theater (GOSET). During World War II was chairman of the Jewish Anti-Fascist Committee. In 1943, Mikhoels and the poet I. Fefer were sent as representatives of the committee to the United States, Canada, Mexico, and Britain to mobilize public opinion and solicit funds among the Jews for the Soviet Union. In those years he became a symbol of the Jewish national body. He was approached as the head of a semiofficial body for Jewish affairs.

Mikhoels was assassinated in Minsk on January 13, 1948. According to the official version, Mikhoels perished as a result of a traffic accident. Alilueva (Stalin's daughter) wrote: "He was assassinated, there was no accident. The traffic accident was an official version suggested by my father when told of the execution" ("One Year only"/"Just One Year", "Only One Year", p. 134), [New York, 1969]. I. Ehrenburg wrote in his memoirs that a Soviet newspaper published in Lithuania stated that Mikhoels was killed by Beria's agents (I. Ehrenburg, *Collected Works* [Moscow, 1967], vol. 9, p. 566).

13. Piotr (Pinhas) Rutenberg, (1879–1924) took part in the Russian revolutionary movement. Engineer by profession. Activist in the Socialist Revolutionary party, organizer of the revolutionary trial and execution of the agent provocateur Father Gapon (1906). After the Revolution of February 1917 he was appointed deputy military governor of Petrograd by A. Kerensky. Lived in Palestine from 1919, where he founded the Palestine Electrical Company.

Isaak Naiditch, (1868–1949), Zionist activist, industrialist. A leader of Russian political Zionism, the founder (1920) and a director of Keren Hayesod.

Margolin—in all probability Arnold Margolin (1877–1956), lawyer, Ukrainian Jewish activist. Spoke at many trials on Jewish pogroms and at the Beilis trial. A founder and leader of the Jewish Territorialist party (1912). In 1918, joined the Ukrainian Social Federalist party; 1918–1920, Deputy Minister of Foreign Affairs and a diplomatic representative of Ukrainian national governments (Central Rada and Directoria). From 1924 lived in the United States.

Yaffe—in all probability Leib Yaffe (1876–1948), Zionist activist, poet (wrote in Russian and Yiddish). Opposed territorialism. An editor of numerous publications. After the 1917 Revolution, was president of the Lithuanian Zionist organization. From 1920, a social activist in Palestine.

14. The so-called Slansky Trial, the main one in a series of Prague Trials in 1952. The first anti-Jewish political show-trial in Eastern Europe after World War II. R. Slansky was at that time Secretary General of the Czechoslovak Communist party. The trial, which was clearly anti-Semitic, took place concurrently with the Doctors' Plot trial in the USSR. Eleven of the fourteen accused were Jews, of whom eight were executed. Israeli citizens were also put on trial, and Israeli diplomats were expelled from Czechoslovakia. The accused were charged with bourgeois nationalism, connections with the Joint, with Zionism, and the State of Israel. Soviet advisers directly supervised the inquiry and trial. All the accused were later exonerated.

15. The cover of the mentioned issue of *Krokodil* features a cartoon entitled "Traces of Crimes." See also above.

16. Correspondence between B. Russell and N. Khrushchev in *Pravda*, March 1, 1963. See *Jews and the Jewish People*, (hereafter cited as *JJP*) vol. 11, no. 148.

17. Yakov Grigorievich Kreyzer, (1905–1969), Soviet military leader (army general). Was given the title Hero of the Soviet Union in the early weeks of the German-Russian war (July 11, 1941). During the war, rose in rank from division commander to army commander. After the war was in command of several military districts.

18. In 1965, the Moskovsky Rabochy Publishing House issued a second edition of P. Gavruto's story *Clouds over the Town (Tuchi nad gorodom)* on the Ukrainian underground during World War II. The publisher's note stated that the book was strictly documentary. P.

Gavruto wrote in his story that the entire Kiev underground had been given away to the Gestapo by one man, namely, the former Komsomol activist Kogan, who became, following his betrayal, Field Marshal Paulus's interpreter. The epilogue read that the "foul traitor Kogan got his punishment all right for his treason."

The first edition (1963) of the book only mentioned the traitor Kogan. The *Literaturnaya gazeta* of August 9, 1966, published an article by Ariadna Gromova, "For the Sake of the Truth," which analyzed P. Gavruto's story. The article provided convincing proof that nobody betrayed "the entire Kiev underground," that all the traitors are known, and that there is no Kogan among them; that Paulus's interpreter is also known by name and he "could by no means be a Jew." The actual A. G. Kogan "never stayed in the occupied city, which he had left with Soviet troops and never even saw Field Marhsal Paulus."

19. The Bund (General Jewish Workers' Union in Lithuania, Poland, and Russia)— Jewish socialist party in Russia, later also in Poland and in the United States, founded in 1897. The Bund was part of the All-Russian Social Democratic Workers party (RSDRP) and was one of its founders (1898). However, representatives of the Bund repeatedly clashed with the RSDRP leadership on issues of Jewish cultural and national autonomy and the position of the Bund in the party structure. The Bund, in full conformity with the views of the RSDRP, regarded Zionism as a "reactionary bourgeois or petit-bourgeois nationalistic movement," diverting Jewish masses from the political struggle in Russia. The Bund was also categorically against Hebrew, supporting Yiddish as the language of Jewish workers.

20. Yevno Fishelevich Azef, (1869–1918), notorious agent provocateur. From 1893 to 1902 was an agent of the Russian secret police (Okhrana) and at the same time one of the organizers of the Socialist Revolutionary (SR) party (1901) and the head (from 1903) of its "Shock Organization," which carried out acts of terror. Prepared the assassination of Pleve, Russia's Minister of Interior (1904), Grand Prince Sergei Aleksandrovich (1905), and other high officials. At the same time he betrayed party activists to the police, and many of them were executed. Was unmasked in 1908. During World War I was arrested in Germany as a Russian agent and died in prison.

21. Yakov Abramovich Zhitomirsky, agent provocateur. From 1901 was among the Social Democrats close to Lenin. Known in their circle by his party nickname, Ottsov. Betrayed Bolsheviks working in the underground, while a member of the party leadership abroad. Was unmasked by the revolutionaries in 1911.

22. *Zubatovshchina*—a policy of the tsarist government with regard to the workers in Russia. Intended as a way of setting up legal workers' organizations which operated under the supervision of the secret police, and of restricting their demands to purely economic issues. Initiated by Colonel S. Zubatov, chief of the secret department of the Moscow Gendarmerie, after whom it was named. In 1901, a number of activists in Minsk and Vilno who had previously been in the Bund, and had been influenced by the Zubatovshchina, organized the Jewish Independent Workers' party, which disbanded in 1903.

23. Khrushchev's speech at a meeting of party and government leaders and literature and art workers on March 8, 1963; for the text, see above.

24. T. Kichko's book was published by the Academy of Sciences of the Ukrainian SSR.

25. Yu. Ivanov's book *Beware: Zionism!* was published as the second edition in 1970 (200,000 copies). It appeared again in 1971, also as a second edition (100,000 copies). It has also been published in the USSR in Ukrainian (1969), Arabic (1970), English (1970), Estonian (1970), Spanish (1971), French (1972), Armenian (1972), and other languages.

26. Heinz Höhne (b. 1926), West German journalist, one of the editors of *Der Spiegel*. In his work as a journalist, Höhne has become an authority on World War II and espionage. Has written *Canaris, Patriot im Zwielicht* (Munich, 1976), *Codeword: Direktor; The Story of the Red Orchestra* (London, 1971), and other books. The quotation is from "Der Orden unter dem Totentkopf," *Der Spiegel*, no. 51 (December 19, 1966). This article was then published as *The Order of the Death's Head: The Story of Hitler's SS* (New York, 1977).

27. Anatoly Andreevich Dimarov, (b. 1922), Soviet Ukrainian writer. "The Paths of Life" was published in the magazine *Dnipro*, and appeared in Russian translation in expanded form under the title *And There will be People* (Moscow: Sovetsky Pisatel Publishing House,

1970). The pages referred to in Moscow Samizdat magazine *Politichesky Dnevnik* [Political diary], no. 9, June 1965, were not included in this edition. The original novel was published as a separate book in 1964 by the Radyansky Pysmennyk Publishing House, Kiev, but the writer of these notes does not have access to a copy.

28. No reference to Harshel Steinschneider (Ganusen) could be found in sources available to us.

29. See *Memories: The Autobiography of Nahum Goldmann* (Jerusalem: Weidenfeld & Nicolson, 1972), pp. 142–150.

30. In all probability, the author of the article used S. Krylov, *Tainoe Oruzhie Sionizma* [Secret weapon of Zionism], (Moscow: Voennoe Izdatelstvo Ministerstva Oborony SSSR, 1972), as a source. This book, however, dates Stern's (Golder's) "penetration" of the Pope's office as 1939 (p. 21), and in contrast to the article, Stern (Golder) is not identified with Avraham Stern. See below, n. 31, and also *The Schellenberg Memoirs* (London, 1969), p. 154.

31. Avraham (Yair) Stern, (1907–1942), organizer and ideologist of Lehi (Fighters for the Freedom of Israel), an underground military organization created in 1940. Unlike other Jewish underground organizations, Lehi refused to suspend military action against the British mandatory authorities during World War II. On Feburary 12, 1942, Stern was killed when the British came to arrest him.

32. Information on Feivel Polkes must have been drawn from the article by Heinz Höhne, *Der Spiegel*, no. 51, December 19, 1966. See above, n. 26.

33. Regarding the author's associating the explosion of the *Struma* with the death of Stern, it should be stressed that Stern was killed during his arrest on February 12, 1942.

The *Struma* with 769 Jewish refugees on board put to sea from the Rumanian seaport of Constantsa in December 1941. The vessel had been damaged by a storm. The Turkish authorities declared they would sanction the repairs on the condition that some state would agree to receive the refugees. The British mandatory authorities refused to admit them to Eretz Israel. On February 23, 1942 the *Struma* was towed off back to the Black Sea by the Turks. The next day there was an explosion on the *Struma*. All its passengers but one drowned. A German author, Rohwer Jurgen, in *Die Versenkung der jüdischen Flüchtling-stransporter "Struma" und "Mefkure" im Schwarzen Meer (February 1942, August 1955)* (Frankfurt/Main, 1965), pp. 81–87, suggested that it was a Soviet torpedo boat which sank the *Struma*. The Soviet Ministry of Defense Publishing House issued in 1978 G. I. Vaneyev's book entitled *The Black Sea Fleet in the Great Patriotic War*. The 299th page of the book informs the reader, based on materials in the Central Navy Archives, that on February 24, 1942, torpedo boat *Shch-213* spotted the enemy transport boat *Struma* . . . which moved without escort. The boat was attacked. . . . The torpedo hit the target, and the boat soon sank." Yet Soviet authors persist in maintaining that the *Struma* was sunk by a German boat (See V. Tarasov, *Have a Rest on a Rock by the Road [Posidi na Kamne u dorogi]* (Novosibirsk, 1981], p. 184).

34. See above, for some excerpts from V. Begun's book. The author of the review, V. Yemelyanov, is also known through his Samizdat publications. His letter to the CPSU Central Committee will be found below.

35. See below, for some excerpts from Yu. Ivanov's book.

36. B'nai B'rith—a Jewish public organization. Was founded in 1843 in New York. Its charter reads: "B'nai B'rith sees its objectives in uniting persons of Jewish faith in efforts directed to satisfying their essential interests and interests of the entire mankind." B'nai B'rith is engaged in educational and philanthropic activities. In 1913, B'nai B'rith organized the Anti-Defamation League, which struggles against all manifestations of anti-Semitism and racial discrimination, for equal civil rights for all, and for mutual understanding between Jews and non-Jews.

37. The frontispiece and title page of E. Evseev's book are shown below.

38. Abram Borisovich Ranovich (Rabinovich) (1885–1948), Soviet historian of antiquity, professor, author of works on early Christianity.

39. I. Tobolsky, "Confession" *(Ispoved)*: Poem, *Ogonyok*, no. 14, 1970, reprinted in vol.

40, no. 273. I. Tobolsky, a Saratov poet, publishes anti-Zionist declarations. See *Pravda*, March 7, 1970, reprinted in JJP, vol. 39A, no. 1914; "There is no middle," *(Serediny net)*. Poem, *Ogonyok*, no. 7, 1979, etc.

40. The author implies *Travel Notes* by A. Vergelis, i.e., *On the Jewish Street: Travel Notes* (Moscow: Sovetsky Pisatel), The Essay "Twenty Days in America," pp. 7–89.

41. The Letter of the Jews of the Ukraine was published in *Pravda*, March 12, 1970, see JJP, vol. 39A, no. 1952.

42. The author refers to the Scroll of Esther.

43. Skurlatov's book *Zionism and Apartheid* was severely criticized by Academician M. A. Korostovtzev; see *Sovietische Heimland*, no. 7, 1978.

44. *Shulchan Arukh*—Jewish religious code compiled by Rabbi Joseph Caro (1488–1578), which was completed by the middle of the sixteenth century.

45. There is no accurate etymology for the word "Sinai." Some scholars connect the word to the name of the moon god, Sin, and others to the word *neh*, the burning bush. The Bible itself mentions a desert named Sin. In the Tractate *Shabbat*, one of many interpretations of the word "Sinai" states that from Mount Sinai there went forth a hatred (*sinah* in Hebrew) for idol-worshippers.

46. The article "Nietzsche and Judaism" by Ahad Ha'am (Asher Ginzberg, 1856–1927), *Ha-Shiloach*, 1898, later published by the author under the title "The Parting of the Ways."

47. V. Jabotinsky, *The Jewish State* (in Russian) (Kharbin, 1938), p. 15.

48. Edward Goldstücker (b. 1913), a Czechoslovakian politician, diplomat, and historian of literature. He was the first Czechoslovak ambassador in Israel (1949–1951). Goldstücker was arrested in 1951. Figured in the Slansky trial, (see above, n. 14). He was released after eight years imprisonment. Afterwards he was professor at Prague University. He was a prominent figure after January 1968: president of the Czechoslovak Writers' Union, a member of the Central Committee of the Communist party, and a member of Parliament. Goldstücker left the country in 1969.

49. The I. S. Narsky letter appeared in the Moscow Samizdat magazine *Political Diary*, no. 75, December 1970.

50. The interview and information about Shimanov were reprinted in full in the *Jewish Samizdat*, vol. 13, pp. 175–188.

Gennady Mikhailovich Shimanov, born in 1937, became known through his *Notes from the Red House* (*Zapiski iz Krasnogo doma*) on his stay in a psychiatric clinic, where he had been placed for his religious and social activity. Having joined the Russian national movement, he became a leader of its religious wing. Shimanov's works were published in Samizdat magazines *Veche*, *Zemlya*, and others, as well as abroad.

51. These critical comments appeared in the Russian Samizdat.

52. V. Yemelyanov's letter to the Central Committee of the party appeared in the Samizdat journal in Moscow, *Jews in the USSR*, no. 16. The editorial board introduced the material with a foreword, which we are publishing here in its entirety.

Valery Yemelyanov has long been known as a most outspoken representative of a militant anti-Semitic clique active for a long time in various scientific institutions, higher-educational establishments, mass-information media, etc. As a matter of fact, in contrast to many others of the same mind, Yemelyanov never exercised even the slightest caution, and his extremism is truly boundless.

We quote in this section V. Yemelyanov's letter to the CPSU Central Committee, dated January 10, 1977. The picture of the "Judeo-Masonic conspiracy" offered by the author of the letter leaves far behind "classical" sources of anti-Semitic propaganda, such as the *Protocols of the Elders of Zion*. All this does not interfere with V. Yemelyanov's remaining a CPSU member. But he is not alone. As seen from the letter, he is backed by a group of people fully sharing his views—the notorious fighters against Zionism Yu. Ivanov, Ye. Yeliseev, V. Begun, D. Zhukov, and others. As a matter of fact, he writes more explicitly and openly things which they express somewhat obscurely in numerous books and articles published in abundance by the central and peripheral press. As for the measures being suggested by Yemelyanov, nearly all of them are being put into practice, although probably less directly or less openly than as he might want. Finally, a few words on the contents of the letter. It is virtually impossible and senseless to refute this whole torrent of traditional lies, as the "Judeo-Masonic conspiracy" theme used to be quite popular in Russian prerevolutionary anti-Semitic literature. Even the linguistic references of Yemelyanov, a linguist, are utterly erroneous. For example, the word "goy" does not derive from the verb "to live," which, incidentally, is *likhiot* rather than *goiti,* and the facts are all invented: Cyrus Vance is not a Jew, Sorensen has never headed the CIA, and Phi Beta Kappa, Delta Kappa Epsilon, etc., are names of traditional students clubs.

Even though we once published a rendering of a lecture by V. Yemelyanov (in no. 8), we find it appropriate to publish this letter expounding an approach which is by no means individual. The more so since this is another point of view on the interrelationships between the Russian and Jewish peoples, and the materials dealing with this theme are traditional for us.

In our book the letter has been reproduced in an abridged version.

Contributors

ABRAMSKY, Chimen (1917–   ). Born Minsk. B. A. Hebrew University, Jerusalem. In England since 1939. M. A. Oxon. Since 1967, Senior Researcher at St. Anthony's College, Oxford. Professor of Hebrew and Jewish Studies, University College, London, since 1974. Many publications and articles on Jewish art, Karl Marx and modern Jewish history.

AZBEL, M., is a Professor of physics. Born in 1932 in Poltava. Studied physics at Kharakov University and received a doctorate at the Institute of Physics in Moscow. In 1977 he came to Israel and joined the staff of Tel-Aviv University.

DIMERSKI-TSIGELMAN, Dr. M., was born in 1929 in Kiev. She graduated from Kiev University in philosophy and has a PhD from the Institute of Philosophy of the Ukrainian Academy of Science. She came to Israel in 1976 and has been a research fellow in the Center for Research and Documentation of East-European Jewry at the Hebrew University since 1977.

DULZIN, Arye (Leon) (1913–   ). Born Minsk. Resident in Mexico, 1928–1956; has lived in Israel since 1956. Secretary and President, Zionist Federation of Mexico, 1931–1944; Treasurer, Jewish Agency, 1968–1978; Israel government minister, 1969; present Chairman, World Zionist Organization and the Jewish Agency.

ETTINGER, Shmuel (1919–   ). Born in Kiev. Rosenbloom Professor and Head of the Department of Jewish History, Hebrew University of Jerusalem. Author of books on modern Jewish history. One of the editors of *Zion* and *Quarterly in Research of Jewish History*. Head of the Centre for Research and Documentation of East-European Jewry, and head of the B. Z. Dinur Center for Research in Jewish History, Hebrew University of Jerusalem.

HIRSH, Shimon, was born in 1925 in Lithuania. During the Second World War he was in the ghetto. He came to Israel in 1978 from Kaunas. Works as an economist in a governmental plant.

IL'IN, M. G., (pseud.), physicist. Since 1977 in Israel.

M. KAGANSKAYA—literary critic and essayist. A graduate of Kiev State University. Arrived in Israel in 1976. Her articles and essays on Russian literature are published in the Israeli and western press.

KOREY, William (1922–   ). Born Chicago. Director, UN office of B'nai B'rith International Council, educated at the Universities of Chicago and Columbia, Professor of History and Social Science. Author of many articles on Soviet affairs and anti-Semitism in Russia and scholarly and popular journals.

LITVINOFF, Emanuel (1915–   ). Born London. English poet and journalist, novelist, playwright and writer of short stories. Director of Contemporary Jewish Library, London. Many publications concerning Diaspora Jewry. Editor of "Insight: Soviet Jews".

LWOFF, Andre Michel (1902–   ). Born Ainay-le-Chateau. French biologist. Co-recipient of the 1965 Nobel prize for medicine and physiology. Awarded Medal of Resistance for his work in the French Underground during World War II.

MAYER, Daniel (1909–   ). Born Paris. French journalist, leader of the Socialist Party (PSU). Member of the Conseil Nationale de la Resistance. Minister of Labour and Minister of Public Health. Many publications on the part the Socialists played in the Resistance during World War II, and also on the history of Socialism and the Left. President of the International Federation of Human Rights (1958–1975).

NUDELMAN, R., a physicist, was born in 1931 in Sverdlovsk. He studied at Odessa and Leningrad Universities, receiving a PhD in Leningrad in 1969. Subsequently he taught physics at various higher learning institutions. From 1973 to 1975 he participated in the publication of the samizdat journal "Jews in the USSR." In Israel since December 1975, he edited, there Russian language journals "Zion" and lately "22," "a social, political and literary journal of the Jewish intelligentsia from the USSR in Israel."

OKUNEVA, Dr. R.—historian and specialist in source material. Graduate of Moscow Historical-Archival Institute. She has been in Israel since 1981. While still in the Soviet Union, she published a series of articles on contemporary problems in the Jewish samizdat.

ROTH, Stephen (1915–   ). Born Hungary. Director of the Institute of Jewish Affairs, London. Executive Director of the European Division of the British W.J.C.; Chairman of Foreign Affairs and Eretz Israel Committees at the Board of Deputies of British Jews; Executive and Trustee of Memorial Foundation for Jewish culture.

SCHWARTZ, Laurent (1915–   ). Born Paris. Since 1953, Professor of Faculty of Sciences of Paris, a Member of the Institute of the Academy of Sciences since 1973; now Professor d'analyse a l'Ecole polytechnic. Was awarded honors and prizes in mathematics.

SOTNIKOVA, E., an art historian. She was born in 1947 in Leningrad and graduated from the Leningrad Art Institute in the faculty of theory and history of art. She was one of the editors of the samizdat journal "Jews in the USSR" in the years 1976-1977. Since 1977 she is in Israel and writes for the Russian language press, as a free-lance journalist.

TARTAKOVSKY, Sofia. Graduated from the Department of Philology at the University of Leningrad. Translated French, Spanish and English publications into Russian. Emigrated to Israel in 1973. Now works as a librarian.

TERRACINI, Umberto (1895–). Born Genoa. Italian Communist and joint founder of the Italian Communist Party. Imprisoned by Mussolini. Liberated in 1943 after the fall of the Fascist government. After the war, he was elected a Deputy in the Italian Parliament, and became its vice-president in 1946 and president in 1947. In 1948, he was elected a senator, and was re-elected until 1963. From 1948 to 1953, was a member of the World Council of Peace. Was also a vice-chairman of the International Federation of Resistance Movements, and of the International Association of Democratic Lawyers.

TIKTINA-SHTURMAN, D., was born in 1923 in the Ukraine. She is a philologist and a historian. In 1944 still as a university student she was sentenced to 5 years in a Soviet concentration camp for "anti-Soviet activity." After her release she graduated from the Kharakov University and worked as a school teacher. She is in Israel since 1977 and is a member of the editorial board of the journal "Time and We," "an international journal devoted to literature and social problems," published in New York and Israel.

TSIGELMAN, Ya.—writer and journalist. Graduate of Leningrad State University. Arrived in Israel in 1974. His article "Anti-Semitism in Soviet Publications (Belles lettres and feature stories)" was published in the first volume of this series.

VOGT, J.—Danish researcher of social phenomena. A graduate of Copenhagen University. Since 1960 she has been living with her husband in Norway. She has published articles about various aspects of anti-Semitism and a book *Historien om et image: antisemitism og antizionisme i karikaturer*, Kobenhavn (Copenhagen), Samleren, 1978, 276 pp.

VORONEL, A., is a Professor of physics at Tel Aviv University. He was born in 1931 in Leningrad, received a degree in physics and mathematics from Kharkov University in 1954. From 1955 until 1972 he worked at the Physco-Technical Research Institute and Radio-Technical Measuring Institute in Moscow. A. Voronel is a founder and one of the first editors of the samizdat journal "Jews in the USSR." Lives in Israel since 1974.

YANAI, Yacob. Was born in 1919 in Riga, Latvia. After World War II was sentenced to 25 years imprisonment for Zionist activity and served in prison from 1946 until 1957. In 1961 he came to Israel and works for an Israeli Governmental Institution.

Index